HARCOURT HORIZONS

The Pledge of Allegiance

I pledge allegiance to the Flag

of the United States of America,

and to the Republic

for which it stands,

one Nation under God, indivisible,

with liberty and justice for all.

HARCOURT HORIZONS
World History

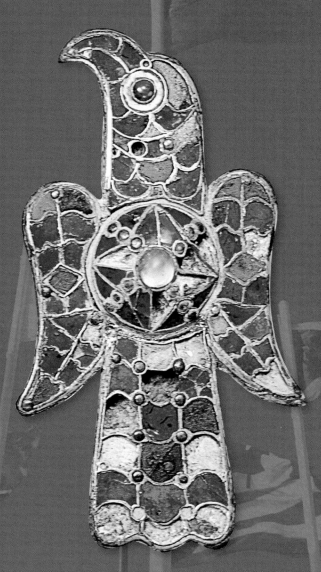

Harcourt
SCHOOL PUBLISHERS

Orlando   Austin   New York   San Diego   Toronto   London

Visit *The Learning Site!*
www.harcourtschool.com

HARCOURT HORIZONS

WORLD HISTORY

General Editor

Dr. Michael J. Berson
Associate Professor
Social Science Education
University of South Florida
Tampa, Florida

Contributing Authors

Dr. Stephen Thornton
Associate Professor of Social Studies
  and Education
Department of Arts and Humanities
Teachers College
Columbia University
New York, New York

Dr. Lawrence W. McBride
Professor of History
Department of History
Illinois State University
Normal, Illinois

Series Consultants

Dr. Robert Bednarz
Professor
Department of Geography
Texas A&M University
College Station, Texas

Dr. Asa Grant Hilliard III
Fuller E. Callaway Professor
  of Urban Education
Georgia State University
Atlanta, Georgia

Dr. Thomas M. McGowan
Chairperson and Professor
Center for Curriculum and Instruction
University of Nebraska
Lincoln, Nebraska

Dr. John J. Patrick
Professor of Education
Indiana University
Bloomington, Indiana

Dr. Philip VanFossen
Associate Professor,
  Social Studies Education,
  and Associate Director,
  Purdue Center for Economic Education
Purdue University
West Lafayette, Indiana

Dr. Hallie Kay Yopp
Professor
Department of Elementary, Bilingual,
  and Reading Education
California State University, Fullerton
Fullerton, California

Content Reviewers

Dr. Richard A. Gerberding
Professor of History
Department of History
The University of Alabama in Huntsville
Huntsville, Alabama

Dr. Ronald H. Sack
Professor
Department of History
North Carolina State University
Raleigh, North Carolina

African History

Dr. Patrick S. Caulker
Assistant Professor
Department of History
Seton Hall University
Seton Hall, New Jersey

Dr. David O'Connor
Professor of Ancient Egyptian Art
Institute of Fine Arts
New York University
New York, New York

European History

Dr. Robert Bast
Associate Professor of History
Department of History
University of Tennessee
Knoxville, Tennessee

Dr. Craige B. Champion
Professor
Department of History
Maxwell School of Citizenship
  and Public Affairs
Syracuse University
Syracuse, New York

Dr. Margery A. Ganz
Professor
Department of History
Spelman College
Atlanta, Georgia

Dr. Richard Pierard
Scholar in Residence
  and Adjunct Professor
Department of History
Gordon College
Wenham, Massachusetts

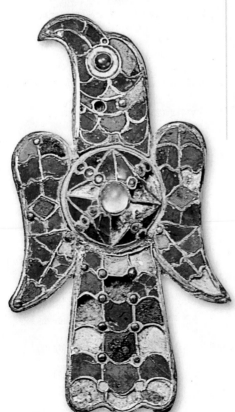

Dr. Kimberly D. Reiter
Associate Professor and Chair
Department of History
Stetson University
Deland, Florida

Dr. Philip M. Soergel
Associate Professor
Department of History
Arizona State University
Tempe, Arizona

Dr. Warren Treadgold
Professor
History Department
Saint Louis University
Saint Louis, Missouri

Modern Times

Dr. Richard Matthew
Associate Professor
International and Environmental Politics
School of Social Ecology
University of California, Irvine
Irvine, California

Dr. Steven Sabol
Assistant Professor of History
Editor-in-Chief, Nationalities Papers
Department of History
University of North Carolina at Charlotte
Charlotte, North Carolina

Southern, Eastern, and Southeastern Asian History

Mrs. Yong Jin Choi
Director, Korean Studies Program
The Korea Society
New York, New York

Dr. Susan Glosser
Associate Professor
Department of History
Lewis and Clark University
Portland, Oregon

Dr. Mark Peterson
Professor
Department of Asian and Near Eastern
  Languages
Brigham Young University
Provo, Utah

Dr. Cynthia Talbot
Associate Professor
Department of History
University of Texas at Austin
Austin, Texas

Southwestern Asian History

Dr. Sandra Alfonsi
Adjunct Assistant Professor
Saint John's University
Language and Literature Department
New York, New York
Chair, Academic Advisory Board
Hadassah Curriculum Watch
(History Specialist)

Dr. Matthew S. Gordon
Associate Professor
Department of History
Miami University
Oxford, Ohio

Shabbir Mansuri
Founding Director
Susan L. Douglass
Affiliated Scholar
Council on Islamic Education
Fountain Valley, California

Classroom Reviewers

Kelly S. Curtright
Social Studies Coordinator
Putnam City Schools
Oklahoma City, Oklahoma

Pamela Fisk
Supervisor of Humanities
Moorestown Township Public Schools
Moorestown, New Jersey

Jennifer Hillis
Teacher
Howard Elementary School
Medford, Oregon

Cathy J. Jackson
Curriculum Coordinator
Calhoun Middle School
Calhoun, Louisiana

Renee Spencer
Teacher
Broadmoor Elementary School
Lafayette, Louisiana

Margaret McLeod Ward
Teacher
Laing Middle School
Mt. Pleasant, South Carolina

Maps
researched and prepared by

MAPQUEST

Readers
written and designed by

TIME FOR KIDS

Take a Field Trip
video tour segments provided by

CNN Turner Le@rning

Copyright © 2005 by Harcourt, Inc.

All rights reserved. No part of this publication may be reproduced or transmitted in any form or by any means, electronic or mechanical, including photocopy, recording, or any information storage and retrieval system, without permission in writing from the publisher.

Requests for permission to make copies of any part of the work should be addressed to:

School Permissions and Copyrights
Harcourt, Inc.
6277 Sea Harbor Drive
Orlando, Florida 32887-6777.
Fax: 407-345-2418.

HARCOURT and the Harcourt Logo are trademarks of Harcourt, Inc., registered in the United States of America and/or other jurisdictions. TIME FOR KIDS and the red border are registered trademarks of Time Inc. Used under license. Copyright © by Time Inc. All rights reserved.

Acknowledgments appear in the back of this book.

Printed in the United States of America

ISBN 0-15-336821-7

4 5 6 7 8 9 10 048 12 11 10 09 08 07 06

Contents

· UNIT ·

1

The World and Early People

· UNIT ·

2

Early Centers of Civilization

· UNIT ·

3

Eastern Civilizations

· UNIT ·

4

Western Civilizations

· UNIT ·

5

The Rise of Later Civilizations

· UNIT ·

6

The Spread of Civilizations

· UNIT ·

7

The Early Modern World

· UNIT ·
8

Toward the Present Day

For Your Reference

Features You Can Use

Skills

CHART AND GRAPH SKILLS

CITIZENSHIP SKILLS

MAP AND GLOBE SKILLS

READING SKILLS

Citizenship

DEMOCRATIC VALUES

POINTS OF VIEW

Music and Literature

Primary Sources

EXAMINE PRIMARY SOURCES

ANALYZE PRIMARY SOURCES

Biography

Geography

Time Lines

Reading Your Textbook

Getting Started

Your textbook is divided into eight units.

Each unit begins with a song, poem, story, or other special reading selection.

Each unit has a Unit Preview that gives facts about important events. The Preview also shows where and when those events took place.

Each unit is divided into chapters, and each chapter is divided into lessons.

The Parts of a Lesson

This statement gives you ideas to help you as you read a lesson.

This statement tells you what the lesson is about.

These are the new vocabulary terms you will learn in the lesson.

Lesson title

This part of the time line shows the period when the events in the lesson took place.

Each new vocabulary term is highlighted in yellow and defined.

Each lesson is divided into several short sections.

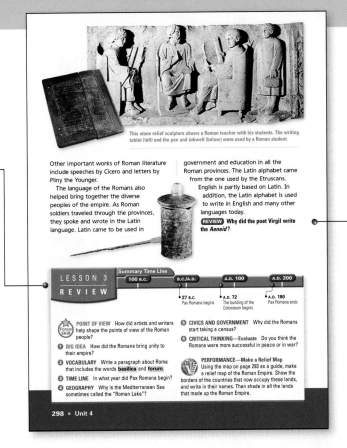

This stone relief sculpture shows a Roman teacher with his students. The writing tablet (left) and the pen and inkwell (below) were used by a Roman student.

Each lesson, like each chapter and each unit, ends with a review. There may be a Summary Time Line that shows the order of the events covered in the lesson. Questions and a performance activity help you check your understanding of the lesson.

Each short section ends with a **REVIEW** question that will help you check whether you understand what you have read. Be sure to answer this question before you continue reading the lesson.

Skills

Your textbook has lessons that will help you build your reading, citizenship, chart and graph, and map and globe skills.

You will be able to practice and apply the skills you learn.

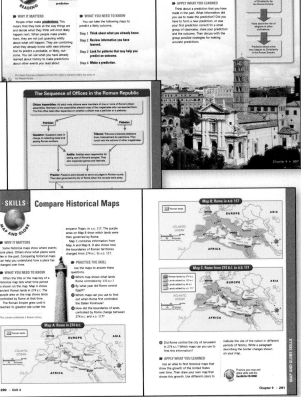

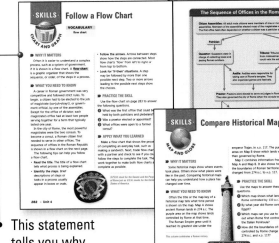

This statement tells you why it is important to learn the skill.

Special Features

The feature called Examine Primary Sources shows you ways to learn about different kinds of objects and documents.

The Visit feature lets you "visit" many interesting places.

Atlas

The Atlas provides maps and a list of geography terms with illustrations.

For Your Reference

At the back of your textbook, you will find the reference tools listed below.

- Almanac
- Biographical Dictionary
- Gazetteer
- Glossary
- Index

You can use these tools to look up words and to find information about people, places, and other topics.

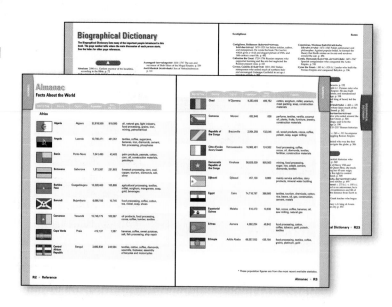

Atlas

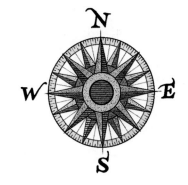

Read a Map

VOCABULARY

grid system	inset map	intermediate direction
map title	compass rose	map scale
locator	cardinal direction	map key

▶ WHY IT MATTERS

Maps provide a visual way to learn about a place and to see where it is in relation to other places. Knowing how to read and understand maps is an important skill for learning social studies.

▶ WHAT YOU NEED TO KNOW

A map is a drawing of some or all of Earth on a flat surface. Mapmakers often include certain features to help people understand and use maps more easily.

- A **map title** tells the subject of the map. The title may also help you identify what kind of map it is.
  - Political maps show cities, states, and countries.
  - Physical maps show kinds of land and bodies of water.
  - Historical maps show parts of the world as they were in the past.

- A **locator** is a small map or picture of a globe that shows where the place on the main map is located.

- An **inset map** is a small map within a larger map.

To help people find places on a map, mapmakers sometimes include lines that cross each other to form a pattern of squares. This pattern of squares is called a **grid system**. Look at the map of Venezuela below. Around the grid system are letters and numbers. The rows, which run left and

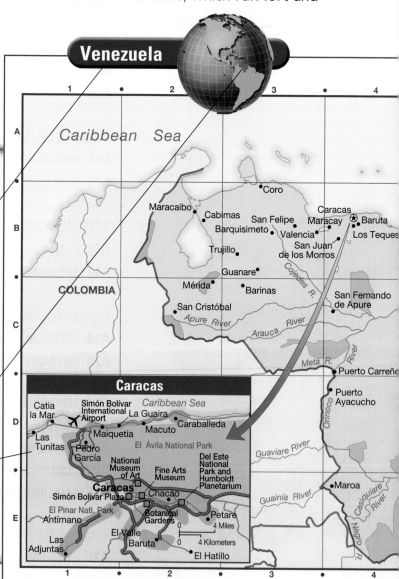

Venezuela

right, have letters. The columns, which run up and down, have numbers. Each square on the map can be identified by its letter and number. For example, the top row of squares in the map includes square A1, square A2, square A3, and so on.

Mapmakers sometimes also include smaller maps called inset maps within larger maps. Inset maps usually show in greater detail an area on the main map. Look at the map of Venezuela below. The inset map of Caracas allows you to see the Caracas area more clearly.

▶ PRACTICE THE SKILL

Use the map of Venezuela to answer these questions.

1. What cities are located in square C5?
2. In what direction would you travel if you went from Valencia to Canaima?
3. Find the map key. What symbol is used to show a national capital?
4. About how many miles is it from Maturín to Ciudad Bolívar?

▶ APPLY WHAT YOU LEARNED

Imagine that you must explain the parts of a map to a younger student. Look in the Atlas maps that follow in this book. Select a country that looks interesting to you. Draw a map of that country. Add all the necessary map parts. Then add a brief explanation of each map part.

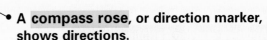

- A **compass rose**, or direction marker, shows directions.
  - The **cardinal directions**, or main directions, are north, south, east, and west.
  - The **intermediate directions**, or directions between the cardinal directions, are northeast, northwest, southeast, and southwest.

- A **map scale** compares a distance on the map to a distance in the real world. It can be used to find the real distance between places on a map.

- A **map key**, or legend, explains the symbols used on a map. Symbols may be colors, patterns, lines, or other special marks.

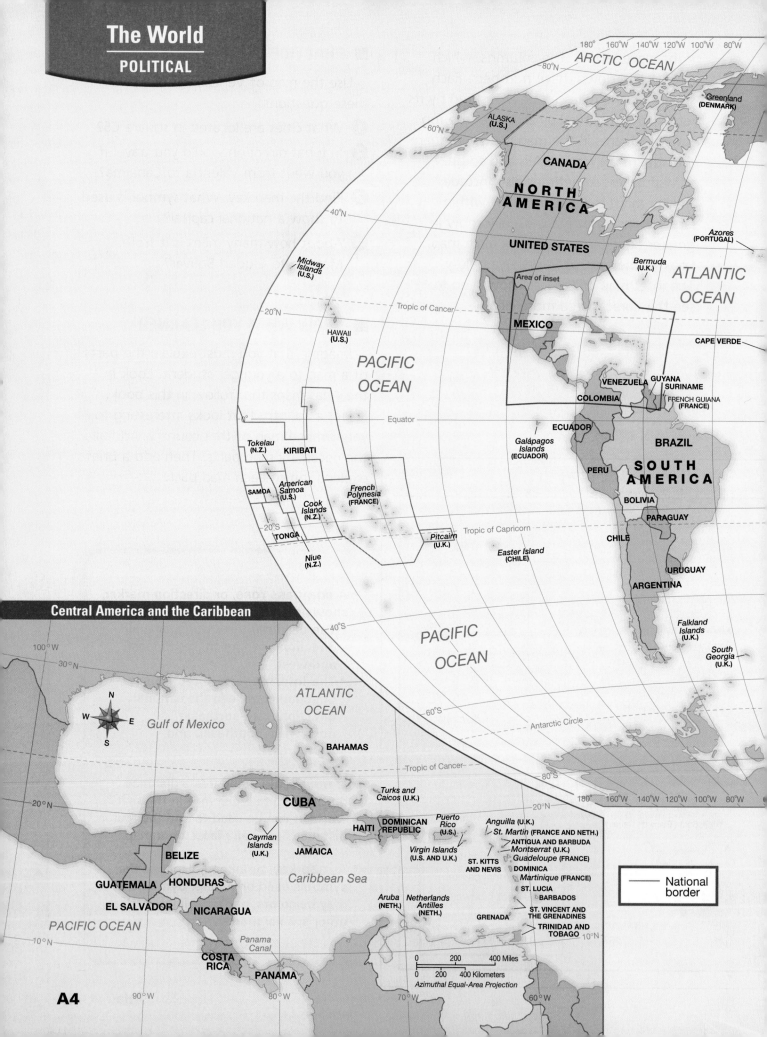

ARCTIC OCEAN

Greenland (DENMARK)

ALASKA (U.S.)

CANADA

NORTH AMERICA

UNITED STATES

Azores (PORTUGAL)

Bermuda (U.K.)

ATLANTIC OCEAN

Area of inset

MEXICO

CAPE VERDE

Midway Islands (U.S.)

Tropic of Cancer

HAWAII (U.S.)

PACIFIC OCEAN

VENEZUELA

GUYANA

SURINAME

COLOMBIA

FRENCH GUIANA (FRANCE)

Equator

ECUADOR

Galápagos Islands (ECUADOR)

BRAZIL

Tokelau (N.Z.)

KIRIBATI

PERU

SOUTH AMERICA

SAMOA

American Samoa (U.S.)

French Polynesia (FRANCE)

BOLIVIA

Cook Islands (N.Z.)

PARAGUAY

Tropic of Capricorn

CHILE

TONGA

Pitcairn (U.K.)

Easter Island (CHILE)

URUGUAY

Niue (N.Z.)

ARGENTINA

PACIFIC OCEAN

Falkland Islands (U.K.)

South Georgia (U.K.)

PACIFIC OCEAN

Antarctic Circle

Central America and the Caribbean

100° W

30° N

N
W   E
S

Gulf of Mexico

ATLANTIC OCEAN

20° N

BAHAMAS

Tropic of Cancer

CUBA

Turks and Caicos (U.K.)

Cayman Islands (U.K.)

HAITI

DOMINICAN REPUBLIC

Puerto Rico (U.S.)

Anguilla (U.K.)

St. Martin (FRANCE AND NETH.)

ANTIGUA AND BARBUDA

Montserrat (U.K.)

Guadeloupe (FRANCE)

JAMAICA

Virgin Islands (U.S. AND U.K.)

ST. KITTS AND NEVIS

DOMINICA

BELIZE

Caribbean Sea

Martinique (FRANCE)

ST. LUCIA

GUATEMALA

HONDURAS

BARBADOS

EL SALVADOR

NICARAGUA

Aruba (NETH.)

Netherlands Antilles (NETH.)

GRENADA

ST. VINCENT AND THE GRENADINES

TRINIDAD AND TOBAGO

PACIFIC OCEAN

10° N

Panama Canal

COSTA RICA

PANAMA

90° W

80° W

70° W

60° W

10° N

200   400 Miles

0   200   400 Kilometers

Azimuthal Equal-Area Projection

| | National border |

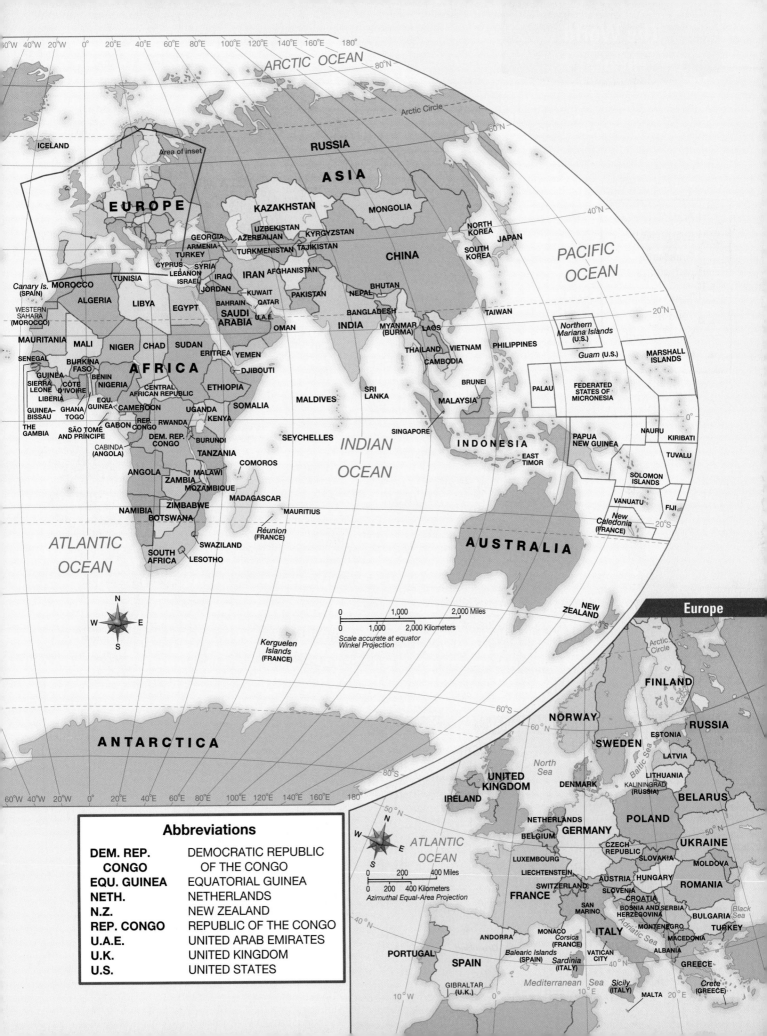

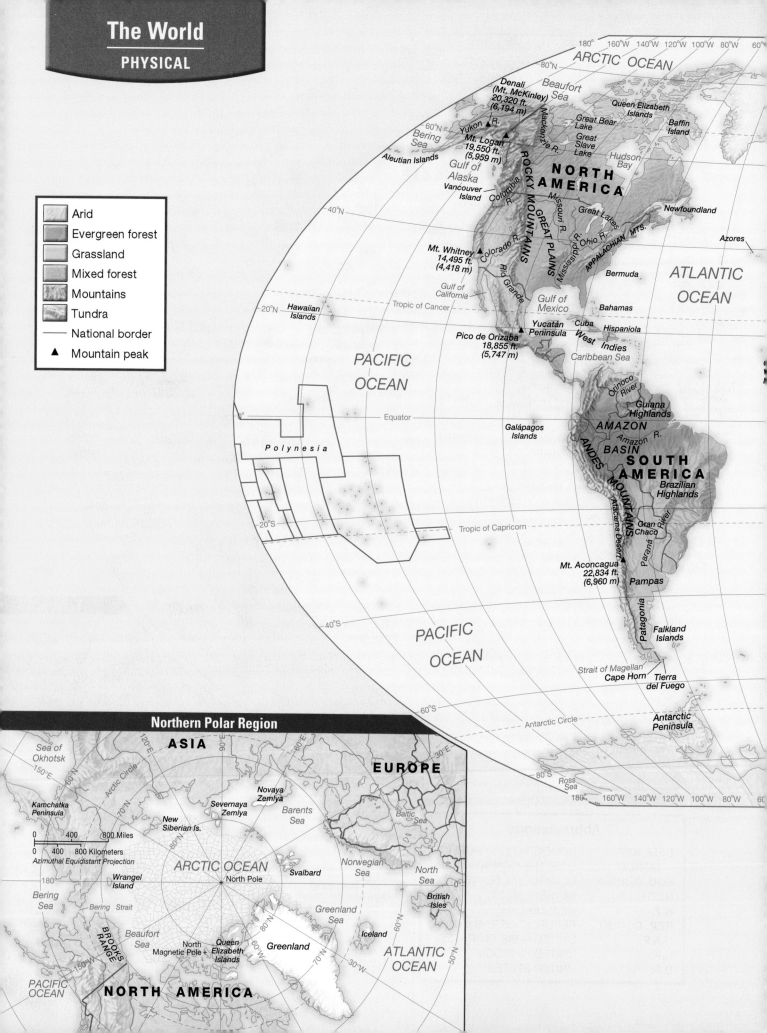

The World
PHYSICAL

Legend:
- Arid
- Evergreen forest
- Grassland
- Mixed forest
- Mountains
- Tundra
- ⎯ National border
- ▲ Mountain peak

ARCTIC OCEAN

NORTH AMERICA

Beaufort Sea
Denali (Mt. McKinley) 20,320 ft. (6,194 m)
Queen Elizabeth Islands
Great Bear Lake
Baffin Island
Yukon R.
Mt. Logan 19,550 ft. (5,959 m)
Mackenzie R.
Great Slave Lake
Hudson Bay
Bering Sea
Aleutian Islands
Gulf of Alaska
Vancouver Island
Columbia R.
ROCKY MOUNTAINS
Missouri R.
Great Lakes
Newfoundland
Mt. Whitney 14,495 ft. (4,418 m)
Colorado R.
GREAT PLAINS
Mississippi R.
Ohio R.
APPALACHIAN MTS.
Azores
Rio Grande
Bermuda
ATLANTIC OCEAN
Gulf of California
Tropic of Cancer
Gulf of Mexico
Bahamas
Hawaiian Islands
Pico de Orizaba 18,855 ft. (5,747 m)
Yucatán Peninsula
Cuba
Hispaniola
West Indies
Caribbean Sea

PACIFIC OCEAN

Equator
Galápagos Islands
Orinoco River
Guiana Highlands
AMAZON BASIN
Amazon R.
SOUTH AMERICA
Brazilian Highlands
Polynesia
ANDES MOUNTAINS
Atacama Desert
Gran Chaco
Paraná River
Tropic of Capricorn
Mt. Aconcagua 22,834 ft. (6,960 m)
Pampas
PACIFIC OCEAN
Patagonia
Falkland Islands
Strait of Magellan
Cape Horn
Tierra del Fuego
Antarctic Peninsula
Antarctic Circle
Ross Sea

Northern Polar Region

ASIA

EUROPE

Sea of Okhotsk
Kamchatka Peninsula
New Siberian Is.
Severnaya Zemlya
Novaya Zemlya
Barents Sea
Baltic Sea
ARCTIC OCEAN
North Pole
Svalbard
Norwegian Sea
North Sea
Wrangel Island
British Isles
Bering Sea
Bering Strait
BROOKS RANGE
Beaufort Sea
North Magnetic Pole
Queen Elizabeth Islands
Greenland Sea
Iceland
Greenland
ATLANTIC OCEAN
PACIFIC OCEAN
NORTH AMERICA

0   400   800 Miles
0   400   800 Kilometers
Azimuthal Equidistant Projection

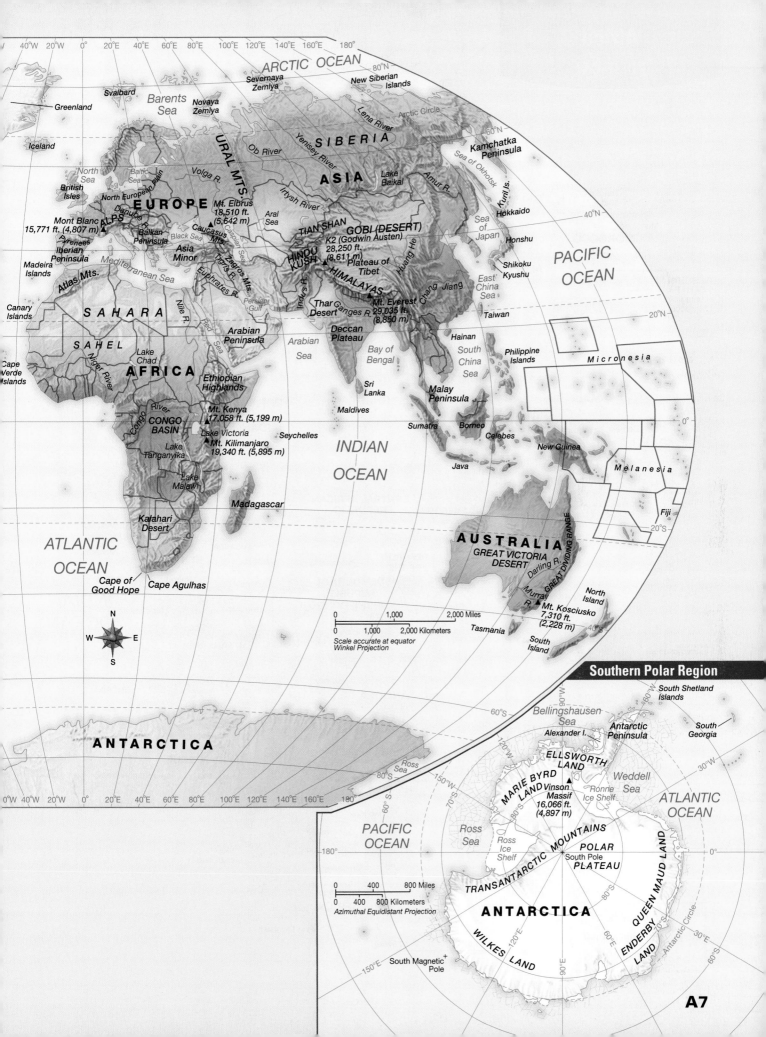

ARCTIC OCEAN

80°N

Arctic Circle

60°N

Greenland

Svalbard

Iceland

Barents Sea

Severnaya Zemlya

Novaya Zemlya

New Siberian Islands

SIBERIA

Lena River

Kamchatka Peninsula

Sea of Okhotsk

Kuril Is.

40°N

British Isles

North Sea

Baltic Sea

North European Plain

EUROPE

URAL MTS.

Ob River

Yenisey River

Irtysh River

ASIA

Lake Baikal

Amur R.

Hokkaido

Sea of Japan

Honshu

PACIFIC OCEAN

Mont Blanc
15,771 ft. (4,807 m)

ALPS

Danube R.

Balkan Peninsula

Black Sea

Mt. Elbrus
18,510 ft.
(5,642 m)

Volga R.

Caspian Sea

Caucasus Mts.

Aral Sea

TIAN SHAN

GOBI (DESERT)

K2 (Godwin Austen)
28,250 ft.
(8,611 m)

Shikoku

Kyushu

East China Sea

Pyrenees

Iberian Peninsula

Madeira Islands

Asia Minor

Mediterranean Sea

Tigris R.

Zagros Mts.

Euphrates R.

HINDU KUSH

Indus R.

Plateau of Tibet

HIMALAYAS

Huang He

Chang Jiang

Taiwan

20°N

Atlas Mts.

SAHARA

Nile R.

Red Sea

Persian Gulf

Arabian Peninsula

Thar Desert

Ganges R.

Mt. Everest 29,035 ft.
(8,850 m)

Canary Islands

SAHEL

Lake Chad

Arabian Sea

Deccan Plateau

Bay of Bengal

Hainan

South China Sea

Philippine Islands

Micronesia

Cape Verde Islands

Niger River

AFRICA

Ethiopian Highlands

Sri Lanka

Maldives

Malay Peninsula

0°

Congo River

CONGO BASIN

Mt. Kenya
17,058 ft. (5,199 m)

Sumatra

Borneo

Celebes

New Guinea

Melanesia

Lake Victoria

Mt. Kilimanjaro
19,340 ft. (5,895 m)

Seychelles

INDIAN OCEAN

Java

Lake Tanganyika

Lake Malawi

Fiji

Madagascar

20°S

ATLANTIC OCEAN

Kalahari Desert

AUSTRALIA

GREAT VICTORIA DESERT

GREAT DIVIDING RANGE

Darling R.

Cape of Good Hope

Cape Agulhas

Murray R.

North Island

Mt. Kosciusko
7,310 ft.
(2,228 m)

N
W E
S

0   1,000   2,000 Miles
0   1,000   2,000 Kilometers
Scale accurate at equator
Winkel Projection

Tasmania

South Island

40°S

ANTARCTICA

Ross Sea

60°S

80°S

0°W   40°W   20°W   0°   20°E   40°E   60°E   80°E   100°E   120°E   140°E   160°E   180°

Southern Polar Region

South Shetland Islands

Bellingshausen Sea

Alexander I.

Antarctic Peninsula

South Georgia

ELLSWORTH LAND

Weddell Sea

ATLANTIC OCEAN

60°S

MARIE BYRD LAND

Vinson Massif
16,066 ft.
(4,897 m)

Ronne Ice Shelf

30°W

PACIFIC OCEAN

180°

Ross Sea

Ross Ice Shelf

TRANSANTARCTIC MOUNTAINS

POLAR PLATEAU

South Pole

0°

QUEEN MAUD LAND

ANTARCTICA

WILKES LAND

ENDERBY LAND

Antarctic Circle

60°S

0   400   800 Miles
0   400   800 Kilometers
Azimuthal Equidistant Projection

South Magnetic Pole

A7

Africa
POLITICAL

ATLANTIC OCEAN

Madeira Islands (PORTUGAL)

EUROPE

Mediterranean Sea

ASIA

Ceuta (SPAIN)
Tangier
Rabat
Casablanca
Marrakech
Fès
Melilla (SPAIN)
Oran
Algiers
Constantine
Tunis
Sfax
Tripoli
Benghazi
TUNISIA
MOROCCO
Canary Islands (SPAIN)
El Aaiún
WESTERN SAHARA (Occupied by Morocco)
ALGERIA
LIBYA
Alexandria
Tanta
Giza
Cairo
Port Said
Suez Canal
Suez
EGYPT
Aswan
Tropic of Cancer
Tropic of Cancer

MAURITANIA
Nouakchott
Dakar
SENEGAL
GAMBIA
Banjul
Bissau
GUINEA-BISSAU
Conakry
GUINEA
SIERRA LEONE
Freetown
Monrovia
LIBERIA
Bamako
Timbuktu
Gao
MALI
Niamey
BURKINA FASO
Ouagadougou
Yamoussoukro
Abidjan
CÔTE D'IVOIRE
GHANA
Accra
TOGO
Lomé
BENIN
Porto-Novo
NIGER
Kano
NIGERIA
Abuja
Ogbomosho
Ibadan
Lagos
CAMEROON
Douala
Malabo
EQUATORIAL GUINEA
Yaoundé
N'Djamena
Lake Chad
CHAD
CENTRAL AFRICAN REPUBLIC
Bangui
Port Sudan
Omdurman
Khartoum
SUDAN
ERITREA
Asmara
DJIBOUTI
Djibouti
Addis Ababa
Dire Dawa
ETHIOPIA
Gulf of Aden
Red Sea

SÃO TOMÉ AND PRÍNCIPE
São Tomé
Gulf of Guinea
Annobón (EQUATORIAL GUINEA)
Libreville
GABON
REPUBLIC OF THE CONGO
Brazzaville
Kinshasa
DEMOCRATIC REPUBLIC OF THE CONGO
Kisangani
Kananga
Mbuji-Mayi
RWANDA
Kigali
BURUNDI
Bujumbura
UGANDA
Kampala
KENYA
Kisumu
Nairobi
Mombasa
Mogadishu
SOMALIA
Kismaayo
Lake Victoria
Mwanza
Dodoma
TANZANIA
Dar es Salaam
INDIAN OCEAN

Equator

ATLANTIC OCEAN

Ascension (UNITED KINGDOM)

CABINDA (ANGOLA)
Luanda
Lobito
ANGOLA
Huambo
Kolwezi
Lubumbashi
Kitwe
ZAMBIA
Lusaka
Lake Tanganyika
Lake Malawi
MALAWI
Lilongwe
Blantyre
COMOROS
Moroni

St. Helena (UNITED KINGDOM)

Harare
ZIMBABWE
Bulawayo
Beira
MOZAMBIQUE
Antananarivo
MADAGASCAR
Mozambique Channel
Tropic of Capricorn
Tropic of Capricorn

NAMIBIA
Windhoek
BOTSWANA
Gaborone
Johannesburg
Kimberley
Pretoria
Mbabane
Maputo
SWAZILAND
Bloemfontein
Maseru
LESOTHO
Durban
SOUTH AFRICA
Cape Town
Port Elizabeth

N W E S

Legend
— National border
⊛ National capital
• Major city

0   500   1,000 Miles
0   500   1,000 Kilometers
Azimuthal Equal-Area Projection

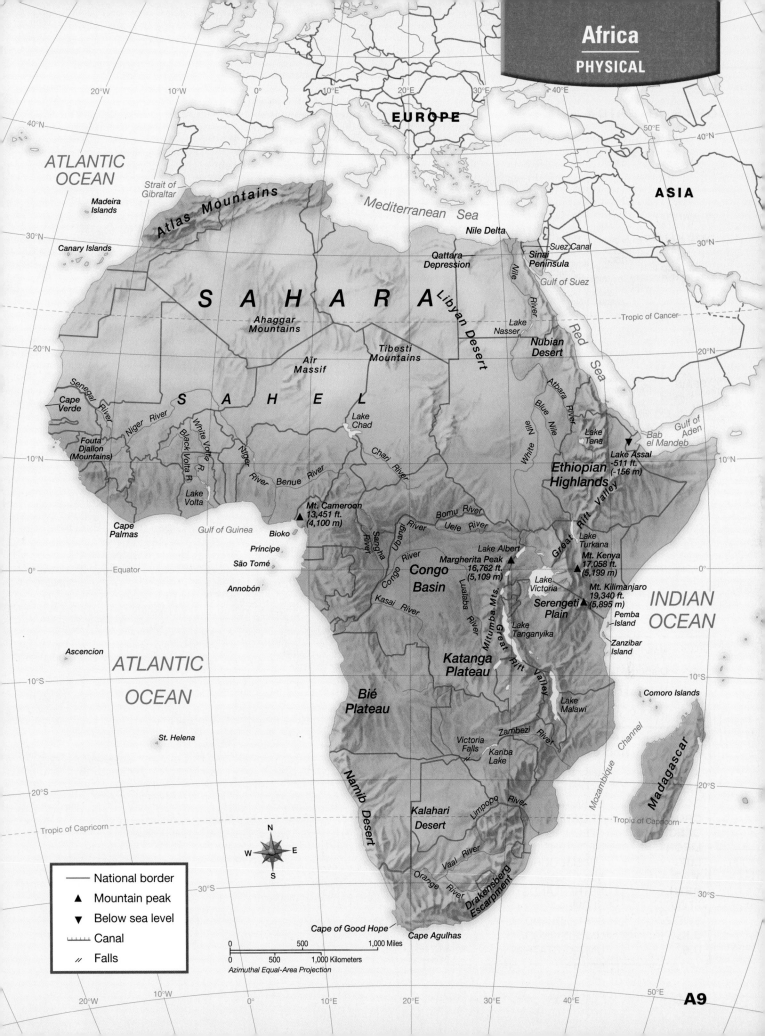

EUROPE

ASIA

ATLANTIC OCEAN

Madeira Islands

Strait of Gibraltar

Canary Islands

Atlas Mountains

Mediterranean Sea

Nile Delta

Qattara Depression

Suez Canal

Sinai Peninsula

Gulf of Suez

S A H A R A

Ahaggar Mountains

Aïr Massif

Tibesti Mountains

Libyan Desert

Lake Nasser

Tropic of Cancer

Nubian Desert

Red Sea

S A H E L

Senegal River

Cape Verde

Niger River

White Volta R.

Black Volta R.

Fouta Djallon (Mountains)

Lake Chad

Niger River

Benue River

Chari River

Atbara River

Blue Nile

White Nile

Nile

Lake Tana

Bab el Mandeb

Gulf of Aden

Lake Assal -511 ft. (-156 m) ▼

Ethiopian Highlands

Cape Palmas

Gulf of Guinea

Lake Volta

Mt. Cameroon 13,451 ft. (4,100 m) ▲

Bioko

Sangha River

Congo River

Ubangi River

Bomu River

Uele River

Great Rift Valley

Lake Turkana

Principe

São Tomé

Equator

Annobón

Congo Basin

Kasai River

Lualaba River

Lake Albert

Margherita Peak 16,762 ft. (5,109 m) ▲

Lake Victoria

Mt. Kenya 17,058 ft. (5,199 m) ▲

Mt. Kilimanjaro 19,340 ft. (5,895 m) ▲

INDIAN OCEAN

Ascencion

ATLANTIC OCEAN

Mitumba Mts.

Great Rift Valley

Lake Tanganyika

Serengeti Plain

Pemba Island

Zanzibar Island

Katanga Plateau

St. Helena

Bié Plateau

Lake Malawi

Comoro Islands

Zambezi River

Victoria Falls

Kariba Lake

Mozambique Channel

Madagascar

Namib Desert

Kalahari Desert

Limpopo River

Tropic of Capricorn

Vaal River

Orange River

Drakensberg Escarpment

N
W   E
S

Cape of Good Hope

Cape Agulhas

	Legend
——	National border
▲	Mountain peak
▼	Below sea level
⊥⊥⊥	Canal
//	Falls

0   500   1,000 Miles

0   500   1,000 Kilometers

Azimuthal Equal-Area Projection

Europe and Asia
POLITICAL

NORTH AMERICA

30°W   15°W   0°   15°E   30°E   *Barents Sea*   45°E   60°E   75°N

Novaya Zemlya   *Kara Sea*

Arctic Circle

ICELAND   *Norwegian Sea*   •Murmansk

Reykjavik

ATLANTIC
OCEAN   Bergen   NORWAY   SWEDEN   FINLAND   •Arkhangel'sk

Glasgow•   Oslo⊛   Stockholm⊛   Helsinki⊛   *Lake Onega*   RUSSIA   *Ob River*

60°N   North Sea   Göteborg   Tallinn⊛   St. Petersburg•   Nizhniy   •Perm   •Yekaterinburg   *Irtysh River*

DENMARK   Riga⊛   ESTONIA   Novgorod•   Kazan•   •Omsk

UNITED   Copenhagen⊛   LATVIA   Moscow⊛   *Kama River*   •Chelyabinsk

KINGDOM   RUSSIA   Vilnius⊛   LITHUANIA   *Volga River*   •Ufa

Dublin•   Amsterdam   •Hamburg   POLAND   Minsk⊛   BELARUS   Saratov•   Samara•   •Astana

IRELAND   NETH.   Berlin⊛   Warsaw⊛   Kiev•   *Don River*   •Qaraghandy

Birmingham•   The   GERMANY   Prague⊛   Kraków•   UKRAINE   Kharkiv•   Volgograd•   KAZAKHSTAN

London•   Hague   LUX.   CZECH   Lviv•   Dnipropetrovsk•   Rostov•   *Lake Balkhash*

Brussels•   REP.   SLOVAKIA   MOLDOVA   Donetsk•   *Aral Sea*

Paris•   BELG.   Munich•   Vienna⊛   Bratislava⊛   Chisinau⊛   Bishkek⊛   Almaty•

FRANCE   LUX.   AUST.   Budapest⊛   HUNGARY   Odessa•   UZBEKISTAN   KYRGYZSTAN

Bern⊛   LIECHT.   ROMANIA   GEORGIA   Tashkent⊛

Lyon•   SWITZ.   Ljubljana⊛   Zagreb⊛   Belgrade⊛   Bucharest•   Tbilisi⊛   Baku⊛   TURKMENISTAN

Bay of Biscay   Turin•   SLOV.   CRO.   Sarajevo⊛   BULGARIA   *Black Sea*   ARMENIA   Dushanbe⊛

45°N   Milan•   SAN   BOS. & HERZ.   SERBIA   Sofia⊛   Yerevan⊛   *Caspian Sea*   Ashgabat⊛   TAJIKISTAN

Marseille•   MARINO   Podgorica⊛   Skopje⊛   Istanbul•   Ankara⊛   AZERBAIJAN   Mashhad•   Islamabad⊛

ANDORRA   MONACO   ITALY   MONTENEGRO   MAC.   Izmir•   Yerevan   Tehran⊛   Kabul⊛

SPAIN   Corsica   Rome⊛   Tiranë⊛   TURKEY   Herat•   AFGHANISTAN

Porto•   Barcelona•   ALBANIA   GREECE   IRAN   Lahore•

PORTUGAL   Madrid⊛   Naples•   Athens⊛   Nicosia⊛   SYRIA   Baghdad⊛   Esfahan•   PAKISTAN

Lisbon•   Valencia•   Sardinia   CYPRUS   Beirut⊛   Damascus⊛   Delhi•

Gibraltar   *Balearic Is.*   Sicily   Crete   LEBANON   WEST BANK   IRAQ   New Delhi⊛

(U.K.)   Valletta⊛   ISRAEL   Amman⊛   Al Basrah•   *Indus River*   Kanpur•

MALTA   *Mediterranean Sea*   Jerusalem⊛   JORDAN   KUWAIT   *Ganges R.*

GAZA STRIP   Kuwait⊛   Manama⊛

EGYPT   BAHRAIN   Doha⊛   Muscat⊛   INDIA

Medina•   Riyadh⊛   Abu Dhabi⊛   Karachi•

Tropic of Cancer   QATAR   OMAN   Ahmadabad•

SAUDI ARABIA   UNITED ARAB EMIRATES   *Arabian Sea*

Jiddah•   Mecca•   Mumbai (Bombay)•

Red Sea   Hyderabad•

15°N   AFRICA   YEMEN   Bangalore•

Sanaa⊛   *Socotra (YEMEN)*   Chennai (Madras)•

Gulf of Aden   INDIAN OCEAN   Colombo•

SRI LANKA

MALDIVES

Male⊛

Legend

— National border
--- Disputed border
⊛ National capital
• Major city

Abbreviations

AUST.	AUSTRIA
BELG.	BELGIUM
BOS. & HERZ.	BOSNIA AND HERZEGOVINA
CRO.	CROATIA
CZECH REP.	CZECH REPUBLIC
LIECHT.	LIECHTENSTEIN
LUX.	LUXEMBOURG
MAC.	MACEDONIA
NETH.	NETHERLANDS
SLOV.	SLOVENIA
SWITZ.	SWITZERLAND
U.K.	UNITED KINGDOM
U.S.	UNITED STATES

N
W   E
S

Diego Garcia (U.K.)

0   500   1,000 Miles
0   500   1,000 Kilometers
Robinson Projection

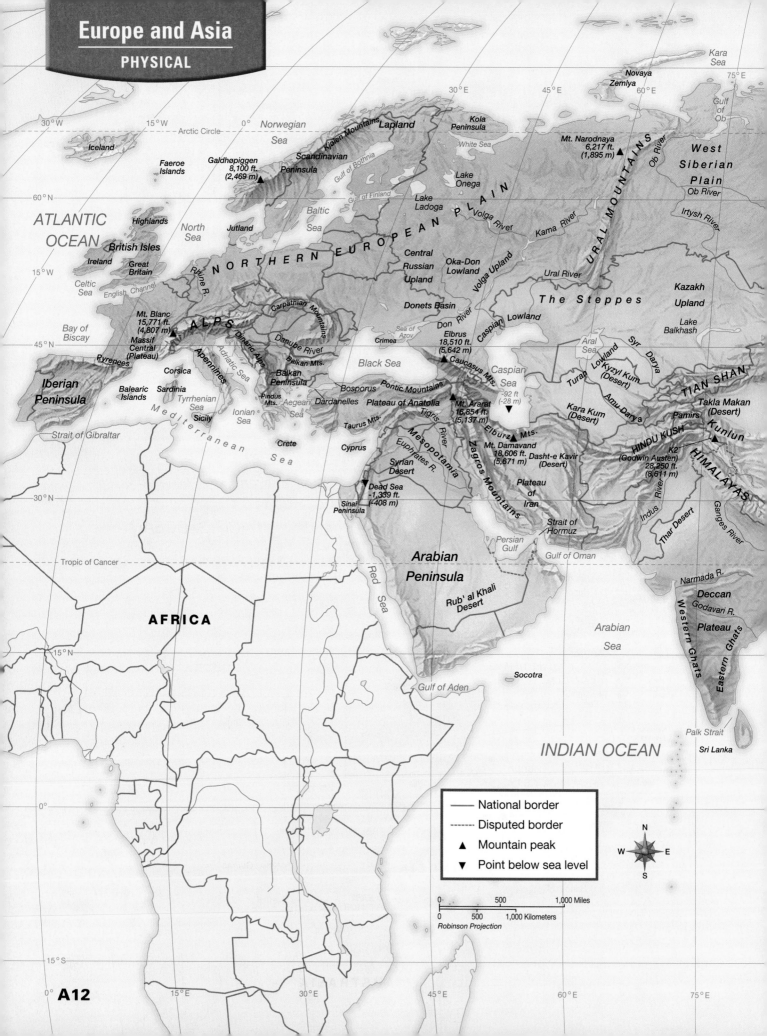

Europe and Asia
PHYSICAL

Kara Sea

Novaya Zemlya

Gulf of Ob

75°E

Arctic Circle

Iceland

Faeroe Islands

Norwegian Sea

Kjølen Mountains   Lapland

Scandinavian Peninsula

Galdhøpiggen 8,100 ft. (2,469 m) ▲

Kola Peninsula

White Sea

Lake Onega

Mt. Narodnaya 6,217 ft. (1,895 m) ▲

West Siberian Plain

Ob River

ATLANTIC OCEAN

Highlands

North Sea

Jutland

Gulf of Bothnia

Gulf of Finland

Baltic Sea

Lake Ladoga

Volga River

Kama River

URAL MOUNTAINS

Ob River

Irtysh River

British Isles

Ireland

Great Britain

Celtic Sea

English Channel

Rhine R.

NORTHERN EUROPEAN PLAIN

Central Russian Upland

Oka-Don Lowland

Donets Basin

Volga Upland

Ural River

The Steppes

Kazakh Upland

Lake Balkhash

Bay of Biscay

Mt. Blanc 15,771 ft. (4,807 m) ▲

Massif Central (Plateau)

Pyrenees

ALPS

Carpathian Mountains

Dinaric Alps

Danube River

Balkan Mts.

Don River

Sea of Azov

Crimea

Caspian Lowland

Elbrus 18,510 ft. (5,642 m) ▲

Caspian Sea -92 ft (-28 m) ▼

Aral Sea

Turan Lowland

Syr Darya

Kyzyl Kum (Desert)

Amu Darya

TIAN SHAN

Iberian Peninsula

Corsica

Balearic Islands

Sardinia

Apennines

Adriatic Sea

Balkan Peninsula

Pindus Mts.

Tyrrhenian Sea

Aegean Sea

Sicily

Ionian Sea

Dardanelles

Bosporus

Pontic Mountains

Plateau of Anatolia

Caucasus Mts.

Mt. Ararat 16,854 ft. (5,137 m) ▲

Tigris River

Elburz Mts.

Mt. Damavand 18,606 ft. (5,671 m) ▲

Dasht-e Kavir (Desert)

Kara Kum (Desert)

Takla Makan (Desert)

Pamirs

HINDU KUSH

K2 (Godwin Austen) 28,250 ft. (8,611 m) ▲

Kunlun

HIMALAYAS

Black Sea

Cyprus

Crete

Mediterranean Sea

Strait of Gibraltar

Taurus Mts.

Euphrates R.

Syrian Desert

Mesopotamia

Zagros Mountains

Plateau of Iran

Strait of Hormuz

Indus

Thar Desert

Ganges River

Dead Sea -1,339 ft. (-408 m) ▼

Sinai Peninsula

Red Sea

Tropic of Cancer

AFRICA

Arabian Peninsula

Rub' al Khali Desert

Persian Gulf

Gulf of Oman

Arabian Sea

Narmada R.

Deccan

Godavari R.

Plateau

Western Ghats

Eastern Ghats

Gulf of Aden

Socotra

Palk Strait

Sri Lanka

INDIAN OCEAN

	National border
	Disputed border
▲	Mountain peak
▼	Point below sea level

N W E S

0   500   1,000 Miles

0   500   1,000 Kilometers

Robinson Projection

A12

ARCTIC OCEAN

Laptev Sea
New Siberian Islands
East Siberian Sea
Taymyr Peninsula
75°N
Kolyma Lowland
Wrangel Island
165°W
Chukchi Sea
North Siberian Lowland
90°E
105°E
120°E
135°E
150°E
165°E
180°
Arctic Circle
Central Siberian Plateau
Verkhoyansk Range
Kolyma R.
Chukchi Peninsula
S I B E R I A
Kolyma Mountains
Bering Strait
Lena River
60°N
Angara River
Korya Range
Central Range
Kamchatka Peninsula
Bering Sea
Stanovoy Range
Dzhugdzhur Range
Sea of Okhotsk
Lake Baikal
Yablonovy Range
Sayan Mountains
Amur River
Sakhalin
Yenisey R.
Greater Khingan Range
Sikhote Alin Range
Kuril Islands
A l t a i M o u n t a i n s
45°N
Junggar Basin
Plateau of Mongolia
Manchurian Plain
Hokkaido
▼ Turpan Depression
-505 ft.
(-154 m)
Gobi (Desert)
Sea of Japan
Tarim Basin
Qilian Shan
Korean Peninsula
Honshu
NORTH PACIFIC OCEAN
Shan
North China Plain
Yellow Sea
▲ Mt. Fuji
12,388 ft.
(3,776 m)
Plateau of Tibet
Huang He
Kanchenjunga
28,208 ft.
(8,598 m)
Kyushu
Shikoku
30°N
Mt. Everest
29,035 ft.
(8,850 m)
Sichuan Basin
Chang Jiang
East China Sea
Ganges R.
Irrawaddy River
Ryukyu Islands
Tropic of Cancer
Taiwan
Philippine Sea
Mekong R.
Gulf of Tonkin
Bay of Bengal
Khorat Plateau
Hainan
South China Sea
Luzon
15°N
Indochina Peninsula
Andaman Islands
Philippine Islands
Andaman Sea
Gulf of Thailand
Palawan
Sulu Sea
Nicobar Islands
Mindanao
Malay Peninsula
Celebes Sea
Strait of Malacca
Halmahera
0° Equator
Moluccas
SOUTH PACIFIC OCEAN
Sumatra
Borneo
Celebes
Ceram
G r e a t e r   S u n d a
▲ Rantekombola
11,335 ft.
(3,455 m)
Banda Sea
I s l a n d s
Java Sea
Lombok
New Guinea
Java
Bali
Sumbawa
Flores
Timor
Lesser Sunda Islands
Timor Sea
Arafura Sea
Sumba
15°S
AUSTRALIA
165°E
90°E
105°E
120°E
135°E
150°E
A13

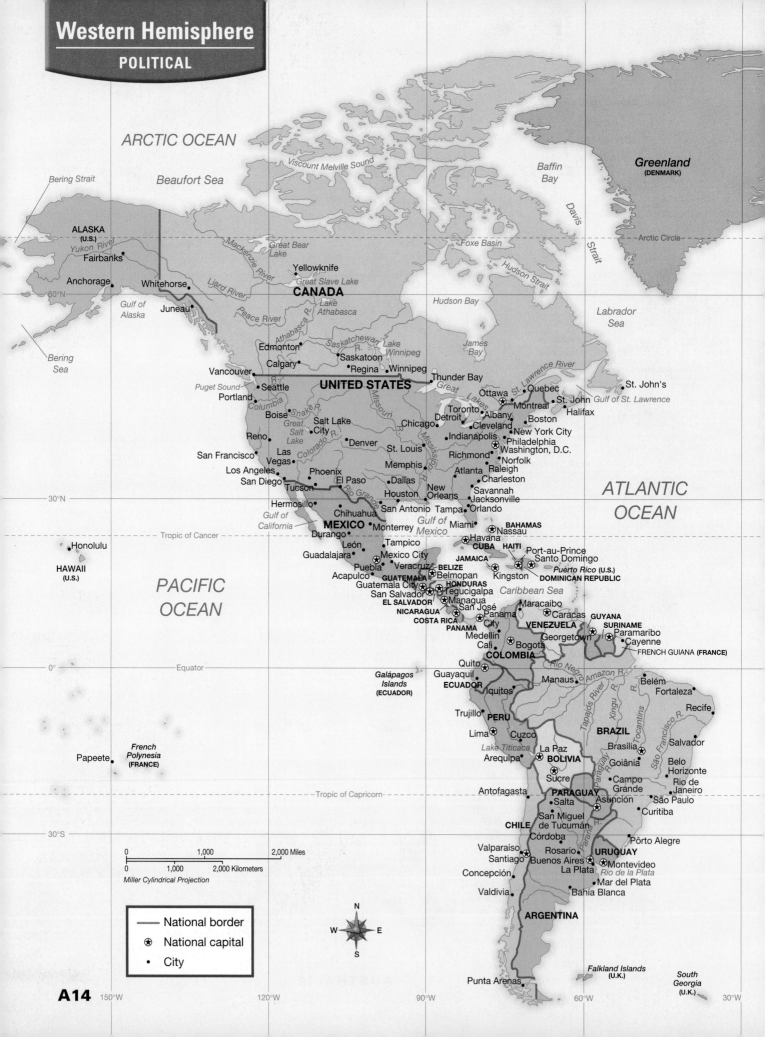

ARCTIC OCEAN

North Magnetic Pole +
Queen Elizabeth Islands

Ellesmere
Island

Melville Island

Devon Island

Viscount Melville Sound

Baffin
Bay

Greenland

Bering Strait
Point Barrow

Beaufort Sea

Banks
Island

B r o o k s   R a n g e

Victoria
Island

Baffin
Island

Davis
Strait

Arctic Circle

Mt. McKinley
20,320 ft.
(6,194 m)

Yukon

River

Great Bear
Lake

C

Great Slave
Lake

Foxe Basin

Hudson Strait

Cape
Farewell

60°N

Yukon
Plateau

Mackenzie Mts.

Mackenzie River

A

Mt. Logan
19,550 ft.
(5,959 m)

Gulf of
Alaska

Liard R.

N

Hudson Bay

James
Bay

A

Labrador
Sea

Alaska Range

Alaska
Peninsula

Kodiak
Island

Bering Sea

Aleutian Islands

Queen Charlotte
Islands

Peace River

Coast Mountains

ROCKY

Athabasca R.

Lake
Athabasca

Saskatchewan
River

D

Lake
Winnipeg

I

A

N

S   H   I   E   L   D

Labrador

Newfoundland

Vancouver Island

Puget Sound

Cascade Range

Coast Ranges

Snake R.

MOUNTAINS

GREAT

NORTH AMERICA

Great Lakes

Niagara
Falls

St. Lawrence R.

Gulf of St. Lawrence

Nova Scotia

Sierra Nevada

Great
Salt Lake

GREAT
BASIN

Black
Hills

PLAINS

Missouri R.

Platte R.

Mississippi

Ohio R.

APPALACHIAN MTS.

Bay of Fundy

Long Island

Mt. Whitney
14,495 ft. (4,418 m)

Death Valley
(lowest point in N.A.)
-282 ft. (-86 m)

Colorado R.

Arkansas

Ozark
Plateau

INTERIOR
PLAINS

R.

River

Cape Cod

Chesapeake Bay

Cape Hatteras

ATLANTIC
OCEAN

30°N

Sonoran
Desert

Rio

Grande

COASTAL   PLAIN

Gulf of
Mexico

Bahamas

Hawaiian Islands

Tropic of Cancer

Baja California

Gulf of California

Sierra Madre Occidental

Sierra Madre Oriental

Pico de Orizaba
18,855 ft.
(5,747 m)

Yucatán
Peninsula

Cuba

Greater Antilles

Hispaniola

Puerto Rico

Lesser Antilles

Lake
Nicaragua

Caribbean
Sea

Lake
Maracaibo

PACIFIC

OCEAN

Isthmus
of Panama

Llanos

Orinoco
R.

Angel Falls

Guiana
Highlands

Chimborazo
20,702 ft.
(6,310 m)

Galápagos
Islands

Equator

Rio Negro

Amazon R.

AMAZON

Cape
São
Roque

Line

Islands

Marquesas
Islands

ANDES

BASIN

Tapajós River

Xingu River

Tocantins R.

São Francisco River

Huascarán
22,205 ft.
(6,768 m)

Mato
Grosso
Plateau

Brazilian

Cook
Islands

Tuamotu

Archipelago

Society
Islands

Lake Titicaca

Altiplano

Atacama Desert

Paraguay R.

Highlands

SOUTH
AMERICA

Tropic of Capricorn

MOUNTAINS

Gran
Chaco

Paraná R.

Iguazú Falls

Uruguay R.

0   1,000   2,000 Miles

0   1,000   2,000 Kilometers

Miller Cylindrical Projection

Mt. Aconcagua
22,834 ft.
(6,960 m)

Pampas

Rio de la Plata

30°S

▲ Mountain peak

▼ Point below sea level

National border

≋ Waterfall

N

W   E

S

Patagonia

Valdés Peninsula
(lowest point in S.A.)
-131 ft. (-40 m)

Falkland Islands

30°W

Strait of Magellan

Tierra del
Fuego

Cape Horn

South
Georgia

A15

150°W

120°W

90°W

60°W

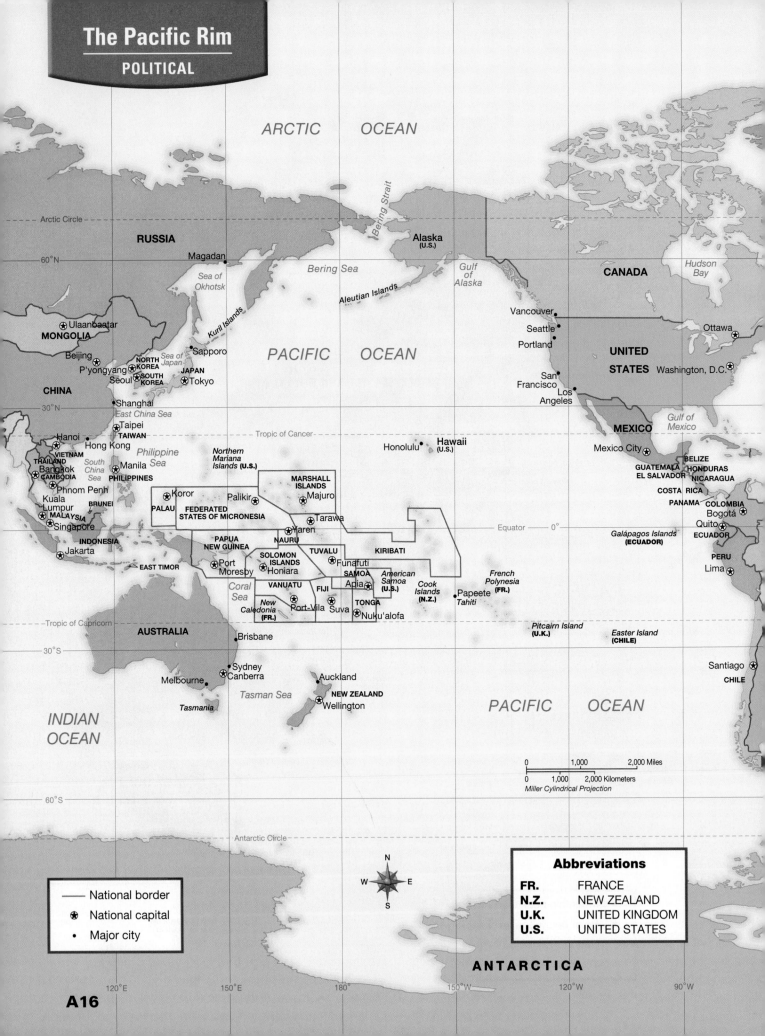

The Pacific Rim
POLITICAL

ARCTIC   OCEAN

Arctic Circle

RUSSIA

60°N   Magadan

Sea of Okhotsk   *Bering Sea*

Aleutian Islands

Alaska (U.S.)

Gulf of Alaska

Hudson Bay

CANADA

Vancouver
Seattle
Portland

⊛ Ulaanbaatar

MONGOLIA

Beijing

CHINA

Kuril Islands

Sapporo

NORTH KOREA
P'yongyang
Seoul
SOUTH KOREA

Sea of Japan

JAPAN
⊛ Tokyo

PACIFIC   OCEAN

San Francisco
Los Angeles

UNITED STATES   Washington, D.C.

30°N   Shanghai

East China Sea

Taipei
TAIWAN

Hanoi
VIETNAM
Hong Kong

Philippine Sea

South China Sea

THAILAND
Bangkok
CAMBODIA
Phnom Penh

Manila
PHILIPPINES

Kuala Lumpur
MALAYSIA
BRUNEI

Singapore

INDONESIA

Jakarta

EAST TIMOR

Tropic of Cancer

Northern Mariana Islands (U.S.)

⊛ Koror
PALAU
Palikir ⊛

FEDERATED STATES OF MICRONESIA

Honolulu • **Hawaii** (U.S.)

MEXICO

Gulf of Mexico

Mexico City ⊛

BELIZE
GUATEMALA   **HONDURAS**
EL SALVADOR   **NICARAGUA**
COSTA RICA
PANAMA   **COLOMBIA**
Bogotá

MARSHALL ISLANDS
Majuro ⊛

Tarawa

PAPUA NEW GUINEA
Port Moresby ⊛

Yaren ⊛
NAURU

TUVALU
Funafuti ⊛

KIRIBATI

Equator   0°

Galápagos Islands (ECUADOR)

Quito ⊛
ECUADOR

PERU
Lima ⊛

SOLOMON ISLANDS
⊛ Honiara

SAMOA
Apia ⊛

American Samoa (U.S.)

Cook Islands (N.Z.)

French Polynesia (FR.)

Coral Sea

VANUATU
Port-Vila ⊛

New Caledonia (FR.)

FIJI
Suva ⊛

TONGA
⊛ Nuku'alofa

Papeete
Tahiti

Tropic of Capricorn

AUSTRALIA

Brisbane •

Pitcairn Island (U.K.)

Easter Island (CHILE)

30°S

Sydney
Melbourne   Canberra ⊛

Auckland

PACIFIC   OCEAN

Santiago •
CHILE

Tasman Sea

Tasmania

NEW ZEALAND
⊛ Wellington

INDIAN OCEAN

0   1,000   2,000 Miles

0   1,000   2,000 Kilometers

Miller Cylindrical Projection

60°S

Antarctic Circle

N
W   E
S

—— National border

⊛ National capital

• Major city

Abbreviations	
FR.	FRANCE
N.Z.	NEW ZEALAND
U.K.	UNITED KINGDOM
U.S.	UNITED STATES

ANTARCTICA

A16

120°E   150°E   180°   150°W   120°W   90°W

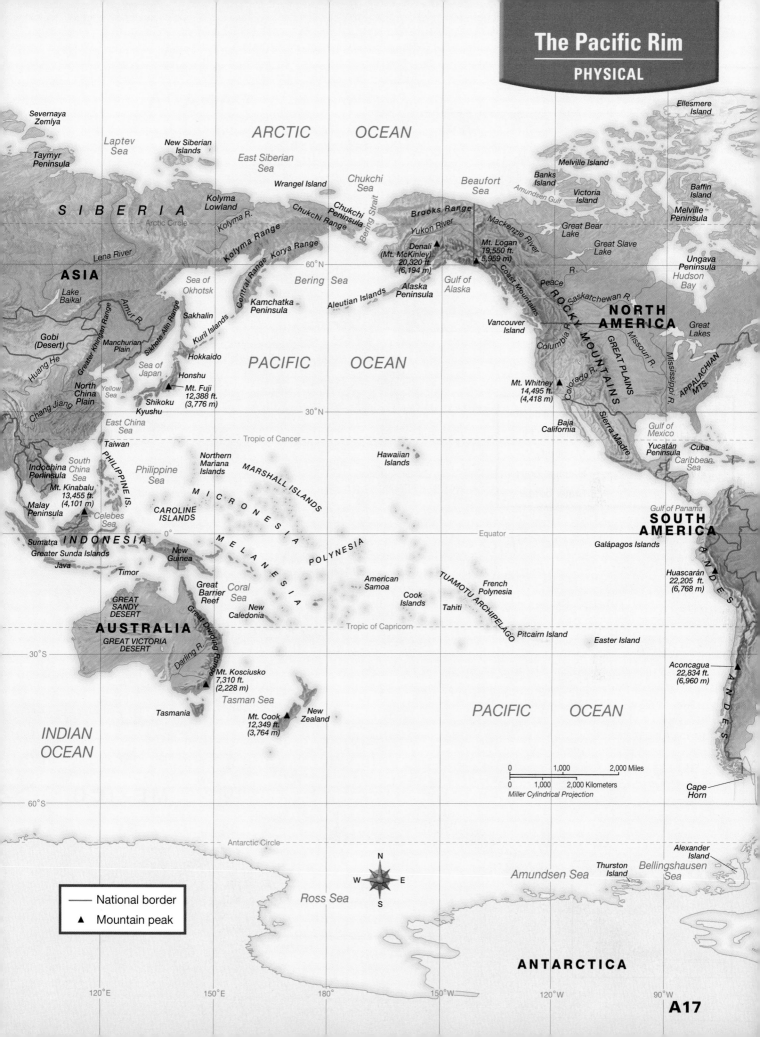

Severnaya Zemlya

Taymyr Peninsula

Laptev Sea

New Siberian Islands

ARCTIC OCEAN

East Siberian Sea

Ellesmere Island

Wrangel Island

Chukchi Sea

Beaufort Sea

Melville Island

Banks Island

Amundsen Gulf

Victoria Island

Baffin Island

Melville Peninsula

SIBERIA

Kolyma Lowland

Arctic Circle

Kolyma R.

Chukchi Range

Chukchi Peninsula

Brooks Range

Yukon River

Mackenzie River

Great Bear Lake

Great Slave Lake

Lena River

Kolyma Range

Korya Range

60°N

Denali (Mt. McKinley) 20,320 ft. (6,194 m) ▲

Mt. Logan 19,550 ft. 5,959 m) ▲

Peace R.

Saskatchewan R.

ROCKY MOUNTAINS

Ungava Peninsula

Hudson Bay

ASIA

Lake Baikal

Amur R.

Greater Khingan Range

Central Range

Sea of Okhotsk

Bering Sea

Kamchatka Peninsula

Aleutian Islands

Alaska Peninsula

Gulf of Alaska

Coast Mountains

NORTH AMERICA

Missouri R.

Great Lakes

Gobi (Desert)

Manchurian Plain

Siknote Alin Range

Sakhalin

Kuril Islands

Vancouver Island

Columbia R.

GREAT PLAINS

Mississippi R.

APPALACHIAN MTS.

Huang He

North China Plain

Yellow Sea

Hokkaido

PACIFIC OCEAN

Mt. Whitney 14,495 ft. (4,418 m) ▲

Colorado R.

Sierra Madre

Chang Jiang

Honshu

▲ Mt. Fuji 12,388 ft. (3,776 m)

30°N

Baja California

Gulf of Mexico

Shikoku Kyushu

East China Sea

Tropic of Cancer

Yucatán Peninsula

Cuba

Caribbean Sea

Taiwan

South China Sea

Indochina Peninsula

PHILIPPINE IS.

Philippine Sea

Northern Mariana Islands

MARSHALL ISLANDS

Hawaiian Islands

Mt. Kinabalu 13,455 ft. (4,101 m) ▲

Malay Peninsula

Celebes Sea

CAROLINE ISLANDS

MICRONESIA

Gulf of Panama

SOUTH AMERICA

Sumatra

INDONESIA

0°

New Guinea

MELANESIA

POLYNESIA

Equator

Galápagos Islands

ANDES

Greater Sunda Islands

Java

Timor

Great Barrier Reef

Coral Sea

American Samoa

Cook Islands

TUAMOTU ARCHIPELAGO

French Polynesia

Huascarán 22,205 ft. (6,768 m) ▲

GREAT SANDY DESERT

AUSTRALIA

New Caledonia

Tahiti

Tropic of Capricorn

Pitcairn Island

Easter Island

GREAT VICTORIA DESERT

Great Dividing Range

Darling R.

Mt. Kosciusko 7,310 ft. (2,228 m) ▲

30°S

Aconcagua 22,834 ft. (6,960 m) ▲

Tasmania

Tasman Sea

Mt. Cook 12,349 ft. (3,764 m) ▲

New Zealand

PACIFIC OCEAN

INDIAN OCEAN

| 0 | 1,000 | 2,000 Miles |
| 0 | 1,000 | 2,000 Kilometers |

Miller Cylindrical Projection

Cape Horn

60°S

Antarctic Circle

Alexander Island

Thurston Island

Bellingshausen Sea

Amundsen Sea

| | National border |
| ▲ | Mountain peak |

Ross Sea

N W E S

ANTARCTICA

120°E   150°E   180°   150°W   120°W   90°W

A17

United States
POLITICAL

RUSSIA

ARCTIC OCEAN

ALASKA

CANADA

Yukon River

• Fairbanks

Bering Sea

• Anchorage

Yukon River

Gulf of Alaska

Juneau ★

PACIFIC OCEAN

0   250   500 Miles
0   250   500 Kilometers

CANADA

Legend:
- Northeast
- South
- Middle West
- West
- ⊛ National capital
- ★ State capital
- • Major city
- National border
- State border

PACIFIC OCEAN

Seattle
★ Tacoma
Olympia   Spokane
WASHINGTON

Portland •   *Columbia River*
★ Salem

• Eugene
OREGON   **IDAHO**

★ Boise

Great Falls •

Helena ★ **MONTANA**

Billings •
Yellowstone R.

Snake River

Pocatello •

WYOMING

Casper •

Cheyenne ★

NEVADA

Lake Tahoe   Reno •
Sacramento ★   ★ Carson City

San Francisco • Oakland •
• San Jose

• Fresno

CALIFORNIA

• Bakersfield

Los Angeles •   • San Bernardino

San Diego •

Great Salt Lake

Ogden •
★ Salt Lake City
• Provo

UTAH

Colorado River

Las Vegas •

Flagstaff •

ARIZONA

★ Phoenix

Tucson •

COLORADO

Denver ★

Colorado Springs •

Pueblo •

Santa Fe ★
Albuquerque •

NEW MEXICO

Roswell •

El Paso •
Rio Grande

MEXICO

Gulf of California

N
W   E
S

0   250   500 Miles
0   250   500 Kilometers
Albers Equal-Area Projection

PACIFIC OCEAN

Honolulu ★

HAWAII

Hilo •

20° N

0   100   200 Miles
0   100   200 Kilometers

A18

CANADA

MAINE
★ Augusta

*Lake Champlain
VERMONT
Burlington ● Montpelier
NEW HAMPSHIRE
● Portland
NEW YORK
Manchester ● Concord
● Boston

NORTH DAKOTA
Grand Forks ●
Fargo ●
● Bismarck

Lake of the Woods

Lake Superior

MICHIGAN

MINNESOTA
Duluth ●

Sault Sainte Marie ●

Lake Huron

St. Lawrence River

Syracuse ●
Rochester ●
● Albany
Hartford ●
MASSACHUSETTS
Providence
RHODE ISLAND
CONNECTICUT

SOUTH DAKOTA
Rapid City ●
● Pierre ★

Sioux Falls ●

St. Paul ★
Minneapolis ★

Green Bay ●

WISCONSIN

Madison ★
Milwaukee ●

Lake Michigan

Grand Rapids ●

Lansing ★

Flint ●

Detroit ●

Lake St. Clair
Lake Erie

Lake Ontario
Buffalo ●

Cleveland ●

PENNSYLVANIA

Newark ●
● New York City
Trenton ●
NEW JERSEY
Philadelphia ●
Wilmington ●
● Dover
DELAWARE

NEBRASKA

Sioux City ●

IOWA
Cedar Rapids ●
Davenport ●

Rockford ●
Chicago ●

ILLINOIS

Gary ●
South Bend ●

Toledo ●
Akron ●

OHIO
Columbus ★

Wheeling ●

Harrisburg ★
Pittsburgh ●

Baltimore ●
Annapolis ★
Washington, D.C. ✪
MARYLAND

Omaha ●

Des Moines ★

Peoria ●
Decatur ●
Springfield ★

INDIANA

Indianapolis ★

Dayton ●
Cincinnati ●

WEST VIRGINIA
Charleston ●

VIRGINIA
Richmond ●

Chesapeake Bay

Lincoln ★

Platte River

Missouri River

Topeka ★

Kansas City ●

St. Louis ●

Louisville ●
Frankfort ★
Lexington ●

Ohio River

Newport News ●
Roanoke ●
Norfolk ●
Virginia Beach ●

KANSAS

Arkansas River

Wichita ●

Jefferson City ★

MISSOURI

Springfield ●

Evansville ●

KENTUCKY

Knoxville ●
Nashville ★
Chattanooga ●

Winston-Salem ●
Charlotte ●

Greensboro ●
● Raleigh ★
NORTH CAROLINA

OKLAHOMA

Tulsa ●

ARKANSAS

Memphis ●

TENNESSEE

Huntsville ●

SOUTH CAROLINA
Columbia ★

Amarillo ●

Oklahoma City ★

Fort Smith ●
Little Rock ★

Birmingham ●

Atlanta ★

GEORGIA

Charleston ●

Lubbock ●

Red River

Lake Texoma

MISSISSIPPI

Arkansas River

ALABAMA

Macon ●

Columbus ●

Savannah ●

Fort Worth ●

Meridian ●

Montgomery ★

Abilene ●
Dallas ●

Jackson ★

Odessa ●

TEXAS

Shreveport ●

LOUISIANA

Mobile ●

Tallahassee ★

Jacksonville ●

Austin ★

Beaumont ●

Baton Rouge ★

Biloxi ●

FLORIDA

Orlando ●

Houston ●

San Antonio ●

New Orleans ●

Tampa ●
St. Petersburg ●

Lake Okeechobee

West Palm Beach ●

BAHAMAS

Laredo ●

Corpus Christi ●

Rio Grande

Miami ●

Gulf of Mexico

ATLANTIC OCEAN

CUBA

Mississippi River

Missouri River

100°W   90°W   80°W   70°W

50°N

40°N

70°W

30°N

80°W

90°W

100°W

A19

United States
PHYSICAL

CANADA

120°W   110°W

Fort Peck
Lake

ARCTIC OCEAN

70°N

120°W

RUSSIA

170°E

Brooks Range

60°N

Seward ALASKA
Peninsula   Yukon   River

Arctic Circle

St. Lawrence
Island

Bering Strait

CANADA

Mt. McKinley
20,320 ft.
(6,194 m) △

Alaska   Range

Yukon River

60°N

Bering
Sea

180°

Gulf of
Alaska

0   250   500 Miles

0   250   500 Kilometers

Kodiak
Island

50°N

Aleutian   Islands

170°W   160°W   150°W   140°W   130°W

40°N

Cape
Mendocino

Legend:

	Arid
	Evergreen forest
	Grassland
	Mixed forest
	Mountains
	Tundra
—	National border
—	State border
▲	Mountain peak
△	Highest point
▽	Lowest point

**PACIFIC
OCEAN**

WA

Mt. Rainier
14,410 ft. (4,392 m) ▲

▲ Mt. St. Helens
8,366 ft. (2,550 m)

Columbia River

▲ Mt. Hood
11,237 ft.
(3,425 m)

Coast Ranges

Cascade   Range

Range

ROCKY

Bitterroot Range

MT

Yellowstone River

Bighorn Mts.

ID

Salmon
River
Mountains

OR

Columbia
Plateau

Snake River

Teton Range

Wind River Range

WY

Great Divide
Basin

Coast Ranges

Sacramento River

Sierra Nevada

Central

San Joaquin Valley

Pyramid
Lake

Donner Pass
Lake
Tahoe

NV

**GREAT
BASIN**

Great
Salt
Lake

Wasatch Range

Uinta Mts.

Mt. Elbert
14,433 ft.
(4,399 m) ▲

**M
O
U
N
T
A
I
N
S**

Front Range

Mt. Whitney
14,495 ft.
(4,418 m) ▲

UT

Colorado River

Lake
Powell

CO

San Juan
Mts.

Sangre de Cristo Mts.

30°N

Point
Conception

CA

Death
Valley

-282 ft. ▽
(-86 m)

Mojave
Desert

Lake
Mead

Grand
Canyon

Colorado
Plateau

Channel
Islands

Salton
Sea

AZ

NM

130°W

Imperial
Valley

**Sonoran
Desert**

Baldy Peak
11,403 ft.
(3,476 m) ▲

Guadalupe Peak
8,749 ft.
(2,667 m) ▲

Rio Grande

MEXICO

N
W   E
S

160°W PACIFIC OCEAN 155°W

Kauai

Niihau

Oahu

Molokai

20°N

HAWAII Lanai Maui
Kahoolawe

Hawaii

Mauna Kea
13,796 ft.
(4,205 m) ▲

0   100   200 Miles

0   100   200 Kilometers

0   250   500 Miles

0   250   500 Kilometers

Albers Equal-Area Projection

20°N

120°W   110°W

Oceans and Rivers of the World

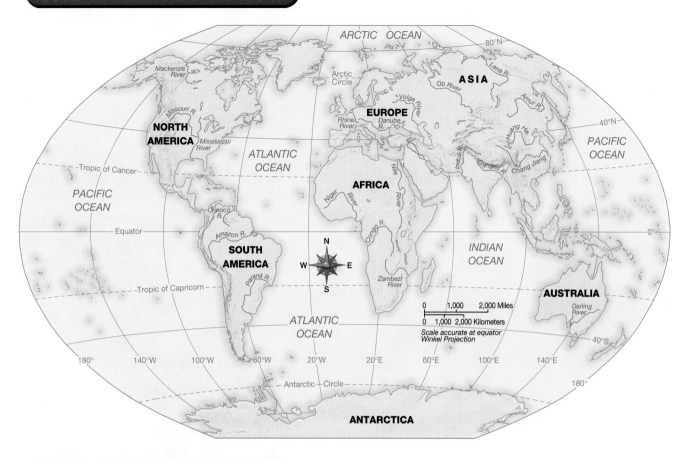

Mountain Ranges of the World

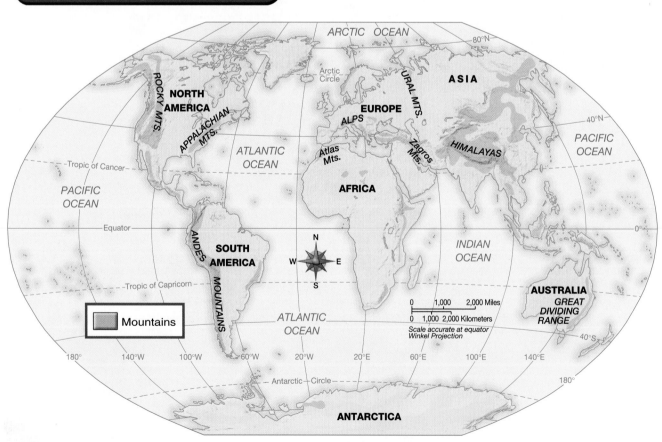

Plains of the World

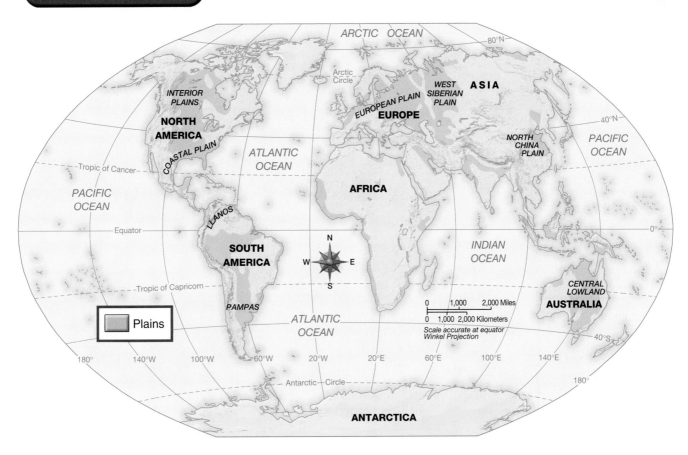

ARCTIC OCEAN

80°N

Arctic Circle

INTERIOR PLAINS

NORTH AMERICA

COASTAL PLAIN

ATLANTIC OCEAN

Tropic of Cancer

40°N

PACIFIC OCEAN

EUROPEAN PLAIN

EUROPE

WEST SIBERIAN PLAIN

ASIA

NORTH CHINA PLAIN

PACIFIC OCEAN

PACIFIC OCEAN

AFRICA

LLANOS

Equator

SOUTH AMERICA

N
W   E
S

INDIAN OCEAN

Tropic of Capricorn

CENTRAL LOWLAND

AUSTRALIA

PAMPAS

ATLANTIC OCEAN

0   1,000   2,000 Miles
0 1,000 2,000 Kilometers
Scale accurate at equator
Winkel Projection

40°S

180°   140°W   100°W   60°W   20°W   20°E   60°E   100°E   140°E   180°

Antarctic Circle

ANTARCTICA

Plains

Deserts of the World

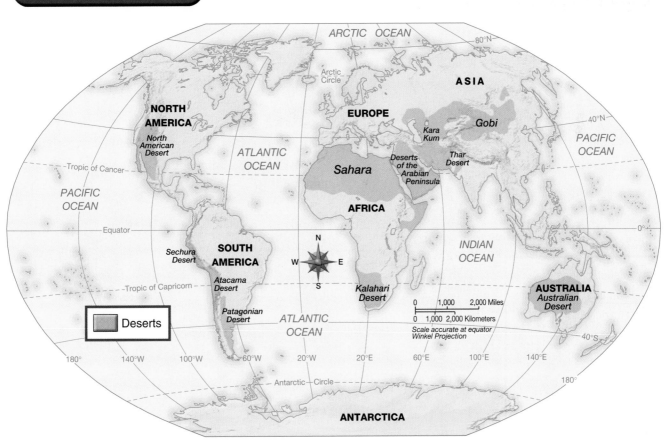

ARCTIC OCEAN

80°N

Arctic Circle

NORTH AMERICA

North American Desert

ATLANTIC OCEAN

Tropic of Cancer

EUROPE

ASIA

Kara Kum

Gobi

40°N

PACIFIC OCEAN

PACIFIC OCEAN

Sahara

Deserts of the Arabian Peninsula

Thar Desert

AFRICA

Equator

Sechura Desert

SOUTH AMERICA

N
W   E
S

INDIAN OCEAN

Atacama Desert

Tropic of Capricorn

Kalahari Desert

AUSTRALIA
Australian Desert

Patagonian Desert

ATLANTIC OCEAN

0   1,000   2,000 Miles
0 1,000 2,000 Kilometers
Scale accurate at equator
Winkel Projection

40°S

180°   140°W   100°W   60°W   20°W   20°E   60°E   100°E   140°E   180°

Antarctic Circle

ANTARCTICA

Deserts

A23

Climates of the World

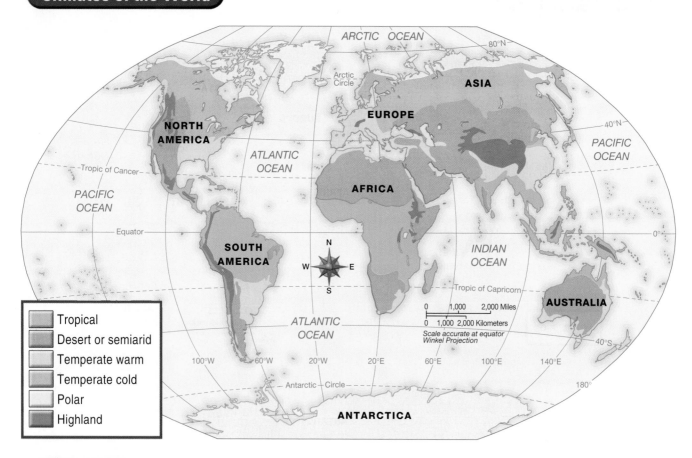

Legend:
- Tropical
- Desert or semiarid
- Temperate warm
- Temperate cold
- Polar
- Highland

ARCTIC OCEAN
80°N
Arctic Circle
ASIA
EUROPE
NORTH AMERICA
40°N
ATLANTIC OCEAN
PACIFIC OCEAN
Tropic of Cancer
PACIFIC OCEAN
AFRICA
Equator
0°
SOUTH AMERICA
INDIAN OCEAN
Tropic of Capricorn
AUSTRALIA
40°S
ATLANTIC OCEAN
100°W 60°W 20°W 20°E 60°E 100°E 140°E 180°
Antarctic Circle
ANTARCTICA

0 1,000 2,000 Miles
0 1,000 2,000 Kilometers
Scale accurate at equator
Winkel Projection

World Land Use

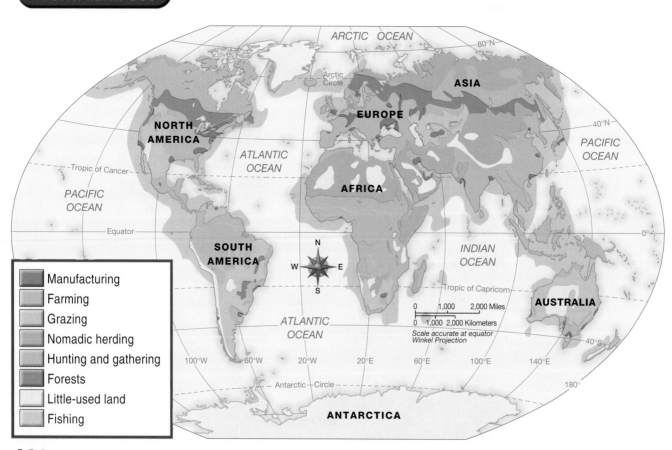

Legend:
- Manufacturing
- Farming
- Grazing
- Nomadic herding
- Hunting and gathering
- Forests
- Little-used land
- Fishing

ARCTIC OCEAN
80°N
Arctic Circle
ASIA
EUROPE
NORTH AMERICA
40°N
ATLANTIC OCEAN
PACIFIC OCEAN
Tropic of Cancer
PACIFIC OCEAN
AFRICA
Equator
0°
SOUTH AMERICA
INDIAN OCEAN
Tropic of Capricorn
AUSTRALIA
40°S
ATLANTIC OCEAN
100°W 60°W 20°W 20°E 60°E 100°E 140°E 180°
Antarctic Circle
ANTARCTICA

0 1,000 2,000 Miles
0 1,000 2,000 Kilometers
Scale accurate at equator
Winkel Projection

World Religions

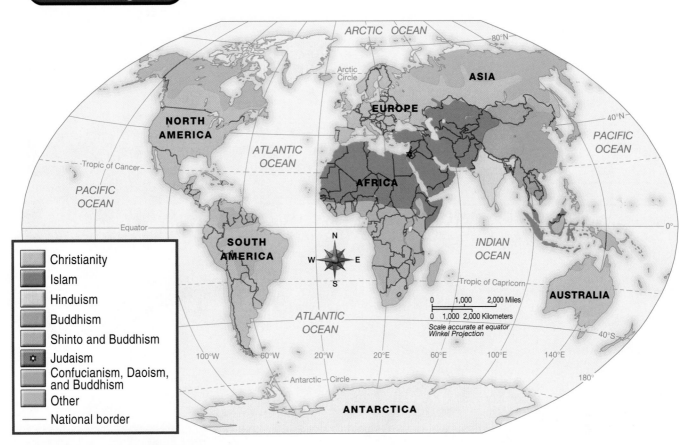

Legend:
- Christianity
- Islam
- Hinduism
- Buddhism
- Shinto and Buddhism
- Judaism
- Confucianism, Daoism, and Buddhism
- Other
- National border

Scale accurate at equator
Winkel Projection

0   1,000   2,000 Miles
0 1,000 2,000 Kilometers

World Languages

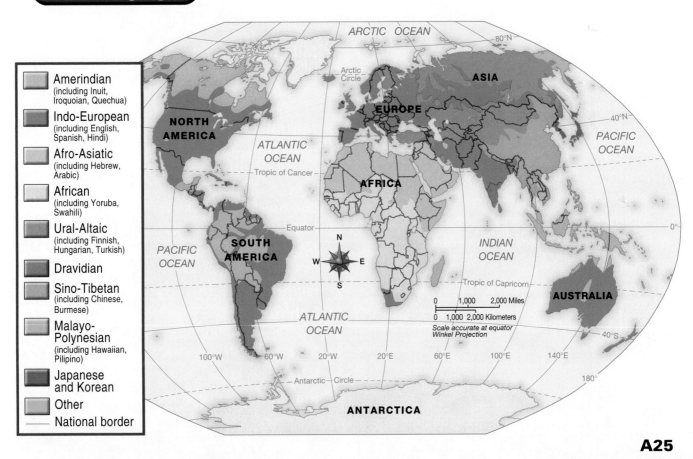

Legend:
- Amerindian (including Inuit, Iroquoian, Quechua)
- Indo-European (including English, Spanish, Hindi)
- Afro-Asiatic (including Hebrew, Arabic)
- African (including Yoruba, Swahili)
- Ural-Altaic (including Finnish, Hungarian, Turkish)
- Dravidian
- Sino-Tibetan (including Chinese, Burmese)
- Malayo-Polynesian (including Hawaiian, Pilipino)
- Japanese and Korean
- Other
- National border

Scale accurate at equator
Winkel Projection

0   1,000   2,000 Miles
0 1,000 2,000 Kilometers

A25

Geography Terms

1. **basin** bowl-shaped area of land surrounded by higher land
2. **bay** an inlet of the sea or some other body of water, usually smaller than a gulf
3. **bluff** high, steep face of rock or earth
4. **canyon** deep, narrow valley with steep sides
5. **cape** point of land that extends into water
6. **cataract** large waterfall
7. **channel** deepest part of a body of water
8. **cliff** high, steep face of rock or earth
9. **coast** land along a sea or ocean
10. **coastal plain** area of flat land along a sea or ocean
11. **delta** triangle-shaped area of land at the mouth of a river
12. **desert** dry land with few plants
13. **dune** hill of sand piled up by the wind
14. **fall line** area along which rivers form waterfalls or rapids as the rivers drop to lower land
15. **floodplain** flat land that is near the edges of a river and is formed by silt deposited by floods
16. **foothills** hilly area at the base of a mountain
17. **glacier** large ice mass that moves slowly down a mountain or across land
18. **gulf** part of a sea or ocean extending into the land, usually larger than a bay
19. **hill** land that rises above the land around it
20. **inlet** any area of water extending into the land from a larger body of water
21. **island** land that has water on all sides
22. **isthmus** narrow strip of land connecting two larger areas of land
23. **lagoon** body of shallow water
24. **lake** body of water with land on all sides
25. **marsh** lowland with moist soil and tall

26 mesa flat-topped mountain with steep sides

27 mountain highest kind of land

28 mountain pass gap between mountains

29 mountain range row of mountains

30 mouth of river place where a river empties into another body of water

31 oasis area of water and fertile land in a desert

32 ocean body of salt water larger than a sea

33 peak top of a mountain

34 peninsula land that is almost completely surrounded by water

35 plain area of flat or gently rolling low land

36 plateau area of high, mostly flat land

37 reef ridge of sand, rock, or coral that lies at or near the surface of a sea or ocean

38 river large stream of water that flows across the land

39 riverbank land along a river

40 savanna area of grassland and scattered trees

41 sea body of salt water smaller than an ocean

42 sea level the level of the surface of an ocean or a sea

43 slope side of a hill or mountain

44 source of river place where a river begins

45 strait narrow channel of water connecting two larger bodies of water

46 swamp area of low, wet land with trees

47 timberline line on a mountain above which it is too cold for trees to grow

48 tributary stream or river that flows into a larger stream or river

49 valley low land between hills or mountains

50 volcano opening in the earth, often raised, through which lava, rock, ashes, and gases are forced out

51 waterfall steep drop from a high place to a

Introduction

"We are not makers of history. We are made by history."

—Dr. Martin Luther King, Jr., *Strength to Love,* 1963

Learning About Our World

This year in social studies, you will be studying the world's past. You will learn not only about events of long ago but also about the people who made those events happen. You will see how both conflict and cooperation between different groups of people have shaped past events. You will also see how new ideas have affected the world. In this way, you will learn about how the past affects the present.

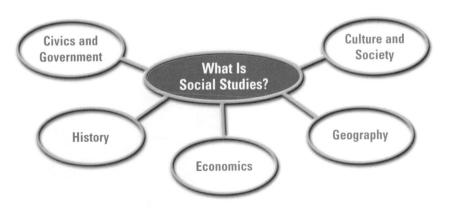

Why History Matters

VOCABULARY

history   oral history   analyze
chronology   perspective
evidence   historical empathy

Many things contribute to the way people live, and one of the most important is **history**, or what happened in the past. History affects all people. In this book you will read about people from the past and the present. You will see how their ways of life have stayed the same or changed over time.

Relating Events in Time

In history, time is the main subject of concern. The time order in which events in history take place is called **chronology** (kruh•NAH•luh•jee). Historians, the people who study history, study the chronology of events to find links between the past and the present.

Finding Evidence

Historians look for **evidence**, or proof, about the past in the objects and records that people have left behind. Historians examine buildings, works of art, photographs, and everyday tools, not just books and papers. They also listen to or read the stories that people tell about the past. A story told aloud by a person who did not write down what happened or who did not have a written language is an **oral history**. By examining the many kinds of historical evidence, historians can often explain when events took place and why they happened as they did.

Historians study sculptures, paintings, photographs, and other objects to learn about people and events of the past. Pictured are a mask of an Egyptian king (top), a painting of England's Queen Elizabeth I (middle), and a photograph of India's Mohandas Gandhi (bottom).

Understanding Perspectives

By reading the words and studying the objects of people in the past, historians begin to understand **perspectives**, or different points of view. A person's perspective often depends on whether that person is old or young, a man or a woman, rich or poor. Perspective is also shaped by what a person believes. Your understanding of the world will grow as you study the perspectives of people around the world.

Historians have their own perspectives as they study the past. They see the past from the present. Because of this, they need to be careful not to judge the actions of people in the past based on the way people act today. In the same way, as you read this book, you must be careful not to judge people in the past and in other places based on your beliefs and point of view. **Historical empathy** is the ability to understand people of the past in terms of the time in which they lived.

These students visiting a museum (above) and these scientists at a dig in Egypt (below) may have different perspectives on history.

Drawing Conclusions

To understand an event in the past, historians need to analyze when, where, and why it happened. When you **analyze** something, you break it into its parts and look closely at how those parts connect with one another. Once you have analyzed an event, you can summarize it or draw a conclusion about how or why it happened.

REVIEW What do you learn when you study history?

SKILLS · READING

Compare Primary and Secondary Sources

VOCABULARY

primary source
secondary source

▶ WHY IT MATTERS

People who study history learn about the past from two kinds of sources—primary sources and secondary sources. By studying and comparing these kinds of sources, you can find evidence of what actually happened.

▶ WHAT YOU NEED TO KNOW

Primary sources are the records made by people who saw or took part in an event. These people may have written down their thoughts about the event in journals, or they may have told their stories in letters or poems.

Primary sources may also be objects or official documents that give information about the time in which they were made or written. Speeches, photographs, and works of art may be primary sources as well. A primary source gives people of today a direct link to a past event.

A **secondary source** is not a direct link to an event. Secondary sources provide information about an event by someone who was not there to see what happened. A magazine article, a newspaper story, or an encyclopedia entry written by someone who only heard about or read about an event is a secondary source.

Some sources can be either primary or secondary, depending on how the event is reported. A newspaper or magazine might print an article containing the exact words of a person who saw the event take place.

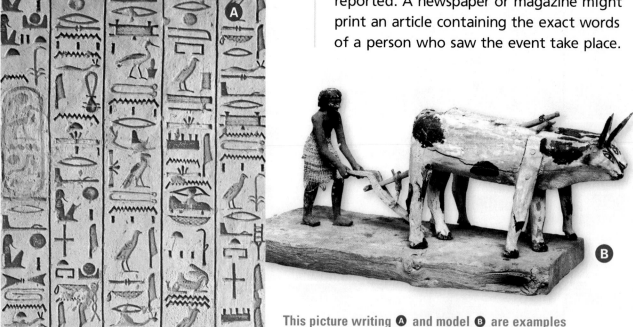

This picture writing Ⓐ and model Ⓑ are examples of primary sources from ancient Egypt.

A newspaper or magazine might also print an article written by a reporter who was not there. Oral histories, textbooks, works of art, films, and online resources can also be either primary or secondary sources.

▶ PRACTICE THE SKILL

Look at the primary and secondary sources on these pages, and answer the following questions.

1 What kinds of information about Egypt do items A and B provide?

2 What kinds of information do items C and D provide?

3 What kind of information might be obtained from item D but not from item A?

▶ APPLY WHAT YOU LEARNED

Find examples of primary and secondary sources in your textbook, and explain to a classmate what makes each source primary or secondary.

This model of the Great Pyramid built in Tokyo ❸ and this Web site about ancient Egypt ❹ are secondary sources.

Why Geography Matters

VOCABULARY

geography	human feature	adapt
relative location	region	cause
absolute location	modify	effect
physical feature		

By studying **geography**, you can find answers to questions about Earth and the people who live on it. Geographers, the people who study geography, try to understand the relationships between people and places on Earth and the relationships between different places.

Themes of Geography

Geographers think about certain topics when they study a place. Five of these topics are known as the five themes of geography. Most of the maps in this book focus on one of these five themes. Keeping the five themes in mind will help you think like a geographer.

Location

Everything on Earth has its own location, or where it can be found. The **relative location** of a place tells where it is in relation to other places. The **absolute location**, or exact location, of a place is its "global address," where it is on the whole Earth.

Human-Environment Interactions

Humans and their surroundings affect each other. People **modify**, or change, their environment by building cities, for example. The environment can cause people to **adapt**, or adjust, to their surroundings, such as by wearing warm clothing in cold places.

Place

Every location on Earth has a place identity made up of unique features. Landforms, bodies of water, climate, and plant and animal life are some of the **physical features** of a place. Buildings, roads, and people are some of a place's **human features**.

Movement

People, products, and ideas move from place to place by transportation and communication. Geography helps you understand how people came to live where they do. It also helps you understand the causes and effects of movement. A **cause** is an action that makes something else happen. An **effect** is what happens as a result of that action.

Regions

Areas on Earth that differ from each other because of their features are called **regions**. Such features can be physical, human, economic, cultural, or political.

Essential Elements of Geography

Geographers also use six other topics to understand Earth and its people. These topics are called the six essential elements of geography. You will find special features in this book that focus on the essential elements.

GEOGRAPHY ESSENTIAL ELEMENTS

• GEOGRAPHY •

The World in Spatial Terms
Geographers organize spatial, or location, information about people and places by creating maps. They also use maps to analyze information.

Human Systems
Geographers study population and human activities, including settlement, trade, and interaction. They also organize these human systems into patterns.

Places and Regions
Geographers identify regions to group together places with similar physical and human features.

Environment and Society
Geographers study ways that physical surroundings and people affect each other.

Physical Systems
Geographers study physical parts of Earth, such as landforms and climate, and organize them into patterns.

The Uses of Geography
Knowing how to think like a geographer and how to use the tools of geography will help you understand the present and plan for the future. For example, citizens might study a region to decide how best to use its resources.

REVIEW In what ways do geographers study Earth and its people?

Why Culture and Society Matter

As you study world history, you will read about the people of the past who have helped to shape the present. You will learn about some of their ideas, skills, arts, tools, and ways of doing things. All these things make up a **culture**, or way of life. Each human group, or **society**, has a unique culture. A society's culture helps set it apart from other societies.

In this book you will discover some of the many societies in the world, both past and present. You will also learn about **heritage**, or those elements of culture that have been passed down through history and continue today. The people in a society share a heritage.

REVIEW What do you learn when you study culture and society?

This painting (left) shows what Chinese culture was like more than 700 years ago. The photograph (below) shows women from a present-day African society.

Why Civics and Government Matter

VOCABULARY

government   civic participation
civics

To keep order and resolve conflicts in a society, people need a government. A **government** is a system of leaders and laws that helps people live safely together in their community, state, or country.

As you read this book, you will discover that there are many different kinds of governments in the world. Most of these were formed long ago and have changed over time. You will find out about the people and events that shaped governments in the past. You will also learn how governments work today.

Civics is the study of citizenship. By studying civics, you will learn about the rights and responsibilities of citizens and how these have changed over time. You will also see how citizens' rights and responsibilities vary from one kind of government to the next. In addition, you will learn about **civic participation**, which means being concerned with and involved in issues related to your community, state, country, or the world.

REVIEW What do you learn when you study government and civics?

These meetings of Greek citizens (above) and the British Parliament (left) are examples of civic participation in government.

Why Economics Matters

VOCABULARY

economy
economics

To support its people, a society must have an **economy**, or a system of using resources to meet needs. The people must be able to make, buy, sell, and trade goods and services to get what they need and want. In this book you will compare and contrast the different economic systems of the past and present.

Economics is the study of the way that goods, services, and wealth are produced, distributed, and used in the world. You will learn how economic systems came to be, how they changed over time, and how they continue to work in today's world.

REVIEW What do you learn when you study economics?

This painting (right) shows how people exchanged goods in Europe in the 1400s. This stock exchange scene in Tokyo, Japan (below), shows part of a present-day economic system.

The World and Early People

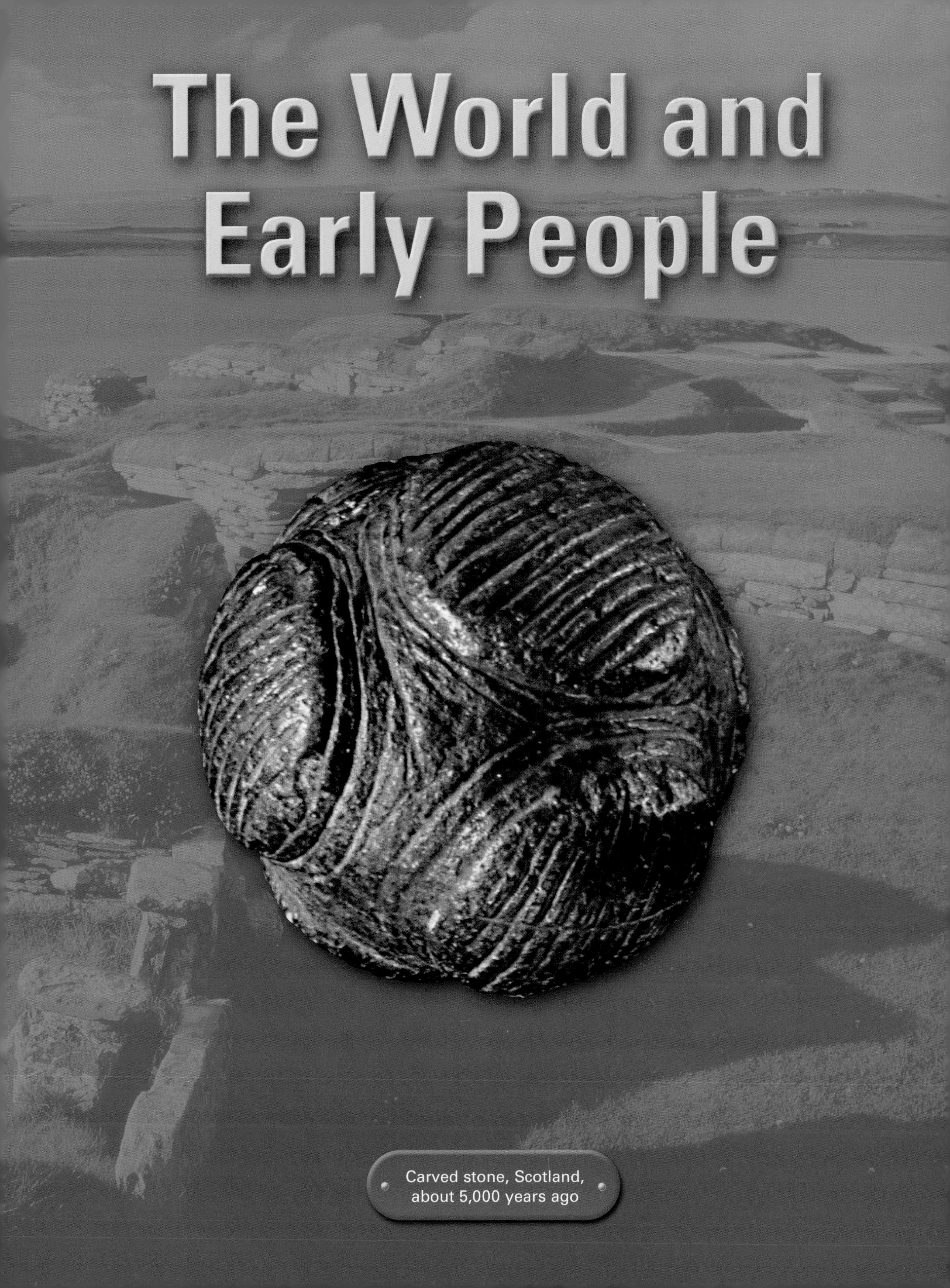

Carved stone, Scotland, about 5,000 years ago

Ruins at Skara Brae, a place of early human settlement, on the Orkney Islands, Scotland

The World and Early People

"To excavate is to open a book written in the language that the centuries have spoken to the earth."

—Spyridon Marinatos, archaeologist, 1972

Preview the Content

Use the titles of the chapters and lessons to fill in the first two columns of a K-W-L chart about geography and early people. After reading the unit, fill in the last column.

K (What I Know)	W (What I Want to Know)	L (What I Have Learned)

Preview the Vocabulary

Compound Words   Compound words are made up of two or more words. Scan the unit to find Vocabulary Words that are compound words. Then write what you think each word means. Check each definition in the Glossary.

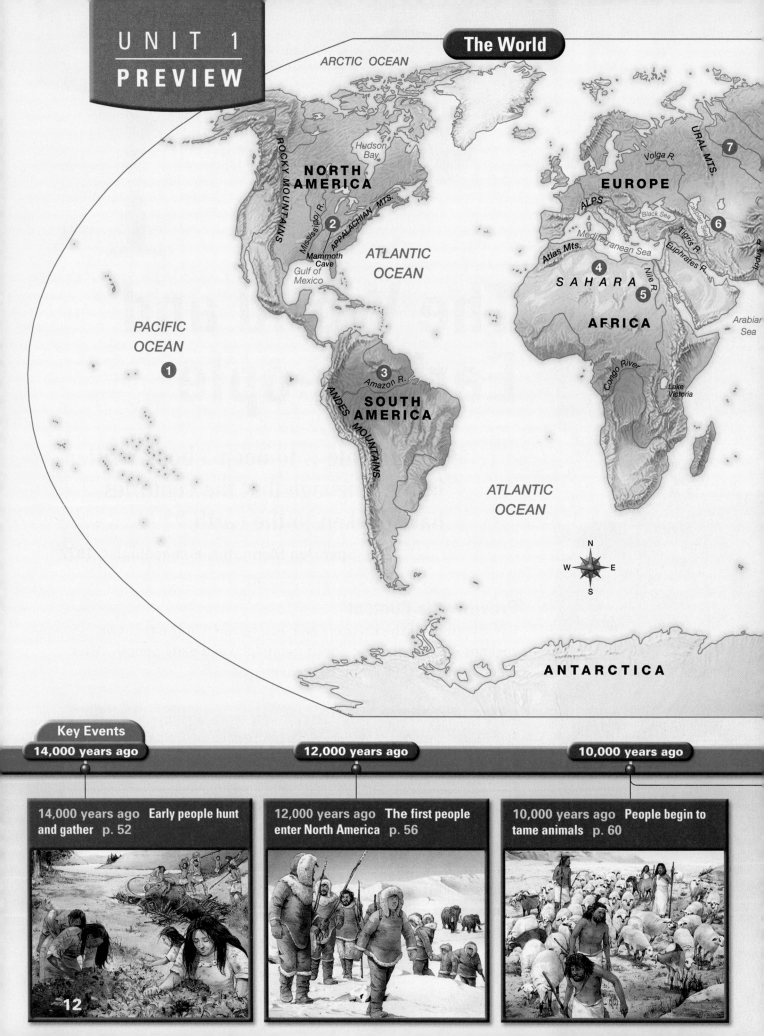

ARCTIC OCEAN

NORTH AMERICA

ROCKY MOUNTAINS

Hudson Bay

Mississippi R.

APPALACHIAN MTS.

②

Mammoth Cave

Gulf of Mexico

ATLANTIC OCEAN

PACIFIC OCEAN

①

③

Amazon R.

SOUTH AMERICA

ANDES MOUNTAINS

ATLANTIC OCEAN

URAL MTS.

⑦

Volga R.

EUROPE

ALPS

Black Sea

Caspian Sea

⑥

Mediterranean Sea

Tigris R.

Euphrates R.

Indus R.

Atlas Mts.

④

SAHARA

Nile R.

⑤

Red Sea

Arabian Sea

AFRICA

Congo River

Lake Victoria

ANTARCTICA

N W E S

Key Events

| 14,000 years ago | 12,000 years ago | 10,000 years ago |

14,000 years ago Early people hunt and gather p. 52

12,000 years ago The first people enter North America p. 56

10,000 years ago People begin to tame animals p. 60

ARCTIC OCEAN

ASIA

Lake Baikal ⑧

GOBI (DESERT)

HIMALAYAS
Huang He
▲ Mt. Everest
Chang Jiang
⑨

Bay of Bengal

South China Sea

PACIFIC OCEAN

INDIAN OCEAN

AUSTRALIA ⑩
GREAT VICTORIA DESERT
GREAT DIVIDING RANGE

0   1,000   2,000 Miles
0   1,000   2,000 Kilometers
Scale accurate at equator
Winkel Projection

Arid
Evergreen forest
Grassland
Mixed forest
Mountains
Tundra
▲ Mountain peak

Facts About World Geography

PHYSICAL FEATURE	NAME	MEASUREMENT
❶ Largest Ocean	Pacific Ocean	70 million sq miles (181 million sq km)
❷ Longest Cave	Mammoth Cave	350 miles (563 km)
❸ Largest River System	Amazon River	2.7 million sq miles (7 million sq km)
❹ Largest Desert	Sahara	3.5 million sq miles (9 million sq km)
❺ Longest River	Nile River	4,160 miles (6,695 km)
❻ Largest Lake	Caspian Sea	143,000 sq miles (370,000 sq km)
❼ Largest Continent	Asia	17 million sq miles (44 million sq km)
❽ Deepest Lake	Lake Baikal	5,315 ft (1,620 m)
❾ Highest Mountain	Mt. Everest	29,035 ft (8,850 m)
❿ Smallest Continent	Australia	3 million sq miles (8 million sq km)

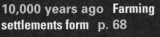

8,000 years ago   6,000 years ago   4,000 years ago

10,000 years ago Farming settlements form p. 68

8,000 years ago Early farmers develop the plow p. 63

5,000 years ago The earliest cities form p. 71

13

PAINTERS OF THE
CAVES
BY PATRICIA LAUBER

Painters of the Caves

by Patricia Lauber

Ever since people first walked on Earth, they have adapted to and changed its physical features. During the Stone Age, ancient artists drew on cave walls scenes of their people hunting animals. This story tells of one discovery of such cave art.

A Great Discovery

One chilly afternoon in December 1994, three old friends met to go exploring. The three—two men and a woman—shared a great enthusiasm: searching for caves in the limestone hills near Avignon, in southeast France.

A scientist (above) examines a Stone Age painting of horses in Chauvet cave in southeastern France.

Avignon (ah•vee•NYOHN) a French city

Limestone is fairly soft rock. Long ago, over many years, the Ardèche River carved deep gorges in these hills, creating cliffs of limestone. The cliffs are honeycombed with caves, some hollowed out by underground rivers, some by rainwater that sank in and dissolved the limestone.

For thousands of years, starting in the Stone Age, people used these caves and left behind traces of themselves. In their exploring, the three friends had found several caves with traces of wall art done by Stone Age painters. They hoped to find more, but what they found that December day was something they had only dreamed about.

Ardèche (ar•DESH) a river that flows through southeastern France

hollowed carved

They followed an ancient mule path up a cliff and arrived at a narrow ledge. An opening in the cliff led to a pile of rocks where they could feel air coming out—the sign of a cave. Tearing away the rocks, they uncovered a small passageway, just big enough for a person to wriggle through.

Exploring caves is dangerous. It is all too easy to get stuck, to take a bad fall, to become lost. But the three had twenty years of experience and they had come equipped with lights, ropes, and a ladder. They pressed ahead.

Stone Age painters used tools and materials like these (right) to make and use paint.

The woman went first, lying on her stomach. At the end of the passageway was a 30-foot drop to the cave floor. Their ladder took them down. The cave was so big that darkness swallowed their lights; they could hardly see the walls. Moving with care, they came to a place where the floor of the cave was strewn with bear bones and teeth, where bears had dug hollows to hibernate in.

Moments later they saw a drawing of a little red mammoth on a spur of rock. As they looked around, a 3-foot-high bear loomed before them on a white wall. Discovery followed discovery—a huge red rhinoceros, a big mammoth, a bear or lion, human handprints stenciled on the walls.

They had made a truly great discovery. The cave, named Chauvet after one of the explorers, holds more than 300 paintings of animals that lived some 32,000 years ago, late in the Stone Age: horses, bears, hyenas, woolly rhinos, mammoths, bison, wild cattle, lions, deer, panthers, mountain goats. Drawn in black, red, and yellow, they parade across rock walls, sometimes leaping or running.

Chauvet is far from the only cave with Stone Age wall paintings. Most such caves lie to the west, in southwest France and northern Spain. Some are found elsewhere in Europe and on other continents from Africa to Australia. But Chauvet is one of the biggest and best, and it is the oldest known. Because its original entrance had been blocked by a rockfall, no one else had visited the cave for thousands of years.

strewn thrown about

mammoth an elephant-like animal that died out long ago

spur a rock sticking out from a mountain

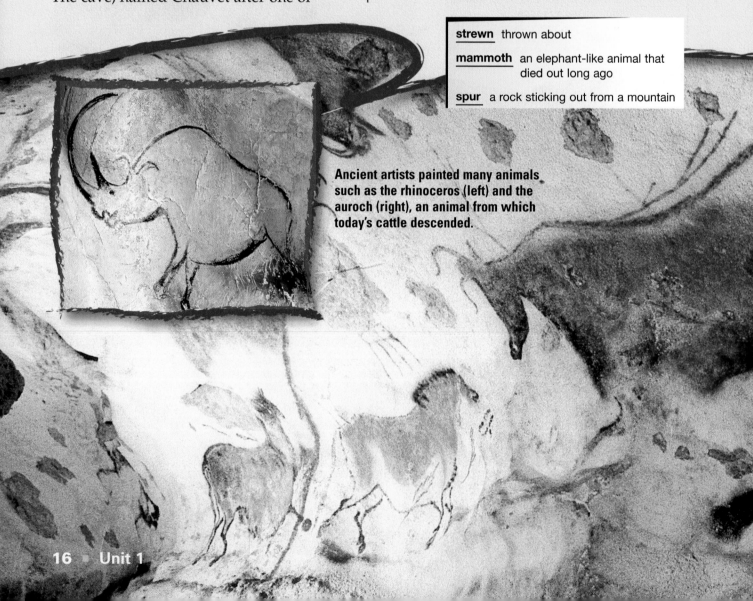

Ancient artists painted many animals such as the rhinoceros (left) and the auroch (right), an animal from which today's cattle descended.

The names of the cave artists are long lost. They could not sign their names, because they lived before writing was invented. But we do know something about them. They were people like us, modern human beings.

Their story has been pieced together by scientists who study ancient peoples. Part of the story is told by fossils, which are traces of ancient life. A fossil can be many things. The footprints of Stone Age artists who worked in the caves are fossils, as are the footprints of children who played there. But most fossils are skulls, bones, and teeth—hard parts of the body that were preserved when rock formed around them. Another part of the story is told by stone tools and other objects that people left behind and that, in time, became buried under dust, dirt, and rock.

Cave painters used this stone lamp to light cave walls as they painted.

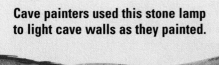

READ A BOOK

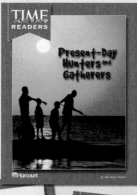

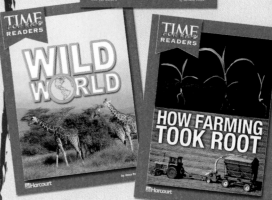

START THE UNIT PROJECT

Create a Scene Create a scene with a group of classmates. As you read this unit, take notes about the world's geography and early people. These notes will help you decide which early people to show in your scene and what kind of land to feature.

Analyze the Literature

❶ What kinds of images did the explorers find on the walls of the Chauvet cave?

❷ Why do you think it is important to study the fossils and artifacts of ancient peoples?

USE TECHNOLOGY

Visit The Learning Site at **www.harcourtschool.com** for additional activities, primary sources, and other resources to use in this unit.

MOUNT ELBRUS, RUSSIA

Mount Elbrus is located in southwestern Russia near the border of the Republic of Georgia. It is part of the high, snow-covered Caucasus Mountains. Because it is the highest point in Europe at 18,510 feet (5,642 m), it attracts mountain climbers from all over the world.

LOCATE IT

RUSSIA

Caspian Sea

Caucasus Mts.

Black Sea

Mount Elbrus

1

The World's Geography

❝ Landscapes have a language of their own, . . . from the mighty peaks to the smallest of the tiny flowers . . . ❞

—Alexandra David-Neel, from *My Journey to Lhasa,* 1927

Main Idea and Details

The **main idea** is the most important thought of a chapter, lesson, or paragraph. The **details** give more information that supports the main idea.

As you read this chapter, be sure to do the following.

• Identify the main idea and supporting details in each lesson and subsection.

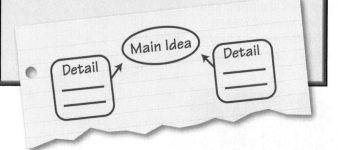

Chapter 1 ▪ 19

MAIN IDEA AND DETAILS

As you read, look for details that support the main idea of each section.

BIG IDEA

Earth's landforms were formed in different ways, and they have been reshaped over time.

VOCABULARY

theory

continental drift

fault

magma

lava

weathering

glacier

erosion

deposition

delta

FAST FACT Earth is not perfectly round. The distance through the planet from the North Pole to the South Pole is 7,900 miles (12,713 km). The distance through Earth at the equator is 7,926 miles (12,755 km).

Earth's Landforms

Although the surface of Earth is mostly water, it is the wrinkled, broken, and worn shapes of land that make studying Earth so interesting. These landforms may be as large as the tallest mountain or as small as a mound in a park. Earth's major landforms—its plains, plateaus, mountains, and hills—came into being through forces of nature.

How Landforms Came to Be

One idea about how Earth's landforms and continents came to be is the plate tectonics (tek•TAH•niks) theory. A **theory** is a possible explanation. According to the plate tectonics theory, Earth's surface is made up of several large, slow-moving slabs, or plates. As these plates move, the sections of continents and ocean floors that they carry move with them.

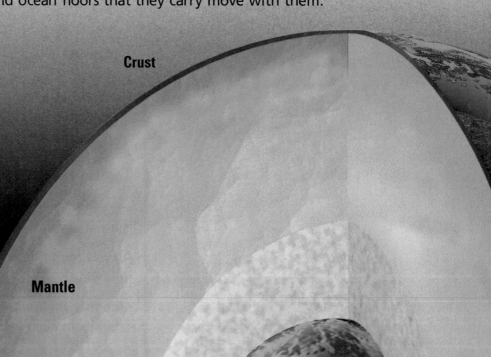

Crust

Mantle

Outer Core

Inner Core

Experts believe that all of Earth's landmasses were once joined as one huge continent. They call this ancient supercontinent Pangaea (pan•JEE•uh). Forces deep within Earth caused Pangaea to break into smaller continents, which drifted apart. This continuing movement is called **continental drift**. The forces that cause it are the result of Earth's inner structure.

Earth is made up of layers. The outer layer, at the surface, is called the crust. Earth's crust is between 10 and 25 miles (16 and 40 km) thick. Beneath the crust is the mantle, which extends about 1,800 miles (2,900 km) below Earth's surface. Experts think that the mantle is made up of hot, rocklike materials.

At Earth's center is a metal core. The core may be as hot as 5,000°F (2,760°C). The inner core is solid. Surrounding the solid inner core is a molten, or melted, outer core.

Heat from the outer core leads to changes on Earth's surface. Sometimes heat causes the mantle to create pressure on the crust, forcing the crust to rise in some places. This pushes large blocks of rock upward, forming mountains and plateaus. The part of the Rocky Mountains between Montana and New Mexico in the United States was formed in this way.

The forces within Earth also cause plates on the surface to move in different ways.

Earth's History

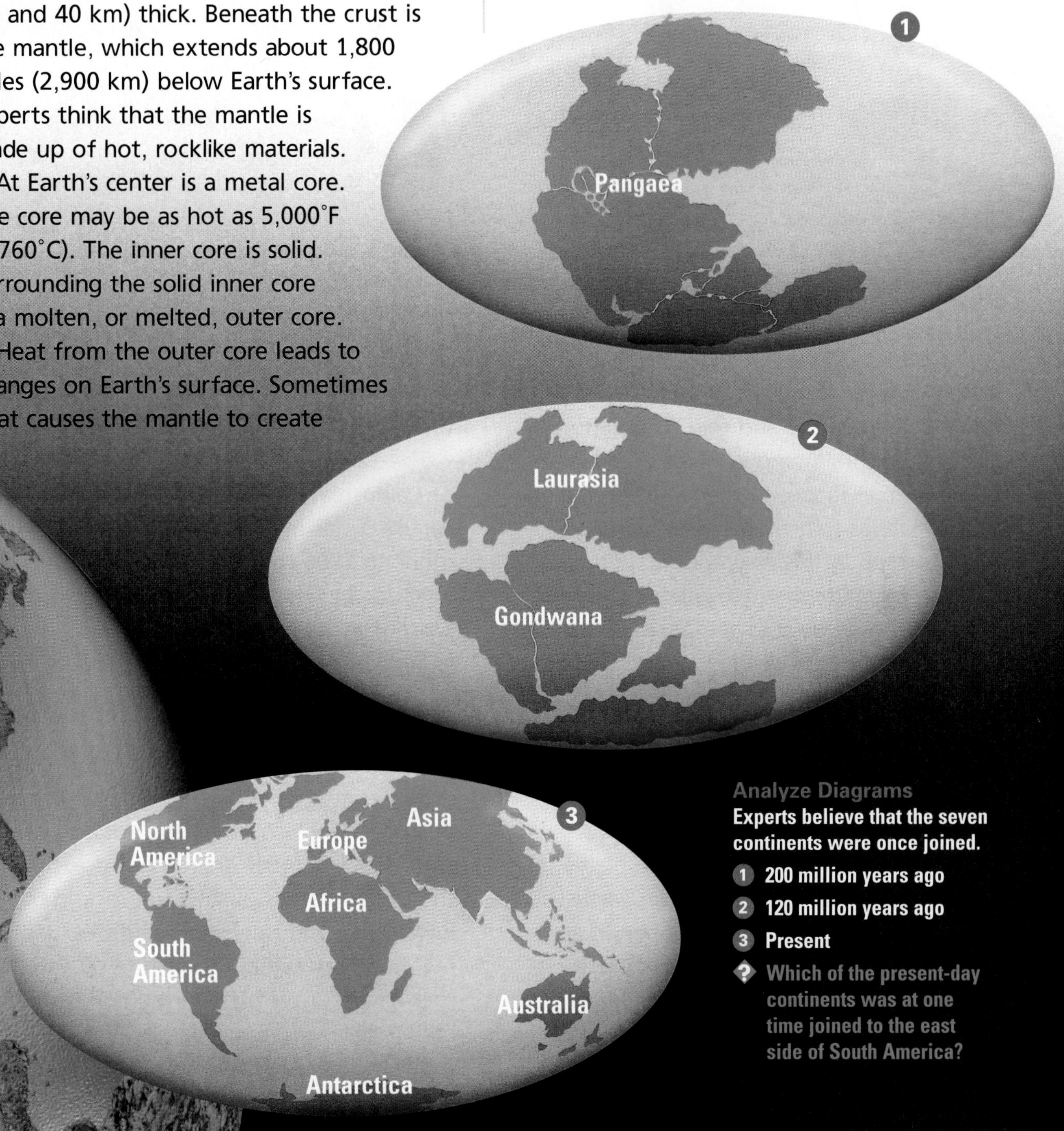

Analyze Diagrams
Experts believe that the seven continents were once joined.

1 200 million years ago

2 120 million years ago

3 Present

❖ Which of the present-day continents was at one time joined to the east side of South America?

These hikers are on the slopes of the second-highest mountain in the world, the peak known as K2, in the Karakoram Range, in Pakistan.

When two plates push together, their edges may crumple and fold. This action creates mountain ranges. Most of the highest mountain ranges in the world, including the Himalayas (hih•muh•LAY•uhz) in Asia, were formed in this way. Mountain ranges are also formed when two plates collide and one moves up over the other. The Cascade Mountains in the western United States were formed by this action.

The same forces that formed mountains and other landforms long ago are still at work today. You may not feel them, but Earth's plates are constantly shifting.

At times, the movement of the plates shakes Earth's surface, causing an earthquake. Earthquakes usually happen in areas along faults and are most destructive there. A **fault** is a crack in Earth's crust along which movement occurs. An earthquake takes place when the movement is sudden. Most faults cannot be seen, but some, like the San Andreas Fault, in the western United States, are visible on the surface.

The San Andreas Fault runs through much of California. It is a line along which two of Earth's plates meet and move past each other. In 1906 these two plates shifted as much as 21 feet (6.4 m), causing a terrible earthquake in San Francisco.

REVIEW How do plates create landforms?

Volcanoes Add Land

Sometimes when two of Earth's plates push against each other, the edge of one plate slides beneath the other. As rock in the upper plate is pushed up, rock in the lower plate is pushed down into Earth's mantle. Heat within the mantle causes the rock in the lower plate to melt. This molten rock is called **magma**.

When rock melts, it produces gases. The gases mix with the magma, causing it to rise to Earth's surface through cracks in the crust. Magma that has reached the surface is called **lava**. Sometimes lava flows slowly. At other times, it erupts in a tremendous explosion.

The openings through which lava escapes are known as volcanoes. Volcanoes have many shapes and sizes. Some are cone-shaped. Others are wide and flat. The size and shape of a volcano depend on the kind of lava that comes from it.

Lava that flows easily can spread over great distances. This kind of lava forms a shield volcano. Mauna Loa (MOW•nuh LOH•uh) in Hawaii is a shield volcano.

Thicker lava may erupt more violently, throwing rock and ash high into the air. When the rock and ash land near the opening, they form a steep-sided, cinder-cone mountain. Paricutín (pah•ree•koo•TEEN), in western Mexico, is a cinder-cone volcano. It began to form in 1943, when a crack opened in a farm field. When the eruptions ended in 1952, the cone was 1,345 feet (410 m) high.

Volcanoes are also classified by how often they erupt. Active volcanoes are those that have continued to erupt since people have been keeping records. Dormant volcanoes have been inactive for some time but may possibly erupt again in the future. Extinct volcanoes have no record of activity and are not expected to erupt again.

REVIEW **How are volcanoes formed?**

Shaping Earth's Surface

Earth's surface can be changed in several ways. One way is by weathering. **Weathering** is the wearing away of rock. All causes of weathering involve motion.

Water is a main cause of weathering. Moving water tumbles rocks against each other, breaking them into smaller and smaller pieces. Fast-moving rivers and streams weather away their banks, producing deep gorges and canyons. Ocean waves weather away sea cliffs, turning them into sand or causing them to fall into the sea.

The movement of glaciers can also change landforms. **Glaciers** are thick masses of ice formed in areas where more snow falls than melts. As glaciers move, they grind down the land below them, weathering it away.

Parincota (PAH•reen•koh•tah) in Chile (above) is a dormant volcano. Mauna Loa (right), Earth's largest volcano, erupts on the island of Hawaii.

Wind is another cause of weathering. A strong, steady wind carrying sand can grind away desert rock. In some places wind has shaped some very unusual formations. Shipton's Arch, in western China, looks like a soaring arch. Other formations look like tall columns or flat tables.

After weathering has broken down rocks into very small bits, erosion may take place. **Erosion** is the carrying away of land by forces of nature. The tiny particles of rock carried by wind, water, and glaciers are called sediment. In time, the sediment is dropped in a new location. This building up of sediment is called **deposition**.

Erosion wears away old landforms, and deposition builds up new ones. Rivers, for example, erode their banks, picking up sediment as they move downstream. When rivers flood, they deposit the sediment in flat land areas. These deposits build up the rivers' floodplains, or low, flat land along the rivers. Rivers also deposit sediment at the point where they flow into another body of water, usually forming a triangle-shaped piece of land called a **delta**.

REVIEW **What details support the idea that water is a main cause of weathering?**

MAIN IDEA AND DETAILS

· GEOGRAPHY ·

China's Karst Pinnacles

Understanding Physical Systems

In southern China unusual rock pillars tower around the city of Guilin (GWEE•LIN). The limestone pillars look like slender mountains, but they are actually pinnacles, or steep peaks, known as karst features. The term *karst* refers to any region of rock layers with features carved by water erosion. Karst features form when water soaks into the ground and breaks apart certain kinds of rock, such as limestone. Over time, water from tropical rainfall carves out these unique features.

CHINA

KARST PINNACLES

Guilin
Liuzhou
Wuzhou
Guangzhou
Nanning
Macao
Hong Kong
VIETNAM
South China Sea
Gulf of Tonkin
Hainan
Hongshui He
Yu Jiang
Xi Jiang

0   100   200 Miles
0 100 200 Kilometers

People Change the Land

Human activities also change Earth. Rivers form floodplains and deltas, but people turn those landforms into farming areas. The sediments that create the floodplains and deltas make excellent soil for growing food. People may also build cities there.

In some places people change land that would otherwise be difficult to use. In Asia some farmers grow rice on mountainsides. They do this by terracing the slopes, or forming a series of flat fields like steps up the mountains. This prevents erosion by keeping the water from rushing downhill and carrying away the soil.

People also reshape waterways and create new ones. They build dams to control the flow of rivers and to produce electricity.

In doing so, they create human-made lakes to store water. These lakes sometimes cover what were once fields and valleys.

People drain water from wetlands to create dry land for cities and farms. They also direct water into dry areas. This makes it possible for people in places such as the western United States to live and work in deserts.

REVIEW **What are some ways in which people change the land?**

Rice farmers in Bali, Indonesia, terrace steep hillsides to grow more crops.

LOCATE IT

INDONESIA

Bali

LESSON 1 REVIEW

 MAIN IDEA AND DETAILS How are landforms created?

① **BIG IDEA** What are two ways that Earth can be reshaped over time?

② **VOCABULARY** What is the difference between **erosion** and **deposition**?

③ **GEOGRAPHY** What is one difference between the inner core and the outer core of Earth?

④ **CRITICAL THINKING—Apply** How would a large storm with heavy rains and high winds off the coast of Alabama affect that state's beaches?

 PERFORMANCE—Make a Scrapbook Page Use the library and the Internet to find an example of people changing a place on Earth. Then make a scrapbook page, using the information you have found. Write a paragraph that tells what the place was like at first. Write another paragraph describing the land after people changed it. Be sure to point out both helpful and harmful effects. Add your page to a class scrapbook titled "People Change Earth."

MAIN IDEA AND DETAILS
Read to find details that support the main idea of each section.

BIG IDEA
Earth's bodies of water are formed in different ways, and they are important to the survival of life on Earth.

VOCABULARY

trench
current
tidal wave
tide
water cycle
tributary
river system
drainage basin
rift
reservoir

Earth's Bodies of Water

Water covers more than 70 percent of Earth's surface. It fills rivers, lakes, and oceans. It is in the ground and in the air we breathe. Without water, there would be no life. People, plants, and animals must all have water to survive.

Earth's Oceans

Earth's oceans are really one large body of water covering much of the planet. Continents and other landmasses divide this great ocean into four parts. In order of size, they are the Pacific Ocean, the Atlantic Ocean, the Indian Ocean, and the Arctic Ocean.

The Pacific is much bigger than the other oceans. It covers about 70 million square miles (181 million sq km), almost double the 36 million square miles (93 million sq km) covered by the Atlantic, the second-largest ocean. The Pacific covers nearly one-third of Earth's surface. At its widest point, it stretches more than 15,000 miles (24,140 km) from the country of Panama in North America to Malaysia, a country in Asia. The Pacific is also the deepest ocean, with an average depth of 12,900 feet (3,932 m).

FAST FACT The ancient Polynesian people of the Hawaiian Islands were surfing long before the arrival of Europeans. Men and women, whether royalty or ordinary people, surfed. Their surfboards were made of solid wood and ranged from about 9 to 18 feet (3 to 5.5 m) in length.

Earth's Bodies of Water

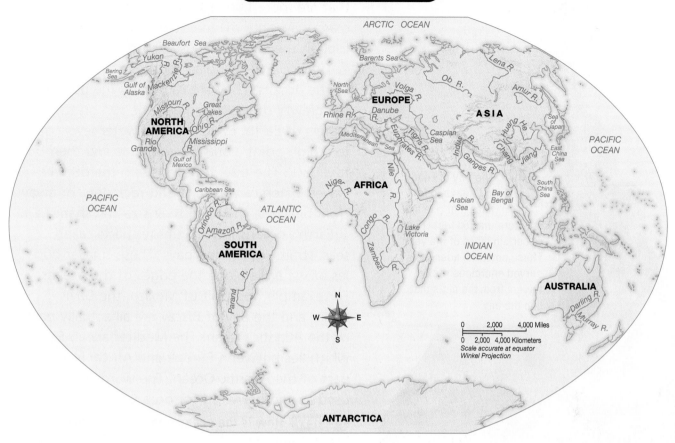

Location **Water surrounds large parts of every continent.**

❖ **Which continents are bordered by the Indian Ocean?**

The ocean floor has physical features like those on land. It has mountain ranges, plains, basins, and valleys. The mid-ocean ridges make up the ocean's largest physical feature, a chain of mountains that runs about 37,000 miles (60,000 km) through the Pacific, Indian, and Atlantic Oceans. Most of the mountain peaks are about 5,000 feet (1,500 m) high. Some of the highest peaks rise above the surface of the water to form islands, such as the country of Iceland in the Atlantic Ocean.

The deepest ocean valley, or **trench**, ever explored is in the western Pacific near the island of Guam. Called the Mariana Trench, it is almost 7 miles (11 km) below sea level.

Deep and vast, the waters of Earth's oceans move constantly. **Currents**, or streams of ocean water, flow through the oceans like giant rivers. Ocean currents are set in motion by the wind. In general, ocean currents move in a clockwise pattern in the Northern Hemisphere and counter-clockwise in the Southern Hemisphere.

Ocean currents tend to carry cold water from near the North and South Poles toward the equator. Warm water near the equator moves toward the poles. These currents greatly affect the temperatures of land areas. They also affect ocean transportation, since it is easier and faster for ships to sail with the ocean currents than against them.

Wind also causes ocean waves, the up-and-down action of the water. Ocean waves can be small ripples or giant waves.

The Bay of Fundy, in Canada, has tides that rise and fall more than 50 feet (15 m) at certain times of the year. These powerful tides have carved enormous rock towers from the cliffs that line the bay.

Earthquakes and severe storms can create waves that are more than 100 feet (30 m) high. These giant waves are often called **tidal waves**, even though they are not caused by the tides.

Tides are the regular, rhythmic rise and fall of the oceans. They are caused by the pull of the gravity of the moon and the sun on the waters of Earth. Every day, the water level rises to a high point along the shoreline and then falls back. The tide, together with the ocean waves, often carries sand and rock onto or away from beaches, changing their size and shape.

Earth's oceans include smaller parts called seas, straits, gulfs, and bays. These smaller bodies of water lie along the edges of the oceans. For example, the Gulf of Mexico, the Davis Strait, and the Bay of Biscay are all actually part of the Atlantic Ocean. The Mediterranean Sea, which lies between Europe and Africa, is also part of the Atlantic Ocean. The word *sea* is also used as another word for *ocean.*

REVIEW How is the ocean floor like the land on Earth's continents?

The Water We Drink

Earth's oceans cover more than 140 million square miles (363 million sq km) and contain about 97 percent of all the water on Earth. With all this water, it may be hard to imagine shortages. Yet more than 99 percent of the total water supply cannot be used for drinking. Ocean water, for example, is too salty to drink.

About 77 percent of Earth's fresh water is frozen in glaciers and in the ice caps at the poles. Some fresh water floats around in the air as water vapor, and some exists as dampness in the soil. Only about 6 percent of Earth's fresh water is in lakes and rivers.

Fortunately, Earth's **water cycle** constantly replaces the supply of fresh water. The sun's heat evaporates water from the sea, leaving the salt behind. Winds carry clouds of water vapor over the land. The vapor cools and condenses, causing rain or other precipitation. As rain falls

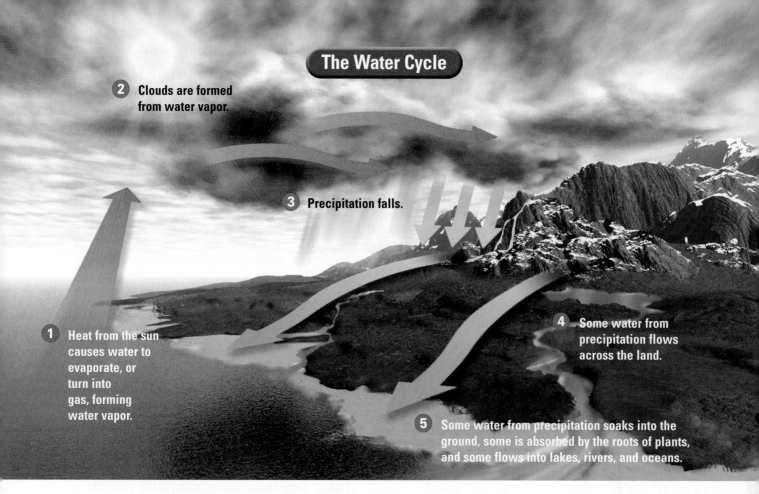

The Water Cycle

2 Clouds are formed from water vapor.

3 Precipitation falls.

1 Heat from the sun causes water to evaporate, or turn into gas, forming water vapor.

4 Some water from precipitation flows across the land.

5 Some water from precipitation soaks into the ground, some is absorbed by the roots of plants, and some flows into lakes, rivers, and oceans.

Analyze Diagrams Earth's water moves continuously from the oceans to the air to the land and back to the oceans again.

◆ How does water get back to the oceans?

on the land, it soaks into the soil and collects underground. Water that is stored within Earth is called groundwater. When heavy rains fall, the soil sometimes cannot soak up all the water. Water that the soil does not soak up is called surface water. Surface water flows across the land and collects in rivers, streams, and other bodies of water. Most of the water that humans use every day comes from surface water in rivers and lakes.

REVIEW How is the supply of fresh water continuously replaced?

Streams and Rivers

Streams and rivers are bodies of water that flow over land in a channel. Most streams begin on high ground, among hills or mountains. The source, or beginning, of a stream may be a melting snowfield or glacier or an overflowing lake. Streams flow from high ground to low ground. A stream ends when it empties into another body of water.

Some streams flow together to form broad, deep rivers. Smaller streams that join rivers are called **tributaries** of the river. As more tributaries empty into a river, it grows larger. Together, a river and all its tributaries make up a **river system**.

Every continent except Antarctica has major rivers. The most important rivers in Africa include the Nile and the Congo. In Asia, the major rivers are the Chang Jiang (CHAHNG JYAHNG) and the Huang He (HWAHNG HUH). Australia's most important river is the Murray, and Europe's is the Danube.

North America's is the Mississippi. South America's is the Amazon. The Nile is Earth's longest river. It flows more than 4,160 miles (6,695 km) from its source in central Africa to its mouth at the Mediterranean Sea. A number of tributaries flow into the Amazon, making it Earth's largest river system. The Amazon carries more water than the Nile, the Chang Jiang, and the Mississippi combined.

River systems drain, or carry water away from, the land around them. The land area drained by a river system is called the river's **drainage basin**. Long rivers usually have large drainage basins. The Amazon River has a drainage basin of about 2.7 million square miles (7 million sq km).

Many of the world's first human settlements were built on the fertile banks of rivers. The rivers also provided sources of drinking water and a way to transport goods. Today many of the world's largest cities are located along rivers for the same reasons.

Some rivers are also valuable energy sources. The fast-moving water at waterfalls along rivers can be used to generate electricity. Rivers are also useful for trade. They were often the first "highways" used by explorers, traders, and pioneers in lands new to them.

REVIEW What details support the idea that rivers are important to humans?

MAIN IDEA AND DETAILS

Lakes

Lakes are bodies of water surrounded by land. The word *lake* comes from a Greek word for "hole." Most lakes form when water fills a low place on Earth's surface.

Lakes exist on every continent of the world. The greatest number can be found in the northern regions of North America, Europe, and Asia. Glaciers there carved huge holes in Earth's surface. When the glaciers melted, water filled the holes, and basins and lakes were formed.

Lakes also form when rainwater collects in holes made in other ways. Crater Lake in the western United States formed in the crater of an extinct volcano. Lake Baikal (by•KAHL), in Russia, is a rift lake. It formed in a huge crack, or **rift**, in Earth's crust. At 5,315 feet

The stilt house shown in both photographs is on the Mekong River floodplain in Vietnam. Heavy summer rains bring annual floods (below) to the region.

LOCATE IT

Mekong Delta

VIETNAM

LOCATE IT

PERU

Lake Titicaca

On Lake Titicaca, high in the mountains of Peru, people build homes and farms on floating islands. They also build boats from reeds.

(1,620 m) deep, it is Earth's deepest lake. Eastern Africa has several large rift lakes, including Lakes Victoria, Malawi, and Tanganyika (tan•guh•NYEE•kuh). The rift along which these lakes and others formed stretches through what is called the Great Rift Valley.

North America has more lakes by far than any other continent. The largest of these are the Great Lakes, on the border between Canada and the United States. One-fifth of all the fresh water on Earth's surface is found in the Great Lakes.

Some bodies of water that are called seas are actually large lakes. These include the Dead Sea, the Sea of Galilee, and the Caspian Sea, all in southwestern Asia. They are called seas because they are very large and contain salt water.

The Dead Sea, between Israel and Jordan, lies about 1,310 feet (400 m) below sea level. It is one of the lowest-lying lakes on Earth. The highest lake is Lake Titicaca (tee•tee•KAH•kah), in South America, at 12,507 feet (3,812 m) above sea level.

Not all lakes are made by nature, however. Some are made when people build dams to control river flooding or to generate electricity. A lake that forms behind a human-made dam is called a **reservoir** (REH•zuh•vwar).

REVIEW How do glaciers form lakes?

LESSON 2 REVIEW

MAIN IDEA AND DETAILS What are some of the ways in which water is important to our survival?

1 BIG IDEA How are rivers formed?

2 VOCABULARY Use the term **current** to describe the movement of water in the oceans.

3 SCIENCE AND TECHNOLOGY What causes ocean tides?

4 CRITICAL THINKING—Analyze What do you think would happen if the glaciers and the ice caps at the poles were to melt?

PERFORMANCE—Draw a Map Find out more about a body of water or a waterway in or near your community, and draw a map of it. Add labels to your map, and write a few sentences describing the body of water.

Use Latitude and Longitude

VOCABULARY	
latitude	longitude
equator	prime meridian

▶ WHY IT MATTERS

When you study geography, it is important to know exactly where places in the world are located. To show absolute, or exact, location, mapmakers draw lines that form a grid system on maps and globes. These lines make it possible for people to describe exact locations on Earth. Of course, the lines do not really exist on Earth's surface.

▶ WHAT YOU NEED TO KNOW

The lines that run east and west on a map or globe are called lines of latitude. **Latitude** is the distance north or south of the equator. Latitude is measured in degrees north or south of the equator.

The **equator** is the line on a globe that circles Earth halfway between the North Pole and the South Pole. The equator, which is marked 0°, divides Earth into the Northern Hemisphere and the Southern Hemisphere. Lines of latitude are parallel, or always the same distance from each other. For this reason, lines of latitude are sometimes called parallels.

Lines of latitude north of the equator are marked N for *north latitude.* Lines of latitude south of the equator are marked S for *south latitude.* For example, 30°N refers to the line of latitude in the Northern Hemisphere 30 degrees north of the equator.

The lines that run north and south on a map or globe are lines of longitude. **Longitude** is the distance east or west of the line that runs north and south through Greenwich, England, near the city of London. Lines of longitude are also called meridians. Unlike parallels, which never meet, meridians meet at the poles and are farthest apart at the equator. Longitude is marked in much the same way that latitude is marked. The meridian running through Greenwich is

Prime Meridian

Equator

This map shows the locations of the equator and the prime meridian.

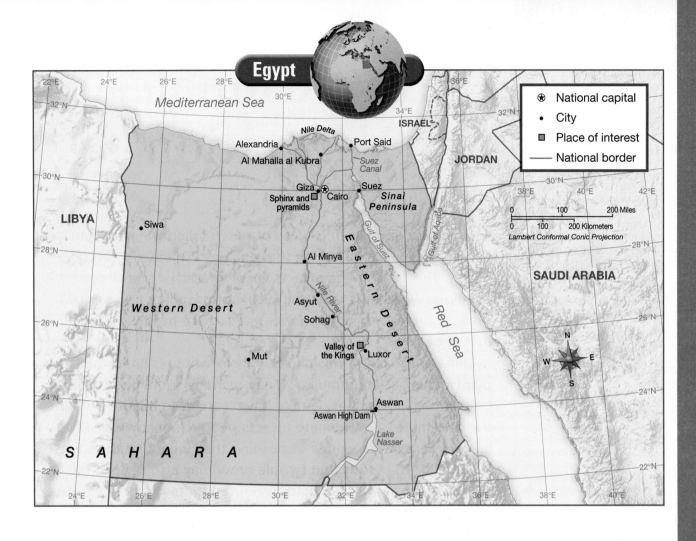

Egypt

National capital
City
Place of interest
National border

Mediterranean Sea
Nile Delta
Alexandria
Port Said
Al Mahalla al Kubra
Suez Canal
ISRAEL
JORDAN
Giza
Sphinx and pyramids
Cairo
Suez
Sinai Peninsula
LIBYA
Siwa
Al Minya
Asyut
Sohag
Mut
Valley of the Kings
Luxor
Western Desert
Eastern Desert
Gulf of Suez
Gulf of Aqaba
Red Sea
SAUDI ARABIA
Aswan
Aswan High Dam
Lake Nasser
S A H A R A
Nile River

0   100   200 Miles
0   100   200 Kilometers
Lambert Conformal Conic Projection

called the **prime meridian**. It is marked 0°. Lines of longitude to the west of the prime meridian are marked *W* for *west longitude.* They are in the Western Hemisphere. Lines of longitude to the east of the prime meridian are marked *E* for *east longitude* and are in the Eastern Hemisphere. The meridian opposite 0° on Earth is 180°. The 180° meridian runs through the Pacific Ocean.

▶ PRACTICE THE SKILL

The map above shows the locations of some of Egypt's physical features, cities, and points of interest. Lines of latitude and longitude on the map form a grid system. Study the map, and then use it to answer these questions.

1 In which sea do the lines 26°N and 36°E cross?

2 Which line of latitude is nearest to the city of Cairo?

3 Between which two lines of longitude is the Gulf of Suez located?

4 Between which two lines of latitude is Lake Nasser located?

▶ APPLY WHAT YOU LEARNED

Using the map, make up five more questions about latitude and longitude. Write them on a sheet of paper. Then exchange papers with a classmate, and answer each other's questions.

Practice your map and globe skills with the **GeoSkills CD-ROM**.

MAP AND GLOBE SKILLS

Earth's Climates and Vegetation

Surrounding Earth is a sea of gases called the atmosphere. These gases make up the air that enables life to exist on the planet. The atmosphere affects Earth's weather and climate patterns. Weather is the state of the atmosphere at a particular time. **Climate** is the kind of weather a place has over a long period of time.

Climate, like landforms and bodies of water, is important to plants, animals, and humans. Many plants and animals can live only in certain climates. People have learned to adapt to a number of climates. Still, climate affects people in many ways. It helps determine the kinds of clothing they wear and the shelters they build. The foods that people grow may also depend on climate. The climate of a place is related to its location. Latitude, nearness to large areas of land or water, and elevation above sea level all affect climate.

The Effect of Latitude

A place's latitude—or distance north or south of the equator—is important in determining its climate. Because the surface of the planet is curved, the sun's rays hit different parts of Earth at different angles. Near the equator the sun's rays hit Earth's surface more vertically than at other latitudes. These direct vertical rays beam a lot of heat into a small area. This makes

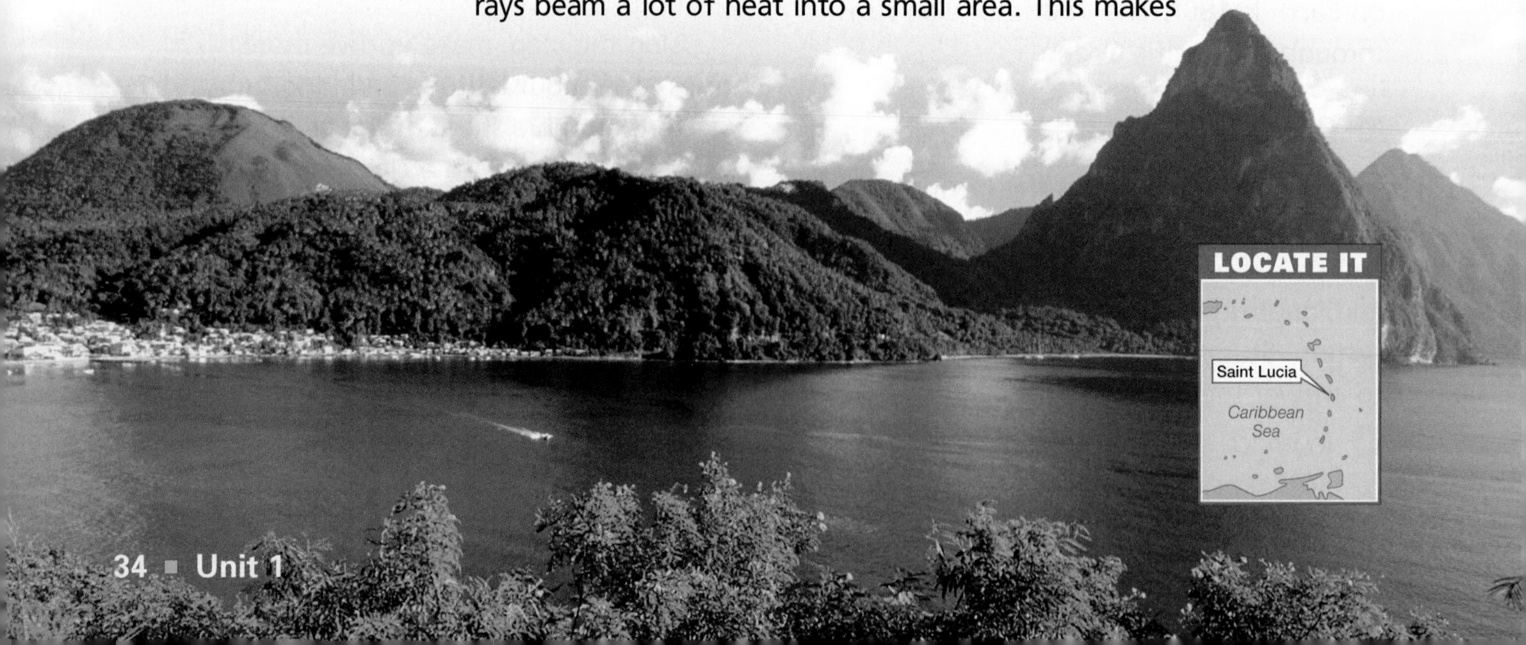

The Caribbean island of Saint Lucia has a tropical climate.

LOCATE IT

Saint Lucia

Caribbean Sea

The Change of Seasons

March 20 or 21
Spring in the Northern Hemisphere

December 21 or 22
Winter in the Northern Hemisphere

June 21 or 22
Summer in the Northern Hemisphere

September 22 or 23
Autumn in the Northern Hemisphere

Analyze Diagrams   As Earth moves around the sun, the seasons change.

When does winter begin in the Northern Hemisphere?

climates near the equator hot or warm year-round. Areas near the poles receive only slanted rays, never vertical ones. As a result, these areas are cool or cold year-round.

Areas in the middle latitudes receive vertical rays of sunlight for part of the year, in their summer season. Their climate is called temperate. A **temperate** climate varies with the seasons. Areas with temperate climates can be hot in summer and cold in winter.

Seasons occur because Earth is tilted on its axis as it travels around the sun. Because of this tilt, the Northern and Southern Hemispheres receive the more vertical rays of the sun at different times of the year. When the Northern Hemisphere is tilted toward the sun, it is summer in that hemisphere and winter in the Southern Hemisphere. When the Southern Hemisphere is tilted toward the sun, it is summer there and winter in the Northern Hemisphere.

About June 22, when the Northern Hemisphere tilts closest toward the sun, vertical rays hit Earth at 23.5° north latitude. Vertical rays never reach places north of this latitude, which is called the Tropic of Cancer. About December 22, when the Southern Hemisphere tilts closest toward the sun, vertical rays hit Earth at 23.5° south latitude, along the Tropic of Capricorn. The word **tropic** refers to the area on Earth between those two latitudes.

REVIEW How does latitude affect climates on Earth?

The Effects of Land and Water

The heating and cooling differences between land and water also affect climate. Land heats faster than bodies of water do. It also cools faster. Water takes longer to warm up, but it stays warm longer. As a result, places in the middle of a large continent experience faster and greater temperature changes than do places along the coast.

Ocean currents also affect the temperatures of some land areas. One example is the North Atlantic Drift. This current brings warm temperatures to western Europe as it flows across the Atlantic Ocean. Without the effect of this ocean current, western Europe would have a much colder climate.

The differences in the heating and cooling of land and water also cause winds. During daylight hours, the air over land is heated more quickly than the air over water. As the warm air rises, cooler air over the water flows in to take its place. This airflow is known as a sea breeze.

At night, the land cools more quickly than the water. The cooler air over the land flows over the water and pushes up the warmer air. This creates a land breeze.

REVIEW **What is the main idea of this section?**
MAIN IDEA AND DETAILS

The Effects of Altitude

The elevation, or **altitude**, of landforms above sea level also affects climate. Going up a mountain is a little like moving from the equator to one of the poles. The air temperature gets cooler the higher you go. For every 1,000 feet (305 m) of altitude, the temperature drops almost 3°F (1.7°C).

Because of the effects of altitude, it is possible to find a place with a cold climate in the middle of a larger region with a warm climate. Tanzania, in eastern Africa, has a mostly warm climate. The top of Mount Kilimanjaro (kih•luh•muhn•JAR•oh), however, is covered in snow and ice year-round. The climate at the mountain's peak is an extremely cold one.

Altitude causes a difference in precipitation on the seaward and landward sides of a mountain. As air from over the ocean moves up the seaward

Analyze Diagrams **Prevailing winds result from the general circulation of air around Earth.**

◈ **Which winds blow across North America from west to east?**

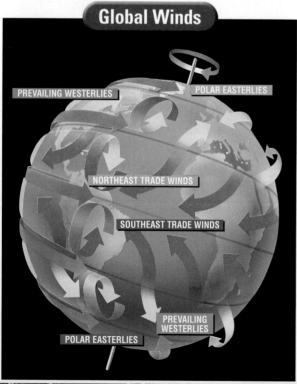

Global Winds

PREVAILING WESTERLIES

POLAR EASTERLIES

NORTHEAST TRADE WINDS

SOUTHEAST TRADE WINDS

PREVAILING WESTERLIES

POLAR EASTERLIES

A sailboat race off the coast of Florida

Amazonia
Understanding Physical Systems

Amazonia is a huge area surrounding the Amazon River. Its plentiful rainfall and warm temperatures provide perfect conditions for many kinds of plant and animal life. One-third of the world's known plant and animal species live in this large region. Some animals live most of their lives in the tree canopy, or the uppermost layer of branches and leaves in a forest. The canopy in Amazonia is so thick that little sunlight gets through to the ground.

Amazonia has a wide variety of plants.

side of a mountain, it cools. Clouds form, and precipitation falls. As a result, the seaward side of the mountain receives a lot of rain or snow. When the air reaches the landward side, it has little moisture left. As a result, that side receives less precipitation. This drier side of the mountain is often said to be in the **rain shadow**. The land east of the Sierra Nevada in the western United States is much drier than the land to the west.

REVIEW How does altitude affect climate?

Climate and Vegetation

No two places on Earth have exactly the same climate. However, Earth can be divided into six major climate regions—tropical, desert, temperate warm, temperate cold, polar, and highland. Each region has its own climate patterns and its own kinds of plant life, or **vegetation**.

Most of Earth's tropical climates are located between the equator and the Tropics of Cancer and Capricorn. Tropical climates are warm all year and receive a lot of precipitation.

Rain forests with thick vegetation and tall trees are found in some tropical regions. The largest tropical rain forests are in the areas around the Amazon River in South America and around the Congo River in central Africa. There are also large tropical rain forests in southeastern Asia. In these places the average year-round temperature is close to 80°F (27°C). Rainfall may measure as much as 100 inches (254 cm) a year.

An area that receives 10 inches (25 cm) or less of precipitation in a year is considered to have a desert climate. Places with deserts can be hot or cold, but all are **arid**, or dry.

To survive in a desert climate, vegetation has adapted to the arid surroundings. Some plants have leaves and stems that store water. Others have root systems that reach water over a large area. Most desert plants grow far apart from each other so they do not compete for the same water.

Temperate climates are found in the temperate zones, areas between the Tropic of Cancer and the Arctic Circle and between the Tropic of Capricorn and the Antarctic Circle. A temperate warm climate is influenced mainly by water, and a temperate cold climate is affected mainly by land.

Areas with a temperate cold climate are often inland, away from coasts. In this kind of climate, big changes in temperature take place from summer to winter. Precipitation is about even year-round. Temperate cold climates support a variety of trees and shrubs that grow in thick forests.

Temperate warm climates are often found along coastal areas. Two kinds of temperate warm climates are marine and Mediterranean. The word *marine* refers to oceans. Marine climates are generally damp or wet. Mediterranean climates are named for the inland sea that borders Asia, Africa, and Europe. The regions around the Mediterranean Sea are warm and fairly dry. Other places that have a Mediterranean

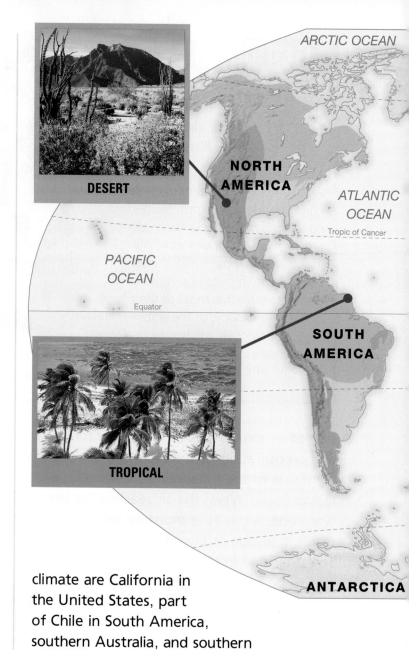

DESERT

TROPICAL

ARCTIC OCEAN

NORTH AMERICA

ATLANTIC OCEAN

Tropic of Cancer

PACIFIC OCEAN

Equator

SOUTH AMERICA

ANTARCTICA

climate are California in the United States, part of Chile in South America, southern Australia, and southern Africa.

North and south of the temperate zones are regions with polar climates. The word *polar* refers to locations near the North and South Poles. In some polar climates, mosses and some grasses grow in the short, cold summers. In other polar climates, there is no vegetation at all.

Hilly and mountainous regions have a highland climate. This kind of climate cannot be defined exactly. Temperature, precipitation, and vegetation depend on altitude, winds, and the rain shadow.

REVIEW What are Earth's six major climate regions?

Climate Regions

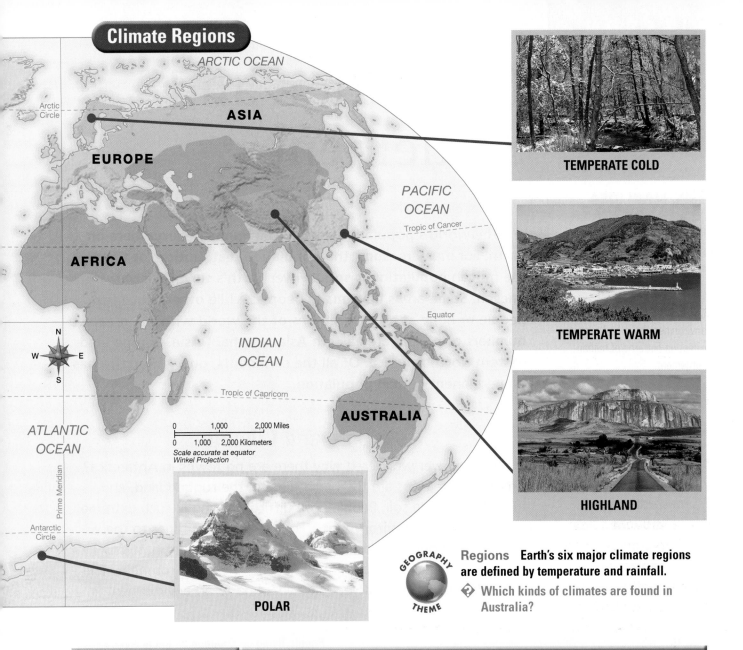

TEMPERATE COLD

TEMPERATE WARM

HIGHLAND

POLAR

Regions Earth's six major climate regions are defined by temperature and rainfall.

❷ Which kinds of climates are found in Australia?

LESSON 3
REVIEW

 MAIN IDEA AND DETAILS What effects does water have on climate?

❶ **BIG IDEA** How does the movement of Earth around the sun affect climate?

❷ **VOCABULARY** What is the **rain shadow** of a mountain?

❸ **GEOGRAPHY** How do the heating and cooling differences between land and water affect people on Earth?

❹ **GEOGRAPHY** Why is it generally warmer near the equator than it is near Earth's poles?

❺ **CRITICAL THINKING—Synthesize** When it is summer in the United States, it is winter in Australia. Why is this so? Use what you know about Earth's path around the sun and the tilt of Earth's axis to explain.

 PERFORMANCE—Make a Brochure
Describe your climate region in a travel brochure that you create. List the kinds of temperature, precipitation, and vegetation common to your region. In your brochure, describe how climate affects life in your region. Draw pictures to illustrate your brochure.

4

Population and Settlement

MAIN IDEA AND DETAILS

Read to find details that support the main idea of each section.

BIG IDEA

Climate and the physical environment have had a major effect on patterns of human settlement.

VOCABULARY

population distribution

environment

irrigation

desertification

drought

migration

urbanization

metropolitan area

The world's population includes all humans everywhere on Earth. For many reasons, the **population distribution**, or the way the human population is spread over Earth's surface, is very uneven. Some areas have many people, while others have few people or none at all. The regions of the world with the greatest numbers of people are eastern Asia, southern Asia, Europe, and eastern North America. Of all the continents, only Antarctica has no permanent human population.

People and Climate

Have you ever wondered why there are no towns in Antarctica? Among the reasons are the harsh climate, the rugged land, and the lack of fertile soil. People have difficulty living in such extreme surroundings, or **environments**. From the earliest times to the present, environment has affected human settlement patterns.

Wherever they live, people must adapt to the environment. The most obvious example of people's adapting to an environment is

People living on Eholmen Island in Norway (below) encounter Arctic temperatures all year. On the island of Grenada (left) in the Caribbean Sea, people face extreme heat from the tropical sun.

Farmers in desert areas use irrigation to make their crops grow.

the clothing they wear. People living in polar and highland climates need to wear heavy coats and boots in winter. People in tropical and desert climates can wear lightweight clothing most of the year.

People also adapt by building different kinds of homes. In Greenland, for example, most homes are built with few windows, to keep out cold winds. In contrast, homes on the tropical island of Samoa, in the Pacific Ocean, have many openings. This allows the cool sea breezes to blow through.

For thousands of years, people in both cold and warm climates have built homes of natural materials that keep out cold or heat. Many homes have thick walls to hold in heat in winter and to block the sun's rays in summer. People have also discovered ways to heat and cool the inside of their homes. Modern electric or gas heaters and air conditioners have allowed greater numbers of people to be comfortable in places where few settled before.

The desert is a good example. Once home to only small numbers of people, some desert areas now support growing cities and large farms. The cities of Phoenix and Las Vegas, in the western United States, are among the fastest-growing cities in the country. Desert cities are also common in the country of Saudi Arabia in southwestern Asia.

To create cities and farms in the desert, people have developed systems of irrigation. **Irrigation** is the use of connected ditches, canals, or pipes to carry water to dry areas.

Making use of desert land is a growing challenge because desert regions are expanding. This is happening because fertile soil, farmland, and forests on the edges of deserts are being lost. These losses are due to the destruction of plant life caused by overgrazing, over-farming, or overlogging. The change of fertile land into desert land is called **desertification**.

People in Bermuda have adapted their clothing to the island's warm climate.

In the 1930s the southwestern United States experienced a severe **drought**, or long period of dry weather. Crops failed, and without plants to hold it, fertile soil blew away in huge dust storms. Many people living in the Dust Bowl, as the region came to be called, chose to move to other parts of the United States.

REVIEW What is the main idea of this section?

MAIN IDEA AND DETAILS

• GEOGRAPHY •

Venice
Environment and Society

Founded long ago at a busy crossroads for European trade, the city of Venice, Italy, is built on 118 small, tightly grouped islands within a lagoon. From earliest times, people used natural waterways to travel between the islands. Over time, the city grew in importance and in population as wealthy sea merchants traded goods from all over the world. Limited available land and a seafaring way of life led to the building of canals throughout the city. The Grand Canal is Venice's main water route.

ITALY

Laguna Veneta

Liberta Bridge

Sacche Canal

Nari Canal

Grand Canal

VENICE

Doge's Palace

St. Mark's Canal

Fusina Canal

Giudecca Canal

N W E S

0   1/2   1 Mile
0   1/2   1 Kilometer

—— Canal

People, Land, and Water

The physical features of land and water also affect population distribution. For example, it is easier for people to live on flat land near water than on mountains.

China in eastern Asia has more people than any other country in the world. Most of China's people live along the three major river valleys of eastern China—the Chang Jiang, the Huang He, and the Xi Jiang (SHEE JYAHNG). Many other people in eastern Asia live on the east coast of China, on the Korean Peninsula, and on the islands of Japan.

India, in southern Asia, has the second-largest population in the world. There the greatest number of people lives in the Ganges River valley in northern India.

Europe is another region with crowded areas. Many people live in central and southern England, a part of Britain.

Populations of Major World Cities

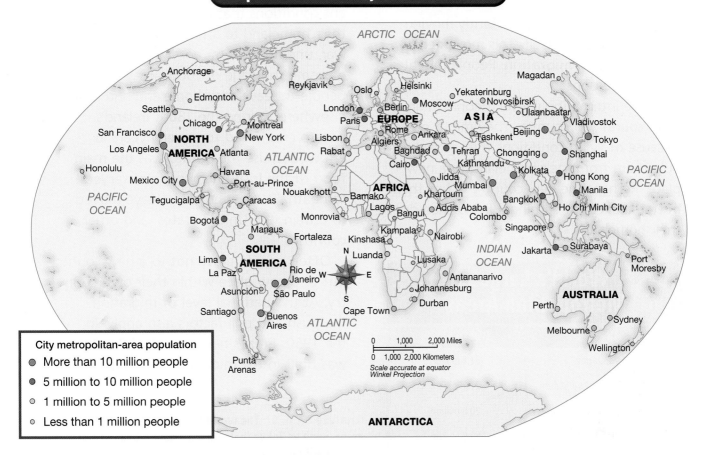

City metropolitan-area population
- More than 10 million people
- 5 million to 10 million people
- 1 million to 5 million people
- Less than 1 million people

Location The world's four largest centers of population are in eastern Asia, southern Asia, Europe, and eastern North America.

❓ What is similar about the locations of these population centers?

Another area with a large population is the Great European Plain. This area begins on the southern coast of the North Sea, in the Netherlands and Belgium, and extends along the Rhine River between France and Germany. People in this group live as far east as the Dnieper (NEE•per) River in Ukraine. Northern Italy and southern France also have large numbers of people.

The largest population group in North America is in the northeastern United States and in southeastern Canada. Population in some of the western parts of the continent is limited by the desert climate and rugged mountains.

Of the remaining continents, Africa has the largest population. One large group of people lives in the Nile River valley. Other groups live around the large lakes of eastern Africa and along the northern, southern, and western coasts.

Most of South America is lightly populated compared to many other areas of the world. Its population mainly follows the edge of the continent. The largest numbers of people in South America are along the southeastern coast where the land is low and flat. A similar settlement pattern occurs in Australia. Most Australians live along the eastern and southern coasts. Few people live in the middle of the continent, which has a largely desert climate.

REVIEW What physical features make places easy for people to live in?

People on the Move

Earth's population is constantly moving and redistributing itself. This movement of people is called **migration**. People migrate for many reasons.

At the international level, people migrate from country to country. They might do so because of living conditions that attract, or pull, them from their homeland to a new place. Perhaps the new country offers them better chances of earning a living than does their homeland.

Other causes for migration are unpleasant conditions that push people out of their homeland to a new country. Drought, war, unemployment, and famine—or an extreme shortage of food—may cause people to leave their homeland and move elsewhere. During the 1800s Ireland's potato crop failed for several years in a row. Because the potato was the main food of the Irish, many people starved to death. Those who could leave moved to Britain, the United States, and other countries.

Often people move not to a new country but to a new place within their own country. At this national level of migration, the push and pull factors also apply. In the 1950s Brazil's new capital of Brasília was built in the middle of the country.

World's Largest Metropolitan Areas

CITY	POPULATION
Tokyo, Japan	31.4 million
New York City, United States	21.2 million
Mexico City, Mexico	20.9 million
Seoul, South Korea	19.9 million
São Paulo, Brazil	18.5 million
Osaka-Kobe-Kyoto, Japan	17.6 million
Jakarta, Indonesia	17.6 million
New Delhi, India	16.7 million
Mumbai (Bombay), India	16.7 million
Los Angeles, United States	16.4 million
Cairo, Egypt	15.5 million
Kolkata (Calcutta), India	13.8 million
Manila, Philippines	13.5 million
Buenos Aires, Argentina	12.9 million
Moscow, Russia	12.1 million

Analyze Tables The world's largest metropolitan areas, such as Tokyo (below), have populations of more than 10 million.

How many more people live in Tokyo than in New York City?

Many people then moved from the southeastern coast to the central region, where few people had lived before. The newcomers were pulled there by the offer of inexpensive land. The same promise of land pulled people in the eastern United States westward in the 1800s.

Migration within countries also takes place from rural areas to urban centers. The movement of people from the countryside to the cities is called **urbanization**. All over the world, people have been moving to cities. Some move because of the difficulty they have in making a living by farming. Others are attracted to city life by the economic opportunities of better jobs and more income for their families.

As a result of urbanization, the largest concentrations of people are now in the world's **metropolitan areas**—the big cities and the sprawling suburbs that surround them. The Tokyo metropolitan area in Japan already has more than 30 million people. Some experts predict that Mexico City in Mexico, São Paulo in Brazil, New York City in the United States, and Mumbai in India will become just as large.

This increase in population is due only partly to migration. More people are born every day, and advances in health care and nutrition are helping people live longer. People who study population estimate that the world's population today is more than 6 billion. They predict that it will grow to more than 8 billion by 2020. Reasons for population growth and patterns of migration will need to be considered in the future.

REVIEW **What are some factors that push and pull people to migrate from place to place?**

LESSON 4
REVIEW

MAIN IDEA AND DETAILS What are four details that support the idea that climate affects where people settle?

1 **BIG IDEA** How do landforms affect where people live in your community?

2 **VOCABULARY** Explain how **migration** and **urbanization** are related.

3 **TECHNOLOGY** What are some ways people have adapted to the climates in which they live?

4 **CRITICAL THINKING—Analyze** Use what you know about climate and landforms to tell which would likely have a larger population— a northern city in the mountains or a coastal city close to the equator. Explain your answer.

PERFORMANCE—Create a Poster Make a poster that tells about your region. In this poster, explain why people would like living where you do. Include pictures or illustrations and a list of your region's good points.

·SKILLS·

MAP AND GLOBE

Read a Thematic Map

▶ WHY IT MATTERS

Sometimes geographers use thematic maps to show different kinds of information. A **thematic map** focuses on one topic or subject. One topic that a geographer might choose to show with a map is population. Knowing how to read a population map can make it easy to see which parts of the world are the most crowded with people and which parts are the least crowded.

▶ WHAT YOU NEED TO KNOW

Look at the map key, or legend, for the map titled World Population on these pages. The map key tells you that the colors on the map stand for different population densities. **Population density** is the number of people who live in 1 square mile or 1 square kilometer of land. A square mile is a square area of land, each side of which is 1 mile long. A square kilometer is a square area of land, each side of which is 1 kilometer long.

The white areas on the map are places where no people live permanently. The tan areas are the least crowded. The population is sparse, which means that people live far apart from one another. The red areas on the map are the most crowded. The population in these areas is dense, which means that the people live close together. The colors in between stand for varying levels of population density.

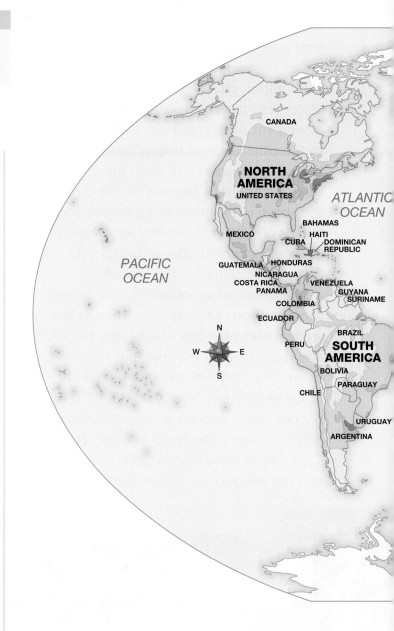

▶ PRACTICE THE SKILL

Use the map to answer the following questions.

❶ Which continent has the highest population density?

❷ On which continent does no one live permanently?

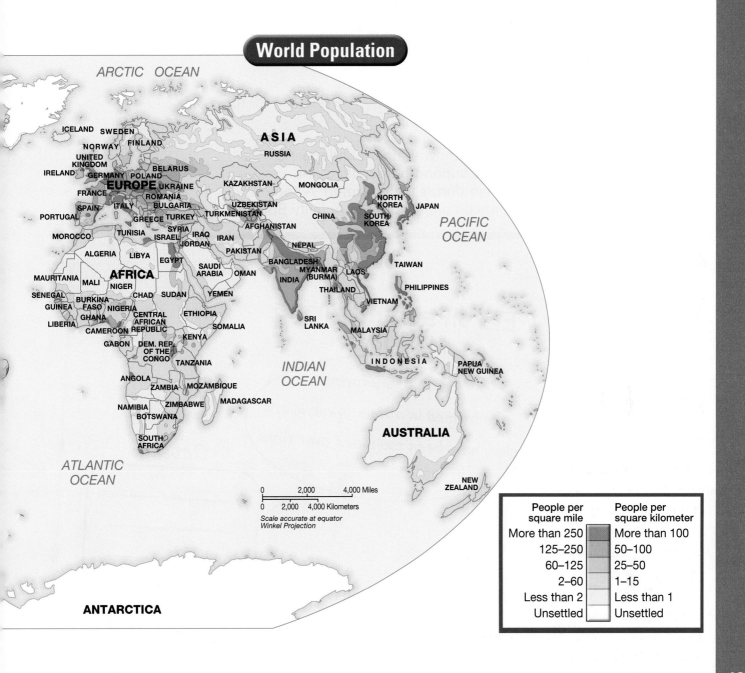

World Population

ARCTIC OCEAN

ASIA

RUSSIA

ICELAND SWEDEN
NORWAY FINLAND
UNITED KINGDOM
IRELAND BELARUS
GERMANY POLAND
EUROPE UKRAINE
FRANCE ROMANIA
ITALY BULGARIA
SPAIN
PORTUGAL GREECE TURKEY
MOROCCO TUNISIA
ALGERIA LIBYA
MAURITANIA MALI
SENEGAL
GUINEA BURKINA
GHANA FASO NIGERIA
LIBERIA CAMEROON CENTRAL AFRICAN REPUBLIC
GABON DEM. REP. OF THE CONGO

KAZAKHSTAN MONGOLIA
UZBEKISTAN
TURKMENISTAN
AFGHANISTAN CHINA
SYRIA IRAQ IRAN
ISRAEL JORDAN NEPAL
EGYPT PAKISTAN
SAUDI BANGLADESH
ARABIA OMAN MYANMAR (BURMA) LAOS
INDIA THAILAND
YEMEN VIETNAM
SRI LANKA MALAYSIA

NORTH KOREA JAPAN
SOUTH KOREA
TAIWAN
PHILIPPINES

PACIFIC OCEAN

AFRICA
NIGER CHAD SUDAN
ETHIOPIA
SOMALIA
KENYA
TANZANIA
ANGOLA
ZAMBIA MOZAMBIQUE
NAMIBIA ZIMBABWE MADAGASCAR
BOTSWANA
SOUTH AFRICA

INDONESIA PAPUA NEW GUINEA

INDIAN OCEAN

AUSTRALIA

ATLANTIC OCEAN

NEW ZEALAND

0   2,000   4,000 Miles
0   2,000 4,000 Kilometers
Scale accurate at equator
Winkel Projection

ANTARCTICA

People per square mile	People per square kilometer
More than 250	More than 100
125–250	50–100
60–125	25–50
2–60	1–15
Less than 2	Less than 1
Unsettled	Unsettled

❸ Not including Antarctica, which continent has the lowest population density?

❹ Does India have a higher or lower population density than Canada?

▶ APPLY WHAT YOU LEARNED

Study the population information given on the map. Then show some of the same information by using a chart, a graph, or a table. For example, you might make a table comparing the population densities of five countries.

Practice your map and globe skills with the **GeoSkills CD-ROM**.

1 Review and Test Preparation

Focus Skill Main Idea and Details

Complete this graphic organizer to show that you understand
how to identify the main idea and supporting details of the
information about how Earth's landforms were formed. A copy
of this graphic organizer appears on page 16 of the Activity Book.

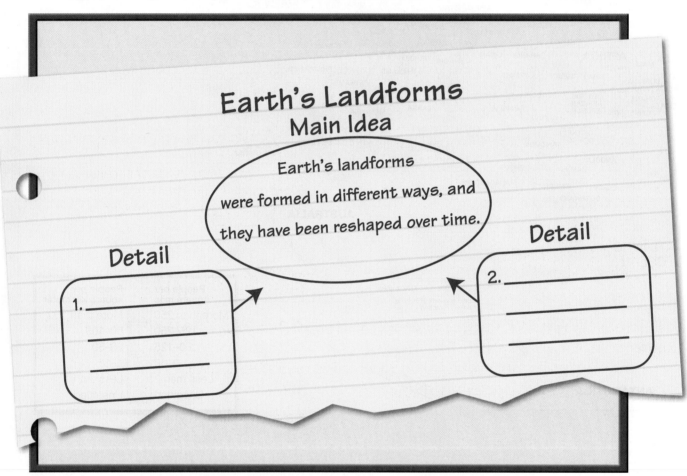

Earth's Landforms
Main Idea

Earth's landforms were formed in different ways, and they have been reshaped over time.

Detail

1. _____

_____

Detail

2. _____

_____

THINK & WRITE

Create an Advertisement Think about
what you learned about population and patterns
of settlement in this chapter. Use this information
to create an advertisement for a place where
people might want to live. The ad should
include attractive images and descriptions.

Write a Tall Tale Tall tales are exaggerated
stories that explain how events happened
or how things were created. Write a tall tale
that explains how mountains or deserts were
formed. Then write a paragraph that explains
how they really were formed.

USE VOCABULARY

Use the terms on the right to complete the sentences.

magma (p. 22)
tributaries (p. 29)
rain shadow (p. 37)
irrigation (p. 41)
metropolitan area (p. 45)

1. Lava is _____, or molten rock, that has reached Earth's surface.

2. Together a river and its _____ make up a river system.

3. People have developed systems of _____ to create farms in desert areas.

4. The Tokyo _____ includes the city and the suburbs that surround it.

5. Because it is in a _____, the land east of the Sierra Nevada is much drier than the land to the west of the mountains.

RECALL FACTS

Answer these questions.

6. What forces cause the weathering of land?

7. Which is the world's largest ocean? How many square miles does it cover?

8. How does Antarctica's environment make it hard for people to live there?

Write the letter of the best choice.

9. **TEST PREP** According to the plate tectonics theory, all of the following statements are true *except*—
   A The movement of Earth's plates sometimes creates magma.
   B Deposition causes earthquakes.
   C Earth's landmasses were once part of the supercontinent Pangaea.
   D The movement of Earth's crust created mountains.

10. **TEST PREP** Which of these is *not* a way people change the land?
    F by terracing mountain slopes
    G by creating faults, or cracks, in Earth's crust
    H by building dams and reservoirs
    J by draining water from wetlands

11. **TEST PREP** Most of Earth's tropical climates are found—
    A near the poles.
    B in Earth's temperate zones.
    C along the drainage basins of rivers.
    D between the Tropics of Cancer and Capricorn.

12. **TEST PREP** People adapt to different kinds of climates by doing all of the following *except*—
    F wearing different kinds of clothing.
    G using heaters and air conditioners.
    H creating larger deserts through desertification.
    J building irrigation systems.

THINK CRITICALLY

13. What kind of climate do you think is the best to live in? Why?

14. How does vegetation affect where people choose to settle?

APPLY SKILLS

Use Latitude and Longitude

15. Use the map on page 33 to find which lines of latitude are nearest to the cities of Aswan and Sohag.

Use a Thematic Map

16. Use the map on pages 46–47 to identify three countries that have a high population density.

LASCAUX CAVE, FRANCE

In 1940 four teenage boys discovered Lascaux Cave near Montignac, France. The cave contains about 600 paintings and drawings—one of the world's most valued collections of art created by early people. To protect the artwork, Lascaux Cave was closed to tourists in 1963. A nearby re-creation of the site attracts about 300,000 visitors every year.

LOCATE IT

Lascaux Cave

FRANCE

Montignac

2

Early People

"[Someone] who has looked with the archaeological eye will never see quite normally again."

—Loren Eiseley, from
The Night Country, 1971

 **Generalize**

When you **generalize**, you make a statement that summarizes a group of facts and shows how they are related.

As you read this chapter, make generalizations.

- **Identify and list important facts.**

- **Use these facts to make generalizations about early people.**

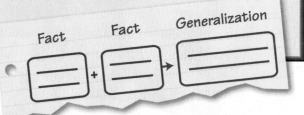

Fact   Fact   Generalization

Hunters and Gatherers

As you read this lesson, make generalizations about the ways that early people met their needs.

BIG IDEA

Early people lived and worked together to survive.

VOCABULARY

descendant
band
consequence
extinct
technology
artifact
specialize

FAST FACT

The last wild European bison died in 1925. In ancient times large herds of bison roamed throughout Europe. Today a few small herds are cared for in eastern Europe.

| 50,000 years ago | 30,000 years ago | 10,000 years ago |

50,000 years ago – 12,000 years ago

Most experts believe that the first modern humans—people like us—lived in eastern and southern Africa more than 100,000 years ago. Generation after generation of these early people lived by hunting and gathering enough food to survive. Over thousands of years, their **descendants**, or children's children, migrated very slowly to other parts of the world.

Living and Working Together

Wherever they lived, early people followed much the same way of life. Most united in **bands**, or small groups of people made up of related families. A typical band had about 30 people.

Early people spent much of their time searching for food. Their search led them through familiar areas that they had visited in the past. At each place they stopped, the women gathered wild fruits, nuts, roots, and seeds for the group to eat. Early people also caught and ate fish, turtles, birds, and small rodents. Experience taught them which animals and plants could be eaten without any unpleasant **consequences**, or results, such as illness.

While the women gathered, the men hunted large animals. Many of these large animals such as woolly rhinoceroses, giant oxen, and elephantlike mammoths and mastodons are now **extinct** (ik•STINGT), or have died out. Other animals, such as bison and deer, still exist. All these animals provided meat for food, skins for clothing and shelter, and bones for tools. To make tools, early people relied not only on bones but also on stone and other natural resources.

Stone carving of a bison, found in France

Early people worked together to hunt large animals (above). These spear points (right) were used in early hunts.

In fact, stone was such an important resource that the time of the hunters and gatherers is now sometimes called the Old Stone Age, or the Paleolithic (pay•lee•uh•LIH•thik) period.

Using resources around them, early people made many kinds of tools. With animal bones they made hooks for fishing and needles for sewing animal skins together. They sharpened animal bones and stones into spear points and tied them to wooden poles for hunting. They also learned to work plant fibers into rope, which they used for making nets and for carrying objects.

From time to time, different groups of early people invented new tools and new weapons. One important weapon was the atlatl (AHT•lah•tuhl), or spear-thrower. With the atlatl early hunters were able to launch their spears at greater speeds to cover longer distances. The atlatl was an important improvement in technology for early people. **Technology** is the use of knowledge and skills to make the work of everyday life easier.

Early people also used special skills and teamwork to hunt. Some early people killed large animals by working together to chase them over a cliff. Others disguised themselves in animal skins and crept close enough to their prey to make a kill. Without such cooperation, the bands most likely would not have survived.

Because early people were always on the move looking for food, they did not have permanent year-round settlements. Instead, they camped near places where they knew animals and plants would be plentiful at different times of the year.

REVIEW How did technology affect the lives of early people? GENERALIZE

DEMOCRATIC VALUES
Common Good

Early people worked together for the common good of their group. During a hunt an entire band would first form a circle around a herd of mammoths or other animals. Shouting and waving sticks or spears, the group would then drive the animals off a cliff or into a pit. Finally, the hunters would throw their spears or large stones at the animals. Afterward, the people skinned the animals and collected the meat. The members of a band also worked together to set up camp, where they rested and cooked. Families helped each other build shelters. They made tents from the bones and skins of animals.

Analyze the Value

1 Why was it important for early people to work together?

2 **Make It Relevant** Identify some people who work together for the common good of everyone at your school. Then write a paragraph that explains how working together helps them do more than they could do separately.

Early People on the Move

Over time some bands of early people grew in number. As a result, they had to go beyond their usual hunting-and-gathering grounds to find enough food. A band's seasonal migration route may have expanded by 2 or 3 miles (3.2 to 4.8 km) each generation. A generation represented about 20 years, the average length of an early person's life, so this movement was very, very slow. In time, however, people spread to almost every part of Earth.

The movement of people throughout the world was made possible mostly by the last Ice Age. At different times in its past, Earth has had long periods of freezing cold. During these periods, known as Ice Ages, Earth's climate became so cold that huge glaciers formed. These sheets of ice covered large parts of Earth. So much of Earth's water was frozen in glaciers that the level of the oceans dropped. This caused "bridges" of dry land to appear between islands and continents.

People probably arrived in southwestern Asia from Africa by way of a land bridge about 90,000 years ago. They most likely

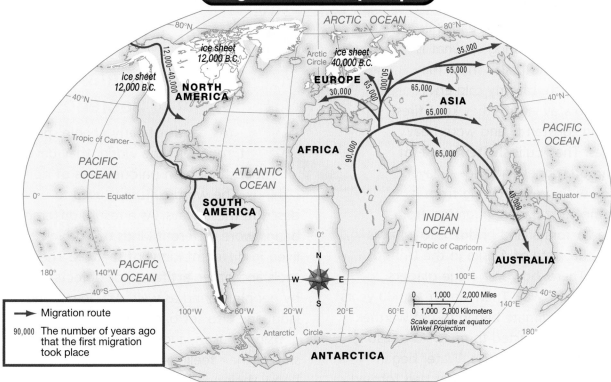

Migrations of Early People

Movement Early people probably began to migrate from Africa about 90,000 years ago.

❓ About when did the first migration to western Europe take place?

followed migrating herds of animals, such as gazelles and deer, from Africa into Asia. Generation after generation, these early people spread out in many directions.

By about 65,000 years ago, early people came to live in eastern Asia, in the land now known as China. Later generations followed herds across land bridges to what is now Indonesia. From there, men, women, and children paddled log rafts across the open ocean in search of new places to hunt and gather food. This most likely was how early people reached Australia about 40,000 years ago.

Early bands may have followed animals from Asia into North America. They used the animals for food, clothing, and shelter, as shown by this mammoth bone hut (in circle on page 54).

By about 30,000 years ago, some early people had already moved into western Europe. Meanwhile, others were migrating to what is now Siberia in Russia. There they faced a harsh, bitterly cold environment. To stay warm, they kept fires burning constantly and wore heavy clothes. They built shelters made of mammoth bones and sod—a layer of soil with grass growing from it.

Some early people migrated from Siberia across a land bridge into what is today the state of Alaska in the United States. There, however, huge glaciers blocked their way. Then, about 12,000 years ago, Earth's climate began to get warmer. Some glaciers started to melt. As a result, the oceans began to rise. Water began covering the land bridges that had formed during the Ice Ages. At the same time, a narrow path opened between two melting glaciers that covered what is now Canada. As a result, later generations of early people were able to make their way farther into North America and, over time, into South America.

REVIEW How did the Ice Ages affect the movement of early people throughout the world?

Found in France, this 22,000-year-old ivory carving shows the face of a woman.

Early Cultures and Societies

As bands of early people spread throughout the world, they developed their own unique ways of doing things. The word *culture* is used to describe these ways. As a result, different bands wore different kinds of clothing and lived in different kinds of shelters. Their tools and other **artifacts**, or objects made by people, varied as well. Art, ideas, and language also set bands apart.

Using spoken language, early people shared their feelings and let each other know their needs. Older members of bands used spoken language to pass on customs, traditions, and history to younger members. The spoken word helped people share new ideas, warn of dangers, and work better as a group. A common spoken language also helped some bands unite to become a society. The word *society* refers to any organized group of people with shared customs, traditions, and ways of life.

The painting (right) shows how an ancient artist may have worked. Below is part of a cave painting from South Africa.

These clay carvings of bison (above) are more than 12,000 years old. The stone-carved wrench (right) is an example of a tool used by early people.

In larger bands and societies, individuals began to **specialize** in their work. Each person did one kind of task, based on his or her skills and the band's needs. By specializing, people were able to work faster and use natural resources more efficiently.

In most large bands, for example, a person who carved well spent most of his or her time making tools for the group. An expert at sewing animal skins became the group's clothing maker. Some tasks were done mainly by women and some mainly by men. Women usually gathered food from plants and cared for children. Men generally were responsible for hunting. The most skilled people in a group often came to be viewed as leaders. In some bands women were leaders. In others, men were leaders.

REVIEW What set apart different groups of early people?

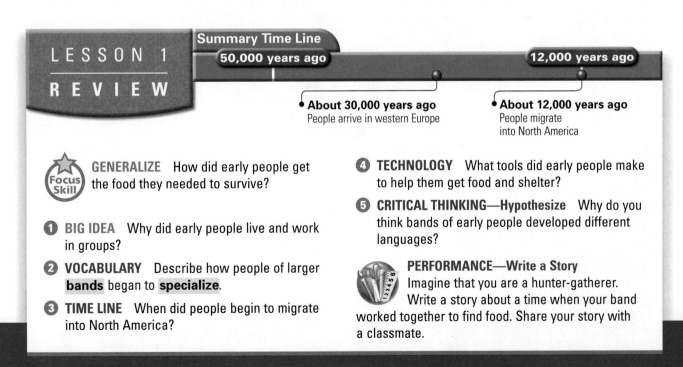

LESSON 1 REVIEW

Summary Time Line

50,000 years ago — 12,000 years ago

• About 30,000 years ago
People arrive in western Europe

• About 12,000 years ago
People migrate into North America

Focus Skill **GENERALIZE** How did early people get the food they needed to survive?

1 BIG IDEA Why did early people live and work in groups?

2 VOCABULARY Describe how people of larger **bands** began to **specialize**.

3 TIME LINE When did people begin to migrate into North America?

4 TECHNOLOGY What tools did early people make to help them get food and shelter?

5 CRITICAL THINKING—Hypothesize Why do you think bands of early people developed different languages?

PERFORMANCE—Write a Story
Imagine that you are a hunter-gatherer. Write a story about a time when your band worked together to find food. Share your story with a classmate.

Studying Early People

Imagine digging through layers of rocks and sand to find out about people and places of the past. That is what **archaeologists** (ar•kee•AH•luh•jists) do to help us learn about what happened before the invention of writing. To find out about this "prehistory," as it is called, archaeologists must look for **evidence**, or proof, other than written words. They must search for clues to piece together the puzzle of life in the distant past.

FROM THE MUSEUM OF ANCIENT HISTORY IN SAINT-GERMAIN-EN-LAYE, FRANCE

Archaeologists study artifacts to gather evidence. For example, they can find out how old the artifacts are. This helps them identify the early people who made the objects. With that information, they can also figure out what the objects were used for.

Early people probably used this stone burin, or chisel, to carve wood and bone.

This harpoon made of bone was used to hunt animals.

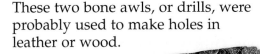

These two bone awls, or drills, were probably used to make holes in leather or wood.

Analyze the Primary Source

1 Why do you think early people made carvings of bison and other animals?

2 How might archaeologists find out how early people used objects such as awls and harpoons?

3 What might early people have made using the needle? What might they have made using the burin?

This spear point is made of flint, a rock that can be broken to form sharp edges.

ACTIVITY

Compare and Contrast Make a list of five everyday items that you think will give future archaeologists useful information about life in the early twenty-first century. Write a paragraph explaining why you made the choices you did.

RESEARCH

Visit The Learning Site at **www.harcourtschool.com** to research other primary sources.

A needle made of bone

Chapter 2 ■ **59**

Early Herders and Farmers

Focus Skill

GENERALIZE
As you read this lesson, make generalizations about how the ways that early people got their food affected their lives.

BIG IDEA
Over time, early people became food producers instead of food collectors.

VOCABULARY

domesticate
livestock
nomad
pastoral society
cultivate
agriculture
slash and burn

12,000 years ago	8,000 years ago	4,000 years ago

10,000 years ago – 8,000 years ago

Different societies of early people throughout the world developed different ways to meet their needs. While most groups migrated seasonally to find food, some stayed in one place all year. These groups settled where there were many animals to hunt and wild plants to gather. When food became harder to find near their settlements, some groups went back to seasonal migrations. Others remained settled.

Pastoral Societies

The groups that stayed settled learned to raise their own food by keeping herds of animals and by farming. By changing from food collecting to food producing, people no longer had to depend only on the food they could hunt or gather. This change marked the beginning of a new age called the New Stone Age, or Neolithic (nee•uh•LIH•thik) period.

Animals were important to Neolithic societies. As early as 10,000 years ago, people began to **domesticate** (duh•MES•tih•kayt) animals, or tame them for human use. People kept cats in their homes to catch rats and mice. They raised dogs to help them hunt

Today many people, such as these herders in Afghanistan (below), still raise animals to meet their needs. This girl from Jordan (left) raises goats.

This ancient cave painting in Algeria, Africa, shows early herders tending their cattle.

and to protect the band. People later began to domesticate other wild animals for the food and the labor they provided.

The first people to domesticate wild animals probably followed migrating herds from place to place. In time some of these people began raising wild animals in pens until the animals came to depend on the people for food and water. The first animals that people domesticated in this way were probably sheep, goats, and pigs. These animals provided people with meat and milk for food and wool and hides for clothing. The term **livestock** refers to domesticated animals that provide such resources.

Many of the early people who raised livestock were **nomads**, or people with no settled home. Like the hunters and gatherers, nomadic herders did not build permanent settlements but lived in temporary shelters. They also traveled in bands, leading their domesticated animals from place to place to find water and grazing areas. When the livestock had eaten all the grass in one place, the band and its herd moved on to fresh grazing land.

In some parts of the world, people still live as nomadic herders, traveling from place to place with their animals. Such nomadic people make up what is known as a **pastoral society**. The word *pastoral* refers to herding.

The Bedouins (BEH•duh•wuhnz) are people who have long been nomadic herders. They live in the deserts of northern Africa and southwestern Asia.

LOCATE IT

Bamian

AFGHANISTAN

Today about 1 million Bedouins still follow their traditional way of life. They live in tents, make woven cloth, and eat mostly meat and dairy products. They trade meat and dairy products from their livestock with people from villages near their camps. In return, they get dates, rice, and factory products from the cities.

REVIEW What livestock animals were probably the first to be domesticated?

Early farmers used these stones to grind wheat into flour.

Farming Societies

Women may have been the first to domesticate wild plants. Since women did most of the food gathering in early societies, they most likely learned that plants produce seeds that grow into new plants. As time passed, they began planting the seeds of plants that grew fast and tasted good.

As years went by, some early societies came to depend less on gathering wild plants. Instead, they began to **cultivate**, or take care of, plants in small gardens. As people became more skilled at cultivating plants, their gardens became larger. Barley and wheat were among the first wild plants to be grown as crops, or domesticated plants.

Cultivating crops meant that people stayed in one place. Planting, caring for, and harvesting crops took many months. Once the crops were harvested, they had to be stored. As a result, permanent shelters were built to store them.

As people began to grow their own crops, they developed new kinds of tools and skills for farming. These were different from the tools and skills people needed for hunting and gathering. For example, early farmers

used sharp sticks, rocks, bones, and shells to break up soil before planting seeds.

About 8,000 years ago, early farmers developed the first plow. They did this by sharpening one part of a large forked branch. The farmer guided the new tool by holding the branch's stump. Another person pulled on the other end of the branch. The sharpened part then dug into the soil, loosening it. Later, cattle and other domesticated animals were used to pull the plow.

Throughout the world, at different times, farming societies developed independently of one another. In southwestern Asia wild barley and wheat were the earliest crops. In northern Africa early people grew such grains as wheat and flax. Rice was grown in southern and eastern Asia.

Early farming societies also developed in the Americas. In what is now southern Mexico, farmers grew squash and other vegetables. Later, maize (MAYZ), or corn, became important. In the mountains of South America, farmers raised beans and corn.

REVIEW What crops were grown by early farmers in Africa, Asia, and the Americas?

🌀 **GENERALIZE**

The Results of Change

The raising of domesticated animals and plants for use by people is known as **agriculture**, or farming. Agriculture changed human societies in many ways.

A CLOSER LOOK
Early Farming Village

The raising of plants and animals caused the first farming communities to develop in southwestern Asia.

1. Oxen and other animals pulled wooden plows. The sharp ends of the plows loosened the soil to plant seeds.

2. Early farmers harvested wheat, barley, and other crops that could feed large populations.

3. Farmworkers stored the harvested crops in permanent buildings. The communities lived off the stored crops for the rest of the year.

❖ How do you think farming led to the development of new kinds of tools?

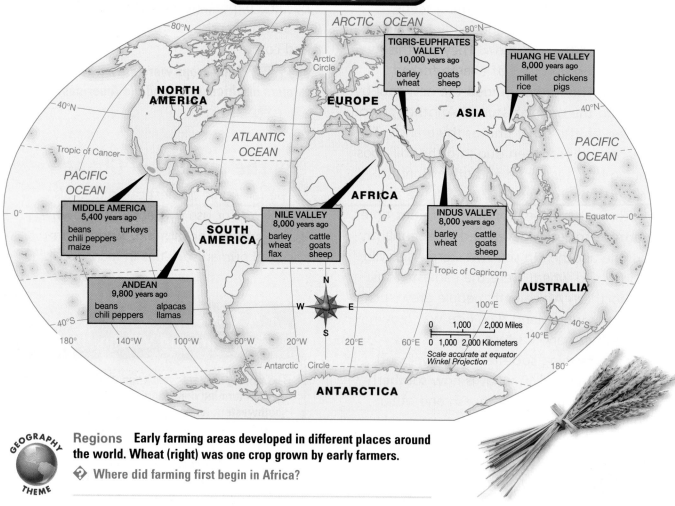

Early Farming Areas

ARCTIC OCEAN

TIGRIS-EUPHRATES VALLEY
10,000 years ago
- barley
- wheat
- goats
- sheep

HUANG HE VALLEY
8,000 years ago
- millet
- rice
- chickens
- pigs

NORTH AMERICA

EUROPE

ASIA

ATLANTIC OCEAN

PACIFIC OCEAN

PACIFIC OCEAN

Arctic Circle

Tropic of Cancer

MIDDLE AMERICA
5,400 years ago
- beans
- chili peppers
- maize
- turkeys

SOUTH AMERICA

AFRICA

NILE VALLEY
8,000 years ago
- barley
- wheat
- flax
- cattle
- goats
- sheep

INDUS VALLEY
8,000 years ago
- barley
- wheat
- cattle
- goats
- sheep

Equator

Tropic of Capricorn

AUSTRALIA

ANDEAN
9,800 years ago
- beans
- chili peppers
- alpacas
- llamas

100°E

N W E S

| 0 | 1,000 | 2,000 Miles |
| 0 | 1,000 | 2,000 Kilometers |

Scale accurate at equator
Winkel Projection

Antarctic Circle

ANTARCTICA

GEOGRAPHY THEME

Regions Early farming areas developed in different places around the world. Wheat (right) was one crop grown by early farmers.

❓ **Where did farming first begin in Africa?**

The most important change was that it provided a reliable food source.

The earliest form of agriculture was subsistence farming, or raising just enough food to meet a group's needs. Once people could subsist on farming, they were less likely to move. They needed to stay near their farmland to take care of their crops. In many places in the world, farming led to the building of permanent homes gathered together in villages.

Some farming societies raised more food than they needed. With more food available, more people could live in one place. As a result, agriculture allowed for larger families. This, in turn, led to population growth. Some farming villages grew to include 100 people or more.

While agriculture made more food available, it also brought problems. Early farmers faced threats to their crops, such as insects, plant diseases, and flooding. When crops failed to grow for any reason, the whole village suffered. In addition, the need for fertile soil in which to grow crops caused fights between some farming societies.

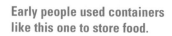

Early people used containers like this one to store food.

The way in which early farmers cultivated crops affected their environment. Many used a method of farming called **slash and burn** to prepare the soil for planting. First, the farmers cleared the trees and brush from the land. Next, they burned the trees and mixed the ashes with the soil to fertilize it. Then they planted different kinds of crops together in the fields. After several years the soil became worn-out and no longer produced healthy crops. When this happened, farmers moved on to new fields and began again.

This method usually worked well for early farmers. Wild plants usually grew back over their old fields. Today, however, such methods can sometimes harm the environment. Pollution and the growth of modern cities can make it difficult for wild plants to grow again in cleared areas.

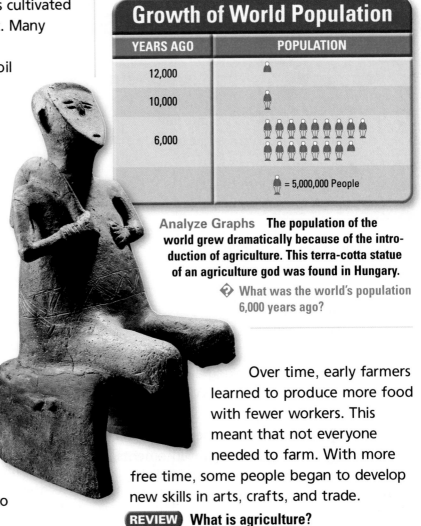

Growth of World Population

YEARS AGO	POPULATION
12,000	👤
10,000	👤
6,000	👤👤👤👤👤👤👤👤👤👤👤👤👤👤

👤 = 5,000,000 People

Analyze Graphs The population of the world grew dramatically because of the introduction of agriculture. This terra-cotta statue of an agriculture god was found in Hungary.

❖ What was the world's population 6,000 years ago?

Over time, early farmers learned to produce more food with fewer workers. This meant that not everyone needed to farm. With more free time, some people began to develop new skills in arts, crafts, and trade.

REVIEW What is agriculture?

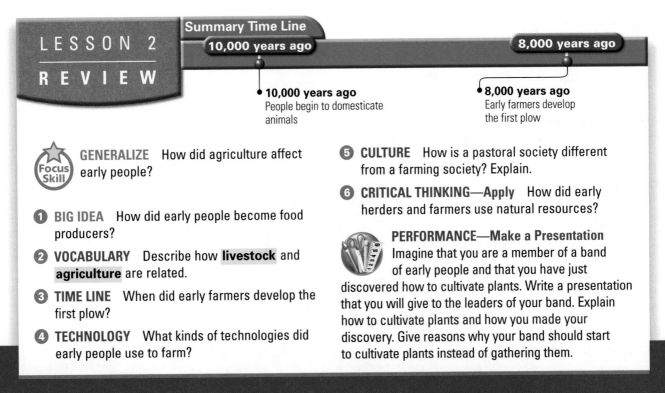

LESSON 2 REVIEW

Summary Time Line

10,000 years ago	8,000 years ago

10,000 years ago
People begin to domesticate animals

8,000 years ago
Early farmers develop the first plow

Focus Skill **GENERALIZE** How did agriculture affect early people?

1 BIG IDEA How did early people become food producers?

2 VOCABULARY Describe how **livestock** and **agriculture** are related.

3 TIME LINE When did early farmers develop the first plow?

4 TECHNOLOGY What kinds of technologies did early people use to farm?

5 CULTURE How is a pastoral society different from a farming society? Explain.

6 CRITICAL THINKING—Apply How did early herders and farmers use natural resources?

PERFORMANCE—Make a Presentation Imagine that you are a member of a band of early people and that you have just discovered how to cultivate plants. Write a presentation that you will give to the leaders of your band. Explain how to cultivate plants and how you made your discovery. Give reasons why your band should start to cultivate plants instead of gathering them.

Read Parallel Time Lines

VOCABULARY	
parallel	A.D.
time line	B.C.E.
B.C.	C.E.

WHY IT MATTERS

Time lines help you understand when events in the past happened and the sequence, or order, in which they occurred. A **parallel time line** is made up of two or more time lines. Each individual time line covers the same period of time for a different place or person. By looking at all the time lines together, you can see what was happening in different places or to different people at the same point in time.

One of the most important advancements of any culture is the development of agriculture. The parallel time line on page 67 helps you compare when different cultures developed agriculture.

WHAT YOU NEED TO KNOW

Look closely at the parallel time line on the next page. Each line covers the same overall time period. Each time line is also divided into the same smaller periods of 2,000 years, beginning at 8000 B.C. and ending at A.D. 2000.

The abbreviation **B.C.** stands for "before Christ." **A.D.** stands for *anno Domini*, a Latin phrase that means "in the year of the Lord." The number that follows the abbreviation A.D. tells how many years have passed since the birth of Jesus Christ.

It is important to remember that with B.C. dates, the greater the number, the longer ago an event happened. For example, an event that happened in 3500 B.C. took place 500 years before an event that occurred in 3000 B.C. It is also important to remember that B.C. always appears after the year and A.D. always appears before the year.

Some time lines are labeled B.C.E. and C.E. rather than B.C. and A.D. The abbreviation **B.C.E.** stands for "before the Common Era," and **C.E.** stands for "Common Era." The abbreviations B.C.E. and C.E. refer to the same years as B.C. and A.D.

No one knows exactly when some events of long ago happened. For this reason, some dates on time lines are only approximate, or more or less correct. Approximate dates are often shown after the Latin word *circa* or after its abbreviation, *c*. The word *circa* means "about."

A farmer in Peru harvests an ancient kind of grain, using traditional methods.

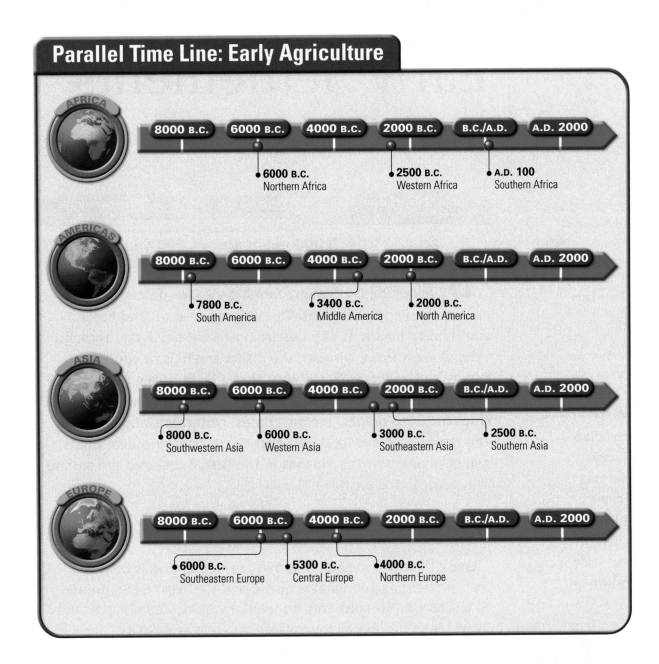

Parallel Time Line: Early Agriculture

AFRICA

8000 B.C. | 6000 B.C. | 4000 B.C. | 2000 B.C. | B.C./A.D. | A.D. 2000

6000 B.C.
Northern Africa

2500 B.C.
Western Africa

A.D. 100
Southern Africa

AMERICAS

8000 B.C. | 6000 B.C. | 4000 B.C. | 2000 B.C. | B.C./A.D. | A.D. 2000

7800 B.C.
South America

3400 B.C.
Middle America

2000 B.C.
North America

ASIA

8000 B.C. | 6000 B.C. | 4000 B.C. | 2000 B.C. | B.C./A.D. | A.D. 2000

8000 B.C.
Southwestern Asia

6000 B.C.
Western Asia

3000 B.C.
Southeastern Asia

2500 B.C.
Southern Asia

EUROPE

8000 B.C. | 6000 B.C. | 4000 B.C. | 2000 B.C. | B.C./A.D. | A.D. 2000

6000 B.C.
Southeastern Europe

5300 B.C.
Central Europe

4000 B.C.
Northern Europe

▶ PRACTICE THE SKILL

Study the parallel time line. Then use it to answer these questions.

1 When did agriculture develop in South America?

2 Did agriculture develop first in northern Europe or in southwestern Asia?

3 In which places did agriculture develop before 3000 B.C.?

4 In which places did agriculture develop after 3000 B.C.?

▶ APPLY WHAT YOU LEARNED

Make a parallel time line comparing important events in your life with important events in the lives of classmates or family members. Make sure that each time line that is part of your parallel time line covers the same months or years. Write three questions for a classmate or family member to answer by using your time line.

GENERALIZE

As you read this lesson, make generalizations about how people's ways of life are influenced by where they live.

BIG IDEA

New ways of life developed when settlements were built in southwestern Asia.

VOCABULARY

obsidian
oasis
import
export
complex society
ziggurat
city-state
civilization

Early Settlements and Cities

12,000 years ago	8,000 years ago	4,000 years ago

9,000 years ago – 4,000 years ago

By about 2000 B.C. many farming villages dotted the rich land of the Fertile Crescent. This curving area of land lies in southwestern Asia. It extends from present-day Israel through Lebanon and Syria, through the plains and hills of southern Turkey and Iraq, and all the way to the head of the Persian Gulf. Among the region's first crops were barley and wheat. Later crops included grapes, melons, dates, pistachios, and almonds. The region also produced the first domesticated sheep, goats, and pigs. Some of the villages in the Fertile Crescent are among the oldest in the world.

Jericho

One of the oldest-known farming settlements was built in southwestern Asia in what is now called the West Bank. Known as Jericho (JAIR•ih•koh), this settlement was located north of the Dead Sea in the Jordan River valley. As early as 8000 B.C., Jericho was an important trading center.

The ancient ruins of Jericho (below) attract thousands of visitors each year. Archaeologists found this clay sculpture with shells for eyes (left) at Jericho.

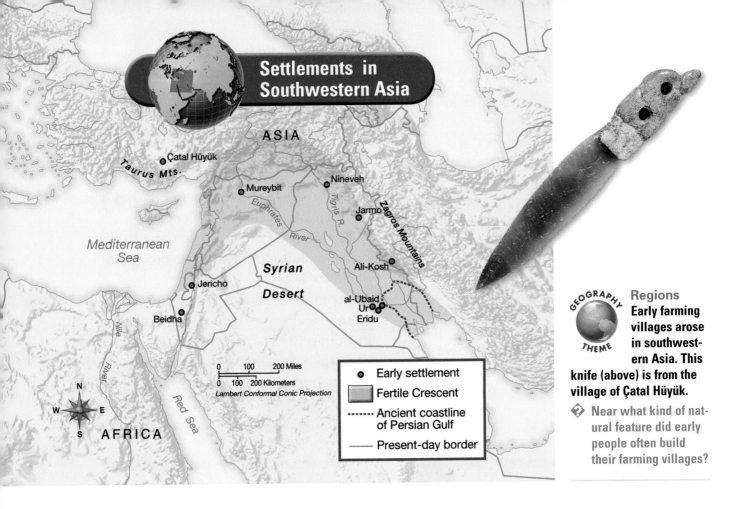

Settlements in Southwestern Asia

ASIA

Çatal Hüyük

Taurus Mts.

Mureybit

Nineveh

Jarmo

Zagros Mountains

Euphrates River

Tigris R.

Mediterranean Sea

Syrian Desert

Ali-Kosh

Jericho

al-Ubaid
Ur
Eridu

Beidha

Nile River

AFRICA

Red Sea

0   100   200 Miles
0 100 200 Kilometers
Lambert Conformal Conic Projection

N W E S

● Early settlement

▨ Fertile Crescent

------- Ancient coastline of Persian Gulf

—— Present-day border

GEOGRAPHY THEME

Regions
Early farming villages arose in southwestern Asia. This knife (above) is from the village of Çatal Hüyük.

❖ Near what kind of natural feature did early people often build their farming villages?

Early people had long been traders. If the farmers of a village grew more barley and wheat than they needed, they traded the extra amount for goods they needed or wanted. In the Fertile Crescent, people traded their extra grain for **obsidian** (uhb•SIH•dee•uhn), a black volcanic rock from the mountains far to the north of Jericho. The razor-sharp obsidian was used as a cutting tool. Polished pieces of obsidian also served as mirrors.

The settlement of Jericho was built in an **oasis** (oh•AY•suhs), a place in the desert that has a dependable supply of water. This oasis provided water for the several hundred people who lived in the settlement year-round. For traders and nomadic herders crossing the desert, Jericho provided water and a place to rest.

Because water was such an important resource for farming in this desert region, the people of Jericho needed to defend

the city's water supply from enemies. To do so, they built thick walls around their settlement. Some of the walls were 20 feet (6.1 m) high and 6 feet (1.8 m) thick.

High walls were built around many early farming villages for protection. In places along rivers and other bodies of water, villagers also built walls to keep floodwaters from destroying their settlements. In Jericho, the large walls were made of stone. The people of Jericho may have also built a stone tower for protection.

Although Jericho was one of the world's oldest-known settlements, it did not last. At some point around 6000 B.C., the people of Jericho abandoned their settlement. Experts do not know why. Since then, two other Jerichos have been built near the location of the original one.

REVIEW Why did people build walls around some early settlements? **GENERALIZE**

Çatal Hüyük

The ruins of another early farming village that was mysteriously abandoned lie in what is now south-central Turkey. That ancient village is known today as Çatal Hüyük (chah•TAHL hoo•YOOK).

Founded around 7000 B.C., Çatal Hüyük grew rapidly and became a prosperous and well-organized community. As many as 6,000 people may have lived in this ancient village. Farmers there grew mainly barley, wheat, and peas. The people also gathered acorns, almonds, and apples to eat.

Domesticated cattle provided meat and milk, but wild animals also seem to have been important sources of food. Wall paintings found in the ruins show the hunting of deer and boars, or wild pigs.

The mud homes of Çatal Hüyük were packed closely together, without streets to separate them. The people entered their homes through holes in the roofs. To reach the holes, they used wooden ladders. Each home had several rooms, the biggest of which was about 12 by 15 feet (about 4 by 5 m). The main room held benches and platforms for sitting and sleeping.

Beyond the farm fields of Çatal Hüyük were volcanic mountains that produced obsidian. Most raw materials, such as obsidian, flint, copper, shells, and timber, were **imports**, or trade goods brought in from other places. The craftworkers of Çatal Hüyük made goods from these materials to be **exports**, or trade goods sent to other places. The goods they made included weapons, tools, sculptures, cloth, and pottery.

Archaeologists know that the lives of people in Çatal Hüyük were short—an average of 34 years for men and 29 years for women. Less is known about the village's government and social life. Nevertheless, Çatal Hüyük shows the important advances in society that resulted from the beginning of agriculture.

REVIEW What raw materials did the people of Çatal Hüyük import?

A CLOSER LOOK
A Ziggurat

Ziggurats were mud-brick structures that towered over early cities like skyscrapers. To build such a structure required teamwork and skill.

1 Builders constructed a ziggurat in layers, each one smaller than the one below.

2 All the walls of a ziggurat sloped. These sloping walls may have been covered with trees and bushes.

3 People built smaller buildings around the base of the ziggurat. Some of these buildings had workshops where workers made clothing, tools, and other items. In others, priests performed religious ceremonies.

❓ Why do you think a ziggurat was built to be the largest structure in a city?

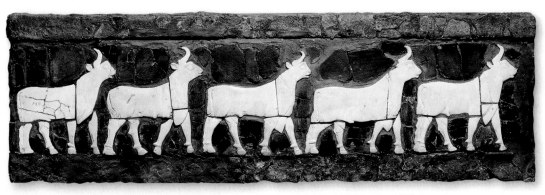

Made about 2600 B.C., this carving once decorated a temple near the city of Ur.

Early Cities

Some of the world's first cities grew up along the banks of the Tigris and Euphrates Rivers in what is now southern Iraq. The area of the Fertile Crescent where the cities were first built came to be known as Mesopotamia, or "the land between two rivers." To be considered a city, a settlement needs more than just a large population. Cities are communities with many people living and working in a complex society. A **complex society** is one with a reliable food source, established laws, customs, and job specialization.

One city in Mesopotamia was Ur. Settled before 3000 B.C., Ur was built along the Euphrates River on the shore of the Persian Gulf. Since that time, the course of the river and the coastline of the gulf have shifted. As a result, the ancient site of Ur is farther inland today than it was long ago.

The people of Ur built an amazing city. At its center was a stepped tower called a **ziggurat** (ZIH•guh•rat). At the top of the ziggurat was a temple dedicated to the city's special god. Even after 5,000 years of erosion, most of the great ziggurat of Ur is still standing today.

Although there were other early cities nearby, such as Eridu (ER•ih•doo) and Lagash (LAY•gash), Ur was the largest, with thousands of people living in it.

Abraham   About 2000 B.C.

Character Trait: Loyalty

The Bible states that Abraham came from Ur. According to tradition, Abraham was the patriarch (PAY•tree•ark), or father, of the Jewish, Christian, and Islamic religions. Abraham's life story is told in the Bible and in the Qur'an (kuh•RAN), the holy book of Islam. No other written records provide further information about this leader. According to the Bible, Abraham remained an obedient follower of God. To reward his loyalty, God made a covenant, or special agreement, with Abraham. The Bible says that God promised Abraham that his family and their descendants would live in Canaan and begin a new nation there. Abraham is a symbol of loyalty because he never broke his covenant with God.

MULTIMEDIA BIOGRAPHIES
Visit The Learning Site at www.harcourtschool.com to learn about other famous people.

The people of Ur had many specialized jobs. Some were skilled in pottery, weaving, or working with leather, copper, or stone. Some, skilled at directing the work of others, acted as leaders and managers. There were also religious leaders, traders, and builders.

The people of Ur lived in rectangular houses built of mud bricks and stones. The bricks were made of clay soil mixed with grass or straw and river water. The wet mixture was molded in wooden frames that shaped it into bricks. The frames were removed and the bricks were baked in the sun to harden. The clay-brick walls kept the inside of a house cool in summer and warm in winter.

Inside many homes, reed mats and wool rugs lay on the floors. Furniture included tables, chairs, and beds, and there were

Today Ur is an archaeological site. The ruins shown in this photograph are all that remain of the ancient city.

baskets made of reeds or wood. A common pet was the mongoose, a small animal that catches rats, mice, and snakes.

Over time many nearby farming villages came under Ur's control, and Ur became a strong city-state. In ancient times, a **city-state** included a city and the area around it. Each city-state had its own government and leaders.

From early city-states in places around the world, large complex societies developed. They produced a population explosion and, many experts say, the beginnings of civilization. A **civilization** is a complex society with developed forms of religion, ways of governing, and centers of learning.

REVIEW What were some of the specialized jobs that the people of Ur did?

What Makes a Civilization?

CIVILIZATION

Developed forms of religion

Developed centers of learning

Developed ways of governing

Analyze Diagrams Large populations are called civilizations after they develop certain characteristics.

Why do you think civilizations need governments?

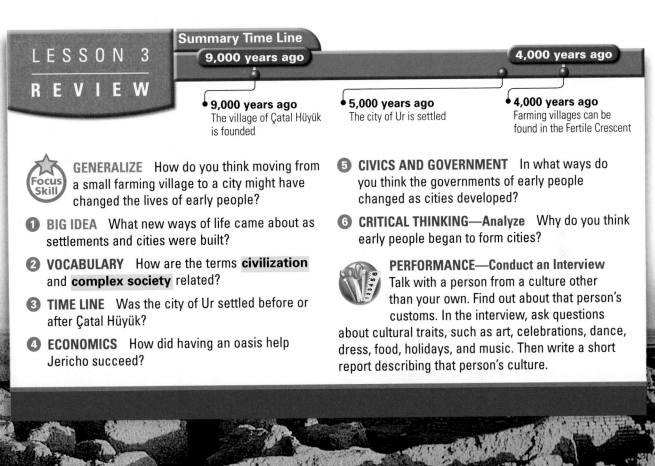

LESSON 3 REVIEW

Summary Time Line

9,000 years ago   4,000 years ago

● **9,000 years ago**
The village of Çatal Hüyük is founded

● **5,000 years ago**
The city of Ur is settled

● **4,000 years ago**
Farming villages can be found in the Fertile Crescent

Focus Skill **GENERALIZE** How do you think moving from a small farming village to a city might have changed the lives of early people?

1 BIG IDEA What new ways of life came about as settlements and cities were built?

2 VOCABULARY How are the terms **civilization** and **complex society** related?

3 TIME LINE Was the city of Ur settled before or after Çatal Hüyük?

4 ECONOMICS How did having an oasis help Jericho succeed?

5 CIVICS AND GOVERNMENT In what ways do you think the governments of early people changed as cities developed?

6 CRITICAL THINKING—Analyze Why do you think early people began to form cities?

PERFORMANCE—Conduct an Interview Talk with a person from a culture other than your own. Find out about that person's customs. In the interview, ask questions about cultural traits, such as art, celebrations, dance, dress, food, holidays, and music. Then write a short report describing that person's culture.

Identify Cause and Effect

▶ WHY IT MATTERS

To find links between events in the past, you need to understand cause and effect. A cause is an event or action that makes something else happen. What happens is the effect. Learning about cause-and-effect relationships is important for understanding both history and current events. It can also help you think about the consequences before you make decisions.

▶ WHAT YOU NEED TO KNOW

The following tips can help you identify cause-and-effect relationships when you read.

- A cause-and-effect relationship can be simple—one cause leads to one effect.

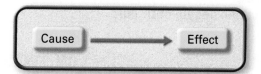

Cause-and-Effect Chart

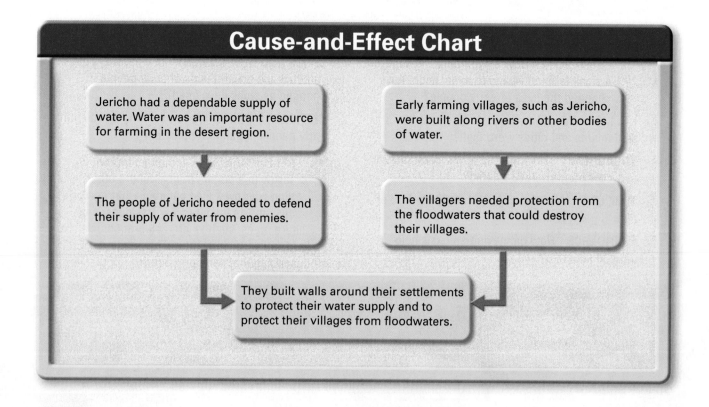

Jericho had a dependable supply of water. Water was an important resource for farming in the desert region.

↓

The people of Jericho needed to defend their supply of water from enemies.

Early farming villages, such as Jericho, were built along rivers or other bodies of water.

↓

The villagers needed protection from the floodwaters that could destroy their villages.

They built walls around their settlements to protect their water supply and to protect their villages from floodwaters.

- In some cause-and-effect relationships, one cause may lead to two or more effects. In others, two or more causes may lead to one effect.

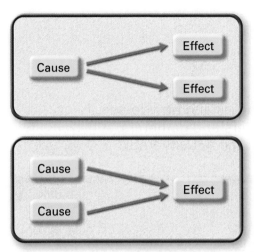

- In some cases, a single cause may lead to a chain of linked effects. Each effect is the cause of another effect.

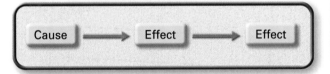

- When you read, look for words that signal cause-and-effect relationships. Examples include *because, as a result, since, consequently, for this reason,* and *in response.* Words such as *also* and *in addition* often signal relationships that have multiple causes or multiple effects.

▶ PRACTICE THE SKILL

Use the cause-and-effect chart on page 74 to answer these questions.

① What kind of cause-and-effect relationship does the chart show?

② What caused the people of Jericho to feel the need to defend their water supply from enemies?

③ What were the two main causes that led people to build walls around their villages?

▶ APPLY WHAT YOU LEARNED

Choose a recent event that took place in your community or one that was reported in the news. Perhaps there was a bad storm or a community celebration. Link the event's causes and effects on a chart like the ones on these pages. Use your chart to explain the event to a classmate or a family member.

The ancient wall of Jericho as it looks today

2 Review and Test Preparation

⭐ (Focus Skill) Generalize

Complete this graphic organizer to show that you understand how to use facts and details to make a generalization about hunters and gatherers. A copy of this graphic organizer appears on page 24 of the Activity Book.

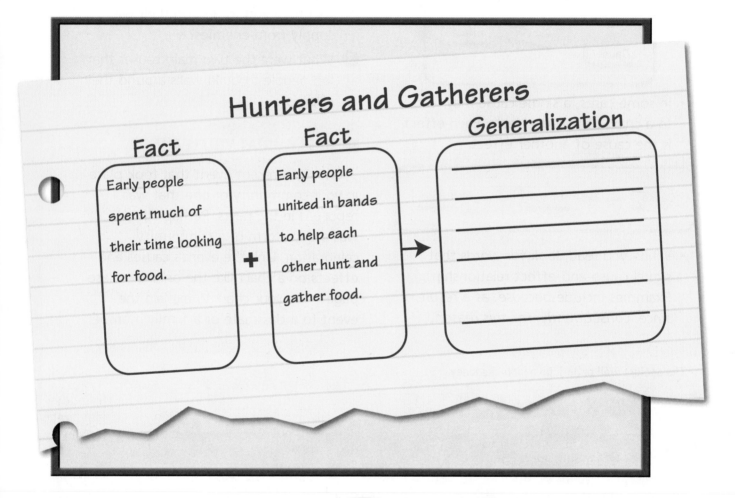

Hunters and Gatherers

Fact

Early people spent much of their time looking for food.

+

Fact

Early people united in bands to help each other hunt and gather food.

→

Generalization

_____
_____
_____
_____
_____
_____

THINK & WRITE

Write a Speech In which kind of society would you rather have lived—hunting and gathering, pastoral, or farming? Why? Write a speech to convince your classmates that your choice is better than the other two. Include at least two reasons that support your choice.

Write a Diary Entry Imagine that you are a member of a hunting and gathering, pastoral, or farming group of early people. Write a diary entry that describes a typical day in your life. Include what you wear, what your home is like, what you eat, and your main activities that day.

8,000 years ago

4,000 years ago

About 9,000 years ago
Çatal Hüyük is founded

About 8,000 years ago
The first plow is invented

About 5,000 years ago
Ur is settled

About 4,000 years ago
Farming settlements can be found in the Fertile Crescent

USE THE TIME LINE

Use the chapter summary time line to answer these questions.

1 About how long ago did early people migrate into North America?

2 Was Çatal Hüyük founded before or after Ur was settled?

USE VOCABULARY

Use each term in a sentence or two to explain both what the term means and how that meaning relates to early people.

3 **extinct** (p. 52)

4 **artifact** (p. 56)

5 **pastoral society** (p. 61)

6 **oasis** (p. 69)

7 **ziggurat** (p. 71)

RECALL FACTS

Answer these questions.

8 Where do most experts believe the first modern humans lived?

9 How did the atlatl make hunting easier for early people?

10 Why was obsidian important to the people of Jericho?

Write the letter of the best choice.

11 **TEST PREP** The time of the hunters and gatherers is sometimes called—
 A the Old Stone Age.
 B the New Stone Age.
 C the Slash-and-Burn Age.
 D the City-State Age.

12 **TEST PREP** A person from Çatal Hüyük entered his or her home through—
 F a door.
 G a hallway connecting other homes.
 H a hole in the roof.
 J a window.

13 **TEST PREP** The city of Ur was located in what is now—
 A the West Bank, in southwestern Asia.
 B southern Iraq.
 C Turkey.
 D Siberia, in Russia.

THINK CRITICALLY

14 What do you think might have been some of the advantages of living in an early city instead of a village?

15 In what ways is your school a complex society? Give at least three examples to support your answer.

APPLY SKILLS

Read Parallel Time Lines

16 What do the abbreviations B.C.E. and C.E. mean? When are they used?

Identify Cause and Effect

17 Think of something good that has happened to you recently. Make a cause-and-effect diagram to show why it happened or other things that happened because of it.

THE BERING LAND BRIDGE
NATIONAL PRESERVE

GET READY

The Bering Land Bridge National Preserve in northwestern Alaska includes part of a landform that once connected Asia and North America. Scientists call this land bridge Beringia (buh•RIN•jee•uh). Today Beringia lies beneath the Bering Strait. The Bering Strait is a narrow body of water between Russia and Alaska.

Many archaeologists believe that the first people to arrive in the Western Hemisphere traveled across Beringia thousands of years ago. Sites throughout the Bering Land Bridge National Preserve provide important clues about these first Americans. At villages in the preserve, visitors can observe Native Americans following the ways of life of their ancient ancestors.

LOCATE IT

ARCTIC OCEAN

RUSSIA

ALASKA

Bering Sea

Bering Land Bridge National Preserve

The Bering Land Bridge National Preserve is a land of beauty. Visitors there can view snow-covered mountains, lakes formed from craters, and plant-covered coastlines.

Ancient tools and spear points used by early people have been found in what is now the state of Alaska.

This archaeologist is studying a spear point from long ago. The spear point was discovered in northern Alaska.

TAKE A FIELD TRIP

GO ONLINE

A VIRTUAL TOUR
Visit The Learning Site at **www.harcourtschool.com** to take virtual tours of other historic sites.

CNN Turner Le@rning

A VIDEO TOUR
Check your media center or classroom library for a videotape tour of an archaeological dig in Alaska.

1 Review and Test Preparation

VISUAL SUMMARY

Write a Paragraph Look closely at the pictures and read the captions to help you review Unit 1. Then choose one development shown in a picture, and write a paragraph that tells why it was important to early people.

USE VOCABULARY

For each pair of terms, write a sentence or two that explains how the terms are related.

1 **altitude** (p. 36), **rain shadow** (p. 37)

2 **migration** (p. 44), **urbanization** (p. 45)

3 **agriculture** (p. 63), **slash and burn** (p. 65)

4 **obsidian** (p. 69), **import** (p. 70)

RECALL FACTS

Answer these questions.

5 What are some factors that can lead to desertification?

6 Why did early people domesticate cats and dogs?

7 Which were nomads, the people in a pastoral society or those in a farming society?

Write the letter of the best choice.

8 **TEST PREP** One idea about how Earth's landforms and continents came to be is the theory of—
  A Pangaea.
  B Laurasia.
  C Gondwana.
  D plate tectonics.

9 **TEST PREP** All of the following reshape Earth's surface *except*—
  F irrigation.
  G weathering.
  H erosion.
  J glaciers.

10 **TEST PREP** The only continent that has no permanent population of humans is—
  A Australia.
  B Antarctica.
  C Asia.
  D South America.

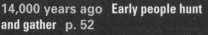

Visual Summary

| 14,000 years ago | 12,000 years ago | 10,000 years ago |

14,000 years ago **Early people hunt and gather** p. 52

12,000 years ago **The first people enter North America** p. 56

10,000 years ago **People begin to tame animals** p. 60

11. What could happen in your community that might cause your family to migrate to another place?

12. How might Earth be different today if the Ice Ages had never happened?

APPLY SKILLS

Read a Thematic Map
Use the population map of India on this page to answer these questions.

13. Which city on the map is in an area that has a population density of between 500 and 1,000 people per square mile?

14. What is the population density around India's capital?

15. What is the population density near India's border with Myanmar?

16. The population density around Kanpur is more than 1,000 people per square mile. How many people per square kilometer is this?

17. What is the population density of much of the land in central India?

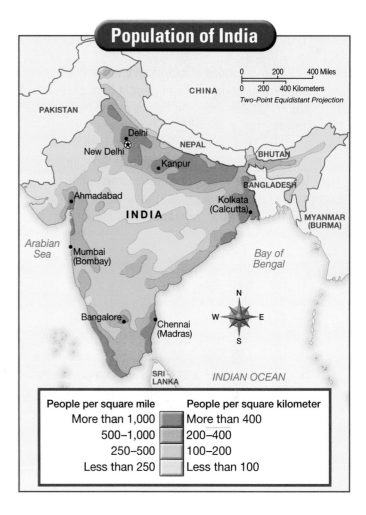

Population of India

People per square mile	People per square kilometer
More than 1,000	More than 400
500–1,000	200–400
250–500	100–200
Less than 250	Less than 100

8,000 years ago	6,000 years ago	4,000 years ago

10,000 years ago Farming settlements form p. 68

8,000 years ago Early farmers develop the plow p. 63

5,000 years ago The earliest cities form p. 71

81

Unit Activities

 GO ONLINE

Visit The Learning Site at www.harcourtschool.com for additional activities.

Draw a Diagram

Find out more about an event that has caused large numbers of people to migrate. You might consider the failure of Ireland's potato crop in the 1800s; movement into the western United States in the 1800s; the Dust Bowl of the 1930s; the building of Brasília, Brazil, in the 1950s; or others. Draw a cause-and-effect diagram that shows why the people migrated or what happened as a result.

Invent a Tool

Early people made tools out of sticks, rocks, and other objects they found. Can you? Use found objects to invent a tool that solves a problem or makes a task easier. In a presentation to your class or a group, explain how you made the tool and what it helps you do.

VISIT YOUR LIBRARY

■ *First Painter* by Kathryn Lasky. DK Publishing.

■ *Ancient Machines: From Wedges to Waterwheels* by Michael Woods and Mary B. Woods. Runestone Press.

■ *Shake, Rattle, and Roll: The World's Most Amazing Earthquakes, Volcanoes, and Other Forces* by Spencer Christian and Antonia Felix. John Wiley & Sons.

COMPLETE THE UNIT PROJECT

Create a Scene Work with a group of classmates to complete the unit project—a scene showing early people and the land in which they lived. Decide which group of early people you want to include in your scene, the activities you want to show them doing, and any landforms and bodies of water they lived near. Use a notecard to caption your scene. As a group, present your scene to the class.

Early Centers of Civilization

Painted funeral mask, Egypt,
about 1300 B.C.

Pyramids of Giza in northern Egypt

Early Centers of Civilization

> **❝**I go into my library, and all history unrolls before me . . . I see pyramids building; I hear the shoutings of the armies . . .**❞**
>
> —Alexander Smith, from the essay "Books and Gardens," 1863

Preview the Content

Use the lesson titles to develop a web for each chapter. Write words and phrases to identify the main topic of each chapter.

Preview the Vocabulary

Suffixes   A suffix is a word part that is added to the end of a root word. Use the root words and suffixes in the chart below to write a possible meaning of each Vocabulary Word.

SUFFIX	ROOT	VOCABULARY WORD	POSSIBLE MEANING
-ation	tax	taxation	_____
-ity	prosper	prosperity	_____
-ize	standard	standardize	_____

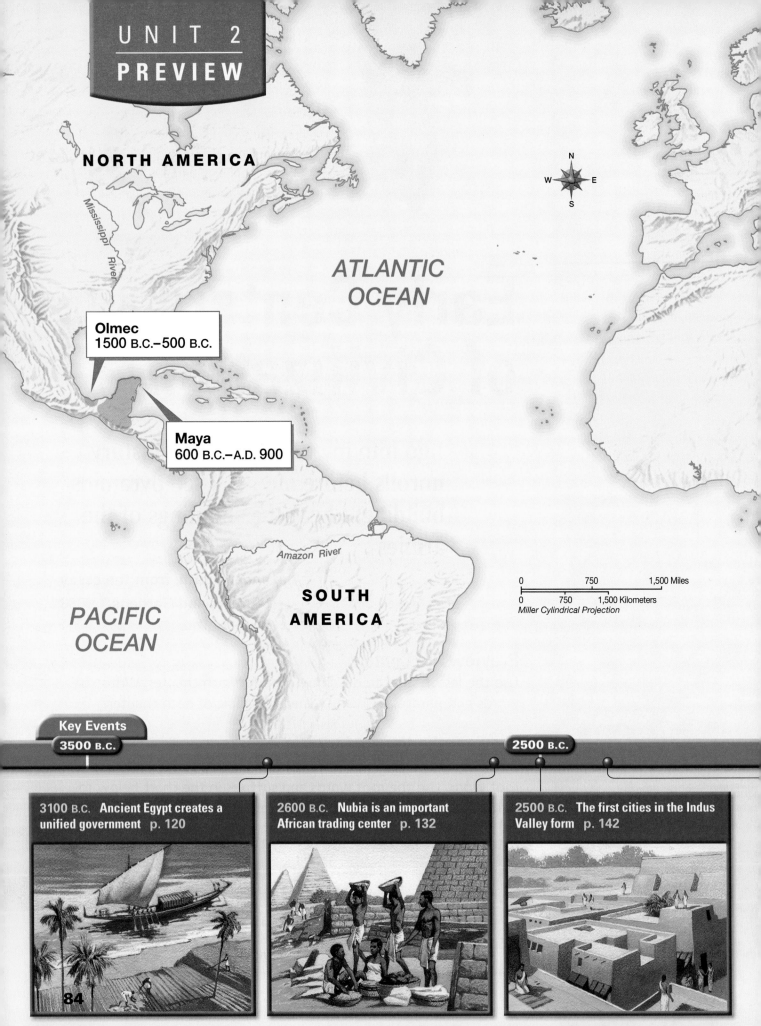

NORTH AMERICA

Mississippi River

ATLANTIC OCEAN

N
W · E
S

Olmec
1500 B.C.–500 B.C.

Maya
600 B.C.–A.D. 900

Amazon River

SOUTH AMERICA

PACIFIC OCEAN

0   750   1,500 Miles
0   750   1,500 Kilometers
Miller Cylindrical Projection

Key Events

3500 B.C.

2500 B.C.

3100 B.C. **Ancient Egypt creates a unified government** p. 120

2600 B.C. **Nubia is an important African trading center** p. 132

2500 B.C. **The first cities in the Indus Valley form** p. 142

Early Civilizations

Shang
1766 B.C.–1122 B.C.

Mesopotamia
3500 B.C.–500 B.C.

Harappa
3000 B.C.–1500 B.C.

Ancient Egypt
3100 B.C.–1069 B.C.

Kush
2000 B.C.– A.D. 350

EUROPE

ASIA

AFRICA

Black Sea

Caspian Sea

Volga River

Tigris River

Euphrates River

Mediterranean Sea

Nile River

Red Sea

Indus River

Huang He

Chang Jiang

INDIAN OCEAN

Early Civilization Names

CIVILIZATION	ORIGIN OF NAME
Olmec	ancient Nahuatl word for "people of the land of rubber"
Maya	based on *Maia*, the name the Maya called their land
Kush	ancient Egyptian name for the region
Egypt	based on *Aegyptus*, the name of a ruler over Egypt in Greek mythology
Mesopotamia	ancient Greek for "the land between the rivers"
Harappa	name of town in present-day Pakistan where city's ruins were found
Shang	Chinese for "above, superior, highest"

1500 B.C.

500 B.C.

2350 B.C. **The world's first empire forms in Mesopotamia** p. 98

1766 B.C. **The Shang dynasty begins to rule in China** p. 150

1500s B.C. **The Olmec civilization begins in the Americas** p. 157

85

Seeker of Knowledge

The Man Who Deciphered Egyptian Hieroglyphs

written and illustrated by James Rumford

Who could not be amazed by the ancient Egyptians? More than 4,000 years ago, they built magnificent structures, painted beautiful pictures on walls, and invented their own picture writing. Perhaps no one has been as fascinated with the Egyptians as Jean-François Champollion (ZHAHN frahn·SWAH shahm·pohl·YOHN), who lived in Grenoble, France, in the early 1800s. He dreamed of unraveling the mystery of hieroglyphics (hy·ruh·GLIH·fiks), the Egyptian picture language. Read on to find out more about Jean-François Champollion's search for the key to understanding hieroglyphics.

There is a roaming, black-as-night jackal in the word "mystery."

There is a sharp-eyed ibis bird in the word "discover."

There is a long-necked, far-seeing giraffe in "predict."

When Jean-François finished school at sixteen, his brother took him to Paris to meet the scholars who were studying a black stone from Rosetta, Egypt. The stone was covered with Egyptian and Greek words and told of a king of Egypt named Ptolemy. By reading the Greek, the scholars hoped to decipher the Egyptian. But the work was difficult—certainly too difficult for a boy—and the scholars turned Jean-François away. They did not see the fire burning bright in his eyes. They did not recognize the genius who had already learned all the known ancient languages. They did not know that he was a seeker of knowledge, one who would not rest until he had found the answer.

Jean-François gathered his notebooks and returned to Grenoble. There he taught school. His students often came to hear him talk about Egypt—her pharaohs and gods and the mysterious writing.

Once, even Napoleon came to Grenoble and sat up all night, listening spellbound as Jean-François told the great man of his dreams.

Napoleon promised to send Jean-François to Egypt when he conquered the world. Napoleon dreamed of glory. Jean-François dreamed of discovery.

But a few months later, Napoleon was defeated at the Battle of Waterloo. France

was now defenseless. Her enemies poured in. They surrounded Grenoble and in the early morning bombarded the city. Jean-François ran to save his notebooks from the flames. . . .

During these troubled times, scholars everywhere were racing to solve the mystery of Egyptian writing. Unbelievable things were said. Ridiculous books were written. No one had the answer. Then an Englishman discovered that a few of the hieroglyphs on the Rosetta Stone were letters, and he deciphered King Ptolemy's name. Everyone said that the Englishman would be the first to unlock the door to Egypt's past—everyone except Jean-François.

Ptolemy	TAH•luh•mee
decipher	determine the meaning of
pharaohs	Egyptian kings
Napoleon	ruler who named himself emperor of France

There is a blue lotus, its center as bright as the yellow sun, in the word "joy."

There are two regal, heads-up-high leopards in the word "glory."

There is an unblinking crocodile lurking in the word "trouble."

When Jean-François was thirty, he gathered up his notebooks and left Grenoble. He made his way back to Paris—to his brother.

In Paris, Jean-François studied the Rosetta Stone and other inscriptions. He compared the Greek letters with the Egyptian hieroglyphs and herded together his own alphabet of eagles and lions and dark-eyed chicks. But this wonderful list of letters was no help in reading the language. There were too many pictures he did not understand. What to make of a fish with legs, a jackal with wings, or an ibis god with a long, curved bill? There had to be a link between the pictures and the Egyptian letters. But what was it? Jean-François slept little. He ate almost nothing.

Then, on a September morning in 1822, Jean-François found a small package on his doorstep—from a friend in Egypt! In it were the names of pharaohs copied from a temple wall. Each name was a jigsaw puzzle of letters and pictures. Jean-François

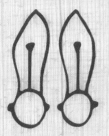

There are strongly woven sandals firmly planted on the ground in "never give up."

There is a jumping free-spirited kid goat in the Egyptian word "imagine."

READ A BOOK

studied the names and saw the link! The pictures were sounds, too. Not single letters, but syllables, even whole words!

One of the names drew him. It began with the hieroglyph of an old, silent friend perched on a sacred staff. This was a picture of the god of writing, Thoth, followed by the letters *m* and *s*.

"Thothmes!" Jean-François suddenly exclaimed, and the rushing sound of the pharaoh's name, as if carried on wings across the centuries, filled the room.

Jean-François raced down the street to his brother's office. He burst through the door, exclaiming, "I have the key!"

Then he collapsed. He had not eaten. He had not slept. For five days, he lay near death.

On the fifth day, he awoke. "Pen and paper," he whispered, and he wrote of his discovery to the world.

Analyze the Literature

1. What discovery did Jean-François Champollion make that helped him unlock the mystery of ancient Egyptian writing?

2. How did scholars hope to decipher ancient Egyptian writing?

3. Do you think it was important that scholars deciphered ancient Egyptian writing? Why or why not?

START THE UNIT PROJECT

Make a Scrapbook   With your classmates, make a scrapbook. As you read this unit, make a list of key people, places, and events. This list will help you select people, places, and events to feature in the scrapbook.

USE TECHNOLOGY

Visit The Learning Site at **www.harcourtschool.com** for additional activities, primary sources, and other resources to use in this unit.

NIPPUR ZIGGURAT, NIPPUR, IRAQ

Once a city in ancient Mesopotamia, Nippur played an important role in the region's religious practices. The ziggurat, or temple, in Nippur was probably used for religious ceremonies. Ziggurats were found in many Mesopotamian cities in ancient times. The city of Nippur was once located on the Euphrates River, but the course of the river changed over time.

LOCATE IT

IRAQ

Nippur

3

The Tigris and Euphrates Valley

"I dug the canal . . . which bringeth copious water to the land of Sumer. . . ."
—Hammurabi, king of the Babylonian Empire, 1792–1750 B.C.

Summarize

Focus Skill

When you **summarize,** you retell briefly what you have read, using your own words.

After you read this chapter, summarize what you have learned.

• Identify the main topic and key facts of each lesson to summarize what you read.

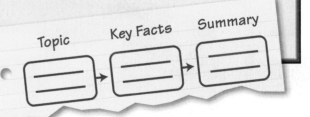

Topic → Key Facts → Summary

1

As you read, summarize advances in civilization that developed in Mesopotamia.

BIG IDEA

City-states in Mesopotamia developed into one of the world's first civilizations by using resources in new ways.

VOCABULARY

innovation
division of labor
surplus
monarchy
absolute authority
bureaucracy
pictograph
cuneiform
social class
merchant

Civilization in Sumer

3500 B.C.	2500 B.C.	1500 B.C.	500 B.C.

3000 B.C.– 1800 B.C.

One of the world's first civilizations formed in the southern part of Mesopotamia in an area called Sumer (SOO·mer). The people there spoke a common language now known as Sumerian. By about 3000 B.C. several cities in Sumer had grown to become large, independent city-states. Each city-state had thousands of people and controlled lands covering hundreds of square miles. Like the many smaller farming settlements in Mesopotamia, the Sumerian city-states depended on agriculture for food.

Advances in Farming

To meet the needs of their growing populations, the city-states in Sumer needed to produce huge amounts of food. In the rich soil along the banks of the Tigris and Euphrates Rivers, Sumerian farmers grew grains such as barley and wheat. They also grew vegetables, including onions and cucumbers, and raised livestock. The need to grow large amounts of food led the Sumerians to many important **innovations**, or new ways of doing things.

LOCATE IT

IRAQ

Nasiriya

In many small villages such as Nasiriya, Iraq, people depend on farming for their survival.

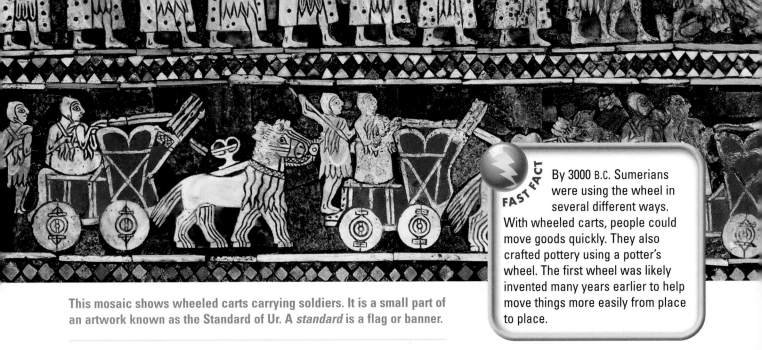

This mosaic shows wheeled carts carrying soldiers. It is a small part of an artwork known as the Standard of Ur. A *standard* is a flag or banner.

By 3000 B.C. Sumerians were using the wheel in several different ways. With wheeled carts, people could move goods quickly. They also crafted pottery using a potter's wheel. The first wheel was likely invented many years earlier to help move things more easily from place to place.

Because Mesopotamia got little rainfall, Sumerian farmers had to find ways to use river water to irrigate their crops. The Sumerians also needed to protect their crops from both flooding and drought. To solve these problems, the Sumerians found ways to change the rivers. They built dikes, or dams made of earth, to control river flooding, and they filled reservoirs, or human-made lakes, with water for later use. The Sumerians built canals to bring water to the fields in dry seasons.

In their farm fields, the Sumerians carefully watched over their plants as they grew taller and taller. Each spring, farmers harvested their crops. After harvesting their grain crops, they threshed, or separated, the grain from the husk, or outer shell, of the plant.

After threshing, farmworkers took the grains to large storehouses in the cities. The Sumerians were among the first to use wheeled carts to carry crops and other heavy loads. They harnessed donkeys and other domesticated animals to pull the carts.

Growing enough food to feed the thousands of people living in a city-state took many workers and a division of labor. **Division of labor** is the sharing of a large job so that each worker does only part of it. In Sumer some workers were in charge of watering the fields. Others planted, cared for, and harvested the crops. Still others took the crops from the fields to the cities. Many more workers helped store and distribute the food. When crops were plentiful, the city-states could trade their surpluses. A **surplus** is the amount of a product that is left after needs have been met.

The Sumerians knew that failure to produce enough food would bring disaster. They learned to depend on organization and cooperation to be successful.

REVIEW What innovations helped the Sumerians grow enough food?

 SUMMARIZE

The Sumerians crafted many humanlike figures, such as this woman and man, from small pieces of marble.

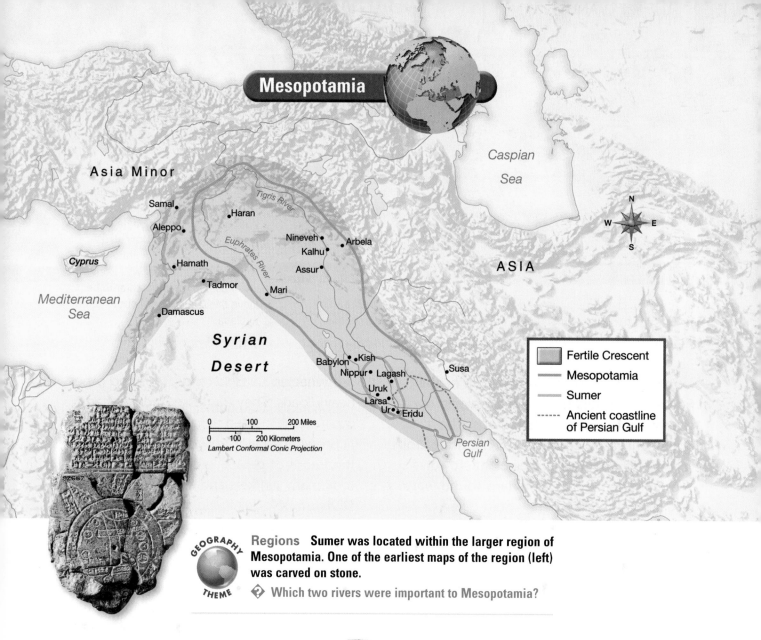

Mesopotamia

Asia Minor

Samal
Haran
Aleppo
Nineveh • Arbela
Kalhu
Hamath
Assur
Tadmor • Mari
Damascus

Cyprus

Mediterranean
Sea

**Syrian
Desert**

Babylon • Kish
Nippur • Lagash
Uruk
Larsa
Ur • Eridu

Caspian
Sea

ASIA

Susa

Persian
Gulf

Tigris River
Euphrates River

	Fertile Crescent
	Mesopotamia
	Sumer
-----	Ancient coastline of Persian Gulf

0   100   200 Miles
0   100   200 Kilometers
Lambert Conformal Conic Projection

N W E S

GEOGRAPHY THEME

Regions Sumer was located within the larger region of Mesopotamia. One of the earliest maps of the region (left) was carved on stone.

◆ Which two rivers were important to Mesopotamia?

Government in Sumer

When large numbers of people live and work in one place, they need a system for making decisions, managing conflict, and keeping order. In other words, they need some form of government. In each city-state one person, the *en*, ruled as king. This means that the Sumerians had a **monarchy**, or a governing system ruled by a king or a queen. In Sumerian city-states the rulers were always men.

The en held **absolute authority**, or complete control, over his city-state. His most important duties included leading the military, arranging trade, settling arguments, and directing public events, including religious ceremonies. Sumerian monarchs were believed to have been chosen by the gods. Because of their leadership, they were called "great men." Some great rulers were honored in Sumerian legends. The story

This carving of the Sumerian King Gilgamesh was made during the 700s B.C.

of the godlike king Gilgamesh has become a part of world literature today.

Sumerian rulers needed help to rule over many people and large areas of land successfully. They created the world's first known bureaucracy. A **bureaucracy** is a governing group made up of nonelected officials. In Sumer most of those in the bureaucracy were priests, or religious leaders. Their duties included choosing and marking lands for farming as well as distributing food to people in the cities.

Sumerian government officials needed a way to keep track of food brought from the farm fields to the storehouses. They also wanted to record the amounts of food given out to the people. In addition, they needed to list any surpluses that were used for trading. The desire to keep such records led to one of the Sumerian civilization's greatest contributions to world history—writing.

REVIEW What form of government did the Sumerians have?

Writing and Other Innovations

Sumerian became the world's first written language. The earliest writings were government lists and records. Using sharpened reeds as writing tools, officials marked numbers and **pictographs**, or picture writing, on wet clay, which dried into hard tablets.

Over time, the Sumerians found ways to improve their writing. They began to use symbols instead of pictures to stand for words. The system came to be called **cuneiform** (kyoo•NEE•uh•fawrm), or wedge-shaped writing. Cuneiform symbols could be combined to stand for words or sounds.

The importance of keeping accurate records also led to other innovations, such as measuring systems. The Sumerians created a standard unit for measuring an area of land, such as a crop field. They called it the *iku*. Today we call it the acre. The containers that held grain became a basic measurement for volume—the quart.

Sumerian Cuneiform

Analyze Primary Sources

Sumerian cuneiform went through major changes over time. The earliest examples of cuneiform date from about 1800 B.C. Many of the clay tablets the Sumerians used still exist today.

❶ The Sumerians mostly wrote on clay tablets. However, they also used materials such as stone, wood, and metal.

❷ Some ancient Sumerian records were illustrated with scenes relating to the messages written in cuneiform.

❸ Over time, the way cuneiform was written changed. At first, cuneiform symbols were written in columns and were read from top to bottom. Later, cuneiform symbols were written so they could be read from left to right.

❖ Why do you think Sumerians used clay for their cuneiform?

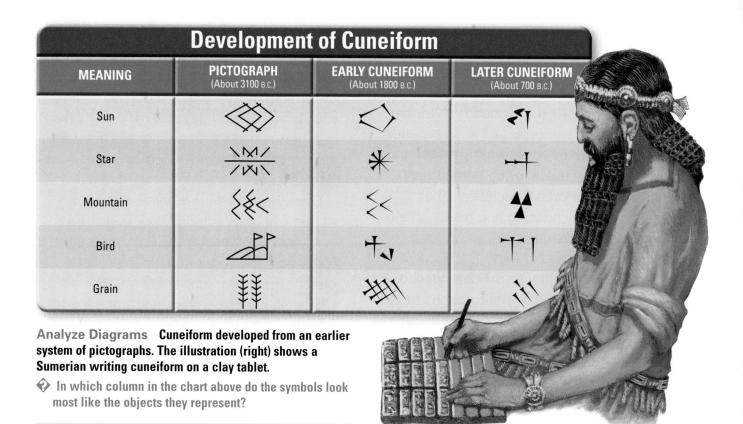

Development of Cuneiform

MEANING	PICTOGRAPH (About 3100 B.C.)	EARLY CUNEIFORM (About 1800 B.C.)	LATER CUNEIFORM (About 700 B.C.)
Sun			
Star			
Mountain			
Bird			
Grain			

Analyze Diagrams   Cuneiform developed from an earlier system of pictographs. The illustration (right) shows a Sumerian writing cuneiform on a clay tablet.

♦ In which column in the chart above do the symbols look most like the objects they represent?

Another innovation made it possible to measure long periods of time. The Sumerians developed a calendar divided into 12 months based on the 28-day cycle of the moon. Since a year made up of 12 lunar, or moon, months is shorter than a solar, or sun, year, an extra month was added every three years.

Today the Sumerians are remembered for other innovations, too. They were the first to build sailboats, which they used to travel along the Tigris and Euphrates Rivers. They were among the first to mix copper and tin to make bronze tools and weapons. The Sumerians also invented the potter's wheel to help them form bowls, vases, and jars from clay.

REVIEW What innovations did the Sumerians develop for measuring?

Divisions in Society

Sumerian society was highly organized. People belonged to different social classes. **Social classes** group people of the same level of importance in their society. The highest, or ruling, class in Sumer was made up of the king, important government officials, priests, and warriors. It also included their families.

Few Sumerians were part of the ruling class. Many were members of the middle class. Some were less-important government officials, craftworkers, farming supervisors, or merchants. A **merchant** is a person who buys and sells or trades goods. Others worked as doctors, carpenters, potters, or bricklayers.

Sumerian musicians played instruments such as this lyre.

Slaves and farmworkers made up the lowest level, or working class, in Sumerian society. Most slaves were prisoners of war. These people had been captured in battle. After the battle, they returned with the Sumerian soldiers to one of the Sumerian city-states. There they were forced to work for a period of time. Some slaves, however, were people who had been enslaved as punishment for crimes or to pay off debts, or money they owed.

Slaves in Sumerian society were not enslaved for life. Those who owed a debt, for example, could gain their freedom when the debt was paid.

In all classes of Sumerian society, men had more authority and independence than women. Men held nearly all of the leadership roles in the Sumerian government. In contrast, family life was matriarchal, or ruled by the oldest woman in the family. Some women were important religious leaders, too.

Sumerian women had more rights and freedoms than women in many other

This carving (above) shows a family celebrating the completion of a building.

ancient civilizations had. Unlike women in some places, the women of Sumer could own property and run businesses. Some were taught to read and write in cuneiform. Most Sumerian women, however, only managed their own households.

REVIEW What were Sumer's social classes?

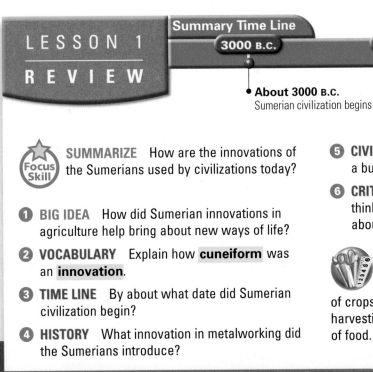

LESSON 1
REVIEW

Summary Time Line

3000 B.C.   2400 B.C.   1800 B.C.

● **About 3000 B.C.**
Sumerian civilization begins

● **About 1800 B.C.**
Sumerians begin to write in cuneiform

(Focus Skill) **SUMMARIZE** How are the innovations of the Sumerians used by civilizations today?

❶ **BIG IDEA** How did Sumerian innovations in agriculture help bring about new ways of life?

❷ **VOCABULARY** Explain how **cuneiform** was an **innovation**.

❸ **TIME LINE** By about what date did Sumerian civilization begin?

❹ **HISTORY** What innovation in metalworking did the Sumerians introduce?

❺ **CIVICS AND GOVERNMENT** In what ways did a bureaucracy help the king?

❻ **CRITICAL THINKING—Evaluate** Why do you think successful changes in farming brought about innovations in other areas of society?

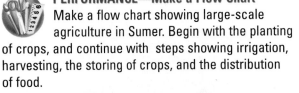

PERFORMANCE—Make a Flow Chart
Make a flow chart showing large-scale agriculture in Sumer. Begin with the planting of crops, and continue with steps showing irrigation, harvesting, the storing of crops, and the distribution of food.

Conquests and Empire Building

3500 B.C.	2500 B.C.	1500 B.C.	500 B.C.

3000 B.C.– 1000 B.C.

Sumerian kings kept order within their individual city-states, but Sumer was not a peaceful place. The city-states were nearly always at war. They fought with one another to gain riches and control of water and other limited resources. Large, powerful city-states competed for control of smaller or weaker cities. The Sumerians wrote about these commonplace struggles, "You go and carry off the enemy's land; the enemy comes and carries off your land."

Sargon the Great

For a brief time around 3000 B.C., the strong city-state of Uruk controlled all of Sumer. However, control of the city-states soon returned to the local kings. Eventually, an enemy from outside of Sumer came to **conquer**, or take over, the Sumerian civilization by force. In about 2350 B.C. the city-states had to battle a people from central Mesopotamia whose leader was known as Sargon (SAR•gon).

Sargon had once served in the army of the king of Kish, a city-state in Sumer. Around 2350 B.C. Sargon killed the king in battle. He then gathered his own army and conquered the other Sumerian city-states. The Sumerians lost control over their city-states and their civilization fell.

This portrait, or likeness, of a ruler (left) is believed to be Sargon. Ancient rulers were often buried with objects of value. This copper axe (below) was discovered in an ancient tomb in present-day Iran.

• BIOGRAPHY •

Sargon of Akkad   About 2370 B.C.
Character Trait: Civic Virtue

Most of what is known about Sargon comes from legends, or stories that have come from the past and that are believed to be partly true. According to legend, Sargon's mother was a priestess in a town on the Euphrates River. She placed her son in a basket on the river soon after he was born. The child was found by a gardener who raised him. As a boy, Sargon became cupbearer to the ruler of Kish and later served in the Kish army. Sargon rose to become a successful army commander and leader of the world's first empire. He was proud that he made his own way in life, and he cared about the well-being of people of every social class.

 MULTIMEDIA BIOGRAPHIES
Visit The Learning Site at www.harcourtschool.com to learn about other famous people.

Sargon continued his conquests beyond Sumer. He gained control of an area from what is now Iran, in the east, to what is now Turkey and the Mediterranean Sea, in the west. By doing this, Sargon built the world's first empire. An **empire** consists of the vast lands and varied people that come under the control of a single government.

As a symbol of Sargon's absolute authority, he ordered that every boundary pillar and city wall be brought down within his empire. The empire was ruled from the capital city of Akkad (AH•kahd) in the central Euphrates River valley. For this reason, the lands united by Sargon became known as the Akkadian (uh•KAY•dee•uhn) Empire.

Carving of Naram-Sin, Akkadian king and grandson of Sargon

Sargon maintained his rule by using the force of his army and by the organization of his government. He was one of the first powerful rulers to keep a **standing army**, an army with paid, full-time soldiers. Before that time, people earned their living from other jobs and served as soldiers only in times of war. Sargon carefully selected people to govern the city-states for him. He chose officials who he knew would remain loyal to the rule of Akkad.

Others in world history who wanted to become powerful leaders would follow Sargon's example. Sargon ruled the Akkadian Empire for 56 years. After his death, the empire lasted more than 200 years. That is why he is remembered as Sargon the Great.

REVIEW How did the Akkadian Empire begin?
 SUMMARIZE

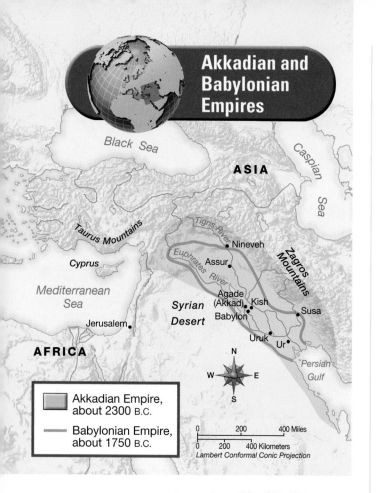

Akkadian and Babylonian Empires

Black Sea

ASIA

Caspian Sea

Taurus Mountains

Cyprus

Mediterranean Sea

Jerusalem

AFRICA

Tigris River

Nineveh

Assur

Euphrates River

Zagros Mountains

Agade (Akkad) Kish

Syrian Desert

Babylon

Susa

Uruk

Ur

Persian Gulf

N W E S

Akkadian Empire, about 2300 B.C.

Babylonian Empire, about 1750 B.C.

0   200   400 Miles

0   200   400 Kilometers

Lambert Conformal Conic Projection

GEOGRAPHY THEME

Regions **Several empires rose and fell in southwestern Asia during ancient times.**

❖ Which empire controlled a part of the Zagros Mountains?

The Rise of Babylon

Later Akkadian rulers found it difficult to keep control over the vast area of their empire. In 2125 B.C. leaders in the Sumerian city-state of Ur rebelled against Akkadian rule. The battles brought an end to the Akkadian Empire.

For a time, Mesopotamia thrived under the rulers of Ur. However, the region drifted back into conflict and disorder. By about 1900 B.C. a group called the Amorites gained control of southern and central Mesopotamia.

The Amorites were led by the mighty king of Babylon. Like the Akkadian Empire, the empire of the Amorites was named for its capital city Babylon. It was called the Babylonian Empire.

The powerful kings of Babylon looked for new ways to govern their empire. They created a system of **taxation**, under which people are made to pay for the running of their government. Officials traveled throughout the empire collecting tax money for Babylon.

REVIEW Who were the Amorites?

FROM THE CODE OF
HAMMURABI

In this part of the Code of Hammurabi, the ruler describes his role as king and gives some reasons for creating the code.

❝I am Hammurabi, noble king. . . . I put an end to wars, I enhanced the well-being of the land. . . . I held the people of the lands of Sumer and Akkad safely. . . . They prospered under my protective spirit, I maintained them in peace, with my skillful wisdom I sheltered them.

In order that the mighty not wrong the weak . . . I have inscribed my precious pronouncements [laws] upon my stela [stone marker] and set it up . . . in the city of Babylon. . . to render the judgements of the land, to give the verdicts of the land, and to provide just ways for the wronged.❞

In addition to putting together a code of laws, Hammurabi introduced the idea of equal justice, or fair treatment, under the laws. His equal justice, however, was limited to equality within each social class. Under the Code of Hammurabi, members of the ruling class were favored over people of other classes. The punishments they received were often lighter than those received by other people. At that time, this was considered fair and just. Today the United States Constitution provides for equal treatment for all people without regard for a person's status in our society.

Analyze the Value

1 Why do you think equal justice for all is important today in the courts of the United States?

2 Make It Relevant   Think about the code of conduct or list of rules your school uses to keep order and resolve conflict. Write a paragraph summarizing how equal justice is carried out in your school.

The Code of Hammurabi

Perhaps the most important innovation of the Babylonian people was their **centralized government**. The Babylonian Empire was governed under a single authority. To help maintain their empire, Babylonian rulers established a set of laws that covered crimes against the empire as well as crimes against people.

The most important set of laws in the Babylonian Empire was put together in about 1790 B.C. It was compiled by the first great Babylonian monarch, Hammurabi (ha•muh•RAH•bee). This new set of laws became known as the Code of Hammurabi. A **code** is a set of laws written down in a clear and orderly way.

Hammurabi based his code of laws on older collections of Sumerian and Akkadian laws. The old laws were complicated and often unfair. Sometimes the laws were not even written down.

Hammurabi carefully revised and expanded the old laws. One **principle**, or important belief, that formed the basis of the Code of Hammurabi is that "the strong shall not oppress [harshly rule] the weak."

The Code of Hammurabi consisted of 282 laws that dealt with almost every part of daily life. The laws covered such matters as private property, military service, land and business deals, family relationships, taxes, trades, loans, and debts.

Some of the laws within the code followed old customs. Others introduced the new principle of "an eye for an eye." These laws stated that anyone causing injury to another person would be punished with the same injury. Under this principle, breaking another person's arm in anger is punished by having your own arm broken. Many laws warned lawbreakers of what to expect.

A lion made of clay, from the time of Hammurabi

For certain crimes people could even be put to death.

The code was carved into stone and placed in public places for all to see. World history's first "lawgiver" wanted the laws to serve as a lasting way to keep order in the present and prevent troubles in the future.

Hammurabi explained that the code would

> 66 Cause justice to prevail . . .
> destroy the wicked . . .
> enlighten the land and . . .
> further the welfare of the people. 99

Hammurabi's code lasted over the years, but his empire did not. By about 1600 B.C. the Babylonian Empire had fallen.

REVIEW What is the principle of an eye for an eye?

The Hittites and the Kassites

After the collapse of the Babylonian Empire, Mesopotamia was conquered by peoples from the north and east. Among these were the Kassites from what is now the country of Iran.

A CLOSER LOOK
Hittite Iron Making

The Hittites were among the first people in the world to make tools and weapons from iron. To do this, the iron had to be extracted from its natural state as iron ore. To extract the iron, the ore must be heated to 3,650°F (2,010°C). The Hittites were able to reach the high temperatures by using a small furnace and pumping air into it. Today, furnaces can heat iron to its melting point. It then can be poured into a mold creating "cast" iron objects. However, the Hittites had to shape iron with tools. They made "wrought" iron objects.

1. Iron ore is mined and hauled to the furnaces for processing.

2. Bellows made from animal skins are pumped to force air into the furnaces, making them burn hotter.

3. As the iron ore is heated, the iron is separated and collected.

4. The iron is reheated and hammered into shape. This may be done many times before the object is ready to be sharpened or polished.

❓ How is cast iron different from wrought iron?

The Kassites tried for many years to take over the city of Babylon, but they were not successful. Then a powerful group called the Hittites came from the north and attacked Babylon.

The Hittites robbed the city of its riches but did not stay long. They were experts in the use of war **chariots**, or carts drawn by horses and used to carry soldiers in battle. The chariots made it possible for Hittite warriors to move quickly and with force. Using such war vehicles, the Hittites captured Babylon easily.

When the Hittites left with their stolen treasure, the Kassites were finally able

The Kassites used stones like this one to mark the borders of their empire.

to conquer Babylon. Their rule lasted for more than 500 years. However, their control of Babylonian lands was not always strong.

The Kassites had an advanced culture. Yet, they adopted the ways of the Babylonians. Even their buildings were created in the style of Babylonian buildings.

By adopting the laws, religion, and literature of the conquered peoples, they continued the long heritage of Babylonian civilization. The Kassites ruled the "land between two rivers" from 1595 B.C. until 1000 B.C., when warriors from another civilization challenged their rule.

REVIEW What event allowed the Kassites to conquer Babylon?

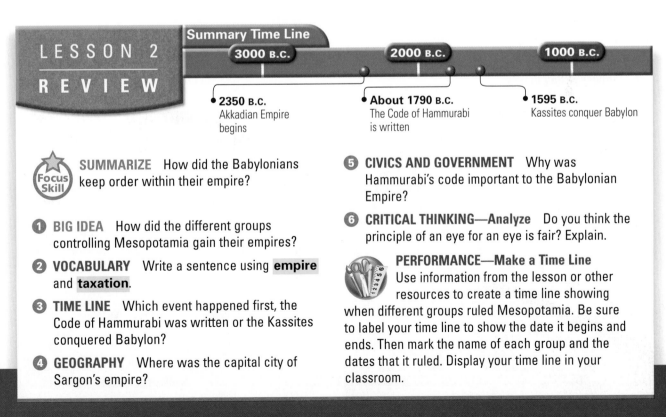

LESSON 2 REVIEW

Summary Time Line

| 3000 B.C. | 2000 B.C. | 1000 B.C. |

2350 B.C.
Akkadian Empire begins

About 1790 B.C.
The Code of Hammurabi is written

1595 B.C.
Kassites conquer Babylon

Focus Skill **SUMMARIZE** How did the Babylonians keep order within their empire?

1 BIG IDEA How did the different groups controlling Mesopotamia gain their empires?

2 VOCABULARY Write a sentence using **empire** and **taxation**.

3 TIME LINE Which event happened first, the Code of Hammurabi was written or the Kassites conquered Babylon?

4 GEOGRAPHY Where was the capital city of Sargon's empire?

5 CIVICS AND GOVERNMENT Why was Hammurabi's code important to the Babylonian Empire?

6 CRITICAL THINKING—Analyze Do you think the principle of an eye for an eye is fair? Explain.

PERFORMANCE—Make a Time Line
Use information from the lesson or other resources to create a time line showing when different groups ruled Mesopotamia. Be sure to label your time line to show the date it begins and ends. Then mark the name of each group and the dates that it ruled. Display your time line in your classroom.

·SKILLS·

Resolve Conflict

VOCABULARY

conflict
compromise

▶ WHY IT MATTERS

Disagreements, or **conflicts**, were common among the ancient city-states. Sometimes the result of conflict was a war. At other times people found peaceful ways to resolve their differences.

Like long ago, many conflicts today can be settled without fighting. When people disagree with one another, there are many ways to settle their differences to avoid fighting with one another. Each side may walk away and let anger or other strong feelings fade. They may explain their ideas and try to get the other person to agree. They may want to compromise.

In a **compromise**, each person gives up some of what he or she wants.

▶ WHAT YOU NEED TO KNOW

Here are some steps that can help you resolve conflicts through compromise.

Step 1 Say clearly and politely what you want. Then listen to the other person's views.

Step 2 Decide which of the things you want are most important to you.

Step 3 Each person makes a plan for a possible compromise.

The Standard of Ur is a two-sided mosaic on wood. This side shows the king (top center) celebrating a victory in war.

On this side of the standard, the king (seated at top left) and others celebrate the benefits of peace. Some experts think the standard was part of a musical instrument.

Step 4 Talk about any differences in the two plans.

Step 5 Continue talking until the two of you can agree on a plan. If either person becomes angry or upset, take a break.

Step 6 To prevent future conflicts, make sure that your compromise plan will work for a long time.

▶ PRACTICE THE SKILL

The different groups living in Mesopotamia often fought with one another over water, natural resources, and borders. Think of an issue about which neighboring groups might have disagreed. With a classmate, role-play a discussion in which each of you represents a leader on a different side of the issue.

Follow the steps to work out a plan that will settle the conflict. After you have reached a compromise, write a paragraph explaining it. Tell whether you think the compromise is or is not fair, and list any ideas you may have for improving it.

▶ APPLY WHAT YOU LEARNED

Identify an issue today about which two countries of the world disagree. Use newspapers or the Internet to research to find out what the most important points are for each side. Then write a report that tells about the conflict and suggests a way to reach a compromise.

A wall carving shows two kings from Mesopotamia shaking hands as they reach an agreement.

SUMMARIZE

As you read, summarize advances in technology and government made by the Assyrian Empire.

BIG IDEA
The Assyrians used both force and innovations to build a large empire.

VOCABULARY

warfare
decree
territory
relief
scribe

Later Empires

| 3500 B.C. | 2500 B.C. | 1500 B.C. | 500 B.C. |

1000 B.C.–500 B.C.

By 1000 B.C. the Babylonian Empire was losing its power. To the north, another empire had started its rise in Mesopotamia. Its most important city was named in honor of its chief god, Assur (uh•SIR), and the empire was called the Assyrian Empire. For hundreds of years the Assyrian people had lived alongside the Babylonian Empire.

The Assyrian Empire

The people of Assur learned **warfare**, or skill in war, from their neighbors to the west, the Hittites. This helped the Assyrians gain an empire. They learned to make iron weapons and to use chariots, as the Hittites had. In addition, the Assyrians developed many of their own innovations in technology and warfare.

The Assyrian army, for example, was among the first to make and use the lance, a spear attached to a long handle. The army also introduced the use of battering rams, or heavy beams for breaking through city walls. These weapons helped make the Assyrian army a fearsome enemy. Tales of bloody battles with the Assyrians made neighbors wary of fighting the mighty warriors.

The Assyrians organized their army by assigning specialized jobs to their soldiers. Skilled chariot drivers carried archers, who used bows and arrows, into battle. Cavalry fought on horseback. There were also foot soldiers, who fought with lances.

This statue represents an Assyrian king who ruled in the 600s B.C.

By the early 700s B.C. the Assyrian army was the largest standing army Mesopotamia had ever seen. It was also one of the most destructive. The Assyrians struck fear in the hearts of their enemies as kingdoms fell one by one.

In 701 B.C. the Assyrian king Sennacherib (suh•NA•kuh•ruhb), stormed the kingdom of Israel, which was near the Mediterranean Sea. He captured more than 40 cities and seized more than 200,000 prisoners as slaves. In 689 B.C. he attacked and destroyed Babylon. Sennacherib bragged, "The city and houses, from its foundation to its top, I destroyed, I devastated, I burned with fire." After destroying the city, he flooded the site.

• SCIENCE AND TECHNOLOGY •

Assyrian Chariots

The Assyrians learned from the Hittites how to make and use chariots. However, the Assyrians used them to win and keep an empire. Assyrian charioteers, or drivers, were experts in managing a team of horses running full-speed into battle. Each chariot carried a driver and a warrior, usually an archer. Horses as well as men wore armor, or protective clothing. These early riders invented bridles, bits, and harnesses, which have changed little in 3,000 years.

Assyrian soldiers wore bronze helmets to protect themselves from arrows.

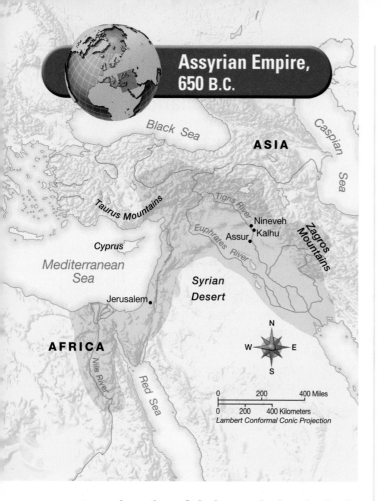

Assyrian Empire, 650 B.C.

Black Sea

ASIA

Caspian Sea

Taurus Mountains

Tigris River

Euphrates River

Nineveh
Assur Kalhu

Zagros Mountains

Cyprus

Mediterranean Sea

Syrian Desert

Jerusalem

AFRICA

Nile River

Red Sea

N
W E
S

0   200   400 Miles
0   200   400 Kilometers
Lambert Conformal Conic Projection

GEOGRAPHY THEME

Location At its largest, the Assyrian Empire stretched more than 1,600 miles (2,575 km).

❖ What landform made up most of the southern border of the Assyrian Empire?

The Assyrians ruled the largest empire in the world at that time. The mighty Assyrian Empire stretched through southwestern Asia. It included not only Mesopotamia but land to the southwest as well. It even included land on either side of the Nile River in northern Africa. The Assyrians had a goal in mind as they claimed more land. They wanted to control all the trade routes in southwestern Asia.

REVIEW What did the Assyrians learn from the Hittites?

Assyrian Achievements

Like the Akkadians and the Babylonians, the Assyrians were challenged by the task of governing an empire. Assyrian kings worked to unite the peoples of their huge empire by improving transportation and communication. The Assyrians built the world's first system of paved roads, linking the major cities of the empire. The roads enabled them to develop the first postal system for carrying messages and decrees. A **decree** is an official order or a decision made by a ruler. Later civilizations would adopt many of these innovations.

The Assyrians were also great builders of large monuments. Many of these structures are covered with finely carved scenes of life in the Assyrian Empire. The Assyrians wanted anyone who saw the huge buildings to know the strength and success of their empire.

Archaeologists have discovered other achievements. The inventive Assyrians were the first to make locks that opened with keys and the first to use a magnifying glass. Some experts believe the Assyrians were the first in Mesopotamia to use plumbing and flush toilets and the first to bring running water to their cities.

King Sennacherib, who ruled Assyria from 705 B.C. to 681 B.C., assembled one of the first libraries. His grandson, King Ashurbanipal (ah•suhr•BAH•nuh•pahl), assembled a second one, which included Assyrian, Babylonian, and Sumerian cuneiform tablets. Much of what is known about the Assyrians comes from the tablets found at Ashurbanipal's library.

The Assyrians used lion-shaped weights to weigh their goods for sale.

This wall relief shows a group of Assyrians with hunting dogs.

One important Assyrian innovation influenced later civilizations even to the present day—organization of the government to control the empire. The Assyrians divided their vast lands into territories. A **territory** is a large division of a country. Local leaders governed the territories and reported to the king. This model for governing large areas continues to this day. People living in the United States are citizens of their country and of a small territory, their state.

REVIEW What innovations helped to unite the peoples of the Assyrian Empire? **SUMMARIZE**

Glorious Nineveh

The Assyrian city of Nineveh (NIH•nuh•vuh) was located on the east bank of the Tigris River, near the present-day Iraqi city of Mosul. In 701 B.C. King Sennacherib made Nineveh the capital of the Assyrian Empire.

FAST FACT
Huge statues of bulls with wings and a human head guarded the entrance to the palace of Sargon II. The statues have eight legs so that when viewed from the front, side, or back, the expected number of legs would be seen.

Before that time, Nineveh was a small city. Most buildings were one story high, built of unbaked mud bricks or of stone, and had flat roofs. Only the temples were taller.

The capital, Nineveh, became a beautiful city with wide boulevards, large squares, parks, and gardens. Throughout the city, many new buildings rose. In about 650 B.C., King Ashurbanipal built a magnificent palace.

The king's palace was spectacular, covered with stone **reliefs**, or wall carvings that stand out from the surface of the building. Some of the finest Assyrian reliefs were at the palace of Ashurbanipal. Scenes of hunting, military victories, and religious ceremonies covered the palace walls.

The Assyrians built temples for their many gods. While their chief god was Assur, they also worshipped Ninurta, the god of war, and Nabu, the god of learning and protector of the scribes. A **scribe** was a person who wrote things for others. Most people in the ancient world could neither read nor write. Yet, Nineveh was home to Ashurbanipal's enormous library.

At its largest, Nineveh was enclosed by a wall that stretched 7.5 miles (12 km) around the city. Each of its 15 gates was named for a god. In time, the great city of Nineveh was destroyed. The mighty Assyrian Empire fell.

In 612 B.C. the Medes attacked Nineveh and killed the king of Assyria. The Medes came from Media, a land that was located in what is now northwestern Iran. A writer of the time described the fall of the city.

66 Woe to the bloody city! . . .
The noise of a whip and the noise
    of rattling wheels,
And of the prancing horses, and
    of leaping chariots.
The horseman lifts up the bright
    sword and glittering spear,
And there is a multitude slain. . . . 99

REVIEW How did Nineveh change after becoming the Assyrian capital?

The New Babylonian Empire

Free of the Assyrians, Babylon again became the center of civilization in Mesopotamia. The New Babylonian Empire stretched beyond Mesopotamia. It is often called the Neo-Babylonian Empire because *neo* means "new." The rebuilt city of Babylon became the empire's capital.

Nebuchadnezzar was one of the Neo-Babylonian Empire's best-known kings. From 605 B.C., he ruled for 44 years. Nebuchadnezzar is remembered for his great building projects. He built a major palace, several temples, and a ziggurat monument that was known in later times as the Tower of Babel. Nebuchadnezzar is

---

• GEOGRAPHY •

Babylon
Places and Regions

Only 11 years after the Assyrians destroyed Babylon, it was rebuilt. During the reign of the Babylonian king Nebuchadnezzar (neh•buh•kuhd•NEH•zer), from 605 B.C. to 562 B.C., Babylon achieved its greatest glory. The mighty king improved protection of the city by building walls almost 85 feet (26 m) thick around the outside of Babylon. Huge inner walls protected the city's main section. A wide moat, or trench filled with water, surrounded the inner walls. People entered and left the city through eight bronze gates. During this time more than 250,000 people may have lived in Babylon and nearby communities.

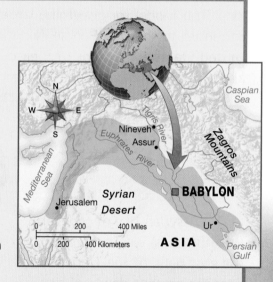

This reconstruction (above left) shows the main entry into Babylon. It was called the Ishtar Gate. The gate was covered with images of lions (above) and imaginary creatures. Today the original Ishtar Gate is in a German museum.

also thought to have built a lovely terraced garden. It came to be called the Hanging Gardens of Babylon. Today the Hanging Gardens of Babylon are remembered as one of the Seven Wonders of the Ancient World.

After Nebuchadnezzar, his son, Awil-Marduk, ruled for just a short time. He was soon replaced by several relatives, none of whom lasted long on the throne. Finally, Nabonidus, from what is today southeastern Turkey, gained control of the New Babylonian Empire. During his time of rule, Nabonidus helped keep his empire strong. He also rebuilt many of the empire's temples to honor the god he worshipped. In time, however, Nabonidus was forced to surrender his land to Persia to the east.

REVIEW By what two names do people today know Nebuchadnezzar's empire?

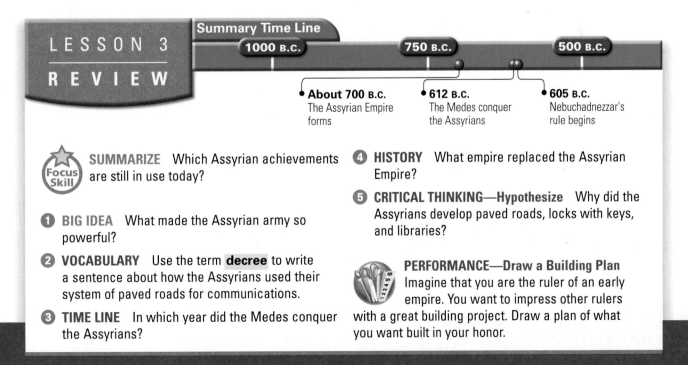

LESSON 3 REVIEW

Summary Time Line

1000 B.C. — 750 B.C. — 500 B.C.

About 700 B.C.
The Assyrian Empire forms

612 B.C.
The Medes conquer the Assyrians

605 B.C.
Nebuchadnezzar's rule begins

Focus Skill **SUMMARIZE** Which Assyrian achievements are still in use today?

1. **BIG IDEA** What made the Assyrian army so powerful?

2. **VOCABULARY** Use the term **decree** to write a sentence about how the Assyrians used their system of paved roads for communications.

3. **TIME LINE** In which year did the Medes conquer the Assyrians?

4. **HISTORY** What empire replaced the Assyrian Empire?

5. **CRITICAL THINKING—Hypothesize** Why did the Assyrians develop paved roads, locks with keys, and libraries?

PERFORMANCE—Draw a Building Plan Imagine that you are the ruler of an early empire. You want to impress other rulers with a great building project. Draw a plan of what you want built in your honor.

Review and Test Preparation

Summary Time Line

3000 B.C.   2500 B.C.

About 3000 B.C.
The Sumerian civilization begins

2350 B.C.
The Akkadian Empire begins

(Focus Skill) Summarize

Complete this graphic organizer to show that you understand how to summarize key facts about civilization in Sumer. A copy of this graphic organizer appears on page 32 of the Activity Book.

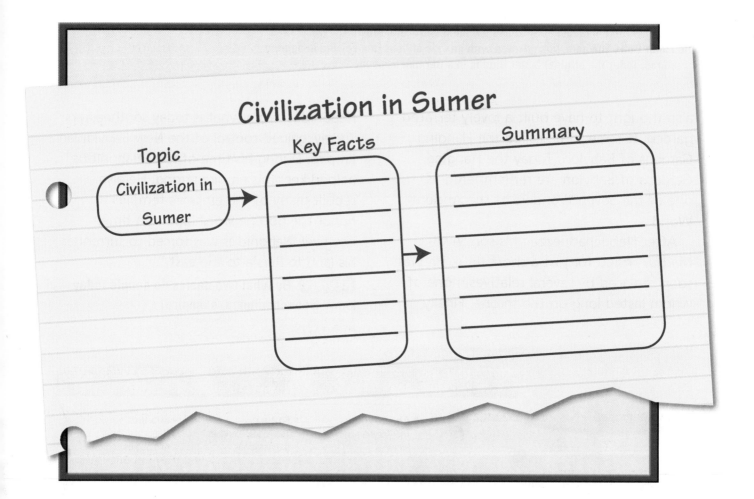

Civilization in Sumer

Topic

Civilization in Sumer →

Key Facts

→

Summary

THINK & WRITE

Write a Speech Which civilization in ancient Mesopotamia do you think made the most important contribution to world history and culture? Write a speech in which you explain the reasons for your choice.

Write an Essay Innovations in ancient Mesopotamia helped bring order to society and improve ways of living. Write an essay in which you describe how innovations today are helping people in our society.

2125 B.C.
The Akkadian Empire ends

1900 B.C.
The Babylonian Empire begins

1595 B.C.
The Kassites conquer Babylon

About 700 B.C.
The Assyrian Empire forms

612 B.C.
The Medes conquer the Assyrians

The Neo-Babylonian Empire begins

USE THE TIME LINE

1 Which group of people controlled an empire first, the Assyrians, the Babylonians, or the Akkadians?

2 About how many years after the Assyrian Empire formed did the Neo-Babylonian Empire begin?

USE VOCABULARY

Identify the term that correctly matches each description.

bureaucracy (p. 95)
cuneiform (p. 95)
merchant (p. 96)
empire (p. 99)
code (p. 101)
decree (p. 108)

3 a person who buys and sells or trades goods

4 a set of laws written down in a clear and orderly way

5 wedge-shaped writing

6 a group of appointed government officials

7 the vast lands and varied people that come under the control of a single government

8 an official order or a decision made by a ruler

RECALL FACTS

Answer these questions.

9 What part of Sumerian society was matriarchal?

10 How did the use of war chariots help the Hittites in battle?

11 How did King Sennacherib and the Assyrians change the city of Nineveh?

Write the letter of the best choice.

12 **TEST PREP** Which civilization's innovations included a system of taxation?
A Sumerian
B Akkadian
C Babylonian
D Assyrian

13 **TEST PREP** Which statement is not true about the Code of Hammurabi?
F It was made up of 282 laws.
G It was created about 2300 B.C.
H It was based on the belief that "the strong shall not oppress the weak."
J It introduced the new principle of "an eye for an eye."

14 **TEST PREP** Assyrian innovations included all of these *except*—
A locks and keys.
B lances and battering rams.
C dikes and reservoirs.
D the first postal system.

THINK CRITICALLY

15 How did the division of labor affect life for the citizens of Sumer?

16 The Akkadian king Sargon created a standing army. How was it an innovation?

17 Why were scribes so important in ancient times?

APPLY SKILLS

Resolve Conflict

18 Find a magazine or newspaper article that describes a conflict between two people or groups. First, identify the issues. Then use the steps on pages 104–105 to brainstorm possible solutions.

CITIZENSHIP SKILLS

AGILIKA ISLAND, ASWAN, EGYPT

In the 1960s the Aswan High Dam was built across the Nile River at Aswan, Egypt. The reservoir created by the dam flooded the island of Philae and its ancient temples, which were important to the ancient Egyptian religion. The temples were later rescued by divers and relocated to the nearby island of Agilika. That island was then reshaped and landscaped to look like Philae.

LOCATE IT

EGYPT

Nile R.

Red Sea

Aswan

4

The Nile Valley

"It flows through old
hushed Egypt
and its sands
Like some grave
mighty thought
threading a dream . . ."
—Leigh Hunt, describing the Nile River, 1818

 **Draw Conclusions**

A **conclusion** is an understanding reached after careful thinking. To draw a conclusion, you use what you already know along with what you read about a subject.

As you read this chapter, draw conclusions about the people of the Nile Valley.

• **Use what you already know and what you read to draw conclusions.**

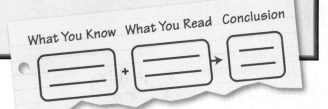

What You Know   What You Read   Conclusion

1

The Gift of the Nile

DRAW CONCLUSIONS

As you read, draw conclusions about the importance of the Nile River to life in Egypt.

BIG IDEA

The Nile River affected the development of Egyptian civilization.

VOCABULARY

predict
inundation
deity
afterlife
mummy
cataract
nation-state
dynasty

| 3500 B.C. | 2500 B.C. | 1500 B.C. | 500 B.C. |

3500 B.C.– 1500 B.C.

In the same centuries B.C. in which civilization was flourishing in Mesopotamia, another civilization was growing in what is now Egypt. Egypt is a country in the northeastern corner of Africa. It is bordered by the Mediterranean Sea on the north and by the vast desert known as the Sahara on the west. Most of present-day Egypt is dry, windswept desert. Through it, however, runs the world's longest river, the Nile. On the fertile land along its banks, one of the world's longest-lasting civilizations developed. It thrived for more than 3,000 years.

The Importance of the Nile

Near the Mediterranean Sea the Nile River divides into several branches and spreads out over a wide area. There it drops the soil it has carried from far upriver. Over time, this soil has formed a huge delta of low-lying land. Around 6000 B.C. early people began

This scene shows ancient Egyptian farmers along the Nile.

FAST FACT

The ancient Egyptians picked the flax plant while it was in full bloom (above). The Egyptians used flax to make clothing and to make oil for foods.

Movement The Nile River flows from higher land in the south to lower land in the north. The model of an ancient Egyptian sailboat (below) is from about 1800 B.C.

❖ Into what sea does the Nile River flow?

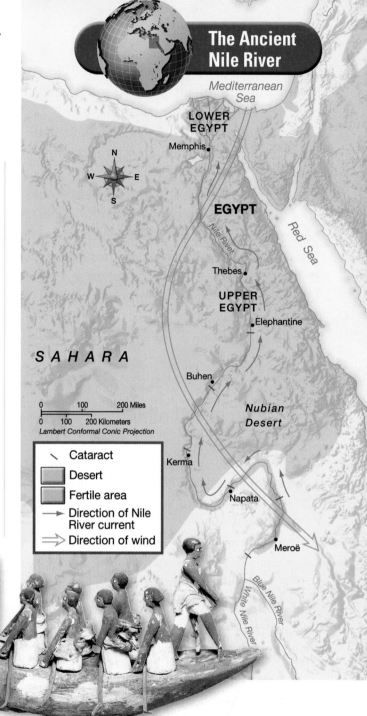

The Ancient Nile River

Mediterranean Sea

LOWER EGYPT

Memphis

EGYPT

Thebes

UPPER EGYPT

Elephantine

SAHARA

Buhen

Nubian Desert

0   100   200 Miles
0 100 200 Kilometers
Lambert Conformal Conic Projection

Kerma

Napata

Meroë

\ Cataract
Desert
Fertile area
→ Direction of Nile River current
⇒ Direction of wind

farming on the delta and in the river valley leading to it.

By 5000 B.C. people had built small farming settlements on the delta and in the valley to the south. Later, people called this place Kemet, meaning "Black Land," because of the rich, dark soil, also called kemet, found along the banks of the Nile. By contrast, the desert beyond Kemet they called Deshuret (deh•SHOO•ret), or the "Red Land."

Every year at about the same time, the Nile River flooded, depositing a fresh strip of rich, black soil along each bank. After the floodwaters drained away, the early farmers sprinkled seeds on top of the soil. Then they led livestock through the fields to walk over the seeds and push them into the ground. In this fertile soil, farmers were able to raise a huge supply of food.

Egypt is a hot country in which little rain falls. The great river provided not only good farmland but also water. Early farmers grew crops through most of the year by irrigating their land. Like the Sumerians, the Egyptians built canals to carry water from the Nile to their fields. They also built dams to form ponds to store floodwater for later use.

The Nile was Egypt's main transportation route. The ancient Egyptians built boats and barges to use the Nile as a river "highway." The first Egyptian boats were made of bundles of reeds, or tall water plants. Later, Egyptians began to make boats and barges out of wooden planks. Some of these were longer than 140 feet (43 m).

At first, the Egyptians used poles to move their boats. Later, they used oars to row them. Around 3000 B.C. the Egyptians developed sails and began to rely on the wind for power. Wind power made it easier for boats to travel upriver against the current. This improvement in transportation brought the many groups living along the Nile River into contact with one another.

REVIEW In what ways was the Nile River important to the ancient Egyptians? They gave special dirt an a gave water.

A Source of New Ideas

Because of the importance of the Nile River to the Egyptians, the ancient Greek historian Herodotus (hih•RAH•duh•tuhs) called Egypt "the gift of the Nile." Without the Nile River, people in Egypt would not have been able to survive.

In some years, though, the Nile also took life away. When the rainy season began in eastern Africa near the Nile's source, the level of the Nile River rose. In most years the river gently overflowed its banks. When too much rain fell upstream, however, the Nile flooded wildly. It washed away crops and drowned people and livestock. When too little rain fell, the river did not flood at all. Then the land along the river lay baked by the sun. Crops dried up, and people went hungry or starved. Usually farmers could depend on regular Nile floods.

Over the centuries, the ancient Egyptians worked out ways to **predict**, or tell ahead of time, when the river would flood. By studying the skies, they observed that the yearly flooding, or **inundation**, began soon after the star Sirius (SER•ee•uhs) reappeared after months of being out of sight. This event occurred on about June 20 each year. Using careful observations such as this, the Egyptians developed a calendar with 365 days in a year.

The Egyptian calendar divided the year into three seasons, based on events along the Nile River and their importance to agriculture. These three seasons were called Inundation, Emergence, and Harvest.

• SCIENCE AND TECHNOLOGY •

A Shaduf

A shaduf (shuh•DOOF) is a device that has been used in Egypt since early times to get water for irrigation. It consists of a container made of animal skins or of pottery attached to a lever and balanced by stones. The container is dipped into a well or river. When full, it is lifted out, and the water is dumped into a canal. Shadufs are still used in rural parts of Egypt.

Some farmers in present-day Egypt (left) still use a shaduf for irrigation like farmers did in ancient times (below).

This calendar is a copy of a design found on the ceiling of the Temple of Hathor in Egypt.

The final season was Harvest, the time when the crops were ready. In most years Egyptian farmers could be certain of a surplus. "It is to be a beautiful year, free from want and rich in all herbs," an Egyptian farmer might say in a year of plentiful crops.

REVIEW **Why did the Egyptians develop a calendar?** DRAW CONCLUSIONS

A Source of Religion

The ancient Egyptians believed in many different **deities**, or gods, each with a different responsibility. The people of ancient Egypt used stories about their gods to explain why flooding, drought, and other acts of nature took place.

The sun god Re (RAY), also known as Ra (RAH), was among the most important of the gods in ancient Egypt. Egyptians believed that Re was born each day and died each night. This explained to them why the sun seemed to come up each morning and go down at night. The sun became a symbol of the life cycle.

Each Egyptian settlement along the Nile also had its special god in addition to Re. People in Memphis, for example, worshipped Ptah, the god of the arts. The people of Hermopolis worshipped Thoth, the god of wisdom and writing. The people of Thebes worshipped Amon, a sun god. Amon was later identified with Re and called Amon-Re. In time Amon-Re became the chief deity of all ancient Egyptians.

Most Egyptians prayed to their gods and believed in a life after death, or **afterlife**. By 1500 B.C. some Egyptian prayers had been collected in what is now known as *The Book of the Dead*. A copy of this book was placed in the tombs of those who had died.

Because the time of flooding was so important to the Egyptians, they considered it to be the start of the new year. During Inundation the land received a fresh supply of kemet from the floodwaters that covered the farmland.

Emergence, or the growing season, followed Inundation. It was the time when the land emerged, or came out, from beneath the waters. As this season began, farmers plowed and seeded the rich soil. The growing season was only long enough to produce one crop of a grain, such as barley or wheat. However, as many as three or four crops of some fruits and vegetables could be produced during this time. Farmers grew lettuce, beans, onions, figs, dates, grapes, and cucumbers. Many also grew flax, which was used to make linen cloth.

A statue of the sun god Re

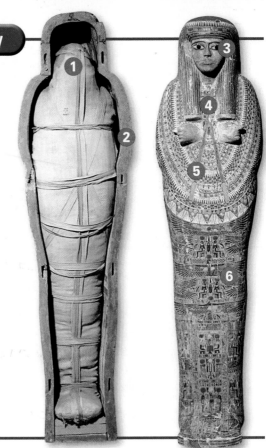

An Egyptian Mummy

Analyze Primary Sources

In ancient times the bodies of wealthy Egyptians were mummified, or preserved, in preparation for the afterlife. The mummies were placed in wooden coffins, or cases, that were covered with pictures of gods and picture writings. The writings were prayers and messages praising the person who had died.

1. Mummy wrapped in linen that protects the body
2. Body of the mummy case
3. Carved likeness of the dead person
4. Lid of the mummy case
5. Red straps to indicate that the person was probably a member of the priesthood
6. Picture of Nut, the sky goddess

❖ Why do you think prayers and images of gods were placed on the mummy's coffin?

The Egyptians believed that it would serve as a guide for the dead in the afterlife.

The ancient Egyptians believed that they would need their bodies in the afterlife. Because of this, they developed ways to preserve dead bodies. Making a **mummy**, or preserved body, took about 70 days. First, the Egyptians removed all the internal organs, except for the heart, and placed them in special containers. They left the heart in the body because they believed that all thinking took place there. Next, they covered the body with powdered salt to dry it out and prevent it from decaying. Then, they rubbed the dried-out body with special oils. Finally, they wrapped the body from head to toe in linen cloth. The mummy was then ready to be placed in its tomb.

REVIEW How did the Egyptians explain events in nature? By making up stories about the gods

A Source of Unity

Most of the small farming settlements in ancient Egypt developed on the Nile Delta and along the Nile River between the delta and the first of six **cataracts**, or waterfalls. The settlements on the Nile Delta became part of a kingdom known as Lower Egypt. The settlements in the Nile Valley to the south of the delta became a part of the kingdom of Upper Egypt.

Stories passed down from generation to generation say that King Menes (MEE•neez) of Upper Egypt conquered Lower Egypt in about 3100 B.C. He then united the two kingdoms and formed the world's first nation-state. A **nation-state** is a region with a united group of people and a single

This statue represents Thoth, the ancient Egyptian god of wisdom and writing.

...ze Illustrations
...uble crown of
...Egypt was formed
...ng the crown of
...Egypt inside the
...of Lower Egypt.

...y do you think the
...owns of Upper and
...wer Egypt were
...mbined?

government. According to ancient Egyptian stories, Menes set up his central government in the capital city of Memphis, in Lower Egypt.

Who really united the two kingdoms is not known. Some experts who study ancient Egypt think that a king named Narmer may have been the one who brought the two regions together. In some ancient artwork, King Narmer is shown wearing the white crown of Upper Egypt and in others, the red crown of Lower

Egypt. Later, pharaohs wore a double crown that combined the two crowns. The double crown stood for unity between the two regions.

Many experts also believe that it was Narmer who began the first Egyptian dynasty. A **dynasty** is a series of rulers who belong to the same family. More than 30 dynasties ruled ancient Egypt in the thousands of years that followed.

REVIEW Why do some historians believe King Narmer may have united Egypt?

LESSON 1 REVIEW

Summary Time Line

3500 B.C. — 2500 B.C. — 1500 B.C.

3100 B.C.
Upper and Lower Egypt are united

3000 B.C.
Egyptians begin to use sails on their boats

1500 B.C.
Egyptian prayers are collected in *The Book of the Dead*

Focus Skill **DRAW CONCLUSIONS** How do you think the Nile River affected the uniting of Upper and Lower Egypt?

1 **BIG IDEA** How did the Nile River affect the development of Egyptian civilization?

2 **VOCABULARY** Use th... and **dynasty** in a sent... civilization.

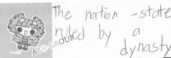

3 **TIME LINE** When were Upper and Lower Egypt united?

4 **ECONOMICS** How did the yearly flooding of the Nile River help shape the economy of Egypt?

5 **CRITICAL THINKING—Analyze** Why do you think settlements developed along the Nile despite the danger of floods?

6 **CRITICAL THINKING—Evaluate** Why do you think the Egyptians united into a single nation-state while the Sumerians did not?

PERFORMANCE—Make a Map Draw a map of ancient Egypt. Be sure to include labels showing the Nile River, Upper Egypt, Lower Egypt, and the location of the cataracts. Use different colors to show the desert and river valley regions. Display your map in the classroom.

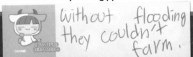

DRAW CONCLUSIONS

As you read, draw conclusions about the dynasties of ancient Egypt.

BIG IDEA

The ancient Egyptians maintained their civilization through many changes.

VOCABULARY

hieroglyphics

papyrus

pyramid

prosperity

vizier

heir

annex

nome

pharaoh

The Dynasties of Ancient Egypt

| 3500 B.C. | 2500 B.C. | 1500 B.C. | 500 B.C. |

3000 B.C.– 1000 B.C.

Most experts trace the beginning of Egyptian civilization to the rule of King Narmer. When Narmer died, rule of the Egyptian nation-state passed on to a member of his family. This continued for several generations, creating Egypt's first dynasty, or family of rulers. When Narmer's descendants lost the authority to rule, a new dynasty took over.

The Early Period

The early period of ancient Egyptian history includes Dynasties 1 and 2, which ruled from about 3100 B.C. to 2686 B.C. During this time, or even earlier, the Egyptians developed irrigation systems and invented plows pulled by animals. The Egyptians also began using **hieroglyphics** (hy•ruh•GLIH•fiks), writing that uses pictures to stand for sounds, words, or ideas. Early Egyptian hieroglyphics had more than 700 pictures. At first the ancient Egyptians used hieroglyphic writing mostly on temples and stone monuments. Highly trained scribes carved religious markings and recorded the words and brave deeds of their kings. Hieroglyphic writing was used by the Egyptians for more than 3,000 years.

As writing became more common, the need developed for a material that would be easier than stone to write on, store, and carry. For this purpose, the ancient Egyptians invented **papyrus** (puh•PY•ruhs), a paperlike material they made from the papyrus plants of the Nile Valley. The English word *paper* comes from *papyrus*. Scribes wrote on dried and woven papyrus with tools made from reeds sharpened to a point. Soot, the fine, black powder from smoke, was mixed with water to serve as ink. Only for the most important words did scribes dip their reeds into ink made from a red powder.

A statue of an ancient Egyptian scribe from about 2400 B.C.

Egyptian Hieroglyphics

HIEROGLYPH	ENGLISH WORD	HIEROGLYPH	ENGLISH WORD
	Female		Male
	Life		Live
	Water		Mouth
	See		Eyes
	You		Peace

Analyze Tables The table (left) lists a few hieroglyphic symbols along with their meanings. The wall carving (above) shows Egyptian pictures and hieroglyphic writing.

◆ Which symbols in the table most clearly show their meaning?

The improvement in communication that resulted from the invention of papyrus helped make united government possible. Today we know about Egypt's early history because of the written records left behind. This history is usually divided into three main periods—the Old Kingdom, the Middle Kingdom, and the New Kingdom. In the times between these kingdoms, competing dynasties ruled parts of Egypt and sometimes fought one another. Today these periods are called intermediate, or in-between, periods.

REVIEW What were the major achievements of Egypt's early period?

The Old Kingdom

The Old Kingdom is also known as the Age of the Pyramids. It lasted from about 2686 B.C. to 2181 B.C. During this 500-year period, the ancient Egyptians developed the technology to build the largest stone structures in the world—the pyramids. A **pyramid** has a square base and usually has triangular sides that come to a point at the top. The Egyptians built pyramids as tombs for their rulers. Built with layer upon layer of stone blocks, they are solid all the way through except for burial rooms and passageways inside.

The architect Imhotep (im•HOH•tep) designed the first Egyptian pyramid as a tomb for King Zoser in about 2650 B.C. King Zoser's pyramid rose about 200 feet (60 m) in six giant stone steps. The resulting "step pyramid" looked somewhat like a Sumerian ziggurat.

Built between 2650 B.C. and 2611 B.C., this pyramid in Sakara was the first in Egypt.

The ancient Egyptians may have built step pyramids to help their kings reach the afterlife. One of their religious writings said, "A staircase to heaven is laid for him [the king] so that he may climb to heaven."

During Dynasty 4 the Egyptians built the Great Pyramid at Giza (GEE•zuh). It still stands across the Nile River from Cairo, the present-day capital of Egypt. The Great Pyramid was built for King Khufu (KOO•foo) by workers who were mostly farmers. As many as 100,000 farmers may have worked on the Great Pyramid during the time each year when the floodwaters of the Nile covered their fields.

To build the Great Pyramid, workers cut and moved more than 2 million blocks of limestone. Each block weighed about 2 tons (about 1,800 kg). The huge stone blocks had to be cut with hand tools and moved on rollers to the construction site. Many archaeologists believe the Egyptians built ramps to help them raise the blocks to each new level of the pyramid. However they did it, the completed pyramid at Giza is huge. It stands about 480 feet (146 m) high and covers 13 acres. Its tip originally was covered with gold to reflect the sun's rays. It was, and still is, the largest pyramid in Egypt.

The Old Kingdom, or Age of the Pyramids, lasted until Dynasty 6 ended. During the next five dynasties, Egyptian kings competed with local rulers for power. Because of this, Egypt's **prosperity**, or economic success, declined. This time is called "the first intermediate period."

REVIEW Why is the Old Kingdom also called the Age of the Pyramids?

The Middle Kingdom

The year 2040 B.C. marks the beginning of the Middle Kingdom, which had its origins in Thebes, in Upper Egypt. It was also the start of the 50-year rule of King Mentuhotep (men•too•HOH•tep) II, who founded Dynasty 11. Mentuhotep II returned more authority to the central government. This brought back Egypt's

A CLOSER LOOK
The Pyramids at Giza

Experts estimate that it took about 20 years to build the Great Pyramid. The architect who designed it included more inner chambers and passageways than in any other pyramid. Because the Great Pyramid was entered by grave robbers, archaeologists cannot be sure exactly what was once inside it.

1. The King's Chamber is hidden close to the center of the pyramid. King Khufu's coffin still remains inside the chamber.

2. Air shafts from the King's Chamber line up with the star constellation, or star pattern, Orion. Egyptians believed the king's soul would ascend, or rise, to the stars.

3. Some secret underground rooms remain mysteries. They look like burial chambers, but for some reason they were never completed.

Why do you think the Egyptians buried treasures and statues with their rulers?

economic and cultural glory. Also during the reign of Mentuhotep II, Egypt began to expand its territory beyond the Nile Valley. The Egyptians under Mentuhotep II conquered parts of what is now Libya to the west, Nubia to the south, and Sinai to the east.

Mentuhotep II was followed by his son, Mentuhotep III, and then by his grandson, Mentuhotep IV. Both continued to rule from Thebes and to build and expand Egypt.

In 1991 B.C. the leader Amenemhet (ahm•uhn•em•HET) took the throne as king. Amenemhet had been the **vizier** (vuh•ZIR), or chief adviser, to Mentuhotep IV. As vizier, he carried out the king's decrees and took care of running the government.

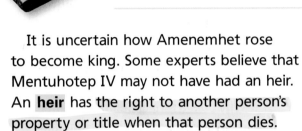

This model shows Egyptians making bread during the Middle Kingdom in about 2000 B.C.

It is uncertain how Amenemhet rose to become king. Some experts believe that Mentuhotep IV may not have had an heir. An **heir** has the right to another person's property or title when that person dies.

One of Amenemhet's first acts as king was to move the Egyptian capital from Thebes back to the area around Memphis. This city provided a more central location between Upper Egypt and Lower Egypt. He then went on to **annex**, or add on, Nubia to Egypt. He also expanded Egyptian influence as far east as the land that is now the country of Syria.

Amenemhet's rule marked the beginning of Dynasty 12, which governed Egypt from 1991 B.C. to 1786 B.C.

LOCATE IT

Cairo
Giza
EGYPT

It was a time when architecture, literature, and other arts flourished in Egypt. During this long period of prosperity, the governors who ruled Egypt's districts, or **nomes**, became less and less important.

In the 1600s B.C. the Hyksos (HIK•sohs) gained control of Egypt. The Hyksos were invaders from the Fertile Crescent who had settled in the Nile Valley in the 1700s B.C. They ruled Egypt until 1570 B.C. During that time they introduced horses, horse-drawn chariots, new weapons, and a new kind of fortification, or building for defense. These changes later helped Egypt expand during the time known as the New Kingdom.

REVIEW Why was a strong central government important in Egypt during the Middle Kingdom?

Focus Skill **DRAW CONCLUSIONS**

The New Kingdom

The New Kingdom was a 500-year period during which ancient Egypt became the world's strongest power. The period began in 1552 B.C., with Dynasty 18. For many years, the Egyptian kings kept a strong hold over Egypt. Then their authority began to weaken. During this dynasty, native Egyptians drove the Hyksos out of Egypt, and Thebes regained its importance as a capital city.

It was at this time that the Egyptian people began to call their king **pharaoh**. The word means "great house" and referred to the king's grand palace. The Egyptians believed that the pharaoh was a god in human form. This belief strengthened the authority of the pharaohs.

At the beginning of Dynasty 18, Egypt developed a full-time standing army. The Egyptians used horse-drawn chariots and other military inventions of the Hyksos. The dynasty's early rulers led military forces into southwestern Asia. Thutmose I (thoot•MOH•suh) reached the Euphrates River. Hatshepsut (hat•SHEP•soot), his daughter, also led armies in battle. Egypt developed a great empire and reached the height of its power during the 1400s B.C. under Thutmose III.

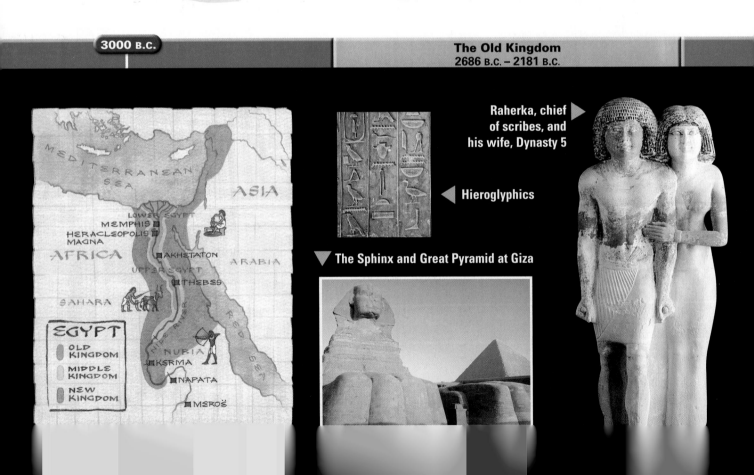

3000 B.C.

The Old Kingdom
2686 B.C. – 2181 B.C.

Raherka, chief of scribes, and his wife, Dynasty 5

Hieroglyphics

The Sphinx and Great Pyramid at Giza

MEDITERRANEAN SEA

ASIA

LOWER EGYPT
MEMPHIS
HERACLEOPOLIS MAGNA

AFRICA

AKHETATON

ARABIA

UPPER EGYPT

THEBES

SAHARA

EGYPT

OLD KINGDOM

MIDDLE KINGDOM

NEW KINGDOM

NUBIA
KERMA

NAPATA

MEROË

Hatshepsut   1503 B.C.–1458 B.C.

Character Trait: Courage

Most pharaohs were men. An exception was Hatshepsut, who ruled as pharaoh during Dynasty 18. When her husband, Thutmose II, died, her stepson Thutmose III inherited the throne. Because he was too young to rule, Hatshepsut served as regent, or temporary ruler. Within a few years she had herself crowned pharaoh alongside her stepson. Hatshepsut knew that the people might not accept a woman as pharaoh, but she was willing to take a chance. Just to be safe, she lived much of her life dressed in the traditional male clothing of the pharaohs. She even wore a false beard like the male pharaohs. Hatshepsut was not the first female ruler in Egyptian history. However, she is the best known because of her achievements and the many monuments built to honor her.

GO ONLINE

MULTIMEDIA BIOGRAPHIES
Visit The Learning Site at www.harcourtschool.com
to learn about other famous people.

Amenhotep IV (ah•muhn•HOH•tep) came to the throne in 1364 B.C., bringing with him great changes for Egypt. He and his wife, Nefertiti (nef•er•TEET•ee), were believers in only one god, the Aton. Amenhotep was so devoted to this god that he changed his own name to Akhenaton (ahk•NAH•tuhn), or "servant of the Aton." Akhenaton declared that the Aton was to replace Amon-Re and all other gods. He also moved the capital to a new city, Akhetaton.

Akhenaton's religious changes led to the making of art that honored the Aton. However, they also brought unrest.

| 2000 B.C. | The Middle Kingdom 2040 B.C. – 1786 B.C. | The New Kingdom 1552 B.C. – 1069 B.C. | 1000 B.C. |

Mentuhotep II, Dynasty 11

A painting of Abu Simbel, a religious site in southern Egypt

Hippopotamus statue

Queen Nefertiti, Dynasty 18

King Tutankhamen, Dynasty 18

Analyze Primary Sources

Discovered in A.D. 1799, the Rosetta Stone helped scientists decode the hieroglyphic writing of ancient Egyptians. On the stone's shiny surface were three different kinds of writing—two ancient Egyptian and one ancient Greek. The ancient Greek gave scholars the key to one of the Egyptian scripts, but the Egyptian hieroglyphics still could not be understood. Then, in 1822, Jean-François Champollion decoded the hieroglyphics, using the other forms of writing as a guide. *There were 3 writings.*

1 This is hieroglyphic writing.

2 This writing, also used by the ancient Egyptians, is called demotic writing. Demotic writing was a short form of hieroglyphic writing.

3 This writing is ancient Greek.

❖ Why do you think decoding hieroglyphic writing was such an important discovery?

Some Egyptians feared that worshipping the Aton might anger the other gods.

Akhenaton's heir ended the unrest. King Tutankhaton (too•tang•KAH•tuhn) allowed Egyptians to once again worship the old Egyptian deities as well as the Aton. He also removed the *aton* from his name and became Tutankhamen (too•tang•KAH•muhn).

Throughout the rest of Dynasty 18 and most of Dynasty 19, Egyptian rulers kept the empire prosperous. During Dynasty 20, power struggles developed between kings, priests, and officials. After Dynasty 20, Egypt began to split up into smaller parts.

Egypt's weakness attracted a series of invaders. During the next 700 years, more than ten dynasties ruled Egypt. Most were formed by Nubians and other outsiders. Although outsiders ruled Egypt, the many achievements of the ancient Egyptians were not forgotten.

REVIEW Who was Akhenaton?

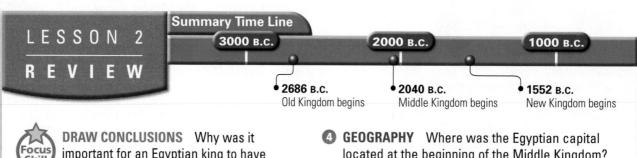

LESSON 2 REVIEW

Summary Time Line

3000 B.C. | 2000 B.C. | 1000 B.C.

2686 B.C.
Old Kingdom begins

2040 B.C.
Middle Kingdom begins

1552 B.C.
New Kingdom begins

Focus Skill **DRAW CONCLUSIONS** Why was it important for an Egyptian king to have an heir?

1 BIG IDEA Do you think that the dynasties helped Egypt maintain its civilization? Why or why not?

2 VOCABULARY Use the term **annex** in a sentence about Egypt.

3 TIME LINE Did the Middle Kingdom begin before or after the Old Kingdom?

4 GEOGRAPHY Where was the Egyptian capital located at the beginning of the Middle Kingdom?

5 CRITICAL THINKING—Evaluate What do you think was the Egyptians' most important invention? Why?

PERFORMANCE—Draw a Mural Learn more about the building of the pyramids at the library or on the Internet. Then draw a mural that shows how this task was done.

Solve a Problem

➡ WHY IT MATTERS

People everywhere and throughout history have had to solve problems. In fact, people still have to solve all kinds of problems every day. Some problems are bigger than others, but most are easier to solve if you have a plan. Knowing how to solve problems is a skill you will use all your life.

➡ WHAT YOU NEED TO KNOW

Imhotep, the architect of the Great Pyramid at Giza, had a big problem. He had to plan the largest structure ever built at that time. He also had to figure out a way to move the huge limestone blocks without pulleys or wheels, which were still unknown to the Egyptians at the time. Here are some steps you can use to solve problems, big or small.

Step 1 **Identify the problem. Get a clear idea of what is needed.**

Step 2 **Think of possible solutions. Come up with at least two that you think might work.**

Step 3 **Look at the facts of the situation and think about how each of your ideas might work. After comparing the possible solutions, you can rule out those that are not the best choices.**

Step 4 **Choose the best solution, and plan a way to carry it out.**

Step 5 **Try your solution, and think about how well it solves the problem.**

➡ PRACTICE THE SKILL

1. What problem did Imhotep face?
2. What are two possible solutions to this problem?
3. Which of the solutions is the better choice? Why?
4. How would you carry out this solution?
5. How well do you think the solution would solve the problem?

➡ APPLY WHAT YOU LEARNED

Identify a problem in your community or school. Use the steps to write a plan for solving the problem. What solution did you choose? Explain why you think it will best solve the problem.

Statue of Imhotep

Treasures of Tutankhamen

Tutankhamen ruled Egypt for only 9 years and died at the age of 18. The "boy king" was buried in a solid-gold coffin, and his tomb was filled with gold and jewelry. The tomb of Tutankhamen lay hidden in Egypt's Valley of the Kings for more than 3,300 years. In November 1922, Howard Carter, an expert in the study of ancient Egypt, discovered it. Today the golden coffin still contains the young pharaoh's remains, hidden from view inside two outer coffins. The Egyptian Museum in Cairo displays many of Tutankhamen's treasures to show Egypt's great wealth during the height of its civilization.

Tutankhamen's golden mask

 FROM THE EGYPTIAN MUSEUM IN CAIRO

Golden hieroglyphics

This highly decorated jewelry chest was found in Tutankhamen's tomb.

Analyze the Primary Source

1. What do the objects on these pages tell you about the economy of Egypt during Tutankhamen's rule?

2. Why do you think it was important to hide the location of Tutankhamen's tomb?

3. Why might Egyptians have placed pictures of enemies on the soles of the pharaoh's sandals?

These leather and gold sandals were decorated with pictures of Egypt's enemies in Asia and Africa.

The crook and flail were royal staffs, or rods carried as symbols of authority. They were symbols of the pharaohs and of Osiris, the Egyptian god of the underworld.

This golden fan once held ostrich feathers. It was meant to fan the pharaoh and restore the breath of life to him in the afterlife.

ACTIVITY

Research and Explain

Tutankhamen's tomb served as a time capsule for items that represent ancient Egyptian culture. Make a list of items that represent your culture to place in a time capsule. Then write a paragraph to explain why you chose these items.

RESEARCH

Visit The Learning Site at **www.harcourtschool.com** to research other primary sources.

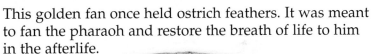

3

As you read, draw conclusions about how the civilizations in Nubia and Egypt influenced each other.

BIG IDEA

The people of Nubia and the people of Egypt influenced each other.

VOCABULARY

ceramic
trade route
mineral
obelisk
independence
ally
trading network
decipher

Nubia and Kush

3500 B.C.	2500 B.C.	1500 B.C.	500 B.C.

3500 B.C.–500 B.C.

The ancient land of Nubia stretched south along the Nile River between the first and sixth cataracts. It occupied the valley from Egypt's southern border almost to where the city of Khartoum (kar•TOOM), in Sudan, stands today. For the ancient Egyptians, Nubia was a source of trade goods and natural resources from central Africa. Although Egypt had a strong influence over Nubia, the Nubians kept their own culture. They worshipped their own gods, and they had their own forms of architecture.

Early People in Nubia

Nubian culture began as early as the 7000s B.C., when people settled along the upper Nile Valley in what is now the northern part of Sudan. By about 4000 B.C. they had built villages and had begun to grow crops and raise livestock.

The Nubians were among the first people to make **ceramic**, or baked clay, pottery. In time the Nubians began to offer ceramic bowls and jars as trade items. Nubian merchants also traded goods that came from places in central and southern Africa. These items included hardwoods and animal products desired by the Egyptians.

Nubia's location between Egypt and central Africa made it an ideal trading center. Nubian merchants served as go-betweens for trade between northern and central Africa. Among the many trade

LOCATE IT

Meroë Pyramids

SUDAN

This ring (above left) belonged to a Nubian king. These Nubian pyramids (below) are located in what is today Sudan.

items the Nubians sent north were leopard skins, ostrich eggs, bird feathers, ivory tusks and horns, spices, gold, and ebony wood.

Egypt and Nubia traded peacefully at first. Then the Egyptians realized that they could gain greater wealth if they controlled Nubia's **trade routes**. These were the waterways, paths, and trails that traders used to move goods for exchange from one place to another. By about 2600 B.C. Egypt had brought Nubian trade under its control.

In addition to controlling trade, the Egyptians also took over Nubia's natural resources. Beneath Nubia's rocky soil were gold and other minerals. A **mineral** is a natural resource found in rocks. Rising high above the landscape were cliffs of granite and other kinds of rocks. The Egyptians cut blocks of these rocks to use for buildings and, during the time of the New Kingdom, for monuments called obelisks (AH•buh•lisks). An **obelisk** is a tall, slender stone pillar with four sides and a pointed top.

After 2000 B.C. the Egyptians annexed northern Nubia, which was called Wawat, and made it part of Egypt. The Egyptians built forts near the second cataract of the Nile and mined gold for themselves. The Nubians fled southward, where they formed a kingdom known as Kush. They set up their capital at Kerma, which became the center for Kushite civilization.

REVIEW Why did Egypt want to control Nubia?

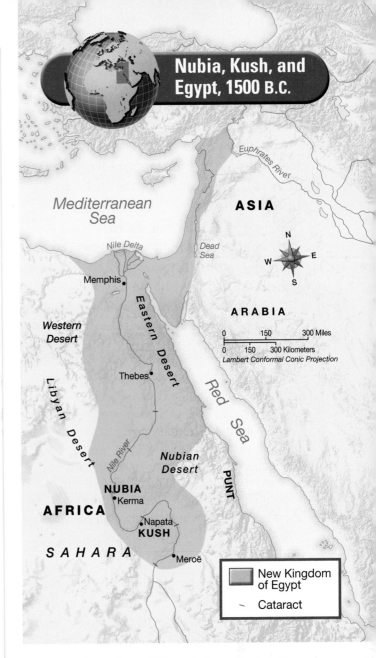

Nubia, Kush, and Egypt, 1500 B.C.

Location This map shows the locations of ancient Egypt, Nubia, and Kush.

❖ Why do you think these civilizations developed along the Nile River?

Freedom and Reconquest

Egyptian control of ancient Nubia lasted about 300 years. By the time the Hyksos gained control of Egypt in the 1600s B.C., the Nubians had already regained their **independence**, or the freedom to govern themselves. Free from Egyptian rule, the kingdom of Kush flourished, or grew.

The ancient burial grounds of Kerma provide evidence of the Kushite people's prosperity. To bury a king, the people of Kerma dug a large round pit. They then placed a gold-covered wooden funeral bed at the bottom. They dressed the king in his finest clothes and laid him on the funeral bed. All around him they placed weapons and treasures. Then they covered the pit with a mound of earth and outlined the mound with the skulls of cattle, as a sign of the king's wealth.

During this time, Kushite kings gained power as well as wealth. Over time they took control of much of what is today northern Sudan and even of parts of southern Egypt. The Kushites gained power at the same time that the Egyptians lost theirs to the Hyksos. The Kushite leaders decided that it would be better for Kush to be an **ally**, or supporter, of the Hyksos than an enemy. After all, the Hyksos controlled most of the land north of Kush. The Kushite leaders did not know that the Egyptians would regain the land.

By the 1500s B.C. the powerful pharaohs of Egypt's New Kingdom had forced out the Hyksos and had begun building their own new empire. The Egyptians invaded Nubia and took more land than they had

CITIZENSHIP

DEMOCRATIC VALUES
Common Good

In about 1938 B.C. the Egyptians conquered northern Nubia. Southern Nubia became known as Kush. The Egyptian pharaohs forced the Nubians in the northern parts to adopt Egyptian customs. Nubian leaders worked hard for independence. By about 1600 B.C. parts of northern Nubia had regained their freedom and reunited with Kush. Nubian culture flourished as Kush became a wealthy and powerful kingdom. Later, the Nubians of Kush would conquer Egypt.

Analyze the Value

1. Why do you think it was important for the Nubians to gain independence from Egypt?

2. **Make It Relevant** Use the library or the Internet to find a recent example of a conflict caused by one culture ruling another.

An army of wooden Nubian soldiers, made about 2100 B.C.

This wall carving (left) shows Nubian princes paying respect to Egyptian King Tutankhamen in about 1310 B.C. This Nubian gold jewelry (above) has Egyptian hieroglyphics engraved on it.

controlled before—almost to the fourth cataract of the Nile. As a show of strength, the Egyptians built cities all across Nubia.

Egypt's rule of Kush lasted for about 550 years. Under Egyptian rule, the Kushites were encouraged to become like Egyptians. Many Kushites adopted Egyptian religious beliefs, customs, and ways of dress.

REVIEW Why do you think the Nubians were able to regain their independence by the 1600s B.C.? DRAW CONCLUSIONS

Conquest of Egypt

Beginning about 1075 B.C., several weak dynasties brought the Egyptian Empire into a time of disorder. At the same time, the kingdom of Kush started to regain its strength. In the Kush capital of Napata (NA•puh•tah), near the fourth cataract, Kush's leaders were well aware of Egypt's problems.

In the 700s B.C. the Kushite king Kashta (KASH•tuh) took advantage of Egypt's weakness and invaded it. By 750 B.C. Kashta's armies had taken control of Upper Egypt. Twenty years later Kashta's son Piye (PEE•yeh), also known as Piankhi (PYANG•kee), followed his father's success. He conquered Lower Egypt, bringing all of Egypt under Kushite control.

The writing on a stone obelisk repeats Piye's orders to his soldiers in their victory over Egypt:

> **Delay not, day or night. . .**
> **Fight at sight. . .**
> **Yoke the war-horse!**
> **Draw up the line of battle.**

After Piye's death his brother Shabaka (SHA•bah•kah) claimed the throne of the Egyptian pharaoh. For about 70 years Kushite pharaohs ruled Egypt as Dynasty 25, or the Kushite dynasty.

This Kushite sphinx, which has the head of a ram, was made during Piye's reign as ruler of Egypt.

In this illustration (right), conquered princes declare loyalty to the Kushite king Piye. This Nubian bracelet (above) was probably owned by a member of the royal family.

The Kushite rule lasted for about 100 years and helped restore some of Egypt's glory. Many old temples were enlarged, and new temples were constructed. The Kushite pharaohs brought back long-forgotten religious ceremonies and ordered scribes to copy and save ancient Egyptian writings.

The pharaohs of the Kushite dynasty learned to write using Egyptian hieroglyphics. For the first time, the people of ancient Nubia began to write about themselves. They began to record their achievements in writing on temple walls and obelisks. Their writing provides a firsthand look into their ancient way of life.

REVIEW How was Dynasty 25 different from other Egyptian dynasties?

This cup from the city of Meroë is decorated with the image of a crocodile.

The Kushites

Kushite rule of Egypt ended in 671 B.C., when the Assyrians invaded the Nile Valley. Threatened but not defeated, the Kushite leaders moved their capital city farther south to Meroë (MAIR•oh•wee), where Kushite civilization prospered again.

In Meroë, merchants set up a trading network. A **trading network** is a system in which buyers and sellers from different places can exchange goods. Goods came to Meroë from the Fertile Crescent, from southern Africa, and from India. Along with gold and spices, the Kushite merchants offered iron products, including spears, plows, and wheel rims.

The land around Meroë was rich in iron ore. It also had many trees that supplied firewood so that the iron could be heated and reshaped.

Using these resources, the Kushites turned Meroë into an iron-making center as well as a center for trade. Today huge heaps of slag, the waste from separating iron from iron ore, provide evidence of this ancient economic activity.

For 600 years Meroë prospered. The Kushites built many stone buildings and a great stone temple to their most important god, Amon. In royal cemeteries, pyramids marked the burial sites of Kushite kings and queens. Carved stone and painted ceramics showed scenes from Kushite life. Words were also carved on monuments and obelisks, but today we cannot read what they say. Archaeologists have not yet **deciphered**, or determined the meaning of, Meroitic writing.

REVIEW What happened to the Kushites after they were forced out of Egypt?

• **HERITAGE** •

The Queens of Kush

Queens played an important role in Kushite society. While men usually were the rulers of Kush, the Kushites traced their family lines through their mothers. Because of this, the queen mother in the Kushite monarchy held a position of great respect and influence. When a king died, the queen mother and the leaders of the kingdom chose the next ruler from among the members of the royal family. If the chosen ruler was too young to govern, the queen mother ruled as regent for him. Ruling queens in Kush were known as Kandakes (kahn•dah•KAYZ). Some queens ruled together with their husbands. Queen Shanakdakhete, one of the most powerful rulers of Meroë, ordered the building of many temples and palaces.

The silver-and-gold mask (left) shows Queen Malakaye of Kush. The mask was made about 2,600 years ago.

	1500 B.C.	500 B.C.
...00 B.C.	750 B.C.	671 B.C.
...ypt takes control ...Nubian trade	Kushite rule of Upper Egypt begins	Kushite rule of Egypt ends

GEOGRAPHY In which present-day country was Nubia once located?

CRITICAL THINKING—Hypothesize How might Kushite history be different if the Assyrians had not driven the Kushites from Egypt?

PERFORMANCE—Write a Journal Entry Imagine that you are a trader from Asia who has just arrived at Meroë. Write a ...urnal entry that describes activities taking place in ...e city. Exchange journal entries with a classmate ...d compare your descriptions.

② **VOCABULARY** Writ... relationship between... **trading network**.

③ **TIME LINE** When di... Nubian trade?

Summary Time Line
3500 B.C.

• **About 3100 B.C.**
Upper Egypt and Lower Egypt
are united into the world's
first nation-state

Focus Skill — Draw Conclusions

Complete this graphic organizer to show that you understand how to draw conclusions about the early Egyptians. A copy of this graphic organizer appears on page 41 of the Activity Book.

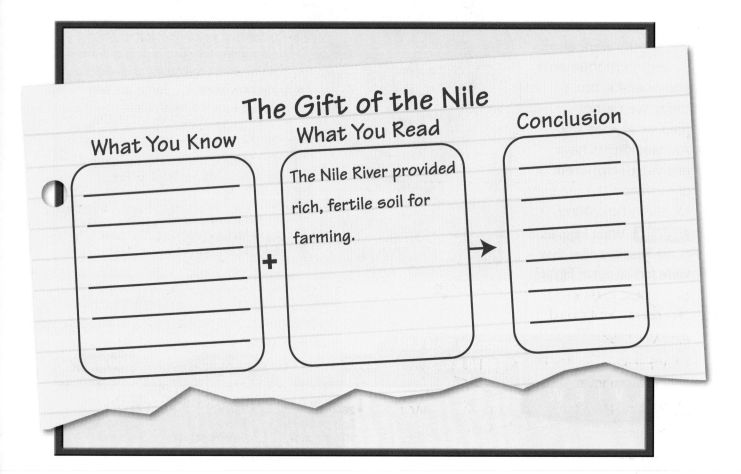

The Gift of the Nile

What You Know

_____
_____
_____
_____
_____

+

What You Read

The Nile River provided rich, fertile soil for farming.

→

Conclusion

_____
_____
_____
_____
_____

THINK & WRITE

Write an Invitation   Imagine that you are the pharaoh of an Egyptian dynasty of your choice. Write an invitation to another leader to encourage him or her to travel to your kingdom. Include a list of sights the leader will see during his or her two-day visit.

Write a News Report   Imagine that you are a news reporter covering a battle in ancient Egypt. In your report, describe the two sides and what they are fighting over. Predict which side will win the battle. Discuss how life in the region might change as a result.

2500 B.C.   1500 B.C.   500 B.C.

2686 B.C.
Egypt's Old Kingdom begins

2040 B.C.
Egypt's Middle Kingdom begins

1552 B.C.
Egypt's New Kingdom begins

750 B.C.
Kushite rule of Upper Egypt begins

671 B.C.
Kushite rule of Egypt ends

USE THE

1 When did Upp
to become the

2 When did the
begin?

USE VOC

For each pair o
two to explain

3 predict (p. 118

4 afterlife (p. 11

5 dynasty (p. 121,

6 pyramid (p. 123

7 trade route (p. 1

8 mineral (p. 133),

RECALL FA

Answer these qu

9 What were the
that the early E

10 Why did New K
change his nar

11 Why did the Nu
of Kush?

Write the letter of the best choice.

12 **TEST PREP** Which time in Egyptian
history is also called the Age of the Pyramids?
A the Early Period
B the Old Kingdom
C the Middle Kingdom
D the New Kingdom

13 **TEST PREP** The word *pharaoh* means—
F "great house."
G "wise leader."
H "godlike one."
J "brave warrior."

14 **TEST PREP** Which kinds of writing were
found on the Rosetta Stone?
A Greek, Hebrew, and Phoenician
B Sumerian and Greek
C ancient Egyptian and Greek
D Latin and Hebrew

15 **TEST PREP** Egyptians and Nubians
battled over all of these *except*—
F control of trade routes.
G control of gold and other minerals.
H control of land.
J control of the way pharaohs were selected.

THINK CRITICALLY

16 In general, civilizations in Egypt prospered
during peaceful times and suffered during
times of conflict. Why, then, do you think they
chose to battle each other so often?

17 How do you think Egyptian civilization might
have been different if Egyptians had not made
a paperlike material from papyrus plants?

APPLY SKILLS

Solve a Problem

18 Read a recent print or online article
to find out about a problem that
exists in your community or another
place in the world. Use the problem-solving
steps on page 129 to come up with possible
solutions to this problem.

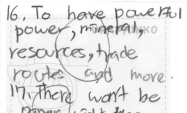

Handwritten notes:
1. 3100 B.C.
2. 750 B.C.
3. They predicted when to inundation.
4. They believed in afterlife, so they made mummies.
5. To have a dynasty they needed a heir.
6. They made pyramids for their pharaohs.
7. Trade routes lead to prosperity.
8. They made obelisk out of mineral.
9. The Red land was the Sahara dessert and the Black land was the land along the Nile.
10. Because how he believed in other gods too.
11. Because they regained their independance.
12. B
14. C
15. J
16. To have powerful power, mineral, resources, trade routes and more.
17. there won't be paper right now.

Chapter 4 ◼ 139

MAYAN RUINS, TULUM, MEXICO

The Mayan ruins of Tulum are located near the entrance of the Mexican national park Sian Ka'an, on the Yucatán Peninsula. The ruins sit on top of limestone cliffs that overlook the Caribbean Sea. Tulum, which means "wall" or "fence" in the Mayan language, was a city surrounded by walls. It was the largest Mayan city built on the coast.

LOCATE IT

MEXICO

Tulum

PACIFIC OCEAN

5

Asia and the Americas

"In the midst of these tall forests through which we passed there is a great variety of ancient buildings."

—Avendaño, Spanish explorer, 1696

Compare and Contrast

Focus Skill

When you **compare and contrast** people, places, events, or ideas, you analyze how they are alike and how they are different.

As you read this chapter, compare and contrast the information you read about.

• Look for similarities and differences among people, places, events, and ideas.

• Record them in a Venn diagram.

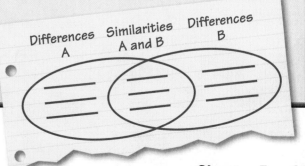

Differences A   Similarities A and B   Differences B

Focus Skill

COMPARE AND CONTRAST

As you read, compare and contrast key details about the Indus Valley civilization.

BIG IDEA

The Indus Valley civilization made many advances in technology.

VOCABULARY

subcontinent

regulate

commercial

artisan

inscription

urban planning

citadel

granary

assimilate

monsoon

FAST FACT

The source of the Indus River is at an elevation of more than 17,000 feet (5,182 m). From there, the river travels about 1,800 miles (2,900 km) to empty into the Arabian Sea.

The Indus Valley

| 3500 B.C. | 2500 B.C. | 1500 B.C. | 500 B.C. |

3000 B.C.– 1500 B.C.

The present-day countries of India, Pakistan, and Bangladesh are located on the large peninsula that extends southward from southern Asia. Geographers call the peninsula a **subcontinent** because of its large size and its separateness from the rest of the continent. The Indian subcontinent is separated from the rest of Asia by a long wall of rocky, snow-capped mountains called the Himalayas. The two great rivers of the Indian subcontinent, the Indus and the Ganges (GAN•jeez), begin in the snowy peaks of the Himalayas and flow southward. It was along the Indus River that the subcontinent's earliest civilization developed.

Early Civilization

Fed by melting mountain snow, the Indus River tumbles from the high mountains onto the hot, dry floodplain in present-day Pakistan. Each spring for thousands of years, the Indus River has flooded, leaving rocks, gravel, and sediment along its banks. In this fertile soil, early farmers grew barley and other grains. These cultivated crops supplemented, or added to, the food that the people got by hunting animals and gathering wild plants.

The first farming villages were built on top of large mounds made from mud and stones. The purpose of the mounds was to keep the villages above the flood level. Some of these villages grew in size and population to become cities. Over time, one of the

The Indus River flows through the Karakoram Range in what today is Pakistan.

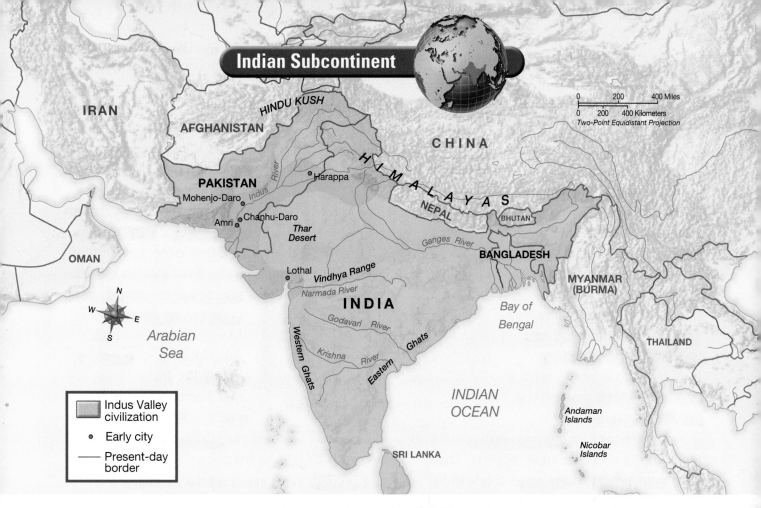

Indian Subcontinent

IRAN

AFGHANISTAN

HINDU KUSH

PAKISTAN

• Harappa

Mohenjo-Daro •

Indus River

CHINA

HIMALAYAS

Amri • • Chanhu-Daro

Thar
Desert

NEPAL

BHUTAN

Ganges River

BANGLADESH

OMAN

Lothal •

Vindhya Range

Narmada River

INDIA

Godavari River

MYANMAR
(BURMA)

Bay of
Bengal

Arabian
Sea

Western Ghats

Krishna River

Eastern Ghats

THAILAND

INDIAN
OCEAN

Andaman
Islands

Nicobar
Islands

SRI LANKA

0   200   400 Miles
0   200   400 Kilometers
Two-Point Equidistant Projection

N
W   E
S

☐ Indus Valley
civilization

• Early city

— Present-day
border

Regions This map shows the Indian subcontinent and the location of some early cities in the Indus Valley region.

❓ Which present-day countries make up the Indian subcontinent?

GEOGRAPHY THEME

largest ancient civilizations formed in what today are Afghanistan, Pakistan, and northwestern India. It is often called the Harappan civilization after the first discovered city, Harappa (huh•RA•puh).

Harappa is named after a Pakistani town where the first evidence of an Indus Valley civilization was found in the 1920s. There, archaeologists uncovered the ruins of a palace. Archaeologists also found at least five mounds, two of which had large walls around them.

These walls were built not only for defense but also to help regulate trade that took place there. To **regulate** means to control according to a set of rules.

Harappa is one of at least eight important ancient cities that flourished in the Indus Valley between 3000 B.C. and 2000 B.C. Others were Mohenjo-Daro (moh•HEN•joh DAR•oh), in what is now Pakistan, and Lothal, in what is now India. All were located on rivers or near the western coast of the Indian subcontinent. All were **commercial**, or trade, centers.

REVIEW What were Harappa and Mohenjo-Daro?

This clay jar, made in about 2000 B.C., was found at Mohenjo-Daro.

The Indus Economy

The people of the Indus Valley cities traded with people in nearby farming villages and with distant mining communities. Goods that people traded most likely included cotton, lumber, grain, and livestock. For transportation, people used pack animals, river barges, and animal-drawn carts.

The Indus people also traded with other civilizations. As early as 2300 B.C., Indus Valley merchants traded with people in central Asia, Mesopotamia, and the Persian Gulf region.

Indus **artisans**, or craftworkers, produced many useful and decorative objects. They used bone, shell, and ivory to create jewelry, game pieces, and trimmings for furniture.

Stone seals, from about 2000 B.C.

They used copper and bronze, a metal made by combining copper and tin, to make pots, pans, and tools. Artisans also worked with silver and clay. They made clay figurines of animals and people, probably for use in religious ceremonies. They also made small limestone figures that may have represented their gods or their leaders.

Other objects found at Indus sites include square stone seals engraved with drawings of animals. Many of the seals had **inscriptions**, or written messages. Indus Valley merchants marked their goods with these seals. The seals were either stamped onto the goods or tied to them.

REVIEW What goods did the Harappan people trade?

The City of Mohenjo-Daro

Mohenjo-Daro is probably the best known of the Indus cities. It was a model of **urban planning**, or thoughtful design of a city. The fact that Mohenjo-Daro was so carefully planned shows that the city must have had a strong government. Leaders must have directed others to plan and build the city's buildings and streets.

Mohenjo-Daro was built using a grid system, just as some modern cities are. Straight, wide streets crisscrossed the city. Some were as wide as 30 feet (about 9 m). The planners laid out these streets to form rectangular blocks for houses and other buildings. The builders used exact measurements as they constructed the city.

Mohenjo-Daro and several other cities were divided into two parts. The eastern part was where most of the homes were

Gold jewelry found in Mohenjo-Daro shows evidence of the city's wealth.

located. The western part was where government and religious activities took place. A **citadel** (SIH•tuh•duhl)—or large, fortlike structure—contained government buildings and palaces. It also had places for religious ceremonies and for storing grain. The builders of Mohenjo-Daro added layers of mud to the western part of the city so that it stood at least 20 feet (6 m) higher than the eastern part, or the "lower city."

Most of the grain-storage buildings, or **granaries**, stood 30 feet (about 9 m) tall and were 1,200 feet (about 366 m) long.

A CLOSER LOOK
Mohenjo-Daro

Archaeologists believe that more than 30,000 people may have lived in Mohenjo-Daro.

1. The citadel had a large public bathhouse.
2. The streets were laid out in a grid system.
3. Artisans made items for everyday use and for decoration.
4. The people stored their grain in large buildings called granaries.
5. People often met outside the city to trade for goods from other places.

❓ Why do you think the people often met outside the city to trade for goods from other places?

Each granary held more than enough grain to feed Mohenjo-Daro's population, which by 2500 B.C. was as high as 35,000. The grain was also used to pay many of the workers in the city.

Most of the buildings in Mohenjo-Daro were made of bricks. Instead of drying bricks in the sun, as the Egyptians and Mesopotamians did, the Harappan people baked their bricks in ovens. Fire-baked bricks were harder and could not be washed away by water like sun-dried bricks, which can be used only in very dry regions. Because brickmakers used exact measurements, each brick was the same size and shape.

Only the wealthiest families lived in houses in the city. The rest of the people lived in small mud huts in villages outside the city. Some city houses were two stories high and had courtyards and servants' rooms. The doors of most city houses opened onto back alleys rather than onto the busy main streets. The fronts of the houses, which had no windows, looked much alike.

While most village huts had only one large room, even the smallest city houses had separate rooms for cooking and for sleeping. Some of the city houses had rooms for bathing, which included water

wells inside. Family members showered by pouring jugs of fresh water over themselves. The runoff water flowed through brick drainpipes into a drainage system along the city's streets. The main drains had covered openings so that workers could repair damaged pipes.

The government of Mohenjo-Daro provided trash collection as a service. At scheduled times, families placed all their trash outside, near the street.

Within Mohenjo-Daro's citadel was a large public bathhouse. The main tank was 40 feet (12 m) long and 8 feet (2 m) deep. Besides bathing there, people may have used the bathhouse for religious purposes. They may also have gathered there to exchange news and conduct business.

An interesting fact about Harappan cities is that they were all very much alike. Their street layouts were similar. People in each city used the same weights, measures, and tools. This probably means that the Harappans had a strong central government to control such things.

REVIEW How were Harappan bricks different from those used by the Mesopotamians and Egyptians? **COMPARE AND CONTRAST**

The remains of Mohenjo-Daro are located in what is today southern Pakistan.

The Mysterious End of the Harappan Civilization

Why the Harappan civilization ended is still a mystery. One theory is that by 1700 B.C. the Indus civilization was slowly breaking up into smaller cultures. The breakup may have been caused by changes in the course of the Indus and other rivers. This could have caused some cities to be flooded and other cities to lose their sources of water and transportation. As a result, many people left the cities of the Indus Valley. In time they may have been **assimilated** (uh•SIH•muh•lay•tuhd) into, or made a part of, other cultures.

Another theory is that the end of the Harappan civilization came because of a natural disaster, such as an earthquake, a flood, or a monsoon. A **monsoon** is a seasonal wind shift that brings heavy rains.

What we know about the Harappan civilization comes from the ruins and artifacts that archaeologists have found.

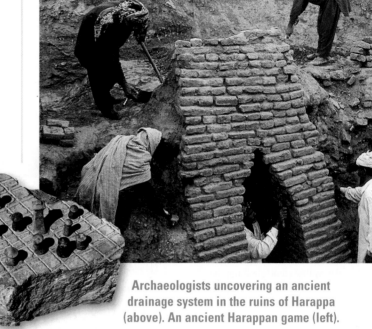

Archaeologists uncovering an ancient drainage system in the ruins of Harappa (above). An ancient Harappan game (left).

Archaeologists have also found examples of Harappan writing, but no one has been able to decipher them. When that happens, we may learn much more.

REVIEW What are some possible causes of the end of the Harappan civilization?

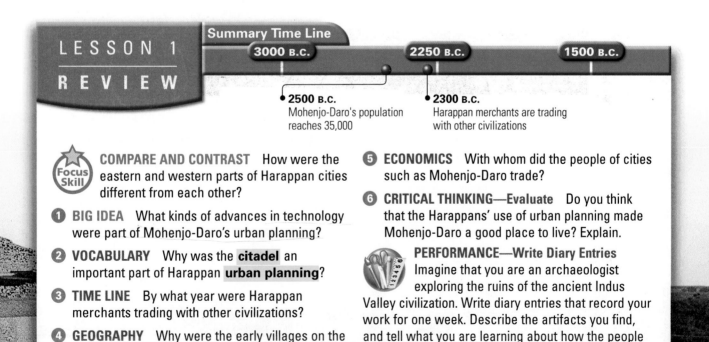

LESSON 1 REVIEW

Summary Time Line

3000 B.C.	2250 B.C.	1500 B.C.

2500 B.C.
Mohenjo-Daro's population reaches 35,000

2300 B.C.
Harappan merchants are trading with other civilizations

Focus Skill **COMPARE AND CONTRAST** How were the eastern and western parts of Harappan cities different from each other?

1 **BIG IDEA** What kinds of advances in technology were part of Mohenjo-Daro's urban planning?

2 **VOCABULARY** Why was the **citadel** an important part of Harappan **urban planning**?

3 **TIME LINE** By what year were Harappan merchants trading with other civilizations?

4 **GEOGRAPHY** Why were the early villages on the Indian subcontinent built on mounds?

5 **ECONOMICS** With whom did the people of cities such as Mohenjo-Daro trade?

6 **CRITICAL THINKING—Evaluate** Do you think that the Harappans' use of urban planning made Mohenjo-Daro a good place to live? Explain.

PERFORMANCE—Write Diary Entries Imagine that you are an archaeologist exploring the ruins of the ancient Indus Valley civilization. Write diary entries that record your work for one week. Describe the artifacts you find, and tell what you are learning about how the people made use of natural resources.

2

The Huang He Valley

COMPARE AND CONTRAST

As you read, compare and contrast information about the early civilizations of China.

BIG IDEA

The influence of the Huang He valley civilization can be seen in present-day Chinese culture.

VOCABULARY

loess

legend

ancestor

oracle bone

character

standardize

tyrant

virtue

mandate

3500 B.C.	2500 B.C.	1500 B.C.	500 B.C.

2000 B.C.–500 B.C.

The ancient civilization that developed in China's Huang He (HWAHNG•HUH) valley has direct links to present-day China. The Huang He, or Yellow River, gained its name because it carries large amounts of soft, sandy yellow soil called **loess** (LOH•uhs). The fertile loess deposited in the floodplain has made the region nearly perfect for farming. For centuries, farmers have used the Huang He for water to make the rich but dry soil come alive with plentiful crops. Even so, the Huang He has been called "China's Sorrow." Its floods have often brought death to the people who lived along its banks.

China's Origins

The story of Yu the Great and the Great Flood is one of the most famous of all Chinese legends. A **legend** is a story handed down from earlier times. This legend tells of a time when a great flood covered much of the Huang He valley. It covered even the hills, so that the people could find no food.

According to the legend, King Shun ruled over several villages along the Huang He. The legend tells that King Shun ordered Yu,

FAST FACT In 1887 the Huang He flooded an area of more than 50,000 square miles (129,500 sq km). This was the worst flood in the recorded history of the river.

Loess gives the Huang He, or Yellow River, its name.

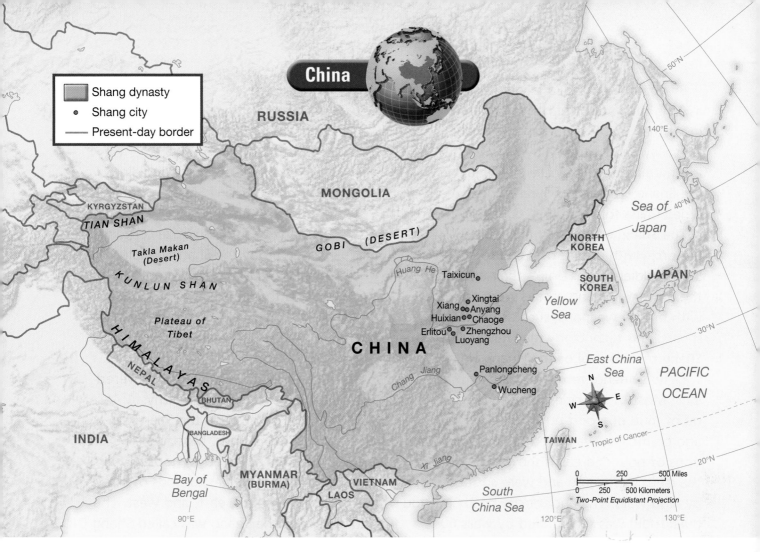

China

Shang dynasty
• Shang city
— Present-day border

GEOGRAPHY THEME

Human-Environment Interactions The Shang claimed land in what is today eastern China.

❖ Why do you think other groups may have wanted the land controlled by the Shang?

a government official, to control the flood. To do so, Yu organized the leaders of the villages. They all ordered their people to cut channels to drain the waters away to the sea. Yu worked for 13 years before bringing the flooding under control. King Shun was so impressed by Yu's accomplishment that he passed his throne on to Yu. Yu the Great has long been known as a legendary ruler of ancient China. Many Chinese people still say,

❝If it were not for Yu the Great, we would all be fishes.❞

Today some experts believe that Yu was a real person. He may have been the first

king of the Xia (SYAH) dynasty. For thousands of years, stories about the Xia dynasty were passed down from generation to generation. The Xia dynasty, if it really existed, would have ruled China from about 2000 B.C. to about 1766 B.C.

So far no evidence, such as Xia artifacts, has been discovered. Because of this, many archaeologists and historians do not accept the Xia as China's first dynasty. That title, they feel, belongs to the Shang dynasty.

REVIEW How is the Xia dynasty different from other dynasties in China?

🔴 **COMPARE AND CONTRAST**

The Shang Dynasty

By about 1766 B.C., a leader known as Tang the Successful had conquered more than 1,800 villages in the Huang He valley. Tang began a dynasty that is remembered in Chinese history as the Shang. The Shang dynasty governed China for more than 600 years.

The Shang established their rule by force, with armies of 3,000 to 5,000 soldiers each. Unlike their enemies, the powerful Shang armies were equipped with bronze weapons, such as bronze-tipped spears. This technology may have helped the Shang take control of the Huang He valley.

Little evidence remains of Shang buildings. Most of the cities, which were made up of mud or wood buildings, have long ago crumbled away. Even so, their foundations of pounded earth show that some of the cities were large and were surrounded by high walls. The ancient city of Zhengzhou (JUHNG•JOH) was surrounded by walls 60

This owl-shaped bronze drinking container is from the Shang dynasty.

feet (18 m) wide and 30 feet (9 m) high.

While few Shang buildings remain, many Shang artifacts still exist. Archaeologists have located many beautiful bronze containers crafted by the Shang people. The Shang made these by melting bronze and pouring the liquid metal into molds.

Archaeologists have found many other kinds of artifacts as well. These include carved marble and jade and silk fabrics. Many of these artifacts were discovered within the graves of the wealthy.

Whether rich or poor, the Shang people believed in many gods. Most were nature gods. The Shang prayed to gods of wind, rain, and fire, as well as to gods of directions—north, south, east, and west. The chief god of the Shang was called Shang Di,

---

• BIOGRAPHY •

Xilingshi about 2700 B.C.
Character Trait: Inventiveness

According to a Chinese legend, in about 2700 B.C. the ruler Huang Di ordered his wife, Xilingshi (SEE•LING•SHIR), to find out what was damaging the mulberry trees in their garden. Xilingshi found white worms eating the leaves and making cocoons. She accidentally dropped a cocoon into hot water. When she lifted it out, she found that one slender thread was unwinding itself from the cocoon. She had discovered silk. It is said that Xilingshi invented a way to join silk threads to make them thick and strong enough for weaving. Some stories say that she also invented the first silk loom, or weaving machine.

In the painting, a weaver uses a loom to make silk fabric. Silk fabric can be made into clothing items, such as these silk slippers.

MULTIMEDIA BIOGRAPHIES
Visit The Learning Site at www.harcourtschool.com
to learn about other famous people.

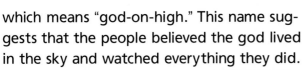

Analyze Primary Sources

During the Shang dynasty, oracle bones were used in religious ceremonies. On the oracle bones, a diviner wrote questions asking the Shang gods about the future.

❶ tortoise shell

❷ ancient Chinese writing

❸ crack from heat

❖ What does the writing carved into the shell represent?

which means "god-on-high." This name suggests that the people believed the god lived in the sky and watched everything they did.

The Shang believed that their **ancestors**, deceased relatives who lived longer ago than grandparents, could plead with the gods for them. They believed that the spirits of their ancestors were wise and could guide the lives of the living.

The most important evidence of Shang rule is the writing found carved on animal bones and turtle shells. The bones and shells, known as **oracle bones**, were used in ceremonies to answer questions about the future. Shang kings would visit a diviner, or person through whom the gods were believed to speak. The diviner would carve the king's question on a bone, make a small hole, and then place a hot metal rod against the bone. The heat caused cracks to spread from the hole. The diviner then gave the bone to the king. The Shang king "read" the cracks to find out the answers to the questions.

Jade figure of a kneeling woman from the Shang dynasty

Archaeologists have found thousands of oracle bones near the last known Shang capital, which is near present-day Anyang. The oracle bones provide much information about the topics that most interested the Shang kings. The writings refer to hunting, wars, weather, and the selection of days for religious ceremonies.

REVIEW For what did the Shang people use oracle bones?

Early Chinese Writing

The system of writing used by the Shang people had many **characters**, or symbols. Some characters in Shang writing look like those of present-day Chinese writing.

The characters used in Shang writing represent whole words. They are not like the letters of the Latin alphabet, which represent sounds. Shang characters are more like Egyptian hieroglyphic writing. Like hieroglyphics, many Shang characters began as pictographs, or drawings of the things they named. The character for *sun*, for example, looked much like the sun. Over time, these characters developed into the form of Chinese writing used today.

Chinese Writing

WRITING FROM SHANG PERIOD	ENGLISH WORD	CURRENT CHINESE WRITING
⊙	Sun	日
☽	Moon	月
木	Tree	木
雨	Rain	雨
山	Mountain	山
水	Water	水

Analyze Tables Chinese writing today has its roots in writing from the Shang period. This Chinese student (below) is learning to write Chinese characters.

◈ Which current Chinese characters look most like the ancient Shang characters?

Inscriptions on oracle bones and bronze containers show that the Shang people used more than 3,000 characters. Only about 1,000 of them have been deciphered, or figured out.

Each of the many city-states in the Huang He valley had its own style of writing. That meant that Shang writing was not always understood from place to place. In 221 B.C., during the Qin dynasty, writing became **standardized** for all Chinese people. That is, one style of writing was decided upon for everyone to use. This was an important event in Chinese history because it made it easier for people to communicate with one another.

Chinese writing has not changed very much over time. As Chinese civilization developed new ideas and made contact with other peoples, some old characters were changed and new ones were added. Even so, present-day Chinese writing has strong roots in the Shang characters.

REVIEW How are Shang characters different from letters in the English alphabet?

The Fall of the Shang

The Shang dynasty lasted more than 600 years, with 31 kings ruling over 17 generations. The last Shang king was said to be a **tyrant**, or a ruler who controls through cruelty. Later Chinese historians wrote that King Zhouxin (JOH•SHIN) and his wife, Daji, made many laws that were cruel to slaves and to the common people. They built expensive palaces and gardens and did nothing for the people they ruled.

By the end of the Shang dynasty, King Zhouxin favored only the nobles who were friendly to him. This made the other nobles angry and caused serious disagreements. Taking advantage of the situation,

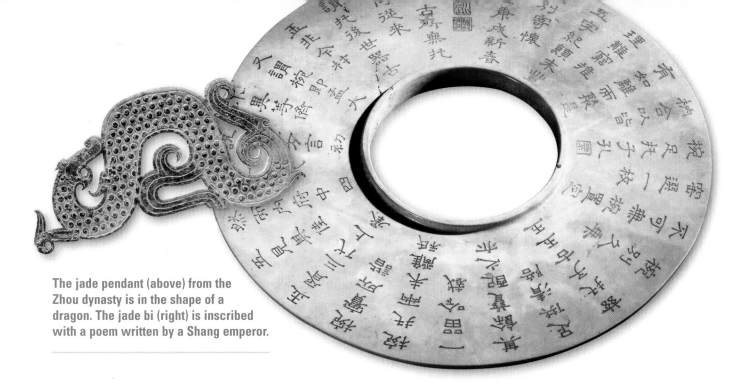

The jade pendant (above) from the Zhou dynasty is in the shape of a dragon. The jade bi (right) is inscribed with a poem written by a Shang emperor.

a tribe called the Zhou (JOH) attacked and overthrew the Shang dynasty.

The Zhou claimed that Heaven had ordered Wu, their leader, to conquer the Shang and to begin a new dynasty. The Zhou thought that the Shang did not have the **virtues**, or right actions and thinking, needed to lead the people.

An early Chinese text called *The Book of Documents* calls Heaven's order to claim rule over China the Mandate of Heaven. The Zhou kings believed that they would be able to keep the **mandate**, or right to rule, as long as they continued to be virtuous rulers. The Zhou believed that only a ruler with virtues could keep order in society. To the Zhou, a virtuous leader was one who looked out for the well-being of the people.

REVIEW What was the Mandate of Heaven?

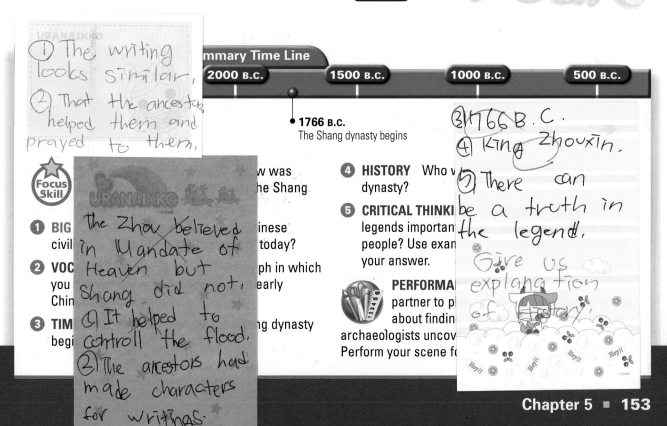

Summary Time Line

2000 B.C. — 1500 B.C. — 1000 B.C. — 500 B.C.

1766 B.C.
The Shang dynasty begins

(handwritten notes)
① The writing looks similar.
② That the ancestors helped them and prayed to them.

the Zhou believed in Mandate of Heaven but Shang did not.
① It helped to controll the flood.
② The ancestors had made characters for writings.

③ 1766 B.C.
④ King Zhouxin.
⑤ There can be a truth in the legend.
Give us explanation of it!

Focus Skill

① **BIG** ... civil...

② **VOC** ... you ... Chin...

③ **TIM** ... begi...

④ **HISTORY** Who ... dynasty?

⑤ **CRITICAL THINKI** ... legends important ... people? Use exam... your answer.

PERFORMA ... partner to p... about findin... archaeologists uncov... Perform your scene fo...

Read a Relief Map and an Elevation Map

VOCABULARY
relief map   contour line

▶ WHY IT MATTERS

Different kinds of maps provide different information. To find the height of physical features in a region, you would look at an elevation map. It shows the elevation, or height of the land in relation to sea level. To get an idea of the physical features of a region, you would look at a relief map. A **relief map** shows the differences in height or depth of hills, valleys, and other physical features.

▶ WHAT YOU NEED TO KNOW

On an elevation map (Map B), the land is measured from sea level. The elevation of land at sea level is 0 feet (0 m). Find sea

level on Drawing A in the Reading Contour Lines diagram below. The lines that circle the hill are contour lines. A **contour line** connects all points of equal elevation. On Drawing A, the 100-foot (30-m) contour line connects all points that are 100 feet (30 m) above sea level.

On a relief map (Map A), shading is often used. Heavy shading shows steep rises and drops in the land. Light shading is used where the land rises or falls gently. No shading shows land that is mainly flat.

Like the shading on a relief map, the red and green lines on Drawings A and B below show how sharply the land rises and falls. Drawing B shows the hill from above. On the steeper side of the hill, the contour

Reading Contour Lines

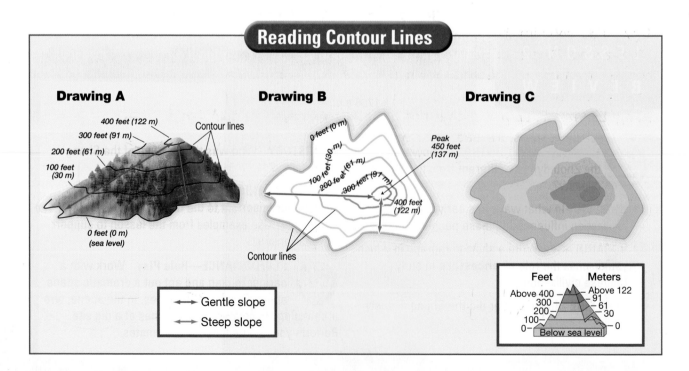

Drawing A

400 feet (122 m)
300 feet (91 m)
200 feet (61 m)
100 feet (30 m)
0 feet (0 m) (sea level)

Contour lines

Drawing B

0 feet (0 m)
100 feet (30 m)
200 feet (61 m)
300 feet (91 m)
400 feet (122 m)

Peak 450 feet (137 m)

Contour lines

Drawing C

⟷ Gentle slope
⟶ Steep slope

Feet		Meters
Above 400		Above 122
300		91
200		61
100		30
0	Below sea level	0

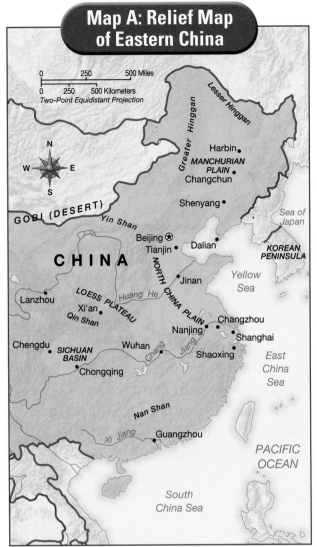

Map A: Relief Map of Eastern China

0   250   500 Miles
0   250   500 Kilometers
Two-Point Equidistant Projection

Greater Hinggan
Lesser Hinggan
Harbin
MANCHURIAN PLAIN
Changchun
Shenyang
Sea of Japan
GOBI (DESERT)
Yin Shan
Beijing ✪
Tianjin
Dalian
KOREAN PENINSULA
CHINA
Yellow Sea
Lanzhou
LOESS PLATEAU
Huang He
Xi'an
Qin Shan
NORTH CHINA PLAIN
Jinan
Changzhou
Nanjing
Shanghai
Chengdu
SICHUAN BASIN
Wuhan
Chang Jiang
Shaoxing
Chongqing
East China Sea
Nan Shan
Xi Jiang
Guangzhou
PACIFIC OCEAN
South China Sea

Map B: Elevation Map of Eastern China

0   250   500 Miles
0   250   500 Kilometers
Two-Point Equidistant Projection

Greater Hinggan
Lesser Hinggan
Harbin
MANCHURIAN PLAIN
Changchun
Shenyang
Sea of Japan
GOBI (DESERT)
Yin Shan
Beijing ✪
Tianjin
Dalian
KOREAN PENINSULA
CHINA
Yellow Sea
Lanzhou
LOESS PLATEAU
Huang He
Xi'an
Qin Shan
NORTH CHINA PLAIN
Jinan
Changzhou
Nanjing
Shanghai
Chengdu
SICHUAN BASIN
Wuhan
Chang Jiang
Shaoxing
Chongqing
East China Sea
Nan Shan
Xi Jiang
Guangzhou
PACIFIC OCEAN
South China Sea

Feet	Meters
Above 13,120	Above 4,000
6,560	2,000
1,640	500
655	200
0	0
Below sea level	

lines are closer together. On the gently sloping side, they are farther apart.

In Drawing C the color between contour lines shows elevation. The land shown in green is between sea level and 100 feet (30 m). Drawing C, however, does not show exact elevations. Instead, the key, or legend, shows the range of elevations for which each color stands.

▶ PRACTICE THE SKILL

Use the maps to answer the following questions.

1 Which city is at a higher elevation, Changchun or Shenyang?

2 How do you know Shanghai has a lower elevation than Lanzhou?

3 How would you describe most of the land of eastern China?

▶ APPLY WHAT YOU LEARNED

Plan a trip between Guangzhou and Beijing. Use the most direct route. Write a paragraph describing the elevations you would cross on your journey. Compare your paragraph with that of a classmate.

MAP AND GLOBE SKILLS

Practice your map and globe skills with the **GeoSkills CD-ROM.**

COMPARE AND CONTRAST

As you read, compare and contrast the ancient civilizations of Mesoamerica.

BIG IDEA
The Maya added to the innovations of the Olmecs and contributed their own.

VOCABULARY

ceremonial center
cultural borrowing
culture trait
glyph
codex
reclaim

Ancient Civilizations in Mesoamerica

3500 B.C. 2500 B.C. 1500 B.C. 500 B.C.

1500 B.C.– 500 B.C.

The land that is known as Mesoamerica, or Middle America, was the home of the Olmecs (OHL•meks), the earliest civilization in the Americas. The Olmecs lived in a region that today includes central and southern Mexico and parts of Central America. The Olmecs are remembered for many innovations that were used and added to by later civilizations. For this reason, the Olmec civilization is called the "mother civilization" of the Americas.

This illustration shows ancient Olmecs playing a ceremonial ball game.

FAST FACT
The word *Olmec* means "people of the land of rubber." The name was given to these people by later civilizations because the Olmecs found many uses for the natural rubber they got from the trees of the rain forest.

The Olmecs

The Olmec people first settled along the coast of the Gulf of Mexico in what are now the Mexican states of Veracruz and Tabasco. By the early 1500s B.C., the Olmecs were living along coastal rivers in villages of small houses made of reeds and grasses. The people fished in the rivers and farmed land made fertile by river flooding.

As in other early farming societies, the Olmecs came to depend on seasonal flooding to water their crops and make the soil rich. They, too, developed a counting system and a calendar to keep track of the flood season. Some scientists believe the Olmecs used a form of picture writing to record dates and events and to tell stories.

The Olmecs are probably best known today for their carvings and artworks. Many of these objects, both large and small, were made for religious purposes. Like the people of other early civilizations, the Olmecs based their religion on the forces of nature that affect the growing of crops. The Olmecs worshipped many gods, but the most important was a god in the form of a jaguar that they believed brought rain.

Some Olmec villages became centers of religion, or **ceremonial centers**. Over time, these centers grew to the size of cities. In the middle of each Olmec city were large temples made of huge stones. Olmec artists decorated the temples with carved stone faces, some more than 9 feet (2.7 m) tall and weighing 36,000 pounds (16,330 kg).

Some experts say the huge stone faces may have been carved to look like Olmec rulers or priests. Others think they portray warriors.

Many experts believe that the Olmec builders moved some of the

This large stone head can be seen near present-day Veracruz, Mexico.

giant stones more than 50 miles (80 km). No one knows exactly how they did it. Their technology did not include the wheel.

Although the Olmecs were hard workers, they found time to play a ceremonial ball game. Two teams competed in the ancient game, which was played on an outdoor court with rubber balls. A game played in Mexico today is much like the Olmec game. In today's game, players may not hit the ball with their hands or feet. They may use only other parts of their bodies such as their hips. Because the ball is very hard and travels at high speeds, all players wear protective clothing. The Olmec players also wore heavy padding to protect themselves from injury.

A jade figure representing the Olmec jaguar god

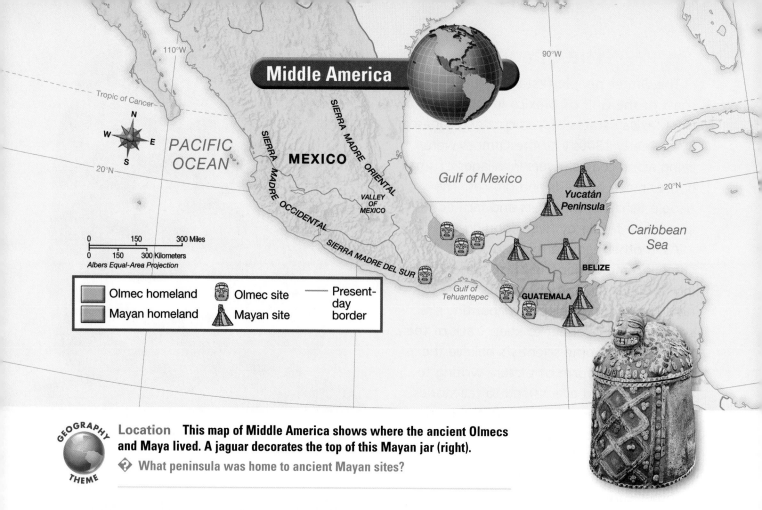

PACIFIC OCEAN

MEXICO

Gulf of Mexico

Yucatán Peninsula

Caribbean Sea

BELIZE

Gulf of Tehuantepec

GUATEMALA

SIERRA MADRE ORIENTAL

SIERRA MADRE OCCIDENTAL

SIERRA MADRE DEL SUR

VALLEY OF MEXICO

Tropic of Cancer

20°N

110°W

90°W

20°N

| 0 | 150 | 300 Miles |
| 0 | 150 | 300 Kilometers |

Albers Equal-Area Projection

Olmec homeland   Olmec site   Present-day border

Mayan homeland   Mayan site

Location   This map of Middle America shows where the ancient Olmecs and Maya lived. A jaguar decorates the top of this Mayan jar (right).

❖ What peninsula was home to ancient Mayan sites?

In 1989 archaeologists found three rubber balls in a bog near San Lorenzo, the oldest known Olmec city. Each of the ancient balls is 3 to 5 inches (7.6 to 12.7 cm) across. These balls are believed to be the only ones to have survived from Olmec times, which lasted from 1500 B.C. to 500 B.C.

REVIEW How was the Olmec civilization similar to and different from other early civilizations? **COMPARE AND CONTRAST**

The "Mother Civilization"

In many parts of Mexico and Central America, far from Olmec cities and ceremonial centers, some traces of Olmec civilization have been found. In southwestern Mexico, cave paintings show Olmec gods. In El Salvador, 500 miles (about 800 km) southeast of what were Olmec lands, a boulder is carved in the Olmec style.

Since the first discovery of Olmec artifacts and artworks, archaeologists have tried to figure out how Olmec ideas spread throughout Middle America. Most believe that the Olmecs' religious ideas, art, architecture, and technology spread through **cultural borrowing**. When societies interact, they sometimes take ideas from one another and use them as their own.

Throughout history many factors have contributed to cultural borrowing. Migration is one, but there is no evidence of a migration out of or into Olmec lands. Nor has evidence been found to suggest that the Olmecs conquered a large area and forced other peoples to follow their ways. Instead, Olmec ideas most likely spread as different cultures came

A statue of an Olmec woman found near present-day La Venta, Mexico

A man uses a tumpline to carry a heavy load in Yucatán, Mexico.

in contact with the Olmecs through trade. People may have borrowed many Olmec ways because they admired them or found them useful.

Some Olmec innovations are still used in present-day Mexico. The early people of Middle America did not use animals or wheeled carts to carry loads. Instead, workers used tumplines (TUHM•plynz). A tumpline is a kind of sling that makes it easier to carry heavy loads. A strap placed over the forehead helps support the load carried in the sling on the person's back.

In many ways other Middle American cultures that followed were based on the Olmec culture. Richard E. W. Adams, who studies and writes about ancient Middle America, notes, "Olmec culture did not die out but was absorbed and passed on."

The way in which Olmec culture was passed to other cultures is one reason experts call it the "mother civilization" of the Americas. The Mayan civilization was the first to borrow and learn from the Olmecs.

REVIEW How did Olmec culture spread?

POINTS OF VIEW
Olmec Writing Controversy

CITIZENSHIP

In 1998 a team of archaeologists, led by Mary Pohl of Florida State University, discovered an ancient Olmec stone cylinder and fragments of a stone tablet in Tabasco, Mexico. After studying the artifacts for more than four years, the team concluded that the symbols on the artifacts are the earliest evidence of writing in North America. Still, many scientists believe that the Maya developed the first writing system in North America.

RICHARD DIEHL, archaeologist, University of Alabama

❝This is the oldest writing. It's the mother and father of all later Mesoamerican writing systems.❞

STEVEN HOUSTON, epigrapher [a person who studies ancient writing], Brigham Young University

❝A few isolated emblems . . . fall well below the standard [guidelines] for first writing.❞

Analyze the Viewpoints

① What view about the Olmec stone cylinder does each person hold?

② **Make It Relevant** Find out if there is a historical debate in your state or community. Identify the different viewpoints about the debate, and explain why the people disagree.

The stone tablet (above) shows ancient Mayan writing. This Olmec stone cylinder (left) may contain writing.

The Maya

The Maya started as a simple farming culture in the rain forests of what are now Belize, Guatemala, Honduras, and southern Mexico. By about 600 B.C., however, Mayan civilization began to take shape. Borrowing many Olmec **culture traits**, or characteristics, the Maya cleared the forest to farm more land and to build cities. By about A.D. 300 they had built more than 100 cities.

The largest ancient Mayan city was Tikal (tih•KAHL), with as many as 100,000 people. In the center of Tikal stood six large temples. A jaguar is carved on top of Tikal's largest temple. It is a religious symbol borrowed from the Olmecs.

The Maya also borrowed other Olmec innovations and added to them. They developed two kinds of calendars. One had 260 days and was used to keep track of religious events. The other had 365 days, just like our modern calendar. The Maya used this calendar to keep track of planting, harvesting, and seasonal flooding.

To record information about trade, the Maya improved on the Olmec number system by adding a symbol for zero—an important idea in mathematics. The Maya also improved on Olmec picture writing.

Mayan writing consisted of a kind of hieroglyphics called glyphs (GLIFS). **Glyphs** are picture-symbols that represent objects, ideas, and sounds. Archaeologists have only recently begun to decipher the ancient Mayan glyphs.

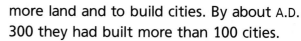

• GEOGRAPHY •

Tikal
Understanding Places and Regions

Tikal began in about 600 B.C. as a small farming village in what is today Guatemala. By A.D. 100 Tikal had grown into an important trading and religious center, with large, pyramid-shaped temples. The tallest of these temples is more than 200 feet (61 m) high. In the A.D. 800s, the city's population began to decline. By A.D. 1000 the city was abandoned.

MEXICO

MEXICO
Paxbán
Tikal National Park ☐TIKAL
Belize City
San Pedro River
Usumacinta River
Lake Petén-Itzá ●Flores
★ Belmopan
●La Libertad
BELIZE
Pasión River
N W E S
GUATEMALA
San Luis●
Chixoy R.
Chinajá
Sarstún River
Lake Izabal
●Cobán

0 20 40 Miles
0 20 40 Kilometers

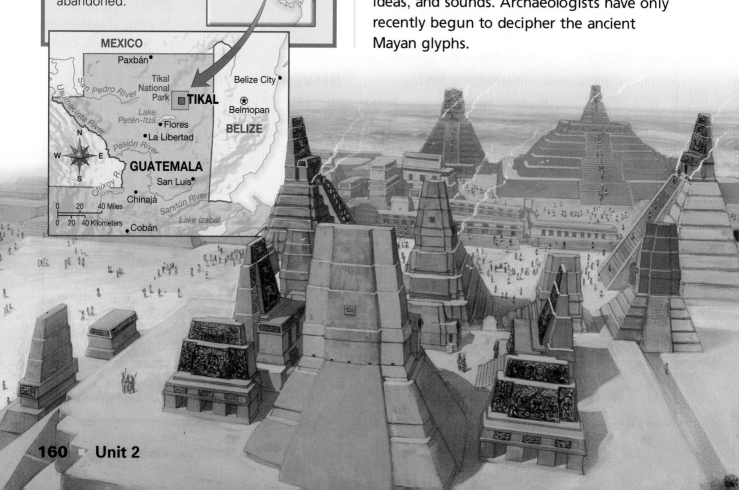

A Mayan marketplace in the country of Guatemala (left). Traditional Mayan dolls like these (above) are sold there.

For writing materials, the ancient Maya made paper from the bark of wild fig trees. Using this paper, a Mayan scribe could make a **codex**, or hand-lettered book, of glyphs. Only four such books of Mayan writing have survived. They tell about such subjects as Mayan religion and learning.

Experts who study early civilizations know that the Mayan civilization lasted more than 600 years. After A.D. 900, some of the Mayan cities were abandoned and were **reclaimed**, or taken back, by the rain forests. Some experts believe the cities became too crowded. Others think that wars among Mayan cities caused the civilization to collapse.

Some Maya migrated north and west. During the A.D. 900s a new Mayan civilization grew in the northern part of the Yucatán Peninsula, in what is now Mexico. Over time, the Mayan civilization declined, but it did not disappear. Today nearly 3 million Maya live in Central America and southern Mexico.

REVIEW How was the Olmec civilization important to the Maya?

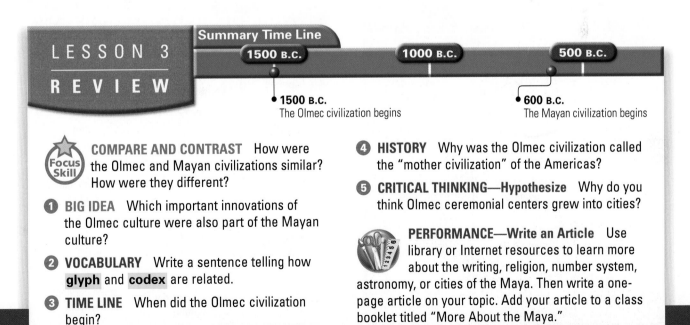

LESSON 3 REVIEW

Summary Time Line

1500 B.C. — 1000 B.C. — 500 B.C.

1500 B.C.
The Olmec civilization begins

600 B.C.
The Mayan civilization begins

Focus Skill **COMPARE AND CONTRAST** How were the Olmec and Mayan civilizations similar? How were they different?

1 BIG IDEA Which important innovations of the Olmec culture were also part of the Mayan culture?

2 VOCABULARY Write a sentence telling how **glyph** and **codex** are related.

3 TIME LINE When did the Olmec civilization begin?

4 HISTORY Why was the Olmec civilization called the "mother civilization" of the Americas?

5 CRITICAL THINKING—Hypothesize Why do you think Olmec ceremonial centers grew into cities?

PERFORMANCE—Write an Article Use library or Internet resources to learn more about the writing, religion, number system, astronomy, or cities of the Maya. Then write a one-page article on your topic. Add your article to a class booklet titled "More About the Maya."

Compare Tables to Classify Information

VOCABULARY

classify

▶ WHY IT MATTERS

Knowing how to **classify**, or group, items of information can make facts easier to find.

▶ WHAT YOU NEED TO KNOW

When you read about the early civilizations of Asia and Middle America in this chapter, you were given a lot of information. Some of this information can be classified by using a chart called a table.

Tables organize information in rows and columns. A row is horizontal, and a column is vertical. On Tables A and B, each row is labeled with a category for comparison. Each column is labeled with the name of an early civilization.

Tables C and D on page 163 classify the same information in different ways. In Table C, the civilizations are classified alphabetically. In Table D, the civilizations are classified according to the order in which they were founded.

▶ PRACTICE THE SKILL

Use the tables on these pages to answer the following questions.

1 In which table is it easier to find out when the earliest civilizations began in Asia and Middle America? Why?

Table A: Early Asian Civilizations		
	SHANG	**HARAPPAN**
Location	Huang He valley, present-day China	Indus Valley, present-day Pakistan and India
Major Cities	Anyang	Harappa, Mohenjo-Daro
Kinds of Cities	government centers	commercial centers
Writing System	characters	picture-symbols
Innovations	silk	urban planning

Table B: Early Middle American Civilizations		
	MAYAN	**OLMEC**
Location	parts of Mexico and Central America	present-day eastern Mexico
Major Cities	Tikal	San Lorenzo
Kinds of Cities	ceremonial centers	ceremonial centers
Writing System	picture-symbols	picture-symbols
Innovations	calendar, number system, writing	stone carvings, artwork

Table C: Early Civilizations of Asia and Middle America

CIVILIZATION	REGION	APPROXIMATE DATES
Harappan	Asia	3000 B.C.–1500 B.C.
Mayan	Middle America	600 B.C.–A.D. 900
Olmec	Middle America	1500 B.C.–500 B.C.
Shang	Asia	1766 B.C.–1122 B.C.

Table D: Early Civilizations of Asia and Middle America

APPROXIMATE DATES	CIVILIZATION	REGION
3000 B.C.–1500 B.C.	Harappan	Asia
1766 B.C.–1122 B.C.	Shang	Asia
1500 B.C.–500 B.C.	Olmec	Middle America
600 B.C.–A.D. 900	Mayan	Middle America

2 In which table is it easier to compare and contrast information about the Indus Valley and Huang He valley civilizations? Why?

3 In which table is it easier to compare and contrast information about the Olmec and Mayan civilizations? Why?

4 What are the advantages and disadvantages of each table in showing facts about these early civilizations?

➡ APPLY WHAT YOU LEARNED

Make a table that compares the early civilizations you have learned about in this chapter. Provide information about the civilizations of the Indus Valley, the Huang He valley, and Middle America. Do research to find out more about the government, economics, and societies of each early civilization. Use the library or the Internet to gather your facts.

These artifacts are from early Asian and Middle American civilizations. From left to right are Harappan horse statues, a Mayan mask, and a Shang cooking vessel.

5 Review and Test Preparation

Summary Time Line

3000 B.C. ————————————————— 2500 B.C.

● **3000 B.C.**
Harappan and other Indus
Valley civilizations begin

 Compare and Contrast

Complete this graphic organizer to show that you understand
how to compare and contrast different groups and cultures, such
as the Harappans and the Shang. A copy of this graphic organizer
appears on page 51 of the Activity Book.

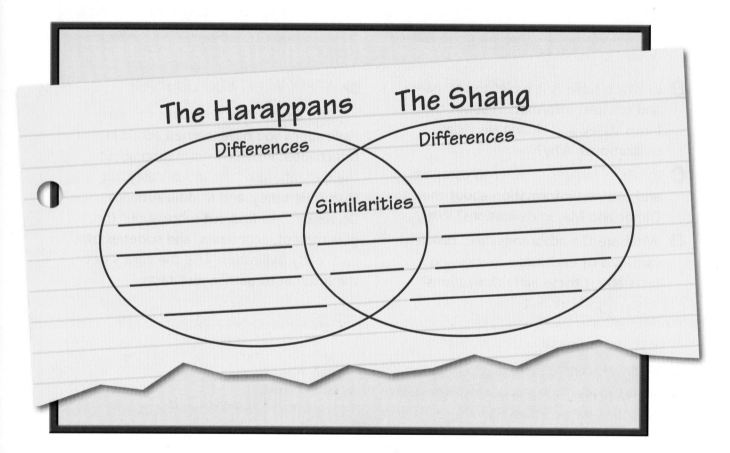

The Harappans   The Shang

Differences   Differences

Similarities

THINK & WRITE

Write a Newspaper Story   Think about
some of the innovations made by the people of
the Indus Valley, the Huang He valley, and
Mesoamerica. Write a newspaper headline
about one of these innovations. Then write a
newspaper story describing the innovation and
why it is important.

Write an Archaeological Journal Entry
Imagine that you are an archaeologist who has
found an item left behind by an ancient culture
described in Chapter 5. Write a journal entry
that describes your discovery. Describe where
you found the item. Tell what it looks like and
what you know about its history.

1700 B.C.
Harappan civilization
starts to disappear

Shang dynasty begins

1500 B.C.
The Olmec civilization begins

600 B.C.
The Mayan civilization begins

500 B.C.
The Olmec civilization ends

USE THE TIME LINE

1 About how long did the Harappan civilization last?

2 How many years passed between the beginning of the Olmec civilization and its end?

USE VOCABULARY

Use each term in a sentence or two to explain both what the term means and how that meaning relates to the civilizations described in this chapter.

3 subcontinent (p. 142)

4 inscription (p. 144)

5 urban planning (p. 145)

6 tyrant (p. 152)

7 virtue (p. 153)

RECALL FACTS

Answer these questions.

8 What was Mohenjo-Daro?

9 How were the endings of the Indus Valley civilization and the Huang He valley civilization different?

10 According to a Chinese legend, what did Yu the Great do to save China from the Great Flood?

Write the letter of the best choice.

11 **TEST PREP** The Olmecs and the Maya used each of the following innovations *except*—

A picture writing.

B a calendar.

C the wheel.

D a counting system.

12 **TEST PREP** All of these are true about oracle bones *except*—

F they were believed to help diviners speak for the gods.

G they are closely associated with the Xia dynasty.

H archaeologists have learned from studying the questions carved on them.

J patterns of cracks in the bones revealed the answers to questions.

THINK CRITICALLY

13 Why is good urban planning important to some societies?

14 Why do you think the standardizing of Chinese writing was such a big achievement?

15 China's Zhou tribe believed that only a virtuous ruler could keep order in a society. Do you agree? Why or why not?

APPLY SKILLS

Read a Relief Map and an Elevation Map

16 Study the maps on page 155. Which has the lower elevation, the area around Beijing or the area around Chongqing?

Compare Tables to Classify Information

17 Make a table to compare the characteristics of three after-school activities that interest you. Arrange the rows, columns, and categories so they best represent what is important to you. Some of the categories may include the activity's cost, time, or effort. Decide how to classify the activities in the best way.

Copán

The ancient city of Copán (koh•PAHN) in western Honduras took nearly 400 years to build. The Maya lived in Copán between 2000 B.C. and A.D. 1200. The city began as a farming community. Over time Copán became a center for religion and art.

Visitors to the site of Copán can see amazing works of art and architecture. Ancient stone carvings decorate the ruins. The Hieroglyphic Stairway has more than 1,000 symbols carved into its 63 stone steps. Nearby is the Ball Court, where the Maya played games with a rubber ball. The Great Plaza may have been used for public events, such as religious ceremonies. A pyramid rises on each side of the plaza. Beneath the two pyramids is a maze of tunnels, in which visitors can explore tombs.

LOCATE IT

MEXICO

Copán

HONDURAS

This sculpture is one of the many rock carvings that visitors can see at the site.

Visitors can see ancient pyramids, plazas, parks, and temples at the site, which was once the home of more than 20,000 people.

The Maya wore jewelry, such as this earring (left) and pendant (right), to honor their gods and rulers.

Many artifacts, such as this sculpted pot, can be seen at the Copán Museum.

Archaeologists continue to discover much about the rich history of Copán. In 1980 Copán became a World Heritage site.

TAKE A FIELD TRIP

GO ONLINE

A VIRTUAL TOUR
Visit The Learning Site at **www.harcourtschool.com** to take virtual tours of other historic sites.

CNN Turner Le@rning®

A VIDEO TOUR
Check your media center or classroom library for a videotape tour highlighting an ancient Mayan city in Guatemala.

2 Review and Test Preparation

Write a Paragraph Study the pictures and captions below to help you review Unit 2. Then choose one of the events shown. Write a paragraph that gives details about what happened and why it was important.

USE VOCABULARY

Use the words from the list to complete the sentences below.

social classes (p. 96)

taxation (p. 100)

inundation (p. 118)

commercial (p. 143)

ancestors (p. 151)

cultural borrowing (p. 158)

1 By studying the skies, the ancient Egyptians learned when the Nile River would have its yearly _____.

2 The highest of Sumer's _____ included government officials, priests, warriors, and their families.

3 The Amorites created a system of _____ to pay for their government.

4 Olmec ways were passed on to other Mesoamerican civilizations through _____.

5 People of the Shang dynasty in early China believed that their _____ could guide their lives and plead with the gods for them.

6 Harappa, Mohenjo-Daro, and other Indus Valley cities were all _____, or trade, centers.

RECALL FACTS

Answer these questions.

7 Who was Nebuchadnezzar?

8 By what other name is the Huang He also known?

Write the letter of the best choice.

9 **TEST PREP** Which Mesopotamian empire did Hammurabi lead?
A the Akkadian Empire
B the Babylonian Empire
C the Assyrian Empire
D the New Babylonian Empire

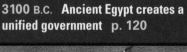

Visual Summary

3500 B.C.

2500 B.C.

3100 B.C. **Ancient Egypt creates a unified government** p. 120

2600 B.C. **Nubia is an important African trading center** p. 132

2500 B.C. **The first cities in the Indus Valley form** p. 142

10 TEST PREP Each of these civilizations created a calendar to keep track of flood seasons *except*—

F the Shang dynasty.

G the Olmecs.

H the Egyptians.

J the Sumerians.

THINK CRITICALLY

11 Which do you think would have been easier to learn and understand, hieroglyphics or early Chinese writing? Why?

12 In which culture of those described in this unit would you rather have lived? Give at least two reasons for your choice.

13 What evidence of urban planning do you see in your community? Describe at least two examples.

APPLY SKILLS

Read an Elevation Map
Use the elevation map on this page to answer the following questions.

14 Which mountain range has a higher elevation overall, the Sierra Madre or the Sierra de las Minas? How can you tell?

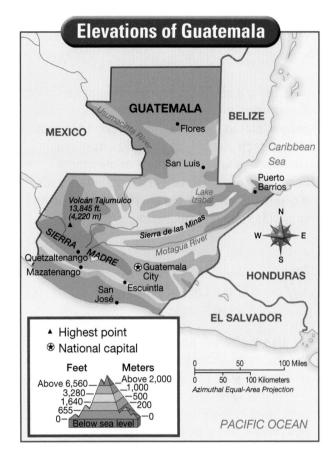

Elevations of Guatemala

GUATEMALA

MEXICO
BELIZE
Flores
Usumacinta River
Caribbean Sea
San Luis
Puerto Barrios
Lake Izabal
Volcán Tajumulco 13,845 ft. (4,220 m)
Sierra de las Minas
Motagua River
SIERRA MADRE
Quetzaltenango
Mazatenango
⊛ Guatemala City
Escuintla
San José
HONDURAS
EL SALVADOR
PACIFIC OCEAN

▲ Highest point
⊛ National capital

Feet	Meters
Above 6,560	Above 2,000
3,280	1,000
1,640	500
655	200
0	0
Below sea level	

0 50 100 Miles
0 50 100 Kilometers
Azimuthal Equal-Area Projection

15 What is the highest point in Guatemala? What is its elevation?

16 Which parts of Guatemala have the lowest elevation?

17 What is the elevation range around Guatemala City?

1500 B.C.

500 B.C.

2350 B.C. The world's first empire forms in Mesopotamia p. 98

1766 B.C. The Shang dynasty begins to rule in China p. 150

1500s B.C. The Olmec civilization begins in the Americas p. 157

169

Unit Activities

Visit The Learning Site at **www.harcourtschool.com** for additional activities.

Create a Set of Pictographs

Create a set of your own pictographs to represent words you use often, including people, places, and activities. Make a key that shows each pictograph and gives its meaning. Then write a letter to a friend or classmate, using your pictographs. Exchange letters with a classmate, and write a short response, using your classmate's pictographs.

Create a Travel Brochure

Use the library and online resources to find out more about the Tower of Babel, the Hanging Gardens of Babylon, the Great Pyramid at Giza, or another great structure described in this unit. Describe who built it and how, when, and why it was important. What have archaeologists learned by studying it? What is still unknown? Does the structure still exist today? Write your brochure so that a person who reads it will want to visit the place you describe.

VISIT YOUR LIBRARY

- **The Sumerians** by Elaine Landau. Millbrook Press.

- **The Indus Valley** by Nadia Kirkpatrick. Heinemann Library.

- **Growing Up in Ancient China** by Ken Teague. Troll.

COMPLETE THE UNIT PROJECT

Make a Scrapbook Work as a group to complete the unit project. Review the list you made during your reading. Then make artwork that portrays the items on your list. You can make drawings and paintings, write poems and essays, and cut out pictures from magazines and newspapers. Combine your artwork with your group's artwork in a scrapbook.

Eastern Civilizations

Ancient Chinese coin,
about 200 B.C.

Great Wall of China

Eastern Civilizations

"To understand the present, examine the past; without the past, there would be no present."

— **Chinese proverb**

Preview the Content
Read the Big Idea statement for each lesson. Work with a partner to identify what you think the focus of each lesson will be.

Preview the Vocabulary
Related Words Related words are words that share a relationship. Make a web like the one below. In the center, write the relationship that the words share.

RELATIONSHIP

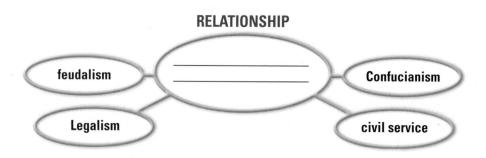

feudalism

_____

Confucianism

Legalism

civil service

Sardis

ASIA

Black Sea

Mediterranean Sea

Caucasus Mountains

Caspian Sea

Legend
- Persian Empire, 500 B.C.
- Han dynasty, A.D. 200
- Gupta Empire, A.D. 400
- —— Silk Road
- ▪▪▪▪ Great Wall
- ● City

Nile River

Berytus
Jerusalem

Euphrates River

Tigris River

Babylon

Zagros Mts.

Persepolis

Red Sea

Arabian Peninsula

Persian Gulf

Arabian Sea

Time Spans of Early Eastern Civilizations

Number of Years

500
400
300
200
100
0

Persian Empire   Han dynasty   Gupta Empire
Name of Civilization

AFRICA

0   400   800 Miles
0   400   800 Kilometers
Two-Point Equidistant Projection

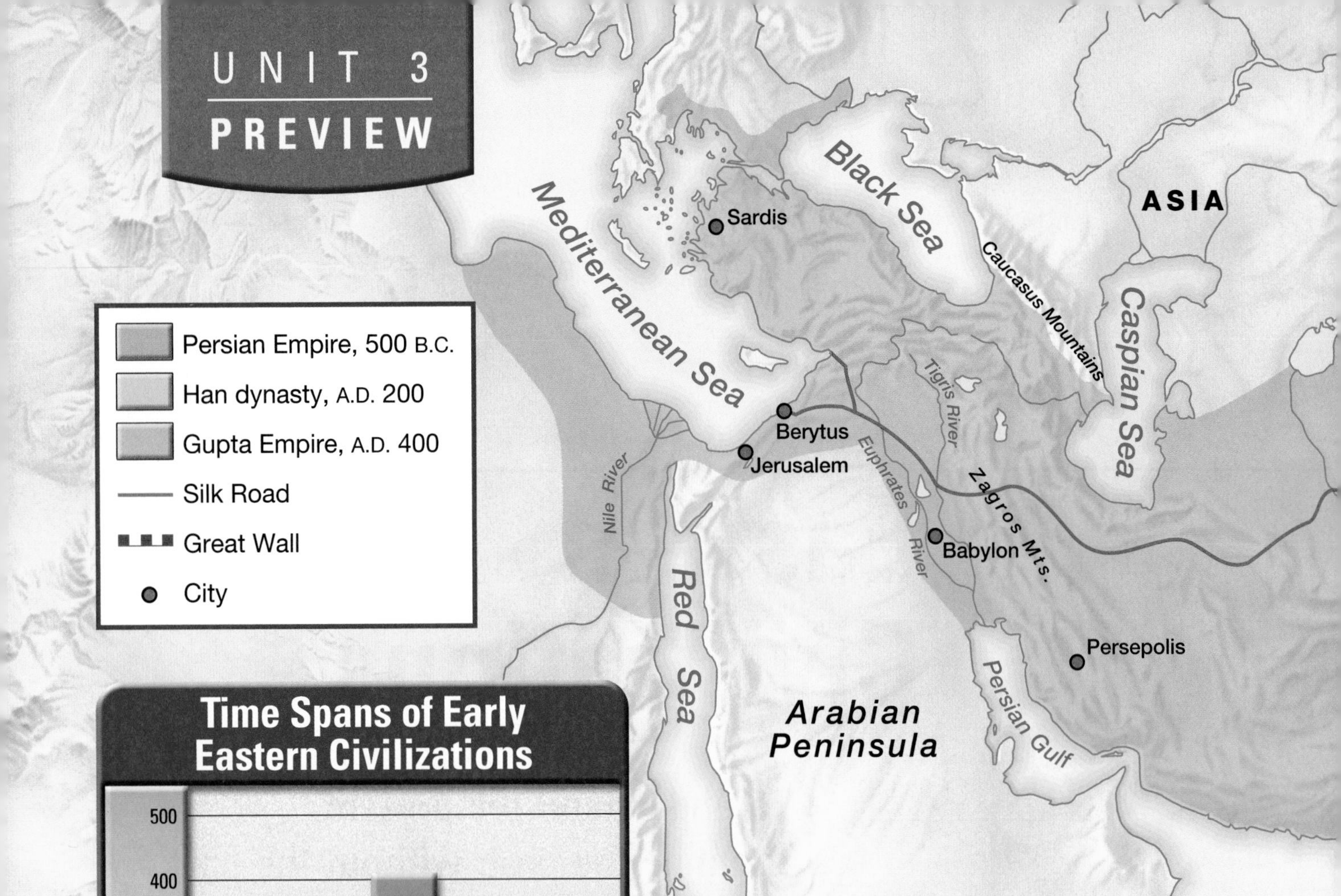

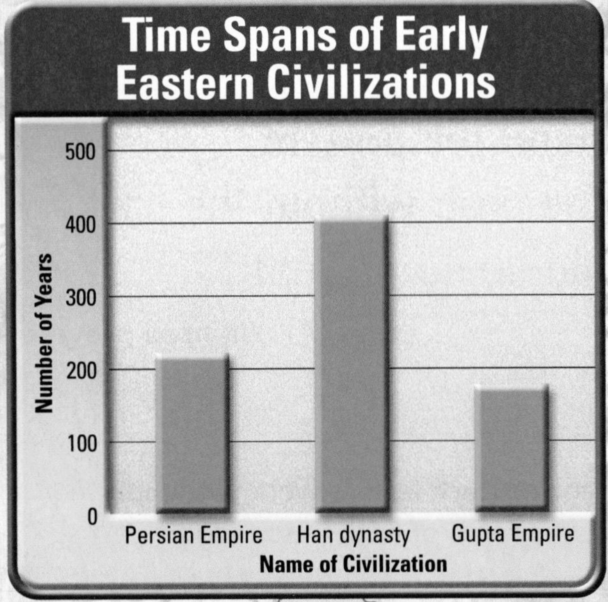

Key Events

2000 B.C.   1500 B.C.   1000 B.C.

2000 B.C. **Aryans migrate to India** p. 206

1100 B.C. **Phoenician city-states reach the height of their power** p. 189

1020 B.C. **The kingdom of Israel is formed** p. 183

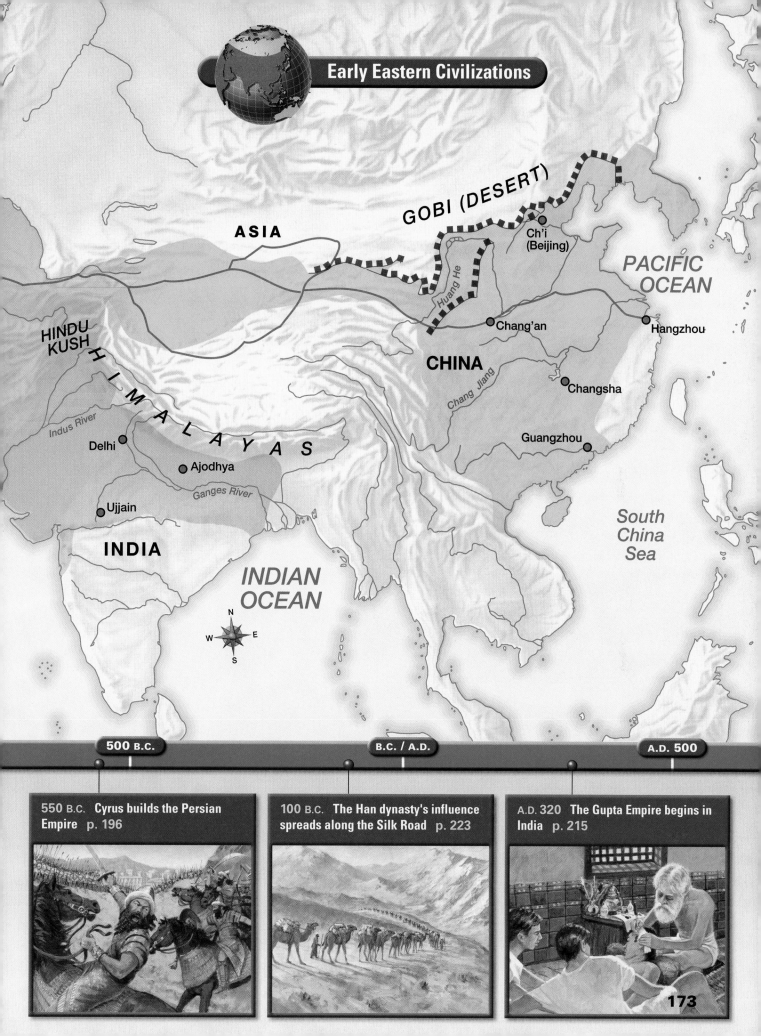

Early Eastern Civilizations

ASIA

GOBI (DESERT)

Ch'i (Beijing)

PACIFIC OCEAN

Huang He

Chang'an

Hangzhou

CHINA

Chang Jiang

Changsha

HINDU KUSH

HIMALAYAS

Indus River

Delhi

Ajodhya

Ganges River

Guangzhou

Ujjain

INDIA

INDIAN OCEAN

South China Sea

N
W E
S

500 B.C.

B.C. / A.D.

A.D. 500

550 B.C. **Cyrus builds the Persian Empire** p. 196

100 B.C. **The Han dynasty's influence spreads along the Silk Road** p. 223

A.D. 320 **The Gupta Empire begins in India** p. 215

173

THE EMPEROR'S SILENT ARMY

▪ ▪ ▪ *Terracotta Warriors of Ancient China* ▪ ▪ ▪

by Jane O'Connor

Civilization in China began many thousands of years ago. As early as 100 B.C., the people of China had developed a written history. Over the years, however, some parts of China's history were lost. Artifacts and other clues about ancient China lay buried, waiting to be rediscovered. In 1974 three farmers made one such discovery. Read on to find out about what they found and the importance of this discovery to experts studying Chinese history today.

This terracotta statue lay buried for more than 2,000 years before being uncovered by archaelogists.

Lintong County, People's Republic of China, March 1974

It's just an ordinary day in early spring, or so three farmers think as they trudge across a field in northern China. They are looking for a good place to dig a well. There has been a drought, and they must find water or risk losing their crops later in the year.

The farmers choose a spot near a grove of persimmon trees. Down they dig, five feet, ten feet. Still no water. They decide to keep on digging a little deeper. All of a sudden, one of the farmers feels his shovel strike against something hard. Is it a rock? It's difficult to see at the bottom of the dark hole, so the farmer kneels down for a closer look. No, it isn't a rock. It seems to be clay, and not raw clay but clay that has been baked and made into something. But what?

Now, more carefully, the men dig around the something. Perhaps it is a pot or a vase. However, what slowly reveals itself is the pottery head of a man who stares back at them, open-eyed and amazingly real looking. The farmers have never seen anything like it before. But they do remember stories that some of the old people in their village have told, stories of a "pottery man" found many years ago not far from where they are now. The villagers had been scared that the pottery man would bring bad luck so they broke it to bits, which were then reburied and forgotten.

The three well-diggers are not so superstitious. They report their discovery to a local official. Soon a group of archaeologists arrives to search the area more closely. Maybe they will find pieces of a clay body to go with the clay head.

In fact, they find much more.

The entrance to the tomb (above) in Shaanxi Province, China

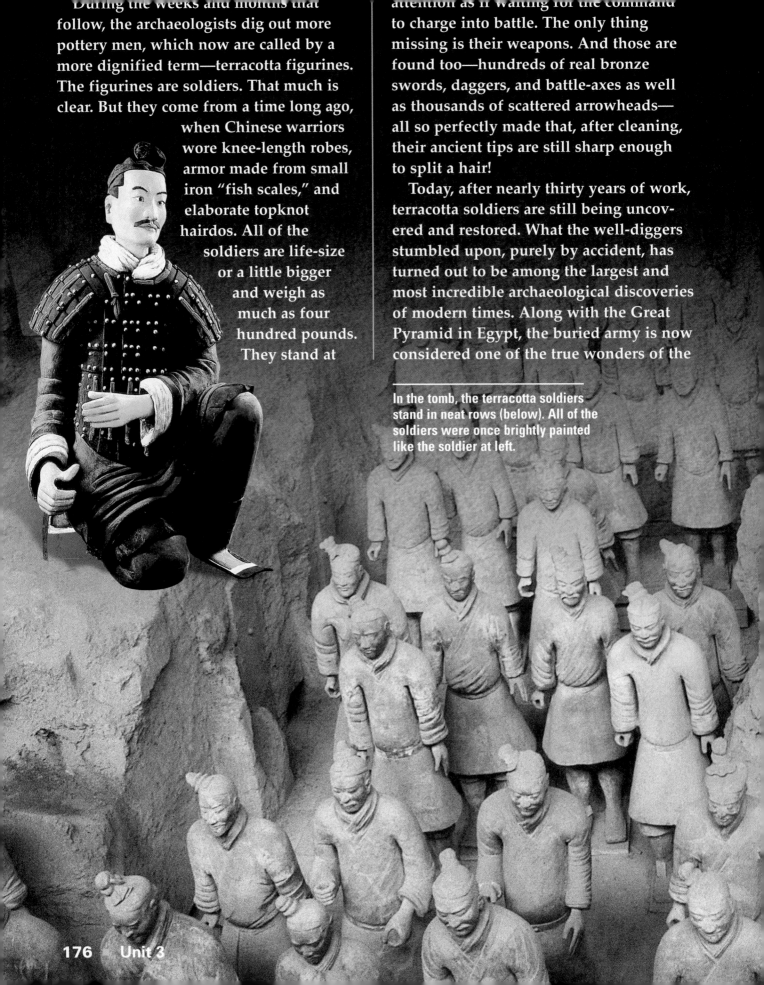

During the weeks and months that follow, the archaeologists dig out more pottery men, which now are called by a more dignified term—terracotta figurines. The figurines are soldiers. That much is clear. But they come from a time long ago, when Chinese warriors wore knee-length robes, armor made from small iron "fish scales," and elaborate topknot hairdos. All of the soldiers are life-size or a little bigger and weigh as much as four hundred pounds. They stand at

attention as if waiting for the command to charge into battle. The only thing missing is their weapons. And those are found too—hundreds of real bronze swords, daggers, and battle-axes as well as thousands of scattered arrowheads— all so perfectly made that, after cleaning, their ancient tips are still sharp enough to split a hair!

Today, after nearly thirty years of work, terracotta soldiers are still being uncovered and restored. What the well-diggers stumbled upon, purely by accident, has turned out to be among the largest and most incredible archaeological discoveries of modern times. Along with the Great Pyramid in Egypt, the buried army is now considered one of the true wonders of the

In the tomb, the terracotta soldiers stand in neat rows (below). All of the soldiers were once brightly painted like the soldier at left.

ancient world. Spread out over several acres near the city Xian, the soldiers number not in the tens or hundreds but in the thousands! Probably 7,500 total. Until 1974, nobody knew that right below the people of northern China an enormous underground army had been standing guard, silently and watchfully, for more than 2,200 years. Who put them there?

One man.

Known as the fierce tiger of Qin, the divine Son of Heaven, he was the first emperor of China.

Analyze the Literature

1 How did archaeologists know that the terracotta statues represented soldiers from long ago?

2 Do you think artifacts are an important tool in learning about cultures of the past? Why?

READ A BOOK

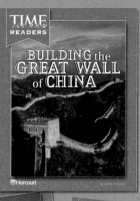

START THE UNIT PROJECT

Prepare a Multimedia Presentation
With your classmates, prepare a multimedia presentation of an early eastern civilization. As you read this unit, you will learn about people, places, and events in early civilizations of Asia. Start to think of ways you will use the information you gather to prepare a multimedia presentation.

USE TECHNOLOGY

Visit The Learning Site at **www.harcourtschool.com** for additional activities, primary sources, and other resources to use in this unit.

Persepolis was the capital of the ancient Persian Empire. The city, with its palaces of early Persian leaders, once covered a large area. When Alexander the Great conquered Persepolis in about 330 B.C., the city was partly destroyed. However, its ruins have provided a wealth of information about Persian culture.

LOCATE IT

IRAN

Persepolis

Southwest Asian Civilizations

"If your actions are upright and good, be assured that they will increase your power and happiness."

—Cyrus the Great, Persian leader,
c. 585–529 B.C.

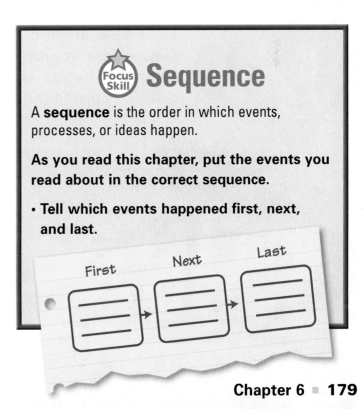

Focus Skill Sequence

A **sequence** is the order in which events, processes, or ideas happen.

As you read this chapter, put the events you read about in the correct sequence.

• Tell which events happened first, next, and last.

First → Next → Last

1

SEQUENCE

Read to learn the sequence of events in the history of the ancient Israelites.

BIG IDEA

The Israelites founded a culture that became the basis for three of the world's major religions.

VOCABULARY

monotheism
covenant
exodus
Ten Commandments
Judaism
exile
Diaspora
synagogue

The Ancient Israelites

| 2000 B.C. | 1500 B.C. | 1000 B.C. | 500 B.C. | B.C./A.D. | A.D. 500 |

2000 B.C. – A.D. 200

Between 2000 B.C. and 500 B.C., several small kingdoms arose in southwestern Asia on the western end of the Fertile Crescent. Among them was the kingdom of Israel. The Israelites were the ancestors of the present-day Jewish people. The Hebrew Bible is the most important source of information about the Israelites. This Bible is named for the Israelites, who were originally known as the Hebrews. Experts using other ancient writings and archaeological evidence have added to our understanding of these people. The ancient Israelites have contributed to the religious and cultural ideas of many people the world over.

Beginnings

The Israelites trace their origins as a people to one man, an important religious figure named Abraham. Experts believe that Abraham lived sometime during the rule of Hammurabi. According to the Bible, Abraham was born near the city of Ur in southern Mesopotamia, in what is now southeastern Iraq.

Like most early people, the Mesopotamians worshipped many gods. They prayed to one god for water, to another for good

This jar (left) from Canaan was made in about 1600 B.C. The ancient Israelites fought many battles at Megiddo (below).

LOCATE IT

Megiddo

ISRAEL

harvests, and to still another for success in love and war. The Mesopotamians also thought of the sun, the moon, and the winds as gods.

Unlike the people of Ur, Abraham believed in only one God. The belief in one God is called **monotheism**. According to the Bible, God spoke to Abraham, telling him to leave Mesopotamia and settle with his family in Canaan (KAY•nuhn), the area that later became Israel.

Leaving Ur, Abraham and his family traveled north along the Euphrates River to the city of Haran. After staying there for a time, they continued their journey into the land of Canaan until they reached a settlement called Shechem (SHEE•kuhm). It was there, according to the Bible, that Abraham heard God say, "I will give this land to your children."

The Bible tells that God made a **covenant**, or special agreement, with Abraham. Because of Abraham's faith in God, God promised to give Abraham's descendants the land of Canaan. Abraham became known as the father of the Jewish people through his son Isaac, and the father of the Arab people through his son Ishmael.

REVIEW How did Abraham's religious beliefs differ from the beliefs of other Mesopotamians?

This painting (above) shows Abraham leading his family to Canaan. This stone carving of a menorah (left) is from about 1600 B.C. The menorah is an important symbol in the religion of the Jewish people.

The Exodus

Abraham's son Isaac had a son called Jacob, who was later known as Israel. Jacob had 12 sons. All of Jacob's descendants, including his sons, became known as Israelites. Each of his sons led a separate Israelite tribe.

When famine came to the land of Canaan, many Israelites migrated to Egypt to find food. The Bible tells that the Israelites lived peacefully in Egypt for many years until a pharaoh enslaved them.

FAST FACT The ancient site of Megiddo contains the ruins of a large network of stables. These buildings once housed hundreds of horses and dozens of war chariots.

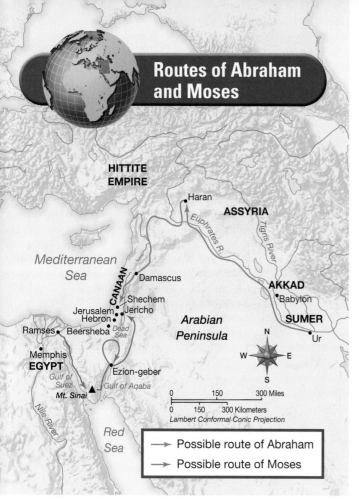

Routes of Abraham and Moses

GEOGRAPHY THEME

Movement Historians believe that Abraham and Moses may have followed the routes shown on this map.

❖ In what region did both Abraham and Moses end their journeys?

HITTITE EMPIRE

Haran

ASSYRIA

Euphrates R.

Tigris River

Mediterranean Sea

CANAAN

Damascus

Shechem
Jericho

AKKAD
Babylon

Arabian Peninsula

SUMER

Jerusalem
Hebron

Ramses
Beersheba
Dead Sea

Ur

Memphis
EGYPT

Gulf of Suez

Ezion-geber

Gulf of Aqaba

N
W   E
S

Mt. Sinai

Nile River

0   150   300 Miles
0   150   300 Kilometers
Lambert Conformal Conic Projection

Red Sea

→ Possible route of Abraham
→ Possible route of Moses

In about 1225 B.C. Moses, a leader of the Israelites, led a revolt against the Egyptians. Many enslaved Israelites followed Moses from Egypt along the Red Sea, through the desert, and back toward Canaan. This journey is known as the Exodus. An **exodus** is a large movement of people from a place.

The Exodus lasted many years and was filled with hardships. The Israelites faced lack of water and food during the journey. They also had disagreements with each other. It was during this time that the Bible says God gave Moses a set of laws for responsible behavior, called the **Ten Commandments**.

The Ten Commandments became an important part of **Judaism**—the religion of the Jewish people—and later of Christianity and Islam. Judaism teaches that God is just and that God's virtues must be imitated. In Judaism, a person's service to God is measured by how many good deeds he or she has done for other people.

The basic laws and teachings of Judaism come from the Torah, the first five books of the Hebrew Bible. The Torah describes God's covenant with Abraham, the Exodus, and how the kingdom of Israel came to be.

REVIEW What set of laws became an important part of three major religions?

Every year during the Passover holiday, Jewish families read the story of the Exodus.

THE TEN COMMANDMENTS

According to the Bible, God spoke to Moses, and these were his words:

1. I am the Lord your God, who brought you out of Egypt, out of the land of slavery. You shall have no other gods before me.

2. You shall not make for yourself an idol in the form of anything in heaven above or on the earth beneath or in the waters below . . . .

3. You shall not misuse the name of the Lord your God, for the Lord will not hold anyone guiltless who misuses his name.

4. Remember the Sabbath day by keeping it holy. Six days you shall labor and do all your work, but the seventh day is a Sabbath to the Lord your God. On that day you shall not do any work . . . .

5. Honor your father and your mother . . . .

6. You shall not murder.

7. You shall not commit adultery.

8. You shall not steal.

9. You shall not give false testimony against your neighbor.

10. You shall not covet your neighbor's house . . . or anything that belongs to your neighbor.

Exodus 20:2-17

The Kingdom of Israel

After the Israelites returned to Canaan, they were opposed by a people to the west known as the Philistines (FIH•luh•steenz). The need to defend themselves against the Philistines led the Israelites to agree to have a king as a single leader for their 12 tribes. Saul became their first king in 1020 B.C. King Saul was followed by King David, who began his rule under the influence of the Philistines. Later, he defeated the Philistines and freed his people from their rule.

The kingdom of Israel reached the height of its power in the 900s B.C. This occurred during the reigns of King David and his son King Solomon. King David captured the city of Jerusalem from the Jebusites and made it his capital. Solomon built a grand temple there. That temple is now remembered as the First Temple. It was the holiest site in all Jerusalem.

After Solomon died in about 928 B.C., disagreements between tribes caused Israel to split into two parts. The northern kingdom, made up of 10 of the 12 tribes, continued to be called Israel. Its capital was Samaria. The southern kingdom, made up of the remaining 2 tribes, kept Jerusalem as its capital. This kingdom was called Judah. The word *Jew* comes from *Judah*, the name of the Israelites' largest tribe.

The kingdom of Israel lasted until about 721 B.C., when the Assyrians conquered it. Judah lasted until about 586 B.C., when the Babylonians conquered it.

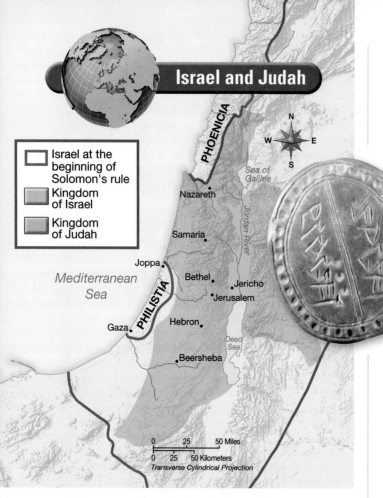

Israel and Judah

Israel at the beginning of Solomon's rule

Kingdom of Israel

Kingdom of Judah

PHOENICIA

Sea of Galilee

Nazareth

Jordan River

Samaria

Joppa

Bethel

Jericho

Jerusalem

Mediterranean Sea

PHILISTIA

Gaza

Hebron

Dead Sea

Beersheba

N W E S

0   25   50 Miles
0   25   50 Kilometers
Transverse Cylindrical Projection

GEOGRAPHY THEME

Regions After the death of Solomon, Israel split into two kingdoms—Israel and Judah. This ancient seal (above right), found near Jerusalem, is engraved with a Hebrew name.

❓ Which of the two kingdoms was larger?

The Babylonians attacked the city of Jerusalem, destroying the temple there. The Babylonians then enslaved the Jews, the people of Judah, and exiled many of them. A person who is **exiled** is forced to leave his or her country and live somewhere else.

In 539 B.C. Babylonia itself was conquered. The following year, the Persians, who took control of Babylonia, allowed the Jews to return to their homeland, then called Judaea. The returning Jews rebuilt their center of worship. By about 400 B.C. the Second Temple in Jerusalem had become the center of worship for all Jews.

REVIEW In what order did the kings of the Israelites rule? SEQUENCE

The Diaspora

In 63 B.C. the Romans, a people from what is now the country of Italy, captured Judaea. They made it a part of the large empire they had built. In about A.D. 66 the Jews revolted against Roman rule and took back control of their capital, Jerusalem. The Romans retook Jerusalem in A.D. 70 and destroyed the Jewish Temple. In doing so, they destroyed an important religious symbol of the Jews as a united people. The Romans also destroyed many of the city's walls. Only part of the Western Wall of the Temple Mount, where both Jewish Temples once stood, remained.

The Jews continued to revolt against Roman rule until A.D. 135, when the Romans drove many of the Jews out of Jerusalem. At about this time, the Romans renamed the area Palaestina, or Philistia. The name *Palaestina* became *Palestine* in English.

Many Jews fled from Palestine and moved to other places outside the region. Through

This stone carving shows Roman soldiers taking items from the destroyed Temple in Jerusalem.

the centuries Jewish people moved to nearly every country in the world. The settling of Jews outside of Palestine is called the **Diaspora**. The word *diaspora* comes from the Greek word meaning "to scatter," as in the sowing of seeds. Although many Jews left Jerusalem, some remained in Jerusalem and elsewhere in Israel.

Strabo, a Greek geographer, wrote this about the world's early Jews of that time:

> 66 [They] are scattered in all the towns, and it is difficult to find a place in all the inhabited world which has not received them. . . . 99

During the Babylonian exile and the Diaspora that followed, the Jews realized that they did not need to be inside the Temple in Jerusalem to worship God. Wherever groups of Jews settled, they built houses of worship known as **synagogues** (SIH•nuh•gahgz). Today synagogues are found in places where Jews have settled.

REVIEW What was the Diaspora?

• HERITAGE •

Klezmer Music

As the Jewish people settled in many parts of the world during the Diaspora, they brought their music and other traditions with them. Their traditions were then influenced by local cultures. The music played by Jews who settled in eastern Europe came to be called klezmer. It combined melodies from traditional Hebrew prayers with local folk music styles. Today klezmer music can often be heard at Jewish weddings and in concerts, played by bands that keep the tradition alive.

The Klezmatics from New York City continue the tradition of klezmer music today.

LESSON 1 REVIEW

Summary Time Line

| 2000 B.C. | 900 B.C. | A.D. 200 |

1225 B.C.
Moses leads the Exodus from Egypt

1020 B.C.
Saul becomes Israel's first king

586 B.C.
Judah is conquered by the Babylonians

 SEQUENCE What happened to the Israelites after Moses led them back to Canaan?

1 **BIG IDEA** What important changes did the Israelites introduce to world culture and religion?

2 **VOCABULARY** Explain the term **synagogue**, using the term **Diaspora**.

3 **TIME LINE** Which event happened first, the Exodus or the fall of Judah?

4 **GEOGRAPHY** What region was offered to Abraham in his covenant with God?

5 **CRITICAL THINKING—Hypothesize** What might have happened if the Temple in Jerusalem had not been destroyed by the Romans?

 PERFORMANCE—Make Flash Cards Make flash cards of the important people, events, and places discussed in this lesson. On the front of each card, write the name of a person, an event, or a place. On the back, provide a brief description. Use your flash cards to quiz a classmate about the history and culture of the ancient Israelites.

Determine Frame of Reference

VOCABULARY

frame of reference   **tradition**

▶ **WHY IT MATTERS**

When you read something that someone has said about an event, you need to consider the person's **frame of reference**, or the point from which that person saw it. A person's frame of reference can influence how he or she sees and understands an event. It can also influence how a person describes that event. By understanding frame of reference as you read about world history, you can gain a better understanding of what happened.

▶ **WHAT YOU NEED TO KNOW**

Time, place, and a person's **traditions**—customs and beliefs—contribute to that person's frame of reference. When reading about people in the past or people in other cultures, historians need to be careful not to make judgments from their present-day frame of reference. You need to be aware that the place you live in, your religion, and your values affect your own frame of reference. When evaluating frame of reference, think about how these factors affect a person's view of the world.

Pictured are a Christian church in West Virginia (below), a Jewish synagogue in California (top right), and an Islamic mosque in Ohio (bottom right).

THE JEWISH FRAME OF REFERENCE

In the frame of reference of the Jewish tradition, the Bible consists of a collection of sacred writings from ancient Israel. The first five books of the Hebrew Bible are referred to as the Torah. Usually the Torah takes the form of a scroll rather than a book.

THE CHRISTIAN FRAME OF REFERENCE

In the frame of reference of the Christian tradition, the Hebrew Bible is referred to as the Old Testament. It is called "old" because Christians view it as the necessary introduction to the New Testament. To Christians, both the Old Testament and the New Testament are holy books.

THE ISLAMIC FRAME OF REFERENCE

In the frame of reference of the Islamic tradition, it is the Qur'an that contains the most sacred writings. In the Qur'an there are accounts of many of the same religious figures as in the Hebrew Bible and the New Testament.

▶ PRACTICE THE SKILL

Read the three descriptions of frames of reference on this page. Then answer the following questions.

1. What three frames of reference are presented?
2. What topic is addressed in all three frames of reference?
3. How are the frames of reference different?
4. How are the frames of reference alike?
5. Why do you think it is important to understand frame of reference?

▶ APPLY WHAT YOU LEARNED

Select a historic event that you have already learned about. Think of the different kinds of people who took part in the event. Write a paragraph that describes the frame of reference of each group.

2

The Phoenicians and the Lydians

Focus Skill

SEQUENCE
Read to learn the sequence of innovations developed by the Phoenicians and the Lydians.

BIG IDEA
The Phoenicians and the Lydians developed innovations that changed the lives of people around the world.

VOCABULARY
commerce
colony
Asia Minor
barter
money economy

2000 B.C.	1500 B.C.	1000 B.C.	500 B.C.	B.C./A.D.	A.D. 500

1200 B.C. – 500 B.C.

Ancient cultures all over southwestern Asia contributed in many ways to the development of present-day civilizations. Between 1200 B.C. and 500 B.C., the Phoenician (fih•NEE•shuhn) and Lydian (LIH•dee•uhn) cultures made important innovations in **commerce**, or the buying and selling of goods. Although their kingdoms never became large empires, their contributions to culture and society continue to be seen today.

Phoenicia

The ancient Phoenicians lived on the narrow strip of land that is now the coastal areas of Lebanon and northern Israel. The region lies between the Lebanon Mountains to the east and the Mediterranean Sea to the west. Phoenicia consisted of separate

FAST FACT

The Phoenicians in the city-state of Tyre were well known for a purple dye they made from a kind of shellfish found in the nearby sea. Kings all around the Mediterranean demanded clothing dyed with Tyrian purple. Purple became known as a royal color.

city-states, such as Byblos, Sidon, Tyre, and Berytus. Berytus is now Beirut (bay•ROOT), the present-day capital of Lebanon. Each city-state had its own king.

Phoenicia was located between Egypt to the south and Mesopotamia to the east. As a result, Phoenicia became a center for commerce. Egypt imported cedar wood from the Lebanon Mountains of Phoenicia. In exchange, the Egyptians exported gold and manufactured goods.

In addition to material goods, the Phoenicians and their trading partners exchanged knowledge and culture. The Phoenicians borrowed Egyptian burial practices and the use of hieroglyphics. The Phoenicians were also influenced by Babylonian culture. The Phoenicians began to write in Babylonian cuneiform.

From about 1100 B.C. to 800 B.C., the Phoenician city-states enjoyed their greatest power and prosperity. During this time the Phoenicians sent out sailors to explore the

A Phoenician jug

Mediterranean Sea as far as the Strait of Gibraltar, near where the sea meets the Atlantic Ocean. From there, they began to explore the open ocean. Sailing north, they reached Britain. The tin mines there provided the Phoenicians with this important raw material. Phoenician sailors also explored the Atlantic to the south, visiting a large part of the western coast of Africa.

A CLOSER LOOK
A Phoenician Port

Phoenician sailors returned home with goods from places as far away as Britain and western Africa. Phoenician port cities, such as Tyre and Sidon, became wealthy centers of trade.

1. Phoenician cloth dyed with Tyrian purple was in great demand.
2. Phoenician trading ships were able to sail on the open seas. They depended mostly on wind power but were equipped with oars in case there was no wind.
3. Merchants shipped cedar logs to Egypt for use in making furniture and building ships.
4. The Phoenicians imported many goods, such as gold, cotton, tin, and ivory.

❓ What kinds of goods did Phoenician merchants trade?

Development of the Alphabet

EGYPTIAN (About 3000 B.C.)	PHOENICIAN (About 1000 B.C.)	GREEK (About 600 B.C.)	LATIN (Present Day)
ᗡ	K	A	A
⊓	Y	B	B
∿∿∿	Y	M	M
X	+	T	T
⊳○⊣	I	Z	Z

Analyze Tables The Phoenician alphabet influenced the development of many present-day alphabets.

❖ Which two sets of letters look most alike?

Soon settlers and traders followed the explorers. The Phoenicians built settlements all around the Mediterranean Sea. They established colonies on the southern coast of Spain, the northern coast of Africa, the western coast of Sicily, and the island of Cyprus. A **colony** is an area of land ruled by a government in another land.

Some Phoenician colonies served as rest stops for sailors traveling on long voyages. Others became important trading ports, part of the vast Phoenician trade network in the Mediterranean.

One such port was Carthage, in what is today Tunisia.

The Phoenicians most likely settled Carthage in 814 B.C. Carthage grew quickly into a successful trading port because of its location on a peninsula and its two excellent harbors. One harbor was large enough to shelter hundreds of ships. Carthage eventually broke away from Phoenician control and created its own empire in the western Mediterranean.

With the rise of the Assyrian Empire in the mid-700s B.C., the Phoenician city-states, one by one, lost their independence to the Assyrians. Later they were controlled by the Babylonians, the Persians, and the Romans.

REVIEW What made Phoenicia important to commerce?

The Phoenician Alphabet

One of the most important innovations of the Phoenicians was their alphabet. The Phoenicians were well aware of other writing systems. The Phoenicians borrowed from

· BIOGRAPHY ·

Dido
Dates unknown
Character Trait: Inventiveness

Dido (DY•doh) was the legendary founder and queen of Carthage. She was the daughter of the king of Tyre. Dido fled from Tyre to northern Africa when her brother, Pygmalion, murdered her husband, Sychaeus (SIH•kee•uhs). There she was offered as much land as could be surrounded by a bull's hide. She cut a hide into thin strips, pieced them together, and laid them out to surround a large area. This area became the site of Carthage.

MULTIMEDIA BIOGRAPHIES
Visit The Learning Site at
www.harcourtschool.com
to learn about other famous people.

these writing systems to create one of the world's first alphabets in about 1000 B.C. The Phoenician alphabet was different from others because it used characters that stood for sounds instead of ideas. Its 22 letters could be combined to form any word. This made the Phoenician writing system simpler than hieroglyphics or cuneiform.

The alphabet made it easier for people to learn to write. Writing could be taught in a week in any Phoenician port. As a result, more and more people began to master the art of writing. No longer was writing limited to scribes.

The Phoenician alphabet also made communication with different cultures much simpler, which was important in trade. Writing was used to record trade agreements and to prepare bills.

Knowledge of the Phoenician alphabet spread quickly among all the Phoenician colonies and other Mediterranean cultures. The Israelites began to use the Phoenician system in about the 800s B.C., adapting it to their own language. The Greeks also adopted it and made their own changes. Later, a people called the Etruscans adopted the Greek alphabet and passed it on to the Romans. The Romans adapted it for their language, Latin. The Latin alphabet is used to write in many present-day languages, including English.

REVIEW What culture adopted the Phoenician alphabet first, the Greeks or the Romans?

SEQUENCE

Lydian Money

The Lydians lived in an area northwest of Phoenicia. The ancient land of Lydia was located on the western end of the peninsula that later became known as **Asia Minor**, or Anatolia (a•nuh•TOH•lee•uh). Today the country of Turkey occupies the peninsula. Lydia was a land rich in natural resources.

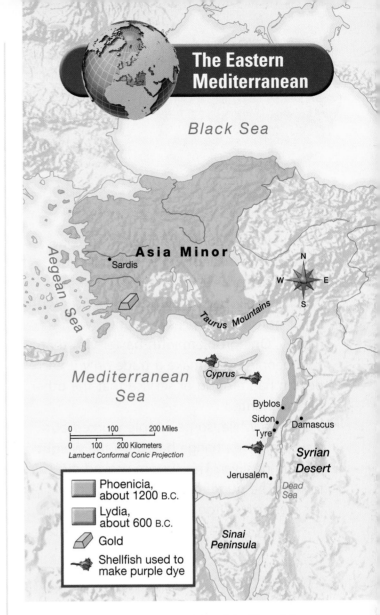

The Eastern Mediterranean

Movement The ideas of the Phoenicians and Lydians influenced the other groups in the Mediterranean region.

❓ Why do you think ideas spread so quickly among groups in this region?

It had fertile soil and abundant minerals, including gold. As a result, the kingdom of Lydia was a very wealthy place.

Like the Phoenicians, the Lydians made a major contribution to life around the Mediterranean. Their contribution, too, was related to commerce. The Lydians became the first people to use coined money put out by their government. Through trade, the Lydians passed this idea to other cultures.

Lydian coin, about 600 B.C.

Phoenician coin, about 300 B.C.

Roman coin, about A.D. 100

Long before coined money, most commerce in the ancient world had relied on barter. **Barter** is a form of exchange in which people pay for goods or services with other goods or services instead of with money. One problem with barter was that two people could make a trade only if each person had a good or service that the other person wanted.

After a while, some people worked out a system of exchange based on the weight of gold or silver. This system proved difficult to use. The nuggets and bars of gold or silver were often too heavy to carry around. The purity of the metals was also uncertain.

In about 600 B.C. the Lydians invented a method for creating coins. They made a die stamp that punched out coins of equal size, weight, and purity. The first Lydian coins were the size of beans. They were made of a natural mixture of gold and silver called electrum. To guarantee the value of each coin, the Lydian government marked it with an official symbol. The first known mark was a lion's head.

The use of coined money allowed Lydian merchants to set prices for their goods and services. As a result, the Lydians developed a **money economy**, an economic system based on the use of money instead of barter.

LOCATE IT

Black Sea

TURKEY

Istanbul

Mediterranean Sea

Today, people along the eastern Mediterranean still gather to trade goods at large markets, such as this one in Istanbul, Turkey.

English coin, A.D. 1658

Early American coin, A.D. 1776

United States quarter, A.D. 2002

After the Lydians, other cultures began to make coins. However, some people began to shave off bits of electrum from the coins. These shaved coins were offered as if they were worth their original value. Yet they were really worth less because they contained less electrum. It was not until centuries later that governments found a way to stop this practice. Then, governments began to require that coins be milled, or cut several times along the edge. People were then able to tell that coins with smooth edges had been shaved.

By the 500s B.C. Lydia, like Phoenicia, had become a center for regional trade. In addition to its natural wealth, its location between growing Greek city-states to the west and the older, richer cities of western Asia to its east helped Lydia prosper. In about 545 B.C., however, Lydia's location also contributed to its downfall. It was conquered first by the Persians, who had expanded their empire into the region. Later, Lydia fell to the Greeks and then to the Romans.

REVIEW How did the use of coined money change the Lydian economy?

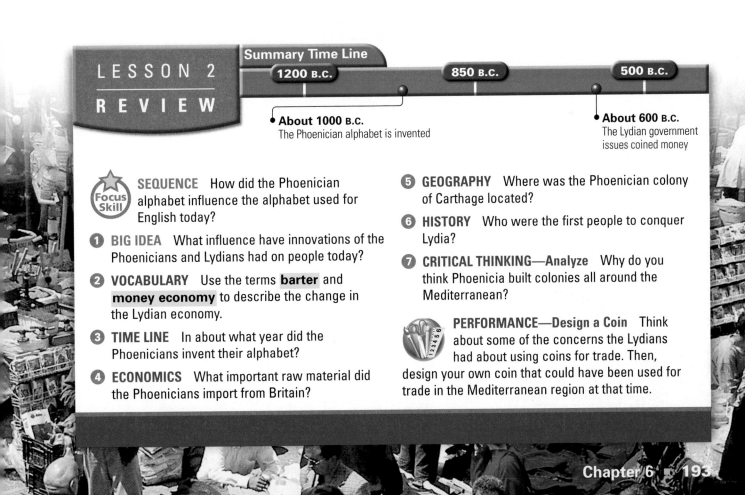

LESSON 2 REVIEW

Summary Time Line

1200 B.C. — 850 B.C. — 500 B.C.

• **About 1000 B.C.**
The Phoenician alphabet is invented

• **About 600 B.C.**
The Lydian government issues coined money

Focus Skill **SEQUENCE** How did the Phoenician alphabet influence the alphabet used for English today?

1 BIG IDEA What influence have innovations of the Phoenicians and Lydians had on people today?

2 VOCABULARY Use the terms **barter** and **money economy** to describe the change in the Lydian economy.

3 TIME LINE In about what year did the Phoenicians invent their alphabet?

4 ECONOMICS What important raw material did the Phoenicians import from Britain?

5 GEOGRAPHY Where was the Phoenician colony of Carthage located?

6 HISTORY Who were the first people to conquer Lydia?

7 CRITICAL THINKING—Analyze Why do you think Phoenicia built colonies all around the Mediterranean?

PERFORMANCE—Design a Coin Think about some of the concerns the Lydians had about using coins for trade. Then, design your own coin that could have been used for trade in the Mediterranean region at that time.

Follow Routes on a Map

▶ WHY IT MATTERS

Some information is easiest to understand when it is shown in a drawing. One way to understand trade and travel routes is to use a map. Maps can also help you understand the ways in which geography affects transportation and the movement of people and goods.

A Phoenician necklace

▶ WHAT YOU NEED TO KNOW

To use a map to follow routes, you first need to understand direction. A direction marker called a compass rose is found on most maps. The compass rose shows the cardinal, or main, directions and the intermediate directions.

The compass rose on the map on this page is located at the top of the

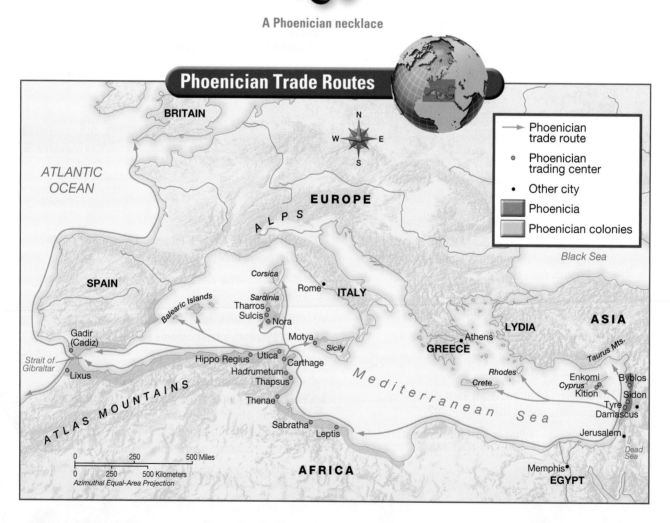

Phoenician Trade Routes

Legend:
→ Phoenician trade route
○ Phoenician trading center
• Other city
▪ Phoenicia
▪ Phoenician colonies

BRITAIN

ATLANTIC OCEAN

EUROPE

ALPS

SPAIN

Black Sea

Corsica
Rome • ITALY
Sardinia
Tharros
Sulcis ○ Nora
Balearic Islands
Gadir (Cadiz)
Motya
Sicily
LYDIA
ASIA
Athens
GREECE
Taurus Mts.
Strait of Gibraltar
Lixus
Hippo Regius ○ Utica ○ Carthage
Hadrumetum
Thapsus
Thenae
Rhodes
Crete
Enkomi
Cyprus
Byblos
Kition
Sidon
Tyre
Damascus
Mediterranean Sea
ATLAS MOUNTAINS
Sabratha
Leptis
Jerusalem
Dead Sea
Memphis
EGYPT
AFRICA

0   250   500 Miles
0   250   500 Kilometers
Azimuthal Equal-Area Projection

This stone carving (above left) shows a Phoenician trading ship. Phoenician artisans produced high-quality crafts, such as these multicolored vases (above right).

map. As is usually the case, the compass rose shows an arrow with *N*, for north, pointing toward the top of the map. This means that south is toward the bottom of the map, east is toward the right, and west is toward the left.

Look at the map and the map key. The arrows show the routes along which Phoenician sailors may have traveled.

Find the scale bar on the map. The map scale compares a distance on the map to a distance in the real world. It can be used to find the real distance between places shown on a map.

▶ PRACTICE THE SKILL

Use the map key, compass rose, and scale bar to answer these questions.

1 A Phoenician ship sets out from Tyre. In which direction will the ship travel to reach Carthage?

2 A Phoenician merchant in Byblos trades goods with a merchant in Enkomi on the island of Cyprus. In which direction must the Phoenician ship travel from Byblos to reach Enkomi?

3 Imagine that you are a merchant in the Phoenician city-state of Sidon. Plan a trading expedition from Sidon to the tin mines of Britain. How far must you travel from Sidon to the Strait of Gibraltar? from the Strait of Gibraltar to Britain? What is the total distance of your trip from Sidon to Britain?

▶ APPLY WHAT YOU LEARNED

Using an atlas, plan a route for a trip you would like to take. Choose where you will begin and end your trip. Use the map key, compass rose, and scale bar to help you. As you plan your route, list the directions in which you will travel and the distances between stops along your way.

Practice your map and globe skills with the **GeoSkills CD-ROM.**

3

Focus Skill

SEQUENCE

Read to learn the sequence of events in the development of the Persian Empire.

BIG IDEA

Strong leaders played a key role in the development of the Persian Empire and its civilization.

VOCABULARY

noble
infantry
cavalry
tribute
courier
polytheism
prophet

The tomb of Cyrus the Great is located in the ruins of the Persian city of Pasargadae (puh•SAR•guh•dee), in present-day Iran.

LOCATE IT

IRAN

Pasargadae

The Persian Empire

| 2000 B.C. | 1500 B.C. | 1000 B.C. | 500 B.C. | B.C./A.D. | A.D. 500 |

600 B.C. – 300 B.C.

In the 500s B.C. one vast empire covered much of southwestern Asia. The Persians, the ancestors of today's Iranian people, built this empire. It was as large as the 48 joined states of the United States. It stretched from eastern Europe and northern Africa in the west to India in the east. It went from the Gulf of Oman in the south to the Caucasus Mountains in the north. Under Cyrus the Great, Darius (duh•RY•uhs), Xerxes (ZERK•seez), and other leaders, Persia became not only the center of an empire but also the home of a great civilization.

Cyrus, the Empire Builder

The one person most responsible for building the Persian Empire was Cyrus the Great. Cyrus was born about 590 B.C. He was the son of a noble Persian family. **Noble** refers to people of high rank or title in a society.

In the year 559 B.C. Cyrus became ruler of Anshan, a part of the Median Empire in southwestern Asia. About 550 B.C. he overthrew the king of the Medes and made Media the center of what would become the Persian Empire.

Cyrus was known as a skilled military leader, determined to conquer his neighbors. He did so with the use of a huge standing army. Its size and advanced weapons overwhelmed Persia's enemies.

The Persian **infantry**, soldiers trained for fighting mainly on foot, were well protected by bronze helmets and shields. This protection helped them in hand-to-hand combat. The Persian **cavalry**, soldiers who fought on horseback, on camels, or from chariots, made swift attacks.

In 539 B.C. Babylonia fell to the Persian army led by Cyrus the Great. Then Assyria, Lydia, Parthia, and Bactria were added to the empire. In less than 20 years, the Persians conquered lands from Asia Minor to what is now northern Pakistan.

Although Cyrus created the Persian Empire by force, he was a somewhat fair ruler. He treated the people he conquered with understanding and respect. For example, he allowed the Jews who had been exiled to Babylonia to return to their homeland. Cyrus also encouraged the Jews to rebuild their temple, the center of their religion and culture.

The only battle Cyrus the Great ever lost was the one in which he died. The battle was fought in central Asia in 530 B.C. The Persian army was warring against people who lived near the Caspian Sea under the rule of Queen Tomyris (tuh•MY•ruhs).

With Cyrus the Great's death, the time of the greatest growth for the Persian Empire came to an end. Cyrus was followed by his son Cambyses (kam•BY•seez). Cambyses conquered Egypt in 525 B.C. but died on his way back to Persia.

REVIEW Who built much of the Persian Empire?

DEMOCRATIC VALUES
Individual Rights

In his day Cyrus the Great was known for his fair and just leadership. This is because he respected the customs and traditions of each part of his vast empire. At the time of his conquest of Babylonia, Cyrus issued a decree listing his goals. This decree was later hailed as the first charter of human rights. This document expressed plans for bringing peace to all people in his empire.

" When I, well-disposed, entered Babylon, I established the seat of government in the royal palace amidst jubilation and rejoicing. . . . My numerous troops moved about undisturbed in the midst of Babylon. I did not allow any to terrorize the land of Sumer and Akkad. I kept in view the needs of Babylon and all its sanctuaries [places of worship] to promote their well-being. The citizens of Babylon . . . I lifted their unbecoming yoke [burden]. Their dilapidated [fallen to pieces] dwellings I restored. I put an end to their misfortunes. "

Analyze the Value

1. Which individual rights did Cyrus include in his decree?
2. **Make It Relevant** Write a paragraph explaining the importance of maintaining individual rights in a society.

This stone cylinder (above left) is carved with Cyrus the Great's decree.

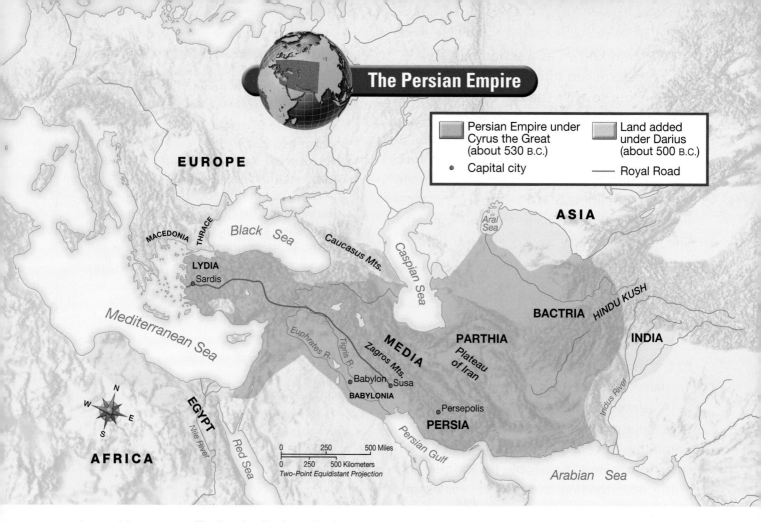

The Persian Empire

Legend:
- Persian Empire under Cyrus the Great (about 530 B.C.)
- Land added under Darius (about 500 B.C.)
- • Capital city
- — Royal Road

EUROPE

ASIA

AFRICA

MACEDONIA
THRACE
Black Sea
Caucasus Mts.
Caspian Sea
Aral Sea
LYDIA
Sardis
Mediterranean Sea
Euphrates R.
Tigris R.
MEDIA
Zagros Mts.
Babylon
Susa
BABYLONIA
Persepolis
PERSIA
PARTHIA
Plateau of Iran
BACTRIA
HINDU KUSH
INDIA
Indus River
EGYPT
Nile River
Red Sea
Persian Gulf
Arabian Sea

0   250   500 Miles
0   250   500 Kilometers
Two-Point Equidistant Projection

GEOGRAPHY THEME

Movement   The Persian Empire gained most of its land under Cyrus the Great.

❖ On which continents did Darius add new territories to the Persian Empire?

Darius, the Organizer

When news of Cambyses's death reached Persia, a struggle for control of the empire followed. In about 522 B.C. Darius I, a relative of Cambyses, became emperor. Darius, who ruled the Persian Empire until his death in 486 B.C., faced the difficult task of ruling a huge empire.

Darius proved to be a successful organizer of the empire. To rule the empire more efficiently, he divided it into 20 territories called satrapies (SAY•truh•peez). Each satrapy was governed by a local official called a satrap.

Satraps ruled like kings over their territories. The emperor, however, was the king of kings, the final and absolute authority in the empire.

Each satrap provided the Persian emperor with tribute. **Tribute** is a required payment from one ruler or country to another, more powerful ruler or country. Most often, the tributes took the form of soldiers for the empire's army or money for the empire's treasury.

This stone carving of Darius I is located in present-day Iran.

Darius used tribute money to build palaces at Persepolis (per•SEH•puh•luhs) and Susa, his two capitals. He also used it for building roads. By about 500 B.C. a royal road connected the cities of Susa, in Mesopotamia, and Sardis, in Asia Minor.

To communicate with his satraps, Darius started a relay system for sending messages. **Couriers**, or messengers, on horseback carried the messages from station to station along major roads. The couriers galloped across the Persian Empire, sometimes covering more than 100 miles (161 km) in a day. "There is nothing in the world that travels faster than these Persian couriers," wrote Herodotus. "Nothing stops these couriers from covering their allotted [assigned] stage in the quickest possible time—neither snow, rain, heat, nor darkness."

Darius also introduced to the Persian Empire the idea of a secret service. Known as the "eyes and ears of the king," members

A goat-shaped drinking vessel found among other treasures in the palace at Persepolis

of the secret service kept Darius informed about events throughout the empire.

Darius died in 486 B.C. while preparing his army for more conquests. He was followed by his son Xerxes, who continued to expand the Persian Empire. Xerxes ruled as his father had until 479 B.C. In that year the Greeks defeated the Persians in a fierce battle at Plataea (pluh•TEE•uh). As a result of this defeat, the Persians were driven out of eastern Europe.

After Xerxes died, the Persian Empire began to decline. However, it continued to exist until 331 B.C. That year the huge Persian army was defeated by the army of Alexander the Great, who had conquered much of Europe and Asia.

REVIEW Who ruled the Persian Empire after Darius? SEQUENCE

This photo shows the ruins of the palace at Persepolis (below). The stone carving of an archer (right) is from Darius's palace at Susa.

A Persian courier carries a message from the city of Persepolis.

A New Religion

Like most ancient people, the earliest Persians worshipped many gods of nature. Belief in many gods is called **polytheism**. The early Persians had no formal ceremonies and built no temples. Each Persian prayed and offered sacrifices to the gods of his or her own choice. By the time of the Persian Empire, however, the royal family of Persia followed a religion called Zoroastrianism (zohr•uh•WAS•tree•uh•nih•zuhm), which was based on a belief in one god. As time passed, more and more Persians practiced Zoroastrianism.

Little is known about Zarathustra (zar•uh•THOOS•truh), also known as Zoroaster, the founder of this religion. He probably lived sometime during the 600s or 500s B.C. Zarathustra was considered a **prophet**, a person who is believed to speak or write with a message from God or a god.

Zoroastrianism teaches a belief in one god, Ahura Mazda, or "Wise Lord," who created all things. The heart of this religion is the belief in a battle between good and evil. "The Earth is a battleground, a struggle between forces of light and forces of darkness," said Zarathustra.

According to Zarathustra's teachings, Ahura Mazda calls upon all believers to fight in this struggle. Each person will be judged at death on how well he or she fought, based on his or her own thoughts, words, and deeds. Zoroastrians believed that nothing in life was possible without the help of their god. Cyrus the Great wrote, "The land of the Persians, which I possess, has been granted unto me by the great god Ahura Mazda."

The prophet Zarathustra (above) taught about Zoroastrianism. The ruins of Zoroastrian altars (left) still stand near what is today Shiraz (shee•RAHZ), Iran.

The holy teachings of Zarathustra are found in several hymns called Gathas. They are part of a sacred book titled *Zend-Avesta.* These hymns provide the only known record of what Zarathustra believed.

Zoroastrianism began losing followers as the Persian Empire declined. About the middle of the A.D. 600s, the Muslims conquered Persia, and Zoroastrianism declined further. However, several groups continued to observe the religion's traditions. These groups have carried the belief into the present in Iran and India. Modern believers of the ideas of Zarathustra are known as Parsis. Most Parsis live in India.

REVIEW **What is Zoroastrianism?**

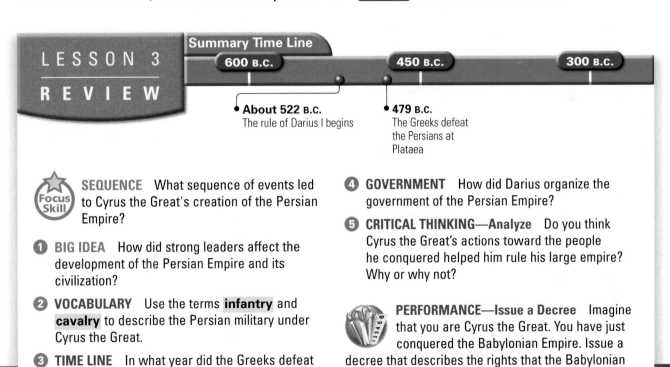

LESSON 3
—————
R E V I E W

Summary Time Line

600 B.C.   450 B.C.   300 B.C.

About 522 B.C.
The rule of Darius I begins

479 B.C.
The Greeks defeat the Persians at Plataea

SEQUENCE What sequence of events led to Cyrus the Great's creation of the Persian Empire?

1 **BIG IDEA** How did strong leaders affect the development of the Persian Empire and its civilization?

2 **VOCABULARY** Use the terms **infantry** and **cavalry** to describe the Persian military under Cyrus the Great.

3 **TIME LINE** In what year did the Greeks defeat the Persians at Plataea?

4 **GOVERNMENT** How did Darius organize the government of the Persian Empire?

5 **CRITICAL THINKING—Analyze** Do you think Cyrus the Great's actions toward the people he conquered helped him rule his large empire? Why or why not?

PERFORMANCE—Issue a Decree Imagine that you are Cyrus the Great. You have just conquered the Babylonian Empire. Issue a decree that describes the rights that the Babylonian people will have under your rule.

6 Review and Test Preparation

• **About 1225 B.C.**
Moses leads the
Exodus from Egypt

Sequence

Complete this graphic organizer to show sequence of events that affected the an this graphic organizer appears on page

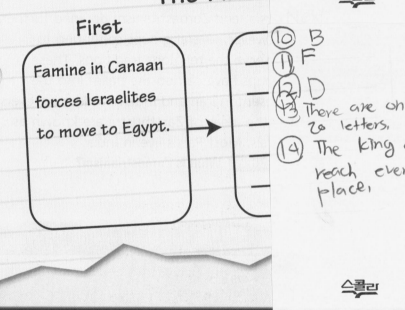

The Ancie

First

Famine in Canaan
forces Israelites
to move to Egypt.

Last

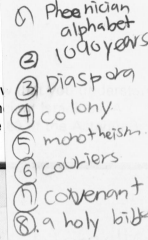

(handwritten notes:)
① Phoenician alphabet
② 1000 years.
③ Diaspora
④ colony.
⑤ monotheism.
⑥ couriers.
⑦ covenant
⑧ a holy bible
스콜라

⑩ B
⑪ F
⑫ D
⑬ There are only 26 letters,
⑭ The king cannot reach every place,

스콜라

THINK & WRITE

Write a Newspaper Article   Imagine that you are a newspaper reporter. Your job is to write a story about a civilization that uses a barter system. Describe how people trade goods and services. Include quotes from interviews in which people talk about the advantages and disadvantages of doing business by bartering.

Create a Campaign Brochure   Imagine that there will be a vote to decide whether Cyrus or Darius will be the newest leader chosen for the World Leaders Hall of Fame. Write and illustrate a persuasive brochure that will explain to the public who your choice is. Persuade your readers to support your choice for this special honor.

928 B.C.
King Solomon dies

The kingdom of Israel splits into Israel and Judah

About 800 B.C.
The Phoenician alphabet begins to spread to Israelites, Greeks, and others

About 600 B.C.
The Lydians make the first coins

530 B.C.
Cyrus the Great dies

A.D. 135
The Jewish Diaspora begins

USE THE TIME LINE

1 Which came first, Lydian coins or the Phoenician alphabet?

2 About how much time passed between the Exodus and the Diaspora?

USE VOCABULARY

Identify the term that correctly matches each definition.

> monotheism (p. 181)
> covenant (p. 181)
> Diaspora (p. 185)
> colony (p. 190)
> couriers (p. 199)

3 a word that comes from the Greek word meaning "to scatter"

4 an area of land ruled by a government in another land

5 the belief that there is only one God

6 messengers

7 a special agreement

RECALL FACTS

Answer these questions.

8 What is the Torah?

9 Who was Zarathustra?

Write the letter of the best choice.

10 **TEST PREP** Which one of these people is considered the father of the Jewish people?
  A Isaac
  B Abraham
  C Ishmael
  D Moses

11 **TEST PREP** Which one of these people was not a king of the united kingdom of Israel?
  F Saul
  G David
  H Jacob
  J Solomon

12 **TEST PREP** All of these people were leaders of the Persian Empire *except—*
  A Xerxes.
  B Cambyses.
  C Darius.
  D Queen Tomyris.

THINK CRITICALLY

13 Why do you think the Phoenician alphabet was easier to learn than earlier forms of writing?

14 Why might ruling a huge empire be more difficult than ruling a smaller one?

APPLY SKILLS

Determine Frame of Reference

15 Find an article about a conflict in your community. Identify who is involved in the conflict and what each side's frame of reference is. Offer possible ways to resolve the conflict. Describe how the different frames of reference might affect each solution.

Follow Routes on a Map

16 Look at the map on page 194. In which direction would you go to travel from Carthage to Jerusalem?

THE GREAT STUPA, SANCHI, INDIA

Sanchi is an excellent destination for those who want to see Buddhist architecture from the first and second centuries A.D. The Great Stupa at Sanchi is among the earliest existing Buddhist monuments. Built of stone, the stupa is 54 feet (16.5 m) high and 120 feet (36.5 m) wide. The art and architecture featured in the Great Stupa represent different stages in the life of the religious leader Buddha.

LOCATE IT

Sanchi

INDIA

Arabian Sea

Bay of Bengal

Asia's Classical Age

❝There is no better work than promoting the welfare of the whole world.❞

—Ashoka, leader of ancient India, *c.* 200s B.C.

Make Inferences

To make an **inference,** use what you already know about a subject and what you read to come to a conclusion.

As you read this chapter, make inferences.

• Write down what you already know about the chapter's topics.

• List details about the people, places, events, and ideas you read about.

• Make inferences about Asia's classical age.

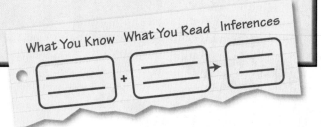

Aryans Bring Changes to India

 MAKE INFERENCES

As you read, make inferences about the changes the Aryans and later religious leaders brought to India.

BIG IDEA

The arrival of the Aryans affected ways of life in ancient India.

VOCABULARY

caste
Hinduism
reincarnation
Sanskrit
enlightenment
Jainism
nonviolence
nirvana
Buddhism

| 2000 B.C. | 1500 B.C. | 1000 B.C. | 500 B.C. | B.C./A.D. | A.D. 500 |

2000 B.C. – 400 B.C.

In about 2000 B.C. groups of herding people began to migrate into the Indus Valley, where the countries of Pakistan and India are located today. They called themselves *arya*, which means "nobles" in Sanskrit. The Aryans (AIR•ee•uhnz) may have come from western Asia. They were a pastoral society, raising cattle, goats, horses, and sheep. Their arrival on the Indian subcontinent brought many changes to the lives of the people already living there. Aryan culture had a lasting effect on the people of India.

The Arrival of the Aryans

The Aryan migration to India took place over hundreds of years. Why the Aryans chose to leave their homeland is not known. They may have been searching for new grazing lands. Perhaps they wanted to escape an overcrowded area.

FAST FACT When groups of Aryans migrated to the Indian subcontinent, they brought the first horses there.

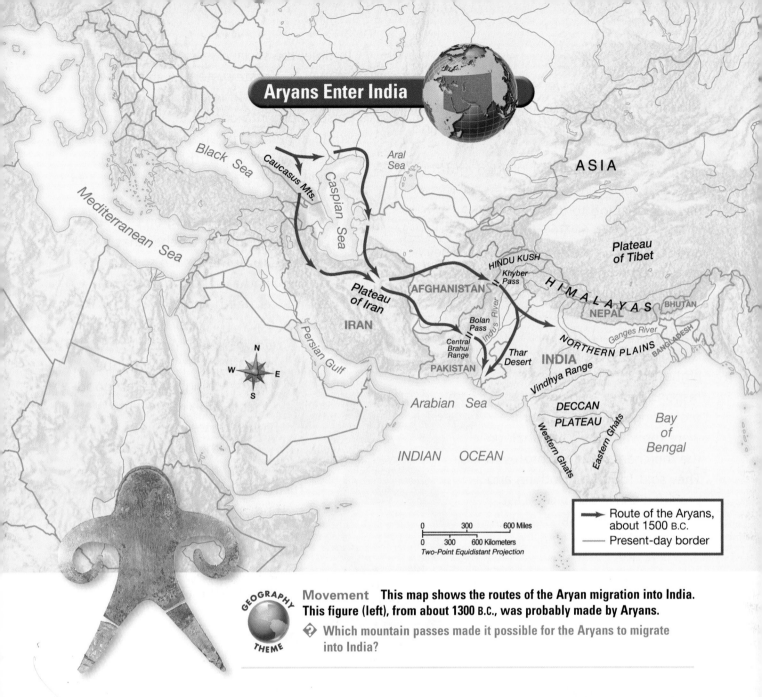

Aryans Enter India

ASIA

Black Sea

Caucasus Mts.

Caspian Sea

Aral Sea

Mediterranean Sea

Plateau of Iran

IRAN

AFGHANISTAN

HINDU KUSH

Khyber Pass

Plateau of Tibet

HIMALAYAS

BHUTAN

NEPAL

Indus River

Bolan Pass

Central Brahui Range

PAKISTAN

Thar Desert

INDIA

NORTHERN PLAINS

Ganges River

BANGLADESH

Persian Gulf

N W E S

Arabian Sea

Vindhya Range

DECCAN PLATEAU

Western Ghats

Eastern Ghats

Bay of Bengal

INDIAN OCEAN

0   300   600 Miles
0   300   600 Kilometers
Two-Point Equidistant Projection

→ Route of the Aryans, about 1500 B.C.
— Present-day border

GEOGRAPHY THEME

Movement This map shows the routes of the Aryan migration into India. This figure (left), from about 1300 B.C., was probably made by Aryans.

❓ Which mountain passes made it possible for the Aryans to migrate into India?

Over several centuries the Aryans may have moved southeast traveling across the Plateau of Iran and into present-day Afghanistan. They then reached the Indian subcontinent by way of mountain passes through the Hindu Kush and the Central Brahui Range.

When the Aryans arrived in the Indus Valley, they found an advanced civilization already living there. The people there lived in villages and grew crops. Some experts believe they were the descendants of the people who earlier had built Harappa,

Mohenjo-Daro, and other cities in the Indus Valley.

In time, the Aryans settled in villages and changed from a pastoral to an agricultural society. As a result, they competed with the native people of India for the most-fertile land. The Aryans, who were the stronger fighters, soon forced some of the native people to leave northern India and move farther south. Many others stayed. Over time, assimilation of ways of life took place between the two peoples.

REVIEW How did the Aryans reach India?

The Origins of Indian Culture

Many traces of Aryan culture can be found in present-day Indian culture. Among these are the Aryan religion, language, and social structure.

Early Aryan society was divided into four different social classes. Each class, or *varna*, had a special job to do.

The Brahmans (BRAH•muhnz), or priests and scholars, were the highest class. They conducted religious services and passed sacred knowledge from one generation to another. The Kshatriyas (KSHAH•tree•uhz), the rulers and the soldiers, were the second-highest class. They were responsible for leading and protecting the people. Third were the Vaisyas (VYSH•yuhz), or the merchants and the professionals. They sold food and clothing and provided various services. Last came the Shudras (SHOO•druhz), the servants of the other classes.

Shiva is one of Hinduism's most important gods.

In time, the social classes in ancient India gave way to a caste system. A **caste** is a group of people within a social class. Often a person born into one caste could not become a member of another caste. Caste members worked within their own group and could only marry others from their caste.

The caste system became part of the teaching of **Hinduism**, a religion of the Indian people. Hinduism teaches that people live many lives until they reach spiritual perfection. Hindus believe that the soul lives on after death and returns to life in a new body. This rebirth is called **reincarnation**. According to Hinduism, those who obey its teachings and lead good lives will be reborn into a higher caste. In time, a person may reach the highest position, *moksha* (MOHK•shuh). Then, no further reincarnation is needed.

Hindus believe that the souls of people who do not lead good lives will return in the bodies of lower life-forms. Hindus believe that all animals have souls just as

A SELECTION FROM THE

Bhagavad Gita

The Bhagavad Gita, or Song of the Lord, is part of the larger ancient Indian poem called the Mahabharata (muh•hah•BAH•ruh•tuh). In this selection, the Hindu god Vishnu speaks to Arjuna, one of the poem's main characters:

There is no doubt that you will know me
  in my total being when you persist
In discipline, and rely on me,
  and when your thought clings to me. Listen.

Without holding back anything, I shall teach you
  wisdom, and explain how it can be attained,
Knowing which,
  there is nothing left to be known.

One out of thousands
  may strive for success.
And even of these only a few
  may know me as I really am.

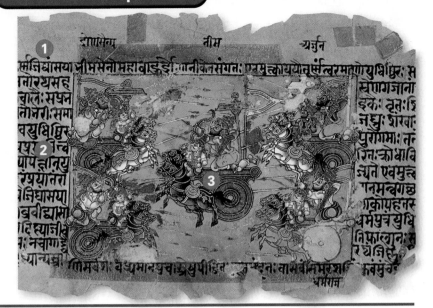

Ancient Indian Epic Poem

Analyze Primary Sources

In this illustrated page from the *Mahabharata,* the Pandavas battle their cousins, the Kauravas, for control of ancient India.

1 This page from a copy of the *Mahabharata* was written and illustrated in the A.D. 1500s.

2 Sanskrit, the language in which the poem was written

3 The Pandavas and Kauravas fought on war chariots.

◆ In what ways is this page like a storybook page today?

---

people do. For this reason, many Hindus are vegetarians.

Believers in Hinduism worship many gods, who are all considered part of one universal being called Brahman. The three main forms of Brahman are Brahma the Creator, Vishnu the Preserver, and Shiva the Destroyer. Below these main gods are many lesser gods.

According to Hinduism, **Sanskrit**, the language of the Aryans, was the language spoken by the gods. The Aryans' holiest books, the Vedas (VAY•duhz), were written in Sanskrit. *Veda* means "knowledge." These collections of knowledge were created beginning in about 1000 B.C.

Through the Vedas, the Aryans developed the foundations for the beliefs and traditions of Hindu society. Over time, people wrote down stories to help people understand the ideas expressed in the Vedas. Later these stories were grouped together in epic poems, such as the *Mahabharata.*

This stone bust shows Buddha meditating.

Many present-day Indian languages are based on Sanskrit. Of these, Hindi is spoken most widely. Most Hindi speakers practice the religion of Hinduism. It was the only religion in India until the 500s B.C., when some religious and social reformers rejected the Vedas.

REVIEW What are the holiest books of Hinduism? MAKE INFERENCES

Jainism and Buddhism

Two religions were founded in India in the 500s and 400s B.C., Jainism (JY•nih•zuhm) and Buddhism. Mahavira (muh•hah•VEE•ruh), an Indian prince, founded Jainism. Siddhartha Gautama (sih•DAR•tuh GOW•tuh•muh), who became known as Buddha (BOO•duh), founded Buddhism. Both religions rejected the Vedas and the authority of the Brahmans. Both religions spread rapidly throughout India.

This painting shows the different stages of Buddha's life.

Mahavira gave up all his possessions to live a religious life. He spent 12 years seeking **enlightenment**, or complete understanding of truth. He then became a religious teacher.

Mahavira organized his teachings into the religion of **Jainism**. It was based on the belief that every living being has a soul and a temporary physical body. Mahavira urged his followers to become vegetarians so that animals would not be killed for food.

Mahavira also believed that the best way to bring about change was through peaceful action. The use of peaceful ways to bring about change is known today as **nonviolence**.

Siddhartha Gautama was born to royal parents about 563 B.C. in northern India. According to ancient stories, Gautama's parents kept him from seeing any kind of suffering.

When Gautama went outside the walls of his palace for the first time, he saw an old person, a sick person, and a dead person. What he saw showed him that aging, sickness, and death come to all people. It also raised many questions for him. Why, he asked, was there suffering? How might suffering be ended? Gautama decided to search for answers to these questions.

For six years Gautama searched for knowledge by studying and praying with Brahman priests. That, however, did not help him find answers. According to tradition, Gautama sat down under a tree one day to rest and think. After several hours of very intense thought, he believed that he understood the meaning of life. He decided that people should seek love, truth, the joy of knowledge, and a calm mind. Others learned of his ideas and began to call him Buddha, which means "Enlightened One."

This stone carving is a Jainist cosmic wheel, which represents the idea of a cycle of birth and rebirth.

Gautama spent the rest of his life teaching his message, which centered on Four Noble Truths:

(1) Suffering is a part of life.

(2) Wanting things brings suffering.

(3) People can find peace by giving up wants.

(4) Following eight basic rules, called the Eightfold Path, can end a person's cycle of reincarnation and lead to **nirvana** (nir•VAH•nuh), or a state of complete bliss that is free from all passion, desire, and suffering.

After Buddha's death in 483 B.C., his followers told others of his teachings. **Buddhism**, the religion based on those teachings, eventually spread across Asia.

Neither Buddha nor his followers formed a religious organization or wrote holy books like the Vedas. Instead, they tried to set an example for others through peaceful behavior.

REVIEW Why did Gautama begin to search for truth?

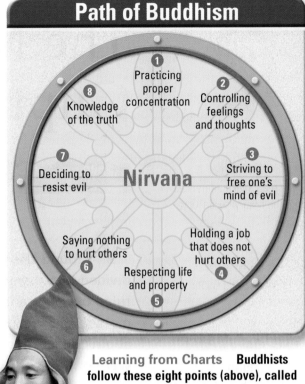

Path of Buddhism

1. Practicing proper concentration
2. Controlling feelings and thoughts
3. Striving to free one's mind of evil
4. Holding a job that does not hurt others
5. Respecting life and property
6. Saying nothing to hurt others
7. Deciding to resist evil
8. Knowledge of the truth

Nirvana

Learning from Charts Buddhists follow these eight points (above), called the Eightfold Path, in their search for nirvana. A present-day Buddhist monk (left) from the Pemayangtse Monastery in India participates in a ceremony.

❖ Why would practicing proper concentration be important?

LESSON 1 REVIEW

Summary Time Line

2000 B.C.   1200 B.C.   400 B.C.

● **About 2000 B.C.**
The Aryan migrations to India begin

● **About 1000 B.C.**
The Aryans begin to write the Vedas

● **About 563 B.C.**
Buddha is born

MAKE INFERENCES Why do you think Jainism and Buddhism spread quickly throughout India?

1 **BIG IDEA** How did the arrival of the Aryans affect the culture of ancient India?

2 **VOCABULARY** How is **caste** related to **reincarnation**?

3 **TIME LINE** Did the Aryans migrate to India before or after writing the Vedas?

4 **CULTURE** What main gods do Hindus worship?

5 **CRITICAL THINKING—Evaluate** For thousands of years, the caste system played a role in the organization of India's society. Do you think this system is a good way to organize a society? Why or why not?

PERFORMANCE—Write a Journal Entry Imagine that you are a farmer in ancient India. In a journal entry, describe the arrival of the Aryans in the Indus Valley. Tell about some of the new ideas the Aryans are introducing to Indian culture. Also describe how the migration of the Aryan people has affected your life.

2

The Maurya and Gupta Empires

MAKE INFERENCES

As you read, make inferences about the Maurya and Gupta Empires.

BIG IDEA

India was united under the rule of Maurya and Gupta leaders.

VOCABULARY

rajah
turning point
edict
missionary
fresco

2000 B.C.	1500 B.C.	1000 B.C.	500 B.C.	B.C./A.D.	A.D. 500

500 B.C. – A.D. 500

Around the time of Buddha, the Indian subcontinent was divided into many small kingdoms. **Rajahs**, or Indian princes, ruled over these lands, which were rich in crops, jewels, and metals. This wealth attracted invaders—first the Persians in about 518 B.C. and then the Greeks in 326 B.C. These invasions were one reason that the individual kingdoms began to unite.

United Rule in India

In about 320 B.C. a ruler by the name of Chandragupta Maurya (chuhn•druh•GOOP•tuh MOW•ree•uh) united nearly all of northern India, Afghanistan, and parts of central Asia into the Maurya Empire. Under Chandragupta, trade flourished, agriculture improved, and weights and measures were made standard. During Chandragupta's rule, money was first used in the Indian subcontinent. Services, such as garbage collection and famine relief, were provided by a central government. To achieve all these things,

During the time of the Mauryas, Buddhists built large stupas, or religious shrines (right). Many of these stupas still stand today. The Mauryas were the first people in India to use money. At left, the front and back of a Maurya coin from about 300 B.C. are shown.

however, Chandragupta ruled in a strict manner. He forced some people to work as slaves for the government. He also demanded high taxes from the people to pay for government services.

What is known about how Chandragupta governed comes from a book published much later, called the *Arthashastra* (ar•thuh•SHAH•struh). The book says that rulers should govern with a firm hand. It states, "Government is the science of punishment." It also says that cruelty is an acceptable way for rulers to reach their goals.

Chandragupta's way of ruling made him many enemies in the empire. Because he feared for his safety, he appeared in public only during a few important festivals. To protect himself from being poisoned, he had servants taste all his food before he ate it. To avoid attackers, he slept in a different room every night. No attack came, however.

In 297 B.C. Chandragupta quietly gave up the throne to Bindusara (bin•doo•SAR•uh), his son. Bindusara extended the Maurya Empire, conquering lands as far south as the present-day city of Mysore (my•SOHR).

REVIEW **What was Chandragupta like as a ruler?**

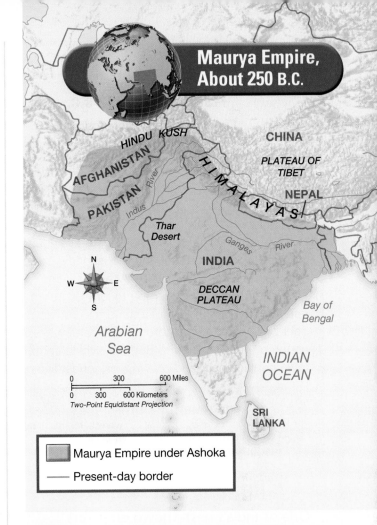

Maurya Empire, About 250 B.C.

HINDU KUSH
AFGHANISTAN
PAKISTAN
Indus River
Thar Desert
CHINA
PLATEAU OF TIBET
NEPAL
HIMALAYAS
Ganges River
INDIA
DECCAN PLATEAU
Arabian Sea
Bay of Bengal
INDIAN OCEAN
SRI LANKA

N W E S

0   300   600 Miles
0   300   600 Kilometers
Two-Point Equidistant Projection

☐ Maurya Empire under Ashoka
— Present-day border

GEOGRAPHY THEME

Place **The Maurya Empire reached its largest size under the rule of Ashoka.**

◈ **What part of the Indian subcontinent was not ruled by the Maurya Empire?**

LOCATE IT

Sarnath
INDIA
Arabian Sea
Bay of Bengal

Ashoka ?–232 B.C.

Character Trait: Responsibility

Ashoka inherited the rule of India from his father, Bindusara. Ashoka enlarged the Maurya Empire to include all of India except the southernmost and southeastern parts. In 262 B.C. Ashoka conquered the kingdom of Kalinga. The War of Kalinga was terrible. About 100,000 soldiers were killed, about 150,000 were wounded, and thousands were captured and forced into slavery. Although Ashoka's army won the war, it seemed to him that both sides had lost. He began to understand that problems could be solved better through peaceful ways. He adopted the teachings of Buddha, which encourage love, nonviolence, and *dharma*, or honest living.

 MULTIMEDIA BIOGRAPHIES
Visit The Learning Site at www.harcourtschool.com to learn about other famous people.

The Reign of Ashoka

One of India's best-known emperors was Chandragupta's grandson Ashoka (uh•SHOH•kuh), also spelled Asoka. Ashoka became emperor in 274 B.C. He began his rule of the Maurya Empire as firmly as his grandfather had. Like his grandfather, Ashoka believed that

> **Any power superior in might [strength] to another should launch into war.**

In 262 B.C. Ashoka ordered his army to invade the kingdom of Kalinga. About 100,000 people were killed.

The high number of deaths made Ashoka regret having gone

These lion sculptures once topped one of Ashoka's pillars.

to war. The invasion of Kalinga became a turning point in the young leader's life. A **turning point** is a single event that causes important change. Ashoka gave up war and turned against violence. He spent the rest of his life spreading a message of nonviolence based on the teachings of Buddha.

To do this, Ashoka issued a number of **edicts**, or decrees. He had these edicts carved on rocks and stone pillars along major roads throughout the empire. One such edict called for people to show "obedience to mother and father." India's national emblem, a group of lions, is taken from the sculptures Ashoka placed on top of these pillars.

Ashoka also sent missionaries to spread the teachings of Buddhism throughout the empire and to other parts of Asia. A **missionary** is a person sent somewhere else to teach about his or her religion.

During the rest of his rule, Ashoka used his authority as emperor to make the lives of his people better. He became known as "the greatest and noblest ruler India has known." Because of Ashoka, the idea of nonviolence spread throughout the empire. Ashoka's view of nonviolence included not killing any living creatures. This inspired many people of the time to avoid eating meat by becoming vegetarians.

After Ashoka's death in 232 B.C., the Maurya Empire began to break apart. Authority was divided among many quarreling kingdoms. For about the next 500 years, there was no unified government. As a result of this weakness, central Asian peoples, including the Scythians (SIH•thee•uhnz) and the Kushans, seized control of northern India. The Kushans established their rule in northern India in about A.D. 50.

REVIEW How did Ashoka's invasion of Kalinga affect the way he governed?

The Gupta Empire

Indian emperors of the Gupta (GUP•tuh) dynasty brought northern India once again under a unified government. In A.D. 320 Chandragupta I, who was not related to the Chandragupta of the Maurya Empire, gained control of a small kingdom in the Ganges River valley. Through marriage and war he expanded his territory across northern India. His son Samudragupta and his grandson

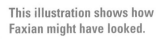

Chandragupta II continued to expand the Gupta Empire, but it never grew as large as the Maurya Empire had once been.

Much of what we know today about life in the Gupta Empire comes from the writings of Faxian (FAH•SHYUHN), a Chinese Buddhist monk. Faxian traveled in India for more than ten years, collecting Buddhist writings to take back to China. Faxian also wrote about his travels. His writings are collected in the book *Fo Kuo Chi*, known in English as the *Record of Buddhist Kingdoms*.

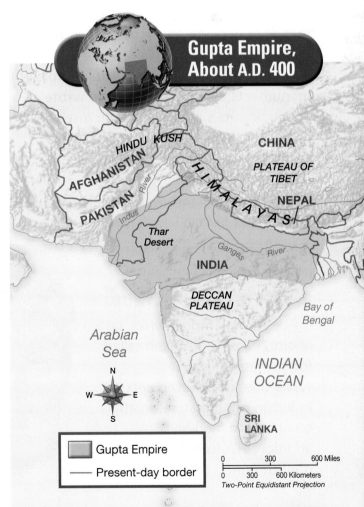

Gupta Empire, About A.D. 400

HINDU KUSH
AFGHANISTAN
PAKISTAN
CHINA
PLATEAU OF TIBET
NEPAL
HIMALAYAS
Indus River
Thar Desert
Ganges River
INDIA
DECCAN PLATEAU
Arabian Sea
Bay of Bengal
INDIAN OCEAN
SRI LANKA

Gupta Empire
Present-day border

0   300   600 Miles
0   300   600 Kilometers
Two-Point Equidistant Projection

GEOGRAPHY THEME

Regions The Gupta Empire once ruled much of the northern Indian subcontinent.

❖ **What present-day countries border what was once the Gupta Empire?**

This elaborately carved structure (left) is the entrance to the Ajanta caves. This fresco (above) of Prince Gautama, later known as Buddha, is one of the many paintings found on the walls of the caves.

The people of India, Faxian observed, were "very well off." They had such freedom that "if they desire to go, they go; if they like to stop, they stop." Faxian marveled at the well-kept roads and beautiful temples, monuments, and palaces. He also wrote of the hospitals in which people received health care. Faxian concluded that India seemed to be a safe and happy place during the Gupta Empire.

REVIEW What might have been different if the Gupta Empire had not been formed?

MAKE INFERENCES

Classical Age of India

The Gupta Empire, which lasted about 200 years, is often called India's classical age. It was a time of achievements in Indian art, literature, mathematics, and medicine. In addition, Hinduism saw new growth during this period.

Chandragupta II supported many writers, including the famous poet and playwright Kalidasa (kah•lih•DAH•suh). One project involved collecting popular folktales from earlier times. In time, this collection, called the *Panchatantra* (pahn•chah•TAHN•truh), became known throughout the world. You may know some of the stories, such as "Sinbad the Sailor" and "Jack the Giant-Killer."

Chandragupta II also supported public art projects. Some Hindu temples were built, and many fine frescoes, especially those at Ajanta, were painted at this time. A **fresco** is a picture painted on wet plaster.

Many important advances in mathematics and medicine were made during this classical age. Indian mathematicians

Gupta sculpture of a bodhisattva, a Buddhist who has attained enlightenment but postpones nirvana to help others

had already developed a base-ten number system—a system that uses the numbers 1 through 9 and the zero. Now known as Arabic numerals, these numerals were used in India before Arab traders later borrowed them for their own use. The Guptas also were among the first people to use decimals and algebra to solve mathematics problems.

Gupta doctors developed ways to set broken bones and to help women give birth more safely. Like surgeons today, doctors during the time of the Guptas used skin from other parts of the body to mend ears and noses. Understanding the need for cleanliness in surgery, they sterilized their cutting tools. Indian doctors at that time also used inoculation. That is, they gave a person a mild form of a disease so that he or she would not get sick with a more serious form.

Traders carried Indian ideas, along with Indian goods, to other lands. Arab traders, for example, took not only spices, cloth, carpets, and jewelry to Europe and Africa but also Indian books and ideas. As a result,

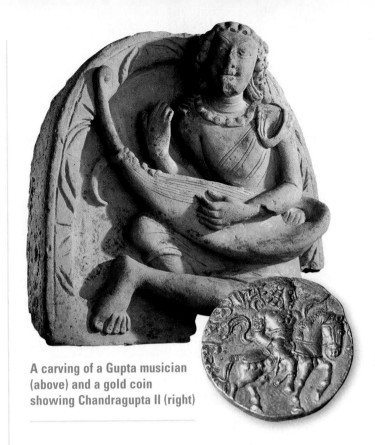

A carving of a Gupta musician (above) and a gold coin showing Chandragupta II (right)

news of India's innovations reached many parts of the world.

REVIEW What important advances in medicine took place during the time of Gupta rule?

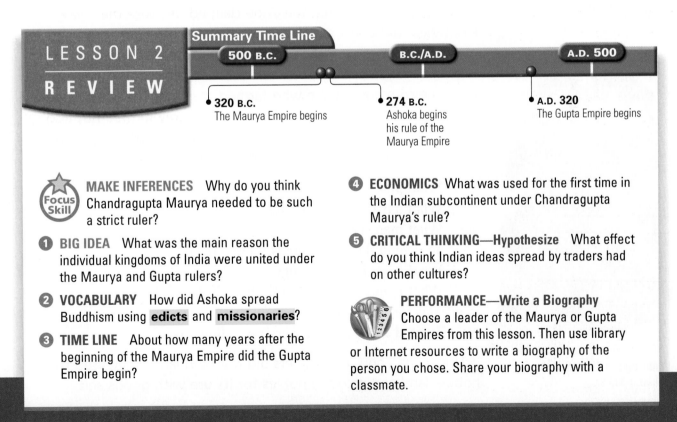

LESSON 2 REVIEW

Summary Time Line

500 B.C. — B.C./A.D. — A.D. 500

320 B.C. The Maurya Empire begins

274 B.C. Ashoka begins his rule of the Maurya Empire

A.D. 320 The Gupta Empire begins

Focus Skill — MAKE INFERENCES Why do you think Chandragupta Maurya needed to be such a strict ruler?

1 BIG IDEA What was the main reason the individual kingdoms of India were united under the Maurya and Gupta rulers?

2 VOCABULARY How did Ashoka spread Buddhism using **edicts** and **missionaries**?

3 TIME LINE About how many years after the beginning of the Maurya Empire did the Gupta Empire begin?

4 ECONOMICS What was used for the first time in the Indian subcontinent under Chandragupta Maurya's rule?

5 CRITICAL THINKING—Hypothesize What effect do you think Indian ideas spread by traders had on other cultures?

PERFORMANCE—Write a Biography Choose a leader of the Maurya or Gupta Empires from this lesson. Then use library or Internet resources to write a biography of the person you chose. Share your biography with a classmate.

3

China's Great Dynasties

MAKE INFERENCES

As you read, make inferences about the Zhou, Qin, and Han dynasties.

BIG IDEA
The Zhou, Qin, and Han dynasties influenced the growth of Chinese culture and society.

VOCABULARY

peasant
feudalism
philosopher
filial piety
Confucianism
Legalism
civil service
Daoism
Silk Road

2000 B.C.	1500 B.C.	1000 B.C.	500 B.C.	B.C./A.D.	A.D. 500

1125 B.C. – A.D. 225

The classical age of China began with the conquest of the Huang He valley in about 1122 B.C. by the Zhou (JOH) people. Under the Zhou and later under the Qin (CHIN) and Han (HAHN) dynasties, China became a great civilization. The Zhou, Qin, and Han dynasties had an influence on Chinese society that has lasted for thousands of years.

The Zhou Dynasty

The Zhou was China's longest-ruling dynasty, lasting from about 1122 B.C. to 256 B.C. The Zhou dynasty began with its conquest of the Shang dynasty. According to the Zhou, Heaven allowed King Wu to conquer the Shang dynasty and begin the new Zhou dynasty. Heaven did this, the Zhou claimed, because the Shang kings were dishonest and cruel.

Zhou rulers set up a social structure with three classes—the king and his family, noble families, and peasant families. The **peasants** were the common people who farmed the land. The life of a peasant was filled with hardships. Peasants not only farmed but also served in Zhou armies. This poem from the *Book of Songs*, written in about 1000 B.C., offers a personal view of a peasant's life:

> **What plant is not faded?**
> **What day do we not march?**
> **What man is not taken**
> **To defend the four bounds [boundaries]?**
> **What plant is not wilting?**
> **What man is not taken from his wife?**
> **Alas for us soldiers,**
> **Treated as though we were not fellow men!**

Under the Zhou, the farmers did not own land. They used the nobles' land and paid the nobles for its use with goods and

This bronze bell was made during the Zhou dynasty, in about 300 B.C.

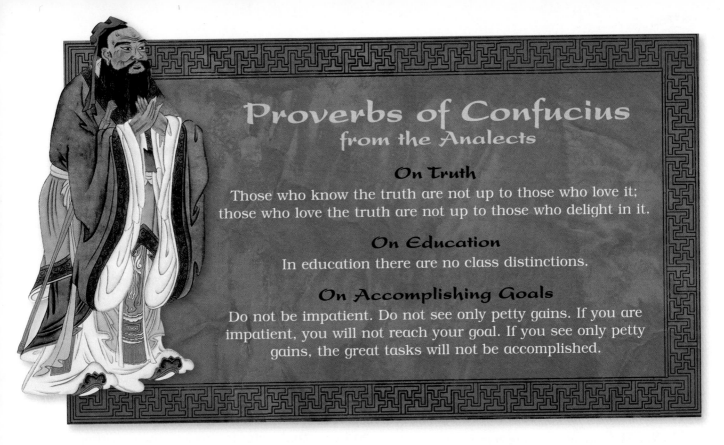

Proverbs of Confucius
from the Analects

On Truth
Those who know the truth are not up to those who love it;
those who love the truth are not up to those who delight in it.

On Education
In education there are no class distinctions.

On Accomplishing Goals
Do not be impatient. Do not see only petty gains. If you are impatient, you will not reach your goal. If you see only petty gains, the great tasks will not be accomplished.

services. In return, the nobles protected the peasants from groups of people not conquered by the Zhou.

The nobles got their land from the king. In return, they were expected to provide the king with military support and other services. This political system of exchanging land for loyalty and protection is known as **feudalism**.

As time passed, some nobles came to rule their own territories, which became independent from the king. The Zhou dynasty was weakened by this, losing its authority. The nobles of several large territories fought to rule China. During about the last 150 years of the dynasty, fighting took place daily. That is why this time is sometimes called the Warring States period.

REVIEW What were the three classes of Zhou society?

The Ideas of Confucius

One of ancient China's most important **philosophers**, or thinkers, lived toward the end of the Zhou dynasty. His name was Kong Fuzi, or Confucius (kuhn•FYOO•shuhs), meaning "Great Master Kong." Confucius spent much of his life thinking about ways to improve society and to restore order in China.

Confucius is remembered as a great teacher. Many people came to Confucius to study the ancient traditions with him. No actual writings of Confucius remain. However, after he died, his students remembered his teachings in the form of short statements.

This statue of Confucius decorates a building in the Chinatown neighborhood of New York City.

POINTS OF VIEW
Confucianism vs. Legalism

Not long after the Zhou dynasty ended, the Qin dynasty began. Emperor Shi Huangdi, the leader of the Qin, opposed the ideas of Confucianism. He felt that the only way to rule his large kingdom was by fear. To do this, he adopted the philosophy of Legalism. Later, the leaders of the Han dynasty saw problems in ruling only by Legalism. They allowed people to study Confucianism and relied on ideas from both philosophies to rule China.

CONFUCIUS, from the *Analects*

❝When a prince's personal conduct is correct, his government is effective without the issuing of orders.❞

HAN FEI, from his book the *Han Fei zi,* which describes the philosophy of Legalism

❝Rewards should be rich and certain so that people will be attracted by them; punishments should be severe and definite so that the people will fear them. The sovereign [king or queen] should show no wavering in bestowing rewards and grant no pardon in administering [giving] punishments.❞

Analyze the Viewpoints

1. What view about government did each person hold?

2. **Make It Relevant** Look at a current newspaper or an Internet news page. Find two different viewpoints about how present-day leaders in the United States should govern. Then write a paragraph that summarizes each viewpoint.

They collected them in a book called *Lunyu* (LUN•YOO) in Chinese. In English it is known as the *Analects.* The Chinese word *lunyu* means "discussions."

Many of Confucius's thoughts about government and society were based on his views about the family. In ancient Chinese culture, children were expected to treat their parents with honor and respect. The ancient Chinese called this kind of treatment of parents *xiao* (SEE•OW), or filial piety.

Filial piety is fulfilling one's duty to one's parents by being respectful to them, following their wishes, and caring for them in their old age. Confucius said that people could use the rules of filial piety to honor and respect their king. Confucius also taught that rulers could gain loyalty from their subjects by treating them with the same love and care that parents show to their children.

The teachings of Confucius were mostly ignored during his lifetime. In time, however, his ideas on government and society spread throughout eastern Asia. **Confucianism** has had one of the longest-lasting influences on the Chinese people.

REVIEW To what did Confucius compare the relationship between rulers and subjects?

The Qin Dynasty

When the Zhou dynasty collapsed in 256 B.C., the Zhou lost the Mandate of Heaven, or their right to rule. The three main kingdoms that remained—the Qi (CHEE), Chu (CHOO), and Qin—fought one another for control. The Qin won in 221 B.C. With this victory, the Qin king was able to unite China under one rule. After establishing the Qin Empire, the Qin king changed his name to Shi Huangdi (SHIR HWAHNG•DEE), or the "First Emperor."

To govern his empire, Shi Huangdi depended on a way of government now known as Legalism. **Legalism** taught that people obeyed their rulers out of fear, not out of respect as Confucius had taught. Under a system of Legalism, people who obey are rewarded. Those who do not obey are punished.

Following the ideas of Legalism, Shi Huangdi ruled the Chinese people harshly. His rule, however, brought important changes to China.

In uniting China, Shi Huangdi ended the power of the nobles and formed a strong central government. To help his government run more smoothly, Shi Huangdi set up a bureaucracy—a network of appointed government officials.

Shi Huangdi not only united China but also extended its borders. As the empire grew, Shi Huangdi organized many building projects to link the people of the empire and protect them from invaders. Prisoners and peasant farmers were forced to work on building new canals, more than 4,000 miles (6,400 km) of roads, and many other projects. Perhaps the best-known building project of the Qin dynasty was its Great Wall.

It took several hundred thousand workers about ten years to build the wall. Many died from hunger and overwork. Some were even buried inside the wall itself.

Shi Huangdi also ordered that many things be made standard across the empire, such as coins, weights, and the Chinese writing system. This helped unite people living in all parts of the empire.

• GEOGRAPHY •

The Great Wall Today
Understanding Human Systems

Visitors to China marvel at the Great Wall. The Great Wall seen today is a result of construction started in A.D. 1368. The Great Wall that stands today is much grander than Shi Huangdi's wall. Much of the Great Wall is 25 feet (7.6 m) high and just as wide. It is made mostly of brick and stone and features tall watchtowers. It extends from the Bo Gulf of the Yellow Sea in the east to the Lop Nur region of western China. Its many sections and branches cover more than 1,500 miles (about 2,400 km).

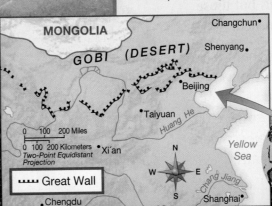

MONGOLIA

GOBI (DESERT)

Changchun•

Shenyang•

•Beijing

•Taiyuan

Huang He

0 100 200 Miles
0 100 200 Kilometers
Two-Point Equidistant Projection

•Xi'an

N
W   E
S

Yellow Sea

····· Great Wall

Chang Jiang

•Chengdu

Shanghai•

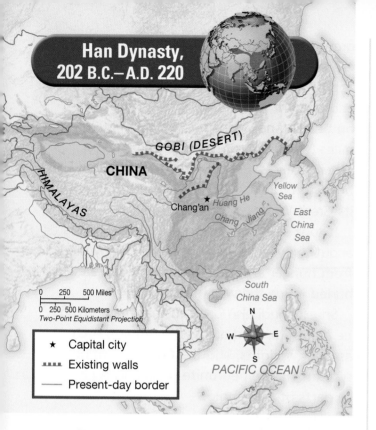

Han Dynasty, 202 B.C.–A.D. 220

GOBI (DESERT)

CHINA

HIMALAYAS

Chang'an ★ Huang He

Chang Jiang

Yellow Sea

East China Sea

South China Sea

PACIFIC OCEAN

0   250   500 Miles
0   250 500 Kilometers
Two-Point Equidistant Projection

★ Capital city
▪▪▪▪ Existing walls
— Present-day border

Movement **The Han dynasty continued to expand the borders of China.**

❖ How do the borders of the Han dynasty compare to the borders of present-day China?

In addition, Shi Huangdi looked closely at education. He wanted to control the books that were used to teach. The books he did not approve of, he ordered burned. An ancient Chinese document reveals the words of Li Si, one of the emperor's trusted advisers.

> **❝I humbly propose that all historical records but those of the Qin be burned.❞**

Many of the books that were destroyed were about Confucianism. Legend says that teachers who refused to give up their copies of the *Analects* were arrested and put to death.

The clay figures that guard Shi Huangdi's tomb

Many people were unhappy with Shi Huangdi's changes. They particularly disliked that Shi Huangdi taxed them heavily. These taxes and other harsh laws led to civil war soon after the First Emperor's death in 210 B.C. By 206 B.C. the Qin dynasty had collapsed.

More than 2,000 years after Shi Huangdi's death, archaeologists uncovered another Qin building project—the clay soldiers that guard Shi Huangdi's tomb. Even today they seem to protect him, as real soldiers guarded him while he lived.

REVIEW **Why did Shi Huangdi destroy copies of the *Analects*?**

⊛ **MAKE INFERENCES**

The Han Dynasty

The Han dynasty gained control of China in 202 B.C. and ruled for about 400 years. The Han relied on the ideas of both Confucianism and Legalism.

Like the Qin emperor, the Han emperor had power over all matters. Under the Han, more people were employed in the **civil service**, or the day-to-day running of the government. Usually, nobles or government officials recommended people for civil service jobs. Sometimes tests were given to make sure that candidates had the skills needed for the positions.

During the time of the Han dynasty, education grew in importance. For example, the Han established a university to train people for civil service jobs. The Han also supported the teaching of the ideas of not only Confucianism but also **Daoism** (DOW•ih•zuhm). Daoism teaches that the key to long life and happiness is to accept life as it is.

There were important inventions during the Han dynasty as well. In A.D. 132 a Han inventor created the world's first seismograph, an instrument that detects and measures earthquakes. Of all their innovations, the Han are perhaps best known for the invention of paper in 105 B.C.

Han influence spread by way of the Silk Road. The **Silk Road** was an overland trade route that linked China with Europe.

The Han dynasty ended in A.D. 220. Han ideas lived on, however, and can still be seen in the culture of the Chinese people today. It is no wonder that the Chinese people still call themselves the children of the Han.

REVIEW **What was the name of the overland trade route between China and Europe?**

Seismograph

In about A.D. 132 Chang Heng invented China's first seismograph. A modern seismograph tells the location and strength of earthquakes. Chang's early seismograph worked in much the same way. A rod inside the seismograph fell toward the dragon's head nearest the earthquake, making a loud noise. A ball then dropped down from the dragon's mouth into a bronze frog below. The direction in which the ball fell showed the general location of the earthquake.

LESSON 3 REVIEW

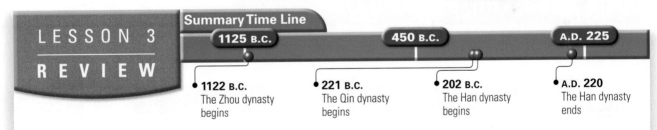

Summary Time Line

1125 B.C.   450 B.C.   A.D. 225

1122 B.C.
The Zhou dynasty begins

221 B.C.
The Qin dynasty begins

202 B.C.
The Han dynasty begins

A.D. 220
The Han dynasty ends

 MAKE INFERENCES Why do you think Chinese people still call themselves the children of the Han?

1 BIG IDEA How did the Zhou, Qin, and Han dynasties affect Chinese culture and society?

2 VOCABULARY Use the terms **filial piety** and **philosopher** in a sentence that describes **Confucianism**.

3 TIME LINE Did the Han dynasty begin before or after the Qin dynasty?

4 CULTURE On what did Confucius base many of his ideas about government and society?

5 CRITICAL THINKING—Evaluate Why might Shi Huangdi have wanted statues of soldiers placed near his tomb?

 PERFORMANCE—Draw a Diagram Read more about the Great Wall of China that stands today. Then draw a diagram that shows how workers built a section of the Great Wall. Share your diagram with a classmate.

·SKILLS·

CHART AND GRAPH

Read a Telescoping Time Line

VOCABULARY

telescoping time line

▶ WHY IT MATTERS

A time line allows you to show events in chronological, or time, order. Sometimes you may want to show more of the details about a certain part of a time line. One way to show these details is to use a **telescoping time line**. Just as a telescope helps you take a closer look at a faraway object, a telescoping time line lets you take a closer look at a time in history.

▶ WHAT YOU NEED TO KNOW

Knowing how to read a telescoping time line can help you learn the details of a period of history. The following tips will help you read a telescoping time line.

- Determine the time period covered by the main time line. The main time line on these pages covers the period from 1200 B.C. to A.D. 300. It is divided into spans of 300 years.

- Look at the telescoping part of the time line, and determine the years it covers. This one covers the years 225 B.C. to 205 B.C. It is divided into spans of 5 years.

- The main time line and the telescoping part cover different amounts of time. The telescoping part of the time line shows more detail about a shorter time period that is part of the main time line.

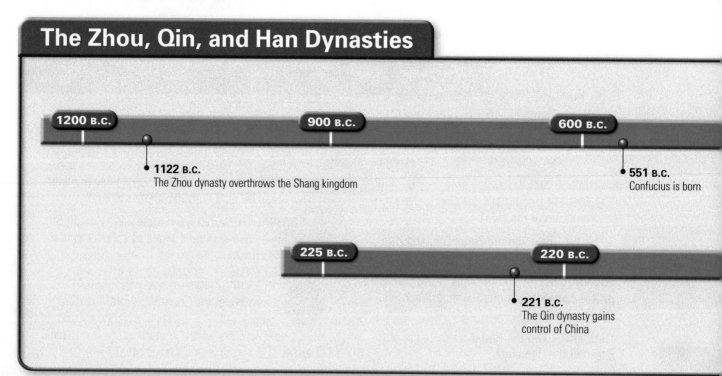

The Zhou, Qin, and Han Dynasties

1200 B.C.   900 B.C.   600 B.C.

1122 B.C.
The Zhou dynasty overthrows the Shang kingdom

551 B.C.
Confucius is born

225 B.C.   220 B.C.

221 B.C.
The Qin dynasty gains control of China

▶ PRACTICE THE SKILL

Use the telescoping time line to answer these questions.

1 Which dynasty had the longest reign?

2 Which event took place first, Confucius's birth or the invention of paper?

3 Which came first, the Warring States period or the Han dynasty?

4 What dynasty does the telescoping part of the time line show?

5 Did Shi Huangdi die before or after the Qin Great Wall was started?

▶ APPLY WHAT YOU LEARNED

Make a time line of your life, using spans of one year. Make a telescoping part for a recent year in your life, showing it in spans of one month. Include at least three events in the telescoping part. Share your time line with a family member.

This illustration shows a Chinese papermaker.

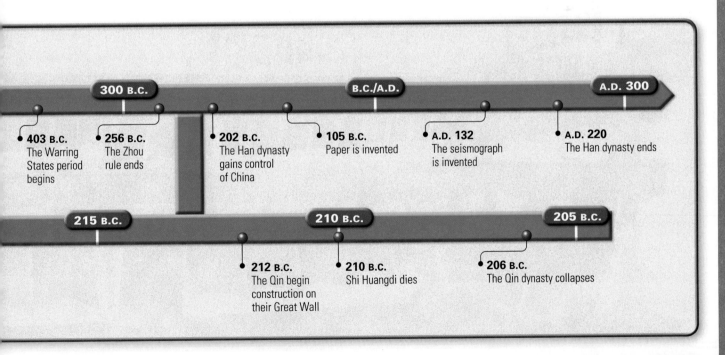

403 B.C.
The Warring States period begins

256 B.C.
The Zhou rule ends

300 B.C.

202 B.C.
The Han dynasty gains control of China

105 B.C.
Paper is invented

B.C./A.D.

A.D. 132
The seismograph is invented

A.D. 220
The Han dynasty ends

A.D. 300

215 B.C.

212 B.C.
The Qin begin construction on their Great Wall

210 B.C.

210 B.C.
Shi Huangdi dies

206 B.C.
The Qin dynasty collapses

205 B.C.

PRIMARY SOURCES

Chinese Designs

The ancient Chinese developed ways to work with bronze and other natural resources to create many beautiful objects. During the Shang dynasty, more than 3,000 years ago, artists learned to carve jade—a green stone—into fine jewelry. They also developed new ways of casting bronze to create elaborate designs. The artists of the Zhou dynasty developed these skills further. In 1977, archaeologists found a tomb belonging to a Marquis Yi of the Zeng state, who died in 433 B.C. Among many fine bronze and jade objects, they found a set of 65 bronze bells. Scientists were amazed to discover that each perfectly tuned bell can sound either of two tones, depending on where it is struck.

The hammers held by this Chinese musician are used to play bronze bells.

 FROM THE HUBEI PROVINCIAL MUSEUM IN CHINA

This rack of 65 bronze bells from Yi's tomb is the heaviest musical instrument in the world.

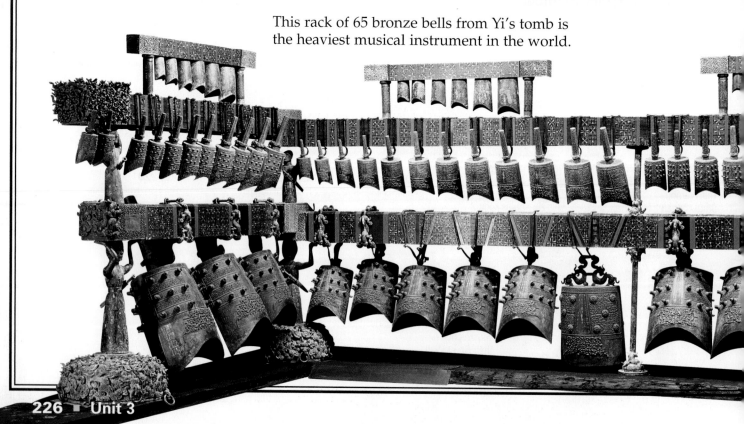

A bronze lamp with a camel and rider made during the late Zhou dynasty

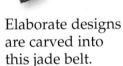
Elaborate designs are carved into this jade belt.

Analyze the Primary Source

1 What can you tell about Yi from the bells found in his tomb?

2 Why do you think the ancient Chinese used bronze and jade in their designs?

3 When do you think the ancient Chinese may have used large bronze instruments like the bells and the drum?

This large bronze drum can be played on both ends.

ACTIVITY

Design and Draw Design a bronze musical instrument that might have been used during the Zhou dynasty. Draw your instrument on a piece of paper. Be sure to decorate your instrument with elaborate designs.

RESEARCH

Visit The Learning Site at **www.harcourtschool.com** to research other primary sources.

Review and Test Preparation

Summary Time Line

2000 B.C.   1500 B.C.

About 2000 B.C.
Aryans from western Asia begin
to migrate into Indus Valley

Make Inferences

Complete this graphic organizer to show that you understand
how to make inferences about ancient India. A copy of this
graphic organizer appears on page 69 of the Activity Book.

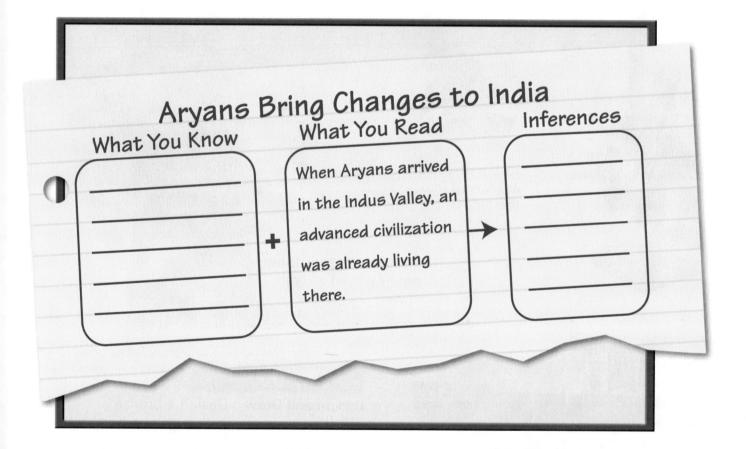

Aryans Bring Changes to India

What You Know + **What You Read** → **Inferences**

When Aryans arrived
in the Indus Valley, an
advanced civilization
was already living
there.

THINK & WRITE

Write a Newspaper Editorial   Write an
editorial, or opinion column, that explains why
you would choose to live in a large nation or
a small one. Discuss the advantages of your
choice as well as the disadvantages of the
other option. Give examples from Chapter 7
to support your opinion.

Write a Personal Journal Entry   Imagine
that you are about to take over control of
a Chinese empire. You can rule your empire
by following the ideas of Confucianism or by
following the ideas of Legalism. Decide which
one will work better and explain your choice in
a personal journal entry.

1122 B.C.
The Zhou dynasty begins

563 B.C.
Buddha is born

About 320 B.C.
The Maurya Empire begins

232 B.C.
Ashoka dies

The Maurya Empire
begins to decline

202 B.C.
The Han Dynasty gains
control of China

A.D. 320
The Gupta
Empire begins

USE THE TIME LINE

1 About how many years passed between the death of Ashoka and the beginning of the Gupta Empire?

2 Which dynasty ruled China first, the Han or the Zhou?

USE VOCABULARY

Use each term in a sentence or two to explain both what the term means and how that meaning relates to the cultures described in this chapter.

3 **Sanskrit** (p. 209)

4 **enlightenment** (p. 210)

5 **nonviolence** (p. 210)

6 **missionary** (p. 214)

7 **feudalism** (p. 219)

8 **philosopher** (p. 219)

RECALL FACTS

Answer these questions.

9 Which mountain ranges did the Aryans pass through to reach the Indian subcontinent?

10 What part of the world did the Maurya Empire control?

Write the letter of the best choice.

11 **TEST PREP** In the caste system, which group worked as servants of the other three classes?
A Brahmans
B Kshatriyas
C Vaisyas
D Shudras

12 **TEST PREP** Which religion is based on Four Noble Truths, including the search for nirvana?
F Hinduism
G Jainism
H Buddhism
J Daoism

13 **TEST PREP** Which leader has been called "the greatest and noblest ruler India has known"?
A Chandragupta Maurya
B Ashoka
C Chandragupta I
D Chandragupta II

14 **TEST PREP** Which Chinese dynasty marked the beginning of China's classical age and ruled China the longest?
F Shang
G Zhou
H Qin
J Han

THINK CRITICALLY

15 Why do you think using standard measuring and writing systems helped unite people under the Qin dynasty?

16 How is the relationship between a leader and a citizen like the relationship between a parent and a child? How is it different?

APPLY SKILLS

Read a Telescoping Time Line

17 Use the information in the time line on pages 224–225 to answer these questions. Why is there a telescoping view of the time period for 225 B.C. to 205 B.C.? What important events occurred in this period?

Xi'an, China

GET READY

The city of Xi'an (SHEE•AHN), formerly Chang'an, is located in the center of China. Xi'an was once the capital of China and a major trade center. Inside the old city walls, visitors can see many historic places. There are also modern universities, museums, and shopping centers to visit.

One popular site is The Big Wild Goose Pagoda, the most famous pagoda in China. Built in A.D. 589, it is seven stories tall. The Bell Tower and Drum Tower, in the center of the city, also attract visitors. The bell and the drum once marked the hours of the day for monks to worship.

LOCATE IT

Xi'an

CHINA

WHAT TO SEE

Each year, the Chinese New Year is represented by one of twelve animals. This Chinese New Year's festival honors the dragon.

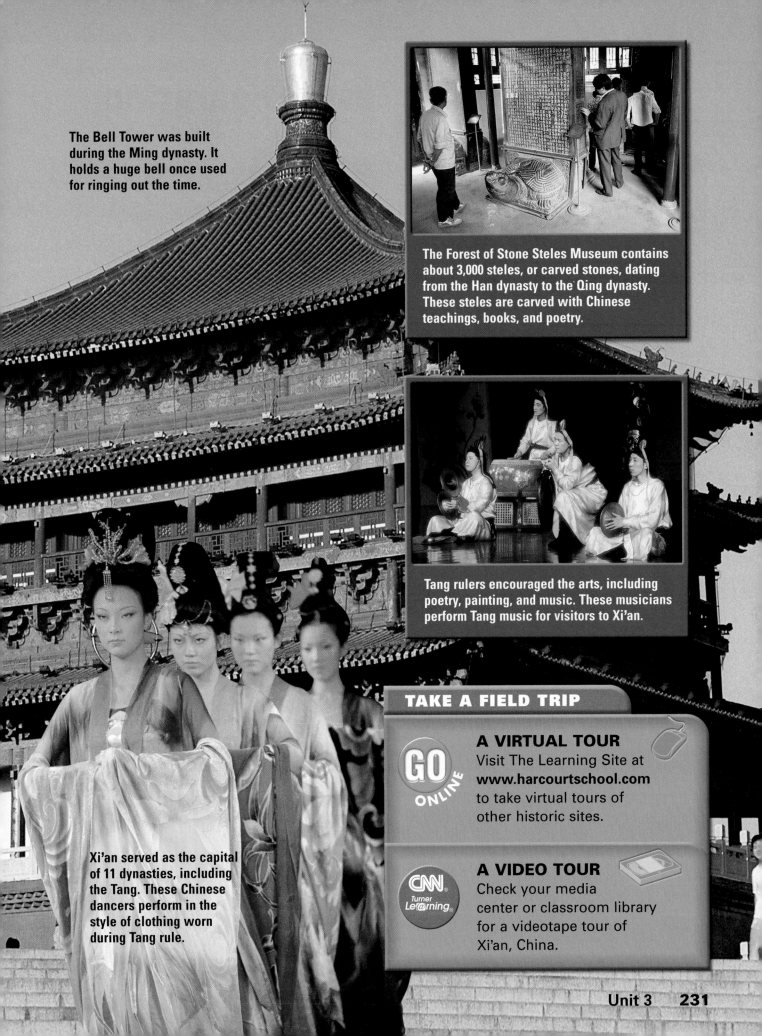

The Bell Tower was built during the Ming dynasty. It holds a huge bell once used for ringing out the time.

The Forest of Stone Steles Museum contains about 3,000 steles, or carved stones, dating from the Han dynasty to the Qing dynasty. These steles are carved with Chinese teachings, books, and poetry.

Tang rulers encouraged the arts, including poetry, painting, and music. These musicians perform Tang music for visitors to Xi'an.

Xi'an served as the capital of 11 dynasties, including the Tang. These Chinese dancers perform in the style of clothing worn during Tang rule.

TAKE A FIELD TRIP

GO ONLINE

A VIRTUAL TOUR
Visit The Learning Site at www.harcourtschool.com to take virtual tours of other historic sites.

CNN Turner Le@rning

A VIDEO TOUR
Check your media center or classroom library for a videotape tour of Xi'an, China.

3 Review and Test Preparation

VISUAL SUMMARY

Write an Outline   Use the picture captions in the time line below as the main headings of an outline of Unit 3. Use Roman numerals to label each main heading. Under each heading, list two or three facts about that event. Label those facts with capital letters A, B, C, and so on.

USE VOCABULARY

For each pair of terms, write two or three sentences that explain what both words mean and how they are related.

1   **monotheism** (p. 181), **polytheism** (p. 200)

2   **exodus** (p. 182), **Ten Commandments** (p. 182)

3   **infantry** (p. 197), **cavalry** (p. 197)

4   **turning point** (p. 214), **edict** (p. 214)

RECALL FACTS

Answer these questions.

5   How did the Persian army under Cyrus the Great overwhelm its enemies?

6   On which two subjects did Confucius focus his ideas and teachings?

Write the letter of the best choice.

7   **TEST PREP**   Each of these has its roots in Indus Valley culture *except*—
   A Hinduism.
   B Buddhism.
   C Jainism.
   D Daoism.

8   **TEST PREP**   Which dynasty had such a lasting influence that today many Chinese people still call themselves "the children of" that dynasty?
   F the Han
   G the Qin
   H the Qi
   J the Chu

THINK CRITICALLY

9   Why do you think that the time of the Gupta Empire became the classical age of India?

10   What do you think was the most important contribution that the ancient Israelites made to world culture?

Visual Summary

2000 B.C.   **1500 B.C.**   **1000 B.C.**

2000 B.C. **Aryans migrate to India** p. 206

1100 B.C. **Phoenician city-states reach the height of their power** p. 189

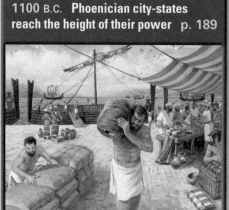

1020 B.C. **The kingdom of Israel is formed** p. 183

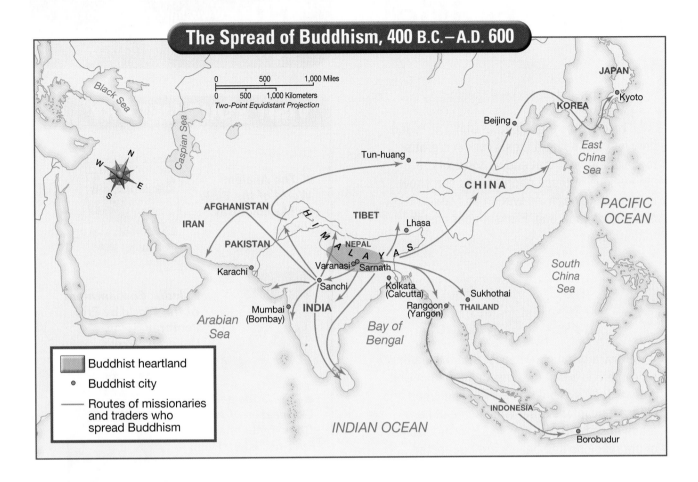

The Spread of Buddhism, 400 B.C.–A.D. 600

0   500   1,000 Miles
0   500   1,000 Kilometers
Two-Point Equidistant Projection

Black Sea

Caspian Sea

JAPAN
Kyoto

KOREA
Beijing

Tun-huang

East China Sea

CHINA

PACIFIC OCEAN

AFGHANISTAN

HIMALAYAS

TIBET

Lhasa

IRAN

PAKISTAN

NEPAL

Karachi

Varanasi
Sarnath

South China Sea

Sanchi

Kolkata (Calcutta)

Mumbai (Bombay)

INDIA

Sukhothai
THAILAND

Rangoon (Yangon)

Arabian Sea

Bay of Bengal

INDONESIA

INDIAN OCEAN

Borobudur

Legend:
- Buddhist heartland
- Buddhist city
- Routes of missionaries and traders who spread Buddhism

APPLY SKILLS

Follow Routes on a Map
Use the map on this page to answer these questions.

MAP AND GLOBE SKILLS

11 Which cities on the map lie within the Buddhist heartland?

12 From which city in central India did Buddhism spread to Pakistan, Afghanistan, and Iran?

13 Which mountain range did Buddhist missionaries and traders cross to reach Tibet?

14 Which country did Buddhism reach first, Korea or Japan?

500 B.C.

B.C. / A.D.

A.D. 500

550 B.C. Cyrus builds the Persian Empire p. 196

100 B.C. The Han dynasty's influence spreads along the Silk Road p. 223

A.D. 320 The Gupta Empire begins in India p. 215

233

Unit Activities

GO ONLINE

Visit The Learning Site at
www.harcourtschool.com
for additional activities.

Make an Innovations Poster

The cultures described in Unit 3 all found new ways of doing things. Work in a group to make a poster that shows some of the innovations of these peoples. You can show people using each innovation or draw a diagram of each one. Present your poster to the class.

Draw a Graphic Organizer

Draw a graphic organizer that names the religions and belief systems described in Unit 3. Give details about each, including when and where it developed and what some of its teachings are. Draw lines to show how some of the religions and beliefs are connected.

VISIT YOUR LIBRARY

- ■ *The Ancient World of the Bible* by Malcolm Day. Viking.

- ■ *India: Enchantment of the World* by Erin Pembrey Swan. Children's Press.

- ■ *The Gods and Goddesses of Ancient China* by Leonard Everett Fisher. Holiday House.

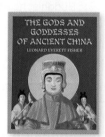

COMPLETE THE UNIT PROJECT

Prepare a Multimedia Presentation

Work with a group to complete the unit project—a multimedia presentation. First, gather the parts of your presentation, such as pictures, costumes, and video. Then, organize all your materials to help you present information about an early eastern civilization. Invite students from other classes to see your presentation.

Western Civilizations

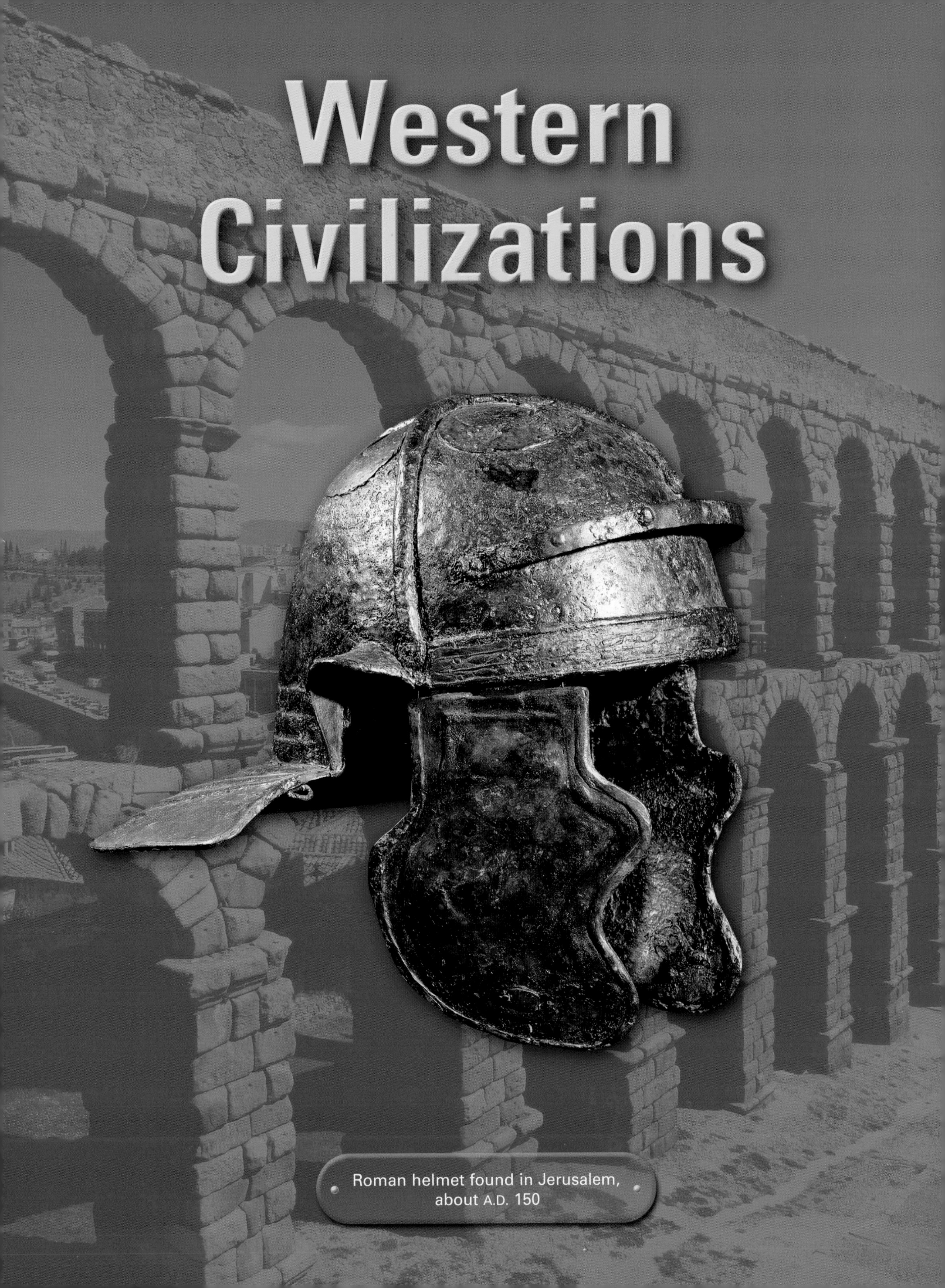

Roman helmet found in Jerusalem,
about A.D. 150

Ancient Roman aqueduct, or structure that carries water, in Segovia, Spain

Western Civilizations

"To the glory that was Greece, And the grandeur that was Rome."

—Edgar Allan Poe, from the poem "To Helen," 1831

Preview the Content

Quickly scan the unit. Use what you see to answer these questions: Who and what is the unit about? When did the events happen? Where are the places shown in the photographs? Why is what happened important? Make a chart to record your responses.

	WHO?	WHAT?	WHEN?	WHERE?	WHY?
Chapter 8	_____	_____	_____	_____	_____
Chapter 9	_____	_____	_____	_____	_____

Preview the Vocabulary

Context Clues   Context clues are the words in sentences that help you figure out the meanings of unfamiliar words. Scan the unit and find the words *oligarchy, aristocracy, democracy, confederation, republic, dictator,* and *triumvirate*. Then use context clues to figure out each word's meaning.

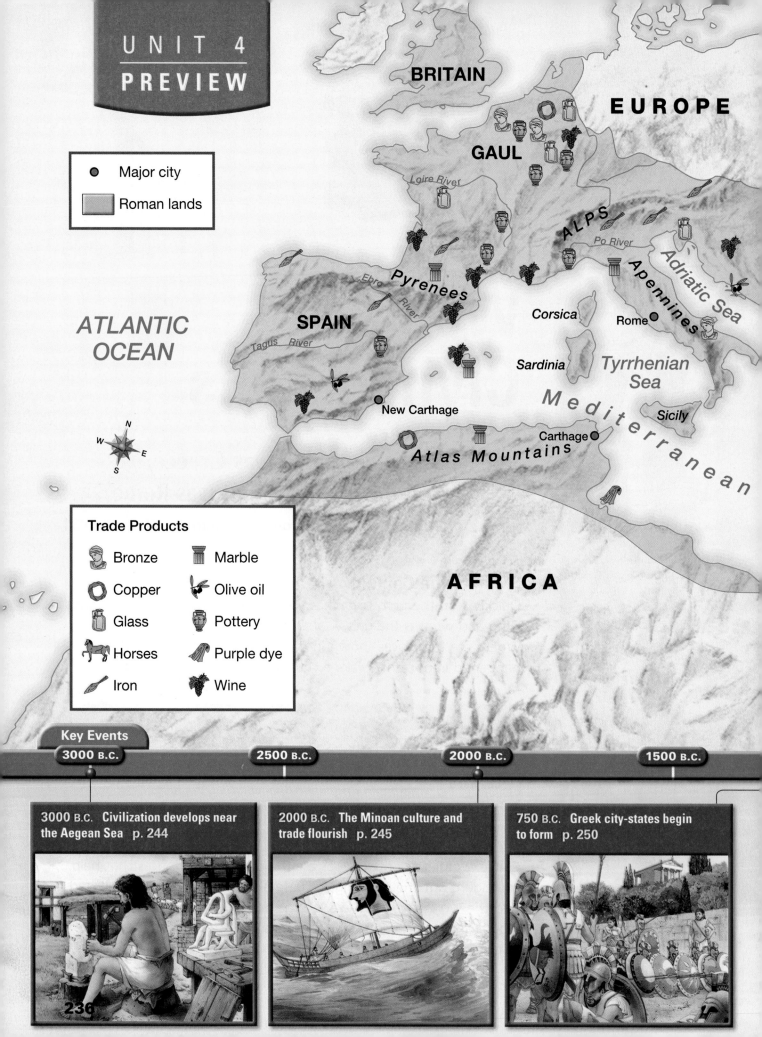

BRITAIN

EUROPE

GAUL

ALPS

Loire River

Po River

Pyrenees

Apennines

Adriatic Sea

Ebro River

SPAIN

Corsica

Rome

Tagus River

Sardinia

Tyrrhenian Sea

ATLANTIC OCEAN

New Carthage

Sicily

Carthage

Atlas Mountains

Mediterranean

AFRICA

N W E S

Major city

Roman lands

Trade Products

Bronze		Marble	
Copper		Olive oil	
Glass		Pottery	
Horses		Purple dye	
Iron		Wine	

Key Events

3000 B.C.   2500 B.C.   2000 B.C.   1500 B.C.

3000 B.C. Civilization develops near the Aegean Sea p. 244

2000 B.C. The Minoan culture and trade flourish p. 245

750 B.C. Greek city-states begin to form p. 250

236

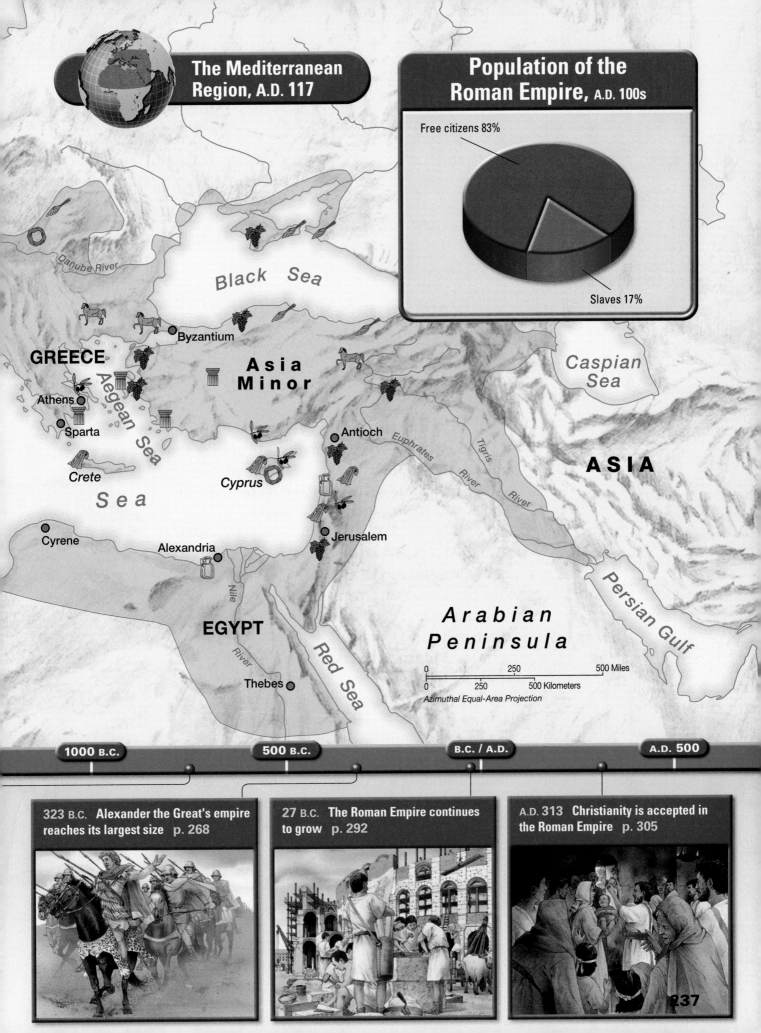

The Mediterranean Region, A.D. 117

Population of the Roman Empire, A.D. 100s

Free citizens 83%

Slaves 17%

Danube River

Black Sea

Byzantium

GREECE

Asia Minor

Caspian Sea

Athens

Aegean Sea

Sparta

Antioch

Euphrates

Tigris River

River

ASIA

Crete

Cyprus

Sea

Cyrene

Jerusalem

Alexandria

Nile River

EGYPT

Arabian Peninsula

Persian Gulf

Red Sea

500 Miles

250

500 Kilometers

250

Azimuthal Equal-Area Projection

Thebes

1000 B.C.

500 B.C.

B.C. / A.D.

A.D. 500

323 B.C. Alexander the Great's empire reaches its largest size p. 268

27 B.C. The Roman Empire continues to grow p. 292

A.D. 313 Christianity is accepted in the Roman Empire p. 305

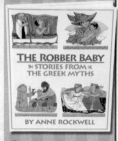

PANDORA'S BOX

from *The Robber Baby:
Stories from the Greek Myths*

by Anne Rockwell

**The ancient Greeks believed in many gods
and goddesses. Greek myths told stories about
how the actions of the gods and goddesses
affected people on Earth. Read on to discover
one of the best-known Greek myths.**

Pandora was made, not born as other people
are. Hephaestus modeled her out of clay. He
made her a young woman as beautiful as his
wife, Aphrodite, the goddess of love and beauty.
Each of the gods and goddesses gave Pandora
a gift. Then Athene, the goddess of wisdom,
breathed life into her. Most of the gifts the gods
gave her were good ones. But unfortunately
Hermes, as always full of tricks and mischief,
gave her more curiosity than was good for her.
Pandora was sent to live on earth. She had no
trouble finding a good husband, for the gods
and goddesses had given her the gifts of smiles
and sweetness and wit and winning ways.
Besides that, she was rich, for as a wedding gift
the gods and goddesses gave her a box that had
been made by Hephaestus. It was as beautiful as
Pandora and very valuable, too.

| **Hephaestus** | Greek god of fire |
| **Hermes** | messenger of the gods |

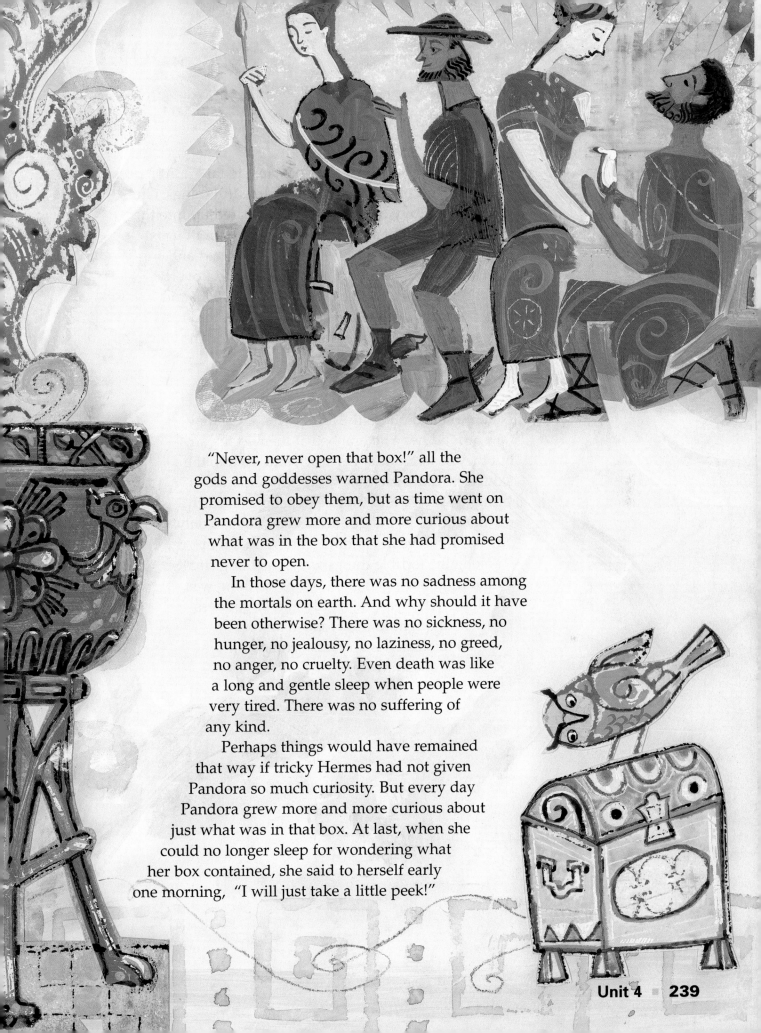

"Never, never open that box!" all the
gods and goddesses warned Pandora. She
promised to obey them, but as time went on
Pandora grew more and more curious about
what was in the box that she had promised
never to open.

In those days, there was no sadness among
the mortals on earth. And why should it have
been otherwise? There was no sickness, no
hunger, no jealousy, no laziness, no greed,
no anger, no cruelty. Even death was like
a long and gentle sleep when people were
very tired. There was no suffering of
any kind.

Perhaps things would have remained
that way if tricky Hermes had not given
Pandora so much curiosity. But every day
Pandora grew more and more curious about
just what was in that box. At last, when she
could no longer sleep for wondering what
her box contained, she said to herself early
one morning, "I will just take a little peek!"

So she opened the box, just to take a little peek.
And out of that box flew dreadful things. Greed
and Envy came out first and soared up into the
clean, bright air. Pandora tried to slam the box
shut, but she could not. Out flew Hatred and
Cruelty with terrible force. Hunger and Poverty
followed. Then Sickness came, and Despair, and
all the other terrible things that the gods and
goddesses knew should remain safely hidden
in that box.

Pandora had set them all free.

"Come back! Come back where you belong!"
Pandora called out to the terrible things as they
flew around her. She grabbed at them in the air,
but they soared out of her reach and up into the
sky. None came back. They are still out there
bringing misery and trouble to people on earth.

But the gods and goddesses had not put only
dreadful things in Pandora's box. Hidden in
among the terrible things was something small
and fragile-winged and good. This thing was
Hope. Who was the kindly god or goddess
who thought to put Hope in among
all the miseries and misfortunes?

No one knows.

But because Hope was hidden in Pandora's box, whenever there is too much trouble and sadness among us mortals, Hope makes us think that tomorrow will be better.

And soon Pandora dried her tears.

"I hope I will never be too curious again!" she said.

And she never was.

Analyze the Literature

❶ What caused Pandora to open the box?

❷ In what ways does the story explain how the actions of the gods affected people on Earth?

❸ Why do you think myths were important to the ancient Greeks?

READ A BOOK

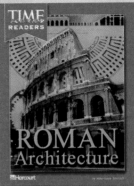

START THE UNIT PROJECT

Plan a Festival As you read this unit, collect information about the cultures of ancient Greece. Start to search the ways people in ancient Greece dressed, the kinds of pastimes they enjoyed, and the art and philosophy they appreciated. Use the information you gather to work with your classmates to plan a Greek culture festival.

USE TECHNOLOGY

GO ONLINE Visit The Learning Site at **www.harcourtschool.com** for additional activities, primary sources, and other resources to use in this unit.

THE ACROPOLIS, ATHENS, GREECE

Ancient cities were often built around a walled fort at the top of a hill so that they could be defended. The highest ground was called the acropolis, a Greek word for "high city." The most famous acropolis of all, the Acropolis in Athens, Greece, was built more than 4,000 years ago. Today, the structure remains an important site in the city.

LOCATE IT

GREECE

Athens

The Ancient Greeks

❝Surely, knowing about excellence is not enough. We must try to possess it and use it.❞

—Aristotle, *The Politics,* 350 B.C.

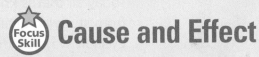

Cause and Effect

A **cause** is an event or action that makes something else happen. An **effect** is what happens as a result of that event or action.

As you read this chapter, list the causes and effects of the key events.

• **Identify and list important events.**

• **Write down the effects of each of these events.**

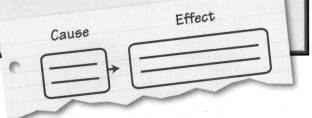

Cause → Effect

CAUSE AND EFFECT

As you read, look for the causes and effects in the rise of the Aegean civilization.

BIG IDEA

Ancient cultures that developed around the Aegean Sea were shaped by sea travel and trade.

VOCABULARY

dominant
mythology
decimal system
strategic
epic

Early Greece

| 3000 B.C. | 2000 B.C. | 1000 B.C. | B.C./A.D. |

3000 B.C.– 1000 B.C.

The present-day country of Greece lies in the southern part of the Balkan Peninsula in southeastern Europe. The Greek mainland is mountainous, with a rugged coastline cut by many inlets and surrounded by as many as 2,000 islands. Between 3000 B.C. and 1000 B.C., four cultures flourished on the Greek islands and the mainland shores. These were the Cycladic (sih•KLA•dik), the Minoan (muh•NOH•uhn), the Mycenaean (my•suh•NEE•uhn), and the Trojan cultures. Together they are known as the Aegean (ih•JEE•uhn) civilization because of their locations in and around the Aegean Sea. Nearly all that is known about the Aegean civilization comes from archaeological studies.

The Cycladic Culture

The Cyclades (SIH•kluh•deez) are a group of about 200 islands located east of the Greek mainland in the southern Aegean Sea. In about 3000 B.C. the Cycladic culture began on these islands. Today all that is known about this culture and its people comes from studying artifacts. Because of this, many questions about Cycladic ways of life may never be answered.

Once home to the Cycladic culture, the Cyclades islands form a circle in the southern Aegean Sea. One of these islands is shown below. This carving of a human head (left) was made in the Cyclades more than 4,000 years ago.

FAST FACT No place in present-day Greece is more than 85 miles (137 km) from the sea. Living close to large waterways affects ways of life today, as it did in the ancient past.

Archaeologists have learned that most Cycladic people made their living by fishing or trading. Others were farmers who grew grapes, olives, and other crops. Highly skilled Cycladic craftworkers made pottery and small marble figures. Most Cycladic artifacts have been found in tombs. However, Cycladic pottery found at sites belonging to other cultures shows that trading took place.

After about 2000 B.C. the Cycladic culture began to weaken. As it did, the people began to follow the customs and traditions of the **dominant**, or more powerful, neighboring cultures.

REVIEW How do archaeologists know about people of the Cycladic culture?

The Minoan Culture

Minoan culture began on the large island of Crete in about 2700 B.C. Crete lies about 60 miles (97 km) southeast of the Greek mainland. Historians named this culture in honor of Minos (MY•nuhs), the king of Crete in Greek mythology. A **mythology** is a collection of myths, or traditional stories, handed down from generation to generation. Myths offer an explanation of how things in nature or human events came to be.

The Minoan culture began as an agricultural society. Over time farming villages grew into cities. The largest of the Minoan cities were Knossos (NAH•suhs), Phaistos (FES•tuhs), Mallia, and Kato Zakro.

This wall painting of dolphins and fish at Knossos shows the importance of the sea to the Minoan way of life.

In about 2000 B.C. the Minoans began to build large, richly decorated palaces. The largest palace was at Knossos. It stood at least three stories high and covered an area about the size of three football fields.

From wall paintings at Knossos, archaeologists have learned that the Minoans were expert sailors. They traded in lands all around the Mediterranean Sea, including Egypt.

LOCATE IT

Cyclades

GREECE

Andros

Kéa

Naxos

Milos

Thira

Mediterranean Sea

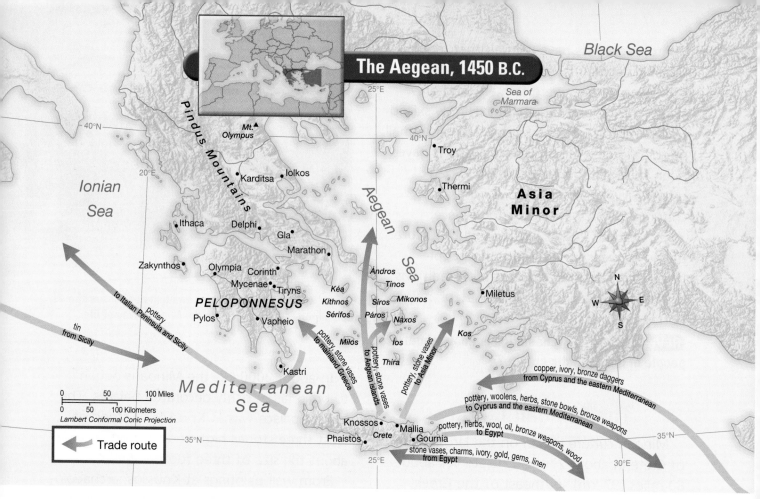

The Aegean, 1450 B.C.

Black Sea

Sea of Marmara

Ionian Sea

Pindus Mountains

Mt. Olympus

Troy

Thermi

Asia Minor

Aegean Sea

Karditsa · Iolkos

Ithaca

Delphi

Gla

Marathon

Zakynthos

Olympia Corinth

Mycenae · Tiryns

PELOPONNESUS

Pylos · Vapheio

Ándros

Tínos

Kéa

Kíthnos Síros Míkonos

Sérifos Páros Náxos

Miletus

Kos

Milos Íos

Thíra

Kastri

Mediterranean Sea

tin from Sicily

pottery to Italian Peninsula and Sicily

pottery, stone vases to mainland Greece

pottery, stone vases to Aegean islands

pottery, stone vases to Asia Minor

copper, ivory, bronze daggers from Cyprus and the eastern Mediterranean

pottery, woolens, herbs, stone bowls, bronze weapons to Cyprus and the eastern Mediterranean

pottery, herbs, wool, oil, bronze weapons, wood to Egypt

stone vases, charms, ivory, gold, gems, linen from Egypt

Knossos · Mallia

Phaistos Crete Gournia

0   50   100 Miles
0   50   100 Kilometers
Lambert Conformal Conic Projection

← Trade route

Location   The Minoan culture on the island of Crete was a center for trade across three seas.

❖ How did the location of Crete help the Minoans trade with other cultures?

GEOGRAPHY THEME

This exchange of goods also led to an exchange of ideas. One idea was an important new technology.

Using a process they learned from civilizations in southwestern Asia, the Minoans mixed copper and tin to form bronze. They made weapons, tools, and bowls from bronze and other metals.

The Minoans had both a counting system and a writing system for keeping records of their trade. To count, the Minoans used a **decimal system**, a system based on the number 10. Their writing system used pictographs

This lifelike carved stone bull was used by the Minoans as a drinking cup.

written on clay tablets to stand for the sounds in words. No one has been able to read the oldest of the Minoan tablets yet. The Minoans may have used a language other than Greek.

Many of the oldest tablets survived a great fire that destroyed nearly all the cities and palaces on Crete in about 1450 B.C. Only the palace at Knossos remained. After the fire a people called the Mycenaeans ruled Crete. By the 1100s B.C. the Minoan culture had disappeared.

REVIEW How did Minoan trading lead to the use of bronze?

🎯 **CAUSE AND EFFECT**

The Mycenaean Culture

The Mycenaean culture takes its name from the city of Mycenae. This city was located on the large southern peninsula of Greece called the Peloponnesus (peh•luh•puh•NEE•suhs). Archaeologists believe that a settlement at Mycenae was started in about 1900 B.C. Other cities that shared this culture were spread throughout the Aegean region. By the 1500s B.C. the Mycenaeans had become the dominant culture in the area.

A gold mask found in a tomb at Mycenae.

As a result of trading, the Mycenaeans learned Minoan ways and adapted them to fit their own culture. For example, they borrowed Minoan art styles and writing. The Mycenaeans adapted the writing to suit their own language, an early form of Greek. The Mycenaeans built palaces in their cities, too. During the 1300s B.C. they built palaces in Mycenae, Athens, Thebes, Pylos, and Tiryns (TIR•uhnz). Mycenaean palaces were much smaller than those built by the Minoans. Many were surrounded by huge walls with a large gateway. This suggests that the palaces were important as places of safety during times of war.

Like the Minoans, Mycenaeans sailed the Mediterranean Sea in all directions. They traveled to trade, to start new settlements, and to make war. Sometimes the Mycenaeans conquered less-powerful peoples, such as the Minoans.

• SCIENCE AND TECHNOLOGY •

Underwater Archaeology

Not all archaeologists work on land. Some work in Earth's oceans and seas. Working underwater is difficult and requires special equipment. Ancient shipwrecks are not often visible from the water's surface. To find these wrecks, archaeologists use sonar—underwater sound waves used to locate objects on the ocean floor. Once a wreck is located, specially trained archaeologists visit the wreck and collect artifacts. To do this, they wear scuba diving equipment. If the wreck lies in water that is too deep for divers, remote-control submarines are sometimes used to collect artifacts.

A diver (right) explores a Mycenaean shipwreck from about 1300 B.C. Artifacts recovered include the world's oldest bookbinding (left) and trade goods such as this medallion (above).

In about 1200 B.C. the Mycenaean culture suddenly came to an end. A large earthquake destroyed many Mycenaean settlements. A few were rebuilt, but the Mycenaeans never regained their earlier power. Some historians believe it was because of weak leaders. Others think that food shortages caused people to move away from the cities. Still others believe that a people known as the Dorians migrated into the area from the north. The Mycenaean people may have chosen to live among the newcomers.

REVIEW What parts of Minoan culture did the Mycenaeans adopt?

FAST FACT

Stories are still told today of the clever weapon used to gain entry to the city of Troy. Because of this, attempting to persuade another person by trickery is sometimes called using a Trojan horse.

The Trojan Culture

The Trojan culture was centered in the ancient city of Troy, in Asia Minor. From as early as 2900 B.C., thick walls surrounded the city. Troy was located on a high point of land near the Dardanelles (dar•duhn•ELZ), a strait that connects the Aegean Sea with the Sea of Marmara (MAR•muh•ruh). This waterway, which separates Asia from Europe, allowed passage to the Black Sea for trading or warfare. Troy's location was therefore **strategic**, or of great importance.

The Trojans farmed, raised horses, and herded sheep. They also traded with the Mycenaeans and other cultures.

Today people can learn about Troy from stories that are a part of world literature.

Troy is described in the *Iliad* (IH•lee•uhd) and the *Odyssey* (AH•duh•see), epics written by the Greek poet Homer. An **epic** is a long poem that tells about important events in the life

of a hero or heroes. Stories about the Trojan War were already hundreds of years old when Homer created his epics in about 750 B.C. Most historians believe that the Mycenaeans invaded and destroyed Troy around 1250 B.C.

Homer's *Odyssey* tells the story of Odysseus (oh•DIH•see•uhs), a legendary Mycenaean hero. For ten years the Mycenaeans tried to capture the city of Troy. The high stone walls of Troy seemed impossible to break through. Homer says that Odysseus ordered workers to build a huge, hollow wooden horse. When the horse was finished, some Mycenaean soldiers hid inside it.

Homer

The Mycenaeans left the horse at the gates of Troy, boarded their ships, and pretended to leave.

Believing the horse to be a peace offering, the Trojans pulled it into their city. That night the Mycenaean soldiers crawled out of their hiding place. They opened the city gates and let in the rest of the Mycenaean army. By morning they had defeated the Trojans and burned down the city of Troy.

Stories of Mycenaean heroes, the Trojan War, and other early legends helped shape the cultures of later Greek peoples.

REVIEW What Greek epics are now a part of world literature?

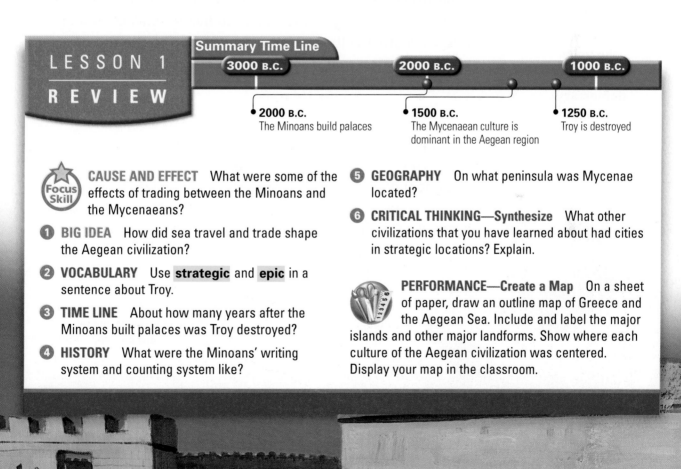

LESSON 1 REVIEW

Summary Time Line

3000 B.C. — 2000 B.C. — 1000 B.C.

2000 B.C.
The Minoans build palaces

1500 B.C.
The Mycenaean culture is dominant in the Aegean region

1250 B.C.
Troy is destroyed

Focus Skill **CAUSE AND EFFECT** What were some of the effects of trading between the Minoans and the Mycenaeans?

1 BIG IDEA How did sea travel and trade shape the Aegean civilization?

2 VOCABULARY Use **strategic** and **epic** in a sentence about Troy.

3 TIME LINE About how many years after the Minoans built palaces was Troy destroyed?

4 HISTORY What were the Minoans' writing system and counting system like?

5 GEOGRAPHY On what peninsula was Mycenae located?

6 CRITICAL THINKING—Synthesize What other civilizations that you have learned about had cities in strategic locations? Explain.

PERFORMANCE—Create a Map On a sheet of paper, draw an outline map of Greece and the Aegean Sea. Include and label the major islands and other major landforms. Show where each culture of the Aegean civilization was centered. Display your map in the classroom.

CAUSE AND EFFECT

As you read, look for the causes and effects in the development of Greek civilization.

BIG IDEA

Independent Greek city-states with different ways of life combined to form Classical Greek civilization.

VOCABULARY

acropolis
agora
oligarchy
aristocracy
democracy
policy
barbarian

City-States and Greek Culture

3000 B.C.	2000 B.C.	1000 B.C.	B.C./A.D.

1200 B.C.–500 B.C.

During the 1100s B.C. the people of what is now Greece entered a period some historians call the Dark Age. During this time many of the developments of the Aegean civilization were lost. People returned to simpler ways of life, living in small farming and herding societies. However, memories of the past were kept alive in songs, myths, and stories about heroes at the time of the Trojan War. The Dark Age lasted until about 750 B.C. At that time people began once again to live in small cities and trade with other cultures. These changes led to the rise of a new civilization that historians call Classical Greece.

The Rise of City-States

The development of Classical Greek civilization began with the rise of city-states. City-states were formed as people living in neighboring villages joined to protect themselves from outside dangers. Many of these groups built walled forts for safety during enemy attacks. Each fort was usually built on a hilltop. It was called an **acropolis** (uh•KRAH•puh•luhs), which means "high-city" in Greek.

The Acropolis of Athens (below) was the site of festivals and religious worship in ancient times. The marble statue of a boy carrying a calf (left) was found on the Acropolis.

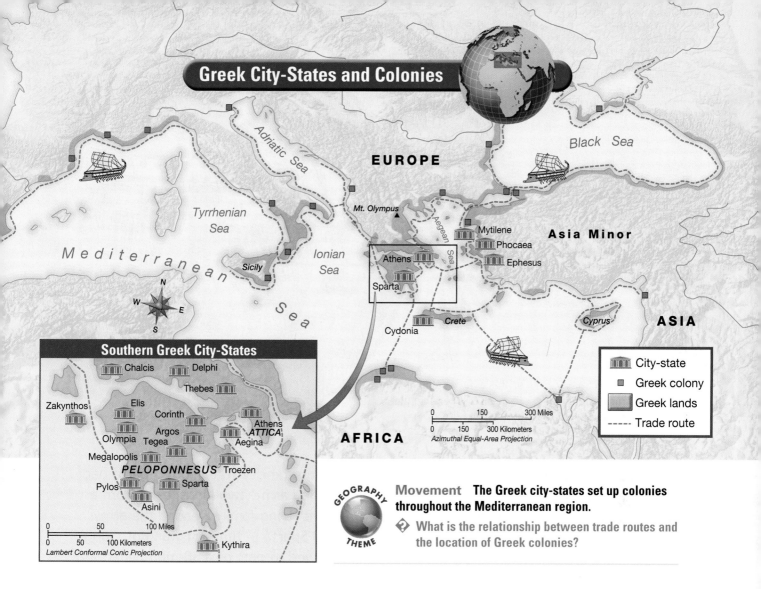

Greek City-States and Colonies

Black Sea

EUROPE

Adriatic Sea

Tyrrhenian Sea

Mediterranean Sea

Ionian Sea

Sicily

Mt. Olympus ▲

Athens

Sparta

Aegean Sea

Mytilene

Phocaea

Ephesus

Asia Minor

ASIA

Cydonia   Crete

Cyprus

AFRICA

N W E S

Southern Greek City-States

Chalcis   Delphi

Thebes

Zakynthos

Elis

Corinth

Argos

Olympia   Tegea

Megalopolis

Athens
ATTICA

Aegina

PELOPONNESUS   Troezen

Pylos   Sparta

Asini

0   50   100 Miles
0   50   100 Kilometers
Lambert Conformal Conic Projection

Kythira

0   150   300 Miles
0   150   300 Kilometers
Azimuthal Equal-Area Projection

🏛 City-state
◼ Greek colony
▨ Greek lands
---- Trade route

Movement The Greek city-states set up colonies throughout the Mediterranean region.

GEOGRAPHY THEME

❓ What is the relationship between trade routes and the location of Greek colonies?

Over time, villages grew into cities around the acropolis. Houses, public buildings, and an open-air market called an **agora** (A•guh•ruh) stood below the acropolis. Beyond these were farmland and smaller villages. Some city-states became overcrowded and did not have enough resources to meet everyone's needs. To ease the overcrowding, Greek colonies were set up in southern Italy, on the island of Sicily, and in other areas.

Neighboring city-states often fought over the lands that lay between them. As a result of these struggles, some city-states grew in size and importance.

Among the best-known and most powerful Greek city-states were Sparta and Athens. Over the years, these two city-states developed very different economies and governments.

REVIEW How did the Greek city-states form?

Sparta

Most city-states were located in coastal areas and had economies based on trade. The city-state of Sparta, however, had an inland location on the Peloponnesian Peninsula. Its inland location caused Sparta to develop a military economy. People in Sparta led simple lives of hard work and physical activity.

A statue of a Spartan female athlete

Chapter 8 ■ 251

Many artifacts from Sparta, such as this carved stone marker (above left), bronze statue (above center), and ceramic plate (right), represent the people's military way of life.

Spartan society was made up of three classes. Only those males in the ruling class were considered to be Spartan citizens. They were the descendants of the Dorians, who had migrated to the Greek peninsula in the 1100s B.C.

The Dorians had enslaved the people already living in the area. These slaves formed the second and largest class in Spartan society. Known as helots (HEH•luhts), they were mainly enslaved farmworkers who belonged to the Spartan city-state. The third class included free people from neighboring communities under Sparta's control. They made goods for Sparta and traded with other city-states.

People in the lower classes outnumbered Spartan citizens by as much as ten to one. This caused citizens to fear the lower classes. Fear of rebellion from within and attack from outside led the Spartan citizens to focus on their military. To prepare for a life as a soldier, Spartan boys began military training at the age of six or seven.

Among the city-states, only Sparta had a standing army. Two kings, each from a different ruling family, headed the army and led Sparta in times of war. Both kings also served as part of a 30-member council that governed Sparta in times of peace.

Other members of the council—all wealthy citizens over the age of 60—were elected to life terms by Sparta's citizens. In addition, five officials called ephors (EH•ferz) were elected to one-year terms. They handled the day-to-day governing. Sparta also had a citizen assembly to vote on new laws, but its members could not suggest them. Only the council or the ephors could do that.

Sparta used a governing system known as an oligarchy. In an **oligarchy** a few people from the ruling class make decisions for everyone. Sparta's system was admired by citizens in other city-states because it was well-ordered and lasting.

REVIEW What led the Spartans to develop their military way of life?

 CAUSE AND EFFECT

Athens

The city-state of Athens was located on Attica (A•tih•kuh), a part of the Balkan Peninsula northeast of the Peloponnesus. After the Dark Age, Athens was ruled by an **aristocracy**, or a small group of leaders from wealthy landowning families who inherit the right to rule. Sometimes the leaders struggled with one another for control of the city-state. In 594 B.C. the Athenians asked a leader named Solon to make reforms, or changes, in their government to end these struggles.

Solon divided the Athenian people into classes based on wealth instead of birth. Those with the most wealth became part of the ruling class. This allowed people to change classes by gaining wealth. A public assembly of all the classes made laws and ran the government. Yet the Athenians wanted a larger role in making decisions.

This coin from Athens shows the goddess Athena on the front and an owl, a symbol of Athena, on the back.

More reforms in 508 B.C. made the Athenian city-state into the world's first democracy. A **democracy** is a system of government in which the people rule. A leader named Cleisthenes (KLYS•thuh•neez) opened the government to all free men 18 years of age or older, not just the wealthiest. He also created a new council. Each year, a drawing was held to select a council of 500 male citizens. The council suggested laws for the assembly and decided on government policies. A **policy** is a plan of action.

Cleisthenes' reforms gave every adult male citizen a chance to serve in the government. They also kept any one person or group from controlling it.

DEMOCRATIC VALUES
Popular Sovereignty

CITIZENSHIP

The government in ancient Athens was a direct democracy. Because the population of the city-state was small, each male citizen could take an active role in making government decisions. Most countries today, such as the United States, have too many people to have a direct democracy. Instead, most present-day democracies are representative democracies. In this kind of government, large numbers of citizens elect other citizens, or representatives, to make government decisions for them. It is the job of representatives to work for the good of the people whom they represent. It is the responsibility of each citizen to learn about different candidates and to vote for the representatives who they feel will best serve their community.

Analyze the Value

1. What might happen in a large democracy if everyone had to vote on every decision made by the government?

2. **Make It Relevant** Research an issue that affects your community or state. Decide whether it would be better for representatives to decide on the issue or whether all citizens should vote on it. Write a paragraph explaining your decision.

These voting ballots were used in Athens in about 470 B.C. Names were scratched onto bits of pottery.

This ancient Greek painted vase shows Olympic athletes in a boxing match.

However, even though the reforms let more people take part in government, they did not include everyone. Women had no voice in government—even those who were citizens. Immigrants and slaves, both male and female, were not allowed to take part in the government.

Most Athenian slaves were people from neighboring areas who had been captured in war. Unlike the Spartan helots, Athenian slaves were owned by private citizens. They could be bought and sold as property.

REVIEW What form of government did Athens have after 508 B.C.?

· HERITAGE ·

The Olympic Games

In about 776 B.C. athletes from many Greek city-states met in the valley of Olympia near the city-state of Elis (EE•luhs). They had come to take part in the first Olympic Games. These games, held every four years, brought the city-states together in peaceful competition. The athletes competed in a single event—a footrace. Later, more events, such as wrestling, boxing, and horse racing, were added.

The spirit of the early Olympic Games is still alive today. Countries from around the world put aside any disagreements they might have to take part in the competitions.

These female athletes are running a race in the Summer Olympics.

To Be Greek

Since the city-states were independent, people did not think of themselves as belonging to a country as Americans do. The different city-states had a cultural identity, or connection, with one another. Over time, this common cultural identity helped people begin to think of themselves as a single civilization.

According to their mythology, the people of all the city-states shared a common ancestor. His name was Hellen. For this reason they called their country Hellas and themselves Hellenes. In English, their language and civilization are known as Greek.

The Greeks believed that their gods, led by Zeus, controlled events both in nature and in human life. Athena, for example, was the Greek goddess of wisdom and of warfare. Aphrodite (a•fruh•DY•tee) was the goddess of love and beauty. Hermes (HER•meez) was the messenger of the gods.

In addition to their language, mythology, and religion, the Greeks were united by other activities. The Olympic Games were held every four years to honor Zeus.

The ancient games were held from about 776 B.C. to A.D. 393.

Writing also helped bring the city-states together. In the 700s B.C. the Greeks developed a writing system based on the one used by Phoenician traders. The word *alphabet* comes from the names of the first two Greek letters, *alpha* and *beta.*

This terra-cotta figurine from the Greek city of Thebes shows a man writing.

A common mythology, religion, activities, and language helped unite the Greeks as a people. It also set them apart from others living in the Mediterranean region. The Greeks thought of themselves as different from all other peoples. They called anyone who could not speak Greek a barbarian. Today a **barbarian** is a person who is considered uncivilized, or rough-mannered.

REVIEW What parts of Greek culture helped form a Greek identity?

LESSON 2 REVIEW

Summary Time Line

1200 B.C.

850 B.C.

500 B.C.

1150 B.C.
The Dorians migrate into the Greek mainland

776 B.C.
The first Olympic games are held

508 B.C.
The Athenians form the first democracy

 CAUSE AND EFFECT What effects did having Hellen as a common ancestor have on the city-states?

1 **BIG IDEA** How did independent city-states develop into the Classical Greek civilization?

2 **VOCABULARY** Use **acropolis** and **agora** in a paragraph about the Greek city-states.

3 **TIME LINE** In what year were the first Olympic Games held?

4 **GEOGRAPHY** On what peninsula is Athens located?

5 **CULTURE** How were the Olympic Games important to Greek culture?

6 **CRITICAL THINKING—Evaluate** What role do you think the Olympic Games play today in shaping cultural identity?

 PERFORMANCE—Give a Speech Imagine that you are a citizen of ancient Athens. Write a short speech in which you discuss why it is important to your city for each citizen to have a voice in government. Present your speech to the class.

CAUSE AND EFFECT

Read to find the causes and effects of the Golden Age in Classical Greece.

BIG IDEA

Defeating the Persian Empire in war led to the Golden Age in Classical Greece.

VOCABULARY

league
patron
tragedy
comedy
plague
demagogue
academy

FAST FACT

The Classical Greeks designed a warship that was fast and easy to move in battle. It was called a trireme (try•REEM) because it had three rows of oars on each side.

The Golden Age

| 3000 B.C. | 2000 B.C. | 1000 B.C. | B.C./A.D. |

500 B.C.–300 B.C.

Historians sometimes use the phrase *Golden Age* to describe the time when a people or civilization was at its best. They judge this based on such things as the civilization's art, architecture, literature, and science. Most historians agree that a Golden Age existed in the Classical Greek civilization for about 100 years, from 490 B.C. to 390 B.C.

The Persian Wars

For hundreds of years the Greek city-states fought over land and trade. Then, beginning in the 500s B.C., a common enemy brought the Greek people together for a time. The common enemy was Persia. During that century Persia built a huge empire that included Assyria, Babylonia, Egypt, and the Greek city-states in Asia Minor. In 490 B.C. Persian king Darius I turned his soldiers toward the Greek mainland.

Citizen-soldiers from Athens met a larger Persian force on the plain of Marathon, not far from Athens. Although the Persians had more soldiers, the well-trained Athenians managed to defeat them in just one day of fighting. Legends about the battle tell

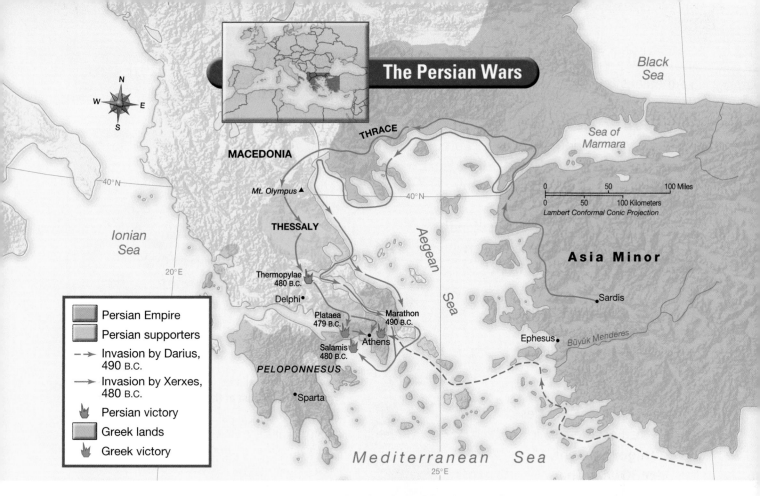

The Persian Wars

Persian Empire

Persian supporters

→ Invasion by Darius, 490 B.C.

→ Invasion by Xerxes, 480 B.C.

Persian victory

Greek lands

Greek victory

Human-Environment Interactions **The Greeks and Persians met in battle on the Balkan Peninsula.**

Who controlled the land on which the Greeks won victories?

of a messenger who ran all the way from Marathon to Athens to report the amazing victory. Athletes today re-create this run in the marathon, a race that covers a distance of 26 miles, 385 yards (42 km, 352 m).

In 480 B.C. the Persians again invaded the Balkan Peninsula. This time Xerxes (ZERK•seez), the son of Darius I, attacked by land and by sea. The Persians were met by Greek forces made up of armies and navies from many city-states, including Athens and Sparta. The Persian forces, as before, outnumbered the Greeks. Yet the Greeks won

once again. They defeated the Persians at sea near the island of Salamis (SA•luh•muhs) and on land at Plataea (pluh•TEE•uh).

Even before fighting the Persians, some Greek city-states had begun to work together in matters of war. To protect themselves, they formed a **league**, or group of allies. Sparta led southern city-states in the Peloponnesian League. After the Persian Wars, Athens made new alliances. City-states from Attica, Asia Minor, and some of the Aegean Islands joined Athens to form the Delian (DEE•lee•uhn) League.

REVIEW What events caused the Greek city-states to unite?

CAUSE AND EFFECT

Greek bronze helmet from about 500 B.C.

The Age of Pericles

Athenians felt great pride in their new leadership position after the defeat of the Persians. This pride led to achievements in other areas. During much of this time, Athens was led by Pericles (PAIR•uh•kleez), a member of the city-state's wealthy ruling class.

Pericles was a relative of Cleisthenes, the Athenian leader who had taken governing authority away from the aristocracy and given it to the city-state's assembly. After the Persian Wars, Pericles wanted to continue the democratic reforms of Cleisthenes.

In about 460 B.C. Pericles was elected as a leader in the Athenian government. Over the next 30 years, he made many important changes. He introduced pay for public officials. At first, only elected officials were paid. In time, all government officials, both elected and appointed, received pay. This allowed people who were not wealthy to serve in the government. As many as 20,000 Athenians may have held government jobs.

In 457 B.C. Pericles gave male citizens of any class the right to hold nearly any government office. He believed that every male citizen, not just wealthy citizens, had a right to take part in government. As Pericles once explained, "No one is prevented from being of service to the state because of [being poor]."

REVIEW How did Pericles change government in Athens?

Population of Athens
about 430 B.C.

Noncitizens 12%

Families of male citizens 33%

Male citizens 19%

Slaves 36%

Learning from Graphs Male citizens with the right to vote made up only a small part of Athens's population. A bust of the leader Pericles (left).

❖ Athens had a population of about 285,000 people. About how many male citizens were there? About how many slaves were there?

Achievements of the Golden Age

Pericles was a **patron**, or supporter, of learning and the arts. He hired the best architects and artists to build and decorate temples—such as the Parthenon—theaters, and other public buildings. The beautiful city of Athens became an important cultural center.

Pericles also supported writers, such as Herodotus (hih•RAH•duh•tuhs), an early historian. Herodotus explained that he wrote

a history of the Persian Wars to record "the astonishing achievements of our own and of other peoples."

Even today many people still read the works of Herodotus and of other writers of the Golden Age. Sophocles (SAH•fuh•kleez) wrote **tragedies**, or serious plays with unhappy endings. Aristophanes (air•uh•STAH•fuh•neez) chose to write **comedies**, or plays designed to make audiences laugh. His comedies usually made fun of political leaders or ideas that he did not agree with.

During the Golden Age, scientists studied nature and human life. Some of their findings changed the way that people viewed their world. One of the great scientists of Greece was Hippocrates (hih•PAH•kruh•teez). He showed that illnesses came from natural causes. Many people at that time believed that illnesses were punishments for angering the gods.

Masks such as this one were used to show different emotions on stage in the ancient Greek theater.

Hippocrates is perhaps best remembered for the rules of behavior that he wrote for doctors. Today doctors still promise to follow these rules when they finish medical school. The promise they make is known as the Hippocratic oath.

REVIEW What contribution did Hippocrates make to science?

The End of the Golden Age

Pericles wanted to make Athens not only "the school of Greece" but also its most powerful city-state. To do this, soldiers were sent to conquer lands in Egypt. Athens also forced its allies from the Delian League to pay tribute as the price for peace and protection. Sparta feared the growing power of Athens and broke off friendly relations.

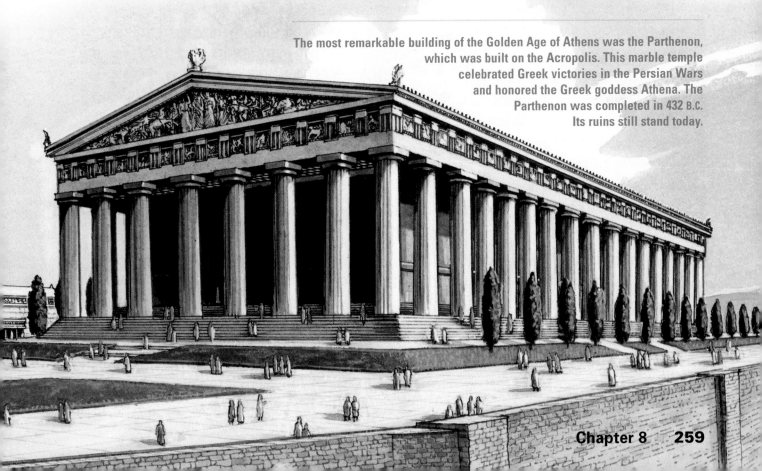

The most remarkable building of the Golden Age of Athens was the Parthenon, which was built on the Acropolis. This marble temple celebrated Greek victories in the Persian Wars and honored the Greek goddess Athena. The Parthenon was completed in 432 B.C. Its ruins still stand today.

POINTS OF VIEW
Democracy

Democracy was an important idea in ancient Athens. Many Athenians believed that citizens should have the right to participate in government. However, not all of the people thought that Athens should be a democracy. Below are two different viewpoints about democracy—one from the Greek philosopher Plato and the other from the Greek leader Pericles.

PLATO, Greek philosopher, from *The Republic,* 360 B.C.

❝Liberty overmasters democracy—the truth being that excessive increase of anything often causes a reaction in the opposite direction; and this is the case . . . above all in forms of government. ❞

PERICLES, Greek leader and general, quoted by the Greek historian Thucydides (thoo·SIH·duh·deez) in *The History of the Peloponnesian War,* 431 B.C.

❝[Our] administration favors the many instead of the few; this is why it is called a democracy. . . . The freedom we enjoy in our government extends to our ordinary life. . . . But all this ease in our private relations does not make us lawless citizens. Against this, fear is our chief safeguard, teaching us to obey the magistrates and the laws. ❞

Analyze the Viewpoints

❶ Why does Plato feel that liberty in a democracy is dangerous? How would Pericles respond to Plato's concerns?

❷ **Make It Relevant** In ancient Athens all male citizens over the age of 18 had a direct voice in government. Describe how democracy in ancient Athens was similar to and different from democracy in the United States.

In 431 B.C. Sparta and its allies in the Peloponnesian League went to war against Athens and its allies. This marked the beginning of the Peloponnesian War.

Pericles called all the people from the countryside into the city while the Spartans and their allies held the surrounding area. In 430 B.C. the **plague**, a deadly disease, broke out and spread quickly through the city. Many people died, including one-fourth of the Athenian army and Pericles himself.

For the next 27 years, the two leagues fought each other. The Athenian navy defended Athens, which was also protected by walls. Without the wise leadership of Pericles, the members of the Athenian assembly began to follow demagogues (DEH·muh·gahgz). A **demagogue** is a leader who stirs up the feelings and fears of people to gain personal power. These new leaders made promises they could not keep. They led the assembly to make poor decisions that began to weaken the city-state.

Faced with ruin, Athens surrendered to Sparta in 404 B.C. Sparta quickly replaced the Athenian democracy with an oligarchy like its own. However, the Athenians soon rebelled, and for a time Athens was a democracy once again.

REVIEW What events brought an end to the Golden Age?

The Greek Philosophers

After the Peloponnesian War there were still many great thinkers and teachers in Athens. They were called philosophers, which means "lovers of wisdom" in Greek. One of them, Socrates (SAH·kruh·teez), called himself the city's "gadfly," after an insect that bites horses and makes them jump. He used criticism of the government to "sting" Athenians into thinking about life and the best way to live it.

This painting from about A.D. 1510 by the Italian artist Raphael is called *The School of Athens*. The two figures in the center represent Plato and Aristotle.

Such criticism would have been more welcome in Pericles' day. Instead, it annoyed the new leaders of Athens. In 399 B.C. an Athenian court found Socrates guilty of teaching dangerous ideas to the city's young people. The court ordered Socrates to end his own life by drinking poison. Friends and family members wanted Socrates to live. They said he should run away. However, Socrates felt that it was important for all citizens to obey the law, so he drank the poison.

One of Socrates' students was Plato (PLAY•toh). Like Socrates, Plato was disappointed in the leaders who came after Pericles. Plato said that a ruler should be a person of good character—someone who is wise. He believed it was possible to become a good ruler by studying hard and by loving wisdom. He felt that philosophers would make the best rulers. In 385 B.C. Plato started a special school, or **academy**, in which future rulers could learn the lessons that they would need to govern well.

Aristotle (AIR•uh•stah•tuhl) entered Plato's Academy at the age of 18. He studied there for about 20 years. Aristotle did not agree with Plato about the kinds of knowledge that were the most important. Plato was mainly interested in how he would like things to be. Aristotle was more interested in how things really were. They disagreed in some areas.

Greek Thought

PHILOSOPHER	IDEAS
Pythagoras of Samos, about 580 B.C.– about 500 B.C.	The inventor of geometry, Pythagoras thought that the world could be understood through mathematical principles.
Socrates of Athens, about 470 B.C.– 399 B.C.	Socrates felt that people must truly understand themselves before they can know right from wrong. He said, "The unexamined life is not worth living."
Democritus of Abdera, about 460 B.C.– about 370 B.C.	Democritus said that the universe is made up of only two things—atoms and space. Much of the modern science of physics is based on this idea.
Plato of Athens, about 428 B.C.– 348 B.C.	Plato believed that a person's reality is a combination of knowledge acquired through learning and opinions based on sense experiences.
Aristotle of Stagira, 384 B.C.– 322 B.C.	Aristotle thought that the physical world is a combination of the elements of fire, air, earth, and water. He believed that all human knowledge comes from sense experiences.

Analyze Tables   This table includes ideas of some important Greek philosophers, including Aristotle (right).

Which philosopher's ideas are a part of the modern science of physics?

However, both Aristotle and Plato thought that the best life was one spent in search of knowledge and truth.

Aristotle's wide search for knowledge covered many subjects, including biology, astronomy, economics, law, science, and sports. He was among the first scientists to study in detail both animals and plants.

REVIEW Why did Socrates end his own life?

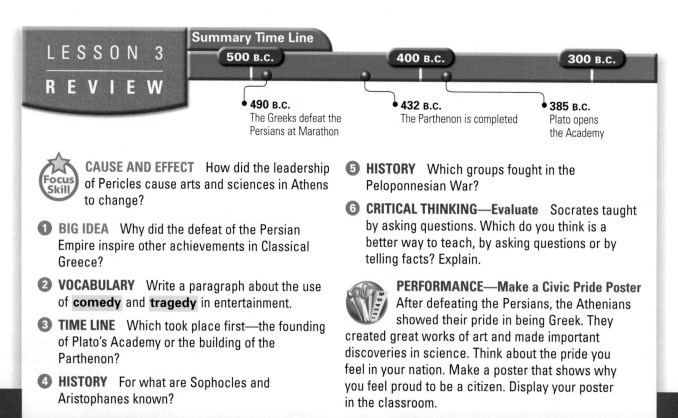

LESSON 3 REVIEW

Summary Time Line

500 B.C.   400 B.C.   300 B.C.

490 B.C. The Greeks defeat the Persians at Marathon

432 B.C. The Parthenon is completed

385 B.C. Plato opens the Academy

Focus Skill **CAUSE AND EFFECT**   How did the leadership of Pericles cause arts and sciences in Athens to change?

1 BIG IDEA   Why did the defeat of the Persian Empire inspire other achievements in Classical Greece?

2 VOCABULARY   Write a paragraph about the use of **comedy** and **tragedy** in entertainment.

3 TIME LINE   Which took place first—the founding of Plato's Academy or the building of the Parthenon?

4 HISTORY   For what are Sophocles and Aristophanes known?

5 HISTORY   Which groups fought in the Peloponnesian War?

6 CRITICAL THINKING—Evaluate   Socrates taught by asking questions. Which do you think is a better way to teach, by asking questions or by telling facts? Explain.

PERFORMANCE—Make a Civic Pride Poster After defeating the Persians, the Athenians showed their pride in being Greek. They created great works of art and made important discoveries in science. Think about the pride you feel in your nation. Make a poster that shows why you feel proud to be a citizen. Display your poster in the classroom.

·SKILLS·

CITIZENSHIP

Act as a Responsible Citizen

■ WHY IT MATTERS

A government depends on its citizens and leaders to act responsibly. To be responsible, citizens must keep informed about what is happening in their nation or community. Leaders must be thoughtful and work to help citizens. When a nation faces problems, its citizens and leaders must work together to solve those problems. Citizens can participate in their nation's government.

■ WHAT YOU NEED TO KNOW

As you have read, the leader Pericles worked to reform the Athenian government. He thought it was important that more Athenian citizens be allowed to take part in government. Here are some steps that people in ancient Athens might have followed to act as responsible citizens:

Step 1 **Stay informed about problems and concerns in your community or nation.**

The Athenian leader Pericles

Step 2 **Think about ways to solve these problems.**

Step 3 **Make a plan to bring about change in ways that would be good for your community or nation.**

Step 4 **Decide how you and other concerned citizens can best help put your plan into action.**

■ PRACTICE THE SKILL

Reread the information about Pericles in Lesson 3 of this chapter. Then answer the questions.

1. What concerns did Pericles have with the Athenian government?

2. How did Pericles work to change the government?

3. In what way was Pericles acting as a responsible citizen for the good of Athens?

■ APPLY WHAT YOU LEARNED

Work with a classmate to identify a problem in your community or your school. Use the steps for acting as a responsible citizen to think of a plan for solving the problem. Present your plan to the class.

CITIZENSHIP SKILLS

4

CAUSE AND EFFECT

Read to learn about the effects that were caused by the actions of Alexander the Great.

BIG IDEA

Alexander the Great built the first empire to begin in Europe and spread Greek civilization to parts of Asia.

VOCABULARY

diffuse
expedition
legacy
scholar

Alexander's Great Empire

3000 B.C.	2000 B.C.	1000 B.C.	B.C./A.D.

400 B.C. – 300 B.C.

For many years after the Peloponnesian War, the Greeks fought small battles with one another. Then in 338 B.C. the Greek city-states came under the control of Macedonia (ma•suh•DOH•nee•uh), a kingdom to their north. A Macedonian leader named Alexander went on to build a huge empire, the first great empire that began in Europe. It covered parts of eastern Europe as well as much of southwestern Asia. Alexander was a leader who respected Greek culture. His actions helped **diffuse**, or spread, Greek culture across the empire he founded.

The Making of an Emperor

Alexander was born in 356 B.C. in Macedonia. His father was Philip II, a Macedonian who had spent part of his boyhood in Greek lands. His mother, Olympias (oh•LIM•pee•uhs), was Greek. Both parents wanted to pass on to their son their love of Greek culture. To do this, they hired the Greek philosopher Aristotle to be Alexander's teacher.

Like his teacher, Alexander was interested in many subjects. He studied literature, philosophy, and politics. He also trained in sports, physical fitness, and warfare. Alexander's schooling ended at age 16, when his father called him away to fight in the army.

From Aristotle, Alexander had learned about other countries and peoples. From his father, he learned to be a fearless warrior.

This bronze statue of Alexander the Great on horseback shows the young leader charging into battle with a sword in his hand. A legend says that Alexander slept with a dagger and a copy of Homer's *Iliad* under his pillow.

This mosaic is a Roman copy of a Greek painting. It was found in the ancient Roman city of Pompeii and shows Alexander (left) charging into battle against King Darius III and the Persians.

In 338 B.C. 18-year-old Alexander commanded the cavalry, or soldiers who fought on horseback, in Philip's army. The Battle of Chaeronea (kair•uh•NEE•uh) brought most of the Greek peninsula under Macedonian control. Philip next prepared to invade the Persian Empire in Asia. Before he could do so, he was killed by one of his bodyguards. In 336 B.C. Philip's rule passed to Alexander, then 20 years old.

After Philip's death some of the Greek city-states under Macedonian rule rebelled. In 335 B.C. Alexander's army attacked the rebelling Greek city of Thebes and destroyed it. About 30,000 people in the city were sold into slavery. Alexander's action against Thebes discouraged other Greek city-states from rebelling.

REVIEW Which Greek philosopher was Alexander's teacher?

The Building of an Empire

With the Greek city-states under his control, Alexander turned to completing his father's plan for attacking the Persian Empire. In 334 B.C. Alexander led an army of more than 35,000 soldiers from southern Europe to Asia Minor. An early victory over the Persians at the Granicus (gruh•NY•kuhs) River gave Alexander more wealth and glory. It also led the way to Alexander's conquest of much of southwestern Asia.

One by one, Alexander conquered the cities along the coast of Asia Minor. Then Alexander and his army marched north to the city of Gordium (GAWR•dee•uhm), in present-day Turkey. A famous legend tells about Alexander's adventures in Gordium.

Alexander the Great may have worn this iron-and-gold vest.

King Gordius had tied a difficult knot to his chariot, stating that whoever untied it would rule all of Asia. When Alexander arrived, he cut the Gordian knot with his sword and was crowned king of the city.

By 333 B.C. Alexander and his army had reached the coast of Syria. From there they marched south into Phoenicia to capture its port cities. Alexander had difficulty taking the port of Tyre because it was on an island about one-half mile (800 m) offshore. A legend says that Alexander ordered workers to build a causeway, or land bridge, out to the island. This changed the island into a peninsula, which it remains today. After seven months of fighting, the people of Tyre surrendered in 332 B.C.

Alexander next went to Egypt, which was under Persian control. The Egyptians

Portrait of Alexander and his mother, Olympias

greeted him warmly because they were thankful to be free from Persian rule. They crowned Alexander as their pharaoh.

From Egypt, Alexander and his army made a long march into the Persian Empire. At Gaugamela (gaw•guh•MEE•luh) Alexander defeated the much larger Persian army and forced the emperor, Darius III, to flee. The victory at Gaugamela ended more than 200 years of Persian rule in southwestern Asia.

Alexander next captured the Persian cities of Babylon and Persepolis (per•SEH•puh•luhs). By 330 B.C. Alexander and his army moved north toward the Caspian Sea to find Darius. The once-mighty Persian emperor had lost so much power that he could not fight. It is said that he was killed by members of his own court. With the death of Darius, Alexander became the most powerful ruler in southwestern Asia. He began to be called Alexander the Great.

REVIEW What early victory led to Alexander's conquests in Asia? CAUSE AND EFFECT

Alexander's rule brought Greek art styles to southwestern Asia. He built a carved-stone city at Petra.

LOCATE IT

JORDAN

Petra

The End of the Empire

Alexander the Great ruled a wide area, but he wanted still more lands. Beyond Persia lay the Indus Valley. Alexander led his army east from Persia into Bactria, now part of northern Afghanistan, and then across the Hindu Kush mountains. While in Bactria in 327 B.C., Alexander married the Bactrian princess Roxane (rahks•AN).

In 326 B.C. Alexander and his army were on the move again. They reached the upper Indus River, and Alexander planned to push on from there to the Ganges River. However, his weary soldiers refused to follow him. Disappointed, Alexander ordered his army to return home.

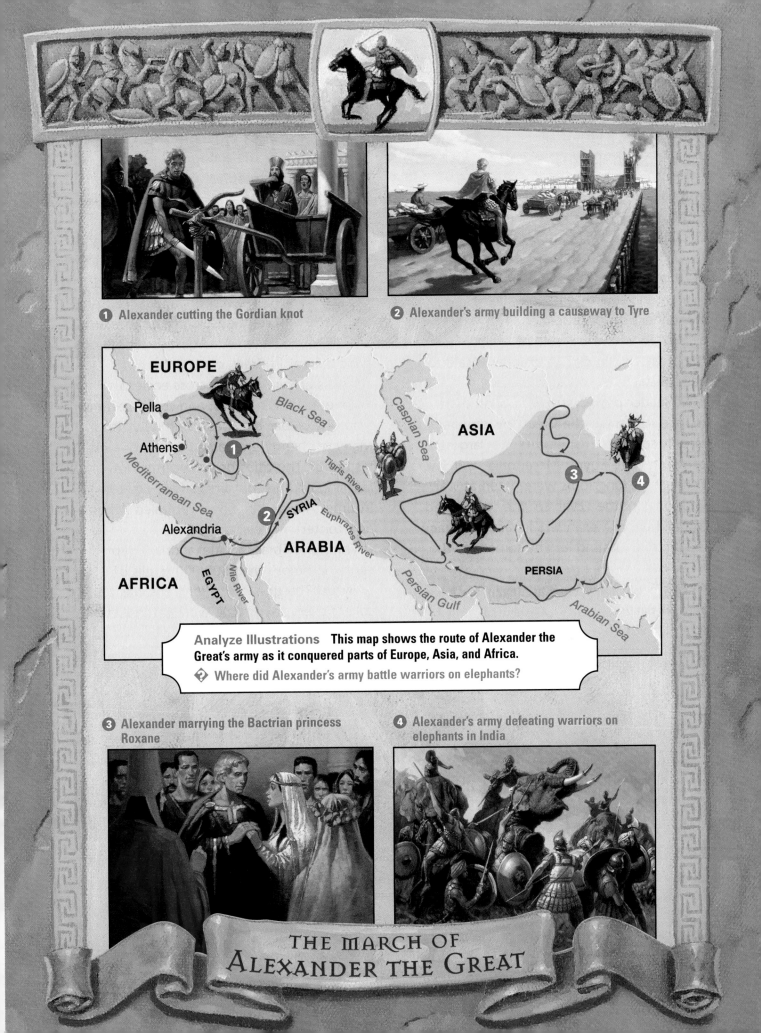

1 Alexander cutting the Gordian knot

2 Alexander's army building a causeway to Tyre

EUROPE

Pella

Athens

Black Sea

Caspian Sea

ASIA

Mediterranean Sea

1

Tigris River

2 SYRIA

Euphrates River

Alexandria

ARABIA

3

4

AFRICA

EGYPT

Nile River

Persian Gulf

PERSIA

Arabian Sea

Analyze Illustrations This map shows the route of Alexander the Great's army as it conquered parts of Europe, Asia, and Africa.

◈ Where did Alexander's army battle warriors on elephants?

3 Alexander marrying the Bactrian princess Roxane

4 Alexander's army defeating warriors on elephants in India

THE MARCH OF
ALEXANDER THE GREAT

By the time he reached Babylon, Alexander was already planning new **expeditions**. He wanted to lead these journeys of exploration deeper into northern Africa and then into the Arabian Peninsula. However, in 323 B.C. Alexander became seriously ill with a fever. He died shortly before his thirty-third birthday.

A legend says that before Alexander's death, a soldier asked, "To whom will rule of the great empire go?" Alexander is said to have answered, "To the strongest!"

No leader proved strong enough to replace Alexander the Great. His empire quickly split into many parts, the largest of which were Egypt, Macedonia, and Syria. These three kingdoms were often at war with one another. Even so, they continued to build upon Alexander's legacy. A **legacy** is something lasting left by someone who has died.

REVIEW What happened to Alexander's empire after his death?

Euclid

Alexander's Legacy

Alexander the Great and his army came into contact with many different cultures. Many of the conquered peoples learned to speak and write in Greek and to follow Greek customs. For this reason, the period of Alexander's rule and several centuries after his death are known as the Hellenistic, or "Greek-like," Age. Like the Golden Age, the Hellenistic Age was a time of achievement in Greek civilization.

As his empire spread across eastern Europe, northern Africa, and southwestern Asia, Alexander the Great built new cities. Many of them were named Alexandria in his honor. The cities became centers of learning and helped spread Greek culture. In time, Alexandria, Egypt, equaled Athens as a center of Greek culture.

The huge library at Alexandria, Egypt, contained more than 500,000 scrolls of papyrus. The goal of its librarians was to collect every text in the world! Connected

The present-day city of Alexandria, Egypt

to the library was a building known as the Museum. There **scholars**, or seekers of knowledge, wrote books and exchanged ideas. Today museums are places that preserve history and offer learning to all people.

Hellenistic scholars worked out new ideas in mathematics. Euclid (YOO•kluhd) of Alexandria, Egypt, did important work in geometry, the study of lines and angles. Archimedes (ar•kuh•MEE•deez) of Syracuse, on the island of Sicily, used mathematics to build many useful machines.

Hellenistic scientists also made use of mathematics as they began to think about the universe. Aristarchus (air•uh•STAR•kuhs) of Samos, an island in the Aegean Sea, used mathematics to suggest that all the planets, including Earth, revolve around the sun. Eratosthenes (air•uh•TAHS•thuh•neez), of Cyrene (sy•REE•nee), in what is now Libya in northern Africa, used mathematics to estimate the distance around Earth.

By 146 B.C. another group of people, the Romans, had gained control of much of the Mediterranean region, including lands held by the Greeks. Yet the knowledge that the

This illustration shows scholars studying at the library of Alexandria.

Greeks had spread to other lands was not lost or forgotten. The Romans borrowed from the art, architecture, philosophy, religion, and literature of the Greeks to build their own civilization. For many years after the Romans took control, Alexandria, Egypt, remained a Greek center for learning.

REVIEW What name is given to the age of Greek achievements started by Alexander the Great?

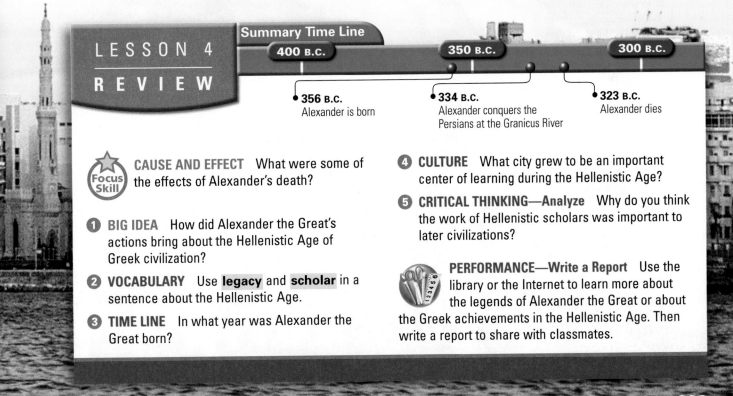

LESSON 4 REVIEW

Summary Time Line

400 B.C. — 350 B.C. — 300 B.C.

356 B.C.
Alexander is born

334 B.C.
Alexander conquers the Persians at the Granicus River

323 B.C.
Alexander dies

Focus Skill **CAUSE AND EFFECT** What were some of the effects of Alexander's death?

1 **BIG IDEA** How did Alexander the Great's actions bring about the Hellenistic Age of Greek civilization?

2 **VOCABULARY** Use **legacy** and **scholar** in a sentence about the Hellenistic Age.

3 **TIME LINE** In what year was Alexander the Great born?

4 **CULTURE** What city grew to be an important center of learning during the Hellenistic Age?

5 **CRITICAL THINKING—Analyze** Why do you think the work of Hellenistic scholars was important to later civilizations?

PERFORMANCE—Write a Report Use the library or the Internet to learn more about the legends of Alexander the Great or about the Greek achievements in the Hellenistic Age. Then write a report to share with classmates.

Greek Architecture

The ancient Greeks built magnificent stone temples and public buildings. They invented new forms of architecture with high roofs supported by strong columns. Sculptures often decorated both the inside and outside of temples. There were three main forms of Greek architecture—Doric, Ionic, and Corinthian. Later, builders in Europe and around the world borrowed ideas from Greek architecture. Many buildings in Washington, D.C., including the White House, the United States Capitol, and the Supreme Court, are based on Greek designs.

FROM THE ARCHAEOLOGICAL MUSEUM IN CORINTH AND THE ACROPOLIS MUSEUM IN ATHENS

Capital, or top, of a
Doric column

Capital of an
Ionic column

Capital of a
Corinthian column

A Doric temple built by the
ancient Greeks

In Greek architecture, pediments are triangle shapes containing sculptures found on the sides of temple roofs. Shown here is part of a pediment with a sculpture of a three-headed creature with a snake's tail.

A tool used by Phidias, a famous Greek sculptor

Analyze the Primary Source

1 What can you tell about the role of religion in Greek society from the temples Greeks built to their gods?

2 How do you think Phidias's tool was used?

3 Why do you think architects chose to borrow from the architecture of the ancient Greeks for the most important buildings of the United States government?

ACTIVITY

Design and Draw Create and draw the front of your own Greek temple. Design columns in any style you wish. Include a pediment at the top of the temple, and decorate it with a scene. Write a paragraph explaining the meaning of the scene.

RESEARCH

Visit The Learning Site at **www.harcourtschool.com** to research other primary sources.

These caryatids (kar•ee•A•tuhdz), or columns in the shape of human figures, support the roof of an ancient Greek temple in Athens, Greece.

271

Review and Test Preparation

 Focus Skill ## Cause and Effect

Complete this graphic organizer to show that you understand how to identify causes and effects relating to early Greece. A copy of this graphic organizer appears on page 79 of the Activity Book.

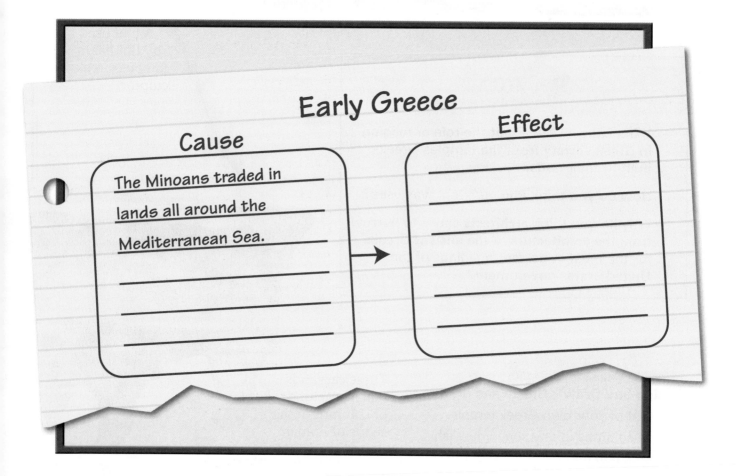

Early Greece

Cause

The Minoans traded in lands all around the Mediterranean Sea.

→

Effect

THINK & WRITE

Write a Description   How were the culture and government of ancient Athens like the culture and government of the United States today? How were they different? Write a paragraph that describes the similarities and differences.

Write a Personal Narrative   A legacy is something lasting left behind by a person who has died. Alexander the Great's legacy shaped the Hellenistic Age. Describe a legacy in your family, school, or community. Why is it important today?

1920 B.C.	1380 B.C.	840 B.C.	300 B.C.

1100 B.C.
The Dark Age of Greece begins

490 B.C.
The Golden Age of Greece begins

338 B.C.
Macedonia conquers
the Greek city-states

334 B.C.
Alexander the Great
begins building his empire

USE THE TIME LINE

Use the chapter summary time line to answer these questions.

1 Which came first, the Golden Age or the Dark Age of Greece? *Golden Age*

2 When did Alexander the Great begin building his empire? *334 B.C.*

USE VOCABULARY

Use each term in a sentence or two to explain both what the term means and how that meaning relates to the ancient Greeks.

3 **decimal system** (p. 246)

4 **epic** (p. 248)

5 **acropolis** (p. 250)

6 **patron** (p. 258)

7 **plague** (p. 260)

8 **academy** (p. 261)

RECALL FACTS

Answer these questions.

9 What is the difference between a tragedy and a comedy? ← *funny* *art*

10 What were the two sides in the Peloponnesian War? When did the war begin?

Write the letter of the best choice.

11 **TEST PREP** Which Aegean culture probably began first?
A Cycladic
B Minoan
C Mycenaean
D Trojan

12 **TEST PREP** Which city-state was the world's first democracy?
F Sparta
G Troy
H Athens
J Macedonia

13 **TEST PREP** Which Greek scientist wrote the medical oath that doctors still take today?
A Socrates
B Herodotus
C Aristotle
D Hippocrates

14 **TEST PREP** Which Greek philosopher started an academy in which future rulers could learn how to govern well?
F Plato
G Herodotus
H Aristotle
J Hippocrates

THINK CRITICALLY

15 According to legend, why did Mycenaean soldiers need to use the Trojan horse to capture the city of Troy?

16 How did Pericles's plan to pay government officials make Athens more democratic?

APPLY SKILLS

Act as a Responsible Citizen

17 Find a newspaper or magazine article about a group of people who solved a problem in their community or country. Write a report describing how these people acted as responsible citizens to solve the problem.

CITIZENSHIP SKILLS

Chapter 8 ▪ 273

THE COLOSSEUM, ROME, ITALY

As many as 50,000 Romans could gather to watch events in the Colosseum after it was opened in about A.D. 72. The stone and concrete building is oval-shaped. It has an open area in its center for games and competitions, and seats on all sides. After about 1,500 years of not being used, the Colosseum was repaired and opened again for public performances in the year 2000.

LOCATE IT

ITALY

Adriatic Sea

Rome

Mediterranean Sea

The Ancient Romans

"My nature is rational and social; and my city and country is Rome . . ."

—Marcus Aurelius, Roman emperor, A.D. 100s

 **Point of View**

To determine someone's **point of view** on a subject, identify that person's way of looking at it.

As you read this chapter, determine the points of view of the people discussed.

- **Make a list of people quoted in the chapter.**

- **Write down what they said and why they said it.**

- **Determine each person's point of view.**

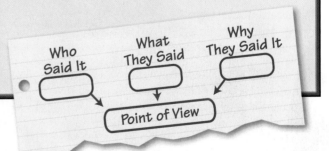

Who Said It → What They Said → Why They Said It → Point of View

1

Early People of Italy

POINT OF VIEW

Read to learn the points of view of the Romans toward the founding of Rome and how their city should be governed.

BIG IDEA

Many cultures contributed to the development of the Roman civilization.

VOCABULARY

confederation
republic
consul
veto
dictator
Senate
patrician
plebeian
tribune

1000 B.C.	500 B.C.	B.C./A.D.	A.D. 500

1000 B.C.–300 B.C.

After the death of Alexander the Great in 323 B.C., control in the Mediterranean region began to move west to the Italian Peninsula. The peninsula is a mountainous land shaped somewhat like a tall, high-heeled boot. From earliest times many different peoples had migrated there. Most of these people spoke Italic (uh•TAH•lik) languages.

Among the Italic-language speakers were the Latins. In about 1000 B.C. the Latins migrated across the Alps from central Europe. Legends tell that in 753 B.C. the Latin people founded a village that became the city of Rome.

The Founding of Rome

The city of Rome was built on a group of seven hills along the Tiber River, near the center of the Italian Peninsula. The steep hills there helped protect the city against enemy attacks by land. Rome was also far enough inland, about 15 miles (24 km) from the Mediterranean, to escape attacks by sea. The area offered fertile soil for farming as well as wood and stones for building.

FAST FACT

The village of Rome was built alongside the Tiber River upon Palatine (PA•luh•tyn) Hill. As Rome grew into a city, it spread across seven hills.

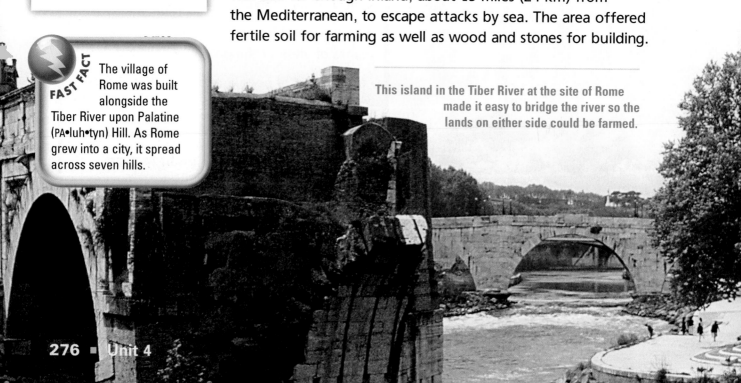

This island in the Tiber River at the site of Rome made it easy to bridge the river so the lands on either side could be farmed.

With the sea nearby, the Latins also had sources of salt and fish.

Rome's location was ideal for trade and for communication with others. The Tiber River provided a nearby route to the sea for trade with other Mediterranean civilizations. In time, Romans were able to gain control of sea-trade routes. The Roman historian Livy (LIH•vee) later wrote about Rome,

> 66 Not without good reason did gods and men choose this spot as the site of a city. 99

Romans told colorful legends to explain the beginnings of their city. One legend told how a Latin king's cruel brother took the throne by force. When the rightful king's daughter gave birth to twin boys, the new king feared the boys would grow up to take back the throne.

The king ordered that the babies be left to die on the banks of the Tiber River. According to the legend, a mother wolf saved the twins. Later, a farmer found the children in the wolf's care and took them home. When the twins, Romulus and Remus, grew up, they defeated their great-uncle and made their grandfather king again.

The legend says that the twins set out to build a new settlement along the Tiber

This mosaic shows the twin babies, Romulus and Remus, and the mother wolf that saved them.

River, near where they had been rescued years before. However, they quarreled about which hill to build on, and Remus was killed. Romulus became the first ruler of the new city, which was named Rome in his honor. Romulus promised that the city would someday rise to greatness. According to the legend, Romulus said, "My Rome shall be the capital of the world."

REVIEW What did the historian Livy think about Rome's location? **POINT OF VIEW**

LOCATE IT

ITALY

Rome

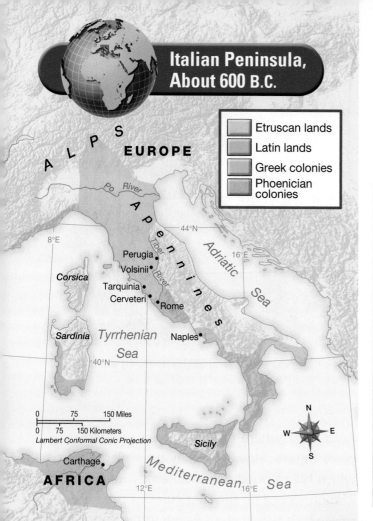

Italian Peninsula, About 600 B.C.

Etruscan lands
Latin lands
Greek colonies
Phoenician colonies

EUROPE

ALPS

Po River

Apennines

Perugia
Volsinii
Tarquinia
Cerveteri
Rome

Corsica

Tiber River

44°N
16°E
8°E

Adriatic Sea

Sardinia

Tyrrhenian Sea

Naples

40°N

0   75   150 Miles
0   75   150 Kilometers
Lambert Conformal Conic Projection

Sicily

N
W   E
S

Carthage

AFRICA

Mediterranean Sea
12°E   16°E

GEOGRAPHY THEME

Regions   **Different cultures existed on the Italian Peninsula in 600 B.C. This Etruscan pitcher (below) was made to look like a woman.**

❓ **Which culture controlled the most lands on the peninsula?**

culture. The Etruscans adapted the Greek alphabet for their own language. Etruscan art styles show Greek influences in pottery and in sculpture. Although the art of the two civilizations looks similar, the subjects represented show differences in the cultures. For example, artifacts suggest that Etruscan women had a more public role in society than Greek women.

Like the Greeks, the Etruscans formed independent city-states. However, the Etruscan city-states shared more than their cultural identity. They all used the same system of government.

Each city-state was governed by a king. Unlike most monarchs, Etruscan kings did not inherit their thrones. The leaders of powerful families within each city-state elected a king. Having similar governments helped the Etruscans unite in a confederation. A **confederation** is a group of governments joined together for a common purpose.

As a result of their confederation, the Etruscan city-states were able to build a strong army. They used their army to control neighboring peoples. Some conquered peoples were forced to work for the Etruscans. By about 600 B.C. the Etruscans controlled large areas of the Italian Peninsula, including Rome. In fact, Etruscan kings ruled the city of Rome for more than 100 years.

REVIEW **In what ways did Greek culture influence the Etruscans?**

The Etruscan Civilization

Across the Tiber River to the north of Rome lived a people whom the Romans called Etruscans. Most archaeologists now believe that the Etruscans were the descendants of an earlier people who spoke a non-Italic language.

The Etruscans lived in the northwestern part of the Italian Peninsula, between the Apennine mountain range and the sea. They had an urban culture, with major settlements between the Tiber and Arno Rivers. In time the Etruscans became the dominant culture on the Italian Peninsula.

Trading with the Greek colonies of the region influenced some parts of Etruscan

The Roman Republic

In about 509 B.C. the Romans rebelled against their Etruscan rulers and started a new form of government. The Romans kept some features of the Etruscan system, including the election of leaders. However, the new Roman government was called a republic. In a **republic**, citizens elect leaders to represent them in an assembly. The assembly makes laws and runs the government.

Two elected leaders called **consuls** headed the republic and led the army. The consuls shared power, but either could **veto**, or reject, the actions of the other. Having two consuls meant that no one person would have too much authority. The consuls served for one year.

In an emergency, the assembly could name a dictator to serve for a six-month term. A **dictator** is a ruler with absolute authority. Every citizen had to obey the orders of the dictator, even the consuls.

This painting (below) shows how the Senate might have looked. In the sculpture (right), a Roman holds carved images of his ancestors.

The most powerful governing body in Rome was the **Senate**. Members of the Senate served for life. They declared wars, made peace treaties, and formed alliances. Senators also passed decrees, or official orders, and handled money matters.

In the first years of the republic, only patricians (puh•TRIH•shuhnz) could serve in the Senate. The **patricians** were wealthy descendants of Rome's earliest settlers. They controlled both the Senate and the assembly, which elected the consuls.

DEMOCRATIC VALUES
Constitutional Government

CITIZENSHIP

In the early republic, Roman laws were based on unwritten customs. In 451 B.C. and 450 B.C., the common people called for the laws to be recorded so that they could be applied equally to all citizens. The laws were posted in Rome's public square on tablets called the Twelve Tables. Some of the laws stated the citizens' rights, such as the right to own property. Other laws stated their duties, such as military service. The Roman Republic did not begin with a written constitution. However, the tradition of recording its laws provided a model for later constitutional governments.

Analyze the Value

1. What were the Twelve Tables?
2. **Make It Relevant** Write a paragraph about why it is important for citizens to know their laws.

All other Roman citizens were called **plebeians** (plih•BEE•uhnz) or common people. Plebeians included craftworkers, farmers, foot soldiers, and merchants. In the early republic, plebeians had a limited voice in government. Later they began to call for a plebeian assembly and their own elected leaders. In 471 B.C. the plebeians stopped all work and marched out of Rome. They refused to return until the patricians agreed to their demands. The plebeians set up an assembly and elected leaders called **tribunes**.

In time a third, larger assembly—the tribal assembly—developed. Unlike the other assemblies, the tribal assembly represented all Roman citizens. Because there were more plebeian citizens, they controlled the tribal assembly. More changes followed, and by 367 B.C. plebeians could also serve as consuls.

REVIEW How did the Roman government change in 509 B.C.?

Roman Society

A Roman's position in society was based on family wealth and history. Patricians dominated the upper class in the early republic. However, by the 400s B.C. wealthy plebeians were also considered part of the upper class.

The upper class enjoyed the best that Rome had to offer. Its members were important government officials. They lived in large and beautiful country homes called villas (VIH•luhz). Often a wealthy family also kept a large home in the city of Rome.

The Roman lower class was made up of all other citizens. Craftworkers, merchants, small-farm owners, and most soldiers belonged to the lower class. These Romans often lived in apartment-style homes, with an entire family living in a few rooms.

Slaves were at the bottom of Roman society. They were not citizens and had little protection under the laws. Treatment

Analyze Illustrations This drawing shows the inside of a Roman villa.

1. The atrium (AY•tree•uhm), or central hall
2. A female slave doing household chores
3. Roman boys with their tutor
4. A kitchen for preparing food

? Why do you think the ceiling of the central hall has an opening?

280

of slaves and their living conditions depended entirely on their owners. Yet, slaves in Rome had more rights than those of other cultures. Many were freed upon their owner's death, and some were able to buy their freedom. Former slaves were granted Roman citizenship.

In all Roman social classes, men were the heads of households. However, Roman women did help in decision making in their own homes.

Statue of a Roman child with a puppy (left)
A dog tag with Latin writing (far left)

In some cases, women could own property, and they offered advice to their sons and husbands. Roman literature and art show that women took an active part in society. However, Roman women were not allowed to participate in government.

REVIEW How was Roman society divided?

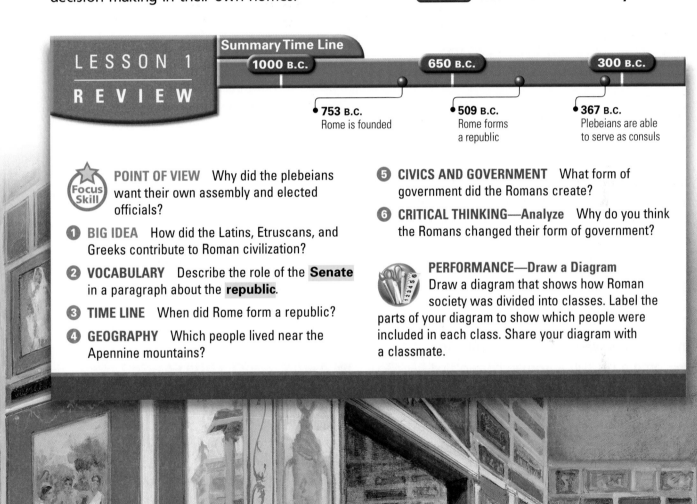

LESSON 1 REVIEW

Summary Time Line

| 1000 B.C. | | 650 B.C. | | 300 B.C. |

753 B.C. Rome is founded

509 B.C. Rome forms a republic

367 B.C. Plebeians are able to serve as consuls

Focus Skill **POINT OF VIEW** Why did the plebeians want their own assembly and elected officials?

1 BIG IDEA How did the Latins, Etruscans, and Greeks contribute to Roman civilization?

2 VOCABULARY Describe the role of the **Senate** in a paragraph about the **republic**.

3 TIME LINE When did Rome form a republic?

4 GEOGRAPHY Which people lived near the Apennine mountains?

5 CIVICS AND GOVERNMENT What form of government did the Romans create?

6 CRITICAL THINKING—Analyze Why do you think the Romans changed their form of government?

PERFORMANCE—Draw a Diagram Draw a diagram that shows how Roman society was divided into classes. Label the parts of your diagram to show which people were included in each class. Share your diagram with a classmate.

Follow a Flow Chart

VOCABULARY

flow chart

WHY IT MATTERS

Often it is easier to understand a complex process, such as a system of government, if it is shown in a flow chart. A **flow chart** is a graphic organizer that shows the sequence, or order, of the steps in a process.

WHAT YOU NEED TO KNOW

A career in Roman government was very competitive and followed strict rules. To begin, a citizen had to be elected to the job of magistrate (MA•juh•strayt), or government official, by one of the assemblies. Except for the office of dictator, each magistrate's office had at least two people serving together for a term that typically lasted one year.

In the city of Rome, the most powerful magistrates were the two consuls. To become a consul, a Roman citizen first needed to serve in other offices. The sequence of offices in the Roman Republic is shown in a flow chart on the next page.

The following tips can help you follow a flow chart.

- **Read the title.** The title of a flow chart tells what process is being explained.

- **Identify the steps.** Brief descriptions of steps or tasks in a process usually appear in boxes or ovals.

- **Follow the arrows.** Arrows between steps show how the steps are connected. Most flow charts "flow" from left to right or from top to bottom.

- **Look for "if-then" situations.** A step may be followed by more than one possible next step. Two or more arrows leading to the possible next steps show the choices.

PRACTICE THE SKILL

Use the flow chart on page 283 to answer the following questions.

1. What was the first office that could be held by both patricians and plebeians?
2. Was a praetor elected or appointed?
3. What offices were open to a former consul?

APPLY WHAT YOU LEARNED

Make a flow chart that shows the process of completing an everyday task, such as making a sandwich. Next, trade flow charts with a partner and check to see if you could follow the steps to complete the task. Then, work together to make both flow charts as complete as possible.

S.P.Q.R. stood for *the Senate and the People of Rome* just as *U.S.A.* stands for *the United States of America.*

The Sequence of Offices in the Roman Republic

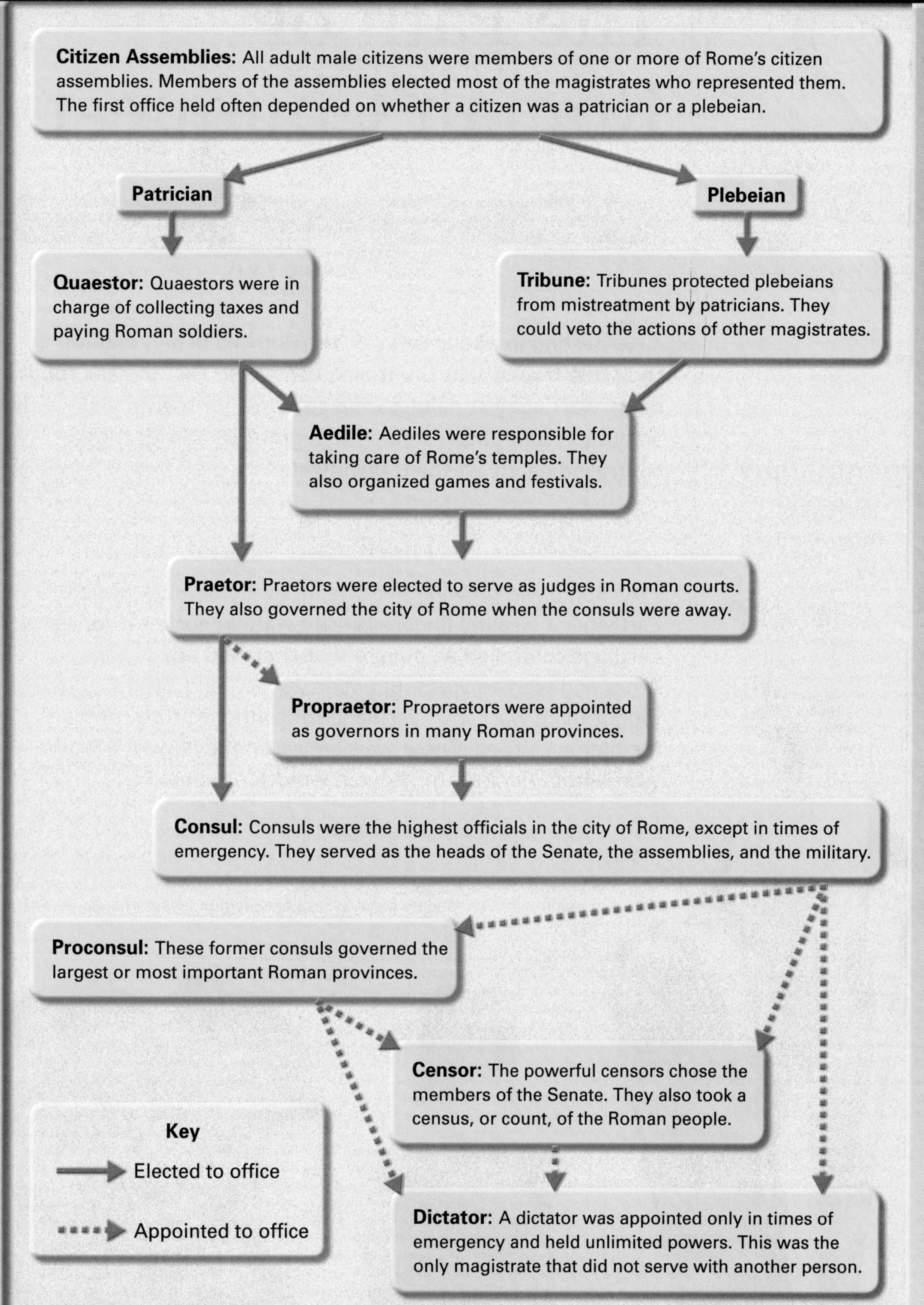

Citizen Assemblies: All adult male citizens were members of one or more of Rome's citizen assemblies. Members of the assemblies elected most of the magistrates who represented them. The first office held often depended on whether a citizen was a patrician or a plebeian.

Patrician

Plebeian

Quaestor: Quaestors were in charge of collecting taxes and paying Roman soldiers.

Tribune: Tribunes protected plebeians from mistreatment by patricians. They could veto the actions of other magistrates.

Aedile: Aediles were responsible for taking care of Rome's temples. They also organized games and festivals.

Praetor: Praetors were elected to serve as judges in Roman courts. They also governed the city of Rome when the consuls were away.

Propraetor: Propraetors were appointed as governors in many Roman provinces.

Consul: Consuls were the highest officials in the city of Rome, except in times of emergency. They served as the heads of the Senate, the assemblies, and the military.

Proconsul: These former consuls governed the largest or most important Roman provinces.

Censor: The powerful censors chose the members of the Senate. They also took a census, or count, of the Roman people.

Key

➡ Elected to office

┅➤ Appointed to office

Dictator: A dictator was appointed only in times of emergency and held unlimited powers. This was the only magistrate that did not serve with another person.

POINT OF VIEW

Read to learn how different points of view in Rome led to civil wars.

BIG IDEA

The Roman government changed as Rome grew into an empire.

VOCABULARY

province
triumvirate

The Path of Roman Conquest

| 1000 B.C. | 500 B.C. | B.C./A.D. | A.D. 500 |

500 B.C.–B.C./A.D.

Starting in about 500 B.C., the Romans began extending their rule throughout the Italian Peninsula. The Romans fought many wars against neighboring cultures. With each victory the amount of land under Roman rule grew. By 264 B.C., Rome controlled nearly all the Italian Peninsula.

The Punic Wars

As Rome was growing in power, a rivalry developed with Carthage, a wealthy Phoenician city-state in northern Africa. Carthage controlled an empire that stretched across northern Africa and west to Spain. Between 264 B.C. and 146 B.C., Rome fought three wars with Carthage for control of trade in the Mediterranean Sea. These wars are called the Punic (PYOO•nik) Wars—from *Punicus*, the Roman word for *Phoenician*.

This bronze statue shows a soldier of the Roman Republic (left) carrying a shield and spear. Fighting groups known as legions carried a standard (below, center), or marker, that let leaders know where each legion was during battle. All Roman soldiers wore protective clothing such as this piece of body armor (below, right).

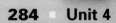

A wall painting shows how an Italian artist in the 1500s thought Hannibal's army looked as the soldiers invaded the Italian Peninsula.

The First Punic War lasted from 264 B.C. to 241 B.C. During that time Rome gained control of Sicily, an island southwest of the Italian Peninsula. Rome sent a governor to oversee its first **province**, or self-governing region. Rome also conquered Sardinia and Corsica, two islands west of the peninsula.

In the Second Punic War, which lasted from 218 B.C. to 201 B.C., Carthage invaded the Italian Peninsula. Starting in what is now Spain, the Carthaginian army marched toward Rome. The general Hannibal led soldiers and

This Roman clay vase shows a Phoenician soldier riding a war elephant.

war elephants over the high, snow-covered Alps into the Italian Peninsula. The Roman historian Livy wrote about Hannibal,

66 No work could tire his body or his spirit. Heat and cold were the same to him. . . . He was always the first into battle and the last to leave. 99

Hannibal's army won several key battles, but the Romans would not give up. Under a general named Scipio, the Romans invaded northern Africa, forcing Hannibal to return to defend his home. In 202 B.C. Scipio's army defeated Hannibal in the Battle of Zama, near Carthage.

In the Third Punic War, from 149 B.C. to 146 B.C., the Romans destroyed the city of Carthage. They left it in ruins and enslaved the people.

Victory in the Punic Wars brought the western Mediterranean Sea and coastal areas of Spain and Africa under Roman control. In the east, Rome had conquered Greece, Macedonia, and parts of southwestern Asia. The Romans divided their vast new lands into more provinces. The conquered peoples had to pay taxes to Rome, and many were taken as slaves.

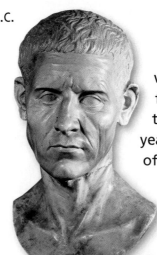

Lucius Cornelius Sulla

Money that came from the provinces made upper-class Romans richer. Slaves who were taken to Rome made many in the lower class poorer. Plebeians lost their jobs or lands as their work was turned over to slaves. This caused terrible conflict between rich and poor Romans.

REVIEW How do you think many people in the lower class viewed slavery?

POINT OF VIEW

The Civil Wars

The provinces brought great wealth to Rome. Yet, the Romans found it difficult to agree on how to govern faraway lands. For 50 years, leaders struggled for control of the republic in a series of civil wars.

A Roman leader named Sulla became dictator in 82 B.C. He ruled for three years, not just for the six months allowed by Roman law during emergencies. Sulla retired in 79 B.C., and leadership returned to the consuls. Romans including Pompey (PAHM•pee) and Cicero (SIH•suh•roh) led as consuls in the years following Sulla's dictatorship.

In 60 B.C. a leader named Julius Caesar (JOO•lee•uhs SEE•zer) was elected consul. Caesar formed an army and captured Gaul (GAWL), a land to the northwest, most of which is now France. Caesar became popular with the citizens of Rome and his soldiers.

Defeated enemy soldiers surrender their weapons to Julius Caesar in this painting created at a later time.

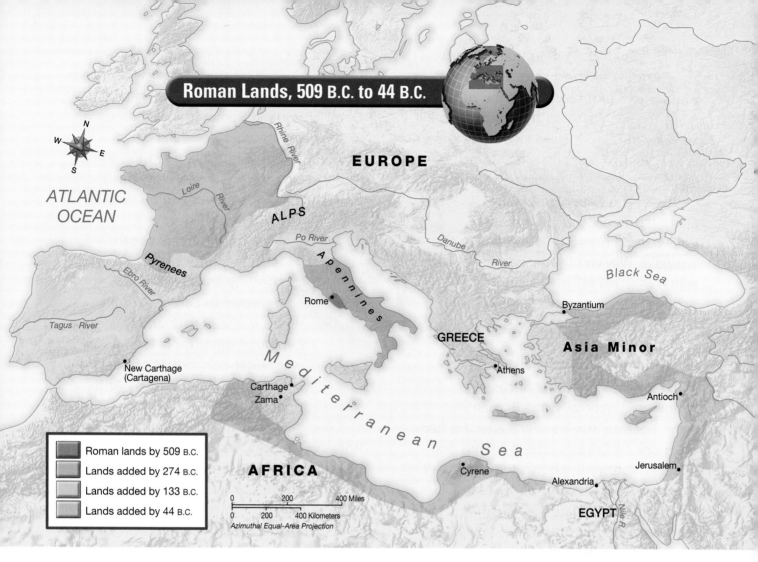

Roman Lands, 509 B.C. to 44 B.C.

EUROPE

ATLANTIC OCEAN

ALPS

Loire River

Rhine River

Po River

Apennines

Danube River

Pyrenees

Ebro River

Black Sea

Rome

Byzantium

Tagus River

GREECE

Asia Minor

Mediterranean Sea

New Carthage (Cartagena)

Carthage
Zama

Athens

Antioch

AFRICA

Cyrene

Jerusalem

Alexandria

EGYPT

Nile R.

Legend:
- Roman lands by 509 B.C.
- Lands added by 274 B.C.
- Lands added by 133 B.C.
- Lands added by 44 B.C.

0   200   400 Miles
0 200 400 Kilometers
Azimuthal Equal-Area Projection

GEOGRAPHY THEME

Movement   **By 44 B.C. Rome controlled lands in Europe, Asia, and Africa.**

❓ **By what year did the Romans control all of Greece?**

By 46 B.C., as Caesar was preparing to return to Rome, some senators began to fear Caesar's return. The senators thought Caesar might try to take over the Roman government. Caesar was warned to give up his army and not bring his soldiers across the Rubicon River, from Gaul into the Italian Peninsula. Caesar ignored the Senate's warning and crossed the river. In just 60 days Caesar conquered the Italian Peninsula.

Julius Caesar with his wife, Calpurnia

Caesar's leadership ability and military victories convinced the Senate that he should rule as dictator for ten years.

As dictator, Julius Caesar proved to be a strong and effective leader. He changed the Senate so it better represented the Roman people. He improved many lives by issuing decrees that helped the poor. He also created new jobs and gave citizenship to more people, including those from the provinces. Caesar's popularity made him very powerful.

Chapter 9 ▪ 287

Some senators worried that Caesar was planning to become a king. These senators wanted to restore control of the government to the Senate, so they plotted to kill Caesar. On March 15, 44 B.C., a day known as the "Ides of March" on the Roman calendar, a small group of senators stabbed Caesar at a Senate meeting. Caesar's death led to another period of civil war and unrest in Rome.

REVIEW Why was Caesar popular with the citizens of Rome?

The End of the Republic

After Caesar's death, Marcus Antonius, a general in the Roman army, became Rome's new leader. He had been one of Caesar's closest friends and advisers. Antonius, known today as Mark Antony, hoped to carry out Caesar's plans for Rome. The Senate named Antony as the new dictator. However, the next year Antony's right to rule was challenged.

Coin showing Antony, Octavian, and Lepidus

Because Caesar had no son of his own, he had adopted his great-nephew, Octavian (ahk•TAY•vee•uhn). Many senators wanted Octavian to lead Rome. In 43 B.C. Octavian, Antony, and another general, named Lepidus (LEH•puh•duhs), agreed to form a **triumvirate** (try•UHM•vuh•ruht), or group of three rulers who share power.

Soon the rulers began struggling for power. At first, Antony and Octavian worked together to defeat Caesar's enemies in the Senate and to remove Lepidus from power. Then a civil war began for control of Rome and its provinces. The army of Antony opposed that of Octavian.

One of the most important Roman provinces was Egypt. Caesar had conquered Egypt and formed an alliance with Egypt's queen, Cleopatra. An agreement with Caesar had allowed Cleopatra to stay in power. Antony met with Egypt's queen and formed a new alliance against Octavian.

The Battle of Actium, 31 B.C.

In 31 B.C. Octavian's forces defeated those of Antony and Cleopatra in a famous sea battle near Actium, in Greece. The next year, Octavian's army conquered Egypt. Both Antony and Cleopatra died within a few days of their defeat. With their deaths Octavian became the unchallenged ruler of all Roman lands.

In 27 B.C. the Roman Senate gave Octavian the title Augustus. The title means "respected one" or "holy one." Octavian has been known ever since as Augustus Caesar, or simply Augustus.

Augustus was Rome's first emperor, but he never used this title. Instead, he adopted the title *princeps*, meaning "first citizen." Augustus knew that the idea of a republic was important to the Roman people. He made sure that in some ways the government remained representative. Even so, the Roman Republic ended when Augustus's rule began.

REVIEW Who was Rome's first emperor?

LESSON 2 REVIEW

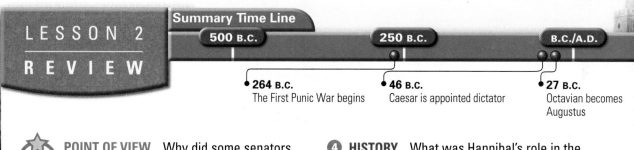

Summary Time Line

500 B.C.	250 B.C.	B.C./A.D.

264 B.C. The First Punic War begins

46 B.C. Caesar is appointed dictator

27 B.C. Octavian becomes Augustus

 POINT OF VIEW Why did some senators fear Julius Caesar?

1 BIG IDEA How did Caesar's term as dictator bring about changes in Roman government?

2 VOCABULARY Use **province** in a sentence describing the expanding borders of Rome.

3 TIME LINE How many years passed between the start of the First Punic War and Caesar's appointment as dictator?

4 HISTORY What was Hannibal's role in the Punic Wars?

5 CRITICAL THINKING—Analyze Why do you think governing the provinces caused problems for the Roman government?

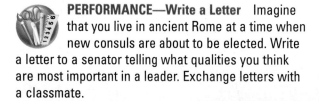 **PERFORMANCE—Write a Letter** Imagine that you live in ancient Rome at a time when new consuls are about to be elected. Write a letter to a senator telling what qualities you think are most important in a leader. Exchange letters with a classmate.

Compare Historical Maps

▶ WHY IT MATTERS

Some historical maps show where events took place. Others show what places were like in the past. Comparing historical maps can help you understand how a place has changed over time.

▶ WHAT YOU NEED TO KNOW

Often the title or the map key of a historical map tells what time period is shown on the map. Map A shows ancient Roman lands in 274 B.C. The purple area on the map shows lands controlled by Rome at that time.

The Roman Empire grew until it reached its greatest size under the

emperor Trajan, in A.D. 117. The purple areas on Map B show which lands were then governed by Rome.

Map C combines information from Map A and Map B. It also shows how the boundaries of Roman territories changed from 274 B.C. to A.D. 117.

▶ PRACTICE THE SKILL

Use the maps to answer these questions.

1. Which map shows what lands Rome controlled by 133 B.C.?

2. By what year did Rome control Egypt?

3. Which maps can you use to find out when Rome first controlled the Italian Peninsula?

4. How did the boundaries of lands controlled by Rome change between 274 B.C. and A.D. 117?

This column celebrates a Roman victory.

Map A: Rome in 274 B.C.

Roman lands

BRITAIN
EUROPE
ASIA
Danube
Aral Sea
ALPS
River
Black Sea
Caspian Sea
ATLANTIC OCEAN
Rome
Tagus R.
Byzantium
New Carthage (Cartagena)
GREECE
Zama
Carthage
Athens
Antioch
Mediterranean Sea
Cyrene
Alexandria
Jerusalem
Tigris River
Euphrates River
0   400   800 Miles
0   400   800 Kilometers
Azimuthal Equal-Area Projection
EGYPT
Nile River
Red Sea
Persian Gulf
AFRICA

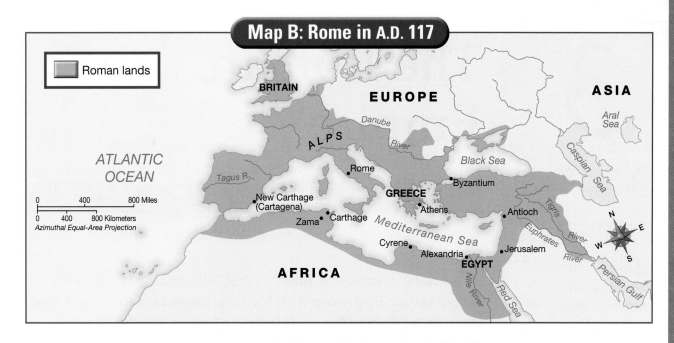

Map B: Rome in A.D. 117

Roman lands

BRITAIN

EUROPE

ASIA

ATLANTIC
OCEAN

0   400   800 Miles
0   400   800 Kilometers
Azimuthal Equal-Area Projection

Aral
Sea

Danube
River

ALPS

Black Sea

Caspian Sea

Rome

Byzantium

GREECE

Athens

Tagus R.

New Carthage
(Cartagena)

Zama • Carthage

Mediterranean Sea

Antioch

Tigris

Euphrates
River

River

Cyrene

Alexandria

Jerusalem

EGYPT

AFRICA

Nile River

Red Sea

Persian Gulf

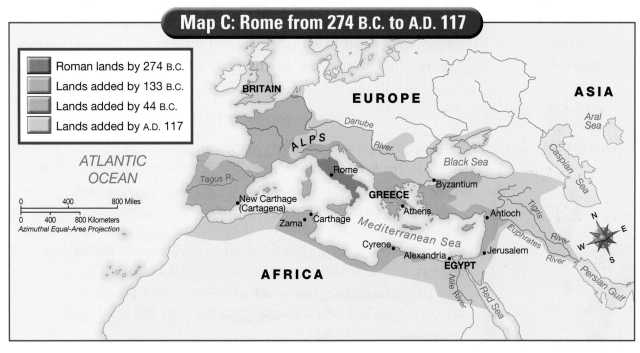

Map C: Rome from 274 B.C. to A.D. 117

Roman lands by 274 B.C.
Lands added by 133 B.C.
Lands added by 44 B.C.
Lands added by A.D. 117

BRITAIN

EUROPE

ASIA

ATLANTIC
OCEAN

Aral
Sea

Danube
River

ALPS

Black Sea

Caspian Sea

Rome

Byzantium

GREECE

Athens

0   400   800 Miles
0   400   800 Kilometers
Azimuthal Equal-Area Projection

Tagus R.

New Carthage
(Cartagena)

Zama • Carthage

Mediterranean Sea

Antioch

Tigris

Euphrates
River

River

Cyrene

Alexandria

Jerusalem

EGYPT

AFRICA

Nile River

Red Sea

Persian Gulf

5 Did Rome control the city of Jerusalem in 274 B.C.? Which maps can you use to find this information?

➡ APPLY WHAT YOU LEARNED

Use an atlas to find historical maps that show the growth of the United States over time. Then draw your own map that shows this growth. Use different colors to indicate the size of the nation in different periods of history. Write a paragraph describing the border changes shown on your map.

Practice your map and globe skills with the **GeoSkills CD-ROM**.

· LESSON ·

3

POINT OF VIEW

As you read, identify points of view of the Romans about their government and culture.

BIG IDEA

The Roman Empire united many different peoples under one government.

VOCABULARY

census
basilica
forum
gladiator
aqueduct
patriotism

The Roman Empire

1000 B.C.	500 B.C.	B.C./A.D.	A.D. 500

100 B.C.– A.D. 200

Like his great-uncle Julius Caesar, Augustus was a strong, skilled leader. Beginning with his rule, Rome was to enjoy a *Pax Romana*, or Roman Peace. This time of peace for the Romans lasted for more than 200 years—from 27 B.C. to A.D. 180. During this period the Roman Empire continued to grow in size. The empire expanded to include lands all around the Mediterranean Sea. For this reason, the sea became known as the "Roman Lake."

Governing the Empire

Millions of people speaking many languages and following different customs lived in the empire. The Roman Empire required a strong government and one that the people would accept.

Augustus carefully chose people to serve as governors for the provinces. He issued decrees that gave Roman citizenship to those who lived in the provinces. Citizenship gave people special protection. One law said that citizens could not be forced to speak against themselves in law courts. This and other principles, or rules, set up by the Romans are important parts of the legal systems of many countries today.

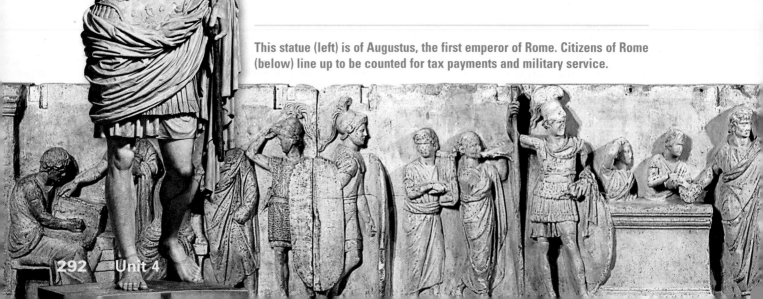

This statue (left) is of Augustus, the first emperor of Rome. Citizens of Rome (below) line up to be counted for tax payments and military service.

292   Unit 4

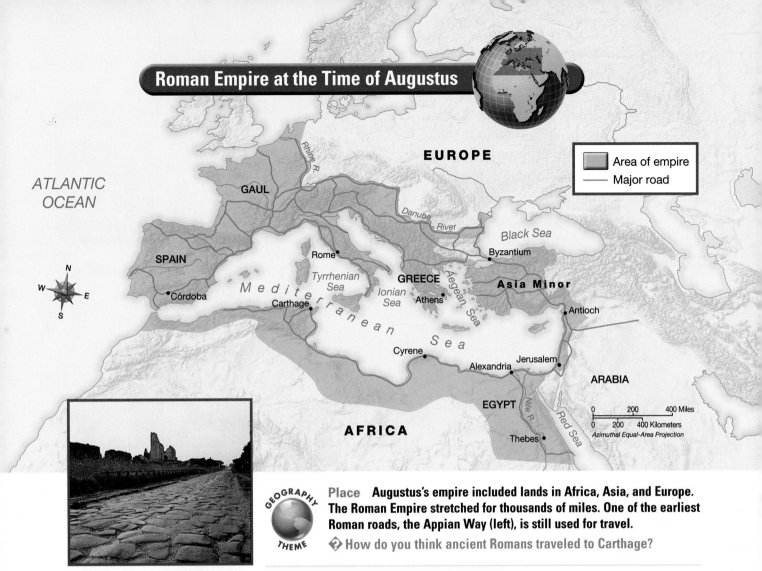

Roman Empire at the Time of Augustus

EUROPE

ATLANTIC OCEAN

GAUL

Rhine R.

Danube River

Black Sea

SPAIN

Rome

Byzantium

Córdoba

Tyrrhenian Sea

Mediterranean Sea

GREECE

Asia Minor

Carthage

Ionian Sea

Athens

Aegean Sea

Antioch

Cyrene

Alexandria

Jerusalem

ARABIA

EGYPT

Nile R.

Red Sea

AFRICA

Thebes

N W E S

Area of empire

Major road

0   200   400 Miles
0   200   400 Kilometers
Azimuthal Equal-Area Projection

GEOGRAPHY THEME

Place Augustus's empire included lands in Africa, Asia, and Europe. The Roman Empire stretched for thousands of miles. One of the earliest Roman roads, the Appian Way (left), is still used for travel.

◆ How do you think ancient Romans traveled to Carthage?

The Romans were the first to take a **census**, or a count of a country's people. The census helped to make sure that Roman citizens paid any taxes or gave any military service that they owed.

Under the early republic the Roman army had been made up only of citizens who owned land. Roman leaders believed that they would fight harder to defend Rome than landless people would. As the borders of Rome grew, more soldiers were needed, so the army was opened to volunteers.

By about 20 B.C. the Roman Empire had a standing army of some 300,000 soldiers. Most were well-trained professionals whose skills made the Roman army one of the most successful military forces in history.

The army's main job was to defend the empire's borders. Many soldiers were sent to regions in central and eastern Europe.

Other important army posts were in Britain, Egypt, Syria, Asia Minor, and northern Africa.

In addition to their military role, Roman soldiers built army posts throughout the empire. They also built about 50,000 miles (about 80,000 km) of roadways. The roads allowed the Roman army to move quickly and made the exchange of goods and ideas possible all over the empire. This led to cultural diffusion, or the spread of ideas, among the provinces.

REVIEW How did Roman roads unite the empire?

The Splendor of Rome

Rome was the capital of the Roman Empire. It was also the empire's largest city, with more than 4 million people. No other city was more splendid.

Augustus ordered new government offices, libraries, temples, and public baths to be built, and existing buildings to be repaired. "I found Rome a city of bricks and left it a city of marble," Augustus said. In the city's center stood huge government buildings called **basilicas** (buh•SIH•lih•kuhz). New temples and other buildings rose beside them.

On a stretch of level ground near the Tiber River was the **forum**, a public place where people could meet for business or recreation. Merchants sold fresh meats, vegetables, pottery, cloth, and luxury goods from the eastern provinces. Public notices were carved in stone there, and papyrus scrolls were filled with writing.

Ideas from Greek architecture could be seen in many buildings. Roman builders admired the beauty of Greek architecture and used Greek styles of columns in their own buildings. They also used arches, as the Etruscans had.

Aqueduct of Claudius

Circus Maximus

A CLOSER LOOK
Ancient Rome

Rome grew from a village of huts to become one of the grandest cities the world has ever known. This illustration shows some of the main structures of Rome around A.D. 320.

1. Circus Maximus
2. Temple of Jupiter
3. Pantheon
4. Trajan's Forum
5. Aqueduct of Claudius
6. Temple of the Divine Claudius
7. Arch of Constantine
8. Temple of Venus and Rome
9. Colosseum
10. Baths of Titus

❓ Which two structures were used for sporting events in ancient Rome?

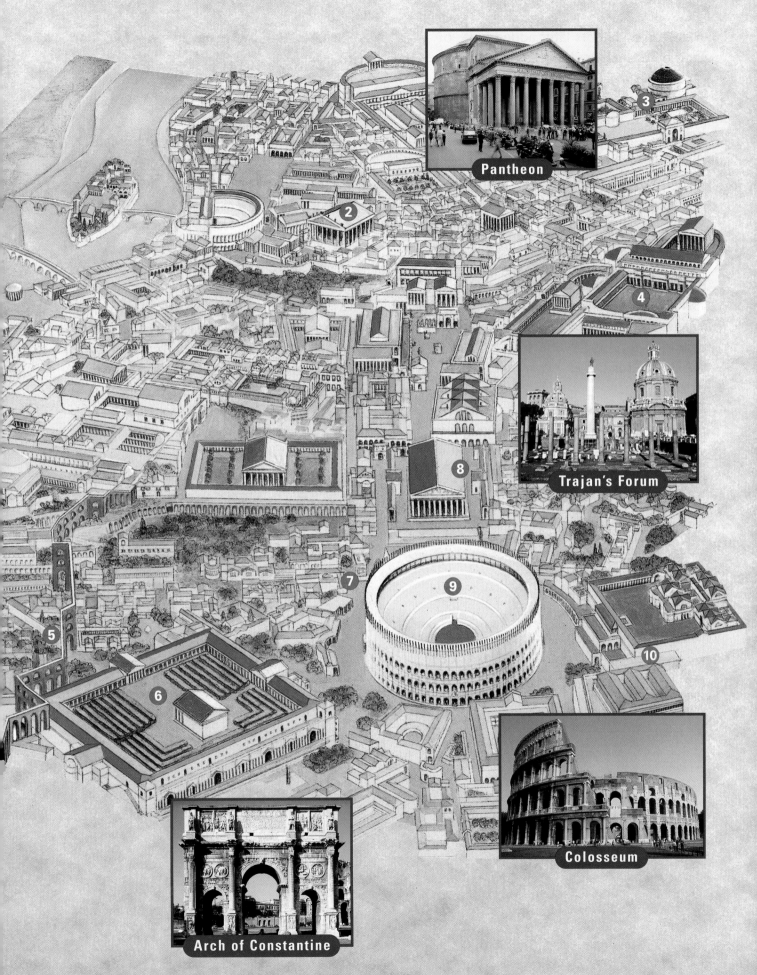

Pantheon

Trajan's Forum

Colosseum

Arch of Constantine

Roman architects later added ideas of their own, such as domes. A famous example is a building known as the Pantheon. *Pantheon* means "temple of all the gods." Built by the emperor Hadrian in A.D. 125, the Pantheon features a dome that is more than 141 feet (43 m) in height.

Some of the new buildings were theaters and sports arenas, where Romans could enjoy entertainment. The largest arena was the Colosseum (kah•luh•SEE•uhm), which could hold 50,000 people. It was built by the emperor Vespasian (ve•SPAY•zhuhn) in about A.D. 72. At the Colosseum, Romans watched battles between gladiators. A **gladiator** was a slave or a prisoner who fought, often to the death, for the entertainment of the citizens.

Because of its splendor, the leaders of provinces in different parts of the empire wanted to remodel their cities after Rome. As far away as Britain and Syria, people built arenas, basilicas, baths, forums, libraries, and temples.

All across the empire the Romans also built aqueducts (A•kwuh•duhkts). An **aqueduct** is a system of bridges and canals used to carry water to a city. The Roman aqueducts carried water from faraway rivers and mountain streams to the cities.

REVIEW What point of view did Augustus have about the work he did for the city of Rome?

POINT OF VIEW

Rome's Cultural Life

Rome often looked to Greece for other cultural ideas besides architecture. Roman artists, sculptors, and writers adopted the Greek styles. The ideas of Greek philosophers such as Aristotle, Plato, and Socrates also spread to Rome. In fact, many wealthy Romans hired Greek scholars to teach their children.

This wall painting shows a gladiator fighting with a lion. This helmet (right) was worn by a gladiator in about A.D. 100.

Mount Vesuvius rises in the background of the ruins of the Roman city of Pompeii (above). A wall painting from Pompeii (left) shows a young married couple.

Roman artists and writers created works that brought out feelings of **patriotism**, or love of country, among the Roman people. Augustus especially wanted an epic that would tell the story of Rome's heroic past. The poet Virgil was asked to write it.

Virgil wrote the *Aeneid* (ih•NEE•uhd), a story about the legendary Trojan hero Aeneas (ih•NEE•uhs), who escapes during the last hours of the Trojan War. Aeneas finds a new home on the Italian Peninsula. In Virgil's retelling of Roman history, Aeneas is the ancestor of Augustus. He is appointed by the gods to create the people of Rome.

The *Aeneid* stirred the patriotic feelings of Romans everywhere. Because of this, it was used for many years as a textbook in Roman schools.

Other Roman writers also made important contributions. Among these were the poets Horace and Ovid (AH•vuhd) and the historians Livy and Tacitus (TA•suh•tuhs).

• GEOGRAPHY •

Pompeii
Understanding Environment and Society

The ancient Roman city of Pompeii (pahm•PAY) was a successful trade and vacation center for many years. Then in A.D. 79 Mount Vesuvius, a volcano near the city, erupted. For nearly two full days, ashes and rocks fell on the city, reaching depths of over 18 feet (5 m). People, homes, and other buildings were completely buried. For 17 centuries the city remained untouched. In the 1700s the Italian military began to dig up Pompeii. They found the ancient Roman city just as it was in A.D. 79. Because Pompeii was trapped in time, we know a great deal about the daily life of the ancient Romans.

ITALY

Adriatic Sea

⊛ Rome

Campobasso

Foggia

Gaeta

Capua

Benevento

Naples

Mt. Vesuvius

POMPEII

Salerno

Ischia

Capri

N W E S

Tyrrhenian Sea

0   25   50 Miles
0   25   50 Kilometers

This stone relief sculpture shows a Roman teacher with his students. The writing tablet (left) and the pen and inkwell (below) were used by a Roman student.

Other important works of Roman literature include speeches by Cicero and letters by Pliny the Younger.

The language of the Romans also helped bring together the diverse peoples of the empire. As Roman soldiers traveled through the provinces, they spoke and wrote in the Latin language. Latin came to be used in

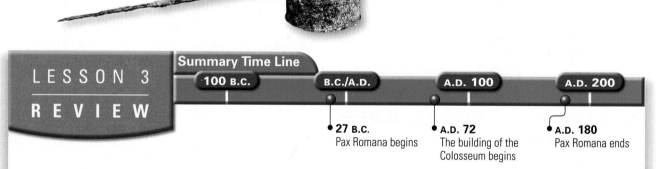

government and education in all the Roman provinces. The Latin alphabet came from the one used by the Etruscans.

English is partly based on Latin. In addition, the Latin alphabet is used to write in English and many other languages today.

REVIEW Why did the poet Virgil write the *Aeneid*?

LESSON 3
REVIEW

Summary Time Line

| 100 B.C. | B.C./A.D. | A.D. 100 | A.D. 200 |

27 B.C.
Pax Romana begins

A.D. 72
The building of the Colosseum begins

A.D. 180
Pax Romana ends

Focus Skill

POINT OF VIEW How did artists and writers help shape the points of view of the Roman people?

1 **BIG IDEA** How did the Romans bring unity to their empire?

2 **VOCABULARY** Write a paragraph about Rome that includes the words **basilica** and **forum**.

3 **TIME LINE** In what year did *Pax Romana* begin?

4 **GEOGRAPHY** Why is the Mediterranean Sea sometimes called the "Roman Lake"?

5 **CIVICS AND GOVERNMENT** Why did the Romans start taking a census?

6 **CRITICAL THINKING—Evaluate** Do you think the Romans were more successful in peace or in war?

PERFORMANCE—Make a Relief Map
Using the map on page 293 as a guide, make a relief map of the Roman Empire. Show the borders of the countries that now occupy these lands, and write in their names. Then shade in all the lands that made up the Roman Empire.

Beginnings of Christianity

| 1000 B.C. | 500 B.C. | B.C./A.D. | A.D. 500 |

100 B.C.–A.D. 400

Parts of the Roman Empire were far from the city of Rome. More than 1,200 miles (1,900 km) from their capital city, the Romans claimed regions of ancient Judaea, Syria, and Palestine. Many Jews, descendants of the ancient Israelites, lived in Judaea and the surrounding areas. Today many people remember Judaea and Galilee, a Roman province to the north, as the areas where Christianity started. **Christianity** was the name given to the religion based on the life and teachings of Jesus.

Jesus is often pictured as a good shepherd, gathering and caring for his flock.

Focus Skill **POINT OF VIEW**

Read to learn how Roman views on religion changed over time.

BIG IDEA
Roman society and the Christian religion affected each other.

VOCABULARY

Christianity
salvation
disciple
messiah
resurrection
apostle
persecute
martyr
Gospels
pope

This painting from the 1400s shows Apollo, the Roman god of music and poetry, dancing with the Muses. The Muses are goddesses who were thought to inspire artists and scientists.

Religion and the Romans

As early as the 500s B.C., Roman religion began to be affected by Greek culture. Roman gods were shown in the humanlike forms of Greek gods and goddesses. Like the Etruscans and Greeks, the Romans built temples to honor their gods and to give them homes to live in. In time, the Roman goddess Juno, who protected women and marriage, came to be identified with the Greek goddess Hera. Jupiter, the most powerful of all the Roman gods, became identified with Zeus.

Worship of the gods was an important part of Roman public and private life. The Romans believed that proper worship of the gods protected the empire from harm. As Rome grew, the government took control of choosing religious leaders and made laws to punish those who did not worship the Roman gods.

In the provinces Romans came into contact with some religious beliefs very different from their own. Often these beliefs were simply adapted to become part of the Roman religion. By A.D. 100 some Romans began to follow religions found in the eastern provinces.

Unlike the Roman religion, some of the other religions promised rewards for believers. Christianity, a new religion, gained many followers because it promised salvation for believers. **Salvation** is the saving of the human soul from evil with a promise of life after death.

REVIEW Why did the Roman government take control of worship?

A statue of the Roman goddess Juno

Jesus and His Teachings

Historians believe that Jesus was born about 4 B.C. For much of his early life, he lived in the town of Nazareth in Galilee. Later, Jesus traveled as a Jewish teacher all over Judaea and Galilee.

Jesus taught belief in one God and in the Ten Commandments, just as other Jewish teachers did. Yet in some ways his teachings were very different from theirs. Jesus told of the coming of what he called the kingdom of God. He called on the Jewish people to turn away from sin, or going against the word of God, so that they could be part of God's kingdom. Jesus explained that God loved them and would forgive those who were sorry for their sins.

Wherever Jesus taught, he gained new followers. Among them were Jesus' **disciples**, a group of men who were his closest followers. Jesus told them to love their enemies as well as one another. He said,

> **" You shall love your neighbor as yourself. "**

One belief of Judaism is that a **messiah** (muh•SY•uh), or a person sent by God, will come to bring justice to the world. Some people began to believe that Jesus was the Messiah.

However, many people did not believe that Jesus was the Messiah, and they did not accept his teachings. Some Jewish leaders argued that Jesus and his disciples did not strictly follow Jewish laws. Often the teachings of Jesus caused great debate among the Jewish people and concern among the Roman leaders in Judaea.

This limestone relief (above) shows two symbols of Christianity—the cross and the fish. This Bible (right) from a later period shows pages from the New Testament.

The Beatitudes

The Beatitudes (bee•A•tuh•toodz) is the name given to a group of statements made by Jesus. The Beatitudes are in the New Testament as a part of Jesus' Sermon on the Mount (Matthew 5:3-12).

Blessed are the poor in spirit, for theirs is the kingdom of heaven.

Blessed are those who mourn, for they will be comforted.

Blessed are the meek, for they will inherit the earth.

Blessed are those who hunger and thirst for righteousness, for they will be filled.

Blessed are the merciful, for they will receive mercy.

Blessed are the pure in heart, for they will see God.

Blessed are the peacemakers, for they will be called children of God.

Blessed are those who are persecuted for righteousness's sake, for theirs is the kingdom of heaven.

Blessed are you when people revile you and persecute you and utter all kinds of evil against you falsely on my account.

Rejoice and be glad, for your reward is great in heaven.

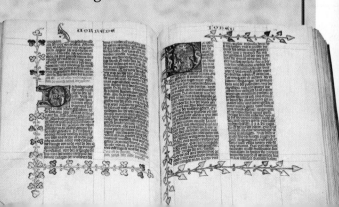

The Roman governor of Judaea, Pontius Pilate, feared that conflicts over Jesus would stir rebellion against Roman rule. Because of this, Pilate ordered that Jesus be put to death by being nailed to a cross and left to die. This was a common form of execution at that time. Jesus is believed to have died in this way in about the year A.D. 30.

Jesus' followers reported that on the third day after his death, Jesus rose from the dead and appeared to them. This convinced them that Jesus was the Messiah. His followers began to tell others of Jesus' **resurrection**, or rising from the dead, and to pass on his teachings.

REVIEW What was Jesus' point of view about how people should treat their neighbors?

 POINT OF VIEW

The Spread of Christianity

Soon the story of the life, death, and resurrection of Jesus spread throughout the Roman Empire. Wherever Jesus' followers traveled, they gained new believers. In lands along the eastern Mediterranean, where people spoke Greek, Jesus came to be known as Jesus Christos, or Jesus Christ. The Greek word for *messiah* is *christos.* The growing number of people who believed in Jesus became known as Christians.

The first to tell others about the life and teachings of Jesus were his disciples. Peter, their leader, became an apostle in the new religion. An **apostle** is a person sent out to teach others. Peter traveled among the Jews

Early Christians often buried their dead in underground tombs called catacombs, such as these on the island of Malta (below). This painting (right) showing Jesus and his twelve apostles is on the wall in catacombs near Rome.

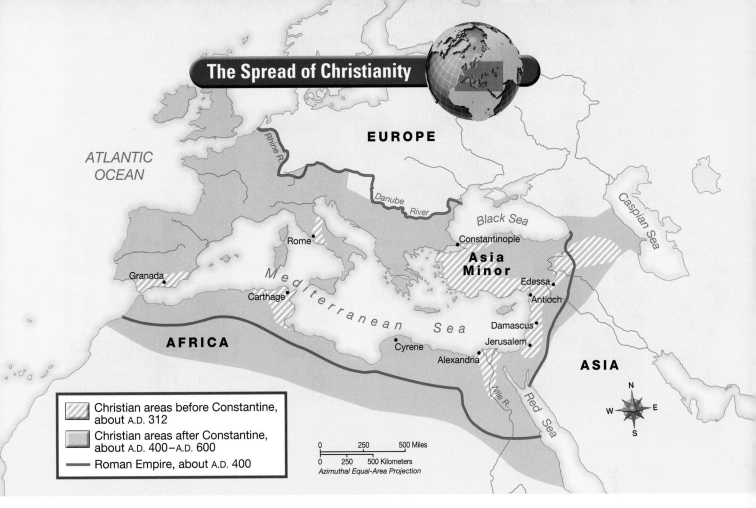

The Spread of Christianity

EUROPE

ATLANTIC OCEAN

Rhine R.

Danube River

Black Sea

Caspian Sea

Rome

Constantinople

Asia Minor

Edessa

Granada

Mediterranean Sea

Carthage

Antioch

Damascus

Cyrene

Jerusalem

Alexandria

AFRICA

Nile R.

Red Sea

ASIA

N
W E
S

Christian areas before Constantine, about A.D. 312

Christian areas after Constantine, about A.D. 400–A.D. 600

Roman Empire, about A.D. 400

0   250   500 Miles
0   250   500 Kilometers
Azimuthal Equal-Area Projection

GEOGRAPHY THEME

Movement   **Constantine helped Christianity grow by making it an accepted religion of the Roman Empire.**

❓ **How many continents did Christianity reach by A.D. 400?**

in Judaea and then among peoples in other parts of the Roman Empire.

Another important apostle of Christianity was Paul of Tarsus, a Roman city in Asia Minor. At first, Paul had opposed the Christians. Later, Paul came to believe in Jesus. He traveled and wrote letters to Christian communities across the Roman Empire. Paul spent the rest of his life as a strong leader of the Christian church.

At times the spread of Christianity caused concern

for Roman leaders. Roman law allowed people to have other religious beliefs as long as they also worshipped the Roman gods. The Christians refused. Some Romans began to fear that their gods might not protect Rome if the Christians did not worship them. That fear led some Romans to **persecute**, or seek out and punish, the Christians for their beliefs.

During times of persecution, many Christians became **martyrs** (MAR•terz), or people who are willing to die for their beliefs. An 86-year-old Christian leader named Polycarp was one such martyr.

A stamp to mark breads used in Christian religious services

The Arch of Constantine (above) still stands in Rome. The head from a huge statue of Constantine I (left) is more than 8 feet (about 2.5 m) tall.

When Polycarp was brought before a Roman governor, he was offered several chances to give up his beliefs. Polycarp refused, saying he had served Jesus for many years and would not stop. By their examples, martyrs helped other Christians remain strong in their beliefs.

Writings by Christians played an important role in the growth of Christianity. Many of the letters that Paul wrote to members of the communities he founded now appear in the Christian Bible. Other Christian writings were grouped to form the **Gospels**, which describe the life, death, and resurrection of Jesus. Paul's letters, the Gospels, and other writings about Jesus were combined to form the New Testament. The first part of the Christian Bible, the Old Testament, contains the books of the Hebrew Bible.

REVIEW Why did some Roman leaders fear Christianity?

Rome and the New Religion

Beginning in A.D. 313, the Romans stopped persecuting Christians for a time. This happened because of the actions of the Roman emperor, Constantine (KAHN•stuhn•teen).

The year before, Constantine had fought an important battle at the Milvian Bridge, near Rome. Just before the battle, something happened that changed Constantine's life. He later reported that the Greek letters for the word *Christos*—*chi* and *rho*—had appeared in the sky above him. Over these letters were written the Latin words for "By this sign [you will] conquer." After ordering his soldiers to paint *chi* and *rho* on their shields, Constantine won the battle.

Early Christian symbol made by combining the Greek letters *chi* and *rho*

Emperor Theodosius I made Christianity the official religion of the Roman Empire.

Because of this victory, Constantine came to believe that the God of the Christians was powerful. In A.D. 313 he issued the Edict of Milan. This edict, or an order from a leader to all the citizens, made Christianity an accepted religion in the Roman Empire. Throughout his reign as emperor, Constantine supported and even helped the growth of Christianity.

In A.D. 392, under the emperor Theodosius I (thee•uh•DOH•shuhs), Christianity became the official religion of the Roman Empire. From this time on, emperors supported Christianity and helped build Christian churches. The number of Christians steadily grew.

From earliest times Christianity was highly organized. Each local church had its own leader called a priest. Nearby churches came together under a single leader called a bishop. Over time, the bishop of Rome became known as the **pope**, or the leader of all bishops. Some Christians believe that Jesus chose Peter to serve as the first pope.

REVIEW How did the support of Roman emperors affect Christianity?

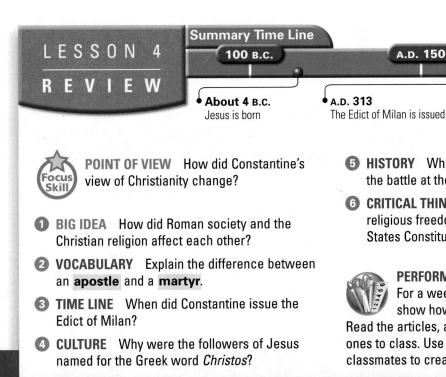

LESSON 4 REVIEW

Summary Time Line

100 B.C. — A.D. 150 — A.D. 400

About 4 B.C. Jesus is born

A.D. 313 The Edict of Milan is issued

A.D. 392 Christianity becomes the official religion of the Roman Empire

Focus Skill **POINT OF VIEW** How did Constantine's view of Christianity change?

1 BIG IDEA How did Roman society and the Christian religion affect each other?

2 VOCABULARY Explain the difference between an **apostle** and a **martyr**.

3 TIME LINE When did Constantine issue the Edict of Milan?

4 CULTURE Why were the followers of Jesus named for the Greek word *Christos*?

5 HISTORY What happened to Constantine before the battle at the Milvian Bridge?

6 CRITICAL THINKING—Analyze Why do you think religious freedom is guaranteed in the United States Constitution?

PERFORMANCE—Make a Bulletin Board For a week, look for newspaper articles that show how religion affects society today. Read the articles, and bring the most interesting ones to class. Use your articles and those of your classmates to create an "In the News" bulletin board.

Predict a Historical Outcome

VOCABULARY

prediction

▶ WHY IT MATTERS

People often make **predictions**. This means that they look at the way things are and decide what they think will most likely happen next. When people make predictions, they are not just guessing wildly about what will happen. They are combining what they already know with new information to predict a probable, or likely, outcome. You can use what you have already learned about history to make predictions about other events you read about.

▶ WHAT YOU NEED TO KNOW

You can take the following steps to predict a likely outcome.

Step 1 **Think about what you already know.**

Step 2 **Review information you have learned.**

Step 3 **Look for patterns that may help you predict an outcome.**

Step 4 **Make a prediction.**

The Santa Francesca Romana church (far right) is located within the ruins of the Roman Forum.

▶ PRACTICE THE SKILL

You have read about the Roman Empire and the beginnings of Christianity. Use the steps on page 306 to predict what happens to Christianity after it is officially adopted by the Romans.

▶ APPLY WHAT YOU LEARNED

Think about a prediction that you have made in the past. What information did you use to make this prediction? Did you have to form a new prediction, or was your first prediction correct? In a small group of classmates, share your prediction and the outcome. Then discuss with the group possible strategies for making accurate predictions.

Make a Prediction About Christianity and the Roman Empire

Facts about adoption of Christianity by the Roman Empire.

⬇

Facts about the rise of religions in other civilizations.

⬇

Prediction about what may happen to Christianity in the Roman Empire.

Review and Test Preparation

(Focus Skill) Point of View

Complete this graphic organizer to show that you understand
different points of view of early people of Italy. A copy of this
graphic organizer appears on page 88 of the Activity Book.

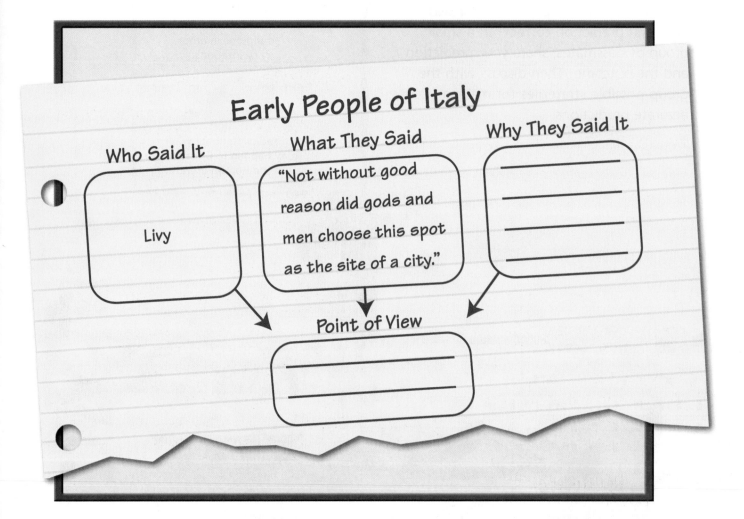

Early People of Italy

Who Said It

Livy

What They Said

"Not without good reason did gods and men choose this spot as the site of a city."

Why They Said It

_____
_____
_____

Point of View

_____
_____

THINK & WRITE

Write a Speech   How did Rome's geography
make it an ideal place to build a city? Write a
short speech to convince others that Rome's
site was a good place from which to rule an
empire.

Write a Children's Book   Retell the story
of Romulus and Remus as if you were writing a
children's book. Tell the story in no more than
ten sentences, and include one sentence and
one illustration on each page.

509 B.C.
Romans form a republic

46 B.C.
Julius Caesar conquers
the Italian Peninsula

27 B.C.
Augustus Caesar becomes
the first Roman emperor

A.D. 30
Pontius Pilate
orders Jesus
put to death

A.D. 392
Christianity becomes
the official religion of
the Roman Empire

USE THE TIME LINE

Use the chapter summary time line to answer these questions.

1 Which leader ruled first, Julius Caesar or Augustus Caesar?

2 About how many years passed between Jesus' death and the date on which Christianity became the official Roman religion?

USE VOCABULARY

For each pair of terms, write a sentence or two to explain how the terms are related.

3 **consul** (p. 279), **veto** (p. 279)

4 **patrician** (p. 279), **plebeian** (p. 280)

5 **dictator** (p. 279), **triumvirate** (p. 288)

6 **persecute** (p. 303), **martyr** (p. 303)

RECALL FACTS

Answer these questions.

7 Who fought in the Punic Wars?

8 How was life for Roman slaves different from life for slaves in other cultures?

Write the letter of the best choice.

9 **TEST PREP** All of the following statements are true about the government of the Roman Republic *except*—
  A Roman citizens elected leaders to represent them in an assembly.
  B In an emergency, a dictator could rule for a period of six months.
  C The Senate was the most powerful governing body.
  D Senators served for a term of six years.

10 **TEST PREP** Which leader transformed Rome into the splendid capital of the Roman Empire?
  F Julius Caesar
  G Mark Antony
  H Augustus
  J Constantine

THINK CRITICALLY

11 Explain the differences between the Etruscan monarchy and the Roman Republic.

12 Do you think the six-month emergency dictator rule in the Roman Republic was a good idea? Why or why not?

APPLY SKILLS

Follow a Flow Chart

13 Create a flow chart showing your daily morning routine before school. In your flow chart, include some unexpected happenings, such as missing your ride to school.

Compare Historical Maps

14 Use the maps on pages 290–291 to understand how the Roman Empire changed from 274 B.C. to A.D. 117. Was Egypt one of the first lands to be controlled by Rome, or one of the last?

Predict a Historical Outcome

15 How might the Christian religion have developed differently if the Edict of Milan had not ended the persecution of Christians?

VISIT

CRETE

Crete, the largest of the Greek islands, lies in the Mediterranean Sea about 60 miles (97 km) south of the Greek mainland. First settled in 6000 B.C., Crete has a rich history that has made it a popular tourist spot.

Crete was once home to the ancient Minoan civilization. Tourists can visit the Minoan ruins at the sites of Knossos and Phaistos. Minoan artifacts, along with objects from other ancient civilizations, can be viewed at the Archaeological Museum in Iráklion, Crete.

Crete's traditional culture can still be seen in the island's country villages. Urban life on the island offers more modern surroundings.

LOCATE IT

GREECE

Crete

WHAT TO SEE

Tourists can buy items made by the island's craftworkers. This shop (bottom) sells handwoven rugs made by weavers (top left). A potter (top right) spins a pot on a wheel.

The palace of the mythological king Minos is located in Knossos. The Minoan civilization was named after the king.

Crete is one of the main olive-producing regions in Greece. Its climate is ideal for growing olives. Much of the olive crop is pressed into olive oil.

Tourists in Crete can enjoy the island's white sandy beaches or see historic artifacts, such as this vase (left), in its many museums.

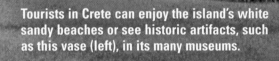

TAKE A FIELD TRIP

GO ONLINE

A VIRTUAL TOUR
Visit The Learning Site at **www.harcourtschool.com** to take virtual tours of other places.

CNN Turner Le@rning

A VIDEO TOUR
Check your media center or classroom library for a videotape tour highlighting Crete, Greece.

4 Review and Test Preparation

VISUAL SUMMARY

Write a Paragraph Look closely at each picture, and read the captions to help you review Unit 4. Then imagine that you are in one of the places shown. Write a paragraph that describes what you see.

USE VOCABULARY

Is each term below associated with the ancient Greeks, the ancient Romans, or both?

1 **aqueduct** (p. 296)

2 **epic** (p. 248)

3 **gladiator** (p. 296)

4 **league** (p. 257)

RECALL FACTS

Answer these questions.

5 Which civilization developed first, the ancient Greek civilization or the ancient Roman civilization?

6 What happened on the Ides of March?

Write the letter of the best choice.

7 **TEST PREP** All of the following people were ancient Greek leaders *except*—
A Mark Antony.
B Cleisthenes.
C Pericles.
D Alexander the Great.

8 **TEST PREP** All of the following are true about ancient Greek civilization *except*—
F Athens became a beautiful cultural center.
G Greek control spread to include all lands around the Mediterranean Sea as well as Britain.
H the Peloponnesian War ended the civilization's Golden Age.
J Greek leaders supported the work of artists, architects, writers, and scientists.

9 **TEST PREP** Which of the following leaders made Christianity an accepted religion in the Roman Empire?
A Constantine
B Marcus Aurelius
C Pontius Pilate
D Augustus

Visual Summary

3000 B.C.	2500 B.C.	2000 B.C.	1500 B.C.

3000 B.C. Civilization develops near the Aegean Sea p. 244

2000 B.C. The Minoan culture and trade flourish p. 245

750 B.C. Greek city-states begin to form p. 250

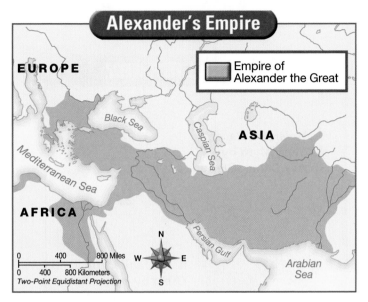

Alexander's Empire

EUROPE

Black Sea

Caspian Sea

ASIA

Mediterranean Sea

AFRICA

Persian Gulf

Arabian Sea

Empire of Alexander the Great

0   400   800 Miles
0   400   800 Kilometers
Two-Point Equidistant Projection

N W E S

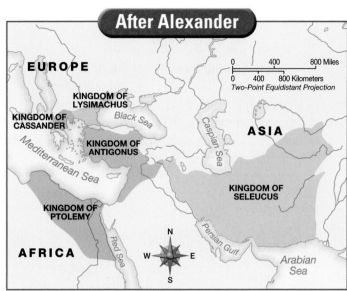

After Alexander

EUROPE

KINGDOM OF LYSIMACHUS

KINGDOM OF CASSANDER

Black Sea

Caspian Sea

ASIA

KINGDOM OF ANTIGONUS

Mediterranean Sea

KINGDOM OF PTOLEMY

KINGDOM OF SELEUCUS

Red Sea

Persian Gulf

AFRICA

Arabian Sea

0   400   800 Miles
0   400   800 Kilometers
Two-Point Equidistant Projection

N W E S

THINK CRITICALLY

10 Why do you think the years from 1100 B.C. to about 750 B.C. were called the Dark Age of Greek civilization?

11 How did the thinkers from the Golden Age of Greece change people's understanding of the world?

12 For a leader, what do you think would be the most difficult thing about uniting people from many different cultures? Explain your answer.

APPLY SKILLS

MAP AND GLOBE SKILLS

Compare Historical Maps
Use the two historical maps on this page to answer the following questions.

13 What kingdoms formed on the land once ruled by Alexander?

14 What kingdom formed in the area of Africa that Alexander once controlled?

15 Why are there more colors on the second map than on the first map?

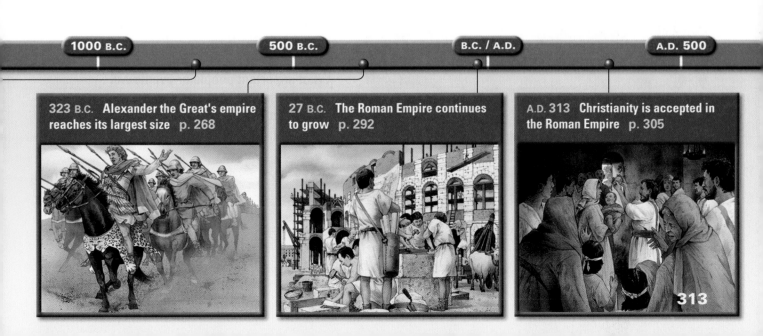

1000 B.C.   500 B.C.   B.C. / A.D.   A.D. 500

323 B.C. Alexander the Great's empire reaches its largest size p. 268

27 B.C. The Roman Empire continues to grow p. 292

A.D. 313 Christianity is accepted in the Roman Empire p. 305

313

Unit Activities

Conduct a Census

First, find out more about the United States census. How often is it taken? What kinds of questions does it ask? How is the information gathered? Then create a list of census questions, and conduct a census of your class or grade. Tally the results, and present them to your classmates.

Create an Informational Poster

Find out more about the Hippocratic oath. What did the original oath say? What was its original purpose? What did Hippocrates think should happen to people who violated it? Do doctors still take an oath today? How have the words changed over time? Present what you learn on a poster to share with your class.

VISIT YOUR LIBRARY

■ *Atalanta's Race: A Greek Myth* by Shirley Climo. Clarion.

■ *Alexander the Great* by Robert Green. Grolier.

■ *The Buried City of Pompeii* by Shelley Tanaka. Hyperion.

COMPLETE THE UNIT PROJECT

Plan a Festival   Work with a group of classmates to complete the unit project— plan a festival. On a piece of paper, create a schedule of activities. When will each activity occur and who will be doing what? On the schedule, also include a description of each activity. How does that activity reflect ancient Greek or Roman life? What important people or events will be represented? Include descriptions of costumes, props, and the roles you and your classmates will play.

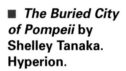

The Rise of Later Civilizations

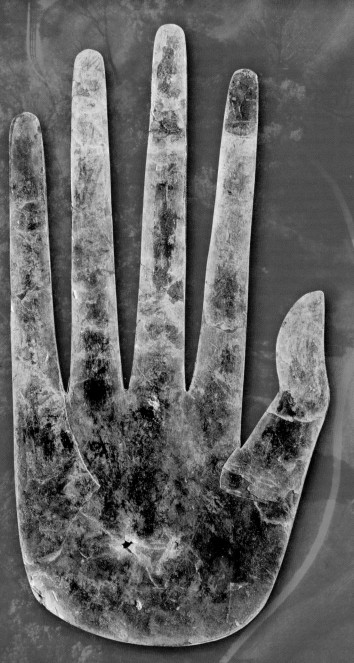

Hopewell Indian mica hand,
southern Ohio, about A.D. 100

Serpent Mound built by the Adena people in the Ohio Valley

5

The Rise of Later Civilizations

❝I am the blue horse that runs in the plain
I am the fish that rolls, shining, in the water❞

—N. Scott Momaday, from
"The Delight Song of Tsoai-Talee," 1975

Preview the Content

Read the titles of the chapters and lessons in this unit. Use them to make an outline about the rise of later civilizations.

Preview the Vocabulary

Compound Words Use the meanings of smaller words to write meanings for the compound words. Record your responses in a chart, and use the Glossary to check your answers.

ORIGINAL WORD		ORIGINAL WORD		COMPOUND WORD	POSSIBLE MEANING
long	+	ship	=	longship	_____
over	+	population	=	overpopulation	_____
long	+	house	=	longhouse	_____

ARCTIC OCEAN

Greenland

ARCTIC

Bering Sea

ARCTIC

SUBARCTIC

ROCKY

NORTHWEST COAST

SUBARCTIC

SUBARCTIC

Hudson Bay

NORTH AMERICA

PACIFIC OCEAN

PLATEAU

MOUNTAINS

GREAT PLAINS

GREAT BASIN

Mississippi River

EASTERN WOODLANDS

CALIFORNIA

SOUTHWEST

ATLANTIC OCEAN

Gulf of Mexico

● Tenochtitlán

Caribbean Sea

0   1,500   3,000 Miles
0   1,500   3,000 Kilometers
Miller Cylindrical Projection

Amazon River

ANDES

Machu Picchu ●● Cuzco

SOUTH AMERICA

MOUNTAINS

PACIFIC OCEAN

World Population
A.D. 1000

AREA	POPULATION
World	322 million
Africa	37 million
Asia	197 million
Australia and the Pacific Islands	1 million
Europe	35 million
North America	2 million
South America	50 million

Key Events

| 250 B.C. | B.C. / A.D. | A.D. 250 | A.D. 500 |

250 B.C. The first city in Africa south of the Sahara forms p. 349

100 B.C. The Three Kingdoms begin to form in Korea p. 361

A.D. 500 The early Middle Ages begin in Europe p. 338

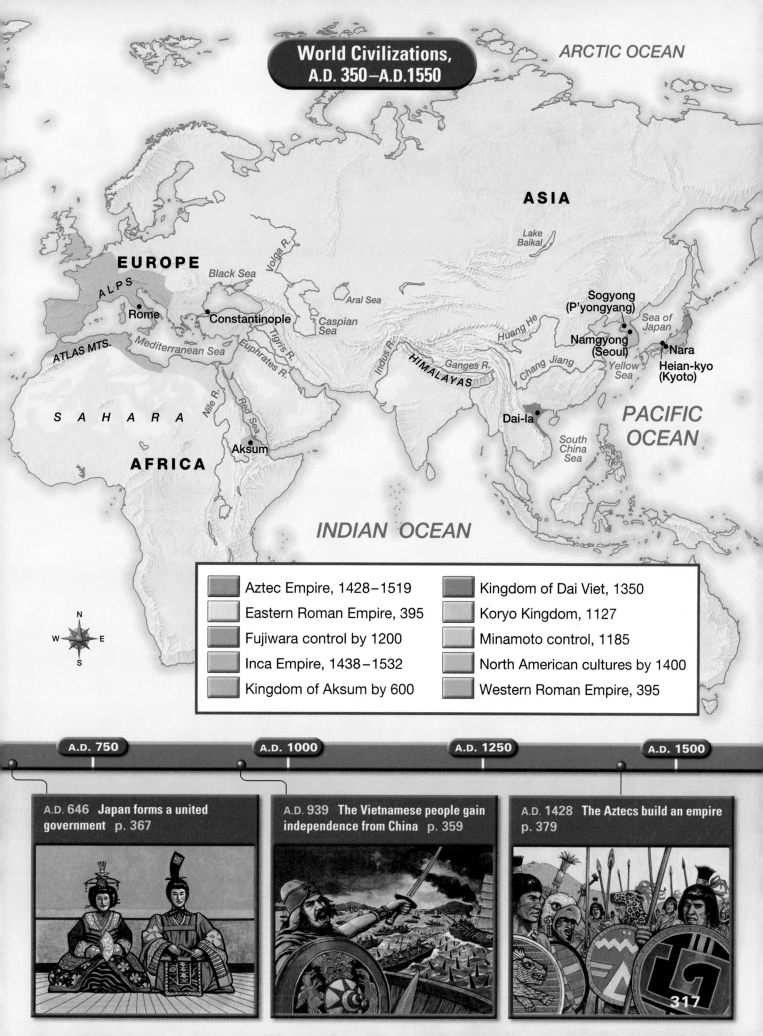

World Civilizations, A.D. 350–A.D.1550

ARCTIC OCEAN

ASIA

Lake Baikal

EUROPE

ALPS

Black Sea

Volga R.

Rome

Constantinople

Aral Sea

Caspian Sea

Sogyong (P'yongyang)

Sea of Japan

ATLAS MTS.

Mediterranean Sea

Euphrates R.

Tigris R.

Huang He

Namgyong (Seoul)

Nara

Heian-kyo (Kyoto)

Nile R.

Red Sea

Indus R.

HIMALAYAS

Ganges R.

Chang Jiang

Yellow Sea

S A H A R A

AFRICA

Aksum

Dai-la

PACIFIC OCEAN

South China Sea

INDIAN OCEAN

Aztec Empire, 1428–1519		Kingdom of Dai Viet, 1350	
Eastern Roman Empire, 395		Koryo Kingdom, 1127	
Fujiwara control by 1200		Minamoto control, 1185	
Inca Empire, 1438–1532		North American cultures by 1400	
Kingdom of Aksum by 600		Western Roman Empire, 395	

N W E S

A.D. 750   A.D. 1000   A.D. 1250   A.D. 1500

A.D. 646 Japan forms a united government p. 367

A.D. 939 The Vietnamese people gain independence from China p. 359

A.D. 1428 The Aztecs build an empire p. 379

The Royal Diaries
Sŏndŏk
Princess of the Moon and Stars
Korea, A.D. 595

written by Sheri Holman

In the A.D. 500s kings ruled over different parts of the world. In contrast, few queens ruled in their own right. Queen Sŏndŏk, of Korea, was an exception. Growing up, young Sŏndŏk knew that one day she would rule the kingdom known as Silla. After all, her father, King Chinp'yŏng, had no sons, and Sŏndŏk was his oldest daughter.

What was it like to grow up in a royal Korean family? We cannot know for certain, but this fictional story gives us an idea. The story is written in the form of diary entries that Sŏndŏk might have written as a princess. Notice that Sŏndŏk does not begin her diary entries with *Dear Diary*, as people might today. Instead, she addresses her entries to her grandmother, who has died.

Last day of the last moon, 16th year of King Chinp'yŏng

All the servants are racing around cleaning the halls from the top to bottom. Remember, Grandmother, for the five days of the New Year they are not allowed to use a broom or they might sweep away our good fortune. From lowest to highest we are making new clothes in which to greet the New Year. We must all bathe our hair tonight, too, so that we won't wash away luck in the New Year.

Tonight we will sit down with all of our relatives and feast in honor of you, Grandmother. And Grandfather, and all of our Kim ancestors.

With no moon in the sky, the heavens are lit only by the milky net of stars. You know how deeply I wish for my own observatory as a New Year's present, Grandmother. Please whisper in Father's ear.

> **observatory** a place for viewing and studying the stars and planets

1st day of the 1st moon, 17th year of King Chinp'yŏng Ipch'un (Spring Begins)

Happy Year of the Rabbit, Grandmother!

I have just returned from performing the *saebae* bow before my parents, and now I bow low to you, Grandmother. We are off to tidy your grave and present you and Grandfather with your New Year's meal. The cooks have prepared more than fifty dishes for you this year. I hope you are hungry.

> **saebae** respect for older people

Later

The festival at Half-moon Fortress was the most elaborate I can remember. All the adults of lesser rank wore their best clothes, with bright, new, wide-sleeved *chogori*, while the children ran around in their happiest colors. We of the royal Holy Bone rank were bedecked in the most costly new clothing—Father in new purple robes, Mother and the girls and I in richly embroidered red silk. I wore my golden shoes (which hurt my feet terribly!) and my beaten gold crown designed to resemble reindeer antlers, which tinkles musically when I walk. I am happy not to have to dress so every day. I was so weighted down with gold rings on every finger and toe, I could barely move.

The court musicians performed their slow and stately dances, but I wandered off to see the peasants' celebration, which was taking place just outside the palace walls. The farmers leaped and sang, beating drums and playing upon pipes. I sometimes yearn to sing and dance along with the common people, Grandmother. It looks like such wonderful sport. But as Chajang says, "Desires are our downfall," so I try not to wish too hard. . . .

2nd day of the 1st moon, 17th year of King Chinp'yŏng

We went to bed last night after feasting on our special New Year's *tuk-tuk*, which every person in Silla, from prince to peasant, eats on this day. It is made from steamed sticky rice, pounded and cut into the shape of coins and half-moons. The soup is stewed with beef and soy sauce and thinly sliced eggs. And as you recall, Grandmother, many say you will not age a year unless you drink this soup. I drank mine and turned fifteen this year. Ch'ŏn-myong turned fourteen, and Sŏnwha thirteen. . . .

---

chogori   a long jacket with wide sleeves

Chajang   a friend of Sŏndŏk

320

5th day of the 1st moon,
17th year of King Chinp'yŏng

Our family went out among our people, who dropped to their knees and touched their heads to the ground when we passed. Mother, the girls, and I rode in our chariot, which only queens and aristocrats of the highest rank are allowed to do. Whenever we dismounted, our servants laid down a river of silk for us to tread upon.

From behind stone walls, our city's black-tiled houses rose gracefully, their flaring roofs looked ready to fly away. While only we of the Holy Bone rank might use the five sacred colors—red, black, white, yellow, and green—to paint our palaces, the natural wood of these houses is still beautiful. Grandmother, you will be happy to know that Kumsŏng does not have the crowded, poor hovels you find elsewhere. We have passed a law that the walls of a city house should be three times as tall as the average man, so that the people are not cramped inside breathing unhealthy air. . . .

hovels small houses in poor condition

Analyze the Literature

1 How was early Korean society similar to and different from that of the United States today?

2 What rights did the wealthy people of early Korea have that other early Koreans did not have?

READ A BOOK

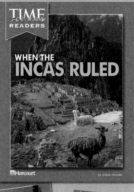

TIME READERS
WHEN THE
INCAS RULED
Harcourt

TIME FOR KIDS READERS
Mount Fuji
Harcourt

TIME FOR KIDS READERS
THE
VIKINGS
Harcourt

START THE UNIT PROJECT

Make Postcards As you read this unit, gather information about the history and geography of the civilizations you read about. Use this information to help you create postcards that show the history and landscape of the civilizations.

USE TECHNOLOGY

GO ONLINE

Visit The Learning Site at **www.harcourtschool.com** for additional activities, primary sources, and other resources to use in this unit.

REPLICA OF VIKING SHIP, ENGLISH COAST

Vikings, or raiders from Scandinavia, once used longships like the one below. The Vikings regularly sailed along the coast of England during the late A.D. 800s, looking for settlements to rob and burn. Viking ships ranged from 45 to 75 feet (about 14 to 23 m) and featured a single square sail. Overlapping floorboards made them sturdy enough to sail in heavy seas.

LOCATE IT

ATLANTIC OCEAN

North Sea

UNITED KINGDOM

English coast

Europe After the Romans

"The number of ships grows, the endless stream of Vikings never ceases . . . "
—Ermentarius of Noirmoutier, Christian monk, A.D. 860

 **Categorize**

To **categorize** information is to classify, or to arrange, the data into similar groups so that it is easier to understand and compare.

As you read, categorize information in the chapter.

• Classify what you read into the following categories: history, geography, economics, and culture.

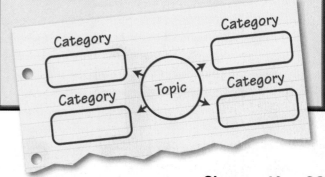

Category

Category

Category

Topic

Category

Focus Skill
CATEGORIZE

As you read, categorize information about the Roman Empire's decline and its legacy.

BIG IDEA
The Roman Empire lost its political power, but its legacy influenced later civilizations.

VOCABULARY

loyalty

portico

 FAST FACT During the Roman Empire's decline, Romans took apart grand buildings, such as amphitheaters, for their stones. They used these stones to build walls to defend their cities from attack.

Rome's Decline and Division

| 500 B.C. | B.C./A.D. | A.D. 500 | A.D. 1000 | A.D. 1500 |

A.D. 100 – A.D. 400

By the middle of the second century A.D., the Roman Empire began to face many problems. Several emperors, including Constantine, tried to keep the empire strong. However, their efforts could not prevent the empire's decline, or downfall.

Trouble in the Roman Empire

The *Pax Romana*, a time of peace for the Romans, ended with Marcus Aurelius's reign as emperor, which lasted from A.D. 161 to A.D. 180. Some troubles began during his rule, such as a rebellion in A.D. 167 that led to a war. At the same time, Aurelius had to defend the empire against invasions along its borders.

Parthians from Asia invaded from the east. Germanic tribes invaded from the north.

Disorder within the empire grew under the harsh rule of Emperor Commodus (KAH•muh•duhs), the son of Marcus Aurelius. Upon the death of Commodus in A.D. 192, the empire became even less stable. Roman leaders fought one another in civil wars, with the winners seizing the throne. Most of them ruled only a short time before being overthrown themselves. From A.D. 235 to A.D. 284, more than 25 leaders served as emperor.

These emperors ruled during uneasy times. Roman citizens were losing respect for the Roman government. Even the soldiers who had fought hard to keep the Roman Empire together felt little **loyalty**, or devotion, toward it. Instead, they were loyal to their generals, who often fought each other.

The political conflicts within the Roman Empire caused its economy to suffer. Trade decreased, and Roman money lost value. Prices rose, bringing hardships to the Roman people. Many people could not even buy enough food.

To make matters worse, a deadly disease called the plague spread through the empire from A.D. 250 to A.D. 265. At one point,

This carving shows a Roman paying taxes to a tax collector. The Roman government needed tax money to pay war costs.

more than 5,000 Romans were dying from it each day.

By the end of the A.D. 200s, the empire was in a serious decline. The historian Dio Cassius, who lived during this time, contrasted life in his day with life during the early days of the empire. "Our history," he wrote, "now plunges from a kingdom of gold to one of iron and rust."

REVIEW What kinds of problems caused the Roman Empire to decline? CATEGORIZE

The Roman Empire included lands as far east as present-day Syria. Ancient Roman columns still lie scattered today in the Syrian city of Palmyra.

LOCATE IT

SYRIA
Palmyra

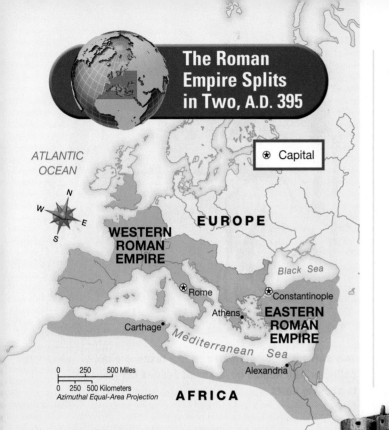

The Roman Empire Splits in Two, A.D. 395

ATLANTIC OCEAN

⊛ Capital

EUROPE

WESTERN ROMAN EMPIRE

Black Sea

⊛ Rome
Constantinople

Athens

EASTERN ROMAN EMPIRE

Carthage

Mediterranean Sea

0   250   500 Miles
0 250 500 Kilometers
Azimuthal Equal-Area Projection

AFRICA

Alexandria

Regions This map shows how the Roman Empire was divided in A.D. 395. The statue (right) shows the Roman leaders Diocletian and Maximian, who had ruled the different parts of the empire before it was officially divided.

◈ In which region was the city of Constantinople located?

The Roman Empire Splits in Two

As the A.D. 200s came to an end, better times briefly returned to the Roman Empire. In A.D. 284 a Roman general named Diocletian (dy•uh•KLEE•shuhn) was named emperor by his troops. Diocletian thought that the Roman Empire had become too large for any single ruler to govern. To bring order to the empire, Diocletian divided the leadership of the empire. He put his trusted friend Maximian (mak•SIM•ee•uhn) in charge of the western part, while he himself ruled the eastern part.

Diocletian's reform stopped the empire's decline for a time. It also led the way for other strong leaders to govern parts of the empire. One of these was Constantine. He not only helped make Christianity an accepted religion in the Roman Empire, but he also helped the empire survive.

Constantine focused his attention on the eastern part of the empire. In A.D. 330 he moved the empire's capital from Rome all the way to the eastern city of Byzantium (buh•ZAN•tee•uhm). Nearly surrounded by water, Byzantium was well located for trade and easy to defend. Renamed Constantinople (kahn•stan•tuhn•OH•puhl) in Constantine's honor, the city replaced Rome as the most important city of the empire.

In A.D. 395 the Roman Empire officially split into two parts. In the years that followed, the eastern part would see the growth of cities and trade. The western part would see further decline, change, and a time of invasions.

REVIEW Why did Diocletian divide the leadership of the Roman Empire?

The City of Constantinople

The city of Byzantium was not Constantine's first choice for his new capital. He had also considered the port cities of nearby Chalcedon (KAL•suh•dahn) and Ilium, formerly Troy. In fact, new capital gates had already been built in Ilium. However, on a visit to Byzantium, across the waters from Chalcedon, Constantine changed his mind. He realized that Byzantium's location was ideal as the center of an empire.

This map (left) from the 1500s shows the city of Constantinople. Constantine (above) holds a model of the city.

Like Rome, Byzantium was built on seven hills. The seven hills lie on a peninsula that reaches into the Bosporus Strait. Important trade routes between Europe and Asia passed through these waters.

Byzantium was a small Greek city when Constantine decided to make it his new capital. To make sure the city honored its role as the new capital, Constantine began many grand construction projects there.

In just a few years, Constantine completely changed the city. New boundaries for the city made Constantinople three times larger than Byzantium had been. The new city had a university, 2 theaters, 52 covered walkways, or **porticos**, 8 public baths, 8 aqueducts, and 153 private baths. It also had 4 law courts, 14 churches, 14 palaces, and thousands of homes with beautiful architecture. Art treasures filled the buildings of Constantinople. Hundreds of statues stood in the city's streets and parks.

Constantine's projects made Constantinople a city of beauty and wealth. It became one of the world's most important capitals. Because of this, the city was often called "the new Rome." Constantinople's greatness lived on for centuries. Today the city is known as Istanbul (is•tuhn•BOOL), Turkey.

REVIEW How was the geography of Rome and Byzantium alike?

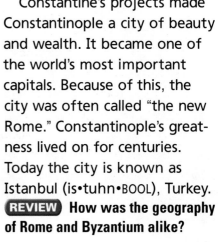

In this carving, Emperor Constantine watches a chariot race in his capital, Constantinople.

Rome's Legacy

Rome lost much of its power and glory when the capital moved to Byzantium. Yet it left a legacy that still lasts today. Roman culture and Roman ideas survived in Constantinople. Later, they regained importance in the lands of the former Western Roman Empire. Over time, they influenced civilizations around the world.

During their rule the Romans introduced new ideas in government, law, city planning, and building. They also borrowed ideas from other ancient cultures, adapting or improving them. Through the Romans, much of Greek culture survived.

The Romans are probably best remembered for their contributions to government and law. The republic they created in ancient Rome was a completely new form of government. The Romans understood the need to limit the power of government. Today, republics are found all over the world. The United States government has been a republic ever since it began, more than 200 years ago.

The Romans developed many kinds of laws that applied to all Roman citizens. Later, they made laws that applied to Romans as well as to others who lived within the empire. The Romans even created laws to provide justice to the people they conquered. Countries around the world now have law systems based on the ideas of Roman law, such as the rights of citizens.

Roman city planners greatly improved city life. They created a level of city cleanliness not seen before that time. Their plumbing and waste-removal systems helped keep the city clean and Roman citizens healthy.

The Thomas Jefferson Memorial (below) in Washington, D.C., features a Roman hollow-dome design as seen on the ancient Pantheon (left) in Rome.

Aqueducts carried water as far as 57 miles (92 km) to Rome. Roman ideas for city planning are still used around the world.

While the Romans imitated the architecture of other cultures, they also left their own legacies in building design. One Roman innovation was the basilica. The Roman basilica was a huge open room, ideal for large groups of people. For the past 1,600 years, many Christian churches have used this design for their places of worship. Another Roman invention was the hollow dome. Before the Romans, domes were solid. The Romans used their knowledge of building arches to figure out a way to build hollow domes.

Latin, the language of the Romans, is another of Rome's legacies. Latin has influenced English as well as other modern languages. Many English words, such as *territory*, *corporation*, *scientific*, and *senate*, have roots that come from Latin.

REVIEW What Roman design have many Christian churches used?

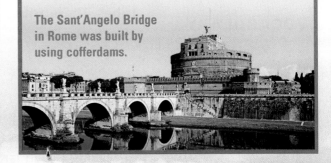
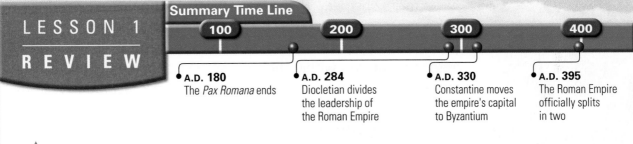

LESSON 1 REVIEW

Summary Time Line

100	200	300	400
A.D. 180 The *Pax Romana* ends	A.D. 284 Diocletian divides the leadership of the Roman Empire	A.D. 330 Constantine moves the empire's capital to Byzantium	A.D. 395 The Roman Empire officially splits in two

 CATEGORIZE The Romans left lasting legacies in government, law, city planning, building, and language. Make a chart listing their innovations in each category.

1 BIG IDEA In what ways did Rome's legacy influence later civilizations?

2 VOCABULARY Write a sentence that includes the word **loyalty**.

3 TIME LINE In what year did Constantine move the Roman Empire's capital?

4 GEOGRAPHY By what name is Constantinople known today?

5 CRITICAL THINKING—Evaluate Which Roman legacy do you think is the most important today? Explain your answer.

 PERFORMANCE—Write a Newspaper Article Imagine that you are a news reporter in Rome in the A.D. 300s. Write a newspaper article announcing the move of the Roman Empire's capital from Rome to Byzantium.

2

Focus Skill **CATEGORIZE**

As you read, categorize information about the peoples involved in one of Europe's most important migrations.

BIG IDEA
A large migration of different peoples through Europe brought many changes.

VOCABULARY

vandal
manor
manor system
serf
self-sufficient

Invasions and Change

500 B.C.	B.C./A.D.	A.D. 500	A.D. 1000	A.D. 1500

A.D. 200 – A.D. 1000

Throughout much of the A.D. 200s, outsiders threatened the Roman Empire from three directions. From the east the Persians invaded Roman provinces in Asia. From the south an African people called the Berbers (BER•berz) attacked Roman lands in northern Africa. From the north came the Germanic tribes. These tribes included the Angles, Franks, Goths, Jutes, Lombards, Saxons, and Vandals.

The Germanic Tribes

The Romans considered the Germanic peoples barbarians because they were not educated in Roman ways. For one thing, they lived in villages, not in large cities as many Romans did. While most people in the Roman Empire were farmers, the Germanic people were mainly herders. Their cattle, sheep, and goats provided them with the resources for their food, clothing, and shelter.

Most Germanic tribes had no form of government. Usually, a respected person within the tribe settled disagreements but had little authority otherwise. The strongest leaders served as military and religious chiefs.

For a time some Germanic peoples were allowed to live peacefully within the Roman Empire. Many of them fought in the Roman army, and some became military leaders. Then, during the late A.D. 300s and the A.D. 400s, the Germanic tribes began entering Roman territory in large numbers. Their

The engraving (far left) shows a Frankish warrior from the A.D. 400s. The belt buckle (left) was worn by a Frank in the A.D. 500s.

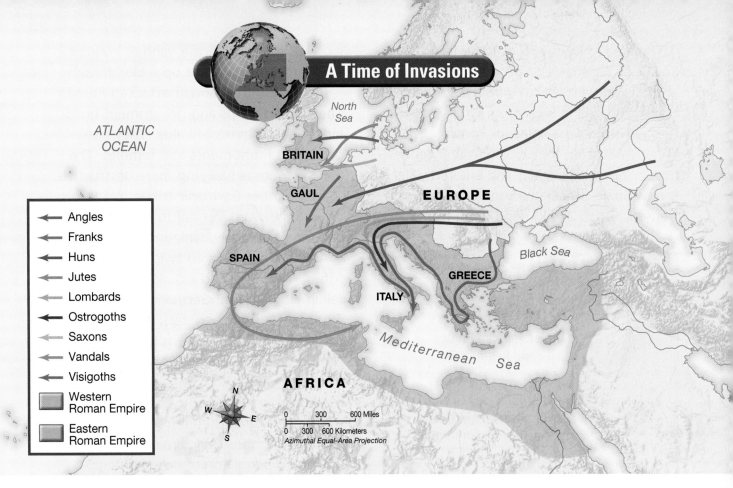

A Time of Invasions

North Sea

ATLANTIC OCEAN

BRITAIN

GAUL

EUROPE

SPAIN

Black Sea

GREECE

ITALY

Mediterranean Sea

AFRICA

N
W   E
S

| 0 | 300 | 600 Miles |
| 0 | 300 | 600 Kilometers |

Azimuthal Equal-Area Projection

Legend:
- ← Angles
- ← Franks
- ← Huns
- ← Jutes
- ← Lombards
- ← Ostrogoths
- ← Saxons
- ← Vandals
- ← Visigoths
- ▮ Western Roman Empire
- ▮ Eastern Roman Empire

GEOGRAPHY THEME

Movement   **Many different Germanic tribes invaded the Western Roman Empire.**

◈ Which tribes invaded Britain? North Africa? Italy?

own lands were being taken over by a people from central Asia called the Huns.

The Huns were a wandering, warlike people. Around A.D. 350 they began moving westward across the Volga River into what is now the country of Hungary. Under Attila (uh•TIH•luh), their greatest leader, they pushed on to the Danube River and as far west as Gaul, which is now mainly France.

By attacking the Germanic tribes, the Huns caused one of the largest migrations of people in world history. The migration of the Germanic peoples into the Western Roman Empire was more than just a movement of people, however. Some historians have called it "the migration of nations." Others consider it a time of invasion.

REVIEW Why did the Germanic peoples begin entering Roman territory in large numbers?

The End of the Western Empire

Some time after A.D. 370, the Huns attacked the Germanic tribes of Goths who lived around the Black Sea. The Goths were divided into two groups. The Ostrogoths (AHS•truh•gahths) lived north of the Black Sea. The Visigoths (VIH•zuh•gahths) lived north of the lower Danube River. In the attack, the Ostrogoths were overrun and absorbed into the Hun Empire. Many of the Visigoths, however, fled into the Western Roman Empire. Under their leader, Alaric (A•luh•rik), the Visigoths invaded the Italian Peninsula and took Rome by force in A.D. 410. Leaders who came after Alaric led the Visigoths into lands that are now Spain and France.

Threatened by the Huns in eastern Europe, a Germanic tribe called the Vandals also moved west. In A.D. 406 the Vandals crossed the Rhine River from what is now Germany into Gaul and took control of it. Three years later, they crossed the Pyrenees (PIR•uh•neez) mountains and entered what is now Spain. Under the Vandal leader Genseric (GEN•suh•rik), who ruled from A.D. 428 to A.D. 477, the Vandals invaded northern Africa and set up a kingdom.

In A.D. 455 the Vandals attacked Rome. They looted shops and government buildings, stealing items of value. They also destroyed monuments and temples. The Vandals were actually no more destructive than the other Germanic tribes. Yet today we use the word **vandal** to describe someone who purposely damages property.

After being attacked twice by Germanic tribes in A.D. 410 and A.D. 455, Rome finally fell in A.D. 476 to a Germanic leader named Odoacer (OH•duh•way•ser). As a young man, he had joined the Western Roman army. He soon became a leader of the Germanic troops serving in the Roman army. When the Roman government would not give his troops land for settlement, he led them in a revolt. With the overthrow of the Western Roman emperor Romulus Augustulus, Odoacer became the first Germanic king of the Italian Peninsula. Many historians consider this event in A.D. 476 the end of the Western Roman Empire.

REVIEW Why do many historians consider A.D. 476 the end of the Western Roman Empire?

• GEOGRAPHY •

The Pyrenees
Understanding Places and Regions

The Pyrenees mountain range forms the border between present-day Spain and France. It is 270 miles (435 km) long and runs from the Atlantic Ocean to the Mediterranean Sea. During the region's early history, the Pyrenees range served as a physical barrier. It cut off Spain and Portugal from the rest of Europe. Trade between the two regions took place by sea. Today modern roads, railways, and tunnels connect the two regions.

Garonne R.

Bay of Biscay

FRANCE

0 50 100 Miles
0 50 100 Kilometers
Azimuthal Equal-Area Projection

Biarritz

Toulouse

Tarbes

P Y R E N E E S

Pamplona

Perpignan

ANDORRA

Pico de Aneto 11,168 ft. (3,404 m)

Andorra la Vella

Ebro River

Zaragoza

Barcelona

SPAIN

Balearic Sea

N W E S

EUROPE

AFRICA

This photograph shows the Pyrenees in the Aquitaine region of France.

This woodcut (above) shows the Saxons landing on the coast of Britain. This helmet (right) is a copy of one found in Britain that belonged to an Anglo-Saxon king.

More Germanic Conquests

After the Western Roman Empire ended, Germanic tribes continued to claim Roman lands in western Europe. Among those to invade Britain during this time were the Angles, Saxons, and Jutes. Together they are known as the Anglo-Saxons.

Legend says that a British king named Vortigern (VAWR•tuh•gern) asked the Anglo-Saxon tribes for help in defending his lands. Vortigern's kingdom was under attack by the Picts, the ancient people of Scotland. The allies quarreled, however, and soon the Anglo-Saxons began to drive out the Britons. By the late A.D. 500s, the Angles, Saxons, and Jutes controlled most of eastern and southern Britain. There they set up a number of small kingdoms. Over time, these and other kingdoms united their territories into one new, larger kingdom. It was called *England,* from Anglo-Saxon words meaning "land of the Angles."

While this was happening in Britain, the Franks invaded northern Gaul and the Lombards took control of the Italian Peninsula. Both Germanic tribes would have a lasting influence on these lands that they invaded.

In A.D. 486 Clovis (KLOH•vuhs), the leader of the Franks, led an invasion of Gaul. He defeated the Gauls, Romans, Visigoths, and others in the territory and set up his own kingdom. By the time Clovis died in A.D. 511, the Franks held firm control from the Rhine River to the Pyrenees mountains. Gaul came to be called France in honor of the Franks.

At about the same time, the Lombards took over what is now Austria. From there they crossed the Alps and invaded the Italian Peninsula. By A.D. 568 they had taken control of much of it. They settled mainly in the part of northern Italy that today is still called Lombardy. Their kingdom lasted more than 200 years.

REVIEW Which Germanic tribes became known as the Anglo-Saxons? **CATEGORIZE**

A CLOSER LOOK
A Manor

A manor was much like a small village. It was home to the lord's family and about 200 to 300 peasants. Most of the peasants were farmers, but some worked as blacksmiths, carpenters, millers, and weavers. Together, they provided almost everything the manor needed.

1. The lord of the manor lived with his family in the manor house.

2. The mill was powered by water. Running water, such as a river or stream, turned the waterwheel. The waterwheel then drove the millstone that ground the grain into flour.

3. The church was a place for religious and social gatherings and for village meetings.

4. The lord of the manor received one-third of the crops grown, the church received nearly one-third, and the rest went to the peasants.

5. The living conditions inside a peasant's home were difficult. Most peasants shared their small house with their animals.

❖ Why do you think the manor house had a wall around it?

Life in a Changing Land

The Germanic invasions destroyed much of what the Romans and earlier civilizations had developed in the lands of the former Western Roman Empire. By the A.D. 800s, art had changed and education had declined there. Industry and trade also suffered greatly. Few people used the system of well-built Roman roads that had united much of the empire.

Cities and towns also lost importance as farming once again became the most important economic activity. Without a strong government to unite it, as the Roman government had done, Europe broke up into many small kingdoms. These kingdoms were divided into large plots of land, or estates, called **manors**. Wealthy landlords, or lords, owned the manors, which were farmed by peasants, or common people.

The manor lands were divided into sections. The peasants paid for the use of their plots with goods and services they provided to the lord. At the same time, the peasants depended on the lord for protection. This economic system for exchanging land use and protection for goods and services came to be called the **manor system**.

Many of the peasants on the manors were **serfs**. The serfs were part of the property. If a lord sold his manor, the new lord would own the serfs as well as the land. Unlike slaves, however, serfs could not be sold without the land.

The serfs lived in small shelters built around a large manor house or castle. Most manors also included a church, a mill for grinding grain into flour, and buildings in which craftworkers worked. Each manor was nearly **self-sufficient**. It was able to produce almost everything the lord and the serfs needed to live.

The manor system lasted in western Europe until the early 1100s, when trade, industry, and cities began to grow again. In central and eastern Europe, it continued into the 1800s.

REVIEW How were serfs different from slaves?

LESSON 2 REVIEW

Summary Time Line

200 — 400 — 600 — 800 — 1000

A.D. 350
Huns move toward
the Roman Empire

A.D. 476
The Western Roman
Empire ends

A.D. 800s
Manor system exists
throughout the former
Western Roman Empire

Focus Skill **CATEGORIZE** Categorize some of the differences between the Romans and the Germanic peoples.

1 **BIG IDEA** How did the migration of people change the government in western Europe?

2 **VOCABULARY** Make a word web that shows how the terms **manor**, **manor system**, and **serf** are related.

3 **TIME LINE** When did the Western Roman Empire end?

4 **HISTORY** What is the origin of the name *England*?

5 **CRITICAL THINKING—Hypothesize** Do you think the Western Roman Empire would have ended if the Huns had not arrived? Explain your answer.

PERFORMANCE—Draw a Scene Draw a scene showing life on a manor. In your drawing, include the buildings, people, and activities common to a manor.

Identify Fact and Opinion

VOCABULARY

fact
opinion

▶ **WHY IT MATTERS**

When you read, it is important to think about whether what you are reading is a statement of fact or a statement of opinion. A statement of **fact** can be proved to be true. An **opinion** is a statement that cannot be proved. It expresses the belief, attitude, or viewpoint of the person making it.

The following statement is a fact: "After the Western Roman Empire declined, the manor system spread throughout Europe." By checking a history book or an encyclopedia, you can prove that the statement is true. The following statement is an opinion. "The manor system was the best economic system in the world at that time." This statement expresses a belief that cannot be proved to be true. Being able to tell the difference between facts and opinions can help you know what to believe when you read.

Many historians believe that the Western Roman Empire came to an end when Romulus Augustulus (right) surrendered to Odoacer (center).

WHAT YOU NEED TO KNOW

The following tips can help you identify whether statements are facts or opinions.

- Ask yourself whether the statement can be proved to be true. Have you personally observed or experienced the events described in the statement? Can the statement be checked in a reliable, up-to-date reference source?

- Certain words may be clues that a statement is an opinion. Words that express feelings or emotions, such as *best*, *worst*, *good*, *bad*, *wonderful*, or *terrible*, are clues that an opinion is being expressed.

- Although you may agree with an opinion, that does not make it a fact. If it cannot be proved to be true, it is an opinion.

PRACTICE THE SKILL

Read the following statements, and decide whether they are statements of fact or opinion.

1. Europe broke up into many small kingdoms after the Western Roman Empire ended.
2. Farming was an important part of the manor system.
3. The Germanic kings were better leaders than the Roman emperors.
4. The serfs were part of the lord's property in the manor system.

This illustrated French manuscript (top) shows serfs building a fence on an early European manor.

5. In the manor system, craftworkers enjoyed much better lives than farmworkers.
6. Europeans should have continued the manor system into the 1900s.

APPLY WHAT YOU LEARNED

Reread the section of the lesson titled "The Germanic Tribes" on pages 330–331. Write six statements about the information in the section—three that state facts and three that are your own opinions. Trade papers with a classmate. Identify which of your partner's statements are facts and which are opinions.

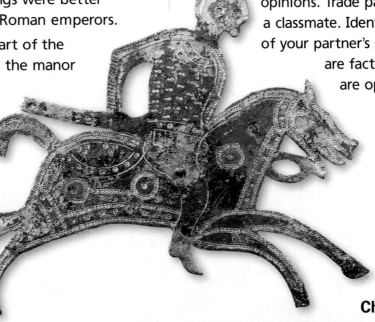

This bronze plaque of a Lombard horseman is from the A.D. 600s.

READING SKILLS

3

Early Middle Ages in Europe

CATEGORIZE

As you read, categorize information about religion and invasions during the early Middle Ages in Europe.

BIG IDEA

The early Middle Ages was a period of great change in Europe.

VOCABULARY

medieval
monastery
Christendom
longship
saga
territorial expansion

500 B.C.	B.C./A.D.	A.D. 500	A.D. 1000	A.D. 1500

A.D. 500 – A.D. 1000

By A.D. 500 much of what is now western Europe was no longer part of any empire. The region consisted of small kingdoms ruled by Germanic leaders or manors owned by lords. It was Christianity, in the form of the Roman Catholic Church, rather than a political ruler, that held the region together. The period from about A.D. 500 to about A.D. 1000 marks western Europe's early Middle Ages, or the early **medieval** (mee•DEE•vuhl) period.

The Growing Influence of the Church

With the end of the Western Roman Empire, no single government had complete control in Europe. Over time, new kinds of authority developed in Europe. The pope, the leader of the Roman Catholic Church, gained more power than any other person at the time.

The pope's authority grew as more people in Europe became Christians. During this time, missionaries traveled throughout Europe teaching Christianity.

Pope Gregory I (left) played an important role in the spread of Christianity to Europe's Germanic tribes. Lindisfarne Monastery (below) was founded on Holy Island in England in A.D. 635.

· BIOGRAPHY ·

Saint Patrick   A.D. 400s

Character Trait: Courage

Patrick was born into a Christian family in England during the early A.D. 400s. When he was 16 years old, Patrick was captured by pirates. He was then taken to Ireland and sold into slavery. During these difficult times, Patrick developed strong Christian beliefs. After 6 years, he escaped and returned to England. Once home, Patrick studied at Christian monasteries. Then he returned to Ireland, where he converted nearly all the Irish to Christianity. After Patrick's death, the pope honored him by naming him a saint. Today, people remember him every year on St. Patrick's Day, March 17.

MULTIMEDIA BIOGRAPHIES
Visit The Learning Site at www.harcourtschool.com to learn about other famous people.

Among the new Christian converts were kings, who helped spread their new religion. In the A.D. 400s the people in what is now Ireland became Christians, mainly through the efforts of the English missionary Saint Patrick. In A.D. 496 Clovis, the ruler of the Franks, became the first Germanic leader to convert to Christianity. This event brought all Gaul into the Church. Soon after that, the Anglo-Saxons in England and the Visigoths in Spain also became Christians.

Pope Gregory I, later known as Gregory the Great, led the Church from A.D. 590 to A.D. 604. Gregory was responsible for developing many important Church teachings.

He created rules of behavior for priests. He also set up **monasteries**, or centers of Christian life, in the lands ruled by the Germanic tribes. Gregory's plan was to make all of Europe a land of Christians, or **Christendom**.

The Roman Catholic Church gained even more power under the Germanic ruler Charles the Great, known as Charlemagne (SHAR•luh•mayn). Under his leadership the Franks brought back unity and order to many of the lands that had been part of the Western Roman Empire.

REVIEW What contributions did Pope Gregory I make to Christianity?

Charlemagne

Historians today know more about Charlemagne than about most rulers of the Middle Ages. This is because of a biography written about him by one of his government officials. Einhard's *Life of Charlemagne* describes the leader as more than 6 feet (1.8 m) tall. This was very unusual at a time when most men were little more than 5 feet (1.5 m) tall. Charlemagne had piercing eyes, fair hair, and a thick neck.

Einhard describes Charlemagne as a great warrior who conquered parts of Spain and central Europe. Charlemagne controlled an

Pendant from Charlemagne's necklace

empire from the Pyrenees mountains in the west to the Danube River in the east. His goal was to unite all the Germanic tribes into a single Christian kingdom.

Charlemagne was the son of Pepin III, a Frankish king. Pepin had helped the pope by defending the city of Rome against the Lombards. Like his father, Charlemagne helped the pope. When the Lombards attacked Rome again in A.D. 774, Charlemagne marched into Italy to protect the pope and to defeat the Lombards.

On Christmas Day A.D. 800, Pope Leo III rewarded Charlemagne by crowning him Augustus, or emperor of the Romans. Charlemagne had reached his goal of uniting Christendom under his rule.

Like Augustus, the first Roman emperor, Charlemagne wanted to make his empire strong. He improved education so that more people could read and write. By granting large estates to loyal nobles, he built a system of officials to govern the lands. In return, the nobles provided military and political services to him as emperor. The nobles also kept up the roads, bridges, and forts on their land. This system became the basis for European feudalism, the political and military system of Europe. Feudalism lasted for the next 400 years, until the end of the Middle Ages.

REVIEW What kinds of changes did Charlemagne make to strengthen his empire? **CATEGORIZE**

DEMOCRATIC VALUES
Justice

Charlemagne wanted his nobles to be wise leaders. He felt it was his responsibility to teach them how to govern fairly. Each spring Charlemagne met with all his nobles. These meetings, called the Fields of May, were held in meadows filled with flowers. Charlemagne set up tents and taught his nobles about law and other subjects. He then sent out teams made up of one noble and one person trained by the Church. The teams traveled to different parts of the empire. Their task was to make sure that all people, including peasants, were receiving equal justice.

Analyze the Value

1 Why do you think Charlemagne wanted equal justice for all people?

2 **Make It Relevant** Think about your school's rules. Write a paragraph about how the students receive equal justice.

A jeweled statue honors Emperor Charlemagne.

A New Wave of Invaders

Charlemagne's rule was the high point of the early Middle Ages. Yet even before Charlemagne's death, his empire faced the challenges of invasions. Arabs and Berbers attacked the empire's Mediterranean coast from northern Africa. Then Magyars and Slavs invaded from the east. From the north came the Vikings from Scandinavia—the present-day countries of Denmark, Norway, and Sweden.

During the A.D. 700s the population of Scandinavia grew quickly. After a while there was not enough fertile land to grow the crops needed to feed all the people who lived there. Many Scandinavians set out in **longships**, or narrow, flat-bottomed boats, to search for food and steal it if necessary.

In one Icelandic **saga**, or adventure story about brave deeds, a young hero says to his father, "Give me a longship and crew therewith, and I go a-viking." The word *viking* meant "fighting as a pirate or warrior." It came to describe these Scandinavian raiders—the Vikings. Others called them Norsemen, or Northmen.

The Vikings were skillful shipbuilders. Their fast-moving longships were powered by large square sails and many strong rowers who served as fighters as well. This allowed the Vikings to reach many of the coastal areas of northwestern Europe and to sail inland along rivers.

The Vikings usually attacked at night or early in the morning in order to take people by surprise. They were fierce fighters, often killing everyone they found and destroying what they did not take. After hearing of a Viking attack in England, one English scholar wrote,

> 66 Never before has such a terror appeared in England. 99

The Vikings began to settle on the lands they attacked. This **territorial expansion**, or adding of new lands, gave the Vikings the resources they believed they needed. The Vikings from what is now Denmark took control of parts of England and France.

Viking helmet

Present-day sailors steer a copy of a Viking longship (left) off the coast of Denmark.

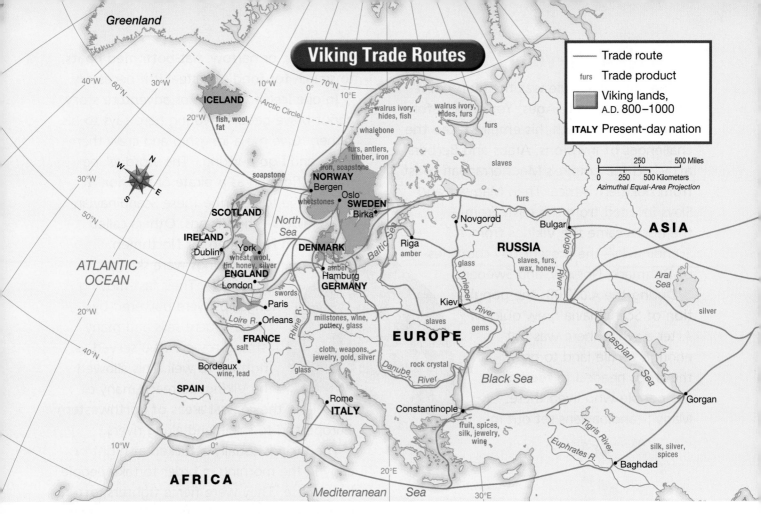

Viking Trade Routes

Greenland

40°W 60°N

30°W

ICELAND
fish, wool, fat

20°W

Arctic Circle

10°W 0° 70°N 10°E

walrus ivory, hides, fish

walrus ivory, hides, furs

furs

whalebone

30°W

furs, antlers, timber, iron

iron, soapstone

soapstone

NORWAY
Bergen

Oslo

whetstones

SWEDEN
Birka

50°N

SCOTLAND

North Sea

IRELAND

Dublin York

ENGLAND
London

swords

Paris

Loire R. Orleans

FRANCE
salt

Bordeaux
wine, lead

SPAIN

10°W 0°

20°W

40°N

wheat, wool, tin, honey, silver

DENMARK

amber
Hamburg

GERMANY

millstones, wine, pottery, glass

cloth, weapons, jewelry, gold, silver

glass

Rome
ITALY

Baltic Sea

Riga
amber

Novgorod

slaves

furs

Bulgar

RUSSIA
slaves, furs, wax, honey

glass

Kiev

Dnieper River

slaves

gems

rock crystal

Danube River

Black Sea

Constantinople

fruit, spices, silk, jewelry, wine

Mediterranean Sea

20°E

30°E

ASIA

Volga River

Aral Sea

silver

Caspian Sea

Gorgan

Tigris River

Euphrates R.

silk, silver, spices

Baghdad

Rhine R.

AFRICA

ATLANTIC OCEAN

Legend:
— Trade route
furs Trade product
▢ Viking lands, A.D. 800–1000
ITALY Present-day nation

0 250 500 Miles
0 250 500 Kilometers
Azimuthal Equal-Area Projection

GEOGRAPHY THEME

The Viking trade routes covered a vast area. The Viking homeland provided many materials and goods for trade, such as animal skins, fish, iron, and timber. The Vikings traded these items for slaves, spices, and silver.

❷ What trade products did the Vikings gain from Iceland?

The Vikings from what is now Norway settled in Iceland, Greenland, and parts of Scotland. They even began a settlement in North America, in what is now the Canadian province of Newfoundland and Labrador.

The Vikings from what is now Sweden settled on the shores of the Baltic Sea in what is now Latvia. They then traveled inland until they reached the Dnieper (NEE•per) and Volga Rivers. They continued up the Dnieper and set up a trading center at Kiev (KEE•ef), in what is now Ukraine.

Erik the Red, a Viking leader

From Kiev, a Viking named Rurik followed the Dnieper north and moved on to the city of Novgorod (NAHV•guh•rahd). In A.D. 862 Rurik invaded the city and established the kingdom of Kievan Rus (ROOS). Many historians believe that the Swedish Vikings became known there as the Rus and that Russia was named for them.

With settlement, *a-viking* became a thing of the past, remembered only in sagas. Over time, trading became the Vikings' main economic activity.

REVIEW What caused the Scandinavians to go a-viking, and why did they stop their raids?

Viking settlements (left) were made up mainly of one-room houses. This Viking jug (above) is made of glazed clay.

Viking Life

While people usually think of the Vikings as seagoing warriors, most actually lived on farms or in villages. They built permanent houses of wood or stone. Farmers grew oats, barley, and rye. Other Vikings worked at woodcarving, metalworking, and fishing. Shipbuilding was important, too.

A king or a chief ruled each Viking community, which was made up of three social classes. These were the nobles, common people, and slaves. The nobles were descendants of important ancestors in the community. The common people included farmers and craftworkers. Most of the slaves were people who had been captured in raids or in battle.

The Vikings lived in simple one-story houses. Indoors, family life centered around an open fireplace. The fireplace was used for light, heating, and cooking.

REVIEW What were the social classes in Viking society?

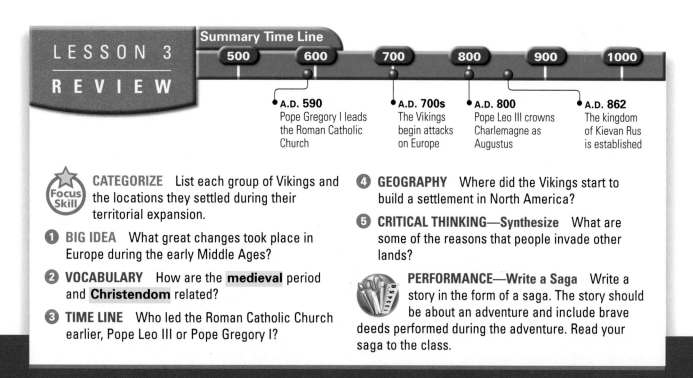

LESSON 3
REVIEW

Summary Time Line

| 500 | 600 | 700 | 800 | 900 | 1000 |

A.D. 590 Pope Gregory I leads the Roman Catholic Church

A.D. 700s The Vikings begin attacks on Europe

A.D. 800 Pope Leo III crowns Charlemagne as Augustus

A.D. 862 The kingdom of Kievan Rus is established

Focus Skill **CATEGORIZE** List each group of Vikings and the locations they settled during their territorial expansion.

1 BIG IDEA What great changes took place in Europe during the early Middle Ages?

2 VOCABULARY How are the **medieval** period and **Christendom** related?

3 TIME LINE Who led the Roman Catholic Church earlier, Pope Leo III or Pope Gregory I?

4 GEOGRAPHY Where did the Vikings start to build a settlement in North America?

5 CRITICAL THINKING—Synthesize What are some of the reasons that people invade other lands?

PERFORMANCE—Write a Saga Write a story in the form of a saga. The story should be about an adventure and include brave deeds performed during the adventure. Read your saga to the class.

10 Review and Test Preparation

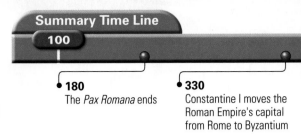
Summary Time Line

100

● 180
The *Pax Romana* ends

● 330
Constantine I moves the
Roman Empire's capital
from Rome to Byzantium

Categorize

Complete this graphic organizer by categorizing information about Rome's legacy. Think about the information, and then choose four categories into which it can be placed. A copy of this graphic organizer appears on page 95 of the Activity Book.

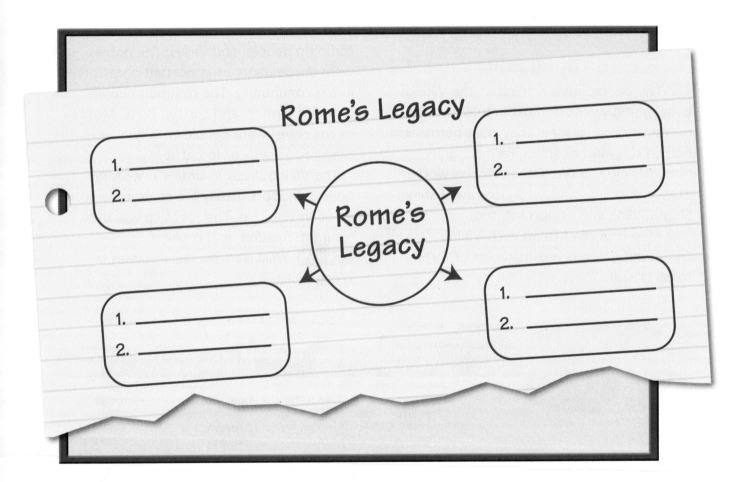

Rome's Legacy

1. _____
2. _____

1. _____
2. _____

Rome's Legacy

1. _____
2. _____

1. _____
2. _____

THINK & WRITE

Write a Biography   Use library or Internet resources to research Diocletian, Constantine, or Charlemagne. Then write a biography that includes a description of the leader's life and accomplishments.

Write a Letter   Imagine that you are a serf living on a manor in the former Western Roman Empire. Write a letter to a friend that describes a day in your life. Share your letter with a classmate.

400		700		1000

395
The Roman Empire officially splits into two parts

476
The Western Roman Empire ends

500
The early Middle Ages begin

700s
Vikings begin attacks on Europe

USE THE TIME LINE

Use the chapter summary time line to answer these questions.

1 In what year did Constantine I move the Roman Empire's capital? *330*

2 In what year did the division of the Roman Empire become official? *395*

USE VOCABULARY

Use one of the terms in the box to complete each sentence.

porticos (p. 327)

vandal (p. 332)

manor system (p. 334)

medieval (p. 338)

longships (p. 341)

saga (p. 341)

3 A _vandal_ is a person who purposely damages property.

4 The Middle Ages are also called the _medieval_ period.

5 Constantine's new capital included 52 covered walkways called _porticos_

6 A _saga_ is an adventure story about brave deeds.

7 In the _manor system_, peasants paid lords in goods and services for protection and for land use.

8 Scandinavian raiders traveled to northwestern Europe in flat-bottomed _longship_

RECALL FACTS

Answer these questions.

9 What was the *Pax Romana*? *Peace of Rome*

10 Who was Odoacer? *Overthrown of*

11 Which present-day countries were home to the Vikings? *Denmark, Sweden, Norway*

Write the letter of the best choice.

12 **TEST PREP** All of these are true about Constantinople *except*—
A it was originally the city of Chalcedon.
B it was renamed in Constantine's honor.
C it became the present-day city of Istanbul, Turkey.
D like Rome, it was located on seven hills.

13 **TEST PREP** Which of the following is *not* true about the manor system?
F Wealthy landlords, or lords, owned the manors.
G Peasants paid the lords with goods and services.
H Peasants provided protection for the lord.
J Some peasants, called serfs, could be sold along with the land.

THINK CRITICALLY

14 Why do you think that having more than 25 different leaders in 49 years—as the Roman Empire did—would cause people to feel less loyal to their government?

15 Why do you think the manor system lasted longer in central and eastern Europe than it did in western Europe?

APPLY SKILLS

Identify Fact and Opinion

16 Find a newspaper or magazine article about a recent event. Read the article, and highlight all statements of opinion in one color and all statements of fact in another color. How much of the article is fact? How much is opinion?

Chapter 10 345

HORYU-JI, NARA, JAPAN

The Horyu-ji is one of the Seven Great Temples of Nara in Japan. These temples, or holy places, were built in about A.D. 607. A fire destroyed the Horyu-ji in A.D. 670, but the temple was rebuilt not long after. The main hall and other parts of the temple have survived. They are among the oldest wooden structures in the world.

LOCATE IT

Sea of Japan

JAPAN

PACIFIC OCEAN

Nara

Africa and Asia

"Who in the future
Will recall me in the scent
Of orange blossoms
When I, too, shall have become
A person of long ago?"

—Shunzei, Japanese poet, 1114–1204

 ## Compare and Contrast

To **compare and contrast** people, places, or ideas, analyze how they are alike and different.

As you read this chapter, compare and contrast the information you read about.

• Record in a Venn diagram similarities and differences among people, places, and ideas.

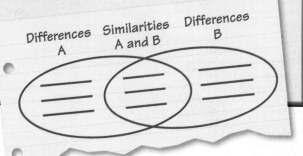

Differences A   Similarities A and B   Differences B

Chapter 11 ■ **347**

1

As you read, compare and contrast eastern Africa with the rest of Africa south of the Sahara.

BIG IDEA
The migration of people affected the history of Africa south of the Sahara.

VOCABULARY

savanna

smelt

overpopulation

FAST FACT

The southern border of the Sahara lies next to a semiarid region called the Sahel. Over time, the boundary between the Sahara and the Sahel shifts back and forth like a slow-moving ocean wave. In fact, the word *Sahel* is an Arabic word meaning "shore."

Africans South of the Sahara

500 B.C. | B.C./A.D. | A.D. 500 | A.D. 1000 | A.D. 1500

500 B.C. – A.D. 600

Most early Africans living south of the Sahara had little contact with people north of the vast desert. However, some early Africans south of the Sahara learned of important innovations in technology made by people farther north. They carried these innovations, along with their language and culture, across the region.

Early Peoples

Many scientists agree that humans like ourselves have lived on the continent of Africa longer than on any other continent. The earliest humans like ourselves lived in the part of Africa south of the Sahara. From there, these early people spread all over the continent of Africa and to the other continents.

As early Africans spread out through the continent, each group had to adapt to its environment. Sometimes, however, the environments they lived in changed.

Between 6,000 and 11,000 years ago, the Sahara in Africa was not a desert but a grassland. During that time the region had a wetter climate, lakes and streams, and plenty of wildlife.

Then, around 4,000 B.C., desertification began as the climate became drier. As the desert area grew larger and larger, it pushed people who lived there to the south. In time, the Sahara separated the lands that lay to the south of it from northern Africa and Europe. Travel across the desert was so difficult that information and new ideas could not be exchanged easily. The barrier formed by the Sahara had a major effect on the societies that developed in Africa south of the Sahara.

Since Africa south of the Sahara has a variety of landforms, many different ways of life developed there. People learned to live in its deserts, grasslands, and rain forests. Each environment had its challenges.

Survival was easiest for the early peoples of western Africa. Much of western Africa was a grassy plain, or **savanna** (suh•VA•nuh). The Niger (NY•jer) River flows across the region. When the Niger River flooded, it brought fertile soil and plenty of water for growing crops such as sorghum and millet. Because of this, western Africa's population grew quickly. One settlement along the Niger River grew into the first known city south of the Sahara—Jenne-Jeno (jeh•NAY juh•NOH). It was located in what is now the country

of Mali. The city formed around 250 B.C. and lasted for more than 1,000 years. During that time it became the region's first trade center. The people of Jenne-Jeno were known for using iron to make tools and weapons. However, they were not the first people to use iron in the region.

Africa South of the Sahara, A.D. 100

SAHARA

Sahel

Jenne-Jeno

Nok

Niger R.

Nile R.

Red Sea

Arabian Peninsula

Adulis

Aksum

Ethiopian Highlands

ATLANTIC OCEAN

Congo Basin

Congo River

Great Rift Valley

Lake Victoria

INDIAN OCEAN

Namib Desert

Madagascar

0   500   1,000 Miles
0   500   1,000 Kilometers
Azimuthal Equal-Area Projection

N
W   E
S

- Rain forest
- Savanna
- Semiarid
- Desert

GEOGRAPHY THEME

Regions Savannas cover more than 40 percent of Africa. Millet (left) grows in the savanna of western Africa.

❓ What is the name of the region that lies between the Sahara and the savanna?

LOCATE IT

Aïr Massif

NIGER

Workers in Ghana use a traditional furnace fueled by wood to work with glass. The Nok probably used furnaces similar to this one to make pottery and smelt iron.

The earliest iron use in Africa may be traced to the Nok culture. The name *Nok* comes from the village in what is today Nigeria (ny•JIR•ee•uh) where Nok artifacts were found. The Nok people flourished between 500 B.C. and A.D. 200. In about 300 B.C. they learned how to smelt iron ore, a mineral containing the metal iron. To **smelt** is to melt an ore to remove its metal. Then the Nok people heated the iron until it was soft enough to shape. Modern experts are not sure how the Nok people gained this technology.

Ancient Nok sculpture showing the face of a woman

Iron had been in use in parts of Asia and Europe since 1200 B.C. However, it is not clear how the idea for smelting iron crossed the barrier of the Sahara. The Nok people may have made this discovery on their own.

Working with iron changed the lives of the Nok people. It gave them stronger weapons for hunting and fighting. Iron tools also made it easier for them to clear land and grow crops. Because of these advantages, the Nok people and other iron users grew powerful. Before long, information about the use of iron began to spread to groups of people in neighboring areas.

REVIEW How did working with iron change the lives of the Nok people?

The Bantu Migrations

The early Bantu-speaking people were among those who learned about iron use. They lived in what is now the country of Cameroon. The name of the people comes from their languages—the Bantu languages. The Bantu speakers were farmers and cattle herders. They probably learned about using iron from their neighbors, the Nok people. Like the Nok people, the Bantu people used iron to make weapons for hunting and warfare and tools for agriculture. Iron tools allowed the Bantu people to produce more food. More food, however, may have led to a problem with **overpopulation**, or too many people living in one place.

Facing overpopulation, groups of Bantu speakers left their homeland in search of more land. Earlier groups had migrated by 500 B.C. However, overpopulation caused the migrations to begin to increase in the A.D. 100s. As groups of Bantu spread across Africa south of the Sahara, they carried their knowledge of farming and iron with them. Many groups took their cattle, too.

From the Bantu homeland the migration generally followed two routes, each avoiding the Sahara to the north. One route went toward the east through what are now the Central African Republic and the Democratic Republic of the Congo. This route turned south along the Great Rift Valley in eastern Africa. The other route went south and followed the coastline of western Africa. It stopped in what is now northern Namibia (nuh•MIH•bee•uh). The Namib Desert there blocked any further migration southward.

Bantu Population Growth

YEAR	POPULATION
400 B.C.	👤👤
A.D. 1	👤👤👤👤👤
A.D. 800	👤👤👤👤👤👤👤
A.D. 1000	👤👤👤👤👤👤👤👤

👤 = 2,000,000 people

Analyze Graphs The Bantu-speaking population grew rapidly as their farming technology improved.

❖ Between which years did the Bantu population more than double?

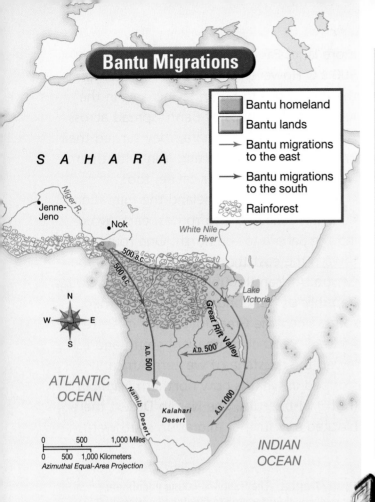

Bantu Migrations

Legend:
- Bantu homeland
- Bantu lands
- → Bantu migrations to the east
- → Bantu migrations to the south
- Rainforest

SAHARA

Niger R.

Jenne-Jeno

Nok

White Nile River

500 B.C.
500 B.C.

Congo River

Great Rift Valley

Lake Victoria

A.D. 500

A.D. 500

ATLANTIC OCEAN

Namib Desert

Kalahari Desert

A.D. 1000

INDIAN OCEAN

0   500   1,000 Miles
0   500   1,000 Kilometers
Azimuthal Equal-Area Projection

GEOGRAPHY THEME

Regions The Bantu migrations continued for about 1,500 years.

◆ Which route covered the longest distance, the east or the south?

Both routes avoided the dense rain forests of the Congo River region in western and central Africa. Tsetse (TSET•see) flies live in that area along riverbanks and lakeshores. They carry diseases that can kill people and livestock, such as cattle.

As the Bantu-speaking people migrated, they met other groups of Africans. These groups were herders, hunters and gatherers, or farmers. None of them were iron users.

The Bantu-speaking people settled among many of these groups and, over time, mixed with them. The Bantu-speaking people taught the other Africans how to work with iron, how to farm better, and how to speak Bantu. Each group developed its own dialect, or way of speaking the Bantu language. Today there are more than 500 dialects, and Bantu is the main language family spoken by Africans south of the Sahara.

REVIEW How were the two Bantu migration routes alike? (Focus Skill) **COMPARE AND CONTRAST**

The Kingdom of Aksum

South of the Sahara, one area in eastern Africa had a lot of contact with places outside the region. Around 500 B.C. people from the southern Arabian Peninsula crossed the Red Sea and settled along the African coast. They mixed with African people in the area and spread inland to the highlands of what is now Ethiopia. There they set up a kingdom around A.D. 50. The capital of the kingdom was a city called Aksum (AHK•soom).

Aksumite kings gained control of several seaports along the Red Sea. The busiest was Adulis (AH•joo•luhs). Africans brought ivory, gold, incense, animal skins, and slaves to Adulis to trade for Mediterranean olive oil, cloth, iron and brass, and tools and weapons.

Obelisks, like the one on the left, and coins (below) were made to honor the rulers of Aksum.

All this trade soon made Aksum a wealthy city. People from many parts of the world lived there. Aksum became a crossroads for many different cultures. King Zoscales (zohs•KAL•eez), who ruled Aksum during the first century A.D., read Greek literature. Many people spoke Greek as well as the local language, Geez (gee•EZ).

Over the next 200 years, Aksum kings took control of the countries known today as Somalia and Djibouti (juh•BOO•tee). They also conquered what is now Yemen on the Arabian Peninsula. During the A.D. 300s, King Ezana (AY•zah•nah) led the Aksumite army against the kingdom of Kush, in the Nile Valley. This warlike king defeated the Kushites and destroyed their capital, Meroë.

In his later years King Ezana made Aksum a Christian state. Soon, Aksum became an important center for Christian learning.

Aksum lost control of its Red Sea ports in the A.D. 600s when traders from southwestern Asia took over the region. Aksum's rulers moved farther from the coast where they formed the kingdom of Ethiopia.

REVIEW Which king made Christianity the religion of the kingdom of Aksum?

• HERITAGE •

Ethiopian Christian Art

Art is one way that Christians in Ethiopia preserve their past. The style of Ethiopia's Christian art developed over the past 1,000 years. It includes both Christian and Islamic influences from Africa, Asia, and Europe. Ethiopian Christian paintings often illustrate stories from the Bible, using bright colors and geometric shapes. Characters in the paintings have round heads, large eyes, and long, straight noses. Today, as in the past, Ethiopian Christians use these paintings in their worship services.

Ethiopian Christian painting

LESSON 1 REVIEW

Summary Time Line

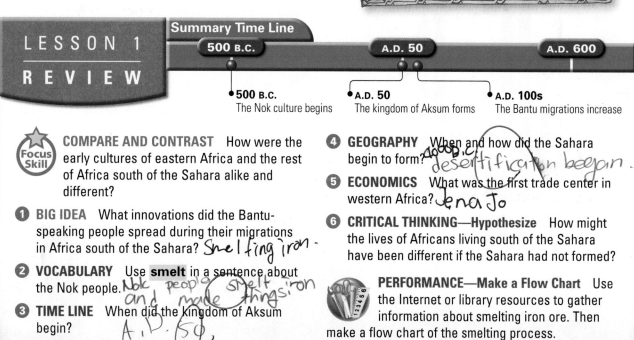

500 B.C. — A.D. 50 — A.D. 600

500 B.C.
The Nok culture begins

A.D. 50
The kingdom of Aksum forms

A.D. 100s
The Bantu migrations increase

COMPARE AND CONTRAST (Focus Skill) How were the early cultures of eastern Africa and the rest of Africa south of the Sahara alike and different?

1 **BIG IDEA** What innovations did the Bantu-speaking people spread during their migrations in Africa south of the Sahara? *Smelting iron*

2 **VOCABULARY** Use **smelt** in a sentence about the Nok people. *Nok people smelt iron and made things iron*

3 **TIME LINE** When did the kingdom of Aksum begin? *A.D. 50*

4 **GEOGRAPHY** When and how did the Sahara begin to form? *4000 B.C. desertification began.*

5 **ECONOMICS** What was the first trade center in western Africa? *Jena Jo*

6 **CRITICAL THINKING—Hypothesize** How might the lives of Africans living south of the Sahara have been different if the Sahara had not formed?

PERFORMANCE—Make a Flow Chart Use the Internet or library resources to gather information about smelting iron ore. Then make a flow chart of the smelting process.

Read a Climograph

VOCABULARY

climograph

▶ WHY IT MATTERS

The routes of the Bantu migrations passed through different climates in Africa south of the Sahara. They began in what is now the country of Cameroon. In Cameroon's capital city of Yaoundé (yown•DAY), the average temperature remains nearly the same all year-round. The rainfall, however, changes during the year.

One way to learn about the climate of a place is to study a climograph. A **climograph** is a kind of graph that shows average monthly temperature and precipitation. Knowing about the climate of a place can help you understand more about that place and its people.

▶ WHAT YOU NEED TO KNOW

A climograph is a line graph and a bar graph combined. The months of the year are shown along the bottom. Along the left-hand side is a temperature scale. Along the right-hand side is a precipitation scale.

Temperatures are shown as a line graph. A dot is placed to show the average temperature for each month. These dots are connected with a line. By studying the line, you can see which months are hotter and which are colder.

The low mountains around Yaoundé, Cameroon, help keep the city's temperatures mild all year.

Climograph of Yaoundé, Cameroon

Average Monthly Temperature

Average Monthly Precipitation

Average Monthly Temperature (in °F)

Average Monthly Precipitation (in inches)

Month

Jan | Feb | Mar | Apr | May | June | July | Aug | Sept | Oct | Nov | Dec

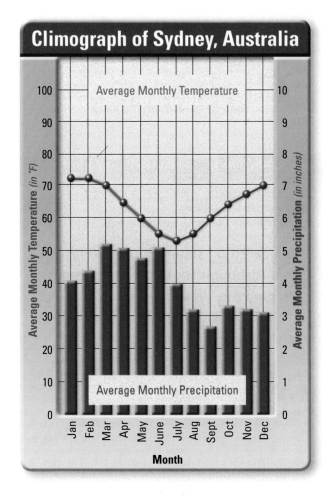

Climograph of Sydney, Australia

Average Monthly Temperature

Average Monthly Temperature (in °F)

Average Monthly Precipitation (in inches)

Average Monthly Precipitation

Jan Feb Mar Apr May June July Aug Sept Oct Nov Dec

Month

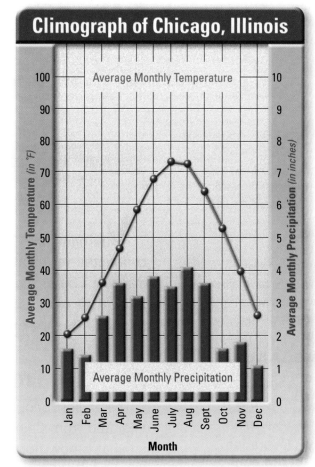

Climograph of Chicago, Illinois

Average Monthly Temperature

Average Monthly Temperature (in °F)

Average Monthly Precipitation (in inches)

Average Monthly Precipitation

Jan Feb Mar Apr May June July Aug Sept Oct Nov Dec

Month

Precipitation is shown as a bar graph. A bar is drawn up to the average amount of precipitation for each month. By studying the heights of the bars, you can see which months are drier and which months have more rain or snow.

▶ PRACTICE THE SKILL

The climographs on these pages show weather averages for Yaoundé in Cameroon, Sydney in Australia, and Chicago in the United States. Use the climographs to answer these questions.

1 Which are the warmest and coldest months in Yaoundé? in Sydney? in Chicago?

2 Which are the wettest and driest months in Yaoundé? in Sydney? in Chicago?

3 Which city has the lowest average temperature in January? Which city has the highest average temperature in August?

4 Which city has the most precipitation in January? Which city has the most precipitation in September?

5 Among the three climates shown on the climographs, which would you rather live in? Explain your choice.

▶ APPLY WHAT YOU LEARNED

Use an almanac to create a climograph for your city or a city near you. Compare your climograph with those in this skill lesson. Share your climograph with a family member. What does the climograph tell you about the area where you live?

2

Read to find out how the early societies of Vietnam and Korea were alike and different.

BIG IDEA

Vietnam and Korea had some of the same influences during the development of their early cultures.

VOCABULARY

animism
staple
clan
federation

LOCATE IT

VIETNAM

Halong Bay

Vietnamese and Korean Cultures

| 500 B.C. | B.C./A.D. | A.D. 500 | A.D. 1000 | A.D. 1500 |

500 B.C. – A.D. 1400

Vietnam and Korea are located on separate peninsulas connected to mainland China. Although these two peninsulas are near China, the early people who lived there were able to build their own unique cultures. Yet, through the years, China had an influence on both Vietnamese and Korean culture.

From Myths and Legends

The earliest people of Vietnam were later joined by people who migrated from China. Together, they settled on the Red River delta in what is now northern Vietnam. On the fertile lands of the delta, these ancient people began forming Vietnam's earliest civilization.

Historians believe that an early civilization existed on the Red River delta by 1400 B.C. Other cultures in southeastern Asia influenced the culture of these early Vietnamese. The people of Vietnam learned ideas about festivals, marriage ceremonies, and animism from other people living in the region. **Animism** is the religious belief that natural objects, such as rocks, have spirits.

According to Vietnamese legend the island peaks of Halong Bay were created by a dragon as it descended from the mountains to the sea. In Vietnamese, *Halong* means "descending dragon."

The first Vietnamese kingdom, called Van Lang, formed on the delta. Myths and legends say that Van Lang began around 2900 B.C. However, most experts believe that Van Lang developed around 1000 B.C. under the Vietnamese dynasty of Hung.

The people of Van Lang discovered how to irrigate their rice fields. As for many other Asians, rice was, and still is, a staple of the Vietnamese. A **staple** is any food or common item that is used regularly. The people of Van Lang also raised chickens and pigs. They made tools, weapons, and drums from bronze.

The Hung dynasty ended when the ruler of a neighboring kingdom conquered Van Lang in about 258 B.C. The conquering ruler added Van Lang to his kingdom and called the new kingdom Au Lac (OH LAK).

Beginning in 207 B.C. the Chinese made historical writings about Vietnam. These records state that the northern half of what is now Vietnam, including Au Lac, became a kingdom within the Chinese empire. In time, the governor of the kingdom wanted independence from the Chinese empire. He killed all government officials within the kingdom who were loyal to the Chinese emperor. Soon after that, he took control of the kingdom from the Chinese empire and named it Nam Viet.

Under China's Han dynasty, the Chinese took back control of Nam Viet in 111 B.C.

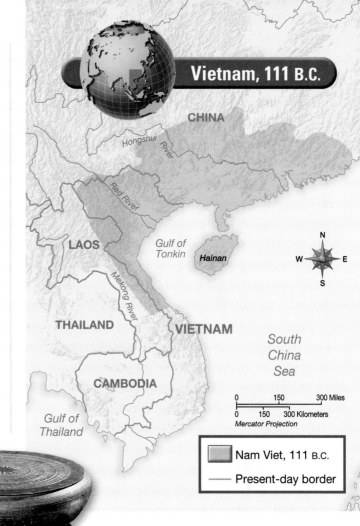

Vietnam, 111 B.C.

CHINA

Hongshui River

Red River

LAOS

Gulf of Tonkin

Hainan

Mekong River

THAILAND

VIETNAM

CAMBODIA

South China Sea

Gulf of Thailand

0   150   300 Miles
0   150   300 Kilometers
Mercator Projection

☐ Nam Viet, 111 B.C.
— Present-day border

GEOGRAPHY THEME

Regions Nam Viet was shifting from the Bronze Age to the Iron Age in 111 B.C. This bronze drum (left) is from this period.

❖ Which present-day countries have lands that were part of Nam Viet?

This event marks the beginning of more than 1,000 years of Chinese rule over what is now northern Vietnam.

REVIEW Where did the earliest civilization form in Vietnam?

Chinese Rule in Vietnam

Under Chinese rule the early people of Vietnam learned many new ideas about the arts, technology, and governing. The Vietnamese used Chinese innovations in irrigation to grow more rice in the Red River delta. They also began to use Chinese farming tools, such as iron plows, and to harness animals to pull them.

Ancient Vietnamese sculpture

In addition to introducing new ideas, the Chinese built waterways and roads across the Vietnamese lands that they ruled. These projects improved transportation and communication and also helped the Chinese keep control over the Vietnamese people.

At first, the Chinese allowed local rulers to take part in governing Vietnamese lands. However, by the first century A.D., the Han dynasty wanted to control the waterways of these lands. Ports along the coast were valuable for trade with other countries, so China began to make its rule over the Vietnamese stronger.

To strengthen its rule, China began forcing the Vietnamese people to follow Chinese customs. The Vietnamese had to study the teachings of the Chinese philosopher Confucius, wear Chinese clothing, and speak the Chinese language. The Vietnamese, however, refused to give up their language. The more firmly the Chinese insisted, the more strongly the Vietnamese resisted.

In A.D. 40 the Vietnamese defeated the Chinese army. They then formed a new Vietnamese kingdom, but Vietnamese rule did not last long. The Chinese army took back control in A.D. 43.

REVIEW Under Chinese rule, how did the Vietnamese culture change?

COMPARE AND CONTRAST

During the Chinese rule of Vietnam, parts of the country received Indian influences. This Hindu temple was built in central Vietnam in the A.D. 300s.

LOCATE IT

Hoa Lu VIETNAM

This site was the capital of Vietnam from A.D. 968 to 1010.

Vietnamese Independence

For the next 900 years, China continued to rule over the Vietnamese people. Chinese rule was sometimes strong and sometimes weak, depending on the strength of the Chinese emperor.

Chinese control over Vietnamese lands finally ended under China's Tang dynasty. In the early A.D. 900s the Tang dynasty began to decline. It became more difficult for the Tang leaders to keep control over lands far from their capital. In A.D. 939, not long after the Tang dynasty fell, the Vietnamese people became independent again.

Through more than 1,000 years of Chinese rule, the Vietnamese had kept much of their early culture. They had not given up the Vietnamese language or lost their culture's influences from southeastern Asia.

The Vietnamese had gained independence, but their lands were not stable. Warlords fought one another for control, rose to power, and quickly fell. Finally, the Ly (LEE) dynasty unified the people in 1009. The new Vietnamese kingdom was called Dai Viet (DY VYET).

· HERITAGE ·

Vietnamese Water Puppets

About 1,000 years ago heavy rains flooded the Red River delta in northern Vietnam. The farmers of the delta could not work in their flooded fields, so they developed water puppets to entertain themselves. The farmers carved puppets from wood and painted them. Next, they connected strings to move the parts of each puppet. Then, they attached the puppets to long bamboo poles. Using a flooded field or a pond as a stage, the farmers presented puppet shows to the villagers. Water made an ideal stage. The performers stood in waist-deep water behind a curtain. The strings and bamboo poles attached to the puppets were hidden under the water. This made the puppets appear to move on their own. Village life and legends were favorite subjects of Vietnamese water puppet shows. Today water puppets are still a part of Vietnamese traditions.

The Three Kingdoms, A.D. 400

CHINA

0 50 100 Miles
0 50 100 Kilometers
Conic Projection

⊛ Tonggu

KOGURYO

East Sea
(Sea of
Japan)

• P'yongyang
NORTH
KOREA

SOUTH
KOREA

SILLA
Kongju
⊛
PAEKCHE Kyongju
⊛

Yellow
Sea

⊛ Capital
— Present-day
  border

GEOGRAPHY THEME

Regions Silla was the smallest of the Three Kingdoms. This crown (right) is from the Silla kingdom.

❓ What was Koguryo's capital?

The capital was established at Hanoi, which is the capital of present-day Vietnam.

The Ly rulers of Dai Viet set up a strong central government. As in China, special schools were built to teach government officials how to govern. Buddhism, which had arrived under Chinese rule, grew during this period. The Ly kingdom lasted until the thirteenth century.

REVIEW What event in China helped the Vietnamese gain independence?

Early Korea

Several thousand years ago, nomadic travelers from northeastern Asia made their way to the Korean Peninsula. Korea's mountains, wild animals, and water resources led the nomads to stay there.

The early people of Korea lived in **clans**, or groups of related families. Some clans lived along Korea's coast, where they fished for food. Other clans lived in the valleys of Korea's mountains. There they hunted deer and other animals and gathered wild plants. Later, they developed the peninsula's earliest farming in the rich soil of the valleys.

The early Koreans were later joined by people from China, who sailed east to Korea. The Chinese people mixed with the people already there.

Over time, clans became parts of tribes, which in turn joined together to form states. By the 300s B.C. the most powerful state was Old Choson (CHOH•son). The people of Old Choson began to use iron tools and weapons. They also used horse-drawn chariots and irrigated their fields. They may have gotten these ideas from the Chinese.

With these new technologies, Old Choson grew to be a large **federation**, or union, of states. Its capital city was P'yongyang (pyawng•YAHNG), which is the present-day capital of North Korea.

In 108 B.C. China's Han army defeated Old Choson. China set up four districts there. As a result, many Chinese influences, including art and architecture, spread across the peninsula. Chinese rule angered the Koreans. After some time, the Koreans regained control of three districts.

REVIEW What was Old Choson?

New Kingdoms

After the Koreans drove the Chinese from much of the Korean Peninsula, new federations of states formed. Beginning in the first century B.C., three of these federations grew into what became known as the Three Kingdoms. They were called Koguryo (koh•gur•YOH), Paekche (PAK•chuh), and Silla (SIH•luh). Koguryo occupied a large area in the northern part of the Korean Peninsula. Paekche and Silla, both much smaller than Koguryo, were located in the southern part.

By A.D. 313 the Koguryo people had completely forced the Chinese out of the Korean Peninsula. Even so, Chinese influences remained strong. Buddhism from India arrived through China. Buddhism went on to become the state religion of all three kingdoms. Along with Buddhism, the early Koreans adopted Chinese characters for writing the Korean language. They used these for more than 1,000 years before they developed their own alphabet to write their language.

For centuries the Three Kingdoms fought among themselves for control of the peninsula. In the A.D. 660s Silla and the Chinese Tang dynasty joined their armies to conquer Paekche and then Koguryo. As a result, Silla controlled much of the peninsula by A.D. 668.

Even after Silla forced the Chinese out of the kingdom's lands, Chinese influences continued. A long period of peace and unity followed. During this time the people of Silla became very interested in science and the arts. More Buddhist temples were built, and Confucianism became another important religion in Korean society.

REVIEW **What kingdoms made up the Three Kingdoms?**

• SCIENCE AND TECHNOLOGY •

Korea's Chomsongdae Observatory

In astronomy, an observatory is a place for viewing and studying the stars and planets. Chomsongdae (chohm•suhng•DY), Asia's oldest observatory, was built in Korea during the seventh century A.D. Its design is fascinating. The observatory stands on 12 large stones, one stone for each month of the year. Its walls are made of stones stacked 30 layers high, one layer for each day of the month. In total, there are 366 stones, roughly one stone for each day of the year. Korean astronomers used the 30-foot-tall (9.2-m-tall) observatory for astronomy and weather studies.

The Changdeokkung palace was the residence of many Choson kings. The painting from the Choson kingdom (right) shows a tiger, a symbol of Korea.

Koryo and Choson Kingdoms

During the late A.D. 800s Silla began to face troubles. Unity within the government declined. At the same time, powerful warlords rose up within the kingdom. They wanted to take control of large areas of the kingdom's lands. In the end, warlords won control of the lands of the former kingdoms of Koguryo and Paekche.

Briefly, the Korean Peninsula was divided into the original kingdoms that made up the Three Kingdoms. Today these new kingdoms are known as the Later Three Kingdoms.

The Later Three Kingdoms did not last long. By A.D. 936 a rebel Koguryo general had gained control of all three kingdoms. He reunited the Korean Peninsula and called it the

Koryo (KOR•yoh) kingdom. The present-day name *Korea* comes from the name *Koryo*.

Koryo leaders did not want Korea to be just like China. They allowed Chinese ideas, particularly those that improved their ways of living and working. However, they encouraged the people of Korea to keep their own customs and traditions.

Under the Koryo kingdom, the families of nobles had power and wealth. They held most of the important government positions. The central government also gave land to some of these officials. This land created even more wealth for the nobles. The nobles followed both Buddhism and Confucianism, and

Bronze water sprinkler from the 1100s

the government gave support to these religions in the Koryo kingdom.

The nobles lived well, but the kingdom's military leaders were treated badly. They received none of the privileges that the nobles received from the government. This situation led to a military uprising in 1170. The military leaders won control of Koryo for more than 200 years. During this time they faced many difficulties, including peasant rebellions and invasions from outsiders.

The kingdom was able to survive these struggles. However, over time it grew weaker. In 1392 a general named Yi set up a new kingdom on the Korean Peninsula. General Yi's kingdom was named Choson in honor of Old Choson.

To create a money economy, the Choson government introduced paper money and coins into the kingdom in the 1400s. Even so, most people continued to use cloth for trade for many years. Buddhism declined under Choson rule as rich landowners began to favor Confucianism. As a result, Choson society developed the strict social classes

This temple holds the Tripitaka, a collection of more than 80,000 wood blocks engraved with Buddhist scriptures during the Koryo kingdom.

found in the teachings of Confucius. The Choson kingdom lasted for more than 500 years.

REVIEW Which Chinese ideas did Koryo leaders accept?

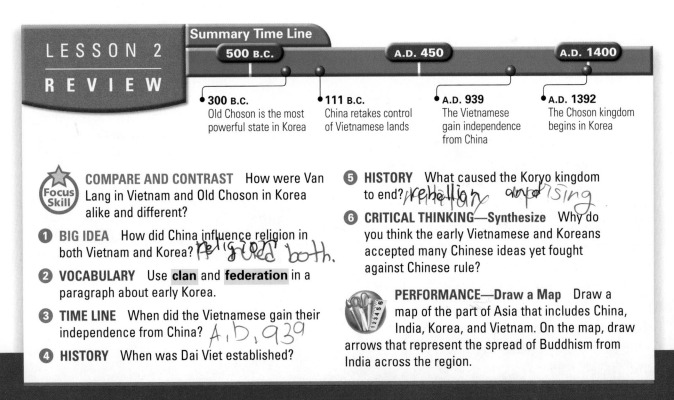

LESSON 2 REVIEW

Summary Time Line

| 500 B.C. | | A.D. 450 | A.D. 1400 |

300 B.C. Old Choson is the most powerful state in Korea

111 B.C. China retakes control of Vietnamese lands

A.D. 939 The Vietnamese gain independence from China

A.D. 1392 The Choson kingdom begins in Korea

Focus Skill **COMPARE AND CONTRAST** How were Van Lang in Vietnam and Old Choson in Korea alike and different?

1 **BIG IDEA** How did China influence religion in both Vietnam and Korea? religion both.

2 **VOCABULARY** Use **clan** and **federation** in a paragraph about early Korea.

3 **TIME LINE** When did the Vietnamese gain their independence from China? A.D. 939

4 **HISTORY** When was Dai Viet established?

5 **HISTORY** What caused the Koryo kingdom to end? military uprising

6 **CRITICAL THINKING—Synthesize** Why do you think the early Vietnamese and Koreans accepted many Chinese ideas yet fought against Chinese rule?

PERFORMANCE—Draw a Map Draw a map of the part of Asia that includes China, India, Korea, and Vietnam. On the map, draw arrows that represent the spread of Buddhism from India across the region.

COMPARE AND CONTRAST

As you read, compare and contrast Japanese culture before and after it received important influences.

BIG IDEA

The early Japanese borrowed from other cultures and developed their own ideas.

VOCABULARY

paddy
Shinto
kami
emissary
regent
daimyo
samurai
shogun

Early Japan

500 B.C.	B.C./A.D.	A.D. 500	A.D. 1000	A.D. 1500

500 B.C. – A.D. 1400

The many islands that make up Japan lie near the east coast of the Asian mainland. This location allowed the early Japanese to have much contact with their Chinese and Korean neighbors to the west. At that time, the Japanese did not know of the lands and peoples that were far to the east. They only saw what appeared to be the endless Pacific Ocean. This led the early Japanese to believe that they were the first people to see the rising sun every day. Because of this, the Japanese call their island country Nippon, or "land of the rising sun."

Japan's Early Cultures

American scientist Edward S. Morse visited Japan in the 1800s to study its sea life. As Morse traveled on a train near the city of Tokyo, he noticed unusual mounds, or small hills, not far from the train tracks. The next day he took a closer look at the mounds.

Inside them Morse found pottery and tools made of bone and stone. The pottery had patterns that looked like rope marks pressed into the clay. Morse named the pottery *jomon* (JOH•mon), which means "rope marks" in the Japanese language. The culture of the ancient people who made the pottery became known as the Jomon culture. On just his second day in Japan, Morse had made one of the country's most important archaeological discoveries!

The Jomon people lived from 10,500 B.C. to 300 B.C. in small settlements all over the Japanese islands. They made some of the earliest clay pottery in the world. They used the pots for storing water and food.

The Jomon people survived by hunting, gathering, and fishing. Since the Jomon people did not know how to weave cloth, they wore tree bark and animal skins as clothing. They also wore seashell bracelets, stone earrings, and bone necklaces.

Over time, a new culture—the Yayoi (ya•YO•ee)—spread across Japan and replaced the Jomon culture. The Yayoi period lasted from 300 B.C. to A.D. 250.

Japan

CHINA

RUSSIA

NORTH KOREA

SOUTH KOREA

Sea of Japan

East China Sea

Hokkaido

Honshu

JAPAN

Mt. Fuji ▲

Shikoku

Kyushu

PACIFIC OCEAN

0   150   300 Miles
0   150   300 Kilometers
Two-Point Equidistant Projection

GEOGRAPHY THEME

Regions Japan is made up of four major islands and about 6,000 smaller islands.

❓ **Which Japanese island is the largest?**

A CLOSER LOOK
Jomon Village

People of the Jomon culture lived in villages such as this one about 4,000 years ago. They constructed buildings suited for the hot, humid summers and snowy winters that exist across much of Japan. This method of building is still used in many parts of Japan.

① Buildings with floors raised above the ground held food supplies. The raised floors allowed air to flow underneath them to reduce humidity.

② The village leader lived in the largest house.

③ Tall platforms were used for ceremonies.

④ Villagers lived in houses with floors made of clay or stone and walls and roofs made of straw.

❓ **How might raised floors have been useful during Japan's snowy winters?**

Analyze Primary Sources

Archaeologists often study ancient pottery to better understand past cultures. They look for changes in the materials, the design, and the methods a society used for making its pottery. Over time, these changes often mean the culture is also changing.

1 The pottery on the left was made during the Jomon culture. The Jomon people handmade their pottery, adding a ropelike pattern for decoration. They baked their pottery in open pits.

2 The pottery on the right was made during the Yayoi culture. The Yayoi people shaped their pottery on a pottery wheel, using simpler designs. They baked their pottery in closed pits.

◈ Which information about the Yayoi pottery might show that it came from a more advanced culture than the Jomon pottery?

The Yayoi period was a time of new ideas. Many of the ideas developed within Japan. Other new ideas began to reach Japan from the mainland of Asia.

The Yayoi were the first people in Japan to use iron. They probably learned about iron from China and Korea. They shaped iron into arrowheads, axes, hoes, and swords. Iron tools helped them grow more food, and more people began to live in farming settlements.

As in Vietnam and Korea, irrigation methods discovered in China helped improve rice farming in Japan. Wet rice fields replaced dry rice fields. Yayoi farmers began building low earth walls around flooded fields to keep the water from flowing away. These walled wet fields are called **paddies**. Rice grows better in a paddy than in a dry field.

At about this time the early Japanese began forming a system of beliefs. They developed a religion called **Shinto**, or "the way of the gods." Animism is part of the Shinto religion. People who follow the religion believe that spirits called **kami** (KAH•mee) live in all natural things, such as stones, trees, and animals. They believe the kami guide them through their life.

REVIEW How was the Yayoi culture different from the Jomon culture?

🔎 **COMPARE AND CONTRAST**

Even today, Japanese farmers use paddies for rice farming.

China's Influence on Japan

The earliest known records about Japan were made by the Chinese in A.D. 57. These ancient documents contain writings about a queen who ruled over a large area of Japan. The queen sent **emissaries**, or representatives, to China. In return, China sent emissaries to Japan. The queen and the ruler of China exchanged information about their lands and people.

Chinese records show a well-developed Japanese culture by the A.D. 200s. At that time, Japan had markets, social classes, and a system for collecting taxes. It also had struggles for power among clans.

Under the leadership of powerful clans, the Yamato kingdom began to emerge in the A.D. 400s. It was during this time that the role of emperor began to develop in Japan. However, the emperor's authority was limited to religious matters. Legends say that the first emperor of Japan was not just a human but also a descendant of the sun goddess. Because of this, the Japanese treated their emperors as godlike leaders for centuries.

During Yamato rule, a number of people from the Asian mainland migrated to Japan. Many of these people carried with them knowledge from Chinese civilization, such as weaving and metalworking. The new arrivals also brought Chinese writing with them. The Japanese had no written language of their own. So they began using Chinese characters to write the Japanese language. The Japanese still use Chinese characters as part of their writing system.

In the A.D. 500s Chinese missionaries arrived in Japan from Korea. The missionaries brought not only Buddhism but also many Chinese customs. They introduced

the Japanese to Chinese art, architecture, law, clothing, and manners. The Japanese accepted many of these Chinese ways.

In A.D. 646 laws called the Taika (TY•kuh) reforms set up a central government for Japan based on Chinese government. The Japanese, however, changed some of the Chinese ways of governing to meet their own needs. For example, the Chinese Mandate of Heaven passed from one dynasty to another. In contrast, the Japanese emperor's family claimed the right to rule for all time.

Origin of Japanese Writing

ENGLISH WORD	CHINESE WRITING	JAPANESE WRITING (KANJI)
Sun	日	日
Moon	月	月
Tree	木	木
Rain	雨	雨
Mountain	山	山
Water	水	水

Analyze Tables The early Japanese based their way of writing on Chinese characters.

❓ Based on the examples above, do you think an ancient Chinese reader could have read Japanese writing?

Statue of a Shinto goddess

THE TALE OF GENJI

The Tale of Genji provides a detailed view of life in the Japanese court as it existed 1,000 years ago. The main character of the novel is Genji, one of the emperor's sons. The following passage from the novel describes the birth of Genji. ". . . she bore the emperor a beautiful son, a jewel beyond compare. The emperor was in a fever of impatience to see the child, still with the mother's family; and when, on the earliest day possible, [the child] was brought to court, he did indeed prove to be a most marvelous babe. The emperor's eldest son was the grandson of the Minister of the Right. The world assumed that with this powerful support he would one day be named crown prince; but the new child was far more beautiful. On public occasions the emperor continued to favor his eldest son. The new child was a private treasure, so to speak, on which to [give unlimited] affection."

A scene from *The Tale of Genji*

As Japan began to follow China's system of governing, the role of the emperor of Japan changed. Once simply a religious leader, the emperor now also became a political leader, as Chinese emperors were. For the first time, the people of Japan united under the emperor.

Like China's Tang rulers, the Japanese emperors encouraged their people to create works of art. For example, Lady Murasaki Shikibu (MUR•ah•SAHK•ee SHEE•kee•BOO) wrote the world's first novel, called *The Tale of Genji* (GEN•jee). Even today *The Tale of Genji* is considered one of Japan's finest pieces of literature.

REVIEW **What were the Taika reforms based on?**

Feudal Japan

In the A.D. 800s Chinese influence over Japan declined. Under the Tang rulers China grew weak. Buddhists in China began to be treated badly. These events caused the Japanese to lose the respect they once held for Chinese ways. Japanese society began to develop its own ways.

One change that took place was in the way Japan was governed. The powerful Fujiwara (FOO•jee•WAH•rah) family gained the right to rule in the emperor's name as regents. **Regents** are people who govern in place of the official ruler. Even so, the Fujiwaras were unable to gain authority over Japan's most distant lands. These lands were governed by noble families.

As nobles claimed different parts of Japan, a system of feudalism began to form. The most powerful nobles were known as **daimyos** (DY•mee•ohz), or "great names." They formed their own armies to defend and expand their lands. The soldiers, who were known as **samurai** (SA•muh•ry), promised loyalty to their daimyos. The daimyos then gave each samurai some of the land won in battle.

Peasants lived on and farmed the land owned by the samurai. The peasants gave the samurai part of their crops. In return, the samurai agreed to protect the peasants.

Only the sons of nobles could become samurai, and their training was long and hard. As part of their training, they hiked barefoot in freezing weather. Sometimes they went for days without eating. This helped them accept pain and hunger. Their training also taught them to be ready at all times for battle and not to fear death.

In time, the daimyos took part in governing Japan. Late in the 1100s a daimyo named Minamoto Yoritomo (MEE•nah•moh•toh yoh•REE•toh•moh) set up a military government. In 1192 he convinced the emperor to give him the title **shogun** (SHOH•guhn), or "leading general." The shogun was supposed to be the emperor's chief army officer, but he really held all the authority.

Built in the A.D. 600s, the Horyu-ji Buddhist temple is the world's oldest wooden building. Samurai armor is shown at left.

Yoritomo and the shoguns who came after him built on the feudal system. They gave land to loyal daimyos. In return, the daimyos sent soldiers to the shoguns in times of war. This system began to weaken in the 1330s. Soon Japan was divided by civil war.

REVIEW What events caused the Japanese to lose respect for Chinese ways?

LESSON 3 REVIEW

Summary Time Line

| 500 B.C. | A.D. 450 | A.D. 1400 |

300 B.C.
Yayoi culture replaces Jomon culture

A.D. 800s
Feudalism begins in Japan

A.D. 1192
Minamoto Yoritomo becomes shogun

COMPARE AND CONTRAST After the Taika reforms, how were the roles of the Japanese and Chinese emperors alike and different?

1 BIG IDEA How did Asian immigrants to Japan influence the Japanese culture?

2 VOCABULARY Use **daimyo** and **samurai** in a sentence about the feudal system in Japan.

3 TIME LINE What happened in A.D. 1192? *Minamoto Yoritomo becomes shogun*

4 CULTURE What knowledge helped the Japanese develop farming settlements? *Usage of paddies.*

5 ECONOMICS What was the relationship between the peasants and the samurai under Japan's feudal system? *Peasants lived on and farmed the land owned by samurai.*

6 CRITICAL THIINKING—Evaluate How might early Japanese culture have been different if Japan were farther from the Asian mainland?

PERFORMANCE—Make Pottery Create a design for a piece of pottery. In doing so, think of a use for your pottery. Then, using your hands, mold your pottery design out of modeling clay. Display your pottery in the classroom.

Japanese Musical Instruments

Music was an important part of life in Japan's royal courts from the 500s to the 1500s. At first, music at court consisted of a single musician singing a story while playing along on a stringed instrument. In Japan these musicians were often blind priests. Later, groups of musicians and others performed *gagaku*, or elegant music, at the emperor's court. *Gagaku* featured storytellers, dancers, acrobats, and the world's first orchestras. All members of the court learned to play the instruments used in *gagaku*.

FROM THE NATIONAL MUSEUM OF JAPANESE HISTORY IN SAKURA, JAPAN

A *biwa*, or Japanese lute

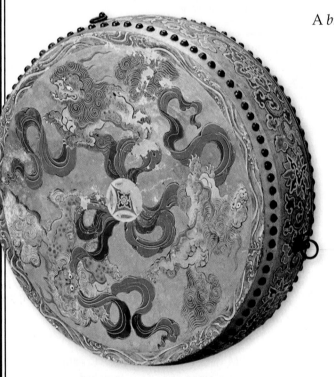

This large drum is called a *taiko*. It is hung from a stand and struck with two large sticks.

❶ What do the instruments and the text tell you about the importance of music to the Japanese during this period?

❷ Do you think musicians made their own instruments, or were they made by special instrument makers? Explain.

❸ Compare the *biwa* to a stringed instrument you are familiar with. How is it similar? How is it different?

A *hichiriki*, or bamboo flute, was used to play the main melody in Japanese court music.

This print shows a woman with a *shamisen*, or long-necked lute.

A *sho* is a mouth organ made of 17 bamboo pipes.

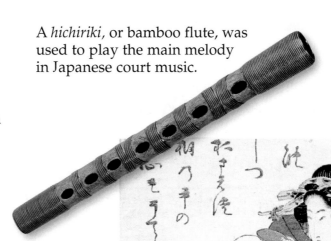

ACTIVITY

Collect and Compile Find out about musical instruments from around the world. Then write about how they are similar and how they are different.

RESEARCH

Visit The Learning Site at **www.harcourtschool.com** to research other primary resources.

11 Review and Test Preparation

Summary Time Line

500 B.C.   **120 B.C.**

250 B.C.
The first known city in Africa
south of the Sahara forms

111 B.C.
China begins its long rule
over northern Vietnam

(Focus Skill) Compare and Contrast

Complete this graphic organizer to show that you understand
how to compare and contrast different topics, such as the early
cultures of Africa south of the Sahara. A copy of this graphic
organizer appears on page 101 of the Activity Book.

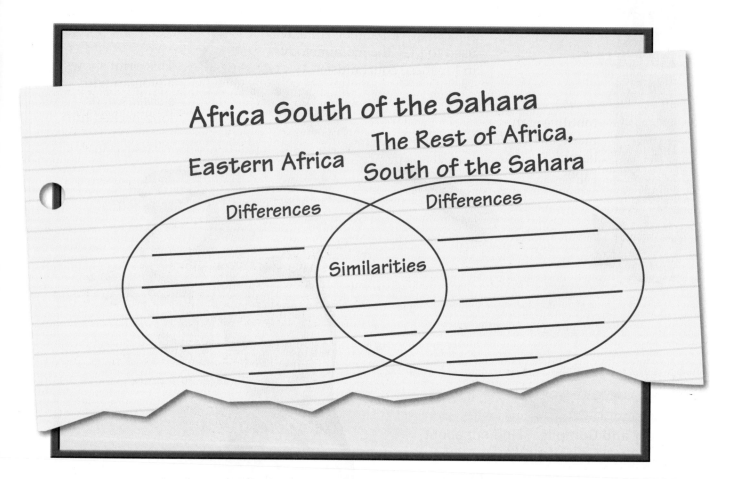

Africa South of the Sahara

Eastern Africa   The Rest of Africa, South of the Sahara

Differences   Differences

Similarities

THINK & WRITE

Write a Help-Wanted Ad   Write a
newspaper help-wanted ad that describes the
job of a samurai. Include information about the
requirements for the job, the training a samurai
receives, the responsibilities of the job, and the
pay or other benefits.

Write a Journal Entry   Imagine that you
are an assistant to scientist Edward S. Morse.
You are traveling with him through Japan.
Where are you, and what is the date? Describe
what Morse finds, and include how he names
the people whose artifacts he discovers.

A.D. 260   A.D. 640   A.D. 1020   A.D. 1400

• A.D. 100s
The Bantu migrations
begin in Africa

• A.D. 800s
A feudal system
begins in Japan

• A.D. 939
The Vietnamese gain
independence
from the Chinese

• A.D. 1392
The Korean Choson
kingdom begins

USE THE TIME LINE

Use the chapter summary time line to answer these questions.

1 What event began in Africa in about A.D. 100?

Bantu migrations began.

2 When did a feudal system begin in Japan?

A.D. 800s

USE VOCABULARY

Identify the term that correctly matches each description.

savanna (p. 349)

smelt (p. 350)

animism (p. 356)

staple (p. 357)

paddy (p. 366)

regent (p. 368)

daimyo (p. 368)

3 any food or common item that is used regularly   *regent*

4 a grassy plain   *savanna*

5 to melt an ore to remove its metal   *smelt*

6 a name for the most powerful nobles in the Japanese feudal system   *daimyo*

7 a person who governs in place of the official ruler   *staple regent*

8 a walled wet rice field   *paddy*

9 the religious belief that natural objects, such as rocks, have spirits   *animism*

RECALL FACTS

Answer these questions.

10 On which continent do many scientists believe humans have lived for the longest time?   *Africa*

11 Who are believed to be the first Africans south of the Sahara to use iron?   *Nok*

12 How are Shinto, animism, and kami related?

Anism is part of Shinto. And they believe kami gods.

Write the letter of the best choice.

13 **TEST PREP**   All of these statements are true about the kingdom of Aksum *except*—

A Adulis was the busiest of its port cities.

B the kingdom's control spread into what are today Somalia, Djibouti, and Yemen.

C King Aksum became a Christian and made Aksum a Christian state.

D southwestern Asian traders took over its seaports in the A.D. 600s.

14 **TEST PREP**   Which of these statements is *not* true about the feudal system in Japan?

F Daimyos were the most powerful nobles.

G Samurai were soldiers who were loyal to the daimyos.

H Peasants lived on samurai land and were protected by them.

J It lasted until the 1630s.

THINK CRITICALLY

15 How did the Bantu migrations change Africa south of the Sahara?

16 Look at the map on page 357. How might the geography of Vietnam have affected the country's relationship with China?

APPLY SKILLS

Read a Climograph

17 Use the climographs on pages 354–355 to draw conclusions about the climates in Yaoundé, Cameroon; Sydney, Australia; and Chicago, Illinois. Write a paragraph describing what the climate in each place is probably like.

CHART AND GRAPH SKILLS

MACHU PICCHU, PERU

Machu Picchu, a city of the Inca people, has stood in the mountains of Peru since about the mid-1400s. It was discovered again in 1911 and is now an important tourist attraction in Peru. Some visitors reach Machu Picchu by walking up thousands of stone steps known as the Inca Trail.

LOCATE IT

PERU

PACIFIC OCEAN

Machu Picchu

· CHAPTER ·

The Americas

> **"And so the birds down on the coast are singing,** *Qosqota riy,* **'Go to Cuzco,'** *Qosqopi riy,* **'In Cuzco is the king.'"**
>
> —From an Inca legend, *c.* 1500s

 **Sequence**

A **sequence** is the order in which events, processes, or ideas happen.

As you read the chapter, put events that you read about in the correct sequence.

- Identify the events that happened.

- Tell which events happened first, next, and last.

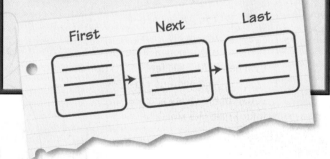

SEQUENCE

As you read, look for the sequence of events that led to the creation of the Aztec Empire.

BIG IDEA

The Aztecs built the first empire in Mesoamerica.

VOCABULARY

Mesoamerica
causeway
chinampa

The Aztecs

500 B.C.	B.C./A.D.	A.D. 500	A.D. 1000	A.D. 1500

A.D. 1000 – A.D. 1500

Neither the Olmecs nor the Maya built empires. It was not until the 1400s that a large empire formed in Mesoamerica. **Mesoamerica**, which means "Middle America," includes Mexico and Central America. The people who built this empire were the Aztecs. The Aztecs were feared warriors who won battle after battle. In less than 200 years, Aztec rule grew from a small island in a lake into a mighty empire.

The Aztecs Settle

For many years the Aztecs lived a nomadic life in what is now northern Mexico. Then around 1200 they began to travel south in search of a new homeland. According to an ancient legend, the war god they believed in promised that they would know they had reached this homeland when they saw an eagle with a snake in its mouth, sitting on a cactus.

This drawing tells the story of the Aztecs' search for a new homeland.

FAST FACT

The Aztecs settled in the Valley of Mexico, a large oval basin. At 7,500 feet (2,300 m), the average elevation of the valley is more than 1 mile (1.5 km) high!

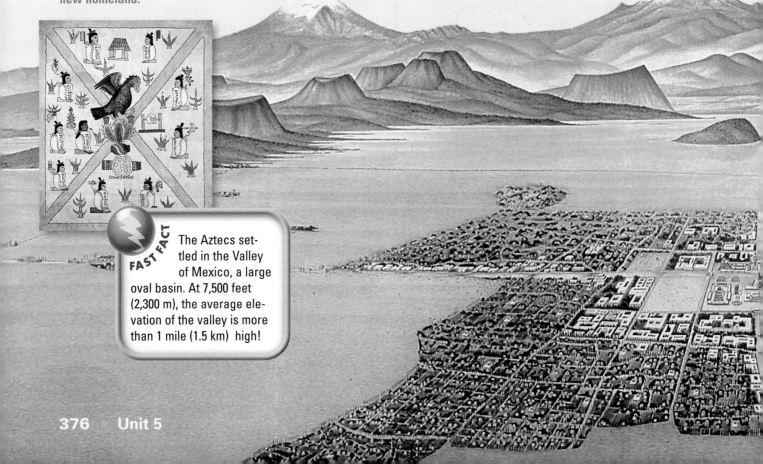

In search of this sign, the Aztecs entered what is now called the Valley of Mexico in central Mexico. There they found cultures that were more advanced than their own.

The Aztecs settled near other cultures in the center of the valley. Their neighbors thought they were uncivilized and did not welcome them. The Aztecs spoke Nahuatl (NAH•wah•tuhl), a language unknown to the peoples in the valley. They wore animal skins instead of clothes woven from cotton. The Aztecs were also warlike. They used bows and arrows to help them gain whatever they wanted. Their weapons helped make them better warriors than most other groups of people in the valley.

After some time, one group forced the Aztecs out. Again, the Aztecs searched for a homeland. This time, they saw what their god had promised them. In the valley, on a small, swampy island in Lake Texcoco (tes•KOH•koh), was an eagle with a snake in its mouth, sitting on a cactus. The Aztecs had finally found their homeland.

The Aztec people called themselves the Mexica. Because of this, their land became known as Mexico. Today the Aztecs are an important part of Mexican heritage. The eagle with the snake is a symbol of Mexico and appears on the Mexican flag.

REVIEW **Why did the Aztec people settle on an island in Lake Texcoco?**

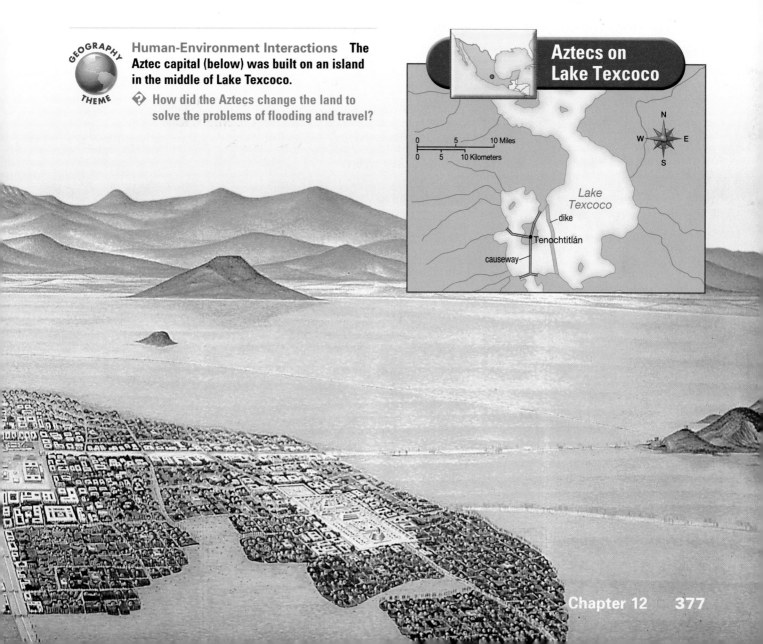

GEOGRAPHY THEME

Human-Environment Interactions **The Aztec capital (below) was built on an island in the middle of Lake Texcoco.**

◆ How did the Aztecs change the land to solve the problems of flooding and travel?

Aztecs on Lake Texcoco

Lake Texcoco

dike

Tenochtitlán

causeway

0 5 10 Miles
0 5 10 Kilometers

N W E S

The Island Capital Tenochtitlán

In about 1325 the Aztecs began building a capital city on the island in Lake Texcoco. The Aztecs called their new capital Tenochtitlán (tay•nohch•teet•LAHN). In many ways the place said to be chosen by their god was a good one. Having water all around made the island city easy to defend. Also, the lake offered fish, waterbirds, and frogs for food. In addition, no other people lived on the island.

The island location did have some problems. The island was separated from the mainland. There was no farmland and no wood or stone for building. Flooding, too, was a problem.

Aztec pottery

The Aztecs found ways to solve all the problems caused by their capital city's location. First, they built **causeways**, or land bridges, to connect the island to the mainland. Then, they made a dike, or wall of earth, 10 miles (16 km) long to protect the city from floods. To get the wood and stone they needed for building palaces and temples, they traded with other peoples.

To solve the problem of not having enough farmland, the Aztecs built **chinampas** (chee•NAHM•pahz) in the lake around their city. Chinampas were human-made islands. To create them, the Aztecs first wove branches together to make huge underwater baskets. Next, they planted trees around the baskets to keep them in

The illustration (below) shows Aztecs building a chinampa. The photo (left) shows a present-day chinampa in Mexico City, Mexico.

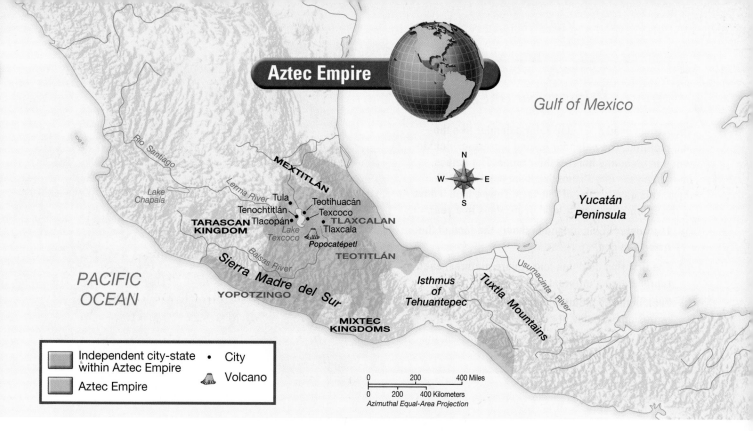

Aztec Empire

Gulf of Mexico

Rio Santiago

Lake Chapala

MEXTITLÁN

Lerma River

Tula

Teotihuacán

Tenochtitlán
Texcoco

TARASCAN KINGDOM

Tlacopán

TLAXCALAN

Lake Texcoco

Tlaxcala

Popocatépetl

TEOTITLÁN

Yucatán Peninsula

PACIFIC OCEAN

Sierra Madre del Sur

Balsas River

YOPOTZINGO

Isthmus of Tehuantepec

Usumacinta River

Tuxtla Mountains

MIXTEC KINGDOMS

| | Independent city-state within Aztec Empire | • | City |
| | Aztec Empire | ⛰ | Volcano |

0   200   400 Miles
0   200   400 Kilometers
Azimuthal Equal-Area Projection

Regions The Aztecs built an empire by conquering the city-states of neighboring peoples.

◆ How many city-states shown on the map were independent within the Aztec Empire?

place. Then they filled the baskets with mud from the lake's bottom. New islands of farmland rose above the water. On these "floating gardens," farmers grew beans, peppers, and maize, or corn. Some farmers even lived on the chinampas.

All these changes to the environment helped the Aztec capital grow. Over time, Tenochtitlán became a city of more than 140,000 people. As their city grew in size, the Aztecs grew in power. In about 1428 they formed an alliance with two nearby cities—Texcoco and Tlacopán (tlah•koh•PAHN).

The Aztecs and their allies quickly became the strongest fighting force in the Valley of Mexico. Led by an Aztec ruler, the alliance built an empire.

REVIEW What was the first step in building a chinampa? **SEQUENCE**

The Empire Develops

The Aztecs were the most powerful of the allies. Under the Aztec ruler Motecuhzoma (maw•tay•kwah•SOH•mah) I, also known as Montezuma, the empire grew. For this reason, it is often called the Aztec Empire.

Motecuhzoma came to power in about 1440. He led Aztec warriors in a march across the Valley of Mexico. They continued over the mountains to the south and the east. All along the way, the Aztecs conquered other native peoples.

The Aztecs demanded tribute, or forced payment, from the people they conquered.

This ceramic figure is of an Aztec eagle warrior.

Analyze Primary Sources

The Aztecs used a 365-day solar calendar like the one pictured. The calendar helped the Aztecs decide when to plant and harvest their crops. The Aztecs divided a year into 18 months. Each month had 20 days. This gave a total of 360 days. They added 5 days to the calendar to give a total of 365 days in a year.

1 The center of the calendar shows the face of the Aztec sun god.

2 The first ring contains four square pictures, each representing a different sun god of the past.

3 Each of the 20 pictures in the second ring represents one day of each month.

❖ Why do you think the Aztec calendar placed the sun god at the center?

The tribute brought large amounts of food, precious stones and metals, and clothing into the Aztec capital of Tenochtitlán. Corn, beans, chilies, cotton, rubber, jaguar skins, feathers of tropical birds, gold, silver, jade, and cacao (kuh•KOW) were all part of the tribute. The Aztecs also learned new ways of doing things that would help them build a stronger empire.

The Aztec Empire reached its greatest power under Motecuhzoma II. By 1519 the empire included more than 400 small city-states. It covered more than 80,000 square miles (207,200 sq km) of central and southern Mexico. As many as 5 million people lived under the rule of the Aztecs.

REVIEW How did the Aztecs gain their power and wealth?

A mask thought to be a likeness of the Aztecs' sun god

Aztec Society

In many ways Aztec civilization was like the civilization of the Maya. Like the Maya, the Aztecs had a calendar and a number system. They developed a system of hieroglyphic writing, as the Maya had done, and they built many large cities.

The Aztec emperor ruled over both military and religious matters. He was assisted by a council of four high-ranking officials. The emperor made all laws for the Aztecs and saw that they were followed.

The emperor was at the top of Aztec society. In fact, the Aztecs believed that the emperor talked with the gods. People were not allowed to turn their backs on him or to look directly at his face.

Below the emperor in society were nobles, who helped the emperor rule, priests, and soldiers. Then came the farmers, craftworkers, and merchants. Aztec women in these classes were allowed to own property and manage

The shield made of feathers and gold (below) belonged to Motecuhzoma II (right, seated at center).

businesses. Many Aztec girls, as well as boys, attended school. Some grew up to become religious leaders, while many others farmed.

At the bottom of Aztec society were the slaves. Some Aztecs became slaves because their parents were too poor to support them. Others were enslaved as adults because they had broken Aztec laws. Often, captured enemies also became slaves. Some captives were sacrificed, or killed as offerings, to the Aztec gods.

Like other early cultures, the Aztecs worshipped many gods. One of the most important gods was Quetzalcoatl (ket•zahl•koo•WAH•tuhl), the god of knowledge and creation. The Aztecs believed that the world would end if they did not make sacrifices to their gods. Thousands of people died each year as sacrifices. Because human sacrifice was so important to the Aztecs, the goal in battle was to capture enemies, not to kill them.

The Aztec Empire lasted less than 100 years. In 1519 the Aztecs met their most fearsome enemy—the Spanish who had come across the ocean from Europe.

REVIEW What was the connection between religion and war in Aztec life?

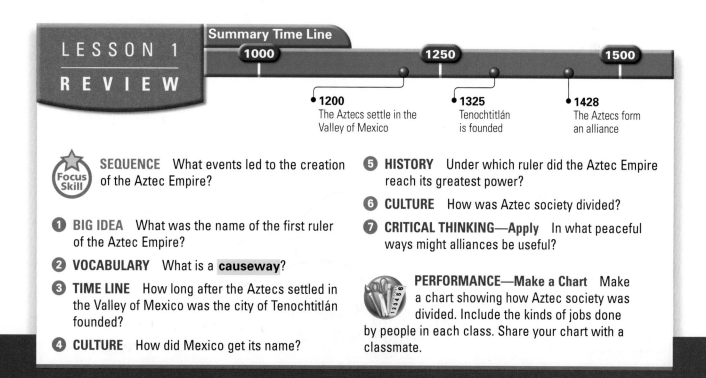

LESSON 1
REVIEW

Summary Time Line

1000 — 1250 — 1500

• **1200** The Aztecs settle in the Valley of Mexico

• **1325** Tenochtitlán is founded

• **1428** The Aztecs form an alliance

Focus Skill

SEQUENCE What events led to the creation of the Aztec Empire?

1 BIG IDEA What was the name of the first ruler of the Aztec Empire?

2 VOCABULARY What is a **causeway**?

3 TIME LINE How long after the Aztecs settled in the Valley of Mexico was the city of Tenochtitlán founded?

4 CULTURE How did Mexico get its name?

5 HISTORY Under which ruler did the Aztec Empire reach its greatest power?

6 CULTURE How was Aztec society divided?

7 CRITICAL THINKING—Apply In what peaceful ways might alliances be useful?

PERFORMANCE—Make a Chart Make a chart showing how Aztec society was divided. Include the kinds of jobs done by people in each class. Share your chart with a classmate.

Compare Maps with Different Scales

▶ WHY IT MATTERS

Look at the maps on these pages. Notice that all three maps show the Aztec city of Tenochtitlán. Each map is different, however. This is because they all have different scales.

Scale refers to the size of a map in relation to what it shows. Places are drawn larger or smaller on maps, depending on how much area is to be shown. Maps that show a large area must use a small scale, since places must be drawn small for everything to fit. Maps that show only a small area can use a larger scale. Drawing places large allows more details to be shown. For example, more cities and towns can be shown. Knowing about maps of different scales can help you choose the best map for gathering the information you need.

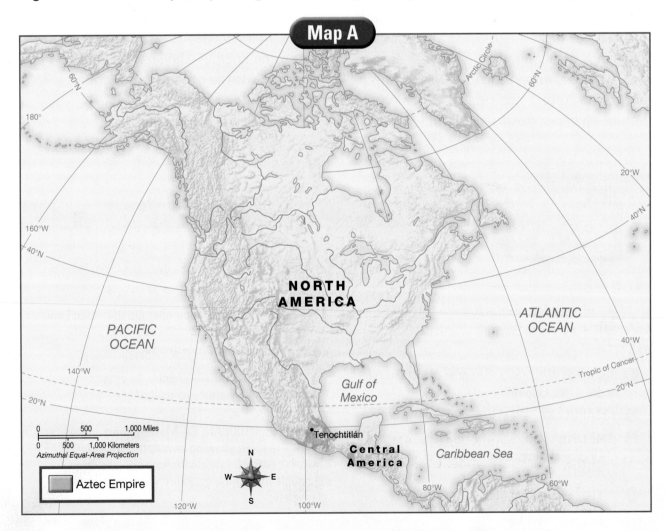

Map A

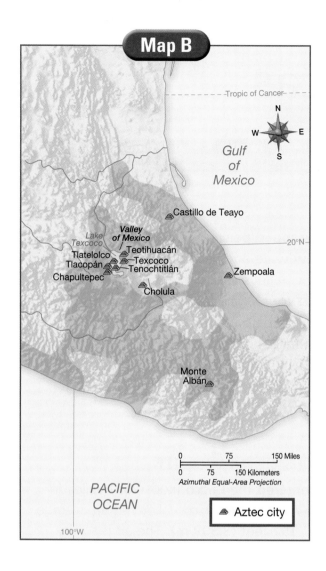

Map B

Gulf of Mexico

─ Tropic of Cancer ─ ─

Castillo de Teayo

Valley of Mexico
Lake Texcoco
Tlatelolco — Teotihuacán
Tlacopán — Texcoco
Chapultepec — Tenochtitlán
Cholula
Zempoala

─20°N─

Monte Albán

PACIFIC OCEAN

100°W

| 0 | 75 | 150 Miles |
| 0 | 75 | 150 Kilometers |

Azimuthal Equal-Area Projection

🔺 Aztec city

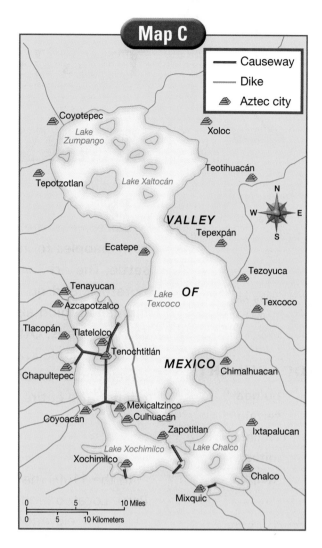

Map C

— Causeway
— Dike
🔺 Aztec city

Coyotepec
Lake Zumpango
Xoloc
Teotihuacán
Tepotzotlan
Lake Xaltocán

VALLEY

Ecatepe
Tepexpán

Tenayucan
Azcapotzalco
Lake Texcoco
OF
Tezoyuca
Texcoco

Tlacopán
Tlatelolco
Tenochtitlán
MEXICO
Chimalhuacan
Chapultepec

Mexicaltzinco
Coyoacán
Culhuacán
Zapotitlan
Ixtapalucan

Lake Xochimilco
Lake Chalco
Xochimilco

Chalco
Mixquic

| 0 | 5 | 10 Miles |
| 0 | 5 | 10 Kilometers |

▶ WHAT YOU NEED TO KNOW

The maps on these two pages show how scale can change depending on whether the map shows a close-up or faraway view of an area. Map A is a small-scale map. It shows a large area of land with little detail. Map C is a large-scale map. It shows a small amount of land with a lot of detail. Map B has a larger scale than Map A and a smaller scale than Map C. A map scale compares distance on a map to distance in the real world.

▶ PRACTICE THE SKILL

Use the maps to answer the questions.

1 Which map shows the most cities of the Aztec Empire?

2 If you planned to cross Lake Texcoco, which map would you use? Tell why.

▶ APPLY WHAT YOU LEARNED

Find two road maps with different scales. One might be a road map of your state, and the other might be a road map of a large city within your state. Write a sentence explaining when it might be more helpful to use the state map, with the smaller scale. Then write another sentence explaining when it might be more helpful to use the city map, with the larger scale.

MAP AND GLOBE SKILLS

Practice your map and globe skills with the **GeoSkills CD-ROM**.

SEQUENCE

As you read, look for the steps the Incas took to create a strong empire.

BIG IDEA
The Inca Empire was composed of many different groups of people.

VOCABULARY

quinoa
terrain
Quechua
mitima
quipu

The Incas

500 B.C.	B.C./A.D.	A.D. 500	A.D. 1000	A.D. 1500

A.D. 1000 – A.D. 1500

Between the snow-capped peaks of the high Andes, early peoples found a few wide and fertile valleys in which to settle. The rich land in the valleys was perfect for growing corn, potatoes, and quinoa (KEEN•wah), a grain high in protein. This highland region also provided stones for building and llamas for carrying loads. Other animals there supplied wool for clothing. In time, people known as the Incas moved into the area and developed a remarkable civilization. Over the years, they claimed the entire area, forming a large empire.

Building an Empire

In the 1100s the Incas entered the Cuzco (KOOS•koh) Valley in Peru. Located high in the Andes, the Cuzco Valley has an average elevation of 11,152 feet (3,399 m). The air is so dry that frost rarely forms in the coldest months.

Manco Capac, the Incas' legendary first ruler, is pictured (left) holding the sun. The Incas believed he was the son of their sun god. Today the ruins of once-flourishing Inca cities stand (below).

The Incas took their name from their ruler, who was known as the Inca. Legends tell of the founding of the city of Cuzco—the Inca capital—by the first Inca, Manco Capac (MAHNG•koh KAH•pahk). One legend says that the Inca sun god sent his sons and daughters to bring civilization to the world. The Incas believed that their first ruler was one of these sons and therefore a living god.

The Incas began to farm in their new home and to build communities. For years they lived much like the other native peoples around them. After a time, however, they no longer lived peacefully in their valley. A shortage of land and other resources, such as water, probably led the Incas to begin attacking other villages.

About 1438 the Incas began to build an empire. They conquered their neighbors and made them pay tribute. Under the leadership of Pachacuti (pah•chah•KOO•tee), Inca rule spread far beyond the Cuzco Valley. Pachacuti conquered some groups by military force. Others he won over through peace talks.

Pachacuti's son and grandson expanded the empire even farther. By the time the Spanish arrived in Peru in 1532, the Inca Empire covered an area of almost half a million square miles (1.3 million sq km). It reached through parts of what are today the countries of Argentina, Bolivia, Chile, Ecuador, and Peru. The Incas ruled more than 9 million people. The conquered peoples spoke at least 20 different languages and belonged to many different cultural groups.

REVIEW What events led to the growth of the Inca Empire?

 SEQUENCE

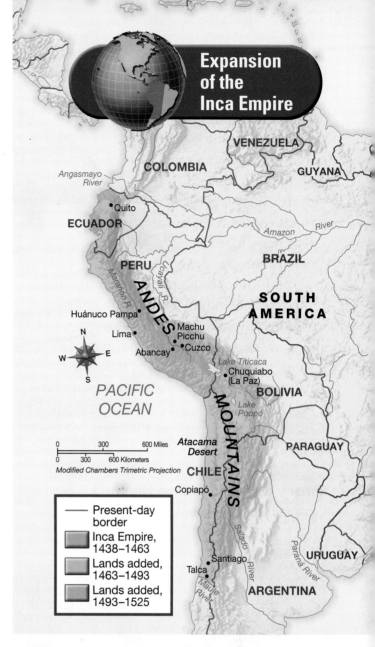

Expansion of the Inca Empire

VENEZUELA

COLOMBIA

GUYANA

Angasmayo River

•Quito

ECUADOR

Amazon River

PERU

Ucayali R.

Marañón R.

BRAZIL

SOUTH AMERICA

Huánuco Pampa•

ANDES

Lima•

Machu Picchu

•Cuzco

Abancay•

Lake Titicaca

•Chuquiabo (La Paz)

BOLIVIA

PACIFIC OCEAN

Lake Poopó

MOUNTAINS

Salado River

0   300   600 Miles

0   300   600 Kilometers

Modified Chambers Trimetric Projection

Atacama Desert

PARAGUAY

CHILE

Copiapó•

Paraná River

— Present-day border

Inca Empire, 1438–1463

Lands added, 1463–1493

Lands added, 1493–1525

Talca•

Santiago•

Maule River

ARGENTINA

URUGUAY

GEOGRAPHY THEME

Regions The Inca Empire was located along South America's Pacific coast. This Inca container (left) represents a jaguar.

❓ How would you describe Cuzco's location within the Inca Empire?

Under Inca Rule

The Inca Empire stretched through three very different environments. These were the dry Pacific coast, the hot and humid eastern foothills of the Andes, and several highland plateaus surrounded by rugged mountains.

To connect the different parts of their empire, the Incas built more than 14,000 miles (22,530 km) of roads. Two main roads ran the length of the empire. One passed through the mountains. The other followed the coast. Many smaller roads connected the two main roads along the way.

The Inca roads were built in different ways depending on the **terrain**, or physical features of the land. Stone causeways led over swampy areas along the coast. On steep mountainsides, roads took the form of stone steps. In the highlands, swaying rope bridges hung across deep canyons. Inca roads were built so well that parts of them still exist today.

Inca roads made the empire strong in many ways. They helped improve communication across the empire. Runners used the roads to carry messages. The roads helped the empire's economy by providing good transportation. People walked beside llamas carrying trade goods. Because of this trade, Incas in Cuzco, which is far from the sea, could enjoy fish caught in the Pacific Ocean.

These roads also helped the Inca military. By using the roads, Inca soldiers could move quickly to all parts of the empire.

The roads connected many parts of the empire, but roads alone could not bring the people together. To win loyalty, the Incas showered newly conquered peoples with gifts of cloth and food. They also allowed the former chiefs of conquered people to take part in governing.

To keep their culture strong, the Incas made sure that the conquered people learned Inca ways. They brought the sons of conquered chiefs to Cuzco. Then, they taught them Inca ways to take back to their people. **Quechua** (KEH•chuh•wuh), the Inca language, became the official language throughout the empire. In fact, it is still an official language of present-day Peru. People were free to worship their own gods, but only after saying that the Inca gods were more powerful.

To support Inca rule, each family in the empire had to pay a labor tax. As payment, all men in the empire had to work for the government for part of each year. They served in the army, cared for government-owned farms and herds, and built roads, bridges, and cities.

Most conquered people were able to stay in their homelands. However, some were sent to live in new places. This practice was known as **mitima** (MID•ah•mah). Mitima helped the Incas begin new communities. It also prevented rebellion by breaking up large groups of conquered people and scattering them to different parts of the Inca Empire.

REVIEW How did the Inca Empire share power with newly conquered peoples?

A CLOSER LOOK
Machu Picchu

High in the Andes mountains lie the Inca ruins of Machu Picchu. The site is located about 50 miles (80 km) from Cuzco, Peru. Built in the mid-1400s, Machu Picchu includes about 200 well-preserved buildings made from stone.

1. The warehouse was used to store food brought from nearby sites by llamas.

2. This small, open area and its temples were connected by stairs to Machu Picchu's highest point, the Intiwatana (een•tee•wah•TAH•nah).

3. This structure, carved from rock, reached a height of 6 feet (1.8 m). It was made to look like the top of a nearby mountain. Seen from the Intiwatana, surrounding peaks align with the cardinal directions and the movements of the sun and stars.

4. On all sides of the royal estate, terraced farming was used to grow herbs, flowers, potatoes, and corn.

5. Most experts believe that Machu Picchu was used as a palace by Inca royalty when they were away from the capital.

❓ How do you think Machu Picchu's location in the mountains affected life there?

Inca Ways of Life

In the center of each Inca city was a main square, with large government buildings all around it. To construct their buildings, Inca workers cut large stone blocks and stacked them to form walls. They fit the blocks so closely that cement was not needed to hold them together. Many Inca walls still stand in areas where earthquakes have toppled newer buildings. This way of building can still be seen in the ruins of the Inca city of Machu Picchu (MAH•choo PEE•choo), in present-day Peru.

Inside the government buildings, nobles and others did many jobs. Accountants kept track of the numbers of people and goods in the empire. They also kept lists that told who was required to work to pay their labor taxes and where and when they would work. All of this information was stored on groups of colored, knotted strings known as **quipus** (KEE•pooz). The

The Incas used quipus to store information, such as the number of llamas owned by the empire.

different colors and knots on the quipus stood for words or ideas. The color yellow, for example, meant "gold." The color white meant "peace."

The Inca people wore beautiful, finely made clothing. Some of the clothing was made from cotton. Some was woven from yarn made from the wool of animals called alpacas (al•PAH•kuhz) and vicuñas (vih•KOON•yuhz). Only Inca nobles could own jewelry made of gold or silver.

Away from the busy streets of the city's center were the Incas' homes. Three generations of the same family usually lived together. Most people lived in small mud houses with thatched roofs. The richest nobles lived in palaces.

Some Incas were craftworkers, traders, or merchants. Most, however, worked on

A present-day Inca weaver makes traditional-style blankets (right) from the wool of animals such as these vicuñas (below).

Terraced fields, such as those at Machu Picchu (left), were used to grow crops such as maize (above).

government-owned farms. The Incas developed a way to make the mountainsides suitable for farming. First, they built terraces—flat ledges cut into hillsides and edged by stone walls. Then, using both irrigation and fertilizer, the Incas raised beans, corn, squash, tomatoes, and many kinds of potatoes on these terraces.

Most of the food grown went to government storehouses. It was used to feed the Inca armies and was given to anyone who needed it. In return for this food, the Inca rulers expected the people to work for them on their many building projects.

REVIEW **What were some of the jobs in Inca society?**

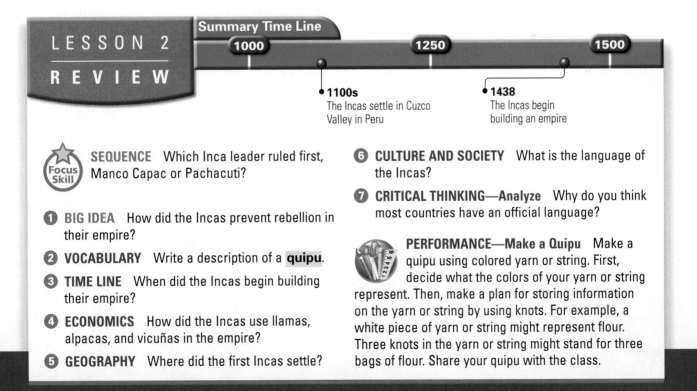

LESSON 2 REVIEW

Summary Time Line

1000 — 1250 — 1500

1100s The Incas settle in Cuzco Valley in Peru

1438 The Incas begin building an empire

Focus Skill **SEQUENCE** Which Inca leader ruled first, Manco Capac or Pachacuti?

1. **BIG IDEA** How did the Incas prevent rebellion in their empire?

2. **VOCABULARY** Write a description of a **quipu**.

3. **TIME LINE** When did the Incas begin building their empire?

4. **ECONOMICS** How did the Incas use llamas, alpacas, and vicuñas in the empire?

5. **GEOGRAPHY** Where did the first Incas settle?

6. **CULTURE AND SOCIETY** What is the language of the Incas?

7. **CRITICAL THINKING—Analyze** Why do you think most countries have an official language?

PERFORMANCE—Make a Quipu Make a quipu using colored yarn or string. First, decide what the colors of your yarn or string represent. Then, make a plan for storing information on the yarn or string by using knots. For example, a white piece of yarn or string might represent flour. Three knots in the yarn or string might stand for three bags of flour. Share your quipu with the class.

North American Cultures

SEQUENCE
As you read, look for the sequence of developments in the early Native American cultural regions of North America.

BIG IDEA
Different environments affected the development of the North American cultures.

VOCABULARY
wigwam
longhouse
palisade
earth lodge
mesa
totem pole
tundra

| 500 B.C. | B.C./A.D. | A.D. 500 | A.D. 1000 | A.D. 1500 |

100 B.C. – A.D. 1500

Experts are not sure how many Native Americans lived in North America before A.D. 1500. They estimate that about 1 million to a few million lived there. These Native Americans lived in hundreds of different tribes, or groups. As the Native Americans adapted to different environments, different cultural regions were formed.

The Eastern Woodlands

Most early Native American cultures shared some common features. They all used stone tools, and nearly all of them had religious beliefs based on nature. Most believed that spirits lived in plants and in animals as well as in the sun, rain, and wind. They had much in common, but there were some differences. Many of these differences developed from the varied environments in which the groups lived. The early Native Americans of different geographic regions made up separate cultural regions.

One such cultural region is called the Eastern Woodlands. It includes much of the land east of the Mississippi River. The people of the Eastern Woodlands used many of the resources of their region's land.

One important resource was the thick forests of hardwood trees found in the Eastern Woodlands. The tribes of this area

This toad artifact of the Hopewell culture was found at an early Eastern Woodlands settlement such as the one pictured below.

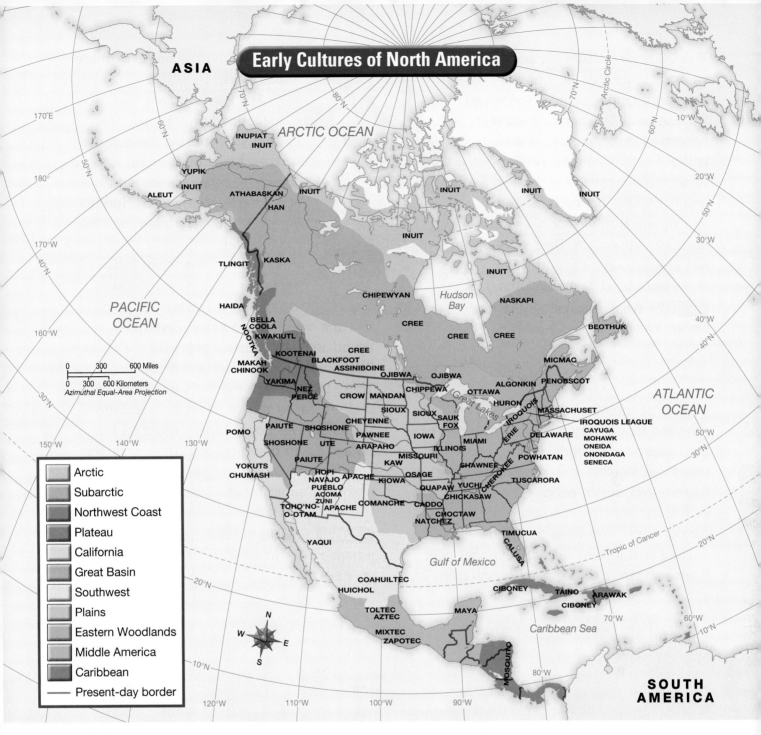

Early Cultures of North America

ASIA

ARCTIC OCEAN

PACIFIC OCEAN

ATLANTIC OCEAN

Hudson Bay

Great Lakes

Gulf of Mexico

Caribbean Sea

SOUTH AMERICA

Legend:
- Arctic
- Subarctic
- Northwest Coast
- Plateau
- California
- Great Basin
- Southwest
- Plains
- Eastern Woodlands
- Middle America
- Caribbean
- Present-day border

0 300 600 Miles
0 300 600 Kilometers
Azimuthal Equal-Area Projection

GEOGRAPHY THEME

Location   Throughout North America, native peoples formed unique cultures. Each culture was influenced in some ways by its land and resources.

❓ How do you think location affected the foods the Native Americans of North America ate?

found uses for almost every part of a tree. Some tribes built **wigwams**, or round, bark-covered shelters. Other tribes constructed long, wooden buildings called **longhouses**, in which several families lived. The Eastern Woodlands people also made canoes from tree bark. They

carved clubs, bows, and the shafts of arrows from tree branches. Trees even provided nuts and sap for food.

The Eastern Woodlands had other useful plants and plentiful rainfall. These resources allowed the Eastern Woodlands people to settle in villages and grow crops for food.

Chapter 12 ■ 391

The fields lay outside the **palisade**, a tall, wooden fence that surrounded a village. This fence helped protect the village from attacks. Women planted and harvested crops of corn, squash, and beans in the fields. While women did most of the farming and gathering, the men hunted and fished. Hunting for deer was especially important. Deer were not only a source of food. Their hides were used to make clothing.

REVIEW What resources did the Eastern Woodlands people use?

Iroquois turtle artifact

The Plains

West of the Mississippi River lies an environment that is very different from that of the Eastern Woodlands. This region is made up of vast treeless, grassy plains. Like the Eastern Woodlands people, the early people of this cultural region adapted to their surroundings, known as the Plains.

The Plains Indians settled in villages near rivers and streams. There they grew crops in rich soil along the banks of these waterways.

The Plains Indians also depended on the few trees that grew beside these water sources. Many built round log homes that they covered with packed earth. These **earth lodges** were their homes during the long, cold winter.

In summer the Plains Indians left their villages and followed, on foot, the herds of buffalo. Like the deer hunted in the Eastern Woodlands, the buffalo provided the Plains Indians with food and clothing. These Indians even made their temporary shelters, called tepees, from buffalo skins stretched over poles. Tepees could be put up and taken down quickly. These shelters were easy to carry from place to place, making it easier for the Plains Indians to follow the buffalo.

REVIEW How did the shelters of the Plains Indians change from season to season?
SEQUENCE

Like many Plains Indian villages, this village was made up of earth lodges and built close to a river.

The Anasazi Cliff Palace (above) is today part of Mesa Verde National Park in Colorado. The ceramic artifacts (right) are Anasazi pitchers.

The Desert Southwest

To the west of the Plains, some Native Americans adapted to living in the desert Southwest. This region is located in what are now parts of the southwestern United States and northern Mexico.

The landscape of the desert Southwest is made up of mountains, canyons, and mesas (MAY•sahz). A **mesa** is a flat-topped hill with steep, sloping sides. Farther west the land gets flatter and drier. The intense heat of the day can be followed by bitter cold at night. Rain might not fall for weeks. Even with all these challenges, Native Americans developed one of the most advanced civilizations in North America there.

One of the earliest civilizations in all of North America was that of the Anasazi (ah•nuh•SAH•zee) of the desert Southwest. The Anasazi civilization began about 100 B.C.

The Anasazi style of housing was an important cultural development. Houses of stone and adobe, sun-dried bricks of clay mixed with straw, were joined next to and on top of one another.

In the A.D. 700s the Anasazi began to build under cliff overhangs. For protection from attack, there were no windows or doors on the first floor. Instead, the people used ladders to get to entrances on the roof. During attacks, the ladders were removed.

Later tribes, known as the Pueblos (PWEH•blohz), used the Anasazi method of building. *Pueblo* is the Spanish word for *village.* It describes their houses, which are actually communities.

The climate of the desert Southwest provided little rainfall, yet the Pueblo Indians managed to farm. They built villages near rivers and learned to irrigate their crops. They grew beans, corn, squash, and cotton. From cotton, Pueblo women made thread and wove cloth for clothing.

A kachina doll from the Hopi, a Pueblo Indian group

POINTS OF VIEW
Makah Whaling

In an 1885 treaty, the Makah tribe gave up its lands to the United States government. In return, the government gave the Makah tribe the right to hunt whales. Today in the state of Washington, the Makah tribe are allowed to hunt whales. While some people disagree with whale hunting, many Makahs believe it is an important tradition.

BRIAN GORMAN, National Fisheries Service

66 The Makahs have an absolute treaty right to whale [hunt whales]. 99

JACK METCALF, former United States Representative

66 . . . the majority of United States citizens . . . believe that whales should be protected. 99

Analyze the Viewpoints

1 What views about whaling does each person hold?

2 **Make It Relevant** Think about an issue that is important to your community. What is your viewpoint on that issue?

Over time, other tribes with different ways of life moved into the region. These tribes were nomadic hunters and gatherers. In their search for food, they often attacked Pueblo villages. Unlike the Pueblo people, they wore animal skins for clothing. In time, however, they adopted some of the ways of the Pueblo people.

Tribes that lived farther west, outside the desert Southwest cultural region, were called Seed Gatherers. They lived in the deserts of what is now California. The land was so dry that crops could not be grown. The Seed Gatherers wandered the desert in search of nuts and seeds. Like other Native Americans, they learned to survive in their environment.

REVIEW How were the Pueblo Indians able to grow crops in the desert Southwest?

The Northwest Coast and the Arctic

The Northwest Coast borders the Pacific Ocean from northern California to Alaska. Unlike the desert Southwest, the Northwest Coast has plentiful rainfall and many useful resources.

The early people of the Northwest Coast lived mostly by fishing, both in the ocean and in the rivers of the region. The waters were filled with salmon and other sea life.

This painting shows a Northwest Coast village. The women are hanging salmon, which were smoke-dried for food.

Successful whale hunts supplied not only food but also oil for burning in lamps. Hunting for deer, elk, and bears in nearby mountains gave the tribes animal skins for clothing as well as more meat to eat. The region's many trees provided wood suitable for building houses and making dugout canoes.

With resources so easy to find, the people of the Northwest Coast had time for other activities. They became expert woodcarvers who made beautiful masks. They carved and painted human and animal faces on tall wooden posts called **totem poles**. They used totem poles to identify their tribes.

The Northwest Coast people were among the few early tribes in North America north of what is now Mexico

An Inuit comb

to use metal. They made decorated plaques, or display plates, from copper found in the region. These copper plaques had value, like money. A single plaque might be worth 7,500 blankets!

Survival was more difficult for the native peoples living near the Arctic Circle. There the land is mainly **tundra**, a flat and treeless plain of frozen ground. Since farming was not possible on the tundra, the people hunted caribou, seals, and other animals to survive. These animals provided food, clothing, shelter, and bones for toolmaking. Some people of the Arctic today still follow some of the old ways of life.

REVIEW Why was survival difficult for early people living near the Arctic Circle?

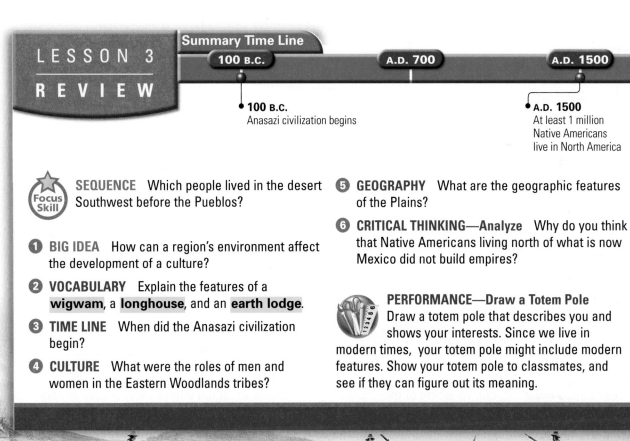

LESSON 3
REVIEW

Summary Time Line

| 100 B.C. | A.D. 700 | A.D. 1500 |

100 B.C.
Anasazi civilization begins

A.D. 1500
At least 1 million Native Americans live in North America

Focus Skill — **SEQUENCE** Which people lived in the desert Southwest before the Pueblos?

1 **BIG IDEA** How can a region's environment affect the development of a culture?

2 **VOCABULARY** Explain the features of a **wigwam**, a **longhouse**, and an **earth lodge**.

3 **TIME LINE** When did the Anasazi civilization begin?

4 **CULTURE** What were the roles of men and women in the Eastern Woodlands tribes?

5 **GEOGRAPHY** What are the geographic features of the Plains?

6 **CRITICAL THINKING—Analyze** Why do you think that Native Americans living north of what is now Mexico did not build empires?

PERFORMANCE—Draw a Totem Pole
Draw a totem pole that describes you and shows your interests. Since we live in modern times, your totem pole might include modern features. Show your totem pole to classmates, and see if they can figure out its meaning.

Summary Time Line

100 B.C.   A.D. 300

● 100 B.C.   ● A.D. 1200
The Anasazi   The Aztecs settle in
civilization   the Valley of Mexico
begins

 Sequence

Complete this graphic organizer by putting events related to the Aztecs in the correct sequence. A copy of this graphic organizer appears on page 109 of the Activity Book.

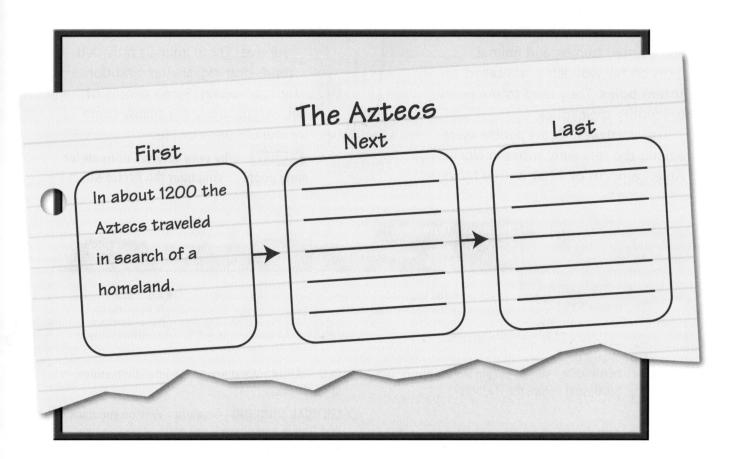

The Aztecs

First

In about 1200 the Aztecs traveled in search of a homeland.

Next

Last

THINK & WRITE

Write an Opinion The Incas used a process called *mitima* to control some of the people they conquered. What was mitima? Do you think it was a good system or a bad one? Would you feel differently if you had been part of a group the Incas had conquered? Write a paragraph that explains your opinion.

Write a Journal Entry Choose a North American region where early Native Americans lived. Imagine that you are a member of a Native American group living in that region. Write a journal entry that describes a day in your life. Include details about how the region's geography affects your daily activities.

A.D. 700   **A.D. 1100**   **A.D. 1500**

A.D. 1428
The Aztec Empire forms

A.D. 1438
The Incas begin
building an empire

A.D. 1500
At least 1 million
Native Americans are
living in North America

A.D. 1519
The Aztec Empire is
at its greatest power

A.D. 1532
The Inca Empire is
home to more than
9 million people

USE THE TIME LINE

Use the chapter summary time line to answer these questions.

1 About how many years passed between when the Aztec Empire formed and when it was at its greatest power?

2 In what year did the Incas begin building their empire?

USE VOCABULARY

Use one of the terms in the box to complete each sentence.

> **Mesoamerica (p. 376)**
>
> **causeways (p. 378)**
>
> **terrain (p. 386)**
>
> **quipus (p. 388)**
>
> **palisades (p. 392)**
>
> **mesa (p. 393)**

3 The Aztecs built _____, or land bridges, to connect Tenochtitlán to the mainland.

4 A _____ is a flat-topped hill with steep slopes.

5 Eastern Woodlands Native Americans often surrounded their villages with tall _____ for protection.

6 Incas built roads in different ways, depending on the _____.

7 _____ is a region that includes Mexico and Central America.

8 Incas kept records on _____, groups of colored, knotted strings.

RECALL FACTS

Answer these questions.

9 Why was the combination of the Aztec, Texcoco, and Tlacopán cultures called the Aztec Empire instead of the Texcoco or Tlacopán Empire?

10 What is Quechua?

11 Who were the Seed Gatherers? How did they get that name?

Write the letter of the best choice.

12 **TEST PREP** All of these statements are true about the Eastern Woodlands Indians *except*—
  A the men followed herds of buffalo in the summer.
  B the women farmed and gathered.
  C their hunters used bows and arrows.
  D they lived in bark wigwams and wooden longhouses.

13 **TEST PREP** What was one of the first regions north of Mexico where Native Americans used metal?
  F the Eastern Woodlands
  G the Plains
  H the Desert Southwest
  J the Northwest Coast

THINK CRITICALLY

14 How did roadways help keep the Inca Empire strong?

15 Which early North American culture would you rather have been a part of? Give at least two reasons for your choice.

APPLY SKILLS

Compare Maps with Different Scales

16 Draw a map of your school. Then draw a map that includes your school and the entire neighborhood around it. Which map is a small-scale map? Which is a large-scale map? For what purposes might you use each one?

MAP AND GLOBE SKILLS

Hue, Vietnam

GET READY

The city of Hue (hoo•AY) is located in the center of Vietnam. It is a city rich in history and tradition. Sometimes called the Imperial City, Hue was the home of many emperors. Before World War II, Hue was the capital of Vietnam. Today, visitors can see both the city's architecture and scenic countryside while taking a boat ride on the Perfume River.

Near the banks of the river stands the Citadel, a walled city in which the emperors lived long ago. On the other side of the river is the Thien Mu (TEE•en MOO) Pagoda, a seven-story Buddhist temple. In Hue you can also see tombs, palaces, theaters, and gardens. All help show visitors the history of this ancient city.

LOCATE IT

Hue

VIETNAM

WHAT TO SEE

The Citadel was built in 1804 to protect the emperor who lived in it. During World War II, many parts of the Citadel were damaged too badly to be repaired.

The Thien Mu Pagoda is the oldest pagoda in Hue. It is located on Ha Khe Hill near the Perfume River.

People can visit the royal tombs of the emperors in the countryside surrounding the city. There are seven tombs in all. Each one contains monuments and statues that honor the emperor buried there.

This food vendor sells fresh produce. Others offer favorite regional dishes, including rice pudding and *pho ga,* or chicken noodle soup.

TAKE A FIELD TRIP

GO ONLINE

A VIRTUAL TOUR
Visit The Learning Site at **www.harcourtschool.com** to take virtual tours of other historic sites.

CNN. Turner Le@rning.

A VIDEO TOUR
Check your media center or classroom library for a videotape tour of Vietnam.

5 Review and Test Preparation

Write Newspaper Headlines Look closely at each picture below, and read the captions to help you review Unit 5. Then write newspaper headlines describing each of the events listed. Include the names of people, places, or groups in your headlines.

USE VOCABULARY

For each pair of terms, write two or three sentences that explain what each term means and how the two terms are related.

1. **manor system** (p. 334), **self-sufficient** (p. 335)

2. **longship** (p. 341), **territorial expansion** (p. 341)

3. **causeway** (p. 378), **chinampa** (p. 378)

4. **Quechua** (p. 387), **mitima** (p. 387)

5. **wigwam** (p. 391), **longhouse** (p. 391)

RECALL FACTS

Answer these questions.

6. How are the cities of Constantinople and Rome related?

7. How did the country of England get its name?

8. What event marked the end of the Western Roman Empire?

Write the letter of the best choice.

9. **TEST PREP** The manor system was—
   A a political system.
   B an economic system.
   C a military system.
   D a social system.

10. **TEST PREP** Which of the following statements is true about early Africa south of the Sahara?
    F Jenne-Jeno, in what is now Mali, was the region's first known city.
    G Life was easiest and populations grew quickly in the savannas of eastern Africa.
    H The Bantu-speaking people migrated because of a climate change in their homeland.
    J The kingdom of Aksum included parts of what are now Morocco, Algeria, Tunisia, and Libya.

11. **TEST PREP** Which culture first practiced the Shinto religion?
    A early Africans south of the Sahara
    B the Vietnamese
    C the Koreans
    D the Japanese

Visual Summary

| 250 B.C. | B.C. / A.D. | A.D. 250 | A.D. 500 |

250 B.C. **The first city in Africa south of the Sahara forms** p. 349

100 B.C. **The Three Kingdoms begin to form in Korea** p. 361

A.D. 500 **The early Middle Ages begin in Europe** p. 338

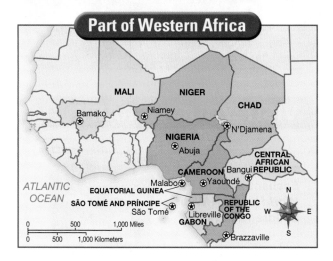

Part of Western Africa

MALI

NIGER

Bamako ⊛ ⊛ Niamey

CHAD

⊛ N'Djamena

NIGERIA

⊛ Abuja

CENTRAL AFRICAN REPUBLIC

CAMEROON Bangui ⊛

ATLANTIC OCEAN

Malabo ⊛ ⊛ Yaoundé ⊛

EQUATORIAL GUINEA

SÃO TOMÉ AND PRÍNCIPE

São Tomé ⊛

REPUBLIC OF THE CONGO

⊛ Libreville

GABON

⊛ Brazzaville

N W E S

0 500 1,000 Miles
0 500 1,000 Kilometers

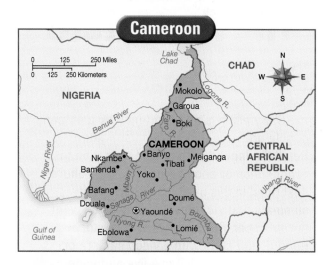

Cameroon

0 125 250 Miles
0 125 250 Kilometers

Lake Chad

NIGERIA

CHAD

Mokolo •

Garoua •

Ogone R.

Benue River

• Boki

Niger River

CAMEROON

Nkambe• • Banyo •Meiganga

Bamenda• •Tibati

Yoko •

Bafang•

Doumé •

Douala• Sanaga River

⊛ Yaoundé

Boumba R.

Nyong R.

Gulf of Guinea

Ebolowa•

• Lomié

CENTRAL AFRICAN REPUBLIC

Ubangi River

N W E S

⑫ **TEST PREP** All of the following statements are true *except*—

F The Inca Empire included much of present-day Peru.

G The Anasazi lived in what are now the southwestern United States and northern Mexico.

H The Plains Indians lived in North America east of the Mississippi River.

J The Aztecs lived in what is now central Mexico.

THINK CRITICALLY

⑬ When the Western Roman Empire ended, why was the pope the most powerful person in Europe?

⑭ Why was the African kingdom of Aksum a crossroads for different cultures?

APPLY SKILLS

MAP AND GLOBE SKILLS

Compare Maps with Different Scales

Use the two maps on this page to answer these questions.

⑮ Suppose you want to describe the location of Cameroon to a friend. Which map would better show the country in relation to other countries?

⑯ Find Cameroon on both maps. Which map shows more cities in Cameroon?

⑰ Suppose you want to travel from Yaoundé, Cameroon, to Mokolo, Cameroon. On which map can you measure the distance between the two cities? Why do you think Mokolo is not shown on the other map?

⑱ On which map can you find the names of rivers?

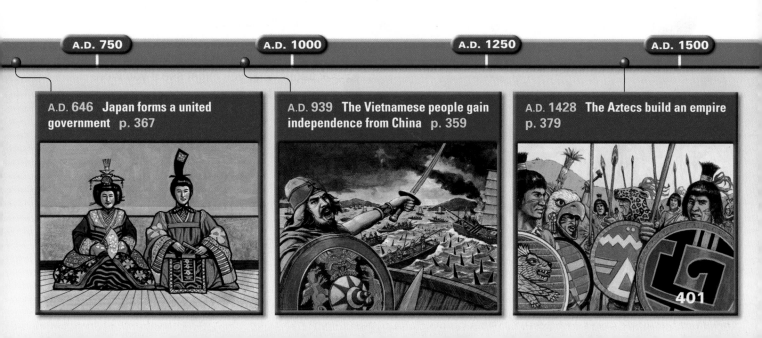

A.D. 750   A.D. 1000   A.D. 1250   A.D. 1500

A.D. 646 **Japan forms a united government** p. 367

A.D. 939 **The Vietnamese people gain independence from China** p. 359

A.D. 1428 **The Aztecs build an empire** p. 379

401

Unit Activities

Tell a Story

Storytelling is an important way that many people preserve and share their culture. Retell the legend of the Aztec migration to Tenochtitlán or another story from a culture described in this unit. First, write a story summary that includes the details you want to remember. Practice telling your story. Record your story with a video camera or tape recorder, or tell it to a live audience of your classmates.

Design a Totem Pole

Find out more about totem poles. What kinds of symbols were used on the totem poles? Use what you learned to help you as you design a totem pole. Use symbols on your totem pole that represent you, your family, or a group to which you belong.

VISIT YOUR LIBRARY

■ *Vietnam: Enchantment of the World* by Terri Willis. Children's Press.

■ *World Book Encyclopedia Presents Old Japan* by Andrew Haslam and Clare Doran. World Book.

■ *Crafts from the Past: The Aztecs* by Gillian Chapman. Heinemann Library.

COMPLETE THE UNIT PROJECT

Make Postcards Work to complete the unit project. First, decide which places you want to show on your postcards. Then, draw or find pictures to decorate one side of each postcard. These pictures should relate to historical sites and to the culture of the early people who lived there. On the other side of each postcard, write to a friend about what you might see if you were visiting this place.

The Spread of Civilizations

Gold-decorated platter from
Tang dynasty, China, about A.D. 750

Nomads traveling on the Silk Road in Bamain Valley, Afghanistan

The Spread of Civilizations

66 Civilization is a movement and not a condition, a voyage and not a harbor. **99**

— A. J. Toynbee, British historian, 1958

Preview the Content

Read the title and the Big Idea statement for each lesson. Then write a paragraph for each lesson, telling what you think the lesson is about.

Preview the Vocabulary

Synonyms Synonyms are words that have similar meanings. Look through the unit to find Vocabulary Words you can match to the synonyms below. Then use each Vocabulary Word in a sentence.

SYNONYM	VOCABULARY WORD	SENTENCE
1. hurricane	_____	_____
2. tax	_____	_____
3. trade ban	_____	_____

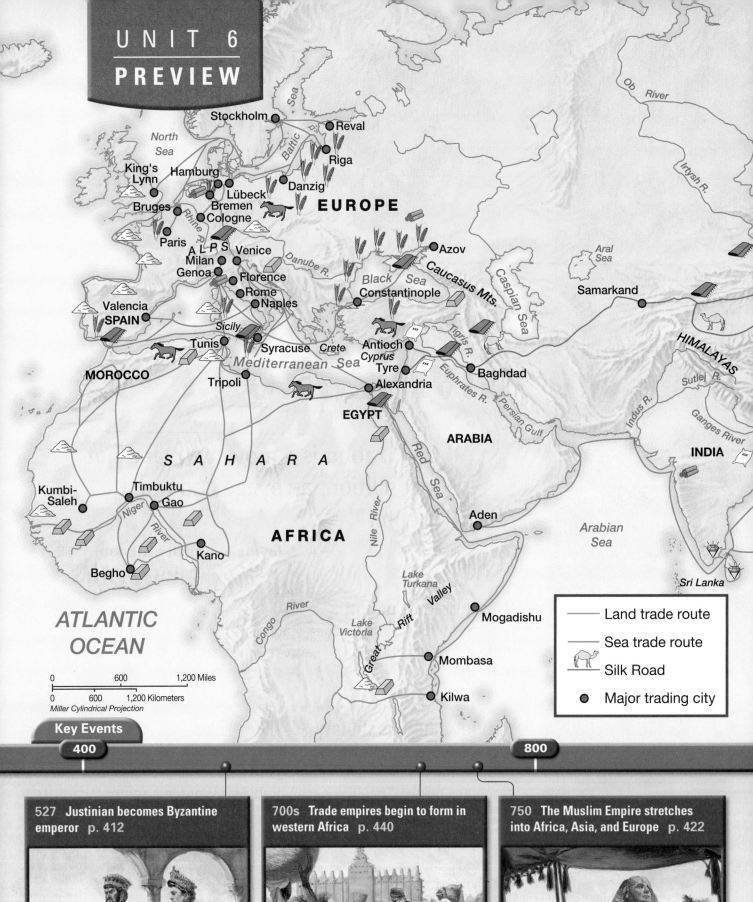

Stockholm
Reval
North Sea
Riga
Danzig
King's Lynn
Hamburg
Bremen
Lübeck
Cologne
EUROPE
Azov
Bruges
Rhine R.
Paris
A L P S
Milan
Venice
Genoa
Florence
Rome
Naples
Danube R.
Black Sea
Constantinople
Caucasus Mts.
Samarkand
Valencia
SPAIN
Sicily
Crete
Antioch
Cyprus
Tyre
Tigris R.
HIMALAYAS
Tunis
Syracuse
Mediterranean Sea
Alexandria
Euphrates R.
Baghdad
Caspian Sea
Aral Sea
Ob River
Irtysh R.
MOROCCO
Tripoli
EGYPT
ARABIA
Persian Gulf
Sutlej R.
Indus R.
Ganges River
INDIA
S A H A R A
Red Sea
Nile River
Kumbi-Saleh
Timbuktu
Gao
Niger River
Kano
Begho
AFRICA
Aden
Arabian Sea
Sri Lanka
ATLANTIC OCEAN
Congo River
Lake Victoria
Lake Turkana
Great Rift Valley
Mogadishu
Mombasa
Kilwa

| 0 | 600 | 1,200 Miles |
| 0 | 600 | 1,200 Kilometers |

Miller Cylindrical Projection

	Land trade route
	Sea trade route
🐪	Silk Road
●	Major trading city

Key Events

400 — 800

527 Justinian becomes Byzantine emperor p. 412

700s Trade empires begin to form in western Africa p. 440

750 The Muslim Empire stretches into Africa, Asia, and Europe p. 422

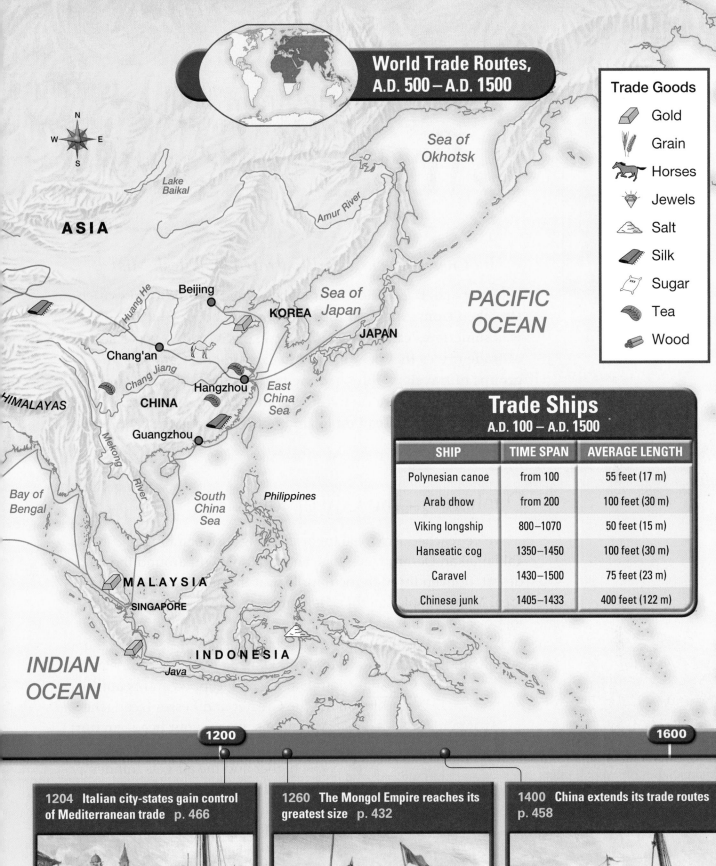

World Trade Routes, A.D. 500 – A.D. 1500

ASIA

Sea of Okhotsk

Lake Baikal

Amur River

Huang He

Beijing

KOREA

Sea of Japan

JAPAN

PACIFIC OCEAN

Chang'an

Chang Jiang

CHINA

Hangzhou

East China Sea

HIMALAYAS

Mekong River

Guangzhou

South China Sea

Philippines

Bay of Bengal

MALAYSIA

SINGAPORE

INDONESIA

Java

INDIAN OCEAN

Trade Goods

Gold	
Grain	
Horses	
Jewels	
Salt	
Silk	
Sugar	
Tea	
Wood	

Trade Ships
A.D. 100 – A.D. 1500

SHIP	TIME SPAN	AVERAGE LENGTH
Polynesian canoe	from 100	55 feet (17 m)
Arab dhow	from 200	100 feet (30 m)
Viking longship	800–1070	50 feet (15 m)
Hanseatic cog	1350–1450	100 feet (30 m)
Caravel	1430–1500	75 feet (23 m)
Chinese junk	1405–1433	400 feet (122 m)

1200

1600

1204 Italian city-states gain control of Mediterranean trade p. 466

1260 The Mongol Empire reaches its greatest size p. 432

1400 China extends its trade routes p. 458

Stories from
The Silk Road

Stories from
The Silk Road

by Cherry Gilchrist • illustrated by Nilesh Mistry

Long ago, trade often took place along the Silk Road, which stretched from Asia to Europe. The Silk Road, or Silk Route as it was sometimes called, was not just a single road. It was a series of trade routes that people used to carry goods. Caravans, or groups of travelers, followed the trade routes, stopping at cities along the way. There they rested at inns called caravansaries and exchanged goods. Read on to find out what traveling along the Silk Road was like.

Dunhuang—The City of Sands

We've reached Anxi, the town marking the beginning of the Taklamakan Desert. Here you can go left or right around the desert, or even through the middle. But this isn't always a good idea. Many people say that "Taklamakan" means "He who goes in, does not come out."

Travelers have always given special names to places along the Silk Road. Just to the north of the Taklamakan Desert, for instance, are the Celestial Mountains—snow-capped and beautiful. Near Khotan are the Greater and Lesser Headache Mountains, where your head can hurt badly as you climb higher and higher and the air gets thinner and thinner.

Water is a vital resource on the Silk Road. The caravans need to know where their next watering place will be, and the names of

Celestial heavenly

the oases give a clue as to the kind of water they offer. One Cup Spring, Bitter Well Halt and Mud Pit Hollow all warn us not to expect too much. Sometimes it's very hard to find the springs, and travelers have to search around for a tiny dip in the ground, marked by a single stone. Even when they find the water, it may be bitter and brackish and not quench their thirst.

If we turned right at Anxi, we could go to the city of Turpan—twelve days' hard travel, with only nasty-tasting water on the way. But in Turpan itself there is delicious cool water. It's brought there through underground channels from the mountains, and flows around the town and its gardens. That's why they can grow such lovely fruit and vegetables there.

If you come to Turpan at a pleasant time of year, you'll probably call it the "Bright Pearl of the Silk Road." In a biting cold winter, though, you might use the name "Storehouse of the Wind." And on a summer's day you

may prefer to join the locals, who retire to the underground rooms in their houses to escape the blistering heat. Some travelers have complained about the terrible insects there—jumping spiders and poisonous cockroaches. But most people like Turpan and stroll around, shaded from the heat by awnings of reed matting, resting up before tackling the next stage of their journey.

But we're going to turn left around the desert and visit Dunhuang, the City of Sands. Here are the famous Thousand Buddha caves, filled with statues and offerings to the deities. For hundreds of years travelers have worshipped here and prayed for protection before they set off across the desert. Here artists work by the rays of the morning sun or by the light of smoky lamps, painting new images to bring good fortune to nervous travelers.

oases	watering holes in the desert
brackish	somewhat salty
awnings	covers that give protection from the sun

Kashgar Caravanserai

We have left the desert behind us now and climbed up to the ancient city of Kashgar. This is a real crossroads, where the folk of the mountain and the plain meet. We'll see all sorts of people in the market. Over there are some weary traders from China who have reached the end of their journey. They will sell their goods and will go home with a new load. Here are some merchants from far-off Samarkand—sharp-eyed, richly dressed, always ready to spot a bargain. Over there are two Buddhist monks from India, carrying scrolls from one monastery to another. Those rosy-cheeked, black-eyed girls are Tajiks, and you might spot a few fair heads among the dark-haired people from the Hindu Kush. Some of their ancestors were Greeks, who came with the army of Alexander the Great.

The locals here are the Uighurs. They manage the trade routes skillfully. The older men among them like to grow long gray beards.

You might wonder how all these people manage to understand each other. But many of them speak one of the Turkic languages, which have a common root, so it's just about possible. The first person begins by saying something like, "I'm going to speak about sheep today," so that the second person knows what the conversation will be about.

People often grumble about taxes. Greedy rulers and officials along the Silk Road charge the caravans "protection" or "duty" and if you don't pay up, your goods won't go any further. No wonder the price of silk is hundreds of times higher in the West than in China!

In the bigger places, most travelers stay at an inn or "caravanserai," with a courtyard for the animals, usually two-humped camels, which can travel for long periods without water and food. Horses are useful too, for fast travel over shorter distances. Mules and donkeys can carry heavy loads in the mountains, and you'll also see yaks, which are at home in the highlands. Caravans have to change their pack animals when they tire, and lots of arguing goes on as the team drivers bargain for the best replacements.

People also stock up on provisions. Those going west need warm wraps, sheep skins and furs for the hard climb into the snowy mountains. There are harsh times ahead; they may suffer fierce blizzards and altitude sickness. Pack animals may tumble over the edge of a precipice, and nights may be spent shivering on a mat laid down on the ice.

Some caravans wait here for months until the highest mountain passes open again. When they get bored, they scratch poems and messages on the walls of the inns—like this one:

Jewels and gems, they are but stones;

Barley and beans, they strengthen your bones.

When you're suffering from cold and hunger, you don't care much for your precious cargo. You'd trade it all in for a bowl of warm gruel!

precipice   a very steep place

Analyze the Literature

❶ What is the most important resource on the Silk Road?

❷ What is special about the names of some of the places along the Silk Road?

❸ Why do you think trade routes like the Silk Road are not used much today?

READ A BOOK

START THE UNIT PROJECT

Make a Travel Guide   As you read this unit, take notes about the historical sites you would like to visit in one of the regions you read about. Include these sites in a travel guide of the region.

USE TECHNOLOGY

Visit The Learning Site at **www.harcourtschool.com** for additional activities, primary sources, and other resources to use in this unit.

HAGIA SOPHIA, ISTANBUL, TURKEY

In about A.D. 537 the Roman emperor Justinian built this church called the Hagia Sophia. Its domed ceiling was a common feature of religious sites built in the Eastern Roman Empire at that time. Visitors to Istanbul can visit the church, which is now a museum.

LOCATE IT

Istanbul
Black Sea
TURKEY
Mediterranean Sea

New Empires

"This then the city by the wide world desired."

—Constantine the Rhodian, poet, A.D. 800s

Summarize

When you **summarize,** you retell briefly what you have read, using your own words.

After you read this chapter, summarize what you have learned.

• **Identify the main topic of each lesson.**

• **List the key facts of the events you read about.**

• **Summarize what you read.**

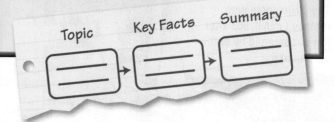

Topic   Key Facts   Summary

SUMMARIZE

As you read, summarize the major events of the Byzantine Empire.

BIG IDEA

Byzantine rulers continued many Roman ideas to shape their empire's culture.

VOCABULARY

Justinian Code
envoy
monopoly
orthodox
icon
patriarch
Catholic

The Byzantine Empire

| 400 | 800 | 1200 | 1600 |

500 – 1500

Roman civilization continued to develop in the eastern part of the former Roman Empire, even after it declined in the western part of the empire. The eastern part became known as the Byzantine Empire. At its greatest size, the Byzantine Empire extended into parts of eastern Europe, western Europe, south-western Asia, and northern Africa. Its capital was the city of Constantinople. A strong army and a well-run government helped the Byzantine Empire last for more than 1,000 years.

Justinian I and Theodora

In A.D. 527 Justinian I became emperor of the Byzantine Empire. He wanted to make the empire as powerful as the Roman Empire had once been. During Justinian's rule, the Byzantine Empire grew to its greatest size.

Justinian sent powerful armies into northern Africa and western Europe. He reclaimed many of the lands that Rome had lost. By A.D. 565 much of the land along the Mediterranean Sea was part of the Byzantine Empire.

FAST FACT The church of Hagia Sophia (ah•YEE•uh soh•FEE•uh), or "Holy Wisdom," was the world's largest church during the time of the Byzantine Empire. The church was built from A.D. 532 to A.D. 537, during the rule of Emperor Justinian I. The large dome was replaced in A.D. 563 after it was damaged by an earthquake.

Empress Theodora
About A.D. 497–A.D. 548

just christian ✎

Character Trait: Justice

Most empresses of the Mediterranean region came from noble families. Theodora did not. Her father worked at the Hippodrome, a huge open-air stadium in the city of Constantinople. He took care of bears and other animals for the circus. Theodora became a circus performer and theater actress. In her early twenties, she met Justinian and married him. When Justinian became emperor, she became empress. As empress she worked to make the laws of the Byzantine Empire fairer to women and to people of different social classes.

 MULTIMEDIA BIOGRAPHIES
Visit The Learning Site at **www.harcourtschool.com** to learn about other famous people.

To better control the empire, Justinian ordered a code, or set of written laws, to be assembled. This new code, known as the **Justinian Code**, organized the old code of Roman laws. The Justinian Code gathered these laws into one book and made them easier to understand.

Some laws in the code were influenced by the empress Theodora, the wife of Justinian. She was one of the first rulers to work for the rights of women. Among the laws she supported were several that advanced women's rights to own property.

Theodora's intelligence and political skills made her Justinian's most trusted adviser. She shared in many of the duties usually performed only by the emperor. For example, Theodora met with **envoys**, or official visitors from other lands. She also wrote letters to the leaders of other governments.

Empress Theodora took part in choosing government leaders as well. She and Justinian believed that jobs should be given based on a person's ability, not on his or her social class. Because of this, Justinian chose a man named Belisarius (beh•luh•SAR•ee•uhs) to lead the Byzantine army. Belisarius was the son of a farmer and had little military training. However, he had proved his skills in battle. Under Belisarius's command, the Byzantine army won important battles in Asia, Africa, and Italy. These victories helped the empire grow.

Justinian realized that the economy of the empire also needed to grow. He welcomed traders into Constantinople and encouraged the start of new businesses and industries.

The Byzantine silk industry was started by Justinian himself. He had silkworm eggs smuggled out of China. The empire was then able to produce silk. This ended China's **monopoly**, or complete control, of the silk trade.

A gold coin showing Emperor Justinian

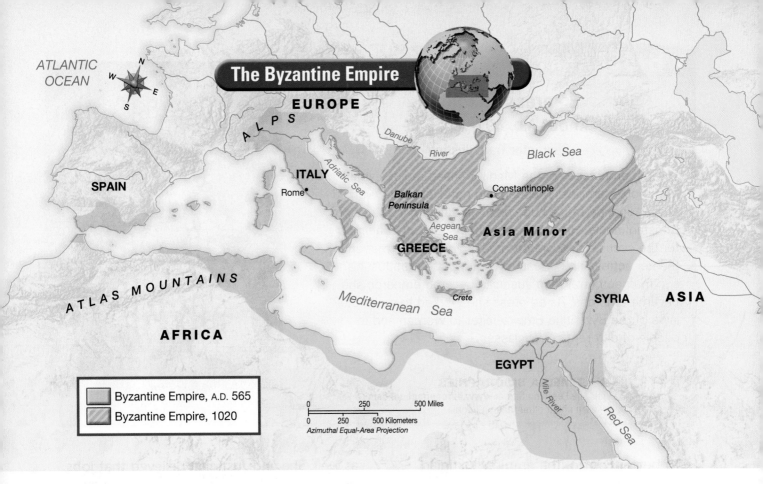

The Byzantine Empire

ATLANTIC OCEAN

EUROPE

ALPS

Danube River

Black Sea

SPAIN

ITALY

Rome

Adriatic Sea

Balkan Peninsula

Constantinople

Asia Minor

GREECE

Aegean Sea

ATLAS MOUNTAINS

Mediterranean Sea

Crete

SYRIA

ASIA

AFRICA

EGYPT

Nile River

Red Sea

Byzantine Empire, A.D. 565
Byzantine Empire, 1020

0   250   500 Miles
0   250   500 Kilometers
Azimuthal Equal-Area Projection

GEOGRAPHY THEME

Regions   Justinian's empire grew to include much of the old Roman Empire. By 1020 the Byzantines had lost some of these lands.

❖ In 1020 did the Byzantine Empire include the city of Rome?

Money from trade and taxes allowed Justinian to make Constantinople a "New Rome." Buildings, roads, bridges, and aqueducts were built throughout the city. Even so, Justinian was not popular among all the people of the empire. In A.D. 532 the people of Constantinople rebelled. Some government officials wanted Justinian to leave the city. He was persuaded to stay by Theodora, who said,

66 . . . one who has been an emperor cannot endure to be a fugitive. 99

The Byzantine army under Belisarius soon ended the rebellion, and Justinian remained emperor.

REVIEW How were the old Roman laws improved by Justinian and Theodora?

The Division of the Christian Church

Christianity was important to the people of the Byzantine Empire. However, different branches of Christianity developed over time, which led to conflicts between Christians.

Even Theodora and Justinian, who were both Christians, disagreed about Christianity. Justinian wanted all people in the Byzantine Empire to follow **orthodox**, or officially accepted, Christianity. Theodora did not follow orthodox Christianity. As a result, she wanted to protect Christians who were not orthodox.

A Byzantine bracelet from the A.D. 500s

Justinian and Theodora never completely agreed about Christianity. However, they worked together to keep all Christians loyal to the empire.

One of the arguments within Christianity centered around **icons**, holy artwork depicting Jesus and the saints. Some Christians liked to look at icons as they prayed. Other Christians felt that using icons in this way was like worshipping idols, which is forbidden in the Ten Commandments.

The argument over icons divided Christians. In western Europe few people could read or write. Church leaders there believed icons were helpful in teaching Christianity. Some Byzantine emperors banned the use of icons. They believed that it went against God's laws.

Disagreement over the use of icons continued for many years. Other religious issues caused further division within the Christian Church.

These conflicts eventually caused the Christian Church to split into two parts in 1054. The Christian Church in the Byzantine Empire became the Eastern Orthodox Church, based in Constantinople. The leaders of this church were called **patriarchs**. The Christian Church in western Europe became the Roman Catholic Church, based in Rome. The church's followers are called **Catholics**. Over time, the

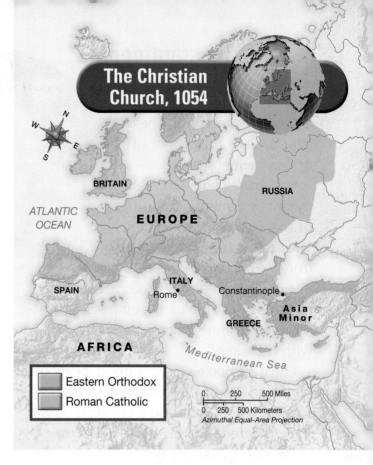

The Christian Church, 1054

Eastern Orthodox
Roman Catholic

Regions Long-lasting conflicts split the Christian Church into two parts in 1054.

❓ Which branch of Christianity did most Russians follow in 1054?

two branches of the Christian Church gained political power and wealth. Both churches contributed to the cultures of their societies.

REVIEW How did the Christian Church change in 1054? **SUMMARIZE**

Begun in 1063, the Roman Catholic Cathedral of Pisa (foreground) in Italy includes the famous Leaning Tower of Pisa (background, right).

Life in Constantinople

The word *Byzantine* comes from Byzantium, the name of an ancient Greek city. The city later became the capital city of Constantinople.

The many people of the Byzantine Empire did not think of themselves as Byzantines. They called themselves *Romaioi* (roh•MY•oy), which meant "Romans." Their mighty capital city, Constantinople, served as the base of the empire's government. Like Rome, Constantinople was filled with treasures.

Constantinople was in a good location to be the center of the empire. Because it was surrounded by water on three sides, it was easy to defend. It was also close to major trade routes. The city became an important gateway between the lands bordering the Mediterranean Sea in the west and regions near and beyond the Black Sea in the east.

This stone relief shows an emperor presenting a crown to the winner of a chariot race at the Hippodrome.

The main road that crossed Constantinople—the Mese, or Middle Street—was filled with traders and merchants from many lands. Because of this, many different languages were spoken in the city. Still, the common language of the empire was Greek.

As in the Roman Empire, the wealthy were mainly government leaders, owners of large farms, and merchants. Most people worked long hours and earned just enough for food, clothing, shelter, and taxes.

Public events were an important part of life for both rich and poor. The Hippodrome in Constantinople was a huge stadium modeled after the Circus Maximus in Rome. It could hold more than 60,000 people.

Constantinople is now the busy port city of Istanbul, Turkey. The woodblock print (left) shows how Constantinople might have looked long ago.

The sword on this Ottoman flag (above) shows the Ottoman Turks' power after the capture of Constantinople (left).

The word *Hippodrome* means "horse racetrack." Chariot races, shows, religious ceremonies, and government events were held in the Hippodrome.

The chariot races and other events at the Hippodrome were only for men. Women—except for the empress—were not allowed to attend. Women were also not allowed to hold public office. While the Justinian Code did much to improve the lives of Byzantine women, they still had fewer rights than men. Yet, women ruled over the empire at different times.

Though Constantinople's location brought much wealth to the empire, the city was also a target for invaders. For almost 1,000 years, different groups tried to conquer the city. The Ottoman Turks finally captured Constantinople in 1453, ending the Byzantine Empire.

REVIEW How was the Hippodrome related to Roman culture?

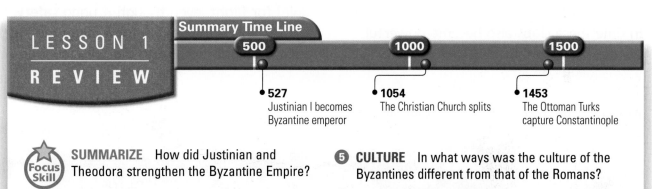

LESSON 1 REVIEW

Summary Time Line

500 — 527 Justinian I becomes Byzantine emperor

1000 — 1054 The Christian Church splits

1500 — 1453 The Ottoman Turks capture Constantinople

SUMMARIZE How did Justinian and Theodora strengthen the Byzantine Empire?

1 BIG IDEA How did the people of the Byzantine Empire build on the ways of the Roman Empire?

2 VOCABULARY Use the term **monopoly** in a sentence.

3 TIME LINE When did the Ottoman Turks capture Constantinople?

4 ECONOMY Explain why the location of Constantinople was good for the economy of the Byzantine Empire.

5 CULTURE In what ways was the culture of the Byzantines different from that of the Romans?

6 CRITICAL THINKING—Analyze Why might some people living in the Byzantine Empire have disliked Justinian I?

PERFORMANCE—Make a Time Line Draw a time line that shows the major events in the Byzantine Empire from A.D. 527 to 1453. Your time line should begin with the rule of Justinian and end with the fall of Constantinople. Add illustrations of key people, places, and events to your time line.

Determine Point of View

VOCABULARY

point of view

▶ WHY IT MATTERS

A person's **point of view** is the set of beliefs he or she holds. A point of view may be shaped by a person's age, gender, culture, religion, race, nationality, and social status. Studying points of view and how they change is the key to understanding how people and ideas shape history.

▶ WHAT YOU NEED TO KNOW

In the Byzantine Empire, chariot racing was a popular sport. Thousands of people attended these races. People formed clubs to support their chariot-racing teams. These clubs took their names from the teams' racing colors—Reds, Whites, Blues, and Greens. In time these clubs also became powerful political organizations.

By A.D. 532 Justinian's tax laws and other policies had angered many Byzantines. That year, some members of the Blues and the Greens were arrested and found guilty of murder. When Justinian refused their requests for mercy, the Blue and Green groups joined to start a riot. For about a week the people of Constantinople rioted, setting fire to parts of the city. When attempts to make an agreement with the rioters failed, Justinian considered leaving the city. He was persuaded to stay by Theodora, his wife. The Byzantine historian Procopius recorded her speech to Justinian:

"My opinion then is that the present time, above all others, is inopportune [not favorable] for flight, even though it bring safety. For while it is impossible for a man who has seen the light not also to die, . . . one who

Musicians perform outside the gates of Constantinople.

has been an emperor cannot endure to be a fugitive. May I never be separated from this purple [royal power], and may I not live that day on which those who meet me shall not address me as mistress. If, now, it is your wish to save yourself, O Emperor, there is no difficulty. For we have money, and there is the sea, here the boats. However, consider whether it will not come about after you have been saved that you would gladly exchange that safety for death. For as to myself, I approve a certain ancient saying that royalty is a good burial-shroud [condition in which to die]."

To determine points of view, you can use the following steps.

Step 1 **Identify the speaker or writer. You may be able to find biographical information that will help you better understand the person's reasons for his or her statements.**

Step 2 **Think about the situation in which the statements were made. When you read about the past, look for clues that tell what life was like then. When you read about the present day, look for references to people or issues in the news. How might the situation have influenced the person's point of view?**

Step 3 **Look for words that help you find a person's point of view. Statements giving points of view may contain phrases such as _I think, I believe, I hope,_ and _in my opinion._**

Empress Theodora

➡ PRACTICE THE SKILL

Refer to Theodora's speech to answer these questions.

1 What is Theodora's point of view about leaving Constantinople?

2 Why do you think she holds this point of view?

3 Which of Theodora's sentences best summarizes her point of view? Why?

➡ APPLY WHAT YOU LEARNED

Look at the Letters to the Editor section in a newspaper or magazine. Find a letter about an issue familiar to you. Cut out or print the letter. Determine the writer's point of view by using the steps described in "What You Need to Know." Highlight any words or phrases in the letter that signal point of view. Then write a summary of the issue and the writer's point of view.

2

The Rise of Islam

| 400 | 800 | 1200 | 1600 |

500 – 900

SUMMARIZE

As you read, think of ways to summarize the history and development of Islam.

BIG IDEA

Beginning in the late A.D. 500s, Islam developed on the Arabian Peninsula and later spread throughout the world.

VOCABULARY

steppe
Islam
Qur'an
Muslim
caliph
Sunni
Shi'i
mosque
minaret

As the **Byzantine Empire was reaching its height near the end of the** A.D. **500s, changes were taking place in the lands to the east of it. Within 100 years, the Persian Empire would be defeated by peoples from the Arabian Peninsula south of Persia. Over time in this region, an empire formed that grew in strength and challenged the Byzantine Empire.**

The Arabian Peninsula

Desert covers more than two-thirds of the Arabian Peninsula. Some parts of the desert are dunes of shifting sand. Other parts are dry plains called **steppes**. Some grasses and plants grow on the steppes, but most of this land is too dry to raise large crops. In the A.D. 500s, many Arab tribes lived on the steppes. They raised camels, sheep, and goats, traveling from place to place to graze them on the sparse grasses.

Some towns formed on the Arabian Peninsula, or Arabia, near oases where there was underground water. Farming was possible near these towns because crops could be watered. The towns became stopping points for travelers on desert trading routes.

One of the largest towns in Arabia was Mecca (MEH•kuh), also known as Makkah, in what is today Saudi Arabia. Goods from Asia and Africa passed through Mecca on their way to lands around the Mediterranean Sea. Trade helped Mecca grow.

Mecca also held an important place of worship. Each year Arabs from all over Arabia came to Mecca to worship at the Kaaba (KAH•buh), a holy shrine. At that time, the Kaaba

Goods like this jade camel (left) may have been exchanged along the Arabian trade routes. Camel caravans (below) still follow these routes.

Thousands of Muslims pray at the Kaaba—Islam's holiest shrine. Muslims around the world face in the direction of the Kaaba when they pray.

hi hao

held statues of the gods that the Arabs had come to believe in. With so many Arabs visiting Mecca to worship at the Kaaba, the city grew in power and wealth.

REVIEW **Why was Mecca an important place of worship?**

Muhammad and Islam

About A.D. 570 an Arab boy named Muhammad was born in Mecca. Muhammad's parents died when he was a child, and relatives cared for him. He grew up to be a respected member of his tribe. He became a trader and married a wealthy widow named Khadija (kah•DEE•juh).

Muhammad was unhappy about his tribe's worship of many gods and idols. He often spent time deep in thought in a cave out-side of Mecca. Muhammad reported that he

had an amazing experience during a visit to the cave. According to Muhammad, the angel Gabriel told him that he would become a messenger to humankind. This experience confirmed to Muhammad that there is no god but God, or *Allah* in Arabic. Over the next 23 years, Muhammad received more messages. The religion based on these messages is **Islam** (is•LAHM).

The messages given to Muhammad make up the **Qur'an** (kuh•RAN), or Koran, the holy book of Islam. For a **Muslim** (MUHZ•luhm), or follower of Islam, the Qur'an is God's word. Muhammad's family and close friends became the first Muslims.

As Islam spread among the Arab tribes, leaders in Mecca worried that people would stop worshipping at the Kaaba. The leaders persecuted the Muslims and tried to force them to give up their beliefs.

Muhammad and his followers did not resist the persecutions. Instead, in A.D. 622 Muhammad led them to settle in the town of Medina, in what is now Saudi Arabia. His journey, called the Hijra (HIJ•ruh), was a new beginning for Muslims. While in Medina, Muhammad reported receiving a message from the angel Gabriel that allowed Muslims to fight their persecutors. Soon after, Medina became the Muslim capital.

REVIEW What is the Qur'an made up of?
SUMMARIZE

The Muslim Empire

In A.D. 630, eight years after the Hijra, the Muslims captured the city of Mecca. Upon his return to the city, Muhammad ordered that all the idols in the Kaaba be destroyed. He then dedicated the Kaaba to the worship of Allah only.

An Islamic house of worship

The Kaaba remains the most holy shrine for Muslims to this day.

Muhammad and his followers worked to spread the message of Islam. After Muhammad's death in A.D. 632, Muslim leaders chose a **caliph** (KAY•luhf), or "successor," to Muhammad. A caliph governed the Muslim community according to the Qur'an and Muhammad's example.

Within a few years the first caliphs united the people of the Arabian Peninsula under Muslim rule. Then Muslim armies carried the teachings of Islam to neighboring peoples in Mesopotamia, Syria, and Egypt. Many people welcomed the Muslims. They felt that Muslim rule would free them from the heavy taxes and religious persecution of their own rulers. The Muslim Empire grew dramatically in the 200 years following the death of Muhammad.

By A.D. 750 the empire stretched

THE FIVE PILLARS OF ISLAM

The Islamic religion is based on five acts of worship known as the Five Pillars. The pillars help shape the lives of Muslims and their communities.

Testify, or say, that there is no god but God, and Muhammad is God's prophet.

Make five prayers at specific times each day.

Give part of one's earnings to take care of the needy.

Fast [do not eat or drink] from dawn to sunset during Ramadan, the ninth month in the Muslim calendar.

Make a hajj (HAJ), or religious visit to Mecca, during one's lifetime if financially able.

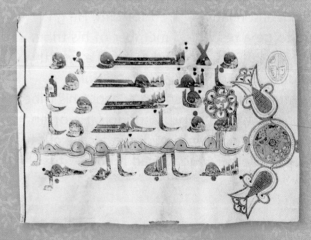

A page from a ninth-century Qur'an

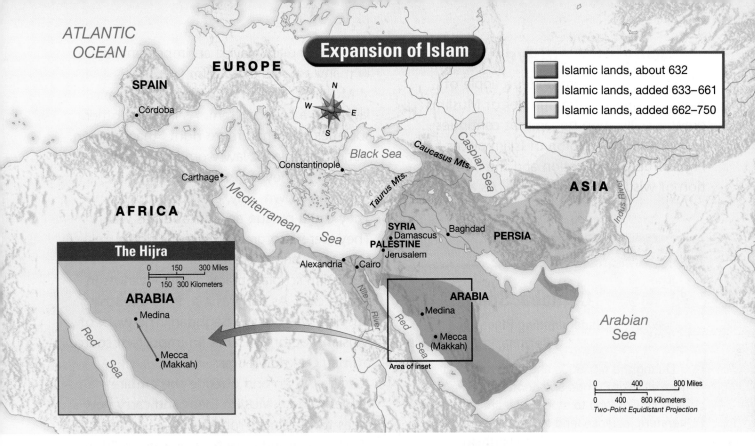

Expansion of Islam

Islamic lands, about 632
Islamic lands, added 633–661
Islamic lands, added 662–750

ATLANTIC OCEAN
EUROPE
SPAIN
Córdoba
Carthage
AFRICA
Mediterranean Sea
Black Sea
Constantinople
Taurus Mts.
Caucasus Mts.
Caspian Sea
ASIA
Indus River
SYRIA
Damascus
Baghdad
PERSIA
PALESTINE
Jerusalem
Alexandria
Cairo
Nile River
Red Sea
ARABIA
Medina
Mecca (Makkah)
Area of inset
Arabian Sea

0   400   800 Miles
0   400   800 Kilometers
Two-Point Equidistant Projection

The Hijra
0   150   300 Miles
0   150   300 Kilometers
ARABIA
Medina
Mecca (Makkah)
Red Sea

GEOGRAPHY THEME

Regions   By A.D. 750, Islam had reached many different peoples and cultures.

❖ During which period did Islam reach the city of Alexandria?

from Spain and northern Africa through Arabia and Persia into parts of the Indus River valley.

As the Muslim Empire grew, powerful families in Mecca argued over who should control it. In A.D. 661 a member of the Umayyad (oo•MY•yuhd) family became caliph and moved the capital from Medina to the city of Damascus in Syria. The Umayyads ruled from the new capital until A.D. 750, when the Abbasid (uh•BA•suhd) family claimed the right to rule. The Abbasid family founded a new capital in A.D. 762 in what is today the city of Baghdad, Iraq.

A member of the Umayyad family started his own government in

Córdoba, Spain. Later, descendants of Muhammad's daughter Fatima formed still another government, with its capital in Cairo, Egypt. As time passed, rival caliphs ruled different parts of the Muslim Empire. The Muslim community split into several groups.

Among the most important of the Muslim groups were the **Sunni** (SOO•nee) and the **Shi'i** (SHEE•uh). Sunni Muslims accepted the changing dynasties within the empire. Shi'i Muslims stayed loyal to the descendants of the fourth caliph, Ali. They did not want either the Umayyad or Abbasid family as rulers. These groups share the basic beliefs of Islam but disagree on some issues.

REVIEW What area did the Muslim Empire cover by A.D. 750?

Box from the Umayyad dynasty

Muslim Achievements

The Muslim Empire united people of many cultures. As the number of Muslims grew, a civilization began that continues to this day. The religion of Islam places a high value on education and the preservation of wisdom for the future. As a result,

• GEOGRAPHY •

Córdoba, Spain
Understanding Places and Regions

During the A.D. 800s and 900s, people from all over Europe and northern Africa went to Córdoba to study subjects such as literature, science, and religion. Moors, who were Muslims originally from northern Africa, controlled Córdoba. The city had a huge Muslim library with more than 400,000 books. It also had a university, more than 60 smaller libraries, and many bookshops. Visitors to Córdoba were amazed by the city's paved and lighted streets.

Muslim scholars played an important role in many aspects of Muslim life.

Muslim scholars helped develop Islamic laws and a court system. As in many other societies, men had more rights than women. Yet, under Islamic law women enjoyed rights that they did not have elsewhere. They could own, buy, and sell property. They could pursue an education as well. They were also granted specific rights in the family and in society.

Muslim scholars made many advances in health care. As early as A.D. 900, a teaching hospital was built in Baghdad. The work of Muslim doctors became an important source of medical knowledge.

Trade within and outside the empire helped spread Muslim ideas and carry new ideas to Muslims. From the Chinese, the Muslims learned how to make paper. From the people of India, Muslims borrowed a system of numbers made up of nine digits and a zero. The Muslims called these Indian numerals. Later, as traders spread their use

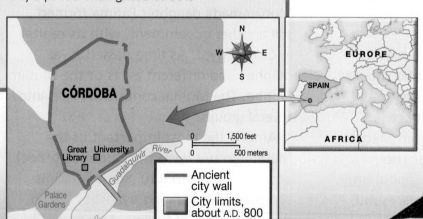

CÓRDOBA

Great Library
University
Guadalquivir River
Palace Gardens

0 — 1,500 feet
0 — 500 meters

— Ancient city wall
▨ City limits, about A.D. 800

N W E S

EUROPE
SPAIN
AFRICA

Built in A.D. 785, the Great Mosque in Córdoba (below) has both Roman and Islamic architecture.

This medical illustration (left) and prayer compass (above) show early Muslim advances in science.

across the Muslim Empire and into Europe, they became known as Arabic numerals. We use Arabic numerals today.

Among the Muslims' most beautiful works of art are their **mosques**, or Islamic houses of worship. The design of a mosque is simple, and the building has little furniture. A mosque has one or more towers called **minarets**, from which the call to

prayer is given five times a day. The walls of mosques are often decorated with rich designs and verses from the Qur'an.

Many Muslim artists also created beautiful paintings and works of literature. They used elements of Persian and Indian music to form their own style of music.

REVIEW How did trade influence Muslim ideas?

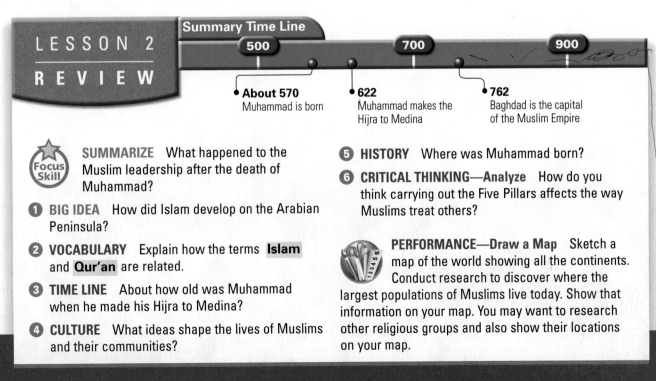

LESSON 2 REVIEW

Summary Time Line

500   700   900

About 570
Muhammad is born

622
Muhammad makes the Hijra to Medina

762
Baghdad is the capital of the Muslim Empire

Focus Skill

SUMMARIZE What happened to the Muslim leadership after the death of Muhammad?

❶ **BIG IDEA** How did Islam develop on the Arabian Peninsula?

❷ **VOCABULARY** Explain how the terms **Islam** and **Qur'an** are related.

❸ **TIME LINE** About how old was Muhammad when he made his Hijra to Medina?

❹ **CULTURE** What ideas shape the lives of Muslims and their communities?

❺ **HISTORY** Where was Muhammad born?

❻ **CRITICAL THINKING—Analyze** How do you think carrying out the Five Pillars affects the way Muslims treat others?

PERFORMANCE—Draw a Map Sketch a map of the world showing all the continents. Conduct research to discover where the largest populations of Muslims live today. Show that information on your map. You may want to research other religious groups and also show their locations on your map.

Compare Circle Graphs

VOCABULARY

circle graph

▶ WHY IT MATTERS

You have read about the spread of Islam from the Arabian Peninsula to other parts of the world. Islam, like other religions, deeply affected the cultures and governments in the places where it was accepted.

In most countries today, people follow a number of different religions. One way to show the religions of a country and the number of people who follow them is by drawing a circle graph. A **circle graph** shows information by means of a circle divided into parts. Circle graphs are often called pie charts, because they look like pies with slices of different sizes. The larger a slice is, the greater its percentage.

▶ WHAT YOU NEED TO KNOW

Listed below are some tips that will help you compare circle graphs.

- Read the titles of the graphs to find out what is being compared.

- The slices of a circle graph add up to 100 percent. The size of each slice represents part of the whole 100 percent. For example, if a slice takes up exactly half of the graph, it equals 50 percent. It is not always easy to estimate how large a slice is just by looking at it, so it is often labeled with its percentage.

- To find out what each slice represents, look for a label within or next to each

Muslims pray at the Badshahi Mosque in Lahore, Pakistan.

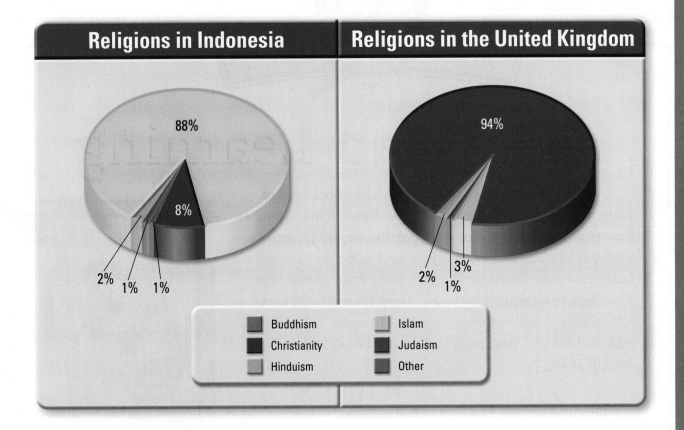

Religions in Indonesia

88%

8%

2% 1% 1%

Religions in the United Kingdom

94%

2% 3%
1%

Legend:
- Buddhism
- Christianity
- Hinduism
- Islam
- Judaism
- Other

slice. Sometimes circle graphs use a legend, or key, instead of labels. For example, the legend on the graphs above tells you that the color yellow represents the percentage of people who practice Islam.

- One of the most useful features of circle graphs is their ability to show information at a glance. For example, just by glancing at the "Religions in Indonesia" graph, you can easily tell that Islam is the most widely practiced religion there.

▶ PRACTICE THE SKILL

Study the circle graphs, and then answer the following questions.

1 Which country has a higher percentage of people who practice Islam?

2 Which country has a higher percentage of people who practice Christianity?

3 Which religion is the most widely practiced in the United Kingdom?

4 Which religion has the same percentage of followers in both countries?

5 In Indonesia, what is the percentage of people who do not practice Islam?

▶ APPLY WHAT YOU LEARNED

Make your own circle graph that shows information about your classmates, such as gender, eye color, or hair color. First, find out what percent of your classmates are in each category. For example, take the number of boys in your class, and divide it by the total number of students in your class. If there are 18 boys in a class of 30, then 60 percent of the students are boys (18 ÷ 30 = 0.6, or 60 percent). Use the percentages you find to make a circle graph.

Books and Learning

The world's first books did not look like books today. Early people copied books by hand and used materials other than paper to write on. For example, the ancient Egyptians used papyrus, made from plants found along the Nile River. Later, Europeans used parchment, made from animal skins. The Chinese were the first to use paper for books, in about A.D. 105. Early books took a long time to make. Often they included colorful drawings, and no two books looked exactly alike.

FROM THE BRITISH LIBRARY IN LONDON

Drawing of Saint Matthew writing

Pages from a highly decorated Qur'an written in Arabic, from northern Africa, 1256

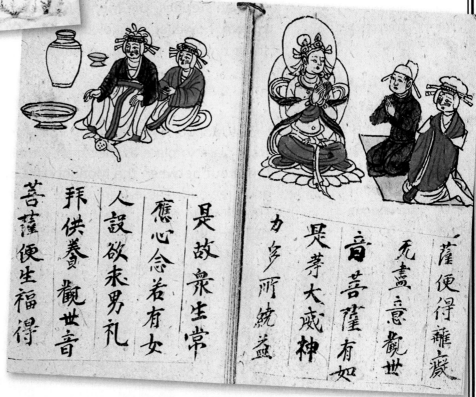

Analyze the Primary Source

❶ Compare the drawings and decorations on the three books. How are they alike? How are they different?

❷ In what way is the subject matter for the three books similar?

❸ What inferences can you make about books at this time by the subject of the books shown here?

Written in Greek, this page was made by monks in Constantinople in 1066. The text is Psalm 26 of the Bible. In the drawing David cares for his sheep. One, however, has been snatched by a wolf.

The pages from this Buddhist book, the Lotus Sutra, were painted in China in the 1100s. The illustration shows Quan Yin, the Buddhist goddess of mercy.

ACTIVITY

Design and Draw Find a poem. Using colored pencils or markers, copy it onto a page. Make your writing beautiful. Decorate the page with colorful drawings. At the bottom of the page, note how long it took you to make this one page. Then, think about how long it might take to make a 100-page book.

RESEARCH

Visit The Learning Site at **www.harcourtschool.com** to research other primary sources.

SUMMARIZE

As you read, summarize the history of the Mongol Empire and the lives of the people connected with it.

BIG IDEA

Trade during the time of the Mongol Empire led to greater contact between Europe and Asia.

VOCABULARY

khan
plunder
siege
khanate
typhoon
travelogue

The Mongol Empire

| 400 | 800 | 1200 | 1600 |

1200 – 1300

The Mongol people lived in a region of steppes in the part of central Asia that is now Mongolia. Like the people of the Arabian steppes, the Mongols were herders. They were best known, however, as skilled horse riders and warriors. In a very short time, the Mongols created a mighty empire.

Genghis Khan

The Mongols were nomads. They lived in small clans, moving from place to place as they grazed their animals. Fighting often broke out between the Mongol clans over grazing lands, water, and firewood. These were scarce resources in the Asian steppes. From time to time a strong leader, or **khan**, brought some of the clans together.

For hundreds of years, Mongolian herders lived in tentlike dwellings called yurts (left). Some herders still use yurts on the steppes (right).

LOCATE IT

CHINA

Mongolia

Even as a young man, Temujin (TEM•yuh•juhn) was among the fiercest Mongol warriors. Temujin was admired and feared for his ambition and skill. At a meeting of the Mongol clans in 1206, he was made leader of the Mongols. He took the name Genghis Khan (JENG•guhs KAHN), which means "Universal Leader."

Genghis Khan began to make conquests to live up to his name. In 1210 he led about 130,000 Mongol warriors into China. In 1215 they captured the capital city and renamed it Khanbalik (kahn•buh•LEEK).

Genghis Khan also pushed west of Mongolia into Muslim lands. In 1220 the Mongols first invaded what is today Iran. Before his death in 1227, Genghis Khan told his sons, "A deed is not glorious until it is finished." The sons of Genghis Khan took these words as an order and continued to expand the empire.

REVIEW What is the meaning of the name Genghis Khan?

The Empire Grows

Batu, one of Genghis Khan's grandsons, led a daring expedition into Europe in 1236. His Mongol army swept through parts of what are now Russia, Poland, and Hungary. Batu and his warriors **plundered**, or took goods by force, everywhere they went.

The Mongols were an almost unstoppable fighting force. They made surprise attacks and learned to strike quickly in large numbers. Mongol soldiers were among the most well-trained and disciplined soldiers of their time.

Mongol forces often killed the people in the places they conquered or sold them into slavery. As word of the Mongols' cruelty spread, many people became terrified of them. The Mongol invaders became known to Europeans as the Golden Horde. *Golden* was for the riches they stole, and *horde* meant "army."

The Mongol army was made up completely of cavalry, or soldiers on horseback. The army could therefore move quickly to defeat other armies on battlefields.

From their enemies, the Mongols learned how to capture cities and forts through siege. A **siege** is a military blockade of a city or fort to force it to surrender. Siege battles could last months or even years.

Over time, the Mongols claimed much of eastern, central, and western Asia. In 1256 they again invaded Iran. By 1258 they had pushed into what is today Iraq and conquered the city of Baghdad. Many of the lands once under Muslim control fell to the Mongols. By about 1260, the Mongols had created the largest empire the world had ever known. It reached from the shores of the Black Sea to the Pacific Ocean.

REVIEW How did the Mongol forces defeat their enemies? 🎯 SUMMARIZE

Kublai Khan

The Golden Age of the Mongol Empire

In 1260 another grandson of Genghis Khan became leader of the Mongol Empire. He took the title of Kublai Khan (KOO•bluh KAHN), or "Great Khan."

By 1260 the Mongol Empire was divided into **khanates**, or smaller regions that were much like states. The khanates were independent in some ways. Each had its own leader and government. All the khanates, however, remained loyal to Kublai Khan.

The Mongol Empire began to change under the rule of Kublai Khan. People in the khanates in western and central Asia continued to live much as the Mongols always had. In the khanates in eastern Asia, the Mongols began to take on Chinese ways. Kublai Khan set up his own capital, named Ta-tu, inside what is today the city of Beijing.

A CLOSER LOOK
Mongol Warriors

Mongol children learned to ride a horse before they learned to walk. Males who were the most skilled with horses served as soldiers in the Mongol army.

❶ An armor made of layers of leather protected each soldier.

❷ Soldiers rode well-trained horses that were able to make quick movements and reach high speeds.

❸ Besides a sword, an axe, and a dagger, a Mongol soldier often used a spear in battle.

❖ What other advantages would riding horses in battle give the Mongol soldiers?

Kublai Khan had several Chinese advisers. One of his advisers told him,

> **I have heard that one can conquer the empire on horseback, but one cannot govern it on horseback.**

Kublai Khan took this to mean that the Mongols would have to adopt some Chinese ways to govern China. For this reason, he acted and dressed as a traditional Chinese emperor.

The Mongols claimed the Mandate of Heaven in 1271, forming the Yuan (yoo•AHN) dynasty. The Mongols tried to control China and took measures to keep peace with the people. In many ways, the Chinese lived as they always had. Most were allowed to practice their own religions.

The Yuan dynasty brought the people of China together again under one government. Even so, many Chinese did not like being ruled by the Mongols. The Chinese had to pay high taxes, and the most important jobs were given to people who were not Chinese.

DEMOCRATIC VALUES
Individual Rights

Rule across the Mongol Empire was harsh. Yet, most Mongol leaders allowed the people within the empire certain individual rights. One important individual right was freedom of religion. While the Mongols had their own religious practices, they never tried to force them on those they ruled. People within the empire could practice their own religions. Allowing freedom of religion did provide an advantage for Mongol rulers. This freedom made it easier to keep peace within the empire. Mongol leaders such as Kublai Khan had a strong interest in different religions. Besides studying different religions, Kublai Khan sought advice from Buddhists, Christians, Muslims, and Daoists. He also supported the teachings of Confucius.

Analyze the Value

1. How was freedom of religion important as an individual right in the Mongol Empire?

2. **Make It Relevant** Read the Bill of Rights to the United States Constitution. Which amendment provides citizens of the United States with freedom of religion?

A Buddhist statue (above) from the Yuan dynasty

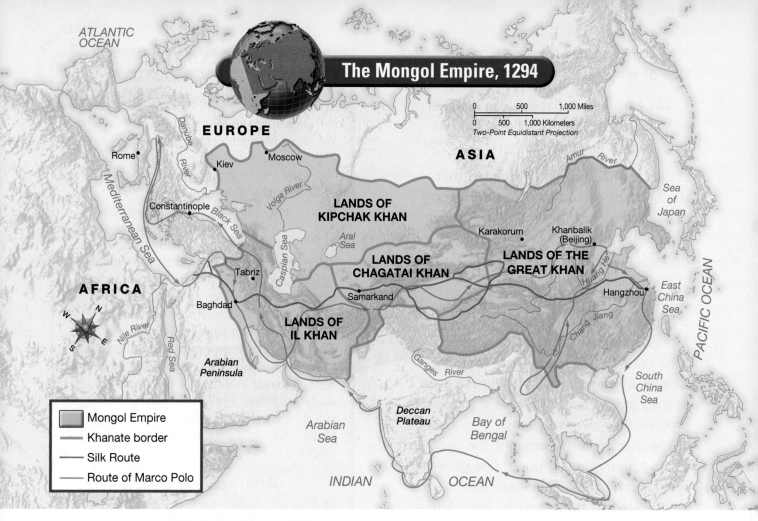

The Mongol Empire, 1294

ATLANTIC OCEAN

EUROPE

ASIA

AFRICA

Rome

Danube River

Kiev

Moscow

Constantinople

Black Sea

Volga River

Mediterranean Sea

Caspian Sea

Aral Sea

LANDS OF KIPCHAK KHAN

Tabriz

LANDS OF CHAGATAI KHAN

Karakorum

Khanbalik (Beijing)

LANDS OF THE GREAT KHAN

Amur River

Sea of Japan

Baghdad

Samarkand

Huang He

Hangzhou

East China Sea

LANDS OF IL KHAN

Nile River

Red Sea

Arabian Peninsula

Chang Jiang

PACIFIC OCEAN

Arabian Sea

Ganges River

Deccan Plateau

Bay of Bengal

South China Sea

INDIAN OCEAN

500 1,000 Miles
500 1,000 Kilometers
Two-Point Equidistant Projection

Mongol Empire
Khanate border
Silk Route
Route of Marco Polo

Regions In 1294 the Mongol Empire was made up of four main parts.

❓ Which was the largest part of the Mongol Empire?

Many improvements were made in China during Kublai Khan's rule. The Grand Canal was made longer, and roads were repaired. A mail service with more than 200,000 riders connected all parts of the empire. Merchants again felt it was safe to travel and trade.

Like earlier khans, Kublai Khan tried to extend the empire. His attempts to conquer Japan and parts of southeastern Asia were unsuccessful. In 1274 and 1281, Mongol warships on their way to Japan were destroyed by **typhoons**, huge storms with heavy rains and high winds. After invading parts of southeastern Asia, the Mongols were unable to keep the region under their rule.

REVIEW How did Kublai Khan change the Mongol Empire?

East and West

Kublai Khan made the Mongol Empire larger, and his strong rule brought peace to it. A stable government led to a time of increased trade. The Mongol Empire was soon part of a trade network with Europe and northern Africa. Soon ideas as well as goods were being exchanged between East and West.

One of the most famous visitors to the Mongol Empire was Marco Polo. At the age of 17, he set out for the lands of Kublai Khan with his father, Niccolò, and his uncle, Maffeo.

The Polos were from Venice, in what is now northern Italy. During this time Venice was a very powerful trading state in the

Mediterranean region. Niccolò and Maffeo were traders who had traveled to China earlier. When they decided to return to China in 1271, they took young Marco with them.

The Polos decided to make the long journey from Europe to Asia over land. After traveling for four years, they reached the summer palace of Kublai Khan in 1275, when Marco Polo was 21 years old.

Marco Polo was amazed by Chinese inventions such as gunpowder and the compass. He also held paper money for the first time. Marco, Niccolò, and Maffeo stayed in China for 16 or 17 years. They were guests of Kublai Khan and probably served as advisers to him. Marco was sent by Kublai Khan to explore and report on distant parts of the empire.

Marco Polo (right) and a description of his father and uncle's travels (far right)

Marco Polo returned to Europe in about 1295. His descriptions of Asia were collected in a book titled *Il Milione*, which means "The Million." The book soon became the most popular **travelogue**, or travel book, of his day. Marco Polo's book led even more Europeans to become interested in China and its riches.

The Mongols wanted to learn more about the lands from which Marco Polo had come. Rabban Bar Sauma of China traveled to Europe to visit kingdoms there. Everywhere he went, he gathered goods and wrote reports of what he saw.

The reign of Kublai Khan encouraged trade between Europe and Asia. Today the Mongol leader is remembered for bringing East and West together. Less than 100 years after his death in 1294, the Mongol Empire came to an end.

REVIEW What was *Il Milione*?

LESSON 3 REVIEW

Summary Time Line

1200	1250	1300

• **1227**
Ghengis Khan dies

• **1271**
The Mongols claim the Mandate of Heaven

• **1294**
Kublai Khan dies

 SUMMARIZE How did Marco Polo cause Europeans to have a greater interest in China?

❶ **BIG IDEA** How did the Mongol Empire affect people in Asia and in Europe?

❷ **VOCABULARY** What is the difference between **khan** and **khanate**?

❸ **TIME LINE** How many years after the death of Genghis Khan did Kublai Khan die?

❹ **HISTORY** By about what year had the Mongols created the world's largest empire?

❺ **GEOGRAPHY** Why were the Mongols unable to conquer Japan?

❻ **CRITICAL THINKING—Evaluate** How do you think claiming the Mandate of Heaven helped the Mongols govern China?

 PERFORMANCE—Make a Travelogue Research more details about the travels of Marco Polo. Imagine that you are traveling with him. Create your own travelogue, describing the people you meet and the places you visit. You may want to illustrate your travelogue with sketches and maps.

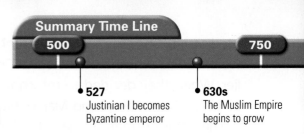

Summary Time Line

500   750

527
Justinian I becomes
Byzantine emperor

630s
The Muslim Empire
begins to grow

Summarize

Complete this graphic organizer to show that you understand how
to summarize key facts about the Byzantine Empire. A copy of this
graphic organizer appears on page 117 of the Activity Book.

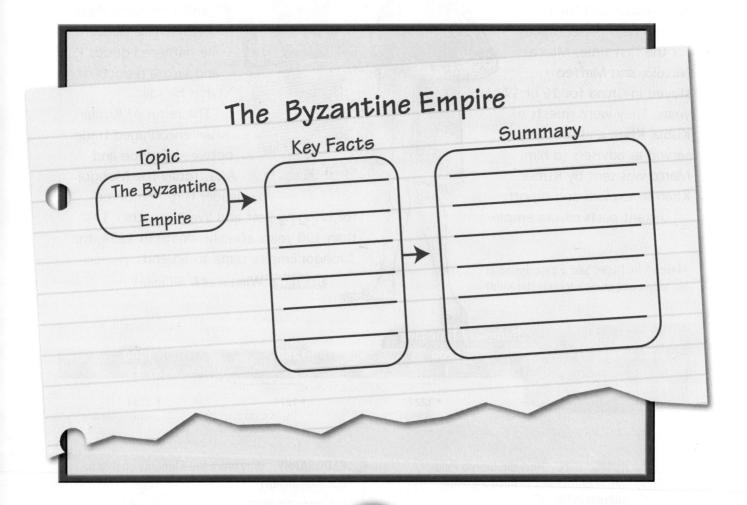

The Byzantine Empire

Topic	Key Facts	Summary
The Byzantine Empire		

THINK & WRITE

Write an Interview   Imagine that you are
a reporter. Your assignment is to interview
Marco Polo, who has recently returned from
the Mongol Empire. Make a list of questions to
ask him. Then write answers to those questions
as if Marco Polo were talking to you.

Write "Who am I?" Questions   Choose
a person introduced in the chapter. Write a list
of "Who am I?" questions that describe the
person you chose. Then exchange lists with
a classmate, and try to guess the person your
classmate has described.

1000	1250	1500

1054
The Christian Church splits

1260
Kublai Khan becomes
the Mongol emperor

1275
Marco Polo reaches
the summer palace of
Kublai Khan

1453
The Byzantine Empire ends

USE THE TIME LINE

Use the chapter summary time line to
answer these questions.

1 In what year did Kublai Khan become Mongol
emperor? *1260*

2 What happened in 1453? *Byzantine Empire ends.*

USE VOCABULARY

For each pair of terms, write a sentence or
two to explain how the terms are related.

3 **orthodox** (p. 414), **icon** (p. 415)

4 **Islam** (p. 421), **Muslim** (p. 421) *Islam is a religion and Muslim is the follower*

5 **mosque** (p. 425), **minaret** (p. 425) *Minaret is a mosque*

RECALL FACTS

Answer these questions

6 What was the Hippodrome? *Circus Maximus Horse race track*

7 What did Marco Polo describe in his
travelogue *Il Milione*? *The million.*

Write the letter of the best choice.

8 **TEST PREP** Which of these was *not* one
of Justinian I's accomplishments as Byzantine
emperor?

   A The Byzantine Empire grew to its greatest
   size during his rule.

   B He rewrote the empire's laws and gathered
   them into a set of three books called the
   Justinian Code.

   C He brought silkworm eggs into the Byzantine
   Empire, ending China's monopoly of the
   silk trade.

   D He and Theodora gave government jobs
   to people based on their ability, not their
   social class.

9 **TEST PREP** Which group captured
Constantinople in 1453 and ended the
Byzantine Empire?

   F the Mongols

   G the Eastern Orthodox Christians

   H the Ottoman Turks

   J the Roman Catholic Christians

10 **TEST PREP** All of these statements are
true about leaders of the Mongol Empire
except

   A Genghis Khan means "Universal Leader."

   B Kublai Khan means "Wise Leader."

   C Mongol forces were known as the Golden
   Horde.

   D Kublai Khan was Genghis Khan's grandson.

THINK CRITICALLY

11 What do you think was the most important
change Kublai Khan made as Mongol
emperor? *follow Chines custom*

12 How do you think Islam helped keep the
Muslim Empire strong? *united people.*

APPLY SKILLS

Determine Point of View

13 Reread the excerpt from
Theodora's speech on pages
418–419. What words does she use
that help you determine her point of view?

Compare Circle Graphs

Look at the circle graphs
on page 427 to answer the
following questions.

14 What percent of people practice Hinduism in
Indonesia?

15 Which country has a higher percent of people
who practice Christianity?

MALI MOSQUE, JENNÉ, MALI

Jenné is an ancient trading city that was founded in A.D. 1300 in the southern part of present-day Mali in western Africa. It lies on the flood plains of the Niger and Bani Rivers. By the 1700s Jenné was a center of Muslim learning. Today it is a small agricultural trading center with several examples of Muslim architecture.

LOCATE IT

ATLANTIC OCEAN

Jenné

MALI

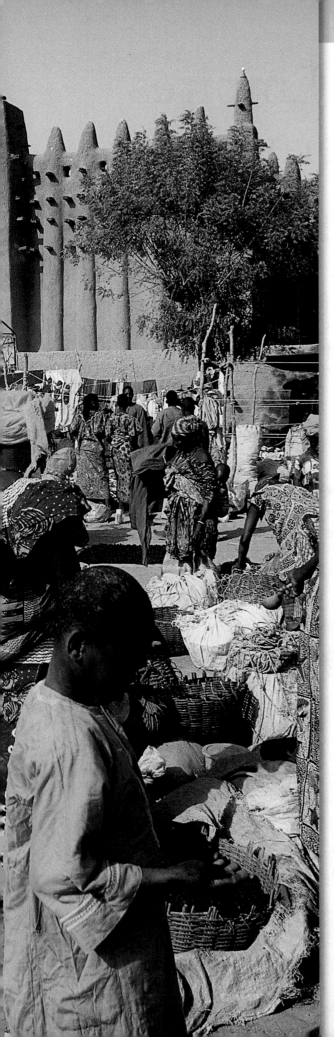

14

The Growth of Trade

❝Along a network of roads . . . flowed communications, tribute, and, above all, gold.❞

—LaVerle Berry, writer, describing trade routes in western Africa, 1995

 Generalize

When you **generalize,** you make a statement that summarizes a group of facts and shows how they are related.

As you read this chapter, make generalizations.

• **Use important facts to make generalizations about the growth of trade.**

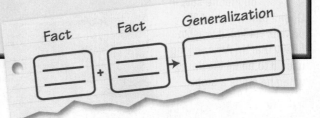

Fact   Fact   Generalization

Trading Empires of Western Africa

400   800   1200   1600

700 – 1600

Focus Skill

GENERALIZE

As you read this lesson, make generalizations about how trade affected the peoples of western Africa.

BIG IDEA

Empires based on trade developed in western Africa.

VOCABULARY

tariff

mansa

From earliest times, the peoples of Africa traded with one another. Trading networks developed in many parts of Africa. These networks linked up with Asian and European trade. In the A.D. 700s empires based on trade began to form in western Africa.

The Soninkes

During the A.D. 700s the Soninke (soh•NING•kay) people lived in what is today the western African country of Mali, along the fertile banks of the Niger River. The Soninkes farmed with iron tools and irrigated their crops with water from the Niger River.

A merchant from western Africa used this spoon (left) to weigh gold dust. Located on the Niger River, the town of Mopti in Mali is a center of trade in western Africa.

FAST FACT

A Muslim writer described a gold nugget he saw in Ghana that weighed 30 pounds (14 kg). It was so heavy that an African king used it to tie up his horse when he made a stop.

The Soninkes were also traders. The key to the Soninkes' success in trade was their location. Their lands were in the grasslands between the Sahara in northern Africa and the rain forests in central Africa.

Northern African merchants crossed the Sahara to trade with the Soninkes. These merchants carried salt and other goods, which they traded with the Soninkes for gold. The gold the Soninkes traded came from the kingdom of Wangara to the south.

The Wangaras needed salt and were willing to trade their gold for it. The Soninkes traded the salt they got from northern African merchants for gold from the Wangaras. They then traded the gold to the northern Africans for more salt.

The Soninkes profited at both ends of this trade cycle—from the northern African merchants and from the Wangaras. The growing wealth and power of the Soninkes led to the forming of an empire. The empire came to be known by the title of its rulers—*Ghana* (GAH•nuh), or "War Chief."

REVIEW How did the Soninkes build a powerful and wealthy trading empire?

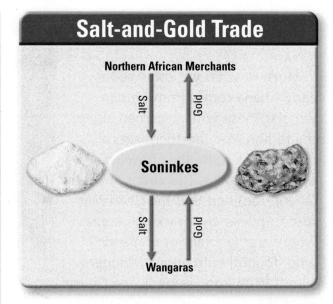

Salt-and-Gold Trade

Northern African Merchants

Salt

Gold

Soninkes

Salt

Gold

Wangaras

Analyze Diagrams The Soninkes were at the center of the salt-and-gold trade.

❖ Who ended up with the salt? Who ended up with the gold?

Ghana

Ghana was located between the Senegal and upper Niger Rivers in parts of what are now Mauritania and Mali. The Ghana Empire began to rise to power in the A.D. 700s. By 1000 it covered more than 100,000 square miles (260,000 sq km).

LOCATE IT

Niger River

A metal and wooden comb from western Africa

Much of what we know about early Ghana comes from Muslim writers. These writers learned about the region from northern African traders or because they traveled there themselves. The writer al-Zuhri (al•ZOO•ree) said that the Ghanaians rose to power by attacking peoples who were "ignorant of iron and who [fought] with ebony [wooden] clubs." With iron weapons, the Ghanaians were able to conquer other kingdoms.

To promote trade, the Ghanaian kings used the army to keep trade routes safe. To increase the empire's wealth, the kings charged **tariffs**, or taxes, on goods entering and leaving Ghana.

• HERITAGE •

Griots

Most western African societies had no system of writing. Their history, laws, religion, and customs were kept alive by people known as griots (GREE•ohz). The griots memorized all this information and passed it on to the next generation by word of mouth. After the northern Africans introduced reading and writing, western African scholars began to write down their history. Even so, the griots of western Africa continued to keep their people's history alive through the spoken word. They are remembered as Africa's storytellers and oral historians.

A griot from Senegal

The eleventh-century Muslim geographer al-Bakri (al•BAHK•ree) explained how the tariffs worked:

> **The king exacts [demands] the right of one dinar [an Arab coin] of gold on each donkey-load of salt that enters his country, and two dinars of gold on each load of salt that goes out.**

The tariffs provided money to feed the soldiers in Ghana's army and to support the empire's government.

Because regions rich in gold became part of the empire, the Ghanaian kings held a monopoly on the gold trade. As al-Bakri wrote, "All pieces of gold that are found in the empire belong to the king of Ghana." By claiming the gold for himself, the king made it difficult for others to buy and sell gold. This kept the price of gold high.

Much of the trading in Ghana took place in the capital, Kumbi-Saleh (KOOM•bee SAH•lay). Kumbi-Saleh was near one of the most important trade routes across the western Sahara.

Northern African merchants brought other goods besides salt to Ghana. They also brought horses, swords, glass, and wool clothing. They traded these goods for gold, ivory, cotton goods, animal skins, and slaves.

During the 1000s Ghana lost a war against one of its trading partners. After that, the power of the Ghana Empire began to weaken. By 1203 the empire had broken up into small kingdoms.

REVIEW How did Ghana's kings keep the price of gold high?

Analyze Primary Sources

This section of a map from the 1300s shows the great Mali Empire. The map is from the *Catalan Atlas*, a reference based on Muslim Sources.

❶ The buildings are symbols for cities.

❷ The lines on the map show the importance of a city. The important cities have more lines than others.

❸ The seated, crowned figure is Mansa Musa.

◈ What do you think the golden wall at the top of the map shows?

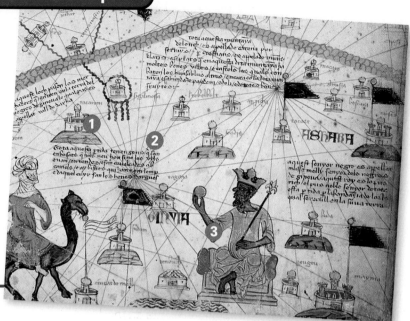

Growth of Islam in Western Africa

Merchants from northern Africa traded throughout western Africa. In the A.D. 800s they began to visit the kingdom of Kanem (KAH•nem), located along the shores of Lake Chad. Merchants also started coming to the trade centers of Jenné (jeh•NAY) and Gao (GOW) along the Niger River.

Contact with northern African merchants began to change the lives of western Africans. The northern Africans showed the western Africans how to use money instead of bartering. The use of money allowed western Africans to trade more easily.

Most of the merchants from northern Africa were Muslims. They spoke Arabic and practiced the religion of Islam. During the 1000s many people in western Africa began to accept Islam. Many of the African empires that rose after Ghana were based both on trade and on the religion of Islam.

REVIEW How did northern Africans change ways of life in western Africa? ◉ **GENERALIZE**

Mali and Mansa Musa

In about 1230 a new empire called Mali formed in western Africa. The people who founded Mali were called Malinkes (muh•LING•kayz). Under their Muslim leader Sundiata (sun•JAHT•ah), the Malinkes conquered many of the same kingdoms and cities that Ghana had once held. Like the Ghana Empire, Mali also became wealthy from the trade of gold and salt.

The Mali **mansas**, or rulers, who came after Sundiata won even more land. The Mali Empire grew to be nearly twice as large as the Ghana Empire had been. Mali's greatest growth came during the time of Mansa Musa, who ruled Mali from 1307 to 1332. Mansa Musa extended the empire to include the rich trading cities of Gao and Timbuktu (tim•buhk•TOO). This addition brought even more wealth to Mali.

In 1324 Mansa Musa made a pilgrimage, or religious visit, to the Muslim city of Mecca. All who saw him were amazed by his wealth.

A gold earring from Mali

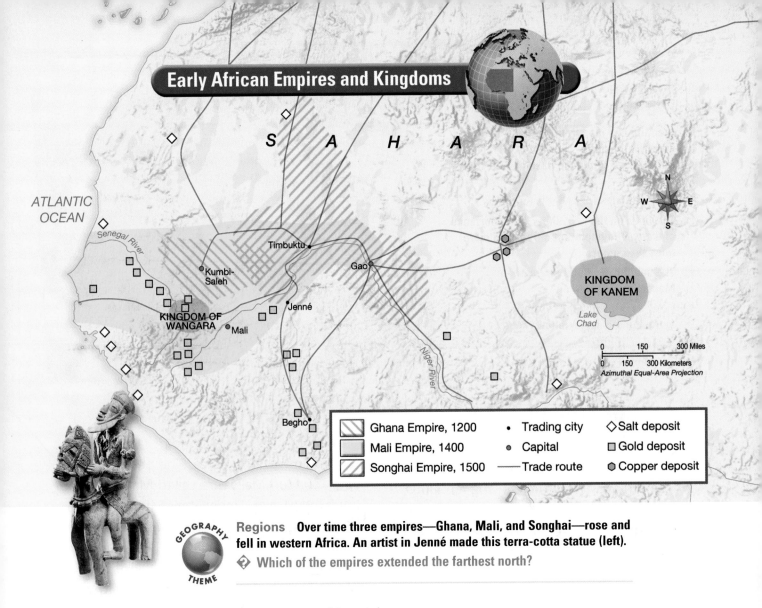

Early African Empires and Kingdoms

ATLANTIC OCEAN

SAHARA

Senegal River

Timbuktu

Gao

KINGDOM OF KANEM

Lake Chad

Kumbi-Saleh

Jenné

KINGDOM OF WANGARA

Mali

Niger River

Begho

▨ Ghana Empire, 1200	• Trading city	◇ Salt deposit
▢ Mali Empire, 1400	• Capital	▢ Gold deposit
▨ Songhai Empire, 1500	— Trade route	⬡ Copper deposit

0   150   300 Miles
0   150   300 Kilometers
Azimuthal Equal-Area Projection

GEOGRAPHY THEME

Regions Over time three empires—Ghana, Mali, and Songhai—rose and fell in western Africa. An artist in Jenné made this terra-cotta statue (left).

◈ Which of the empires extended the farthest north?

All along the way, Mansa Musa gave gold to almost everyone he met.

During Mansa Musa's rule, Mali became known as a center of learning. Mansa Musa invited Arab scholars to come to Mali to teach. After his pilgrimage, Mansa Musa had mosques built in Gao and Timbuktu. A university formed around the mosque at Timbuktu. Students from as far away as Arabia studied there.

Mansa Musa's pilgrimage helped make Mali known far and wide. The trading power of the empire grew. Later rulers, however, were unable to hold the empire together. After Mansa Musa's death, Mali's power began to weaken.

REVIEW Why did people come to Mali during the rule of Mansa Musa?

Songhai

As Mali weakened, another empire in western Africa developed. By the late 1400s much of what had been Mali had become part of the Songhai (SAWNG•hy) Empire. Like the earlier empires of Ghana and Mali, the Songhai Empire grew rich by controlling trade routes across the Sahara. The cities of Jenné, Gao, and Timbuktu were part of this empire as well. Along the Niger River, a fleet of war canoes guarded the trading centers from attacks. A large army of soldiers on horses protected the trade routes.

The Muslim traveler and geographer Leo Africanus (LEE•oh af•rih•KAY•nuhs) visited Songhai in the early 1500s. In Gao he found "rich merchants who travel constantly about the region with their wares [goods]." He saw that people were buying goods imported from Europe, Asia, and northern Africa.

Like Mali, Songhai became a center of learning. African writers published books in Arabic about Islamic law and western African history. Leo Africanus wrote that in Timbuktu "more profit is made from the sale of books than from any other merchandise."

Songhai's control of trade lasted only until the 1590s. In 1591 the ruler of Morocco in northern Africa sent a large army to attack Songhai. The Songhai soldiers fought with swords and spears, but their attackers had new weapons not known before in Africa. The Moroccans had guns, which they had gotten from southwestern Asia.

The people of Songhai could not defend themselves against these new weapons. After the Songhai Empire ended, the Saharan trade routes became less important. European ships sailing along Africa's Atlantic coast created new routes for western African trade.

REVIEW How did the Songhai rulers protect their empire?

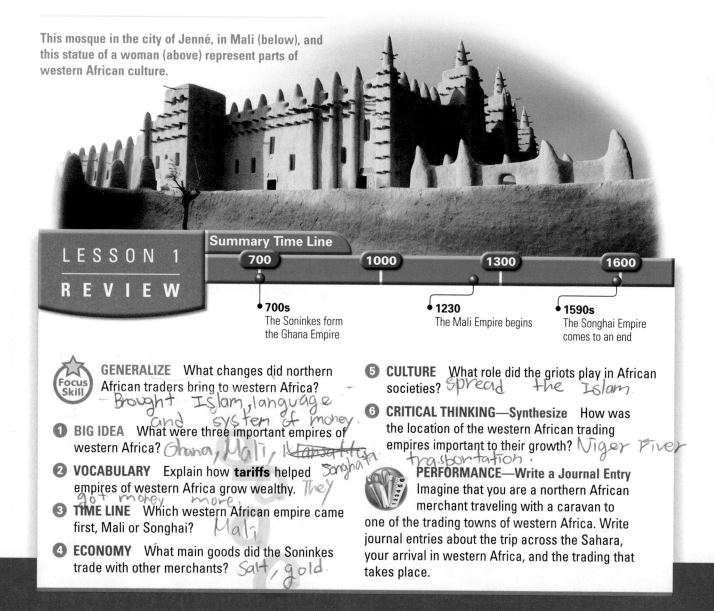

This mosque in the city of Jenné, in Mali (below), and this statue of a woman (above) represent parts of western African culture.

LESSON 1 REVIEW

Summary Time Line

| 700 | 1000 | 1300 | 1600 |

700s The Soninkes form the Ghana Empire

1230 The Mali Empire begins

1590s The Songhai Empire comes to an end

(Focus Skill) GENERALIZE What changes did northern African traders bring to western Africa? — Brought Islam, language and system of money.

1 BIG IDEA What were three important empires of western Africa? Ghana, Mali, Kabasattsa Songhai

2 VOCABULARY Explain how **tariffs** helped empires of western Africa grow wealthy. They got money more.

3 TIME LINE Which western African empire came first, Mali or Songhai? Mali

4 ECONOMY What main goods did the Soninkes trade with other merchants? Salt, gold.

5 CULTURE What role did the griots play in African societies? spread the Islam.

6 CRITICAL THINKING—Synthesize How was the location of the western African trading empires important to their growth? Niger River trasbortation.

PERFORMANCE—Write a Journal Entry Imagine that you are a northern African merchant traveling with a caravan to one of the trading towns of western Africa. Write journal entries about the trip across the Sahara, your arrival in western Africa, and the trading that takes place.

· SKILLS ·
MAP AND GLOBE

Read a Land Use and Product Map

VOCABULARY

land use
raw material

▶ WHY IT MATTERS

Have you ever wondered where the products that people buy are made? For example, people buy cereal at grocery stores, but where was that cereal made and where was the grain for it grown? To find the answers to questions like these, you might use a map that shows where products are made and how land is used.

▶ WHAT YOU NEED TO KNOW

The map on the next page is a land use and product map of western Africa. This is the same area where the ancient empires of Ghana, Mali, and Songhai were located.

Colors on the map show **land use**, or what is done with most of the land in a particular place or region. Study the map key to learn which color stands for each kind of land use.

The picture symbols on the map show some of the products produced in western Africa today. Study the map key to learn which symbol stands for each product. Many of the product symbols on the map are raw materials. **Raw materials** are natural resources that can be made into useful products. The map cannot show exactly how all the land is used in western Africa or every product made there. Instead, the map shows how the land is mainly used and the major products of the region.

▶ PRACTICE THE SKILL

Look at the map and map key to answer these questions.

1 What products are found near Dakar in western Africa?

2 What product is caught in the waters bordering western Africa?

These women harvest rice in the western African country of Senegal.

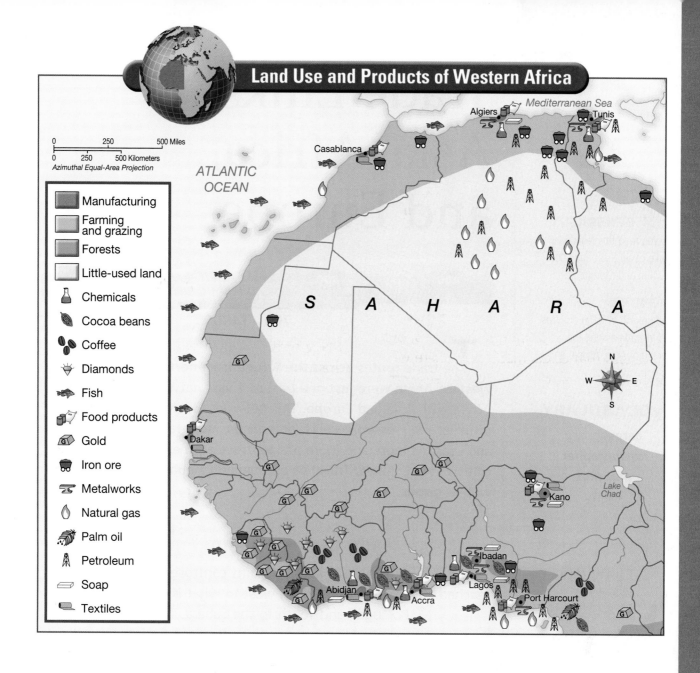

Land Use and Products of Western Africa

Manufacturing

Farming and grazing

Forests

Little-used land

Chemicals

Cocoa beans

Coffee

Diamonds

Fish

Food products

Gold

Iron ore

Metalworks

Natural gas

Palm oil

Petroleum

Soap

Textiles

3 Where is most of the little-used land on the map?

4 Where are most of the diamonds found in western Africa?

➡ **APPLY WHAT YOU LEARNED**

Use the information from the lesson to make a land use and products map of western Africa during the time of the early trading empires. Your map should cover the empires of Ghana, Mali, and Songhai, showing their major trading centers and products. After you have finished your map, compare it with the one above to see if any of the products on the two maps match.

Practice your map and globe skills with the **GeoSkills CD-ROM**.

2

GENERALIZE

As you read this lesson, make generalizations about Muslim and Mongol trade.

BIG IDEA

The growth of large empires led to trade among the people of Asia, Africa, and Europe.

VOCABULARY

caravansary
cartographer
passport
treaty

Trade Links Asia, Africa, and Europe

| 400 | 800 | 1200 | 1600 |

700 – 1400

The trade routes across the Sahara from northern Africa to western Africa were just one part of a vast network that linked Africa with Asia and Europe. This network covered thousands of miles and crossed deserts, grasslands, mountains, forests, and seas. As more and more people traveled these routes, many cultures were linked. Travelers exchanged languages and ideas as well as goods.

Trade in the Muslim Empire

By the end of the A.D. 700s, Muslims controlled lands that reached east to the Indus River, west to what is now Spain and Portugal, and south to the Sahara. The Muslim Empire included many peoples—Persians, Syrians, Egyptians, Berbers, and Spaniards, among others.

Over the next five centuries, the different peoples under Muslim rule came together as one culture. Many of these peoples became Muslims and learned to speak Arabic. The prophet Muhammad is reported to have said, "Whoever speaks Arabic is an Arab."

Roads connected places throughout the Muslim Empire. Many of these roads were built in earlier times by the Romans and the Persians. The Muslims repaired these roads and established new trade routes.

Painting of an Islamic pilgrimage, 1237

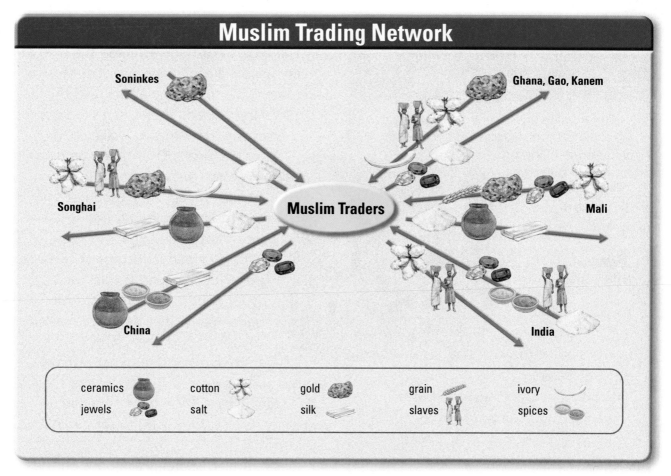

Muslim Trading Network

Soninkes

Ghana, Gao, Kanem

Songhai

Muslim Traders

Mali

China

India

ceramics	cotton	gold	grain
jewels	salt	silk	slaves

ivory

spices

Analyze Diagrams The Muslim traders exchanged goods with people in Africa and Asia. Traders sometimes stopped at caravansaries like the one below.

◆ From where did Muslim traders get gold? spices? ceramics?

On caravan routes in southwestern Asia and in Africa, Muslim merchants used the Arabian camel as their main form of transportation. Well suited for desert travel, this "ship of the desert" can go for four days without water. On a good day a camel caravan could walk about 25 miles (40 km) in ten hours. Every few days, the caravan needed to stop at an oasis to take on fresh water.

Desert travel was dangerous. A caravan could become lost or face huge sandstorms. Sometimes caravans were attacked, and their goods were stolen. The profits that merchants took in by crossing the deserts, however, made the dangers worth facing.

At the watering places along the most-traveled routes, inns called **caravansaries** (kair•uh•VAN•suh•reez) provided protection to travelers. The caravansaries had thick walls and windows with narrow slits, protecting travelers from bad weather and attackers.

REVIEW What helped connect the many peoples of the Muslim Empire?

GENERALIZE

POINTS OF VIEW
What Brought Success to Muslim Traders?

Historians have different opinions about the reasons for the success of the Muslim Empire. The following quotations from two historians show a difference in opinion:

JAMES SIMMONS

❝The domestication of the camel, not the invention of the wheel, liberated [freed] the early Arabs and allowed them to master the vast desert spaces and develop lucrative [profitable] trade routes. Great camel caravans . . . transported ivory, slaves, and exotic skins from . . . Africa, silks from India, and spices from southeastern Asia. ❞

FRANCIS ROBINSON

❝Muslim traders, making good use of the fortunate geographical position of the Islamic heartlands, came in the years before 1500 to control much of the international traffic along the trade routes of the world. These arteries formed natural channels along which Islamic influences flowed . . . non-Muslim trading partners often came to embrace Islam as well, in part because business was so much smoother if men shared a common culture and a common law. ❞

Analyze the Viewpoints

1 How do the two historians differ on how Muslim people became successful traders?

2 **Make It Relevant** Do some research to find out more about Muslim traders. Write a persuasive essay explaining why you think they were successful.

A Time of Cultural Exchange

The growth of trade affected the lives of many people living in and near the Muslim Empire. Gold, for example, changed the way the Muslims traded. The Muslims used gold from western Africa to make coins called dinars. Over time, the dinar became the standard coin for trade. Dinars were used not only in the Muslim Empire but also in the places that traded with the Muslims.

Trade helped industries of all kinds grow. Sugar, paper, textiles, and metal goods were produced for trade. Many cities became known for certain goods. The city of Damascus (duh•MAS•kuhs), in what is today Syria, became known for fabrics, glass, and fine steel blades. The city of Baghdad, in present-day Iraq, was famous for beautiful jewelry.

Ideas traveled as freely as goods on the trade routes. Muslim scholars studied works by scientists and philosophers of ancient Greece. By combining their own ideas with the ideas of the ancient Greeks, Muslim scholars made amazing discoveries. Their knowledge of astronomy, geography, mathematics, science, and medicine was among the most advanced of the time.

From trade with India, Muslims adopted the number system that we know today as Arabic numerals. Using this system, Muslim mathematicians developed the study of algebra, or *al-jabr* in Arabic. Algebra deals with the relationships among numbers. Algebra problems use letters, such as *x* and *y*, to label variables.

By observing the stars and planets, and by using the earlier writings of travelers and of explorers, skilled Muslim **cartographers** (kar•TAH•gruh•ferz), or mapmakers, drew maps with great accuracy. Their maps were used by people in Europe, Africa, and Asia.

This French engraving shows a scene from *The Arabian Nights*.

The Silk Road in Mongol Times

The Mongol invasions in the 1200s brought changes to Asia and Europe. The Mongols destroyed hundreds of cities and took many lives. However, when the Mongols began to govern the lands they conquered, they opened up many new trade opportunities. The Mongol government was often harsh, but it was also stable.

From the Chinese in the southeast to the Russians in the northwest, the Mongols ruled over peoples of many cultures. Under Mongol rule, warring peoples of the central Asian steppes were brought together. Mongol rule also made travel much safer along the trade routes between Europe and China. Merchants were given **passports**, or documents that gave them permission to travel, for use in the Mongol Empire.

Literature, too, owed much to the flow of ideas along the trade routes. Many of the stories in *The Arabian Nights* were originally from India and Persia. People in the Muslim Empire read Arabic poetry, essays, biographies, and tales. Through Arabic literature they also learned about Islamic history, law, and science.

The overland trade routes stayed under control of the Muslim Empire for many years. In the mid-1200s, however, the Muslim trading center of Baghdad was attacked and destroyed by the Mongols. After the destruction of Baghdad, the trade routes fell from Muslim hands until the Mongols later became Muslims.

REVIEW **What were some industries that trade helped to grow?**

During the twelfth century, the Muslim cartographer al-Idrisi drew this map of the world.

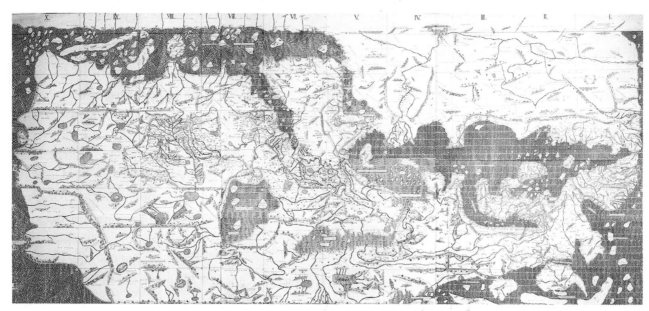

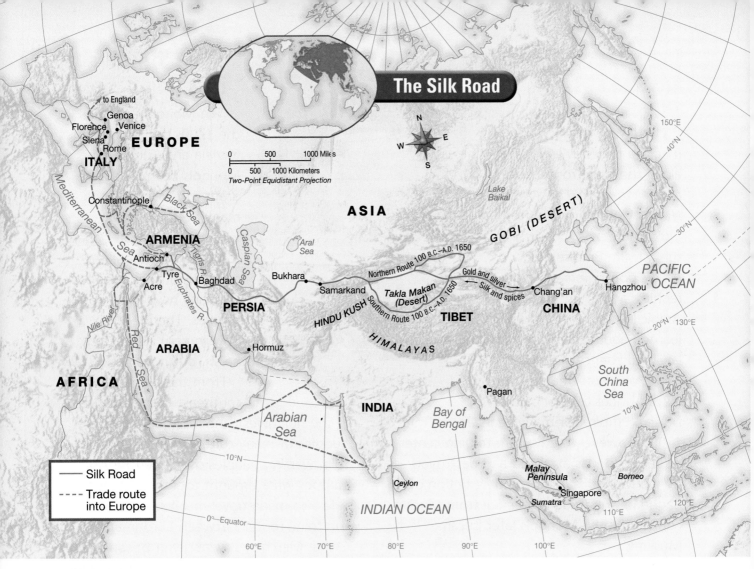

The Silk Road

to England
Genoa
Florence Venice
Siena
Rome EUROPE
ITALY

Mediterranean Sea

Constantinople Black Sea

ARMENIA
Antioch
Tyre
Acre Baghdad

Tigris R.
Euphrates R.

Nile River
Red Sea

AFRICA

ARABIA

PERSIA

Hormuz

Caspian Sea

Aral Sea

Bukhara

Samarkand

HINDU KUSH

Southern Route 100 B.C.–A.D. 1650

ASIA

Takla Makan (Desert)

HIMALAYAS

INDIA

Northern Route 100 B.C.–A.D. 1650

Lake Baikal

GOBI (DESERT)

Gold and silver
Silk and spices

TIBET

Chang'an

CHINA

Hangzhou

PACIFIC OCEAN

Arabian Sea

Bay of Bengal

South China Sea

Pagan

Malay Peninsula
Sumatra Singapore

Borneo

Ceylon

INDIAN OCEAN

— Silk Road
---- Trade route into Europe

0 500 1000 Miles
0 500 1000 Kilometers
Two-Point Equidistant Projection

Movement **The Silk Road provided a way into Asia for European merchants and travelers.**

❓ **Around what desert did the Silk Road split into two routes?**

The Silk Road was the route that merchants used to cross Asia. Marco Polo, his father, and his uncle traveled the Silk Road in the 1270s. When they returned to Europe with stories of China's riches, even more merchants set out for Asia on the Silk Road.

The Italian city-states of Genoa, Venice, Florence, and Siena all signed trade **treaties**, or agreements, with the Mongols. The

Italian city-states grew wealthy from trade on the Silk Road. Merchants such as Marco Polo traveled from the Italian city-states deep into the Mongol Empire to trade.

In the 1300s the Mongol Empire began to weaken, and civil war broke out. Travel along the Silk Road became dangerous again. Without a safe land route, Europeans began to depend more on sea routes to reach Asia.

REVIEW How did the Mongols affect trade along the Silk Road in the 1200s?

This Mongol passport (right) permitted travel through the Mongol Empire.

Trade in Southern Asia

Stories of the riches of India had been heard in southwestern Asia for centuries. One Muslim trader reported that "the Indian rivers are pearls, the mountains rubies, and trees perfumes." Such tales led Muslim traders from central Asia to begin exploring the lands of India.

Beginning in the early 1000s, Persian and Afghan Muslims pushed south through the high mountain passes of the Hindu Kush range. They conquered much of northern India. More Muslims went to northern India after the Mongols destroyed their cities in Persia and central Asia. Many goods began to flow back and forth across the mountains.

Gold, silver, precious jewels, perfumes, indigo, salt, and a scented wood called aloe were among the goods that left India. Horses and Chinese silk traveled south into India from central Asia. In addition to goods, slaves were carried in caravans going in both directions.

REVIEW **What were some of the goods that came from India?**

The painting (above) shows Mongol leader Genghis Khan and his officials meeting with Muslim travelers. Silver ax-shaped coins like this one (left) were used in the Mongol Empire.

LESSON 2 REVIEW

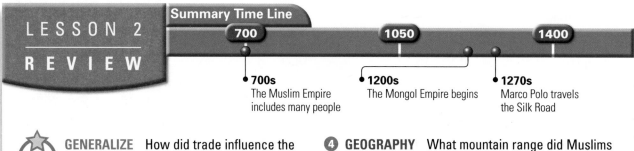

Summary Time Line

700 — **700s** The Muslim Empire includes many people

1050 — **1200s** The Mongol Empire begins

1270s Marco Polo travels the Silk Road

1400

GENERALIZE How did trade influence the lives of people living in the Muslim Empire?
religion , language

1 **BIG IDEA** How did the growth of the Muslim and Mongol empires lead to the trade of goods and ideas? *more ~~east~~ trades*

2 **VOCABULARY** Use the term **caravansary** to describe desert travel in Asia.

3 **TIME LINE** About how many years after the Mongol Empire began did Marco Polo travel the Silk Road?

4 **GEOGRAPHY** What mountain range did Muslims from central Asia cross to reach northern India?

5 **CRITICAL THINKING—Analyze** How did the exchange of goods lead to the exchange of ideas?

PERFORMANCE—Draw a Map Imagine that you have the job of choosing a land route from northern India to western Africa. Using an atlas or other references, make a physical map of Africa and southern Asia. Think carefully about landforms, and draw the route you would take. Explain your decision.

Make Economic Choices

VOCABULARY

trade-off
opportunity cost

▶ WHY IT MATTERS

In the previous lesson, you read about the growth of trade between Asia, Africa, and Europe. As trade grew, merchants had to make economic decisions. The governments within these regions at the time—especially ones that controlled trade routes—also had to make economic decisions.

Merchants had to decide with whom to trade goods. Often, by selecting one person to trade with, the chance to trade with someone else was lost. For example, if a Muslim trader from Persia decided to trade with merchants in western Africa, the chance to trade with merchants in India would be lost. In the same way, governments that decided to favor traders from one region might have lost the chance to trade with those of other regions.

▶ WHAT YOU NEED TO KNOW

When you make an economic choice, you decide to buy one thing instead of another. When you do this, you are making a **trade-off**—you give up one thing to get another. When you make an economic choice, what you decide to give up is known as an **opportunity cost**.

Many Muslim merchants gained prosperity through trade. This art shows a group of Muslim traders celebrating.

This student is buying a new stereo. By spending his money now, he makes the trade-off of not being able to spend that money in the future.

For example, suppose you have just finished playing soccer. You are hungry and thirsty, but you only have enough money to buy either a cold drink or a slice of pizza. If you decide to buy the pizza, the opportunity cost of your economic choice is the cold drink.

Making economic choices can be difficult. Use the following steps to help you think carefully before making an economic choice.

Step 1 **Determine the trade-off you will make.**

Step 2 **Determine the opportunity cost of deciding in favor of each of your choices.**

Step 3 **Decide which choice has the opportunity cost that you can most easily accept, and make your decision.**

▶ PRACTICE THE SKILL

Suppose that school officials are trying to decide whether to buy new computers or new playground equipment.

1 What is the trade-off?

2 If the school officials decide to buy new computers, what is the opportunity cost?

3 If the school officials decide to buy new playground equipment, what is the opportunity cost?

4 What choice would you make? Explain.

▶ APPLY WHAT YOU LEARNED

Write a journal entry titled "The Best Economic Choice I Ever Made." What was the trade-off you made? What was the opportunity cost of your decision? Why do you feel that you made the right economic choice?

GENERALIZE

As you read this lesson, make generalizations about travel and trade in the Indian and Pacific Oceans.

BIG IDEA

Ships traveling the Indian and Pacific Oceans linked peoples through trade and settlement.

VOCABULARY

lateen sail
dhow
junk
diplomat
outrigger
star path
archipelago

Ocean Trade

| 400 | 800 | 1200 | 1600 |

600 – 1500

Water routes opened new lands to trade. Merchants sailed the Indian Ocean to exchange goods at port cities. They also sailed along the Pacific coast of Asia, searching for new places to trade. Merchants also looked for new sources of gold, silk, ivory, and glass. A few daring explorers sailed into the open ocean to explore and settle lands.

From Baghdad to Guangzhou

"This is the Tigris," the Muslim caliph al-Mansur (al•man•SOOR) said in A.D. 762 when he chose Baghdad, on that river, as his capital. "There is no obstacle between us and China. Everything on the sea can come to us on it."

Baghdad did become "the harbor of the world." Boats from Baghdad sailed down the Tigris River to the deep harbor at Basra on the Persian Gulf. At Basra, merchants loaded their goods onto oceangoing ships. They then sailed out into the Indian Ocean, heading for eastern Africa, India, and China.

Merchants planned their voyages around the monsoons, or strong winds that reverse their direction with the changing

The city of Guangzhou (GWAHNG•JOH) in southeastern China is a busy port today (left) like it was in the time of early ocean trade (below).

seasons. Over the Indian Ocean, the winter monsoon blows from the northeast between November and April. The summer monsoon blows from the southwest between May and October.

Because of these steady winds, seagoing peoples along the Indian Ocean had developed the **lateen sail**. This triangle-shaped sail lets a boat or a ship travel into the wind. Arab boats, known as **dhows** (DOWZ), used lateen sails to travel east toward China when the northeast monsoon blew.

The merchants stopped first at Muscat, a trading port located at the tip of the Arabian Peninsula. About a month later, they arrived at the Malabar coast of southwestern India. By late winter, merchants had usually reached the Nicobar Islands in the eastern Indian Ocean.

When the summer monsoon began, southwest winds carried the dhows to Guangzhou, China's major port. After trading in Guangzhou, Arab merchants used the winter monsoon to sail home. They returned with goods from China, India, and the East Indies.

It took about 18 months to complete the entire trip. Arab merchants usually spent 6 months at home between trips, gathering more goods to trade. A new journey then began with the next winter monsoon.

REVIEW How did trade goods from Baghdad reach people in Guangzhou?

Indian Ocean Trade

Until the late 1400s, Arabs were the main traders on the Indian Ocean. However, other merchants also used the ocean trade routes. Jewish merchants from southwestern Asia used the routes to travel from the Persian Gulf to China. Indian traders sailed to ports along the eastern Indian Ocean.

A CLOSER LOOK
The Dhow

The dhow was a wooden boat with one or two sails. The boards it was made of were not held together with nails or wooden pegs, as on European ships. Instead, they were stitched together with cords made of coconut husk. Arab shipbuilders then spread a coating of oil, such as shark oil, over the boards to keep water out.

❶ Each mast supported an efficient triangle-shaped sail.

❷ A curved bow, or front, allowed the dhow to move easily through the water.

❸ The hold, or cargo deck, was the area that held the traders' goods.

❖ Why do you think a dhow had two masts?

Zheng He   About 1371–1435

Character Trait: Courage

Zheng He was born into a Muslim family. When he was about ten years old, the Ming dynasty gained control of China. Zheng He was captured during this time and sent into the army. By 1390 Zheng He had shown his courage in battle. He was selected by the emperor to lead naval expeditions for China. Zheng He first set sail in 1405 with 62 ships and 27,800 men. Over the next 30 years, Zheng He made six more voyages and visited places in southeastern Asia, India, the Arabian Peninsula, and northern and eastern Africa. He died in 1435. Zheng He is remembered as a courageous commander. His naval expeditions strengthened China's power in sea trade in southeastern Asia.

GO ONLINE

MULTIMEDIA BIOGRAPHIES
Visit The Learning Site at www.harcourtschool.com to learn about other famous people.

Starting in the A.D. 800s, Chinese traders sailed to places such as the Malay Peninsula in **junks**, large wooden ships with trapezoid-shaped sails that are strengthened with strips of bamboo.

In the 1100s the Chinese emperor Gao Zong (GOW ZAWNG) decided that getting into sea trade would improve China's economy. He said:

> 66 **Profits from maritime commerce [sea trade] are very great. If properly managed, they can amount to millions [in currency]. Is this not better than taxing the people?** 99

The government provided money to improve both harbors

A Chinese junk

and ships. By the 1200s the Chinese had the fastest ships in the South Pacific. They controlled the waters along the Pacific coast from Guangzhou to Korea and Japan. They had also started to control trade in the South China Sea and westward toward the Indian Ocean.

In the early 1400s Chinese traders began to travel even farther. Under the command of Admiral Zheng He (JUHNG HUH), Chinese ships visited what are now Thailand, Indonesia, Sri Lanka, the Arabian Peninsula, and the coast of eastern Africa.

Zheng He was not only a sailor but also a **diplomat**—a person skilled in developing treaties between nations. Zheng He spoke with leaders in the lands he visited about trading with China. This led to far-reaching trade networks.

REVIEW What did the Chinese do in the 1100s to support sea trade?

Trade Settlements in Eastern Africa

Because their journeys on the Indian Ocean were very long, Arab merchants started communities in some of the ports they visited. Arab settlements were started in Sri Lanka, parts of Indonesia and China, and eastern Africa.

The ways of life in these trading communities soon began to spread to the people living around them. Most Arab merchants were Muslims. Over time, many of the people living in and around the trading communities became Muslims. Some of the earliest Muslim communities started in the trading ports of eastern Africa.

Arab dhows had been sailing southeast from the Arabian Peninsula to the eastern coast of Africa since the A.D. 600s. Arab traders brought cloth, spices, and pottery to eastern Africa. They exchanged these goods for African gold, ivory, animal skins, and sometimes slaves.

Some Arab traders settled in eastern Africa and raised families. The trading ports in eastern Africa eventually grew into independent city-states.

This art shows a giraffe taken to China from Africa in 1419 by Zheng He.

By the 1300s there were as many as 40 trading ports along the eastern coast of Africa. They stretched from Mogadishu (moh•guh•DEE•shoo) in the north to Sofala (soh•FAH•lah) in the south. Reports of the great wealth of these cities brought the Chinese admiral Zheng He to eastern Africa in the 1400s. Among the interesting things he took back to China was something never before seen there—a giraffe.

REVIEW How did Islam spread in lands bordering the Indian Ocean? **GENERALIZE**

Out into the Pacific

Although the Chinese controlled coastal trade along the Asian coast of the Pacific, they did not sail eastward into the open ocean. Had they done so, they would have found people living on thousands of widely scattered islands.

The Pacific Islands had been settled centuries earlier by sailors who set out from the larger islands off the Asian mainland.

Buildings in the port city of Mogadishu, Somalia, in eastern Africa, show a Muslim influence in their architecture.

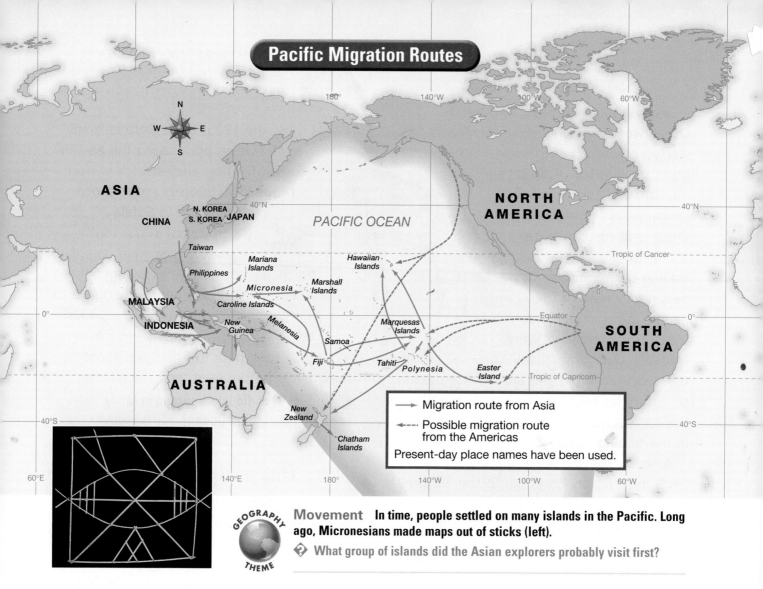

Pacific Migration Routes

ASIA

N. KOREA
CHINA   S. KOREA JAPAN   PACIFIC OCEAN

NORTH
AMERICA

Taiwan

Philippines   Mariana
Islands   Hawaiian
               Islands

Micronesia   Marshall
               Islands

MALAYSIA   Caroline Islands

INDONESIA   New   Melanesia   Marquesas
            Guinea   Islands

            Samoa

            Fiji   Tahiti   Polynesia   Easter
                                           Island

AUSTRALIA

SOUTH
AMERICA

New
Zealand

Chatham
Islands

Tropic of Cancer

Equator

Tropic of Capricorn

→ Migration route from Asia

◄---- Possible migration route
     from the Americas

Present-day place names have been used.

Movement In time, people settled on many islands in the Pacific. Long ago, Micronesians made maps out of sticks (left).

❖ What group of islands did the Asian explorers probably visit first?

As far back as 1500 B.C., seagoing people arrived in Melanesia (meh•luh•NEE•zhuh), or "the dark islands," northeast of Australia. Later generations pushed northward to Micronesia (my•kruh•NEE•zhuh), or "the small islands," and Polynesia (pah•luh•NEE•zhuh), or "the many islands," to the east, including New Zealand.

By about A.D. 800 these people had settled many islands in the Pacific. In doing so, one scholar wrote, they "achieved the greatest feats of maritime [ocean] navigation in human history."

The boats used by these people were small but well suited to ocean travel. **Outriggers**, or wooden frames placed on

People in present-day Polynesia paddle boats along the coast of a Pacific island.

each side, kept the boats from tipping over in rough seas. Large triangle-shaped sails called crab claws powered the boats. These sails, like lateen sails, allowed the boats to travel into the wind.

To navigate in the open sea, the Pacific Islanders used the sun and the stars. They also studied **star paths**, the paths the stars in the night sky seem to follow because of Earth's rotation. Some Pacific Islanders continue to use these navigation skills.

Traders regularly sailed among the many separate islands in an **archipelago** (ar•kuh•PEH•luh•goh),

a group or chain of islands. Archipelagos that were far from each other were soon linked by trade. This included the archipelagos of Tahiti and Hawaii, which are separated by nearly 2,400 miles (3,862 km) of ocean.

For the Pacific Islanders the vast ocean was "a highway, not a barrier." For centuries they had this highway all to themselves. Then, in the 1500s, European explorers entered the Pacific Ocean. Soon after, they began to take control of its waters.

REVIEW **What did the Pacific Islanders use to navigate in the open sea?**

A Maori necklace from New Zealand

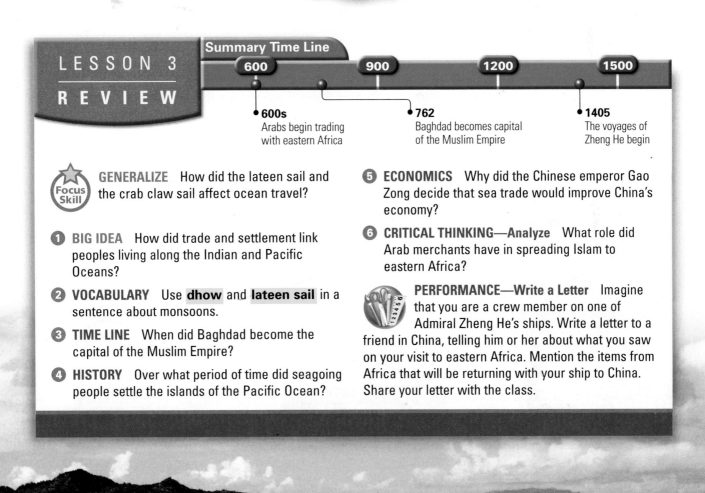

LESSON 3 REVIEW

Summary Time Line

| 600 | 900 | 1200 | 1500 |

600s Arabs begin trading with eastern Africa

762 Baghdad becomes capital of the Muslim Empire

1405 The voyages of Zheng He begin

Focus Skill **GENERALIZE** How did the lateen sail and the crab claw sail affect ocean travel?

1 **BIG IDEA** How did trade and settlement link peoples living along the Indian and Pacific Oceans?

2 **VOCABULARY** Use **dhow** and **lateen sail** in a sentence about monsoons.

3 **TIME LINE** When did Baghdad become the capital of the Muslim Empire?

4 **HISTORY** Over what period of time did seagoing people settle the islands of the Pacific Ocean?

5 **ECONOMICS** Why did the Chinese emperor Gao Zong decide that sea trade would improve China's economy?

6 **CRITICAL THINKING—Analyze** What role did Arab merchants have in spreading Islam to eastern Africa?

PERFORMANCE—Write a Letter Imagine that you are a crew member on one of Admiral Zheng He's ships. Write a letter to a friend in China, telling him or her about what you saw on your visit to eastern Africa. Mention the items from Africa that will be returning with your ship to China. Share your letter with the class.

4

European Sea Trade

Focus Skill **GENERALIZE**

As you read, make generalizations about European sea trade.

BIG IDEA

Groups competed to gain control of trade in the seas around Europe.

VOCABULARY

Greek fire
doge
Hansa
embargo

400   800   1200   1600

500 – 1500

For many centuries the Romans controlled the most important sea routes of Europe. The Mediterranean and Black Seas were both "Roman lakes," and Roman ships sailed along the Atlantic coast as far north as Britain. Over these bodies of water, goods moved back and forth throughout the Roman Empire. When the empire broke up, different groups struggled for control of trade on the seas around Europe.

Byzantine Trade

During the A.D. 500s the Roman emperor Justinian I brought the Mediterranean and Black Seas under Byzantine rule. The capital of the Byzantine Empire, Constantinople, was located between the two seas. "Into her harbors sailed expectantly the vessels of the world's trade," a poet of the time wrote.

Byzantine trade reached far beyond the Mediterranean and Black Seas. Merchants followed land routes to China. Byzantine ships sailed south from Egypt through the Red Sea and across the Indian Ocean to India. Other ships crossed the Black Sea and sailed the

Byzantine glass

Chinese pottery

Russian silver

Dnieper (NEE•per) River to trade with the people of Kiev (KEE•ef) in what is now Ukraine.

Merchants on these routes returned to Constantinople with goods. Furs, salt, wax, and honey came from Kiev. From India and China came pottery, spices, and jewels.

A deadly, secret weapon called Greek fire helped the Byzantine navy control the seas. **Greek fire** was a chemical mixture that burst into flames when it was ignited. With Greek fire, the navy could quickly turn enemy ships into "blazing wrecks."

REVIEW **What route did Byzantine ships take to reach Kiev?**

One shot of Greek fire from a Byzantine ship could set another ship on fire.

Muslim Trade in the Mediterranean

When the Muslim Empire expanded in the A.D. 600s and 700s, the Muslims tried to take control of Mediterranean trade. In 649, Muslims seized the island of Cyprus in the eastern Mediterranean. Later, Muslims from northern Africa and Spain took over the islands of Crete and Sicily.

From these three islands, Muslims were able to protect their trade ships. This kept the western link of their trade network safe. At the time, the Muslim trade

network reached all the way from Spain to China.

In the late A.D. 900s the Byzantine Empire took back Cyprus and Crete. All merchants in the empire were ordered to stop selling wood and iron to Muslim traders. Byzantine leaders hoped that this would stop Muslims from building new trading ships.

Merchants in the Italian cities of Amalfi and Venice paid no attention to the order. These cities had grown rich by trading with the Muslims. Amalfi and Venice were both far from Constantinople. Neither city wanted to lose the wealth gained from trading with Muslims.

REVIEW **Why did Muslims take control of certain Mediterranean islands?**

Chinese jug

Byzantine bowl

Silver cup found in Russia

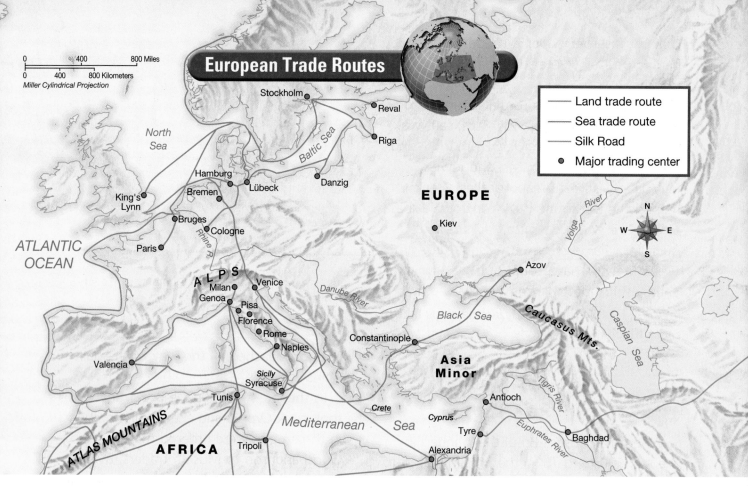

European Trade Routes

0   400   800 Miles
0   400   800 Kilometers
Miller Cylindrical Projection

Legend:
— Land trade route
— Sea trade route
— Silk Road
● Major trading center

Labels on map: Stockholm, Reval, Riga, North Sea, Baltic Sea, Hamburg, Lübeck, Danzig, EUROPE, Bremen, King's Lynn, Kiev, Bruges, Cologne, Volga River, ATLANTIC OCEAN, Paris, Rhine R., ALPS, Milan, Venice, Azov, Genoa, Danube River, Pisa, Florence, Black Sea, Caucasus Mts., Rome, Constantinople, Naples, Caspian Sea, Valencia, Asia Minor, Tigris River, Sicily, Syracuse, Antioch, Tunis, Crete, Cyprus, Euphrates River, Mediterranean Sea, Tyre, Baghdad, Tripoli, AFRICA, Alexandria, ATLAS MOUNTAINS

Movement European merchants traveled by land and water to trading centers throughout Europe, northern Africa, and southeastern Asia.

❖ What kind of routes were traders from Naples most likely to use?

GEOGRAPHY THEME

Viking Descendants

In northern Europe, the Vikings began to settle and trade in lands outside Scandinavia. Vikings from Sweden settled on the Baltic shores of present-day Latvia in eastern Europe and inland along the Dnieper and Volga Rivers. These Vikings became known as the Rus (ROOS).

Stories of the Rus and their trading spread. The Muslim geographer Ibn Rustah noted during the A.D. 900s that the Rus "trade in sable and squirrel skins . . . selling them to those who will buy from them."

Danish Vikings took control of parts of England and France. Viking settlers in France became known as Normans. In the 1000s the Normans of France began a territorial expansion, or adding of lands to their territory.

In 1066 the Normans crossed the English Channel and conquered England. Other Normans set up a kingdom in Sicily and southern Italy. As the Normans grew stronger, they also began to compete for trade across the Mediterranean Sea.

REVIEW Who were the Rus and the Normans?

William the Conqueror became the first Norman king of England.

The Rise of the Italian City-States

Venice, as an eleventh-century document said, was a city-state "that does not plow, sow, or gather vintage [grape crops]." Instead, the Venetians "buy grain and wine in every port." Trade was the most important activity in Venice. Merchants bought goods from western Europe and sold them in the Mediterranean ports of the Muslim and Byzantine Empires.

Ships from Italy carried linen, cotton, jewels, perfumes, and spices south across the Mediterranean. The ships returned with leather goods, animal skins, grain, and other items for further trade.

The Italian port cities acted as independent city-states, without ties to a larger government. Some of the Italian ports, such as Genoa and Pisa, formed strong ties with the Muslim ports of Tunis, Tripoli, and Alexandria.

When the Normans came to the Mediterranean, the Venetians fought against them. As a reward, the Byzantines allowed Venetian traders to carry goods through Constantinople without paying taxes. Soon, the Venetians extended their trading voyages into the Black Sea.

Later, however, the Venetians changed sides and turned against the Byzantines.

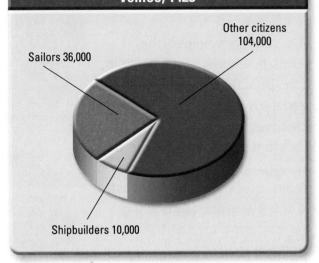

Sea-Related Industry
Venice, 1423

Other citizens 104,000

Sailors 36,000

Shipbuilders 10,000

Analyze Graphs Venice's location on the Adriatic Sea made it an important sea-trade center.

◆ About what percent of citizens were sailors or shipbuilders?

This oil painting by Antonio Canaletto shows the port of Venice.

Venetian ducat (top right)
Florentine florin (bottom right)

The Venetians helped the Normans end Byzantine rule in Italy. In 1204 the **doge** (DOHJ), or leader, of Venice told crusaders on their way to the Holy Land to attack Constantinople. After three days of fighting, the city surrendered. Venice quickly took over most of the Byzantine lands along the eastern shores of the Mediterranean.

Venice now controlled the important trading routes in the eastern Mediterranean and in the Black Sea. Genoa still controlled trade in the western Mediterranean until it was defeated by Venice in 1381.

As Venice grew in power, inland city-states, such as Milan and Florence, also started to trade. In 1252 Florence and other city-states began making their own gold coins. Soon Florentine florins and Venetian ducats replaced the Arab dinars as the coins used for trade in Mediterranean lands.

The Italian city-states, with Venice in the lead, held a monopoly on trade in the Mediterranean for more than 200 years. Then, in 1453, Constantinople was captured by the Ottoman Turks. The eastern Mediterranean and the Black Sea then became Turkish waters.

Most of the trade routes to Asia became unsafe for Europeans to use. Some European countries sent explorers out into the Atlantic Ocean to look for a new route to Asia. These voyages set the stage for a time of worldwide exploration by Europeans.

REVIEW How was trade affected by the fall of Constantinople? **Focus Skill** GENERALIZE

The Hanseatic League

European merchants faced many problems. They were taxed at many ports and cities in which they stopped. They were not always well protected, which left them open to attacks at sea and on land.

In the early 1200s some merchants in northern Europe decided to protect themselves by working together. They formed trade groups called **Hansas** (HAN•suhz). Hansa members shared the costs of trading.

The "Great Crane of Danzig" helped people move heavy cargo at the town of Bruges in northern Europe.

466 ▪ Unit 6

For example, all Hansa members would pay for the rental of ships, or for the hiring of guards to protect trade caravans.

Around 1240 the Hansas of the German ports of Lübeck and Hamburg signed a treaty. In the treaty they agreed to protect each other's merchants. Over the next century the merchants of about 200 towns in northern Europe joined this Hanseatic League.

The members of the Hanseatic League were not like the city-states that wanted trade monopolies in the Mediterranean and Black Seas. They were not interested in taking over one another's lands.

Sometimes the league went to war to protect its members and to gain new trade agreements. Usually the league used **embargoes**, or bans on trade, to get the trade agreements it wanted.

The Hanseatic League controlled trade in both the North Sea and the Baltic Sea for more than 100 years. Then, during the 1400s, trade began to shift to ports on the Atlantic Ocean.

REVIEW **Why was the Hanseatic League formed?**

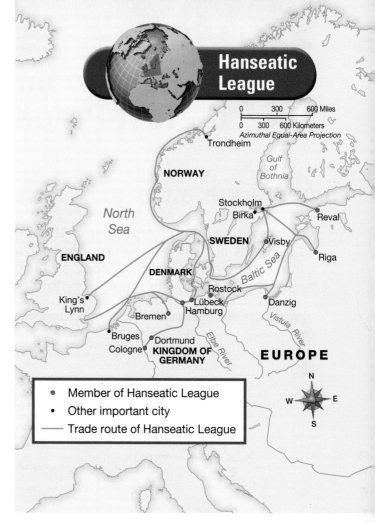

Hanseatic League

Movement **Trade routes connected towns in the Hanseatic League.**

❓ **What might have happened to Riga if it had not joined the league?**

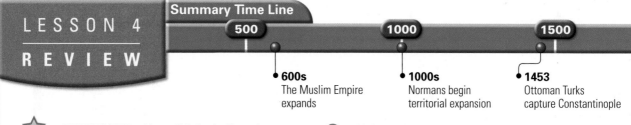

LESSON 4
—————
R E V I E W

Summary Time Line

500   1000   1500

600s
The Muslim Empire expands

1000s
Normans begin territorial expansion

1453
Ottoman Turks capture Constantinople

GENERALIZE How did the Italian city-states become leaders of trade?

1 **BIG IDEA** How did different groups gain control of trade in the seas around Europe?

2 **VOCABULARY** Explain how the **Hansas** used **embargoes** to make trade treaties.

3 **TIME LINE** Which people expanded their territory first, the Muslims or the Normans?

4 **GEOGRAPHY** What made Constantinople's location good for trade?

5 **ECONOMICS** Why did florins and ducats replace dinars in Mediterranean lands?

6 **CRITICAL THINKING—Synthesize** Why do you think that about 200 European towns joined the Hanseatic League?

PERFORMANCE—Make a Presentation
Imagine that you are a leader of the Hanseatic League. You want to get more towns to join the league. Create a presentation that tells the advantages that trade towns would gain by becoming league members.

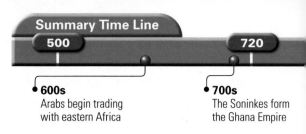

Summary Time Line

500

720

600s
Arabs begin trading
with eastern Africa

700s
The Soninkes form
the Ghana Empire

14 Review and Test Preparation

Generalize

Complete this graphic organizer to show that you understand how to use facts and details to make generalizations about the trading empires of western Africa. A copy of this graphic organizer appears on page 126 of the Activity Book.

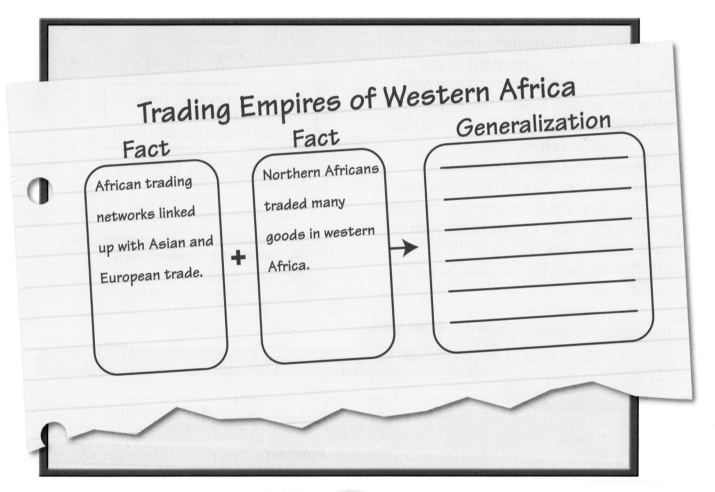

Trading Empires of Western Africa

Fact + **Fact** → **Generalization**

African trading networks linked up with Asian and European trade.

Northern Africans traded many goods in western Africa.

THINK & WRITE

Write a Speech   Imagine that you are trade adviser to one of the groups described in this chapter. Propose to your group's leaders that their empire do all of its trade either by land or by sea. Which do you think is better? Give reasons to support your advice.

Write a "Packing for a Journey" List
Write a list of at least ten items that you might pack if you were traveling with a group of traders along the Silk Road. Next to the name of each item, write a sentence explaining why you would pack that item.

940	1160	1380	1600

1000s
The Normans begin
territorial expansion

1230
The Mali Empire begins

1240s
The Hanseatic League
is formed

Late 1400s
The Songhai Empire begins

1591
Moroccans defeat
the Songhai Empire

USE THE TIME LINE

Use the chapter summary time line to answer these questions.

1 When did the Ghana Empire form?

2 Did the Hanseatic League form before or after the Normans began territorial expansion?

USE VOCABULARY

Use one of the terms in the box to complete each sentence.

tariffs (p. 442)
cartographers (p. 450)
passports (p. 451)
star paths (p. 461)
embargoes (p. 467)

3 Pacific Islanders studied the sun, the stars, and _____ to help them navigate in the sea.

4 People in Europe, Africa, and Asia used maps made by the Muslim Empire's expert _____.

5 Merchants received _____, documents that gave them permission to travel through the Mongol Empire.

6 Ghana's leaders charged taxes, or _____, on goods that passed through their empire.

7 League members used _____, or bans on trade, to get the trade agreements they wanted.

RECALL FACTS

Answer these questions.

8 What did Muslim traders call "the ship of the desert"?

9 What do the names Melanesia, Micronesia, and Polynesia mean?

10 **TEST PREP** Which of the following trading centers was the most powerful of the Italian city-states?

A Florence
B Genoa
C Milan
D Venice

11 By what name did Vikings from Denmark who settled in France become known?

F the Franks
G the Rus
H the Latvians
J the Normans

THINK CRITICALLY

12 Why do you think Baghdad was known as "the harbor of the world"?

13 Why did seagoing traders plan their trips around monsoon winds?

APPLY SKILLS

Read a Land Use and Product Map

14 Look at the land use and product map of western Africa on page 447. Which parts of the region are used mostly for manufacturing? Which areas do you think are probably the most heavily populated? Explain your answer.

Make Economic Choices

15 Think of a time when you made the choice to buy one thing rather than another. What was the opportunity cost of your decision?

VISIT The Silk Road

GET READY

During the A.D. 1200s, traders began to travel a route linking Europe with Asia. Because China's major export was silk, the route became known as the Silk Road.

Merchants from Asia traveled 4,000 miles (6,400 km) along the Silk Road from Chang'an in China to the Byzantine Empire to exchange riches such as silk, gold, and jade. Merchants from Europe also used the route to cross Asia and trade their goods for others along the way.

Trading continues today along parts of this historic route. Tourists and merchants still travel to many trading centers along the Silk Road.

WHAT TO SEE

Travelers along the Silk Road can see the doorway of a ruined caravansary near the city of Khiva, Uzbekistan, in western Asia.

Visitors to Tashkent, Uzbekistan, can buy and trade at a large spice market.

LOCATE IT

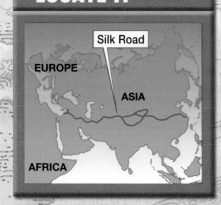

Silk Road

EUROPE

ASIA

AFRICA

Merchants in Kashgar, in western China, sell colorful fabrics (above) and fresh fruit (below).

A camel caravan crosses the Takla Makan desert in western China.

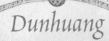

Kashgar

TAKLA MAKAN DESERT

Dunhuang

Chang'an

Visitors to the Magao Caves in Dunhuang, China, can see Buddhist statues, carvings, and wall paintings from as early as the A.D. 500s.

TAKE A FIELD TRIP

GO ONLINE

A VIRTUAL TOUR
Visit The Learning Site at www.harcourtschool.com to take virtual tours of historic sites.

CNN Turner Le@rning

A VIDEO TOUR
Check your media center or classroom library for a videotape tour of a city on the Silk Road.

6 Review and Test Preparation

Write a Description Look closely at each picture, and read the captions to help you review Unit 6. Then write a description of each picture, and tell how it relates to the social studies ideas presented in this unit.

USE VOCABULARY

Identify the term that correctly matches each description.

monopoly (p. 413)

steppe (p. 420)

Qur'an (p. 421)

caravansary (p. 449)

archipelago (p. 461)

Greek fire (p. 463)

1 an explosive powder that Byzantines used in naval battles

2 complete control of a certain product or kind of trade

3 a chain or group of islands

4 dry land where only some grasses and plants grow

5 an inn offering shelter to traveling traders and their animals

6 the holy book of Islam

RECALL FACTS

Answer these questions.

7 What was the Silk Road?

8 What happened to the Christian Church in 1054?

9 Why were Mongol invaders called the Golden Horde?

Write the letter of the best choice.

10 **TEST PREP** Marco Polo wrote about his travels through what empire?
A the Byzantine Empire
B the Muslim Empire
C the Mongol Empire
D the Gupta Empire

11 **TEST PREP** Who was the founder of Islam?
F Genghis Khan
G Mecca
H Muhammad
J Qur'an

Visual Summary

400 ———————————————— 800

527 Justinian becomes Byzantine emperor p. 412

700s Trade empires begin to form in western Africa p. 440

750 The Muslim Empire stretches into Africa, Asia, and Europe p. 422

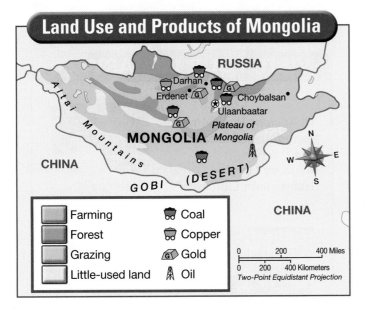

Land Use and Products of Mongolia

RUSSIA

Darhan
Erdenet
Choybalsan
Ulaanbaatar

MONGOLIA
Plateau of
Mongolia

CHINA

GOBI (DESERT)

CHINA

Altai Mountains

Farming
Forest
Grazing
Little-used land

Coal
Copper
Gold
Oil

0   200   400 Miles
0   200   400 Kilometers
Two-Point Equidistant Projection

12 TEST PREP Of what empire were
Justinian I and Theodora leaders?
A the Byzantine Empire
B the Ottoman Empire
C the Muslim Empire
D the Mongol Empire

13 TEST PREP In what part of the world did
great empires grow based on the trading of
gold and salt?
F Africa
G Asia
H Europe
J the Pacific Islands

THINK CRITICALLY

14 For what reasons might people abandon one
trade route for another?

15 What was unusual about the way the
Hanseatic League solved its trade problems?

APPLY SKILLS

Read a Land Use and Products Map

Use the map on this page to
answer the questions.

MAP AND GLOBE SKILLS

16 Where in Mongolia are coal deposits mainly
located?

17 Does Mongolia have more coal deposits
or copper deposits? How can you tell?

18 For what is most of the land in Mongolia
used?

19 What mineral can be found near Erdenet,
Mongolia?

20 Does Mongolia have large areas of
manufacturing? How can you tell?

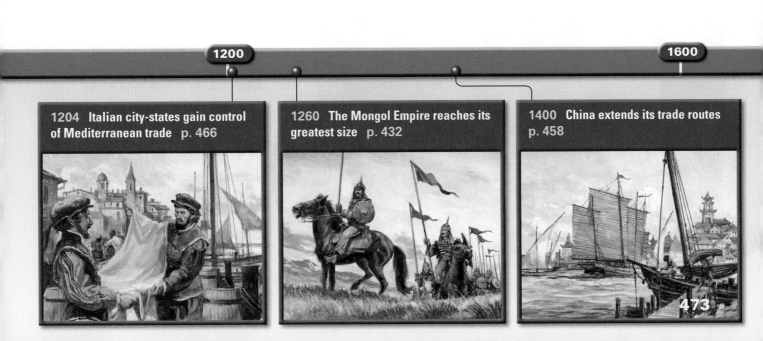

1200

1600

**1204 Italian city-states gain control
of Mediterranean trade** p. 466

**1260 The Mongol Empire reaches its
greatest size** p. 432

1400 China extends its trade routes
p. 458

473

Unit Activities

GO ONLINE Visit The Learning Site at www.harcourtschool.com for additional activities.

Make a Safety Poster

Use library or Internet resources to find out more about monsoons. What are the different kinds? In what directions do they move? What should you do or not do during one? Make a safety poster that includes descriptions of the monsoons and of what you should or should not do during a monsoon.

Draw a Map

Choose a land or water trade route described in this unit, and draw a map of the route. Include information about the route's beginning and end points, the goods a trader might buy or sell along the way, problems the trader might encounter, and land regions or bodies of water on the route.

VISIT YOUR LIBRARY

■ *Ancient West African Kingdoms: Ghana, Mali, & Songhai* by Mary Quigley. Heinemann Library.

■ *Science in Early Islamic Cultures* by George Beshore. Franklin Watts.

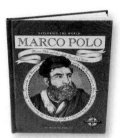

■ *Marco Polo and the Silk Road to China* by Michael Burgan. Compass Point Books.

COMPLETE THE UNIT PROJECT

Make a Travel Guide Work with a group of classmates to complete the unit project—a travel guide about a region you read about in the unit, such as the Mongol Empire. In this travel guide, include information about the region's people, cultures, and landforms. Also include information about historic sites you think people might want to visit. Illustrate your travel guide with your own drawings or with pictures from magazines.

474 ■ Unit 6

The Early Modern World

Medici family shield, Italy, early 1600s

Santa Maria del Fiore, the Cathedral or Duomo of Florence, Italy

The Early Modern World

"*Ancora imparo.*" (I am still learning)

—Motto of Michelangelo Buonarroti (1475–1564)

Preview the Content

Scan the pictures in each chapter and lesson to create a list of topics you will learn about in the unit.

Preview the Vocabulary

Multiple Meanings   A word can have several meanings. Use a dictionary to look up each word in the chart below. Write two dictionary definitions for each word. As you read, check to see if any of your definitions match the definitions in the unit. If not, add definitions from the unit to the chart.

VOCABULARY WORD	MEANING 1	MEANING 2	MEANING IN THE UNIT
Reformation	_____	_____	_____
miniature	_____	_____	_____
projection	_____	_____	_____

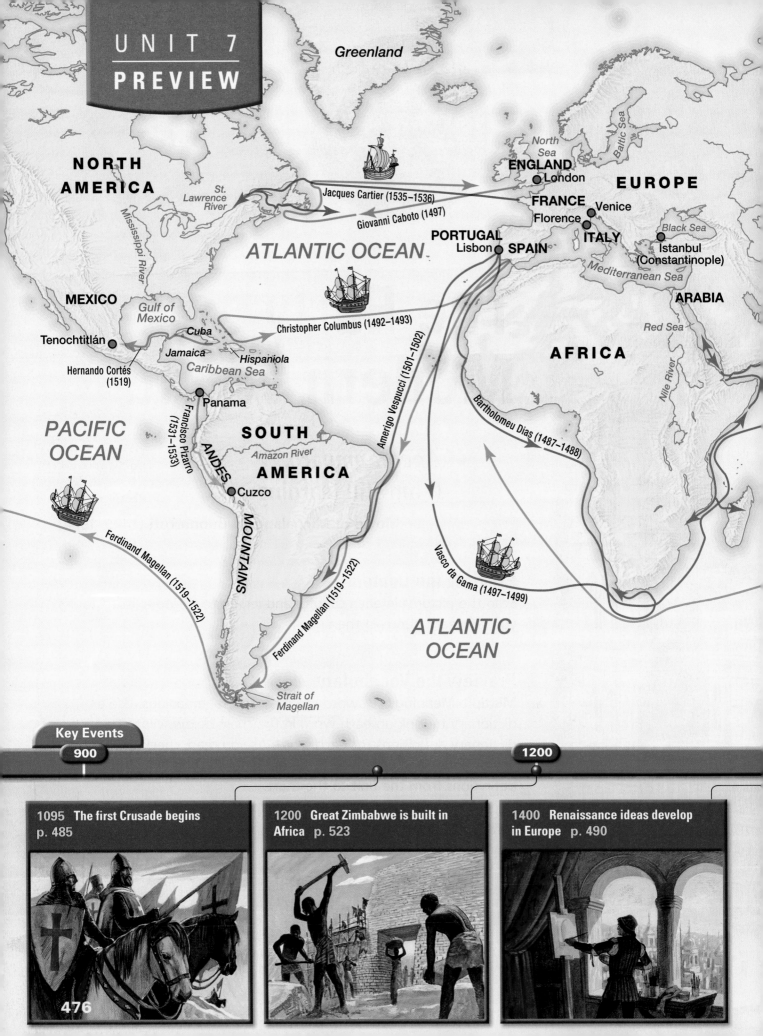

Greenland

NORTH AMERICA

St. Lawrence River

Mississippi River

ATLANTIC OCEAN

Jacques Cartier (1535–1536)

Giovanni Caboto (1497)

North Sea

Baltic Sea

ENGLAND ● London

EUROPE

FRANCE ● Venice

Florence

PORTUGAL **ITALY**

Lisbon ● **SPAIN**

Black Sea

● Istanbul (Constantinople)

Mediterranean Sea

MEXICO

Gulf of Mexico

● Tenochtitlán

Hernando Cortés (1519)

Cuba

Jamaica

Hispaniola

Caribbean Sea

Christopher Columbus (1492–1493)

Amerigo Vespucci (1501–1502)

ARABIA

Red Sea

AFRICA

Nile River

Panama

PACIFIC OCEAN

Francisco Pizarro (1531–1533)

SOUTH AMERICA

Amazon River

● Cuzco

ANDES MOUNTAINS

Ferdinand Magellan (1519–1522)

Bartholomeu Dias (1487–1488)

Ferdinand Magellan (1519–1522)

Vasco da Gama (1497–1499)

ATLANTIC OCEAN

Strait of Magellan

Key Events

900

1200

1095 The first Crusade begins p. 485

1200 Great Zimbabwe is built in Africa p. 523

1400 Renaissance ideas develop in Europe p. 490

World Exploration, 1400s–1500s

ASIA

PACIFIC OCEAN

Beijing

Huang He

CHINA

Chang Jiang

Persian Gulf

HIMALAYAS

Guangzhou

INDIA

Admiral Zheng He (1421–1422)

Calicut

South China Sea

Philippine Islands

Ferdinand Magellan (1519–1522)

Borneo

INDIAN OCEAN

Java

AUSTRALIA

Exploration by
- → China
- → England
- → France
- → Portugal
- → Spain
- ● City

N W E S

| 0 | 1,500 | 3,000 Miles |
| 0 | 1,500 | 3,000 Kilometers |

Miller Cylindrical Projection

Explorers' Ships and Crews

EXPLORER	NUMBER OF SHIPS	SIZE OF CREW
Jacques Cartier	3	110
Giovanni Caboto	1	18
Christopher Columbus	3	87
Hernando Cortés	11	608
Francisco Pizarro	3	about 200
Ferdinand Magellan	5	270
Amerigo Vespucci	3	unknown
Bartholomeu Dias	3	unknown
Vasco da Gama	4	170
Zheng He	62	27,800

1500

1800

1492 Columbus reaches the Americas p. 505

1526 The Mogul Empire is established in India p. 538

1644 The Manchus rule the Qing dynasty p. 530

477

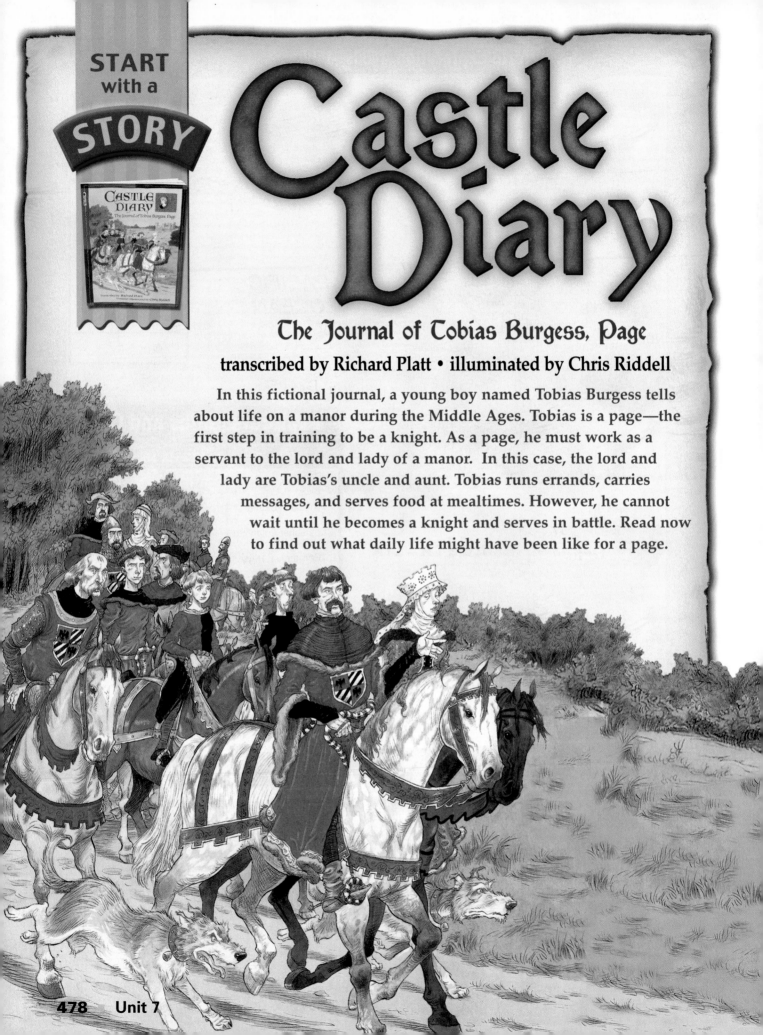

Castle Diary

The Journal of Tobias Burgess, Page

transcribed by Richard Platt • illuminated by Chris Riddell

In this fictional journal, a young boy named Tobias Burgess tells about life on a manor during the Middle Ages. Tobias is a page—the first step in training to be a knight. As a page, he must work as a servant to the lord and lady of a manor. In this case, the lord and lady are Tobias's uncle and aunt. Tobias runs errands, carries messages, and serves food at mealtimes. However, he cannot wait until he becomes a knight and serves in battle. Read now to find out what daily life might have been like for a page.

I Learn My Tasks

January 12th, Friday

I find that everyone calls my uncle and aunt "My Lord" and "My Lady," and that I must do likewise. There are so many strange things to learn and do here that today I have time to write only a line or two. I fear my journal will have many gaps in it!

January 13th, Saturday

Directly after we had broken our fast yesterday, my aunt summoned me and spoke to me of my duties. Pages here serve my aunt and uncle, and thus learn courtesy and the manners and customs of a noble family.

Like the other pages, I am expected to make myself useful by running errands and carrying messages and suchlike. At mealtimes I will learn to serve my aunt and uncle and their guests—to fill their cups and carve them slices of meat which I will place before them in a genteel way.

But as I am her nephew, I am also to be my aunt's personal page and must hold myself ready at all times to attend her. (Though I thought this an honor, Humphrey—who is the oldest of the pages here—scorned it, saying my aunt will have a sharper eye than most for my errors.)

Much of this seemed to me to be dull stuff, so I asked my aunt if I might also ride in a hunt. She did not answer but instead told me of my studies. The castle Chaplain is away at present, for he visits with the Bishop, but on his return I will join the other pages under his tutelage. With this, my aunt bade me make myself familiar with the many buildings and places within the castle walls, and then dismissed me.

January 14th, The Lord's Day

This noon 'twas my task to serve my aunt at table, though I fear that through the nervous shaking of my hand as much food fell to the floor as was placed before her.

The Hall was crowded, for there are many servants here, and it will be some days before I will properly know one from t'other. Only two of them are women, and one is constantly at my aunt's side. This woman, whose name is Isbel, dresses finely in clothes quite like my aunt's. The other is Isbel's maid. She wears clothes of red and blue, the same colors as the uniforms of many of the men servants. . . .

My Uncle Returns

January 15th, Monday

I attended my aunt today in the Great Chamber. At home we call this room the Solar, though ours is smaller by far. My aunt is always busy, for it is she who directs the Steward in the management of the castle household. She jokes that when my uncle is away she must do all her own work and also everything he does—except for shaving!

January 16th, Tuesday

With my aunt again this day and met more of the people who aid her in her daily busy-ness. Within the walls, it is the Constable who minds the castle when my aunt and uncle are both away at their other estates. When my aunt told him who I was, he did not smile or speak, but sighed deeply as if I had already wronged him.

With him also was the Reeve. This man has charge of all the manor—the farms and forest and common lands belonging to the castle. The Reeve collects the rents and taxes which those who dwell on the manor must pay to my uncle regularly for their housing and farms—and for other privileges such as the right to collect firewood in the forest.

January 17th, Wednesday

Today returned my uncle. When I was summoned to greet him, he clapped me firmly on the shoulder and told me that I would make a fine page.

I asked him if I could have a horse (much missing my own pony, which Hugh had taken home) and when I could ride in a hunt. But he laughed and said only: "Patience lad, thou shalt learn of such things in time."

My uncle says I am to study archery and mayhap fighting with a sword, for I shall need these noble skills when I become a squire and learn the craft of knighthood.

Knights serve the King and do battle against his foes. But they must be honorable as well as brave, so squires also study the rules of chivalry—which means doing noble deeds and helping and respecting everyone.

January 20th, Saturday

This day returned the Chaplain to lead our daily worship. He it is who has the task of teaching us pages, as well as writing letters for my aunt when she is busy with her other duties. Now not only must we rise an hour earlier each morn to attend Mass, but schooling will begin again soon!

Analyze the Literature

❶ What are some of the duties of a page?

❷ Do you have duties or responsibilities at home or in your school? Make a list of these duties and responsibilities and share them with the class.

READ A BOOK

START THE UNIT PROJECT

Hold an Art and Science Fair
With your classmates, hold an art and science fair. As you read the unit, take notes about the new kinds of art and new discoveries in science discussed. Your notes will help you decide what to include in your art and science fair.

USE TECHNOLOGY

GO ONLINE Visit The Learning Site at **www.harcourtschool.com** for additional activities, primary sources, and other resources to use in this unit.

BELEM TOWER, LISBON, PORTUGAL

In the 1400s Portugal led the way in the search for new sea routes to Asia. Many Portuguese explorers, such as Vasco da Gama, set sail from the port at Lisbon. In the early 1500s Belem Tower was built in the port at the mouth of the Tagus River. It served as a fortress and as a monument to Portuguese discoveries. Today the tower is a popular tourist attraction.

LOCATE IT

PORTUGAL

Lisbon

15

Europe and the Western Hemisphere

"For knowledge is not given as a gift but by study."

—Laura Cereta, Renaissance scholar, 1469–1499

Focus Skill: Categorize

To **categorize** information is to classify, or to arrange, the data into similar groups so that it is easier to understand and compare.

As you read this chapter, classify what you read into the following categories: history, geography, economics, and culture.

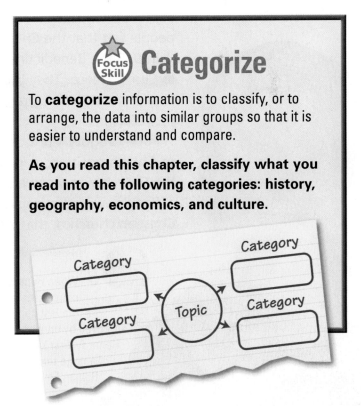

1

Focus Skill **CATEGORIZE**

As you read, think of categories into which the people, places, and events of the high and late Middle Ages can be placed.

BIG IDEA

Changes in medieval Europe led to the decline of feudalism.

VOCABULARY

cathedral

crusader

Crusade

knight

Reconquista

burgher

guild

Magna Carta

Europe's High and Late Middle Ages

| 900 | 1200 | 1500 | 1800 |

1000–1500

By 1000 Europe was made up of many small, independent kingdoms. Even so, most people of medieval Europe were united by Christianity. From 1000 to 1300, culture in medieval Europe reached its highest point in a period called the high Middle Ages. Following this period, great changes took place across Europe as nation-states began to form. This period of change, called the late Middle Ages, lasted from 1300 to 1500.

An Age of Faith

In the Middle Ages the Catholic Church was a powerful institution with its own government, laws, and taxes. The Church used its power mainly to help people. Some Church leaders, however, took advantage of their power. They grew rich and sometimes corrupt. Some Church leaders were not faithful to Church teachings. Many people felt that the Church needed to reform, or make changes.

In 910 the Benedictines, an order of monks, began a monastery in Cluny, France. They lived simply and followed Church teachings. Similar monasteries sprang up across Europe. Together they called for reform.

Pope Gregory VII took up the challenge. He outlawed the selling of Church positions and other corrupt practices. People's faith in the Church was renewed by his actions.

People were also inspired by the building of **cathedrals**, or large Christian churches, that were often located in the middle of town. Replacing the low, dark structures of the past, cathedrals seemed to express the renewed faith and hope of the time.

FAST FACT

When Pope Gregory VII was chosen for his position, he was the last pope in history to be approved by an emperor. The emperor was Henry IV, first king of Germany and leader of a large territory later called the Holy Roman Empire.

Cathedrals also expressed the authority of the Church. The Church had more than religious authority. The pope crowned emperors and sent soldiers to war.

In 1095 Pope Urban II called on all Christians to help retake the holy city of Jerusalem in southwestern Asia. Jerusalem was under the control of the Seljuk Turks, who were Muslims. Excited volunteers stitched red crosses to shirts, cloaks, and banners and set out for what they called the Holy Land. Because they took the cross as their sign, they were called **crusaders**. The wars these Christians fought were called the **Crusades**.

Some saw the Crusades as their religious duty. Others fought for different reasons. Peasants hoped to escape a life of poverty and find riches in the Holy Land. Serfs were freed, and criminals were released from jail if they signed up to fight.

Heavily armored soldiers on horseback, called **knights**, also fought in the Crusades. Before joining the Crusades, most knights provided protection for feudal lords. As part of the Crusades, knights developed a code of behavior based on Christian values.

Between 1095 and 1291, there were eight Crusades. In some, whole families set out for the Holy Land. An army of children marched off on what became known as the Children's Crusade. Most of them died of hunger on the long trip. Thousands of Muslims and Christians lost their lives in the Crusades.

A CLOSER LOOK
Notre Dame Cathedral

Built in the 1100s in Paris, France, Notre Dame Cathedral represented a new architectural style called gothic.

1. **Buttresses press against the cathedral's outside walls to provide support.**
2. **Most cathedrals are shaped like a cross. The spire stands where the building forms the center of the cross.**
3. **Some stained-glass windows on cathedrals are called roses because of their shape.**

❖ What does the size of Notre Dame Cathedral say about religion during this time?

A Moorish king pays tribute to the Spanish king and queen during the Reconquista.

Increased contact with Muslims in Spain and in Sicily brought new scientific ideas to Europeans. At the time, Muslim scholars were more advanced in mathematics and medicine than Europeans. Some were skilled surgeons. Others had invented algebra and created maps of the stars.

The Crusades helped open new trade routes between Europe and Asia. Europeans were introduced to new goods. These goods included spices and silks.

The Crusades inspired attempts in Europe to enforce the teachings of the Church. In Spain, King Ferdinand and Queen Isabella led the **Reconquista** (ray•kohn•KEES•tah), or Reconquest, to drive out the Moors. The Moors were Muslims who had come to Spain from northern Africa. By 1492 Ferdinand and Isabella had claimed all of the land the Moors once held. They forced Spain's Muslim population to leave the country or convert to Christianity. They also drove more than 200,000 Jews from Spain. The country became united under one government and one religion.

The crusaders never gained permanent control of the Holy Land. Still, the Crusades had other far-reaching effects. On their way to the Holy Land, crusaders passed through Constantinople, capital of the Byzantine Empire. There they were amazed by the size of the city. Europe had grown isolated during the Middle Ages. The Crusades brought Europe back into contact with the thriving Byzantine and Muslim civilizations.

REVIEW How did the Crusades change Europe?

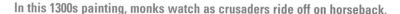

In this 1300s painting, monks watch as crusaders ride off on horseback.

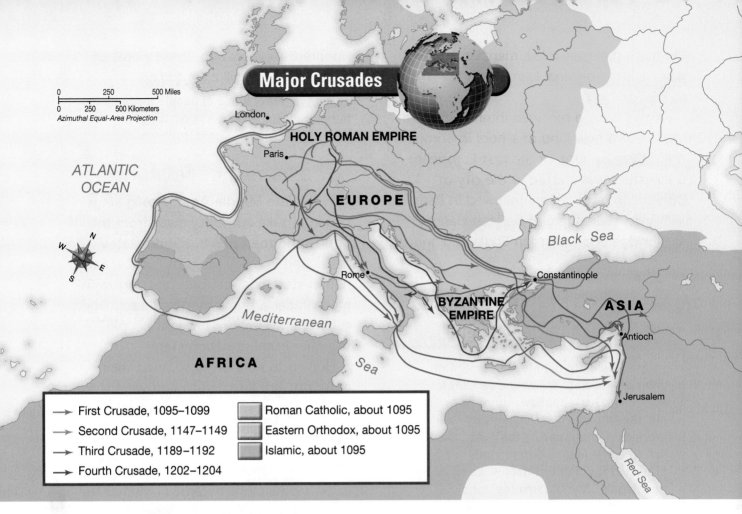

Major Crusades

0 250 500 Miles
0 250 500 Kilometers
Azimuthal Equal-Area Projection

London
HOLY ROMAN EMPIRE
Paris
ATLANTIC OCEAN
EUROPE
Black Sea
Rome
Constantinople
BYZANTINE EMPIRE
ASIA
Mediterranean
Sea
Antioch
AFRICA
Jerusalem
Red Sea

→ First Crusade, 1095–1099
→ Second Crusade, 1147–1149
→ Third Crusade, 1189–1192
→ Fourth Crusade, 1202–1204

Roman Catholic, about 1095
Eastern Orthodox, about 1095
Islamic, about 1095

Movement **The Crusades brought many Europeans into close contact with Muslims of southwestern Asia.**

❖ **About how many miles did the crusaders travel to get from Paris to Constantinople during the Second Crusade?**

Trade and Cities

While some Europeans were away on the Crusades, changes were taking place at home. Improvements in agriculture led to greater food production and a better diet. In turn, this led to a growth in population.

New cities developed in Europe, and with them a new class of people between nobles and peasants. This new class was made up of **burghers** (BER•gers), or merchants and craftworkers. This middle class steadily grew more powerful. By forming **guilds**, or trade associations, burghers made sure that they got fair wages for their work. They also set standards for the quality of their goods. To become guild members, craftworkers had to prove that they were masters of their craft.

Local markets turned into medieval fairs. Spices, silks, and other interesting goods from Asia were sold there. Handcrafted items from all over Europe were also offered for sale.

New forms of banking helped trade flourish. Moneylenders began to provide loans to merchants. Then, merchants used the money to buy goods to sell at the fairs.

An early thirteenth-century seal from a guild of sea merchants

On the last day of a fair, merchants would pay back the original loan plus a fee to the moneylenders.

At this time, a renewed interest in learning led to a new kind of school in Europe—the university. One of the first European universities was started in the city of Bologna in Italy. Others followed in Paris in France, Heidelberg in Germany, and Cambridge and Oxford in England. Founded hundreds of years ago, these places of higher learning still exist today.

REVIEW What kinds of people made up the burgher class? CATEGORIZE

The End of Feudalism

In the late Middle Ages, strong kings began to take authority away from the nobles and the Church. Nation-states developed in many parts of Europe. Each nation-state had a strong central government under a single monarch. Language, culture, and customs brought people together in these nation-states.

Hoping to hold on to some of their authority, nobles tried to find ways to limit the power of kings. In 1215 a group of English nobles presented King John of England with a list of 63 demands. Written as a contract, this document became known as the **Magna Carta**, or "Great Charter." King John was forced to agree to it.

The Magna Carta was written to protect the upper class. However, parts of the charter later became the basis for laws that protected the freedoms of all classes of people. For example, the

In this illustration (below), King John agrees to follow the demands of the Magna Carta (above).

488

Magna Carta gave people the right to trial by jury.

The Magna Carta required that the English monarch have the "general consent of the realm [kingdom]" before ordering new taxes. The assembly of nobles who met to vote on taxes later became known as Parliament. Today the main lawmakers of Parliament are elected by the people.

The document had long-lasting effects. The United States Constitution has its roots in the ideas first expressed in the Magna Carta.

In many ways it seemed that life in Europe was improving. However, two disasters lay ahead. In 1337 a war started between England and France. Known as the Hundred Years' War, it ended when the French drove the English out of France.

At the same time a second disaster hit Europe. In the late Middle Ages, cities were crowded and unhealthy places. They were full of people, animals, and garbage. Between 1347 and 1351 the Black Death, an outbreak of the bubonic plague, struck. This disease, spread by the fleas on rats, killed one-fourth of Europe's population.

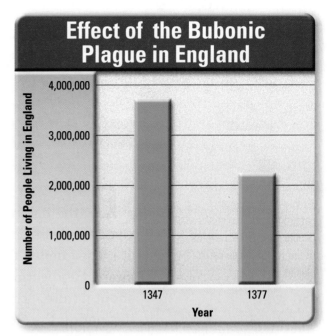

Effect of the Bubonic Plague in England

Number of People Living in England / Year

Analyze Graphs The bubonic plague killed many people in England.

❖ By about how much did the population change in England between 1347 and 1377?

By the mid-1400s feudalism was declining. Many people blamed the kings and the Church for not being able to stop the plague. Europeans were growing tired of war. Peasants wanted to be paid for their work.

REVIEW What was the Magna Carta?
a document

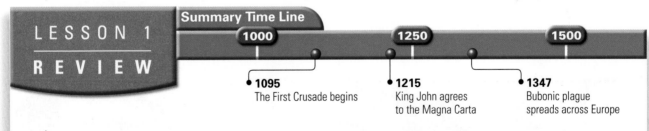

LESSON 1 REVIEW

Summary Time Line

1000 — 1250 — 1500

1095 The First Crusade begins

1215 King John agrees to the Magna Carta

1347 Bubonic plague spreads across Europe

CATEGORIZE What kinds of events occurred in Europe during the high and late Middle Ages?

1 BIG IDEA What changes in medieval Europe led to the decline of feudalism?

2 VOCABULARY Use the terms **burgher** and **guild** in a sentence.

3 TIME LINE When did the First Crusade begin?

4 GOVERNMENT How did the Magna Carta limit the power of the English king?

5 CRITICAL THINKING—Analyze How do you think the growth of trade and cities was related to changes in feudalism?

PERFORMANCE—Form a Guild Work with a group to form a guild. First, decide what kind of work your guild will do. Then, decide on a fair price that all guild members will charge for their products or services. Finally, write a set of standards that all guild members must follow to make sure all work is of high quality.

BIG IDEA

The Renaissance was a time of new ideas and creativity in Europe.

VOCABULARY

Renaissance
humanism
vernacular
scientific method
movable type

The Renaissance

| 900 | 1200 | 1500 | 1800 |

1400 – 1600

By the beginning of the 1400s, Europeans who had survived the wars and plagues of the Middle Ages wanted to enjoy life. They began to look at the world around them with new interest and curiosity. Their creativity burst out with new ideas about nature, art, science, language, and learning. Historians call this period the **Renaissance** (REH•nuh•sahns), which means "rebirth." It began in Italy and then spread into northern Europe. The Renaissance lasted from about 1400 to 1600.

The Cradle of the Renaissance

The Renaissance began in Italy for three main reasons. Italy had bustling urban centers, wealthy merchants, and the heritage of the ancient Roman Empire. Much of the trade between northern Europe and Asia passed through northern Italy. Urban centers sprang up that were home to a rising merchant class. Wealthy merchants and bankers, who wanted to show their power, became patrons, or supporters, of the arts. Patrons often paid artists to create paintings and sculptures for their homes.

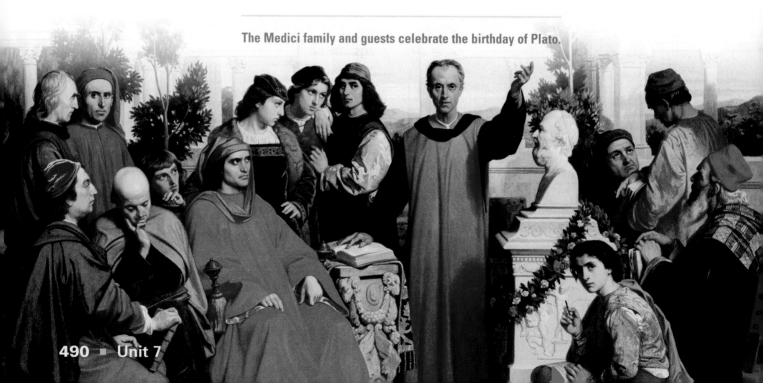

The Medici family and guests celebrate the birthday of Plato.

The members of the powerful Medici (MED•ee•chee) family of Florence were wealthy bankers. Around the year 1434, they gained control of the city-state of Florence. Cosimo de' Medici, who was said to be the richest person of his time, supported many artists. Florence soon became the center for art and artists.

Wealthy merchant families in the city-states of Florence, Venice, Naples, Milan, and Genoa had long competed against each other for control of trade. Now they competed to make their cities centers of art and learning as well. They invited artists, scholars, writers, and philosophers to live and work in their city-states.

The thinkers of this age looked around them and saw the ruins of the ancient Roman Empire. European scholars began to rediscover the writings of the ancient Greeks and Romans. They found that many classical, or ancient, ideas differed from the ideas of the Middle Ages, which revolved around religion. The ancient peoples had studied the workings of nature from small to large. Many of their ideas challenged the way of thinking in the Middle Ages.

Many ancient ideas came to Europe by way of Muslim scholars, who had preserved the ancient texts when few Europeans were interested in them. Others had been stored in European monasteries.

In the Middle Ages the Church had kept learning alive. However, many ideas of the Church did not hold up against the scientific thinking of ancient times. This led Europeans to new ways of thinking about human beings and the world they live in.

REVIEW In what way was the Renaissance a "rebirth" of ancient ideas?

Medici family accounting book

Renaissance Italy

Place During the Renaissance, Italy was controlled by powerful city-states.

❷ Which city-states controlled land that is not part of present-day Italy?

New Ways of Thinking and Seeing

The new ways of thinking during the Renaissance became known as humanism. **Humanism** focused on the ideas and actions of individuals. Renaissance writers wrote about daily life and ways for individuals to be all that they could be. Writers wrote not only in Latin but also in the **vernacular** (ver•NA•kyuh•ler), or the everyday language of the people. This meant that the average person could learn about these new ideas.

Baldassare Castiglione (bahl•das•SAR•ay kahs•teel•YOH•nay) wrote the book *The Courtier* to describe the proper education for young people of the upper class. He explained that young men should be taught to sing, dance, write poetry, and play a musical instrument. They should also be skilled at sword fighting, horseback riding, and wrestling. According to Castiglione, young women should be instructed in art, dance, and music.

In contrast, writer Niccolò Machiavelli (NEE•koh•loh ma•kee•uh•VEH•lee) instructed leaders. In his book *The Prince,* Machiavelli encouraged leaders to use whatever means necessary, including military force, to keep control.

Baldassare Castiglione

Renaissance painters and sculptors began to picture a more realistic view of the world. In addition to painting religious themes, they painted portraits of their patrons and other individuals. They also painted scenes from daily life.

People in paintings from the Middle Ages often appeared flat. People in Renaissance paintings looked like real human beings. Their faces showed expression.

Even the background of the paintings looked real. Renaissance painters discovered how to use perspective. This way of painting allows an artist to show a difference between objects that are close and objects that are far away.

As art changed, the way people viewed artists changed as well. In the Middle Ages,

This fifteenth-century Italian painting (below) illustrates the use of perspective. Notice how all parts of the painting lead the eye to a center point (right).

The Discoveries of Copernicus

In the 1500s Polish astronomer Nicolaus Copernicus (nik•uh•LAY•uhs koh•PER•nih•kuhs) used mathematics to show that Earth revolves around the sun. He also demonstrated that Earth rotates once daily on its axis. Copernicus's heliocentric, or "sun-centered," theory influenced later scientists, such as Galileo (ga•luh•LAY•oh) and Isaac Newton. Before Copernicus most scientists and thinkers accepted the idea that Earth was the center of the universe and that it did not move.

Copernicus (far right) drew this diagram (right) to demonstrate his sun-centered theory.

people thought of artists as craftspeople. Like carpenters or bricklayers, artists worked in guilds, or groups, and their work was anonymous, or unsigned. During the Renaissance, patrons competed to attract the best artists of the time. Many of these artists became famous for developing their own styles.

One of the greatest geniuses of the Renaissance was Leonardo da Vinci (lee•uh•NAR•doh duh VIN•chee). He was a scientist, an engineer, an inventor, a philosopher, and a writer as well as an artist. He filled many notebooks with his ideas and drawings. Some of da Vinci's ideas, such as the parachute and flying machine, were hundreds of years ahead of their time.

Leonardo's paintings stand as some of his greatest works. For centuries people have been trying to guess the secret behind the smile of the *Mona Lisa.* His attention to detail in *The Last Supper* still leaves people amazed.

The Renaissance artist Michelangelo Buonarroti (my•kuh•LAN•juh•loh bwaw•naw•RAW•tee) also showed skill in many fields. His statues of David and Moses show his skill as a sculptor. The magnificent St. Peter's Church in Rome shows his strength as an architect. The glory of his painting can be seen in the ceiling of the Sistine (SIS•teen) Chapel. The painting, which was requested by Pope Julius II in 1508, displays scenes from the Bible.

It took Michelangelo four years to paint the ceiling of the Sistine Chapel. Today, people still visit the chapel to see Michelangelo's work, which is considered a masterpiece of Renaissance art.

The spirit of the Renaissance showed in science as well. Polish astronomer Nicolaus Copernicus made mathematical calculations showing that Earth revolves around the sun.

Michelangelo's sculpture of Moses

One of the Bibles (above) printed on Gutenberg's printing press (right)

This idea went against Church teachings, which said that Earth stayed in one spot at the center of the universe.

In the early 1600s Galileo Galilei (ga•luh•LAY•oh ga•luh•LAY), an Italian scientist, built a telescope and turned his attention to studying the stars. He observed and recorded the movement of the planets. Like Copernicus's findings, Galileo's observations showed that Earth moves around the sun. His way of using observation and experiments to prove ideas became known as the **scientific method**. It is the model still used by scientists today.

Church leaders did not support the new ideas of Galileo and other scientists. After all, their ideas challenged Church teachings. The Church leaders forced Galileo to say that he was

Galileo's telescopes were an improvement over earlier models. His work greatly advanced the field of astronomy.

wrong. Old and ill, Galileo gave in. However, according to legend, Galileo said, as he lay dying, "And yet it [Earth] *does* move."

REVIEW Which Renaissance figures were scientists? CATEGORIZE

The Spread of Ideas

Renaissance ideas spread throughout Europe with the help of an invention from Germany. In about 1450 Johannes Gutenberg (yoh•HAHN•uhs GOO•tuhn•berg) became the first European to print with **movable type**. Gutenberg's printing press used small metal pieces, each with a single raised number or letter of the alphabet. These pieces could be arranged in trays in a printing press to form words and sentences.

Before Gutenberg's invention, printers used blocks of wood carved with words and pictures to print books. The whole block had to be recarved if anything on a page needed to be changed. Movable type made printing books faster and less expensive.

In 1455 Gutenberg printed a 1,200-page Bible, using a printing press with movable type. Soon, printing presses appeared all over Europe. Because books could be printed in large numbers, they became cheaper and more people could afford them. Through printed books Renaissance ideas spread quickly throughout Europe.

Renaissance ideas inspired Dutch artists, such as Pieter Brueghel (PEE•ter BROO•guhl), to create a new style of painting based on the daily life of common people. They led writers Desiderius Erasmus (day•see•DAIR•yuhs ih•RAZ•muhs) of the Netherlands and Thomas More of England to develop ideas about creating a better society.

Renaissance ideas also gave rise to one of the greatest English writers—William Shakespeare. Ordinary people, nobles, and royalty alike crowded into London's Globe Theatre to see Shakespeare's plays. People still enjoy his works today. As English poet Ben Jonson noted, "He was not of an age but for all time."

REVIEW How did movable type help spread Renaissance ideas?

William Shakespeare (left) was one of the greatest English playwrights. His plays are still performed at the new Globe Theatre in London (above).

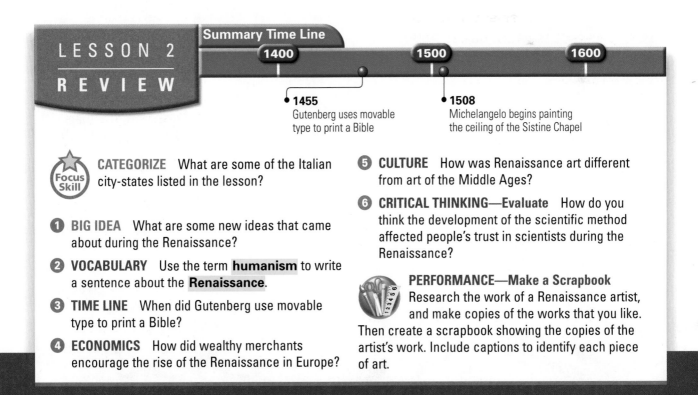

LESSON 2 REVIEW

Summary Time Line

1400 — 1500 — 1600

• **1455** Gutenberg uses movable type to print a Bible

• **1508** Michelangelo begins painting the ceiling of the Sistine Chapel

Focus Skill **CATEGORIZE** What are some of the Italian city-states listed in the lesson?

① **BIG IDEA** What are some new ideas that came about during the Renaissance?

② **VOCABULARY** Use the term **humanism** to write a sentence about the **Renaissance**.

③ **TIME LINE** When did Gutenberg use movable type to print a Bible?

④ **ECONOMICS** How did wealthy merchants encourage the rise of the Renaissance in Europe?

⑤ **CULTURE** How was Renaissance art different from art of the Middle Ages?

⑥ **CRITICAL THINKING—Evaluate** How do you think the development of the scientific method affected people's trust in scientists during the Renaissance?

PERFORMANCE—Make a Scrapbook Research the work of a Renaissance artist, and make copies of the works that you like. Then create a scrapbook showing the copies of the artist's work. Include captions to identify each piece of art.

·SKILLS· CITIZENSHIP

Make a Thoughtful Decision

▶ WHY IT MATTERS

Every action has a consequence, or result. Some consequences are short-term. That is, they last only a short time. Other consequences are long-term. They last a long time. An action can also have either positive or negative consequences—or both. You cannot always predict all the consequences of your actions. However, thinking about possible consequences before you take action is the key to making a thoughtful decision.

Here are some steps you can use to help you make a thoughtful decision.

Step 1 **Know that you have to make a decision.**

Step 2 **Gather information.**

Step 3 **Identify choices.**

Step 4 **Try to predict possible consequences, and weigh those consequences.**

Step 5 **Make the choice that seems best, and put your choice into action.**

Religious themes were common among Renaissance painters. This fifteenth-century Renaissance painting shows Saint Peter kneeling to Jesus Christ.

This painting of a peasant village by Pieter Brueghel shows his interest in the lives of the common people.

▶ PRACTICE THE SKILL

Read the passage below about Renaissance artists. Then answer the questions.

"At the beginning of the Renaissance, writers began to explore the ideas of humanism. Renaissance painters and sculptors also began to explore these ideas. They wanted to show a more realistic view of the world in their works. In addition to painting religious themes, artists made portraits of their patrons and other individuals. They also included subjects from Greek and Roman mythology, ancient stories about heroes and gods, in their art. This style of painting developed in Italy and spread throughout Europe.

"In 1551 Dutch painter Pieter Brueghel traveled to Italy to study Italian paintings. Like other Renaissance artists, Brueghel wanted to show a more realistic view of the world in his art. Although he was influenced by the Italian style, Brueghel would develop his own style.

"Brueghel took the ideas of humanism a step farther. He chose to show the lives of common people in his paintings. Brueghel had often observed the daily lives of peasants, including their festivals and celebrations. In his paintings, he showed a realistic view of common people at the time. Some of Brueghel's most famous paintings include *Peasant Dance, Peasant Wedding,* and *Children's Games.*"

1 What decision did Brueghel make?

2 What information did Brueghel gather?

3 What other subjects could Brueghel have chosen to paint?

4 What are some possible consequences Brueghel may have weighed before making his decision?

5 Do you think Brueghel's choice to create paintings of peasant life was a good choice? Why or why not?

▶ APPLY WHAT YOU LEARNED

Think about a decision you made at school. What steps did you follow? What choices did you make? What were the consequences? Do you think you made a thoughtful decision? Explain.

CATEGORIZE

As you read, think of categories into which the people, places, and events of the Reformation can be placed.

BIG IDEA

The Reformation brought many changes to Europe.

VOCABULARY

indulgence
heresy
Protestant
Reformation

The Reformation

900 — 1200 — 1500 — 1800

1510–1550

During the 1400s and 1500s, many changes were sweeping across Europe. Books were being published in languages spoken by ordinary people. Because of this, more people could read about new ideas. New inventions, such as movable type, were changing the way people did their work. Even the teachings of the Church were being questioned. Some Church leaders were taking advantage of their power. A new period of reform, or change, was about to begin with the actions of one person.

Standing Up for Reform

In 1513 a member of the Medici family of Florence became pope. He took the name Pope Leo X. It is said that he wrote to his brother, "God gave us the papacy [office of the pope]—let us enjoy it." Leo X did indeed enjoy himself. He spent Church money freely on himself and as a patron of the arts. To pay for his projects, Leo sold positions in the Church to whoever could pay the most.

Leo X wanted to rebuild St. Peter's Church in Rome. To raise the money for this huge project, the Church began selling **indulgences**, or pardons for sins. The Church had sold indulgences before, but Leo X's new indulgences were different. They promised forgiveness not only for past sins but also for sins that people might commit in the future.

Pope Leo X (left) encouraged the selling of indulgences to pay for the rebuilding of the dome of St. Peter's Church (right) in Rome.

Martin Luther nails his 95 Theses to the door of the Castle Church in Wittenberg.

A priest named Martin Luther saw the sale of indulgences taking place near the German town of Wittenberg (WIH•tuhn•berg). The idea of selling forgiveness for past sins shocked him. Selling forgiveness for future sins shocked him even more. Luther decided to take action to end the selling of indulgences.

On October 31, 1517, Luther nailed his 95 Theses (THEE•seez), or statements of opinion, to the door of the Castle Church in Wittenberg. The papers listed Luther's complaints against the Church.

In 1521 Luther was put on trial for his beliefs. At the trial, Luther explained that he did not intend to hurt the Church. He only wanted to identify and help solve its problems. He refused to change any of his statements. The court found Luther guilty of **heresy**, or not following the beliefs of the Church. For this the Church excommunicated him, or made him no longer a member of the Church.

REVIEW What caused Martin Luther to call for reforms in the Church?

The Spread of Protestantism, 1618

ATLANTIC OCEAN

SCANDINAVIA

SCOTLAND
IRELAND
NORWAY
SWEDEN
North Sea
RUSSIA
BALTIC STATES
ENGLAND
DENMARK
NETHERLANDS
Baltic Sea
PRUSSIA
GERMANY
FRANCE
POLAND
BOHEMIA
AUSTRIA
TRANSYLVANIA
HUNGARY
PORTUGAL
SPAIN
ITALIAN STATES
Black Sea
OTTOMAN EMPIRE
Mediterranean Sea

Protestant
Roman Catholic
Islamic
Eastern Orthodox

0   300   600 Miles
0   300   600 Kilometers
Azimuthal Equal-Area Projection

GEOGRAPHY THEME

Movement **The earliest Protestants lived in an area known today as Germany.**

❖ **What was the major direction in which the Protestant religion spread?**

The Reformation Takes Hold

In the 1500s Germany was made up of many states united under the name Holy Roman Empire. The emperor, Charles V, declared Martin Luther an outlaw. No one in the empire was to help him. Even so,

a German prince named Frederick the Wise became Luther's patron. He offered Luther protection and a place to live and continue his work.

By now Luther had begun to question the role of priests and the pope. He came to believe that the Bible held all the religious teachings people needed to know. From his safe place Luther translated the Bible from Greek to German, the people's language. In 1534 his translation was published.

Because of the new printing presses with movable type, Luther's translation of the Bible quickly spread. Many German-speaking people now read the Bible in their own language for the first time. They eagerly agreed with Luther's ideas. His followers called themselves Lutherans and formed the Lutheran Church.

Several princes in northern Germany also supported Luther's movement. Some approved of Luther's ideas. Others saw the movement as a way to weaken the power of the Catholic Church.

Emperor Charles V saw this as a challenge to his power. He joined forces with princes in southern Germany who had remained Catholic. Charles V and other Catholic leaders tried to put an end to Luther's movement. Luther's supporters protested these actions. As a result, these supporters became known as **Protestants**.

In the 1600s war broke out across Europe. Called the Thirty Years' War, it began as a religious conflict between Protestants and Catholics.

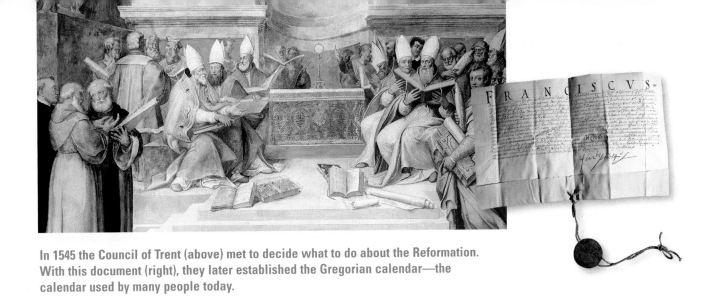

In 1545 the Council of Trent (above) met to decide what to do about the Reformation. With this document (right), they later established the Gregorian calendar—the calendar used by many people today.

Disputes between Catholics and Protestants in Europe continued for many years. The movement started by Luther became known as the **Reformation**, because it began as a call for reforms in the Church. The Reformation spread from Germany to other parts of Europe. In the Netherlands, England, Scotland, and Scandinavia, other reformers founded their own churches.

In 1545 Catholic leaders met to discuss what to do about the Reformation. At the meeting, called the Council of Trent, they supported the beliefs of the Catholic Church but also called for changes. Loyal Catholics welcomed these reforms. Yet they could not undo what had happened. Europe was now divided into Catholic and Protestant states.

The Catholic Church remained strong in Spain, Portugal, Italy, France, Ireland, and parts of eastern Europe. The Protestant movement took hold in Germany, Scandinavia, England, Scotland, and the Netherlands.

REVIEW Who became known as Protestants?

CATEGORIZE

LESSON 3 REVIEW

Summary Time Line

1510 — 1530 — 1550

1513 Leo X is named pope

1517 Martin Luther nails his 95 Theses to a church door

1545 The Council of Trent meets to discuss reforms

CATEGORIZE Which areas of Europe remained mostly Catholic during the Reformation? Which became mostly Protestant?

1 BIG IDEA How did the Reformation bring changes to Europe?

2 VOCABULARY Use the term **Protestant** to describe the **Reformation**.

3 TIME LINE How many years passed between Martin Luther's nailing of his 95 Theses and the Council of Trent?

4 HISTORY Why did Martin Luther decide to write his 95 Theses?

5 CRITICAL THINKING—Hypothesize Do you think the Reformation would have spread throughout Europe without the printing press? Explain.

PERFORMANCE—Write a Journal Entry Imagine you are a citizen of Wittenberg. Write a journal entry explaining what happened on the day Martin Luther nailed his call for reforms to the church door.

4

Focus
Skill
CATEGORIZE
Think of categories into
which the people, places,
and events of the Age
of Exploration can be placed.

BIG IDEA
European nations began to
explore the world in search
of new sea routes to Asia.

VOCABULARY
caravel
astrolabe
circumnavigation
armada

The Age of Exploration

900   1200   1500   1800

1400 – 1600

By the early 1400s Italian and Arab merchants controlled much of the trade between Europe and Asia. Several European countries wanted a part of this profitable trade. If they could trade directly with Asia, they could keep all of the profits. To break the Italian and Arab monopoly in the Mediterranean, many Europeans began to look for new sea routes to Asia. This search led to an Age of Exploration in Europe.

New Routes to Asia

In 1453 Ottoman Turks conquered the city of Constantinople. Constantinople had long served as the gateway for the trade between Europe and Asia. With Constantinople under Ottoman control, the power of Venice and the other Italian city-states began to decline.

The capture of Constantinople shocked Europeans, but they did not feel concerned for the Italian traders. Many European nations had already turned their attention in a new direction. They had begun to look for new water routes to Asia so that they would no longer have to pay Italian traders. The search for new trade routes focused on the Atlantic Ocean. Such routes would allow them to trade directly with Asia.

Many Europeans had read about the travels of Marco Polo, the Italian merchant who had reached China in the 1200s.

Caravels were smaller, lighter, and faster than most other ships of the time.

Navigational tools like this fifteenth-century map (left) and compass (above) made sailing for long distances easier.

Other Europeans may have heard of the Viking explorations across the Atlantic many years earlier. Europeans also returned to an idea first suggested by ancient Greek and Muslim scholars—that Earth is round. Could it be possible that by sailing west from Europe they could arrive in the east in Asia? Were there lands to the west unknown to Europeans?

Ships of the early 1400s were not strong enough to make a long ocean voyage. In the mid-1400s, shipbuilders in Portugal began to build a new kind of ship called a **caravel**. This sturdy craft could travel long distances swiftly and withstand rough seas. It had lateen, or triangular, sails. This kind of sail allowed the ship to travel into the wind. Portuguese shipbuilders adopted the idea for these sails from Arab traders, who had long used them to sail on the Indian Ocean.

At the same time, European sailors became better navigators. They did this in part by studying the ideas of other cultures. They learned to use the **astrolabe** (AS•truh•layb), an instrument to help sailors navigate by the stars. The astrolabe had been developed centuries earlier by Muslims. From Muslim mapmakers, Europeans got more accurate maps of India and southeastern Asia. From China, European sailors learned about the magnetic compass. This device helped sailors identify the direction in which they were sailing. With all these tools European sailors were prepared to search for new sea routes to Asia.

REVIEW What developments allowed European sailors to look for new sea routes to Asia?

Portugal and Spain Take the Lead

Portugal led the way in exploring the Atlantic Ocean. Portugal was a small and fairly poor country. Even so, its leaders dreamed of the profits from trade with Asia. It was through the efforts of one person, Prince Henry the Navigator, that the Portuguese began to work toward their dream.

Around 1419 Prince Henry founded a school for navigators. It was located on a high rocky point that stuck out into the Atlantic Ocean and was known as "The End of the World." Prince Henry brought together the best mapmakers, scientists, and ship designers. He put their ideas into use by paying for voyages of exploration along Africa's Atlantic coast.

Prince Henry died in 1460, but the Portuguese continued their expeditions along Africa's western coast. In 1488 a sailor named Bartholomeu Dias (DEE•ahsh) sailed around the southern tip of Africa and entered the Indian Ocean. Although Dias's crew made him turn back, he had found a new way to Asia.

Ten years later, Vasco da Gama sailed as far as India. He returned to Portugal in 1499 with a cargo of Indian spices and jewels. The sale of his cargo brought Portugal 60 times what the trip had cost!

By the late 1500s Portugal ruled a trade network that extended around Africa, the Indian subcontinent, and China. Portuguese sailors had found the new sea route to Asia. Portuguese leaders realized their dream of becoming rich and powerful.

An Italian sailor, Christopher Columbus, also dreamed of the riches that could be made from trade with Asia. However, Columbus had a new idea about how to reach the continent. He felt sure that he could travel to Asia by sailing west across

Italian sailor Christopher Columbus stands before King Ferdinand and Queen Isabella of Spain. Columbus's coat of arms is at left.

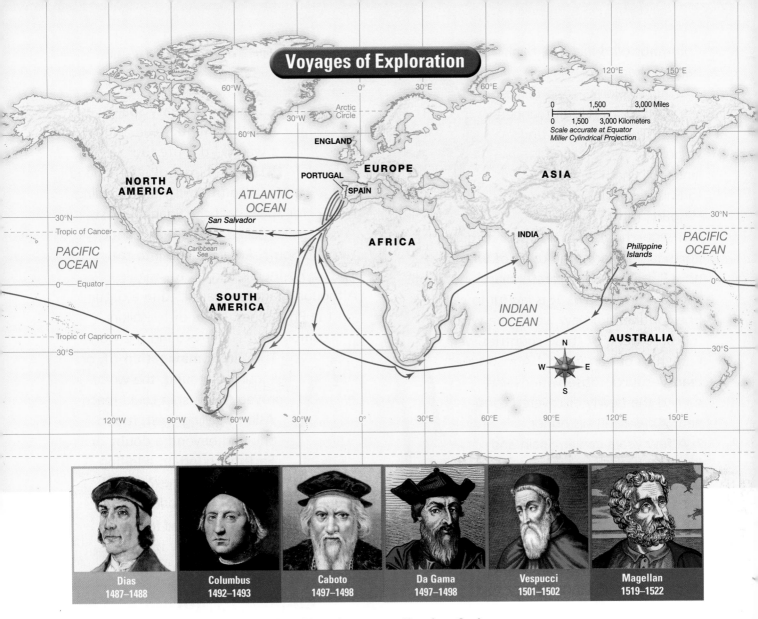

Voyages of Exploration

ENGLAND

EUROPE

PORTUGAL

SPAIN

NORTH AMERICA

ATLANTIC OCEAN

San Salvador

Caribbean Sea

PACIFIC OCEAN

SOUTH AMERICA

AFRICA

ASIA

INDIA

INDIAN OCEAN

PACIFIC OCEAN

Philippine Islands

AUSTRALIA

Arctic Circle

Tropic of Cancer

Equator

Tropic of Capricorn

0   1,500   3,000 Miles
0   1,500   3,000 Kilometers
Scale accurate at Equator
Miller Cylindrical Projection

| Dias 1487–1488 | Columbus 1492–1493 | Caboto 1497–1498 | Da Gama 1497–1498 | Vespucci 1501–1502 | Magellan 1519–1522 |

Movement   At the end of the fifteenth century, sailors from Spain, Portugal, and England set off to explore the world.

❖ Which explorer traveled mainly along the Tropic of Cancer?

the Atlantic Ocean. The king of Portugal was not interested in his idea, so Columbus took it to King Ferdinand and Queen Isabella of Spain. Columbus promised them wealth and new lands. He also promised to spread the Catholic faith in Asia. Ferdinand and Isabella were devout, or faithful, Catholics. They also wanted the riches from trade with Asia. They agreed to pay for Columbus's voyage.

On August 3, 1492, Columbus set sail with three ships. A little more than two months later, on October 12, he

landed on a small island that he named San Salvador ("Holy Savior") in the Caribbean Sea. Columbus was sure he had reached the East Indies in Asia. Because of this, he called the native people Indians. When he returned to Spain in 1493, he received a hero's welcome.

Columbus made three more voyages to the Caribbean. However, he never landed on the North American mainland.

Queen Isabella's scepter

Columbus died in 1506, thinking he had reached Asia.

Other explorers soon realized that Columbus had not landed in Asia. They began to understand that he had found new lands that had been unknown to Europeans. In 1501 Amerigo Vespucci (uh•MAIR•ih•goh veh•SPOO•chee), an Italian sailing for Portugal, explored the coast of what is now Brazil. He drew careful maps and wrote about what he saw. "It is lawful to call [the continent] a new world," he wrote, "because none of these countries were known to our ancestors." A mapmaker read Vespucci's observations and named the newly discovered continent *America* in his honor.

A few years earlier, Spain and Portugal had signed a treaty that divided the unexplored parts of the world between them. They drew an imaginary line north and south on the world as they knew it. Spain gained the right to explore all lands west of the line. Portugal could explore all lands east of the line.

Under this treaty Spain was able to continue searching for a westward route to Asia. In 1519 five ships led by Ferdinand Magellan (muh•JEH•luhn), sailing for Spain, left the Spanish coast. Magellan sailed across the Atlantic, around South America, and into the Pacific. He then sailed on to Asia. Although Magellan was killed in a battle in the Philippines, some of his sailors completed the trip around the world. This **circumnavigation** of, or sea journey around, the world proved that a ship could reach Asia by sailing west. It also showed beyond a doubt that Earth is round. In addition, it gave geographers a new way to figure out the size of the world.

REVIEW Which explorers sailed for Spain?

CATEGORIZE

English Exploration

The English began to search for new trade routes shortly after Columbus's first voyage. King Henry VII paid Italian explorer Giovanni Caboto to search for a western route to Asia. In 1497 and 1498 Caboto sailed along the northeast coast of North America and claimed the land for England.

Henry VII's son, Henry VIII, focused less on exploration. Under his rule England became a Protestant country. It was Henry VIII's daughter, Elizabeth I, who made England a sea power. After she came to the throne in 1558, she gave money to support a group of sea captains, including Francis Drake and Walter Raleigh. Some of the captains were also pirates, who attacked Spanish and Portuguese ships. Queen

This painting shows Francis Drake being knighted by Queen Elizabeth I.

English warships defeated the Spanish Armada (left). England issued these playing cards (above) to celebrate its victory.

Elizabeth was willing to ignore their pirate ways because they filled her treasury with gold and silver.

The acts of English pirates made King Philip II of Spain angry. He also wanted to force Protestant England to return to the Catholic Church. In 1588 Philip sent an **armada** (ar•MAH•duh), or a fleet of warships, to attack England. It seemed that this armada could not be stopped. Yet the smaller, faster English ships sank many of the large Spanish warships. A storm destroyed many of the remaining Spanish ships as they tried to return to Spain. England's victory over the Spanish Armada saved England from invasion. It also showed that Spain was weakening as a world power, and England was gaining strength.

REVIEW What event showed that England was becoming a world power?

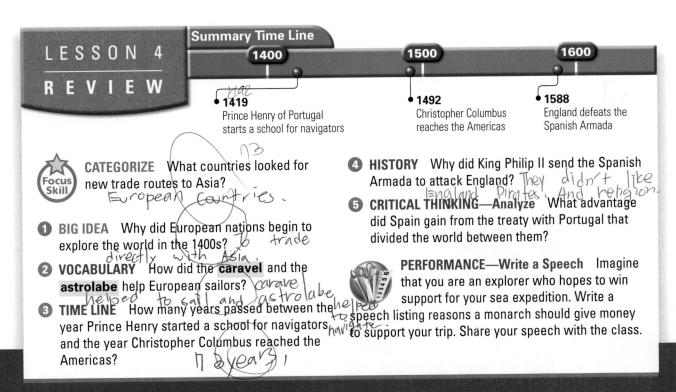

LESSON 4
REVIEW

Summary Time Line

1400 .... 1500 1600

• **1419**
Prince Henry of Portugal starts a school for navigators

• **1492**
Christopher Columbus reaches the Americas

• **1588**
England defeats the Spanish Armada

Focus Skill **CATEGORIZE** What countries looked for new trade routes to Asia?
European countries.

❶ **BIG IDEA** Why did European nations begin to explore the world in the 1400s? To trade directly with Asia.

❷ **VOCABULARY** How did the **caravel** and the **astrolabe** help European sailors? caravel helped to sail and astrolabe helped to navigate.

❸ **TIME LINE** How many years passed between the year Prince Henry started a school for navigators and the year Christopher Columbus reached the Americas? 7 years

❹ **HISTORY** Why did King Philip II send the Spanish Armada to attack England? They didn't like England Pirates. And religion.

❺ **CRITICAL THINKING—Analyze** What advantage did Spain gain from the treaty with Portugal that divided the world between them?

PERFORMANCE—Write a Speech Imagine that you are an explorer who hopes to win support for your sea expedition. Write a speech listing reasons a monarch should give money to support your trip. Share your speech with the class.

Tools for Navigation

Tools for navigation allowed sailors to explore lands far away and find their way back. Most such tools used the sun, moon, and stars to determine location. Beginning in the 900s, Muslim astronomers built astrolabes and quadrants, instruments that used the sun's position to measure latitude. These tools reached Europe through the Muslim-controlled parts of Spain. European navigators were using them widely by the 1400s. Navigators also developed new tools, such as the compass, and a better knowledge of astronomy.

The Italian explorer Amerigo Vespucci using an astrolabe

 FROM THE SCIENCE MUSEUM IN LONDON

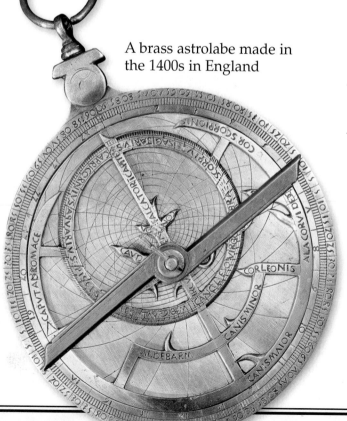

A brass astrolabe made in the 1400s in England

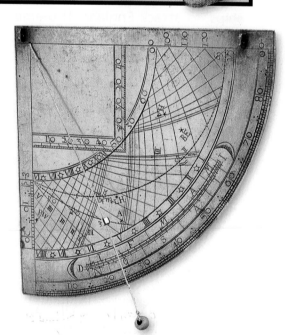

This brass quadrant was made in Europe in the 1600s.

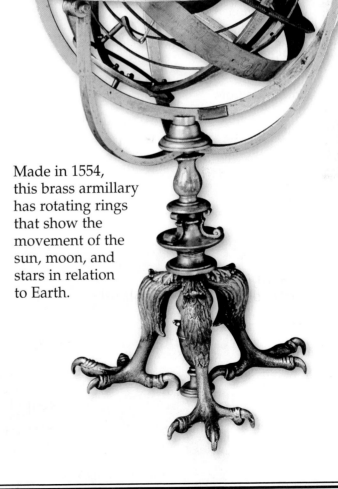

This sundial with a compass was made in northern Europe in 1566.

Analyze the Primary Source

1. How did early navigation tools work?

2. Which navigation tools might be the easiest to use on a ship? Which would be most difficult? Why?

3. In which subject areas do you think most navigators in the 1400s and 1500s received training?

Made in 1554, this brass armillary has rotating rings that show the movement of the sun, moon, and stars in relation to Earth.

ACTIVITY

Compare and Contrast Use the library or Internet to research navigation tools used today. Write a paragraph describing these tools and a paragraph comparing the navigation tools today with those of the 1400s. How are they alike, and how are they different?

RESEARCH

Visit The Learning Site at **www.harcourtschool.com** to research other primary sources.

5

CATEGORIZE

As you read, think of ways to categorize the people, cultures, and events involved with the colonization of the Americas.

BIG IDEA

Europeans, Africans, and Native Americans shaped new ways of life in the Americas.

VOCABULARY

colonization
conquistador
indigenous
immunity
Columbian exchange
encomienda
coureur de bois

Colonization of the Americas

900   1200   1500   1800

1475–1675

From a lookout on the deck of the *Pinta*, one of Columbus's three ships, the cry rang out *"Lumbre! Tierra!"*—"Light! Land!" Columbus's first voyage was one of exploration. On his second voyage in 1493, he set out with 17 ships, more than 1,000 people, and horses, cattle, and sheep. The purpose of the second voyage was **colonization**, or settlement. A flood of settlers followed, beginning a process that brought together cultures from Europe, Africa, and the Americas.

Spain Builds an Empire

The first Europeans came to the Americas looking for gold and other riches. The Spanish called these treasure seekers **conquistadors** (kahn•KEES•tah•dawrz), or conquerors. One of the first conquistadors was Hernando Cortés (air•NAHN•doh kawr•TEZ). Attracted by stories of great wealth to be found, Cortés set out in 1519 to explore Mexico.

Spanish conquistador Hernando Cortés visits Motecuhzoma, the Aztec emperor (below). The feathered headdress (left) was worn by Motecuhzoma.

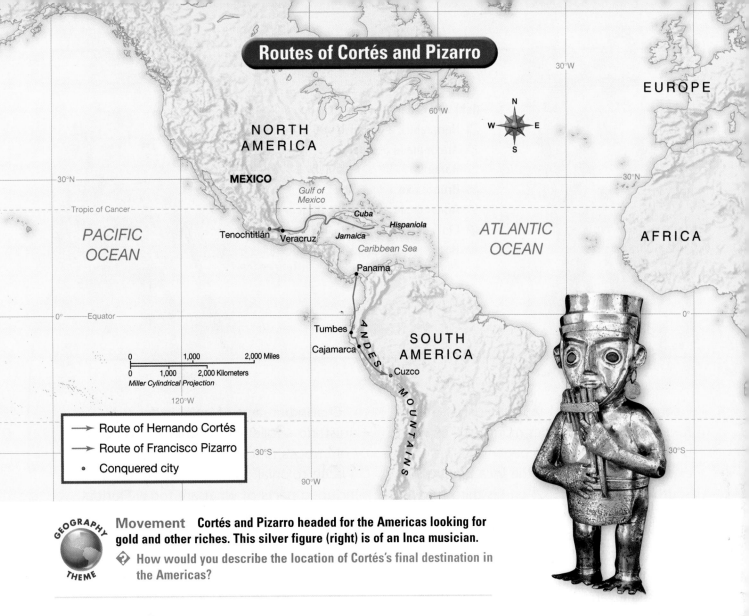

Routes of Cortés and Pizarro

EUROPE

NORTH AMERICA

MEXICO

Gulf of Mexico

Tenochtitlán Veracruz

Cuba

Hispaniola

Jamaica

Caribbean Sea

PACIFIC OCEAN

ATLANTIC OCEAN

AFRICA

Panama

Tumbes

Cajamarca

SOUTH AMERICA

Cuzco

ANDES MOUNTAINS

0   1,000   2,000 Miles
0   1,000   2,000 Kilometers
Miller Cylindrical Projection

→ Route of Hernando Cortés
→ Route of Francisco Pizarro
• Conquered city

Movement Cortés and Pizarro headed for the Americas looking for gold and other riches. This silver figure (right) is of an Inca musician.

❷ How would you describe the location of Cortés's final destination in the Americas?

Motecuhzoma, the Aztec emperor, heard of Cortés's arrival. At first, Motecuhzoma thought that Cortés might be Quetzalcóatl, the Aztec god. An Aztec legend had said that Quetzalcóatl would one day appear as a bearded, light-skinned man, which described Cortés. The legend also said that Quetzalcóatl had sailed away to the east. Cortés arrived from the east. In addition, Cortés and his soldiers rode horses and carried guns—both unknown in the Americas.

When Cortés arrived in the Aztec capital, Tenochtitlán, Motecuhzoma welcomed him and offered gifts of gold. This was the treasure that Cortés had been seeking. He and his army were not interested in Aztec culture, only in Aztec gold.

When Cortés's soldiers began to treat the Aztecs badly, the Aztecs drove the Spanish from Tenochtitlán. Cortés returned a year later with a larger army and burned the Aztec capital. On the ashes of Tenochtitlán, Cortés began to build Mexico City.

Tales of Cortés's gold soon attracted other conquistadors such as Francisco Pizarro (frahn•SEES•koh pee•SAR•oh).

Francisco Pizarro

Spanish Conquistador and Inca Warrior

Analyze Illustrations The Spanish conquistador (left) was better equipped than the Inca warrior (right).

1. Harquebus, a gun invented in the 1400s
2. Armor made of steel
3. Horse
4. Bronze axe
5. Armor made of quilted cotton or leather
6. Cloth shield

❓ How might conquistadors on horseback have had advantages over Inca warriors on foot?

Pizarro heard tales of fantastic riches to be found high in the Andes mountains of what is now Peru. In 1524 he began a series of expeditions to conquer the Inca Empire in South America. In 1532, on his third trip, Atahuallpa (ah•tah•WAHL•pah), the Inca emperor, agreed to meet with Pizarro but was then taken prisoner.

In return for his freedom, Atahuallpa promised Pizarro a large room filled with gold. Even though Atahuallpa kept his word, Pizarro had him killed. By 1532 the Spanish had conquered the Incas and taken control of their lands.

Pedro Cabral's ship

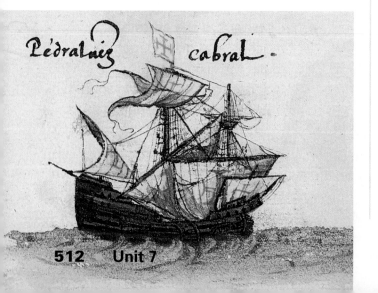

Chasing dreams of gold, other conquistadors followed. Within 100 years of Columbus's first voyage, the Spanish ruled a large colonial empire in the Americas. It included parts of what are today Florida, the southwestern United States, and Mexico, as well as large parts of Central and South America. The Spanish did not control all of South America, however. In 1500 Pedro Cabral (kuh•BRAHL) claimed what is now the country of Brazil for Portugal.

REVIEW How did Spain create an empire in the Americas?

Cultural Change and Exchange

Almost at once, ships began to carry gold, silver, and precious stones from the Americas back to Spain. Spain became the richest and most powerful nation in the world during the 1500s.

As the Spanish moved through the Americas, they ate native, or **indigenous** (in•DIH•juh•nuhs), foods that were unknown in Europe. The Spanish sent these foods to their homeland. Corn, beans, tomatoes, squash, peppers, peanuts, and chocolate soon were added to the European diet. Some foods, such as the peanut, became important food sources in Africa and Asia. Perhaps the food that brought the greatest change to Europe was the potato. Cheap and plentiful, the potato kept many poor Europeans from starving. One nonfood crop—tobacco—also made its way to Europe.

The Spanish settlers who colonized the Americas brought European animals and plants with them. Cattle, pigs, chickens, sheep, chickpeas, sugarcane, and wheat changed the diet and ways of life of many native people in the Americas. The introduction of horses changed transportation, hunting, and warfare.

In this drawing a Spanish noble forces a young Inca woman to weave.

Spanish settlers also brought diseases, such as influenza, smallpox, and measles, with them. The native people of the Americas had never been exposed to these diseases before. Many native people died because they had never developed an **immunity**, or resistance, to the diseases. Some historians believe that as much as 90 percent of the native population may have died from European diseases.

Historians refer to the movement of people, animals, plants, ideas, and diseases between Europe and the Americas as the **Columbian exchange**. People and their cultures were an important part of this.

GEOGRAPHY THEME

Movement   **The effects of the Columbian exchange can still be felt today.**

❓ In what direction did wheat travel—from west to east or east to west?

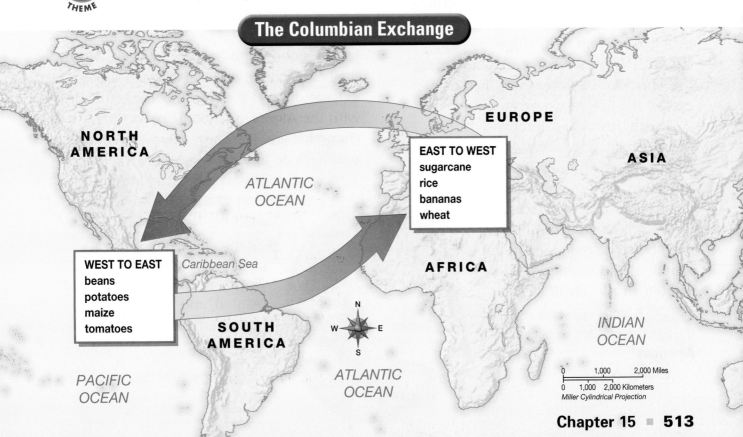

The Columbian Exchange

EUROPE

ASIA

EAST TO WEST
sugarcane
rice
bananas
wheat

NORTH AMERICA

ATLANTIC OCEAN

WEST TO EAST
beans
potatoes
maize
tomatoes

Caribbean Sea

AFRICA

SOUTH AMERICA

ATLANTIC OCEAN

INDIAN OCEAN

PACIFIC OCEAN

0   1,000   2,000 Miles
0   1,000   2,000 Kilometers
Miller Cylindrical Projection

Father Jacques Marquette traveled the Mississippi River, meeting different Native American tribes.

Some Spanish colonists used a system called the **encomienda** (en•koh•mee•EN•dah). Under this system Native Americans were to work for colonists and accept the Catholic faith. In return, colonists would provide them with food and housing.

In truth many Native Americans were treated like slaves. Few colonists questioned the encomienda system. When native people died from overwork and disease, colonists began to bring enslaved Africans to the Americas. The slave trade then became part of the Columbian exchange.

The cultures of the European colonists, African slaves, and Native Americans began to mix in Spanish America. Many Native Americans and Africans became Catholics. Colonists adopted some customs of Native Americans and Africans that were better suited to life in the Americas. This mixing of cultures created a new way of life.

(REVIEW) **What are some diseases the Spanish settlers brought to the Americas?**

(Focus Skill) **CATEGORIZE**

Colonization Grows

Like Spain, other European countries began to claim lands in the Americas. In 1534 French explorer Jacques Cartier (ZHAHK kar•TYAY) claimed land in what is now Canada for France. Cartier reported seeing many fur-bearing animals along the St. Lawrence River. Furs could be sold for high prices in Europe. French traders bartered, or traded, goods with Native Americans. Mostly they exchanged furs for beads and supplies.

Trade grew as the French became friendly with the Algonkin (al•GON•kin) and the Huron Indians. French trappers, known as **coureurs de bois** (koo•RER duh BWAH), or "runners of the woods," lived in Algonkin and Huron villages. The trappers adopted the Native American languages and customs.

French priests, who came to North America to spread their religion, also lived with the Native Americans. They, too,

Captain John Smith, leader of Jamestown

adopted many native ways of life. Father Jacques Marquette traveled nearly the whole length of the Mississippi River. Explorers who followed Marquette's route claimed all this land for France.

In 1585 the first English settlers arrived in North America and established a colony at Roanoke. Although the Roanoke colony failed, the English tried again at Jamestown in 1607. With the leadership of Captain John Smith and the help of Native Americans, Jamestown survived.

Native Americans also helped colonies started by Pilgrims and Puritans, people who had left England to find religious freedom. As more settlers arrived, the colonies grew, pushing Native Americans westward.

In 1609 explorer Henry Hudson claimed the area along the Hudson River for the Netherlands. At the mouth of the river, the Dutch founded the settlement of New Amsterdam, which later became New York. New Amsterdam was a place of religious freedom and cultural diversity. As many as 18 different languages were spoken there.

REVIEW How did Native Americans influence the French who came to North America?

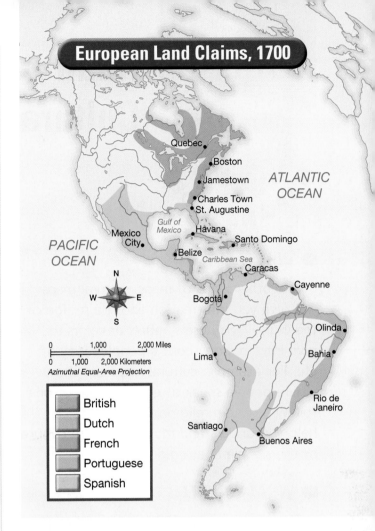

European Land Claims, 1700

British
Dutch
French
Portuguese
Spanish

Regions By 1700 Europeans had claimed lands across the Americas.

❓ Which European country had claimed the most land by 1700?

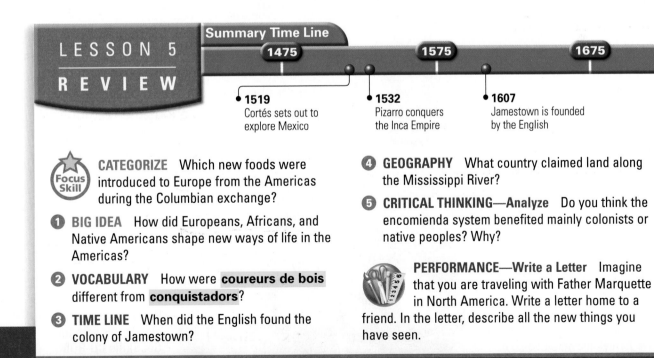

LESSON 5 REVIEW

Summary Time Line

1475 — 1575 — 1675

1519 Cortés sets out to explore Mexico

1532 Pizarro conquers the Inca Empire

1607 Jamestown is founded by the English

CATEGORIZE Which new foods were introduced to Europe from the Americas during the Columbian exchange?

1 **BIG IDEA** How did Europeans, Africans, and Native Americans shape new ways of life in the Americas?

2 **VOCABULARY** How were **coureurs de bois** different from **conquistadors**?

3 **TIME LINE** When did the English found the colony of Jamestown?

4 **GEOGRAPHY** What country claimed land along the Mississippi River?

5 **CRITICAL THINKING—Analyze** Do you think the encomienda system benefited mainly colonists or native peoples? Why?

PERFORMANCE—Write a Letter Imagine that you are traveling with Father Marquette in North America. Write a letter home to a friend. In the letter, describe all the new things you have seen.

· SKILLS ·
MAP AND GLOBE

Read a Map of Cultural Regions

▶ WHY IT MATTERS

Like other kinds of maps, cultural maps can give you information about a region of the world. They use symbols or colors to give information about a people's way of life. For example, cultural maps can show where people speak a certain language or follow a certain religion. These maps can help you understand more about the culture of the people in a region.

▶ WHAT YOU NEED TO KNOW

The map on page 517 is a cultural map showing the languages that people speak in South America today. The colors on the map key stand for the languages spoken in the regions shown on the map. The map key also divides the languages spoken in South America into two groups— official languages and indigenous, or native, languages.

Indigenous languages are spoken mainly by South America's native peoples. These groups were living in South America long before Europeans explored the continent.

When European settlers built colonies in South America, they brought their languages with them. After years of colonial rule, many South Americans spoke European languages, such as Spanish, Portuguese, French, Dutch, and English. Most countries of South America are independent today, but European languages are still the official languages of most countries there.

▶ PRACTICE THE SKILL

Study the cultural map and the map key to answer these questions.

1. In which country do many people speak Portuguese?

2. What languages do people speak in Argentina? Which of these languages is spoken by the most people?

3. In which South American country is the official language Dutch?

4. Which indigenous languages are spoken in Peru?

▶ APPLY WHAT YOU LEARNED

Draw a cultural map of South America. Use an encyclopedia, atlas, or almanac to gather information about the religions practiced by the people of South America. You may use colors or symbols to show where people practice the different religions. Have a classmate use your map to make some generalizations about the religions practiced in South America.

Native Peruvians in traditional dress

MAP AND GLOBE SKILLS

Practice your map and globe skills with the **GeoSkills CD-ROM.**

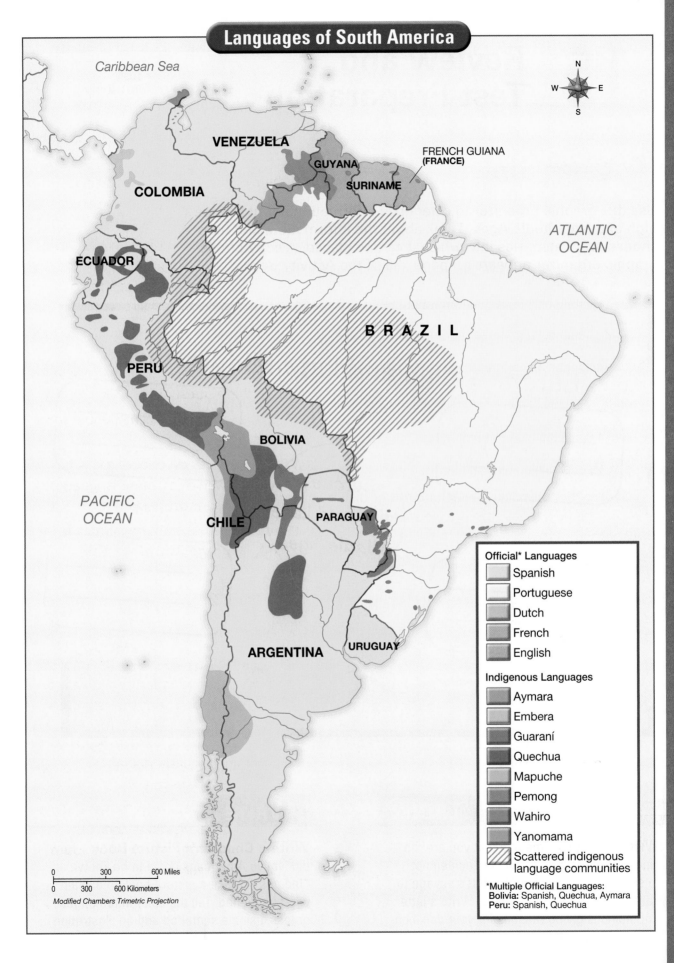

Languages of South America

Caribbean Sea

VENEZUELA

COLOMBIA

GUYANA

SURINAME

FRENCH GUIANA
(FRANCE)

ATLANTIC
OCEAN

ECUADOR

PERU

B R A Z I L

BOLIVIA

PACIFIC
OCEAN

CHILE

PARAGUAY

ARGENTINA

URUGUAY

N
W   E
S

Official* Languages
- Spanish
- Portuguese
- Dutch
- French
- English

Indigenous Languages
- Aymara
- Embera
- Guaraní
- Quechua
- Mapuche
- Pemong
- Wahiro
- Yanomama
- Scattered indigenous language communities

*Multiple Official Languages:
Bolivia: Spanish, Quechua, Aymara
Peru: Spanish, Quechua

0   300   600 Miles
0   300   600 Kilometers
Modified Chambers Trimetric Projection

15 Review and Test Preparation

Focus Skill Categorize

Use this graphic organizer to categorize information about Europe's high and late Middle Ages. Think about the information, and then choose four categories into which it can be placed. A copy of this graphic organizer appears on page 136 of the Activity Book.

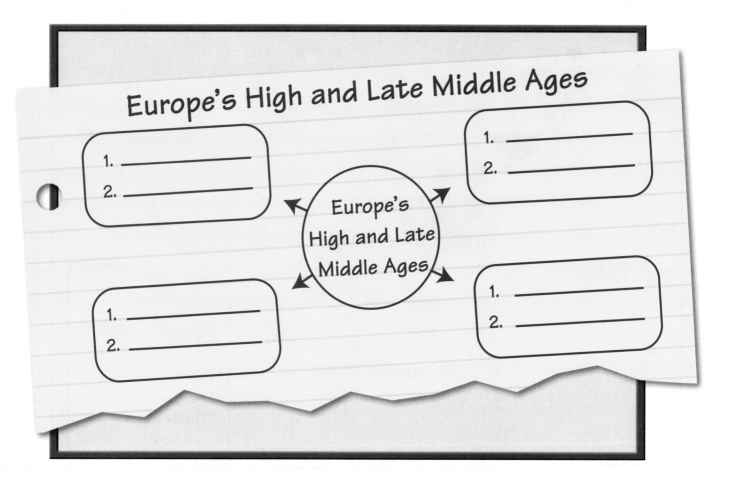

Europe's High and Late Middle Ages

1. _____
2. _____

1. _____
2. _____

Europe's High and Late Middle Ages

1. _____
2. _____

1. _____
2. _____

THINK & WRITE

Write a Letter   Imagine that you are the king of Portugal and you have decided not to support Christopher Columbus's voyage to search for a new route to Asia. Write a letter to Columbus giving reasons for your decision. Compare your letter with a classmate's.

Write a Children's Picture Book   How did Native Americans come to be known as "Indians"? Make a picture book to explain what happened. Tell the story in ten pages or less, using a sentence and an illustration on each page of the book.

1215
King John agrees to
the Magna Carta

About 1400
The Renaissance begins

1492
Columbus reaches
the Americas

1532
Pizarro conquers
the Inca Empire

1607
Jamestown is founded
by the English

USE THE TIME LINE

Use the chapter summary time line to
answer these questions.

1 Which came first, the Renaissance or the
founding of Jamestown?

2 In what year did Pizarro conquer the Inca
Empire?

USE VOCABULARY

Use each term in a sentence to explain its
meaning and how that meaning relates to
the ideas presented in this chapter.

3 **Magna Carta** (p. 488)

4 **Protestant** (p. 500)

5 **armada** (p. 507)

RECALL FACTS

Answer these questions.

6 How did guilds improve the quality of
European goods?

7 For what explorer is America named?

Write the letter of the best choice.

8 **TEST PREP** Who is considered one of
England's greatest playwrights?
A Pieter Brueghel
B Michelangelo Buonarroti
C Leonardo da Vinci
D William Shakespeare

9 **TEST PREP** Which scientist built a
telescope and used it to show that Earth
revolves around the sun?
F Nicolaus Copernicus
G Galileo Galilei
H Johannes Gutenberg
J Niccolò Machiavelli

10 **TEST PREP** Which of these is *not* a reason
Aztec leaders thought Hernando Cortés might
be a god?
A Cortés had red hair.
B Cortés was light-skinned.
C Cortés and his men rode horses.
D Cortés and his men carried weapons that
shot fire.

11 **TEST PREP** All of these are reasons
Ferdinand and Isabella supported Columbus's
voyage to the New World *except*—
F Columbus promised them wealth.
G Columbus promised them lands.
H Columbus promised to map the areas he
explored.
J Columbus promised to spread the Catholic
faith in Asia.

THINK CRITICALLY

12 Why was it important that Martin Luther
translated the Bible into German?

13 Why do you think that many Native Americans
and Africans became Catholics?

APPLY SKILLS

Make a Thoughtful Decision

14 Think about a decision you might
need to make in the future. Then
use the steps on page 496 to
decide which action to take.

Read a Map of Cultural Regions

15 Use the cultural map on page 517
to identify which European
languages are spoken in South
America. List the countries in South
America in which each is spoken.

TAJ MAHAL, AGRA, INDIA

The Taj Mahal is located in the city of Agra, in northern India. Made of white marble, this beautiful tomb is an example of Mogul architecture, which blends Indian, Persian, and Islamic styles. It was built for the wife of the Mogul ruler Shah Jahan. Begun in 1632, it required 20,000 workers and 15 years to finish.

LOCATE IT

Agra

INDIA

Arabian Sea

Bay of Bengal

16

The Eastern Hemisphere

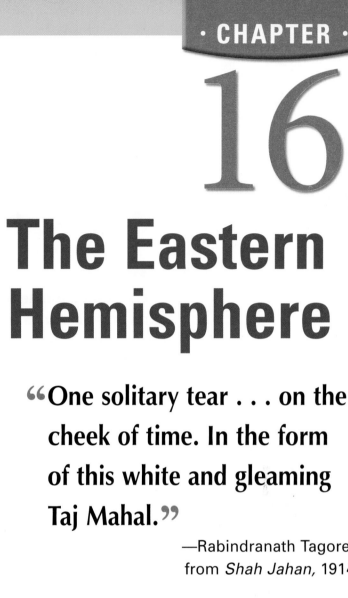

"One solitary tear . . . on the cheek of time. In the form of this white and gleaming Taj Mahal."

—Rabindranath Tagore, from *Shah Jahan,* 1914

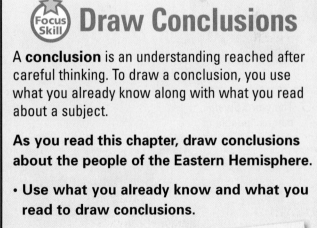

Focus Skill Draw Conclusions

A **conclusion** is an understanding reached after careful thinking. To draw a conclusion, you use what you already know along with what you read about a subject.

As you read this chapter, draw conclusions about the people of the Eastern Hemisphere.

• Use what you already know and what you read to draw conclusions.

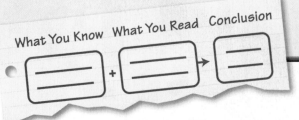

What You Know What You Read Conclusion

1

Later African Kingdoms

DRAW CONCLUSIONS

As you read, draw conclusions about how trade affected kingdoms in Africa.

BIG IDEA

Trade in Africa and around the Indian Ocean linked many peoples.

| 900 | 1200 | 1500 | 1800 |

900–1700

During the time of the Middle Ages in Europe, new kingdoms arose in Africa south of the Sahara. Like the powerful empires of western Africa, these kingdoms grew and gained wealth because of trade. Merchants from the Arabian Peninsula, Asia, and eventually Europe made journeys to trade with many of these African kingdoms.

Swahili City-States

By the A.D. 900s a culture and a language that were part Arabian and part African had formed in eastern Africa. This culture had developed in the trading communities along the coast. The people and the language they spoke were called **Swahili** (swah•HEE•lee). Over time, the Swahili communities became independent city-states that controlled trade in eastern Africa.

Bronze jewelry (left) from Asia has been found at the sites of Swahili city-states. Mosques like this one in Kilwa (KIL•wah) (below) are also among the ruins.

FAST FACT The word *Swahili* means "people of the coast."

Each city-state was governed by a **sultan**, or Muslim ruler. Most Swahilis became Muslims, but they also followed many African traditions and customs.

Kilwa was one of the richest Swahili city-states. Kilwa was as far south as Asian traders could sail in one monsoon season. It was also the center of the region's gold trade. The wealthy lived in tall houses surrounded by walls of coral stone. The Muslim traveler Ibn Battuta wrote that Kilwa was "one of the most beautiful and best-constructed towns in the world."

To the south of Kilwa was the city-state of Sofala (soh•FAH•lah). Gold mined farther inland was shipped first to Sofala and then to Kilwa. A Muslim traveler to Sofala in the 1000s wrote that Sofala had "gold in abundance and other marvels." Besides gold, many of the Swahili city-states were rich in such goods as ivory, animal skins, herbs, oils, and perfumes.

REVIEW How were the Swahili city-states governed? It was governed by a sultan.

Great Zimbabwe

The goods that brought wealth to the Swahili city-states came from regions farther inland. Merchants from central Africa traveled to the coastal cities to trade gold for salt, tools, and cloth.

The ancestors of the central Africans had migrated from western Africa hundreds of years before. These people, whom historians call Bantu speakers, settled in all parts of eastern and southern Africa.

In about 1200 a Bantu-speaking group called the Shonas (SHOH•nuhz) took control of the gold mines in southern Africa. This made the Shonas very wealthy. Another source of wealth for the Shonas was

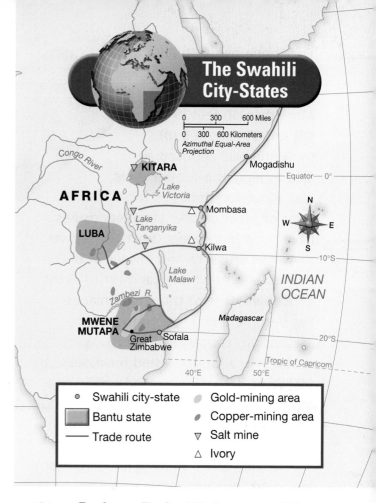

The Swahili City-States

GEOGRAPHY THEME

Regions The Swahili city-states traded with the Bantu states in Africa and with southwestern Asia.

❓ Why do you think the Swahili city-states formed along the coast?

the ivory trade. They also raised large herds of cattle and had large grain houses. To protect their wealth, the Shonas used iron to make swords and other weapons. They also traded iron and goods made of iron.

Over time, the Shonas established an empire. They built their capital at Great Zimbabwe (zim•BAH•bway). The word *zimbabwe* comes from a Shona term meaning "stone enclosure." Archaeologists now believe that as many as 11,000 people may have lived in Great Zimbabwe.

Merchants in Great Zimbabwe traded for Asian goods such as this Chinese bell.

The Shona people built a huge stone wall at Great Zimbabwe around the royal court. More than 30 feet (9 m) tall and 15 feet (4.5 m) thick, the wall enclosed an area as long as a football field and about four times as wide. The ruins of other, smaller stone enclosures have been found near Great Zimbabwe.

African artists carved images of birds into the walls of the royal court of Great Zimbabwe. One of these bird images has become a national symbol of the present-day country of Zimbabwe.

The Shona Empire lasted for more than 200 years, trading with the Swahili city-states. In about 1450 the Shonas abandoned Great Zimbabwe. Why they left is not known.

A leader named Mutota (moo•TOH•tah) led some Shona people north. They settled on a high plain known as the Zimbabwe Plateau, located between the Zambezi and Limpopo Rivers.

These bronze bracelets were found near the ruins of Great Zimbabwe.

Mutota's son Matope (mah•TOH•pay) built a new empire—the Mutapa Empire—by conquering smaller states nearby. Matope's government taxed all goods passing through the empire. In this way he took over the trade that had once been controlled by Great Zimbabwe.

REVIEW Where did the Shonas build their capital? At Great Zimbabwe.

Other African Kingdoms

The kingdom of Kanem developed near Lake Chad in the 800s. Later, Kanem joined with the nearby kingdom of Bornu (BAWR•noo). By 1600 the soldiers of Kanem-Bornu had created a huge empire.

Kanem-Bornu's time of greatest growth came during the rule of Idris Aloma (EE•drees al•OH•muh) in the late 1500s. Idris Aloma was a Muslim who spread

In what is today the African country of Zimbabwe stand the ruins (left) of Great Zimbabwe. Remains of walls (bottom) still surround the ruins of a royal court.

Analyze Primary Sources

Zimbabwe's present-day flag (right) pictures the Zimbabwe bird, an image found in the form of soapstone carvings (far right) at the abandoned city of Great Zimbabwe.

1 Black stripes on the flag stand for the people of Zimbabwe.

2 Green and yellow represent Zimbabwe's agriculture and mineral wealth.

3 Red stripes honor those whose blood was shed during a fight for freedom.

◆ Why do you think the colors green and yellow represent agriculture and mineral wealth?

his faith to the lands he governed. He replaced the old laws of Kanem-Bornu with new ones based on Islamic law. He also strengthened his army by providing them with guns and military training.

To the southwest of Kanem-Bornu, in the forests of western Africa, other trading kingdoms formed. By 1500 Benin (buh•NIN) was among the most powerful of these kingdoms. Benin grew wealthy from trading spices, ivory, cloth, tools, and slaves.

From a palace in the walled city of Benin, the *oba* (OH•buh), or king, ruled a large empire. Its lands lay in what is now southern Nigeria.

To the west of Benin, other kingdoms grew. Among these were Oyo (oh•YOH), which rose in the late 1400s. A king, or *alafin* (ah•LAHF•in), ruled Oyo, but a council of advisers could remove him if they thought he was not a good leader. In Dahomey (duh•HOH•mee), which rose in the mid-1600s, the king controlled everything without question. The king of Ashanti

(uh•SHAHN•tee), founded in the late 1600s, made decisions with a council of chiefs. Women also had a place in Ashanti government. Female relatives of the king advised him and sometimes ruled in his place.

Far to the south, the kingdom of the Kongo arose in the 1400s. The people thought of their king, the *manikongo*, as a god. Like other kingdoms, the Kongo had an economy based on trade.

REVIEW What changes did Idris Aloma bring to Kanem-Bornu?

Europeans in Africa

The Portuguese sailed around the southern tip of Africa in 1488, looking for a sea route to India. They were amazed by the great riches they found in the city-states of Sofala and Kilwa. Instead of trading with these places, the Portuguese wanted to control them.

In 1505 the Portuguese invaded Kilwa. They also took over Sofala and Mombasa. With their advanced weapons, the Portuguese very soon controlled the Swahili city-states.

A bronze statue of a member of Benin's royal family

Next, the Portuguese turned to the gold mines in southern Africa. In 1629 the Portuguese defeated the ruler of the Mutapa Empire. The next ruler gave the Portuguese rights to all the gold, silver, and iron mines in the kingdom.

Other European countries also became interested in African resources and trade. At first, European merchants traded mostly for gold, ivory, and spices. Over time, however, slaves became the main export of African trade.

European settlers had started colonies throughout North, Central, and South America. They built mines and started huge farms, or **plantations**, on which they grew cash crops such as coffee, sugarcane, tobacco, and cotton. Most Europeans would not work on the plantations or in the mines.

European colonists soon looked to Africa for slave labor, but slavery was not new.

Enslaved Africans picked coffee beans from plants like this one.

Many African societies kept slaves long before the arrival of Europeans. However, most African slaves were prisoners of war or criminals. Many had a chance of one day being free. European slavery was different in that slaves were thought of as property. They were bought and sold as their owners saw fit. This kind of slavery was for life. Children of a slave were born slaves and would remain enslaved all their lives.

The sale of people was part of a system called the **triangular trade**. First, traders sailed from Europe to Africa with iron, cloth, guns, and liquor. In Africa these goods were exchanged for enslaved people. Next, the enslaved people were shipped to plantations in the Americas. There, the enslaved people were sold for goods. The goods from the plantations

The Portuguese set up workshops for washing the gold-bearing sand found in Africa (below). They used special spoons and boxes for storing gold dust (left).

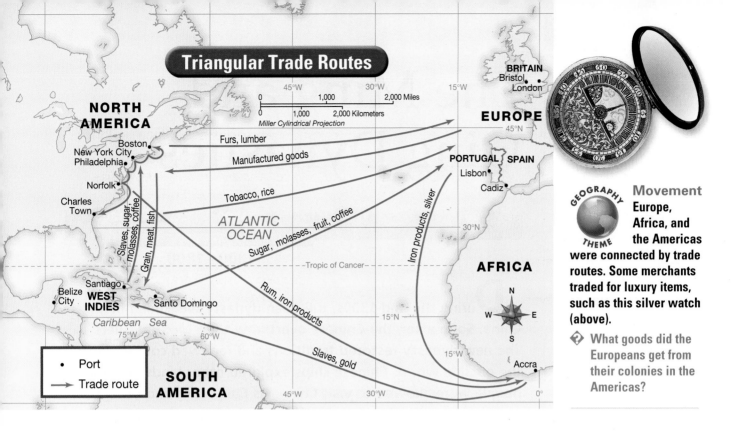

Triangular Trade Routes

NORTH AMERICA
- Boston
- New York City
- Philadelphia
- Norfolk
- Charles Town
- Santiago
- WEST INDIES
- Belize City
- Santo Domingo

Caribbean Sea

SOUTH AMERICA

ATLANTIC OCEAN

-Tropic of Cancer-

EUROPE

BRITAIN
- Bristol
- London

PORTUGAL SPAIN
- Lisbon
- Cadiz

AFRICA
- Accra

Furs, lumber
Manufactured goods
Tobacco, rice
Sugar, molasses, fruit, coffee
Slaves, sugar, molasses, coffee
Grain, meat, fish
Rum, iron products
Slaves, gold
Iron products, silver

Miller Cylindrical Projection

- • Port
- → Trade route

GEOGRAPHY THEME

Movement Europe, Africa, and the Americas were connected by trade routes. Some merchants traded for luxury items, such as this silver watch (above).

❓ What goods did the Europeans get from their colonies in the Americas?

were taken back to Europe, completing the triangle.

For more than 300 years, Africa was the focus of the slave trade. As many as 10 million enslaved Africans were taken to the Americas. Many Africans died on the way to the Americas. The African kingdoms that took part in the slave trade made such large profits that they ignored all other economic activities. When the slave trade and its profits ended, the once-great African kingdoms were left with no income.

REVIEW How did the slave trade deny human rights? 🔵 DRAW CONCLUSIONS

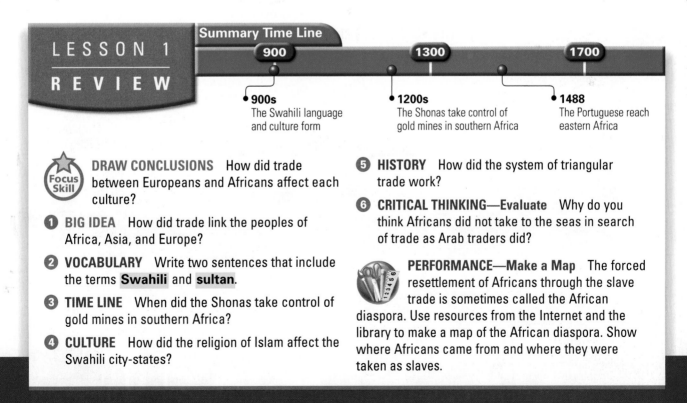

LESSON 1 REVIEW

Summary Time Line

- **900s** The Swahili language and culture form
- **1200s** The Shonas take control of gold mines in southern Africa
- **1488** The Portuguese reach eastern Africa

⭐ **Focus Skill** **DRAW CONCLUSIONS** How did trade between Europeans and Africans affect each culture?

1. **BIG IDEA** How did trade link the peoples of Africa, Asia, and Europe?

2. **VOCABULARY** Write two sentences that include the terms **Swahili** and **sultan**.

3. **TIME LINE** When did the Shonas take control of gold mines in southern Africa?

4. **CULTURE** How did the religion of Islam affect the Swahili city-states?

5. **HISTORY** How did the system of triangular trade work?

6. **CRITICAL THINKING—Evaluate** Why do you think Africans did not take to the seas in search of trade as Arab traders did?

✂️ **PERFORMANCE—Make a Map** The forced resettlement of Africans through the slave trade is sometimes called the African diaspora. Use resources from the Internet and the library to make a map of the African diaspora. Show where Africans came from and where they were taken as slaves.

2

 Focus Skill

DRAW CONCLUSIONS

As you read, draw conclusions about the effects that the Ming and Qing dynasties had on China.

BIG IDEA

The ways in which the Chinese saw themselves in relation to the rest of the world changed over time.

VOCABULARY

isolation

ambassador

The Ming and Qing Dynasties

| 900 | 1200 | 1500 | 1800 |

1300 – 1800

During the mid-1300s, the Yuan dynasty weakened in China. Soon after, the Chinese overthrew their Mongol rulers. The new dynasty restored traditions and renewed contact with the outside world. Chinese ships explored other lands, and many people were allowed to visit China. As Europeans and others hurried to trade with the empire, however, its borders were closed once again to outsiders.

The Ming Dynasty

The Mongol Empire was torn apart by revolts, natural disasters, and fighting among would-be rulers. Believing that the Mongols had lost the Mandate of Heaven, the Chinese people rebelled. One of the rebel leaders, a former Buddhist monk named Hong Wu, took control in 1368. He declared himself emperor of a new dynasty called the Ming.

The Forbidden City in Beijing (below) was the seat of Chinese government from about 1420 until about 1911. Its more than 9,000 rooms hold historic artifacts like this painting of the Forbidden City (left).

Under Hong Wu's leadership, China began to recover. Farms, canals, and roads were repaired. The economy improved, and China's population grew. Later, however, Hong Wu became a tyrant. He had thousands of people thrown into prison or killed.

When Hong Wu died in 1398, one of his sons, Yong Le (YUHNG LEH), became emperor. During his reign, China once again became a major force in Asia. Yong Le personally led attacks against the Mongols to push them farther out of China. He also paid for the ocean voyages of Admiral Zheng He. The Chinese learned much about other places through the voyages of Zheng He. At the same time, those places learned of the wealth and splendor of the Ming dynasty.

Yong Le died in 1424, and China's ocean explorations ended soon after. In 1433 the Chinese government stopped all ocean voyages and destroyed Zheng He's records.

Emperor Yong Le

The reason the Ming government ended ocean voyages is a mystery. Perhaps the ocean voyages became too costly or perhaps Ming officials agreed with an earlier emperor who said,

❝China's territory produces all goods in abundance, so why should we buy useless trifles from abroad?❞

Whatever the reason, the Ming rulers turned to a policy of **isolation**, or cutting oneself off from contact with others. Ming emperors began rebuilding China's strength from within. They made the Great Wall stronger and repaired the Grand Canal. The Ming rulers also offered help to farmers.

Although trade with the outside world was discouraged by the Ming rulers, trade within China was encouraged. Merchants transported farm products, cloth, and valuable metals along China's waterways. Some villages along the rivers became market towns, and many cities grew.

LOCATE IT

Beijing

CHINA

Under Ming rule, there was a flowering, or growth, of Chinese culture. Instead of searching for new ideas, the Chinese focused on their traditions. Chinese scholars wrote histories of earlier dynasties. Ming artists produced masterpieces of calligraphy, the Chinese art of handwriting. They also made beautiful works in porcelain, a very fine china. Ming painters improved upon the art of landscape painting.

For the most part, Ming rulers did not allow non-Chinese people in China. A few Catholic missionaries from Europe were allowed to visit. However, most Chinese showed little interest in European religion.

REVIEW How might the focus on Chinese traditions have affected the Ming people?

 **DRAW CONCLUSIONS**

This porcelain vase is a treasured art object from the Ming dynasty.

Manchurian Rule

The Ming kept tight control over contact between Europeans and the Chinese people. Even so, European merchants did not stop trying to trade with China. In 1557 the Chinese allowed the Portuguese to set up a trading post on an island near Macao (muh•KOW).

By 1600 the Ming had ruled China for more than 200 years. Then bad harvests and poor leadership began to weaken the Ming. In 1644 invaders from Manchuria, in the north, swept into China. The Manchus set up the Qing (CHING) dynasty and claimed the Mandate of Heaven.

The Manchus forced the Chinese people to change many of their customs. However, the Manchus also adopted the values of Confucius, who taught the importance of good behavior in society. This won the Chinese people's respect and brought peace to China.

Saint Paul's Church (below) was built in Macao by the Portuguese in 1602.

 · **GEOGRAPHY** ·

Macao
Understanding Places and Regions

Macao is located along the South China Sea in southeastern China. In the 1550s the region came under the control of Portugal. In 1987 Portugal and China signed an agreement to return Macao to China in 1999. Under this agreement Macao has political and economic freedom under China.

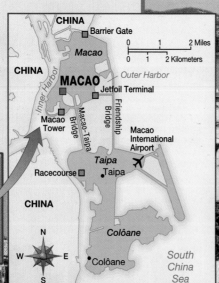

CHINA

CHINA
Barrier Gate
Macao
CHINA
MACAO
Outer Harbor
Inner Harbor
Jetfoil Terminal
Macao Tower
Macao-Taipa Bridge
Friendship Bridge
Macao International Airport
Racecourse
Taipa
Taipa
CHINA
Colôane
Colôane
South China Sea

0   1   2 Miles
0   1   2 Kilometers

N S E W

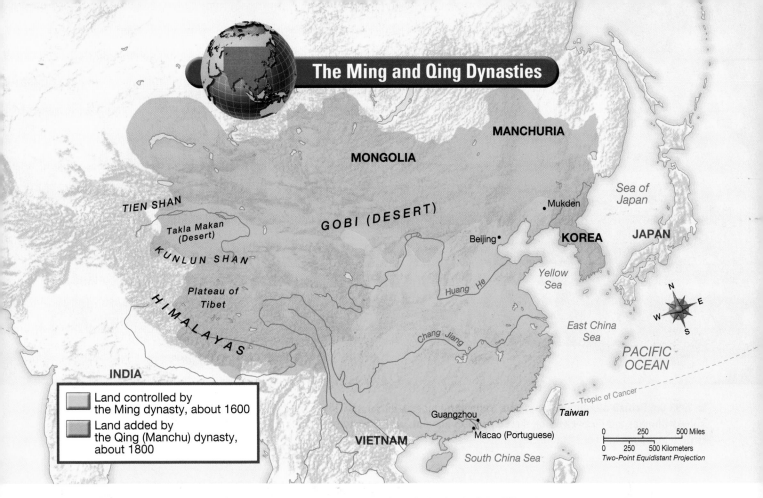

The Ming and Qing Dynasties

MANCHURIA

MONGOLIA

TIEN SHAN

Takla Makan (Desert)

GOBI (DESERT)

KUNLUN SHAN

Plateau of Tibet

HIMALAYAS

INDIA

Mukden

Sea of Japan

Beijing•

KOREA

JAPAN

Huang He

Yellow Sea

Chang Jiang

East China Sea

PACIFIC OCEAN

N E W S

Tropic of Cancer

Guangzhou

Taiwan

VIETNAM

Macao (Portuguese)

South China Sea

0   250   500 Miles
0   250   500 Kilometers
Two-Point Equidistant Projection

Land controlled by the Ming dynasty, about 1600

Land added by the Qing (Manchu) dynasty, about 1800

Regions The empire of the Qing dynasty included all the land of the Ming dynasty as well as much additional territory.

GEOGRAPHY THEME

❔ What natural feature marked the southwestern border of the Qing dynasty?

The Qing emperor **Kangxi** (KAHNG•SHEE) traveled throughout China. He listened to the people's problems and observed the ways that they lived. Kangxi invited Catholic missionaries to teach western mathematics to Chinese students. He also ordered a dictionary of Chinese characters to be created. Kangxi ruled for 60 years.

China reached its greatest size under the rule of Kangxi's grandson, Qianlong (CHYAHN•LUHNG). He became emperor in 1736 and ruled until 1795. Qianlong is remembered mostly for his support of education and the arts.

The people in the neighboring lands that came under Manchu rule had to pay tribute to the Chinese emperor. Under this tribute system, an envoy, or messenger, brought the emperor gifts. The tribute system was used to remind people of the emperor's strength.

REVIEW How did the Qing earn the respect of the Chinese people?

Kangxi (left) was fond of learning. His dictionary (far left) listed 42,000 Chinese characters.

In 1793 the British attempted to set up a trade agreement with China. This engraving shows Chinese subjects carrying the emperor to his tent, where he was to meet the British ambassador, Lord Macartney.

The Collapse of the Qing Dynasty

By the time of Qianlong, the Dutch had replaced the Portuguese as the main European power in the Indian Ocean trade. To be allowed to trade with the Chinese, the Dutch agreed to a number of Chinese rules.

Among these rules was one that limited European trade to one place, the city of Guangzhou. Wealthy Chinese merchants there had been granted permission by the emperor to trade. All the trade between Chinese and European merchants was closely watched by a Chinese official. This official was appointed by the emperor and collected taxes on the sale of all goods.

Foreigners were forbidden to enter some parts of Beijing except to pay tribute. For many years the Dutch and other Europeans accepted the tribute system. They did so because Chinese goods, such as porcelain, silk, and tea, brought high prices in Europe.

The British also wanted to trade with China, but they would not accept China's trade rules or its tribute system. In 1793 Lord George Macartney was sent to China as a British **ambassador**, or official representative. He sailed to China with about 100 men and more than 600 gifts.

Macartney also carried a letter from King George III to Qianlong. In the letter, the British king asked the Chinese emperor for a better trade agreement. The British wanted the right to sell their goods to the Chinese.

The emperor did not grant the British the agreement they wanted.

Qianlong was an emperor, a hunter, and a poet.

In a long reply to King George III, Qianlong wrote,

> **As your Ambassador can see for himself, we possess [have] all things. I set no value on objects strange or ingenious [clever], and have no use for your country's manufactures.**

By the time of Macartney's visit, the population of China had reached about 400 million. China was self-sufficient and had achieved a dazzling level of wealth and splendor. While on a boat trip around the palace, Macartney wrote of the 50 pavilions he visited, each "furnished in the richest manner . . . [so] that our presents must shrink from the comparison."

Macartney's visit did not succeed in getting a good trade agreement from the Chinese. However, his trip changed the way the British viewed the Chinese. The British wanted more than ever to break China's policy of isolation and to open it up to trade.

Emperor Puyi

As the British and other Europeans began demanding trade with China, problems within China began to surface. These problems would eventually cause the collapse of the Qing dynasty.

About 13 years before Macartney visited China, Qianlong began to make poor decisions. The emperor placed his trust in Heshan, a corrupt palace guard. Over time, Heshan stole great amounts of money from the Chinese treasury. In fact, the amount of Heshan's wealth would equal about 1.5 billion American dollars today!

Over the next 100 years, the Qing dynasty slowly fell apart. In 1909 the last Qing emperor, a three-year-old child named Puyi (POO•EE), took the throne. In 1911 the imperial government fell because of a rebellion. After 2,000 years of imperial rule, China had seen its last emperor.

REVIEW **What was the purpose of Macartney's visit to China?**

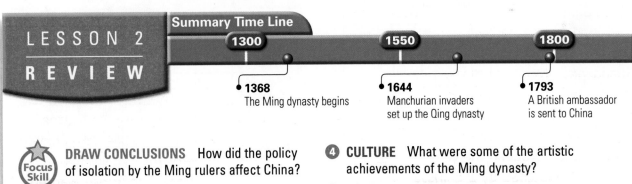

LESSON 2 REVIEW

Summary Time Line

| 1300 | 1550 | 1800 |

• **1368**
The Ming dynasty begins

• **1644**
Manchurian invaders set up the Qing dynasty

• **1793**
A British ambassador is sent to China

Focus Skill **DRAW CONCLUSIONS** How did the policy of isolation by the Ming rulers affect China?

① **BIG IDEA** How did Chinese interaction with the outside world change from the Ming to the Qing dynasties?

② **VOCABULARY** Explain how an **ambassador** might help end a policy of **isolation**.

③ **TIME LINE** When did Manchurian invaders set up the Qing dynasty?

④ **CULTURE** What were some of the artistic achievements of the Ming dynasty?

⑤ **CRITICAL THINKING—Analyze** Why do you think the Ming rulers turned to a policy of isolation?

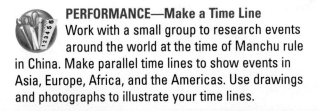

PERFORMANCE—Make a Time Line
Work with a small group to research events around the world at the time of Manchu rule in China. Make parallel time lines to show events in Asia, Europe, Africa, and the Americas. Use drawings and photographs to illustrate your time lines.

·SKILLS·

CHART AND GRAPH

Read a Population Pyramid

▶ WHY IT MATTERS

A **population pyramid** is a graph that shows how a country's population is divided by age. It also shows what part of each age group is made up of males and of females.

A population pyramid's shape depends on the country's birth rate (the number of births each year for every 1,000 people) and its death rate (the number of deaths each year for every 1,000 people). The shape of the pyramid also depends on the number of people moving to or leaving the country. Knowing how to read a country's population pyramid can provide you with a lot of information about that country.

▶ WHAT YOU NEED TO KNOW

The population pyramids on these pages show the populations of the United States, China, South Korea, and Vietnam by age groups. The bars that make up each pyramid show the percent of males and of females in each age group.

Look at the shapes of the four population pyramids. The shape of the United States pyramid shows that its population is growing very slowly. The United States has a higher percent of people over the age of 50, while China, South Korea, and Vietnam have higher percents of young people.

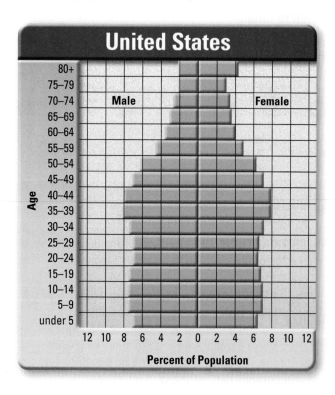

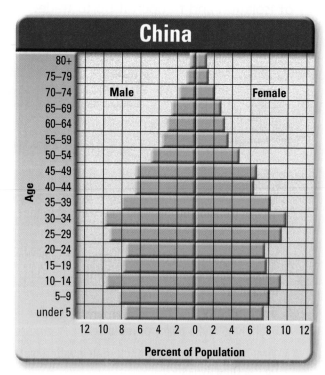

▶ PRACTICE THE SKILL

Use the population pyramids to answer these questions.

1 What percent of the population of the United States is in your age group?

2 Are there more males or more females in this group?

3 Compare the United States' percent for this group to those of the other countries. Are there more or fewer people in your age group in China, South Korea, and Vietnam?

4 Which of the four countries has the largest percent of people between 15 and 19 years old?

▶ APPLY WHAT YOU LEARNED

Think about the similarities and differences in these population pyramids. Write some questions of your own about the populations of these four countries. Make an answer key, and exchange questions with a classmate. Answer your classmate's questions.

A busy city street in Shanghai, China

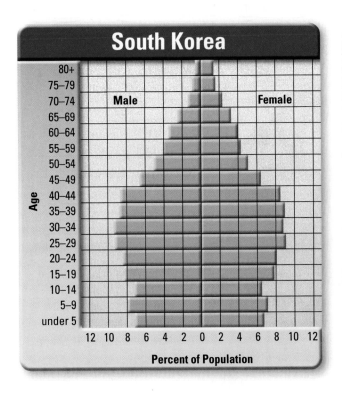

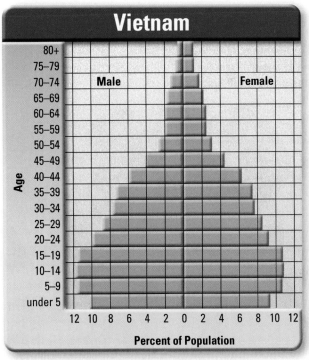

The Ottoman and Mogul Empires

Focus Skill **DRAW CONCLUSIONS**

As you read, draw conclusions about the similarities between the Ottoman and Mogul Empires.

BIG IDEA

The Ottoman and Mogul Empires had lasting effects on the people of the regions ruled by them.

VOCABULARY

jizya
Janissary
miniature
Indochina

900   1200   1500   1800

1450 – 1650

By the mid-1500s, two major Muslim empires controlled lands that reached from southeastern Europe to Tibet in central Asia. Because they shared a common religion—Islam—these empires formed cultures that were similar in many ways.

The Ottoman Empire

The Ottomans were Muslims from central Asia who had migrated to southwestern Asia. In about 1300 they began claiming lands. By 1453 they had defeated the Byzantine Empire and captured the city of Constantinople. The Ottoman Sultan Mehmed (meh•MET) II made Constantinople the capital of the empire and renamed the city Istanbul (is•tuhn•BOOL).

Mehmed wanted to return Istanbul to its former glory as a center of learning. He started colleges and built an amazing library. Christian and Jewish scholars were invited to the city to study and teach. Non-Muslims were allowed to follow their own religions and religious leaders. To do so, they paid a special tax called **jizya** to the Ottoman government.

This painting by an Ottoman artist shows a master philosopher and his students.

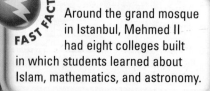

FAST FACT Around the grand mosque in Istanbul, Mehmed II had eight colleges built in which students learned about Islam, mathematics, and astronomy.

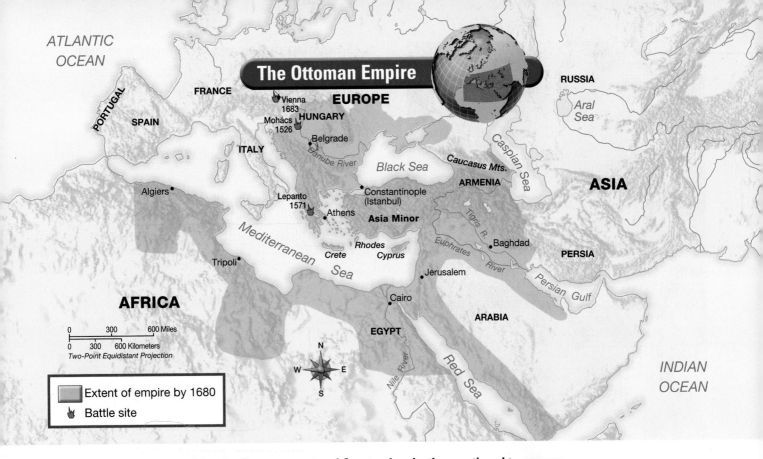

The Ottoman Empire

ATLANTIC OCEAN

EUROPE

RUSSIA

Aral Sea

FRANCE

PORTUGAL

SPAIN

ITALY

Vienna 1683
HUNGARY
Mohács 1526
Belgrade
Danube River

Black Sea

Caucasus Mts.

Caspian Sea

ARMENIA

ASIA

Algiers

Lepanto 1571
Athens

Constantinople (Istanbul)

Asia Minor

Tigris R.

Baghdad

PERSIA

Mediterranean

Crete

Rhodes

Cyprus

Euphrates River

Tripoli

Sea

Jerusalem

Persian Gulf

AFRICA

Cairo

0   300   600 Miles
0   300   600 Kilometers
Two-Point Equidistant Projection

ARABIA

EGYPT

Nile River

Red Sea

INDIAN OCEAN

N
W   E
S

Extent of empire by 1680

Battle site

GEOGRAPHY THEME

Regions After the Ottomans captured Constantinople, they continued to conquer land in Europe.

❓ How might conquering southwestern Europe have benefited the Ottomans?

The sultan also dreamed of re-creating the Eastern Roman Empire under Islamic rule. To achieve this, he raised a large army and created a strong government. The best-trained soldiers in the Ottoman army were called **Janissaries** (JA•nuh•sair•eez). Most were former Christians who had been captured or recruited as boys and then became Muslims. Years of training prepared them for war and also taught them unquestioning loyalty to the sultan. With the Janissaries at its head, Mehmed's army brought much of southeastern Europe under Ottoman control.

REVIEW Who were the Janissaries?

Süleyman I

Süleyman I

Later sultans built on the foundations of Mehmed II. Perhaps the greatest of these was Süleyman (soo•lay•mahn) I, who came to power in 1520.

The people of the Ottoman Empire called Süleyman the Lawgiver. To the Europeans he became known as Süleyman the Magnificent.

Süleyman led his armies into central Europe, capturing the city of Belgrade in 1521. The following year, his navy conquered the island of Rhodes. This gave the Ottomans control of a large part of the eastern Mediterranean. The Ottomans continued, seizing much of Hungary over the next few years.

This painting from the late 1500s shows Ottoman students playing.

Though he often started wars to gain territory, Süleyman also brought peace to the lands he conquered. An ambassador from Venice reported,

> 66 I know of no state which is happier than this one . . . no state can be compared with it. 99

For advice Süleyman depended on Ibrahim Pasha (ih•brah•HEEM PAH•shah), his grand vizier. Süleyman also asked his favorite wife, Roxelana (rahk•suh•LAHN•uh), for her advice. Both Ibrahim and Roxelana had been slaves.

Süleyman did his work honestly and was called the Lawgiver. He tried to make sure that all people under his rule were treated fairly. He encouraged education and was a patron of the arts. Süleyman also had the architect Sinan (suh•NAHN) plan new buildings for Istanbul.

In 1566 Süleyman died, and the Ottoman Empire slowly began to decline. The empire lasted until the twentieth century, but it never regained the same strength.

REVIEW **What might have been an effect of Süleyman's fairness and honesty?**

🌟 **DRAW CONCLUSIONS**

India's Mogul Empire

In about 1000, Muslim Turks gained control of much of northern India. This began a period of unified rule in India that historians call the Delhi sultanate. Under the sultanate many Hindus became Muslims. By 1500 the Delhi sultanate had begun to lose its hold in India. In 1526 Muslims from central Asia swept down through the Khyber Pass and claimed northern India. Their leader, Babur (BAH•ber), founded the Mogul (MOH•guhl) Empire. The greatest Mogul emperor was Babur's grandson, Akbar (AK•ber), who ruled from 1556 to 1605.

Unlike the Delhi sultans, Akbar treated Hindus fairly. He allowed them to practice their own religion. Hindus and other non-Muslims were also allowed to become government officials.

Akbar also worked to improve the economy. He gave farmers more land and lowered their taxes. He encouraged trade with both China and Europe.

Sinan, an Ottoman architect

Akbar supported learning and the arts, such as architecture, painting, and literature. Mogul artists of his time captured great details in small paintings called **miniatures**. In addition to the arts, religion also interested Akbar. He welcomed priests and scholars of many religions to India and talked with them about their beliefs.

A daring military leader, Akbar kept pushing the boundaries of the Mogul Empire south. By 1605 he had united most of India under Mogul rule.

After Akbar's death, his son Jahangir (juh•HAHN•gir) became ruler. He left the ruling of the empire mostly to Nur Jahan (NOOR juh•HAHN), his wife. Jahangir and Nur Jahan rejected Akbar's religious ideas. They tried to make the Mogul Empire completely Muslim.

The next Mogul ruler, Shah Jahan (SHAH juh•HAHN), ruled harshly. He ordered the destruction of several Hindu temples. He also personally directed the construction of many beautiful buildings such as the Taj Mahal (TAHZH muh•HAHL).

By the time Shah Jahan's son Aurangzeb (ow•ruhng•ZEB) seized power in 1658, the empire had weakened. Harsh rule had caused Hindus and Muslims alike to rebel. The loss of Mogul control made it easier for Europeans to gain land in India.

REVIEW Who was Babur?

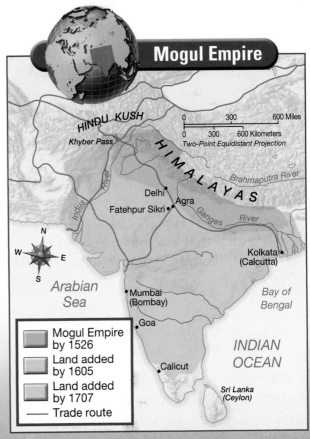

Mogul Empire

HINDU KUSH
Khyber Pass
HIMALAYAS
Brahmaputra River
Indus River
Delhi
Fatehpur Sikri • Agra
Ganges River
Kolkata (Calcutta)
Arabian Sea
Mumbai (Bombay)
Goa
Bay of Bengal
INDIAN OCEAN
Calicut
Sri Lanka (Ceylon)

0   300   600 Miles
0   300   600 Kilometers
Two-Point Equidistant Projection

- Mogul Empire by 1526
- Land added by 1605
- Land added by 1707
- Trade route

GEOGRAPHY THEME

Movement By 1707 most of India had been united by the Moguls. The Taj Mahal (below) was built in honor of Mumtaz Mahal, Shah Jahan's wife. Shah Jahan is buried by her side under the floor of the Taj Mahal.

❓ By about what year had the Moguls gained control of northern India?

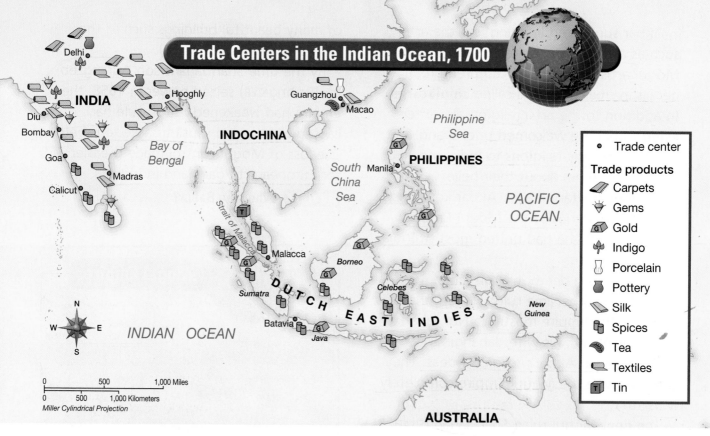

Trade Centers in the Indian Ocean, 1700

Map labels: Delhi, INDIA, Hooghly, Diu, Bombay, Goa, Madras, Calicut, Bay of Bengal, INDOCHINA, Guangzhou, Macao, Philippine Sea, PHILIPPINES, Manila, South China Sea, PACIFIC OCEAN, Strait of Malacca, Malacca, Borneo, Celebes, Sumatra, DUTCH EAST INDIES, New Guinea, Batavia, Java, INDIAN OCEAN, AUSTRALIA

Legend:
- • Trade center

Trade products
- Carpets
- Gems
- Gold
- Indigo
- Porcelain
- Pottery
- Silk
- Spices
- Tea
- Textiles
- Tin

0   500   1,000 Miles
0   500   1,000 Kilometers
Miller Cylindrical Projection

Regions Merchants in trade centers along the Indian Ocean exchanged goods with traders who sailed from Europe.

◆ What product did the Philippines provide for trade?

Europeans in the Indian Ocean

After conquering the Swahili city-states of eastern Africa, the Portuguese moved on. They captured the port city of Hormuz (AWR•muhz), between the Persian Gulf and the Arabian Sea. This gave them control of the Arabian Peninsula. In 1510 they took over Goa and other port cities on India's western coast.

A year later the Portuguese gained control of the Strait of Malacca (muh•LAH•kuh). This strait gave them control of what Europeans called the Spice Islands, in what

became the Dutch East Indies. These were islands rich in valuable spices.

Portugal's success attracted other European nations to the lands of the Indian Ocean. Ferdinand Magellan claimed the Philippine Islands for Spain in 1521. In 1602 the people of the Netherlands, the Dutch, formed the Dutch East India Company to trade with Asia. The Dutch established the headquarters of the trading company on the island of Java. Soon after, the balance of power among Indian Ocean traders began to shift.

From Java, the Dutch won Malacca from the Portuguese, taking over the gateway to the valuable Spice Islands. The Dutch also took control of

The coat of arms of the Dutch East India Company

the Cape of Good Hope on the southern tip of Africa. This success brought great wealth to the Netherlands. Amsterdam, the Dutch capital, became a leading commercial center in Europe.

The English and the French were also building empires. The English set up the English East India Company and focused their attention on India.

The French focused on the area known as Indochina. **Indochina** is a peninsula that includes the present-day countries of Vietnam, Laos, Cambodia, Thailand, Myanmar (formerly Burma), and part of Malaysia.

At first, European control in the Indian Ocean was limited to port cities and coastal areas. However, European influence eventually spread to the inland regions of India and Indochina. During the 1800s the actions of European nations greatly affected the people of these regions.

REVIEW Which European countries were involved in Indian Ocean trade?

• GEOGRAPHY •

GEOGRAPHY ESSENTIAL ELEMENTS

Angkor Wat
Understanding Human Systems

One of the most important and powerful kingdoms in Indochina was the Khmer (kuh•MEHR) Empire. In the A.D. 700s, Khmer princes from the island of Java established a state called Kambuja in present-day Cambodia. In about 1130 the Khmer started building Angkor Wat (AN•kor WAHT), a huge temple complex. Angkor Wat was abandoned in the 1400s after a rebellion. Eventually, Angkor Wat was completely covered by the vines and plants of the rain forest that surrounds it. When the temple complex was rediscovered in 1860, it captured the imagination of the world.

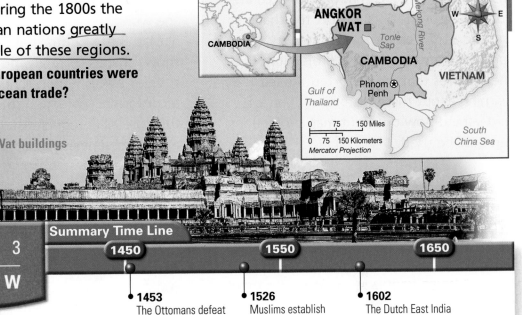

A view of the Angkor Wat buildings

Summary Time Line

LESSON 3 REVIEW

| 1450 | 1550 | 1650 |

1453 The Ottomans defeat the Byzantine Empire

1526 Muslims establish the Mogul Empire

1602 The Dutch East India Company is formed

 DRAW CONCLUSIONS Why were the Ottoman and Mogul Empires similar in many ways?

1. **BIG IDEA** How did the policies of Mogul rulers affect religion?

2. **VOCABULARY** What is a **miniature**?

3. **TIME LINE** About how many years passed between the start of the Mogul Empire and the forming of the Dutch East India Company?

4. **CIVICS** How did Akbar's tolerance of all religions benefit the Mogul Empire?

5. **CRITICAL THINKING—Analyze** How was Akbar's rule of the Mogul Empire different from Shah Jahan's rule?

 **PERFORMANCE—Paint a Mural** Work with a group to research Mogul art under Akbar's rule. Then paint a mural showing a scene from life in the Mogul Empire.

Compare Map Projections

VOCABULARY	
projections	distortions
equal-area projection	conformal projection

▶ WHY IT MATTERS

Cartographers, or mapmakers, have developed different ways to show round Earth in the form of a flat map. These different views of Earth are called **projections**.

To draw maps, cartographers must change the appearance of Earth's shape by splitting or stretching it. Every map projection has **distortions**, or parts that are not accurate. Some map projections distort the shape or the size of the area shown. One way that cartographers classify map projections is by the features that are distorted the least. By learning about these distortions, you will understand how different map projections can best be used.

▶ WHAT YOU NEED TO KNOW

Maps A and B show the same area. Map A shows an equal area on either side of the prime meridian and on either side of the equator. This is an **equal-area projection**. The sizes of regions are correct in relation to one another, but the shapes are distorted. An equal-area projection is useful for comparing information about different parts of the world.

Map B is a **conformal projection**. It shows shapes correctly, but it distorts the sizes of places, especially near the poles. On a conformal projection, the lines of longitude are all an equal distance apart. On a globe, these lines get closer together as they

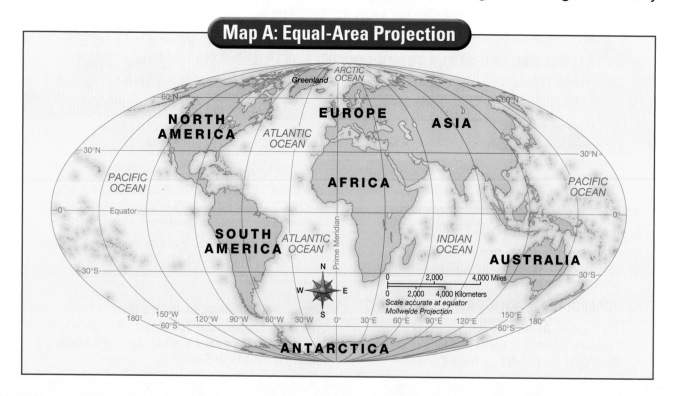

Map A: Equal-Area Projection

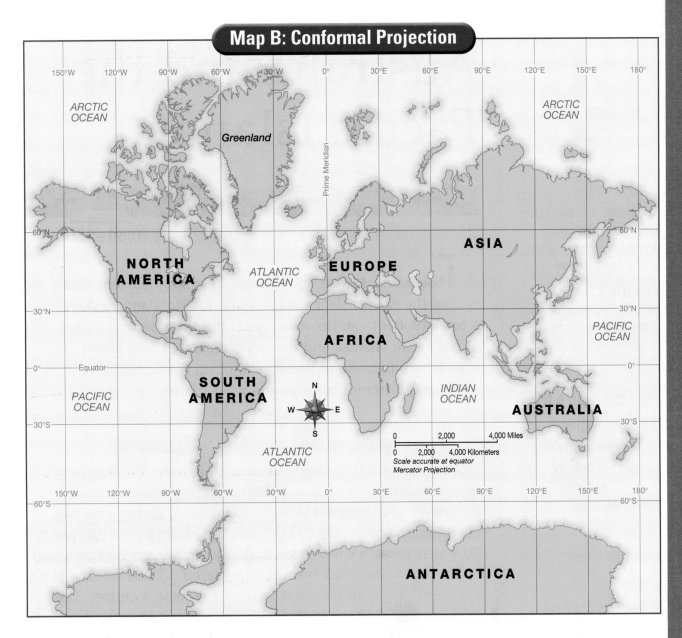

Map B: Conformal Projection

near the poles, where they meet. On a conformal projection, the lines of latitude get farther apart closer to the poles. On a globe they are an equal distance apart.

▶ PRACTICE THE SKILL

Look carefully at both map projections, and notice the differences. Think about the best uses for each projection. Then use the maps to answer these questions.

1 Africa is really much larger than Greenland. Which projection shows Greenland's size more accurately, Map A or Map B?

2 On which map is the shape of Africa more accurate?

3 On which map are all lines of longitude an equal distance apart?

▶ APPLY WHAT YOU LEARNED

Write a paragraph about the advantages and disadvantages of using an equal-area projection map and a conformal projection map.

Practice your map and globe skills with the **GeoSkills CD-ROM.**

4

Australia and the Pacific Islands

DRAW CONCLUSIONS

As you read, draw conclusions about the development of different cultures in Australia and the Pacific Islands.

BIG IDEA

Different cultures developed in the varied environments of Australia and the Pacific Islands.

VOCABULARY

Aborigine
dreamtime
penal colony
tabu
kastom

| 900 | 1200 | 1500 | 1800 |

1650 – 1800

Thousands of years ago, people from southeastern Asia settled the Pacific Islands. As a result, Pacific Islanders share a common heritage. However, great distances separate most of the Pacific Islands, and the environment of each island is different. Because of these conditions, Pacific Islanders developed different cultures and ways of life.

Australia and New Zealand

Scientists think that people from southeastern Asia may have reached Australia as early as 40,000 years ago. These first settlers are known as Aborigines. **Aborigine** means "a person who was here from the beginning." Aborigines were hunters and gatherers. They were nomads who moved from place to place in search of food.

The Aborigines lived in small tribes called clans. A clan is a group of people who share the same ancestors. The clans traded with one another and respected each other's territory. The traditions and history of each clan were passed on from one generation to the next through storytelling.

Aborigines believe that they have been in Australia ever since the **dreamtime**, an ancient time when spirits created the land and all things in it, and then gave them to the people. Each clan's dreamtime spirits made that clan the guardian of its land and all living things forever.

In Australia, Aborigines go on walkabouts to visit their sacred lands.

POINTS OF VIEW
Maori Land Rights

CITIZENSHIP

In 1840 the British government and several Maori tribes signed the Treaty of Waitangi. Under this treaty, Maori lands were to be protected, but much of their land was later illegally sold or seized. In the 1990s the government of New Zealand began returning lands to the Maori or paying the tribes for their losses. In recent years, however, a new debate has started over another part of the Treaty of Waitangi, which gives the Maori sovereignty, or the right to rule, over their lands.

SIR DOUGLAS GRAHAM, Minister in Charge of Treaty of Waitangi Negotiations

66 Here [in New Zealand] Maori do not live on reservations—they are fully integrated . . . . Maori sovereignty is totally inconsistent with today's world. 99

TAU HENARE, Minister of Maori Affairs

66 If we are going to have a treaty, then give us all that . . . [the Treaty of Waitangi] said that Maori would have undisturbed possession of their lands 99

Analyze the Viewpoints

1 What views about Maori sovereignty does each person hold?

2 **Make It Relevant** Think about an issue that is important to your community. What is your viewpoint on that issue? Where do your classmates stand on that issue? Divide into groups, and debate the issue.

A Maori carving

In the late 1600s European explorers began to arrive. In 1770 Captain James Cook claimed Australia for Britain. The British decided to use the faraway continent as a **penal colony**, or prison colony. The word *penal* means "punishment." In 1788 a group of ships landed with 750 prisoners in chains. Over time, Australia was partly settled by prisoners who finished their prison terms and chose to stay.

As in North and South America, contact with Europeans brought hardships for the native people of Australia. European settlers took away much of the land of the Aborigines, and many Aborigines died from diseases brought by Europeans. By 1850 the Aborigine culture had been

Captain James Cook

nearly destroyed. In recent years, Australia's government has made a formal apology for the past mistreatment of the Aborigines.

The first people of New Zealand called themselves Maori (MOW•ree), which means "local people." Unlike the Aborigines, Maori tribes went to war against each other to defend their territories. When Europeans began colonizing New Zealand, the Maoris fought to keep their lands. However, they were unable to stop the European settlers. In later years, New Zealand, like Australia, gained independence as a member of the British Commonwealth.

REVIEW Why might Britain have used Australia as a penal colony?

DRAW CONCLUSIONS

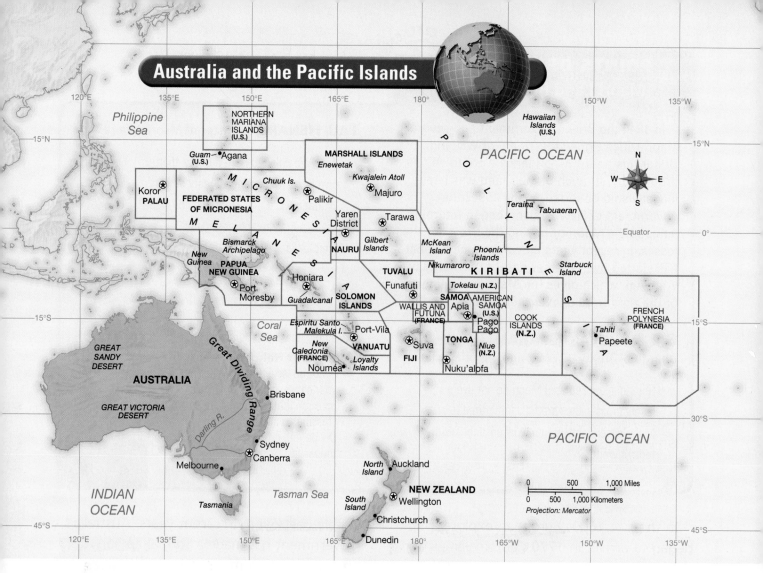

Australia and the Pacific Islands

Philippine Sea

NORTHERN MARIANA ISLANDS (U.S.)

Guam (U.S.) • Agana

MARSHALL ISLANDS
Enewetak
Kwajalein Atoll
Majuro

Koror ⊛
PALAU

Chuuk Is.

M I C R O N E S I A

FEDERATED STATES OF MICRONESIA
⊛ Palikir

M E L A N E S I A

Yaren District ⊛
NAURU

Gilbert Islands

Tarawa

Teraina • Tabuaeran

Equator

McKean Island
Phoenix Islands

KIRIBATI

Starbuck Island

Nikumaroro

P
O
L
Y
N
E
S
I
A

Hawaiian Islands (U.S.)

PACIFIC OCEAN

New Guinea

Bismarck Archipelago

PAPUA NEW GUINEA

Honiara ⊛
Port Moresby ⊛

Guadalcanal ⊛

SOLOMON ISLANDS

TUVALU
Funafuti

Tokelau (N.Z.)

SAMOA
Apia ⊛

WALLIS AND FUTUNA (FRANCE)

AMERICAN SAMOA (U.S.)
⊛ Pago Pago

COOK ISLANDS (N.Z.)

FRENCH POLYNESIA (FRANCE)

Tahiti
• Papeete

Coral Sea

Espiritu Santo
Malekula I.

Port-Vila

New Caledonia (FRANCE)

VANUATU

Nouméa •

Loyalty Islands

Suva ⊛

FIJI

TONGA
Niue (N.Z.)

Nuku'alofa ⊛

GREAT SANDY DESERT

AUSTRALIA

GREAT VICTORIA DESERT

Great Dividing Range

Darling R.

• Brisbane

• Sydney
⊛ Canberra

Melbourne •

INDIAN OCEAN

Tasmania

Tasman Sea

North Island

• Auckland

PACIFIC OCEAN

NEW ZEALAND
⊛ Wellington

South Island

• Christchurch

Dunedin

Scale: 0 — 500 — 1,000 Miles
0 — 500 — 1,000 Kilometers
Projection: Mercator

Regions Early settlers of Australia and the Pacific Islands most likely came from southeastern Asia. The island of Rangiron (below) is in Polynesia.

❓ Into what three groups are the Pacific Islands divided?

Pacific Island Cultures

Beyond Australia is a group of islands known as the Pacific Islands. Geographers have divided these islands into three groups—Melanesia, Micronesia, and Polynesia. Scientists think that some of these islands were settled as early as 40,000 years ago.

The island groups are very far apart and their environments vary. As a result the people of each island developed different customs and cultures. For example, each culture had its own way of choosing and relating to its leaders.

On the Melanesian island of Fiji (FEE•jee), chiefs were considered sacred, and it was **tabu**, or forbidden, to touch them. Most Fijian chiefs were the sons of chiefs, but anyone who showed great skill in warfare or gained wealth could also be a chief.

Elsewhere in Melanesia, such as in Vanuatu, **kastom**, or custom, governed the villages. Village elders passed traditional beliefs from generation to generation.

Micronesians followed a different system, based on clans. People inherited land and a place in society through their clans. On some islands leadership was based on how long a clan's ancestors had lived on the land.

Polynesians also lived in a clan society. The clan chiefs were older men who could show their direct relation to an ancestor. Oral histories were important for a chief to prove his ancestry.

Many Pacific Islanders were skilled craft-workers. They used the resources of their islands—bones, shells, stone, and wood—to make tools and weapons. Also, artists made masks, carvings, and sculptures.

After the arrival of the Europeans, the island cultures declined. Today, however, many descendants of the Pacific Islanders are rediscovering traditional ways.

REVIEW How did the people of Fiji view their chiefs?

• HERITAGE •

Melanesian Art

Because the cultures of the Pacific Islands developed differently, the artwork of each culture had its own style. In Melanesia, craftworkers used art to create a link between daily life and Melanesian history, beliefs, and ancestors. To achieve this, they carved human figures, gods, animals, and masks from wood. These objects were often decorated with shells, feathers, fur, grasses, and flowers. Melanesian art was often made for religious ceremonies. After the art had served its purpose in the ceremony, the art was often discarded and left to decay.

Wooden mask from Papua New Guinea

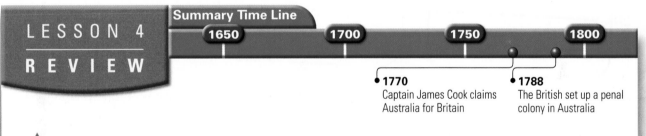

LESSON 4 REVIEW

Summary Time Line

1650 — 1700 — 1750 — 1800

1770 Captain James Cook claims Australia for Britain

1788 The British set up a penal colony in Australia

DRAW CONCLUSIONS How did the locations and environments of Australia and the Pacific Islands affect the cultures that developed there?

1. **BIG IDEA** How were the cultures of Australia and the Pacific Islands different?

2. **VOCABULARY** Use the terms **Aborigine** and **dreamtime** in a sentence.

3. **TIME LINE** How long after the British claimed Australia did they set it up as a penal colony?

4. **CULTURE** Explain the importance of kastom to the people of Vanuatu.

5. **CRITICAL THINKING—Analyze** Compare and contrast the customs of Pacific Islanders.

PERFORMANCE—Tell a Story Work with a small group to research a dreamtime story of the Aborigines. Then work with your group to act out the story for your class. You may want to choose one person to be the narrator. You may want to make props or paint a picture as a backdrop or setting for your story.

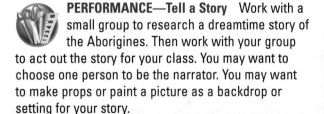

16 Review and Test Preparation

900s
The Swahili culture and language form

Draw Conclusions

Use this graphic organizer to show that you know how to draw conclusions about the later African kingdoms. A copy of this graphic organizer appears on page 146 of the Activity Book.

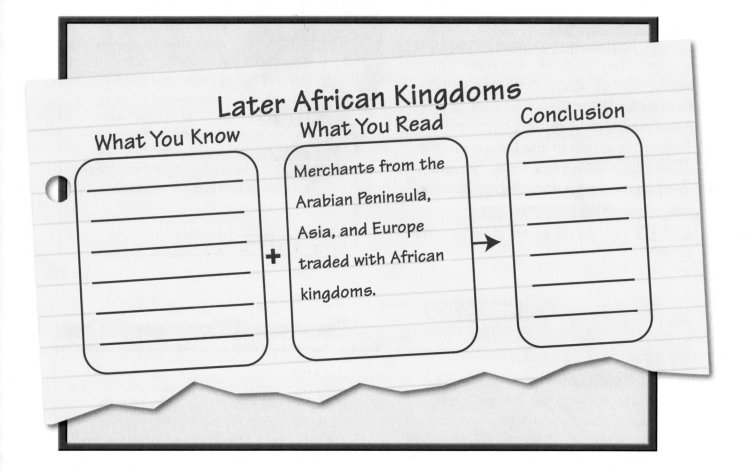

Later African Kingdoms

What You Know

+

What You Read

Merchants from the Arabian Peninsula, Asia, and Europe traded with African kingdoms.

→

Conclusion

THINK & WRITE

Write a Letter   It is the early 1400s, and Ming dynasty leaders are debating whether to adopt a policy of isolation for China. What do you think they should do? Write a letter to the emperor's advisers explaining why you think isolation is or is not a good idea.

Write a List   Africa's Oyo kingdom had a king, but a council of advisers could remove him if they thought he was not a good leader. Write a list of at least five actions that would show good leadership by a king and five actions that would show bad leadership by a king.

1368
The Ming dynasty begins

1453
Ottomans conquer the Byzantine Empire

1526
Muslims establish the Mogul Empire in India

1644
The Qing dynasty replaces the Ming dynasty

1788
The British set up a penal colony in Australia

USE THE TIME LINE

Use the chapter summary time line to answer these questions.

1 When did Muslims establish the Mogul Empire? *1526*

2 Which Chinese dynasty ruled first, the Ming dynasty or the Qing dynasty? *Ming Dynasty*

USE VOCABULARY

Use one of the terms in the box to complete each sentence.

> sultan (p. 523)
>
> plantations (p. 526)
>
> triangular trade (p. 526)
>
> penal colony (p. 545)
>
> tabu (p. 546)

3 European traders took African slaves to America as part of the _____ system. *triangular trade*

4 _____ are huge farms where cash crops are grown. *Plantations*

5 Each Swahili city-state was governed by a _____ *sultan*

6 On the island of Fiji, chiefs were considered sacred and it was _____ to touch them. *tabu*

7 The British used faraway Australia as a _____, or place to send prisoners. *penal colony*

RECALL FACTS

Answer these questions.

8 The blending of which two peoples created the Swahili language and culture? *Arabic African*

9 Which emperor traveled throughout China, listened to people's problems, and observed the ways they lived? *Kangxi*

10 Of which empire was Süleyman I a leader? *Ottoman empire*

Write the letter of the best choice.

11 **TEST PREP**   Who was the greatest Mogul emperor?
  A Babur
  B Akbar
  C Jahangir
  D Shah Jahan

12 **TEST PREP**   Which of these statements is *not* true about the native peoples of Australia and New Zealand?
  F The native people of Australia are called Aborigines.
  G The native people of New Zealand are called Maoris.
  H Aborigines fought each other to defend their territory.
  J *Maori* means "local people."

THINK CRITICALLY

13 Why do you think European countries were so interested in trading with China? *It had many tea and more resource*

14 Of Fiji, Vanuatu, or Micronesia, which Pacific Island culture would you rather lead? Why? *Fiji, chief was sacred*

APPLY SKILLS

Read a Population Pyramid

15 Review the population pyramids on pages 534 and 535. About what percent of each country's population is age 65 or older?

Compare Map Projections

16 Use the maps on pages 542 and 543 to create a quiz about map projections. For this quiz, write three questions that ask students to compare map projections.

VISIT

Venice, Italy

GET READY

The city of Venice is located in northeastern Italy. First settled during the A.D. 400s, Venice is made up of about 120 islands and part of mainland Italy. Venice's seaside location has made it an important trading center. Today it is one of Italy's largest ports.

Venice is probably best known for having canals that serve as streets. Tourists visit Venice for this attraction, as well as for the city's fine art, architecture, and history. Historic sights include Piazza San Marco and the Bridge of Sighs, which is connected to the Doge's Palace. Many museums, such as the Academy of Fine Arts, feature famous works of art.

WHAT TO SEE

Museums in Venice feature many pieces of fine art. Above is an oil painting showing Piazzo San Marco in the 1400s. Below are bronze statues from the 300s B.C.

LOCATE IT

Venice

ITALY

Adriatic Sea

The Grand Canal is the main "street" in Venice. From boats called gondolas, visitors view churches, palaces, and other famous buildings.

San Marco Basilica stands on Piazza San Marco, a center of activity for Venice.

Even during times of flood, Venice receives visitors from around the world.

Tourists can shop at outdoor markets (left) or buy Venetian glass (above) at fine shops in Venice.

TAKE A FIELD TRIP

GO ONLINE

A VIRTUAL TOUR
Visit The Learning Site at **www.harcourtschool.com** to take virtual tours of other cities.

CNN® Turner Le@rning

A VIDEO TOUR
Check your media center or classroom library for a videotape tour highlighting Venice, Italy.

7 Review and Test Preparation

Write a Diary Entry On the Visual Summary Time Line below, find the year Christopher Columbus reached the Americas. Imagine that you are an explorer traveling with Columbus. Write a diary entry describing the day Columbus first reached land.

USE VOCABULARY

For each pair of terms, write two or three sentences to explain what each term means and how the two terms are related.

1 **Renaissance** (p. 490), **humanism** (p. 491)

2 **heresy** (p. 499), **Reformation** (p. 501)

3 **armada** (p. 507), **conquistador** (p. 510)

4 **immunity** (p. 513), **Columbian exchange** (p. 513)

RECALL FACTS

Answer these questions.

5 What changes did the Renaissance bring to Europe?

6 Who invented a printing press that used movable type?

7 How did the Ming and Qing dynasties change China's relationship with the rest of the world?

Write the letter of the best choice.

8 **TEST PREP** Each of these statements is true about the Crusades *except*—
A The eight Crusades lasted nearly 200 years.
B Catholic leaders achieved their goal of retaking the holy city of Jerusalem.
C Volunteer soldiers were called crusaders because they carried the cross as their sign.
D Heavily armored soldiers called knights fought in the Crusades.

9 **TEST PREP** Which country's navy defeated the Spanish Armada?
F France
G Portugal
H England
J the Netherlands

Visual Summary

900

1200

1095 The first Crusade begins p. 485

1200 Great Zimbabwe is built in Africa p. 523

1400 Renaissance ideas develop in Europe p. 490

10 TEST PREP Which of these European countries did *not* claim lands in what is now North America?

A England

B France

C the Netherlands

D Portugal

THINK CRITICALLY

11 In which period would you have rather lived, the Middle Ages or the Renaissance? Why?

12 Suppose China had continued to explore the world in the late 1400s. What effects might this have had on today's world?

APPLY SKILLS

Read a Map of Cultural Regions
Use the map on this page to answer these questions.

MAP AND GLOBE SKILLS

13 In which country is English the official language? Why do you think this might be so?

14 In what country or countries do people speak Miskito?

15 What indigenous languages are spoken in Mexico?

16 What languages are spoken in Panama?

Languages of Mexico and Central America

MEXICO

Gulf of Mexico

PACIFIC OCEAN

Caribbean Sea

BELIZE

GUATEMALA
EL SALVADOR

HONDURAS

NICARAGUA

COSTA RICA

PANAMA

0 200 400 Miles
0 200 400 Kilometers
Azimuthal Equal Area Projection

N W E S

Official Languages
- Spanish
- English

Indigenous Languages
- Mayan
- Miskito
- Kuna
- Garifuna
- Nawan/Spanish
- Mixtec
- Zapotec
- Embera

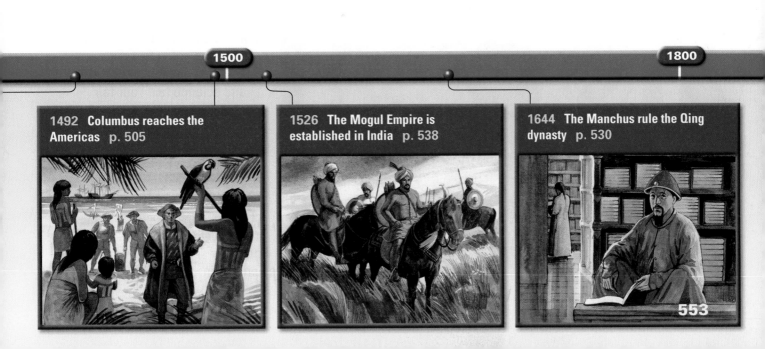

1500

1800

1492 Columbus reaches the Americas p. 505

1526 The Mogul Empire is established in India p. 538

1644 The Manchus rule the Qing dynasty p. 530

553

Unit Activities

Visit The Learning Site at www.harcourtschool.com for additional activities.

Create an Information Pamphlet

Use library or Internet resources to find out more about the human immune system. What is it and how does it work? How did immunity—or the lack of it—affect people described in this unit? Use what you learn to create an informational brochure called "Your Immune System."

Draw a Diagram

Draw a diagram that illustrates the triangular trade system. Use resources from the library or the Internet to find out more about the goods that traveled between Europe, Africa, and the Americas. Include those details on your diagram.

VISIT YOUR LIBRARY

■ *Art and Civilization: Medieval Times* by Giovanni Di Pasquale and Matilde Bardi. McGraw-Hill.

■ *Around the World in a Hundred Years: From Henry the Navigator to Magellan* by Jean Fritz. Putnam.

■ *Mapping the World* by Sylvia A. Johnson. Atheneum.

The Renaissance and The Age of Exploration

COMPLETE THE UNIT PROJECT

Present an Art and Science Fair Work with a group of your classmates to finish the unit project—presenting an art and science fair. Look over your notes describing new kinds of art and new discoveries in science discussed in the unit. Use these notes to decide what to include in your art and science fair. Your fair may feature posters or models representing different art forms and scientific discoveries. You may also wish to have some members of your group dress as artists, explorers, or scientists from the period. Finally, present your art and science fair.

Toward the Present Day

Computer microchip

Changgyeong Palace in Seoul, Korea

Toward the Present Day

❝History is merely a list of surprises. It can only prepare us to be surprised again.❞

—Kurt Vonnegut, author (1922–)

Preview the Content

Read the Big Idea statement for each lesson. Work with a partner to identify what you think the focus of each lesson will be.

Preview the Vocabulary

Parts of Speech   Most sentences have at least one noun and one verb. Use the diagram below to categorize each of the Vocabulary Words listed below as a noun or a verb. If you think a word can be used as both a noun and a verb, write it in the center of the diagram. Use a dictionary to check your answers.

revolution   constitution   demand   armistice   czar   purge

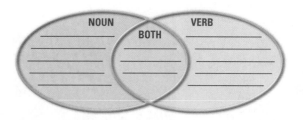

NOUN

BOTH

VERB

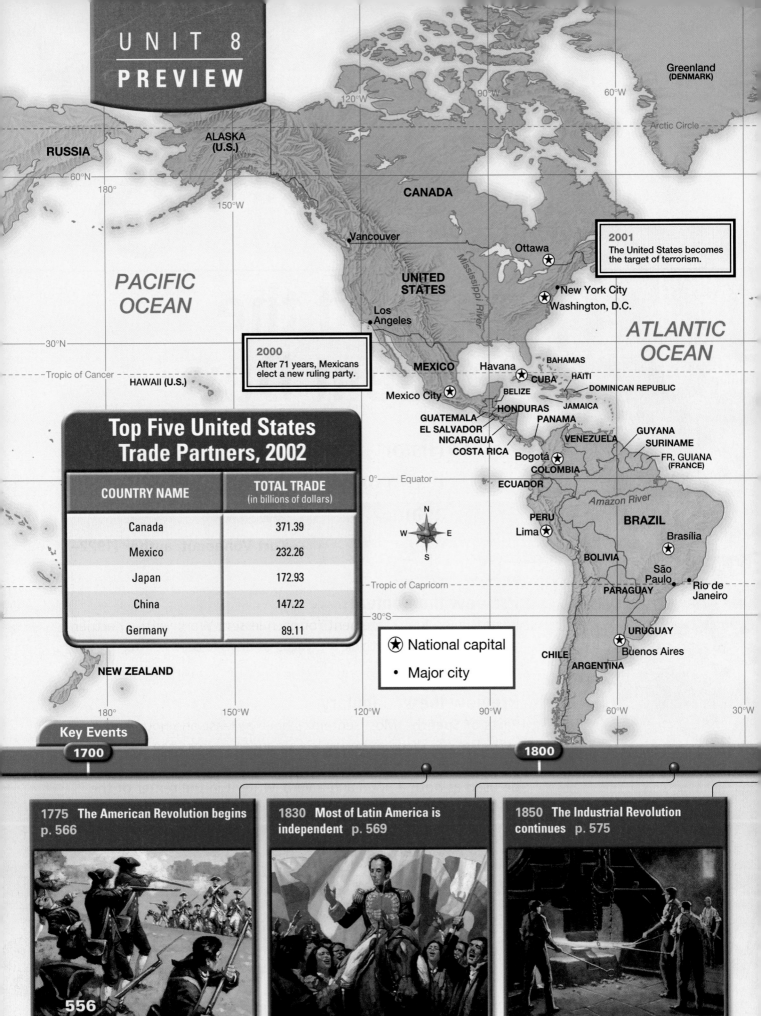

PREVIEW

RUSSIA

ALASKA (U.S.)

CANADA

Vancouver

Ottawa

PACIFIC OCEAN

UNITED STATES

Los Angeles

2001
The United States becomes the target of terrorism.

Greenland (DENMARK)

Arctic Circle

New York City
Washington, D.C.

ATLANTIC OCEAN

2000
After 71 years, Mexicans elect a new ruling party.

HAWAII (U.S.)

Tropic of Cancer

MEXICO   Havana

BAHAMAS

CUBA   HAITI

Mexico City

BELIZE

HONDURAS

DOMINICAN REPUBLIC

JAMAICA

GUATEMALA
EL SALVADOR
NICARAGUA
COSTA RICA

PANAMA

VENEZUELA

GUYANA
SURINAME

FR. GUIANA (FRANCE)

Bogotá
COLOMBIA

Equator

ECUADOR

Amazon River

Top Five United States Trade Partners, 2002

COUNTRY NAME	TOTAL TRADE (in billions of dollars)
Canada	371.39
Mexico	232.26
Japan	172.93
China	147.22
Germany	89.11

PERU
Lima

BRAZIL

Brasília

BOLIVIA

São Paulo

Rio de Janeiro

Tropic of Capricorn

PARAGUAY

NEW ZEALAND

⊛ National capital

• Major city

URUGUAY
Buenos Aires

CHILE   ARGENTINA

180°   150°W   120°W   90°W   60°W   30°W

Key Events

1700

1800

1775 **The American Revolution begins** p. 566

1830 **Most of Latin America is independent** p. 569

1850 **The Industrial Revolution continues** p. 575

556

The World Today

1999
Most European Union countries begin to use a new form of money called the euro.

2002
North Korea reveals that it has a nuclear weapons program.

1999
South Africans elect their second black South African president.

2002
Most African nations are members of the African Union.

ALB.	ALBANIA	LITH.	LITHUANIA
ARM.	ARMENIA	LUX.	LUXEMBOURG
AUS.	AUSTRIA	MAC.	MACEDONIA
AZER.	AZERBAIJAN	NETH.	NETHERLANDS
BELG.	BELGIUM	REP. CONGO	REPUBLIC OF THE CONGO
BOS.-HER.	BOSNIA AND HERZEGOVINA	ROM.	ROMANIA
C.A.R.	CENTRAL AFRICAN REPUBLIC	SEN.	SENEGAL
C.d'I.	CÔTE D'IVOIRE	SERB. & MONT.	SERBIA AND MONTENEGRO
CRO.	CROATIA		
CZH. REP.	CZECH REPUBLIC	S.L.	SIERRA LEONE
DEM. REP. OF CONGO	DEMOCRATIC REPUBLIC OF THE CONGO	SLK.	SLOVAKIA
		SLN.	SLOVENIA
EQ. GUI.	EQUATORIAL GUINEA	SWITZ.	SWITZERLAND
G.B.	GUINEA-BISSAU	U.A.E.	UNITED ARAB EMIRATES
HUNG.	HUNGARY		
LEB.	LEBANON	U.S.	UNITED STATES

0   1,500   3,000 Miles
0   1,500   3,000 Kilometers
Miller Cylindrical Projection

1900   **PRESENT**

1914 World War I breaks out p. 606

1941 The United States enters World War II p. 614

2000 The world population reaches 6 billion people p. 647

WHERE Poppies GROW

A WORLD WAR I COMPANION

by Linda Granfield

The twentieth century was a time of many achievements, but it was also a time of war. In the first 50 years alone, two world wars raged. These wars affected not just the soldiers who fought in them but also their families at home. Read now to find out what life was like in the United States during World War I.

"To make the World Safe for Democracy"

This postcard shows the flags of the Allied countries that fought in World War I.

"Keep the Home Fires Burning"

So began a popular wartime song. The next lines are: *While your hearts are yearning, though your lads are far away they dream of Home.*

Home. Whether a farmhouse on the prairies or a cozy house in one of North America's big cities, it was physically far from the Front, but was tied to Europe nevertheless. Everyone's life was affected by the news that arrived via newspapers, magazines, and public announcements. Every aspect of family business and pleasure was filled with reminders. The war would only be won if *everyone* worked together. Work they did, even the children who created war gardens for food supplies.

> **the Front** the location of a battle
>
> **via** by way of

People at home supported the war effort in many ways. They wore buttons honoring war heroes, planted gardens, and kept track of the food and the fuel they used in ration books. Some even volunteered to help build ships.

Raised 'em myself in my U.S. School Garden

ISSUED BY THE U.S. SCHOOL GARDEN ARMY BUREAU OF EDUCATION, DEPARTMENT OF INTERIOR, WASHINGTON, D.C.

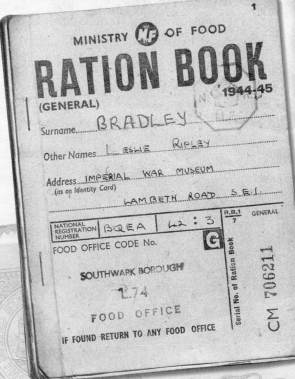

MINISTRY OF FOOD
RATION BOOK 1944-45
(GENERAL)
Surname BRADLEY
Other Names Leslie Ripley
Address IMPERIAL WAR MUSEUM
(as on Identity Card)
LAMBETH ROAD S.E.1

| NATIONAL REGISTRATION NUMBER | BQEA | 42:3 | R.B.1 7 | GENERAL |

FOOD OFFICE CODE No.
SOUTHWARK BOROUGH
L74
FOOD OFFICE
IF FOUND RETURN TO ANY FOOD OFFICE

Serial No. of Ration Book CM 706211

Shipyard [Volu]nteers

Certificate of Enrollment

to Certify That_____ has enrolled in the
Shipyard Volunteers of the Public Service Reserve to aid the Nation
in its imperative need for merchant ships with which to overcome the submarine menace and maintain our forces at the front.

The World War will be won or lost in the American shipyards. Every rivet driven is a blow at the Kaiser. Every ship turned out brings America nearer to victory.

Those who give their strength and their influence to the speedy construction of ships render service that is patriotic and highly essential to the successful termination of the war.

Edward N. Hurley

A Child's World

Fathers, uncles, older brothers—perhaps all had gone to war. Mothers, aunts, and older sisters were busy keeping life as normal as possible and providing for the country's wartime needs. What was it like for a young child during the war?

School, play, and chores filled their young lives, as they had before the Great War began. But school, play, and chores also changed a bit, each reflecting the war that threatened to engulf the world. A new chore would have been packing handkerchiefs, peppermint drops, and pencils in a gift box for a soldier, perhaps their father, at the Front.

De la tranchée et sous la fusillade.
Petit père qu'il n'est plus malade!

232

J. COURCIER

A HAPPY XMAS

A Signal Wish from the
School Children of the Empire
who sent Christmas Gifts to
Our Brave Soldiers & Sailors

PRESENTED TO

Noel Buckle

who has helped to send some Comfort and Happiness to the Brave Men who are Fighting to uphold the Freedom of our Glorious Empire.

Patron
H.M. the King

OVER-SEAS CLUB
General Buildings,
Aldwych, London W.C.

The photograph (left) shows a British soldier with his family just before he had to leave to go to war. The poster (top) shows a French soldier's family thinking of him away fighting in the trenches. The certificate (bottom) was issued to people who helped send Christmas packages to soldiers fighting in the war.

Mum's the Word

Letters and postcards were a soldier's primary link with his family while he was serving his country. Many of the letters repeated the same words: *I'm fine, don't worry about me, how's everything at home?* There wasn't too much more that a soldier could write, because if he mentioned and described where he and his <u>comrades</u> were, there was a chance the enemy would intercept the mail and determine the <u>Allies'</u> locations. "Mum's the word" (I can't tell you anything) was a phrase often repeated. For families missing a loved one, however, just the sight of his handwriting was enough consolation. Every letter received meant he was still alive.

comrades other soldiers, friends

Allies the United States, Britain, France, and the other countries that fought against the Central Powers

A World War I postcard that soldiers sent to their loved ones back home.

Analyze the Literature

❶ How did World War I affect the lives of people at home?

❷ Interview a relative or another adult who lived during wartime. Then write a report that describes his or her experiences. Share your report with the class.

READ A BOOK

START THE UNIT PROJECT

The Hall of Fame With your classmates, create a Hall of Fame about the people in the unit. As you read, take notes on the contributions key people made. Your notes will help you create your Hall of Fame.

USE TECHNOLOGY

Visit The Learning Site at **www.harcourtschool.com** for additional activities, primary sources, and other resources to use in this unit.

IRONBRIDGE GORGE, SHROPSHIRE, ENGLAND

Built over the Severn River, the Iron Bridge is known throughout the world as a symbol of the Industrial Revolution. It was the world's first iron bridge and the result of iron-processing innovations at nearby Coalbrookdale Works. Ironbridge required 378 tons of cast iron before it was finished in 1779.

LOCATE IT

Ironbridge Gorge

UNITED KINGDOM

17

Times of Rapid Change

"Mighty designs in advancing the sciences will leave lasting monuments."
—John Locke, English philosopher, 1690

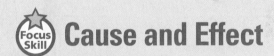

Cause and Effect

A **cause** is an event or action that makes something else happen. An **effect** is what happens as a result of that event or action.

As you read this chapter, list the causes and effects of the key events.

• **Identify and list important events.**

• **Write down the effects of each of these events.**

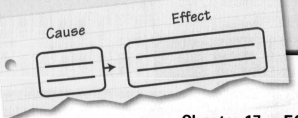

Cause → Effect

1

CAUSE AND EFFECT

As you read, identify the causes and effects of revolutions in Europe and the Americas.

BIG IDEA

Revolutions led to the development of new governments in Europe and the Americas.

VOCABULARY

Enlightenment
revolution
constitutional monarchy
preamble
constitution
federal republic

FAST FACT

The Houses of Parliament in England is also known as the Palace of Westminster. It was the residence of the kings of England during the high and late Middle Ages. Rebuilt in 1834 after a fire, the building has about 1,200 rooms, 100 staircases, and more than 2 miles (3.2 km) of hallways.

A Time of Political Change

1700 – 1850

Beginning in the late 1600s and continuing throughout the 1700s, some European thinkers introduced ideas called the Enlightenment. The **Enlightenment** was a movement that used reason, or thinking things through, to develop ways of improving both science and society. A part of the Enlightenment focused on ways to create a government that would protect individual rights. These ideas led to **revolutions**, or sudden changes in the way people think and act. As a result, political revolutions began to spread across Europe and the Americas. In many cases, the revolutions led to independent nations based on democracy.

Political Changes in England

England was among the first countries to become more democratic. Some people in England believed that powerful monarchs were needed to keep order. However, the philosopher John Locke led others to think very differently. Locke believed that the liberty, or freedom, of all citizens must be protected. He said that citizens had a right to enjoy their property without the government having a say. He also believed that citizens had the right to overthrow a government that tried to take away their liberty.

In 1688 Locke's ideas were tested. English leaders feared that their king, James II, wanted to make England a Catholic country once again. The leaders forced James II to leave the country. Then they invited William of Orange and his wife, Mary, to become England's new rulers. Mary was the daughter of James II. This change of government took place with little bloodshed. That is why the English called it the Glorious Revolution.

John Locke

To become king and queen, William and Mary had to agree to a document that became the English Bill of Rights. This document gave Parliament the right to choose English leaders.

With the English Bill of Rights, England's government became a constitutional monarchy. In a **constitutional monarchy**, the monarch has mostly ceremonial duties. A lawmaking body holds most of the power. England's lawmaking body is Parliament—made up of the House of Lords and the House of Commons.

In England the people began to elect lawmakers to the House of Commons. This meant that the citizens of England had gained a greater voice in their government. As time passed, England, which became part of Britain, became more and more democratic.

REVIEW What document caused England's government to become more democratic? **CAUSE AND EFFECT**

DEMOCRATIC VALUES
Individual Rights

In addition to giving Parliament the right to choose English leaders, the English Bill of Rights protected the individual rights of English citizens. When the United States won independence from Britain, Thomas Jefferson and other leaders pushed for a Bill of Rights to be added to the United States Constitution. As in Britain, United States leaders felt it was important to protect the individual rights of citizens. The United States Bill of Rights guarantees many liberties, including freedom of religion and freedom of speech.

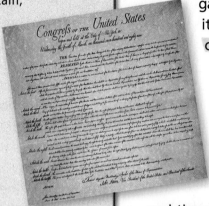

Analyze the Value

❶ Why do you think it is important to have a written document that protects the rights of citizens?

❷ **Make It Relevant** Read a copy of the United States Bill of Rights. Then write a paragraph that explains its effect on your life.

The United States Bill of Rights (above)

The American Revolution

British citizens had gained more rights, but British colonists in North America had not. Since the colonists had no representation in the British Parliament, they had little say in decisions that affected them.

The colonists especially disliked being taxed without their approval. In 1763 the British had defeated the French in the French and Indian War. The British Parliament decided to tax the colonies to help pay for the war. The colonists protested the new taxes.

After a while Parliament ended them. However, the British passed new taxes, so the colonists continued to protest.

In 1775 fighting broke out between the colonists and British soldiers in Massachusetts. The next year, a group called the Continental Congress gathered in Philadelphia. There, its leaders wrote the Declaration of Independence.

The main author of the Declaration of Independence was Thomas Jefferson. In the **preamble**, or introduction, he wrote that all men are created equal and that they have the right to "Life, Liberty, and the pursuit of Happiness."

The Declaration also explained that the British government had tried to take these rights away from the colonists. Therefore, the Declaration continued, the people had the right to create an independent country—the United States of America.

To gain their independence, the American colonists fought the British in a war that became known as the American Revolution. In 1781 the American army, led by George Washington, defeated the British. The war officially ended in 1783.

At first the United States was a confederation, or a loose group of governments working together. However, it soon became clear that a stronger national government was needed.

In 1787 political leaders from the different states met to write a constitution. A **constitution** is a written plan of government. The leaders wanted to

Thomas Jefferson was the main author of the Declaration of Independence.

create a government that would protect liberty and also keep order. That government is described in the document known as the Constitution of the United States of America. The Constitution was approved by the states in 1788.

The government described in the Constitution is a **federal republic**. It has three branches—one to make laws, one to interpret them, and one to enforce them.

A Bill of Rights became part of the Constitution in 1791. These amendments, or additions, prevent the government from taking away individual rights, including freedom of speech and freedom of religion.

The Constitution stated an important idea. It said that the government belonged to the citizens. This idea would soon spread across the world.

REVIEW How did Thomas Jefferson and George Washington contribute to the American Revolution?

The French Revolution

Enlightenment ideas about liberty developed in France, too. The poor people of France complained that they paid almost all the taxes that kept the government running.

The French king, Louis (LOO•ee) XVI, tried to stop this criticism by calling a meeting of the Estates-General. This group included representatives from France's three estates, or social classes. Much of the nobility who made up the First Estate and the Second Estate held the high government positions and paid few taxes. The Third Estate included everyone else, from doctors to merchants to peasants. Its members had little voice in the government but paid nearly all the taxes.

Every time the Third Estate tried to set up a fairer way of taxing, the other Estates voted against it. In 1789 the Third Estate broke away from the Estates-General.

The storming of the Bastille (below) marked the beginning of the French Revolution. The Bastille's key (above) was given to President George Washington as a symbol of liberty.

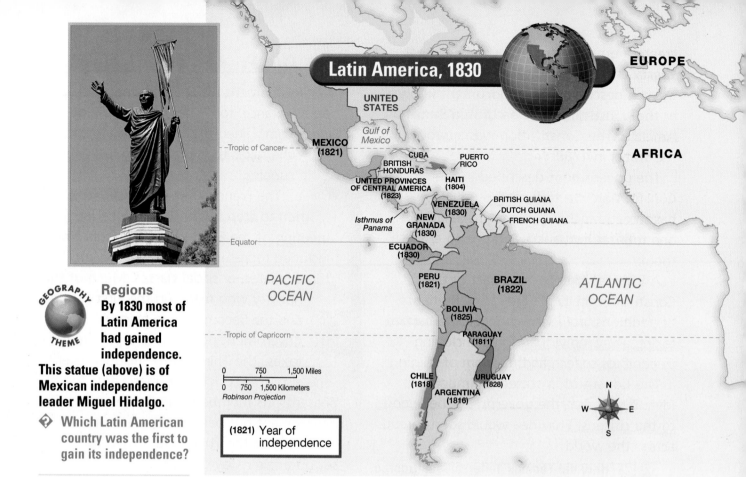

Latin America, 1830

EUROPE

AFRICA

UNITED STATES

Gulf of Mexico

Tropic of Cancer

MEXICO (1821)

CUBA

PUERTO RICO

BRITISH HONDURAS

HAITI (1804)

UNITED PROVINCES OF CENTRAL AMERICA (1823)

VENEZUELA (1830)

BRITISH GUIANA

DUTCH GUIANA

FRENCH GUIANA

Isthmus of Panama

NEW GRANADA (1830)

Equator

ECUADOR (1830)

PACIFIC OCEAN

PERU (1821)

BRAZIL (1822)

ATLANTIC OCEAN

BOLIVIA (1825)

Tropic of Capricorn

PARAGUAY (1811)

0   750   1,500 Miles

0   750   1,500 Kilometers
Robinson Projection

CHILE (1818)

URUGUAY (1828)

ARGENTINA (1816)

N W E S

(1821) Year of independence

Regions
By 1830 most of Latin America had gained independence. This statue (above) is of Mexican independence leader Miguel Hidalgo.

❖ Which Latin American country was the first to gain its independence?

Calling itself the National Assembly, it claimed the right to make laws for France.

Shocked by this action, Louis XVI brought soldiers into Paris. The people of France decided that they needed weapons for protection. On July 14, 1789, French citizens stormed a prison called the Bastille. They grabbed the weapons stored there, freed prisoners, and burned the Bastille. The French Revolution had begun.

In time, a group of young revolutionaries took over France's government. Violence broke out across France. Louis XVI was put to death. So, too, were at least 40,000 other people.

To protect themselves, the revolutionaries raised an army led by General Napoleon Bonaparte (nuh•POH•lee•uhn BOH•nuh•part). After winning many victories, Napoleon declared himself

emperor of France in 1804. Napoleon wanted to spread France's revolutionary ideas across Europe. Britain, Russia, and others joined forces to stop Napoleon. He was defeated in 1815, and the son of Louis XVI became king.

REVIEW Why were many French people unhappy under Louis XVI?

Simón Bolívar

Revolutionary Ideas in Latin America

Ideas about individual rights, revolution, and independence reached Latin America. The first successful revolution in this region occurred in the French colony of St. Domingue (SAN duh•MANG) in the Caribbean.

The French had freed the slaves in St. Domingue after a 1791 rebellion.

A former slave named François Toussaint-Louverture (fran•SWAH too•SAN loo•vair•TYOOR) wanted all the former slaves in St. Domingue to enjoy independence and full citizenship. He led an army that would defeat and push the French out of the colony in 1803. St. Domingue became the independent country of Haiti the following year.

Revolutions also broke out in Mexico, Central America, and South America. Local leaders across Latin America wanted to be independent from European rule. In 1822 Brazilians peacefully broke away from Portugal. Nearby, José de San Martín fought to free Argentina from Spain. To the north, Simón Bolívar fought the Spanish and won independence for Venezuela, Ecuador, and other South American countries. Mexican revolutionaries won independence for their country in 1821.

Revolutions in Latin America continued for years and cost thousands of lives. In many cases, the revolutions helped only the wealthy and did little for everyone else.

REVIEW How were the paths to freedom different for Brazil and Argentina?

LESSON 1 REVIEW

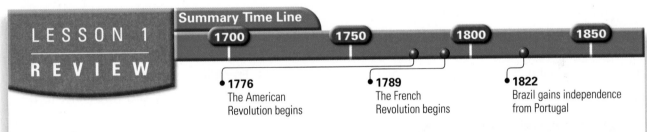

Summary Time Line

| 1700 | 1750 | 1800 | 1850 |

1776 The American Revolution begins

1789 The French Revolution begins

1822 Brazil gains independence from Portugal

 CAUSE AND EFFECT How did the ideas of the Enlightenment influence revolutions in Europe and the Americas?

1 BIG IDEA Which countries formed new governments through revolutions?

2 VOCABULARY Write a sentence using the terms **preamble** and **constitution**.

3 TIME LINE How many years after the American Revolution began did the French Revolution begin?

4 ECONOMICS Why did Britain raise taxes in the American colonies?

5 HISTORY Who fought for independence for Venezuela, Ecuador, and other countries?

6 CRITICAL THINKING—Synthesize Do you think that the leaders of the American Revolution were influenced by John Locke's ideas? Why or why not?

PERFORMANCE—Draw a Portrait Learn more about a leader mentioned in this lesson at the library or on the Internet. Then draw a portrait of the person you chose. On the back of your portrait, write a biography of this person. Share your portrait and biography with the class.

SKILLS · READING

Read an Editorial Cartoon

VOCABULARY

editorial cartoon

▶ WHY IT MATTERS

Many cartoons make us laugh, but some cartoons have a serious message to make us think. A cartoon on the editorial page of a newspaper usually presents the artist's point of view about people, current events, or politics. This kind of cartoon is called an **editorial cartoon**. Knowing how to read an editorial cartoon can sometimes help you better understand political and cultural issues.

▶ WHAT YOU NEED TO KNOW

Benjamin Franklin published one of the first editorial cartoons (cartoon Ⓐ) in 1754. It urged the 13 British colonies in North America to unite for protection against the French and their Native American allies. Franklin's cartoon shows each colony as part of a cut-up snake. The caption *Join, or Die* appears with the cartoon.

As political revolutions began to spread across Europe and the Americas, drawing cartoons became a common way for artists to express their ideas and opinions. Cartoon Ⓑ, below, expresses opinions on the American Revolution. Cartoon Ⓒ on page 571 comments on the many political revolutions that were happening in the world by the late 1700s.

To understand the meaning of an editorial cartoon, you first need to identify its details. Look for a caption or any writing on the drawing that can help you identify the people or the setting.

Many cartoonists use symbols, like Franklin's snake. Symbols often stand for the artist's ideas or opinions. To understand an editorial cartoon, you will need to identify what the symbols stand for. In Franklin's cartoon, the snake represents his view of the colonies. Franklin believed that the colonies needed to unite if they did not want to be

Ⓐ

P.
S.C.
M.
N.E.
V.
N.Y.
N.C.
N.J.

JOIN, or DIE.

Ⓑ

defeated by the French and their Native American allies. The statement below the cartoon reinforces his opinion.

In cartoon **B** the horse represents the American colonies and the "master" riding the horse represents Britain. The horse is throwing his master from his back, which represents America's Declaration of Independence. In cartoon **C** electricity represents the "spark" of new ideas that is causing revolutions throughout the world.

▶ PRACTICE THE SKILL

Look at the cartoons that appear on these pages. Think about how each cartoon uses symbols and other details to get its message across. Then use the cartoons to answer these questions.

1 What opinion do you think the artist of cartoon **B** had about the British? What symbols or details helped you determine your answer?

2 Why do you think that the American colonies are represented by a horse?

3 Do you think the artist of cartoon **B** supported the American Revolution? Explain.

4 What do the people being knocked down by the electricity in cartoon **C** represent?

5 Do you think the artist of cartoon **C** supported the political revolutions that were happening at that time? Explain.

▶ APPLY WHAT YOU LEARNED

Choose a current event that you have a strong opinion about. Write a paragraph describing your feelings about it. Then draw your own editorial cartoon that shows your opinion.

2

The Industrial Revolution

 CAUSE AND EFFECT

As you read, identify the causes and effects of the Industrial Revolution.

BIG IDEA

Technology introduced during the Industrial Revolution changed the way people lived and worked.

VOCABULARY

Industrial Révolution
innovator
crop rotation
textile
factory
patent
entrepreneur

1700 – 1900

In the late 1700s new ideas about government brought about political revolutions. New technology brought about another kind of revolution, the **Industrial Revolution**. This period of advances in technology changed forever the way people lived and worked.

Changes in Agriculture

After 1660 Britain's population increased rapidly. British leaders predicted that the country would not have enough food to feed its people. Scientists, inventors, and other innovators worked together to solve the problem of increasing population. An **innovator** is a person who thinks of new ideas and invents new technologies. These innovators helped Britain find ways to improve farming.

By the mid-1700s farmers were using iron plows instead of wooden ones. Instead of scattering seeds on top of the soil, they used the seed drill invented by a farmer named Jethro Tull. This invention planted seeds in neat rows. British innovators had also found ways to grow stronger plants that produced more and larger fruits and vegetables.

This seed drill (right) from 1790 used the earlier ideas of Jethro Tull (above).

In the 1700s new inventions and discoveries in farming led to increased food production in Britain. These ideas enabled fewer people to produce more food.

A farming method called crop rotation made it possible to use farmland for a longer period of time without wearing it out. **Crop rotation** is the planting of different crops in a field from year to year. Because different crops use and give back different nutrients, the soil remains fertile.

Changes in agriculture during this time were the result of more than new technology. A growing demand for wool created the need for more grazing land for sheep. Wealthy farmers bought up plots of land and fenced in large areas to use as private pastures. Owners of smaller farms could no longer use this land for raising crops or grazing their animals. They had to either rent land from the owners of large farms or stop farming altogether. Many farmers left the countryside to look for work in towns and cities. They arrived just as the Industrial Revolution was beginning.

REVIEW What new ways of farming did British innovators introduce?

The Age of Machines

The Industrial Revolution started quietly with people trying new ways of doing things in workplaces throughout Britain. These experiments resulted in an explosion of new technology.

At first, most new technology developed in the **textile**, or cloth, industry. Until the mid-1700s, families worked at home to make cloth from cotton or wool supplied to them by merchants. The weavers spun the cotton or wool into thread by hand. Then they wove the thread into cloth on wooden looms. Afterward, they brought the cloth to the merchants, who paid them for it.

Soon, people looked for ways to speed up production. The invention of the flying shuttle in 1733 made it possible to weave cloth twice as fast as before. In 1764 James Hargreaves, a weaver, invented the spinning jenny. With the spinning jenny, one worker could spin eight threads at the same time.

Two new inventions, the spinning frame and the power loom, not only increased cloth production but also changed where the work was done. Families could not afford to buy these machines. Instead, rich textile merchants would buy them. They put the machines in **factories**, or large buildings where goods are made. Workers had to move near factories.

Because the large spinning and weaving machines depended on the power of running water, early factories were built near rivers. This changed in 1769, when James Watt built a practical steam engine, which did not require running water.

By 1800 about 1,200 steam engines were in use across Britain. They powered textile machines in factories. Later, they even powered boats and trains. Steam became the power of the Industrial Revolution.

REVIEW How did new technology affect the textile industry? CAUSE AND EFFECT

James Watt

Britain Leads the Way

British innovators such as James Watt and James Hargreaves helped start the Industrial Revolution. Britain continued to encourage experimenting. Business owners ran contests and offered prizes for new ideas on how to improve their operations. Almost every large British city had a science club, where inventors could meet and talk about their projects.

All this led to a rush of inventions. More than 1,000 new machines received patents in Britain between 1760 and 1789. A **patent** is a legal document stating that only the inventor has the right to make and sell the new product.

The British led the Industrial Revolution for several other reasons. First, Britain had many natural resources, such as iron and coal.

A CLOSER LOOK
A Textile Mill

With the invention of the steam engine, textile mills no longer depended on running water as a power source.

1. The steam engine turned the gears that drove the different machines inside the mill.
2. First, machines spun cotton or wool into yarn.
3. Next, machines prepared the yarn for weaving.
4. Finally, machines wove the yarn into cloth.

What powered all of the machines in the mill?

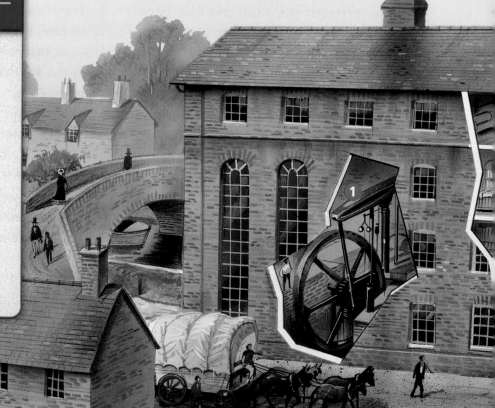

New Ways of Working and Living

Iron was used to make machine parts. Coal was burned to run steam engines. Second, Britain's colonies supplied industries with low-cost cotton, lumber, wool, and other raw materials, or natural resources used to manufacture goods. Also, the growing populations of Britain and its colonies needed more and more manufactured goods. British factory owners had to meet this demand.

Through trade, Britain had become a very wealthy country. British banks had large amounts of money to lend to entrepreneurs (ahn•truh•pruh•NERZ). An **entrepreneur** is a person who starts and runs a business. Many British entrepreneurs did well.

REVIEW What made Britain a leader in the Industrial Revolution?

By the mid-1800s the Industrial Revolution was at its peak in Britain. It had also begun to spread to other parts of western Europe and the northeastern United States. People experienced great changes in how they worked.

The huge factories also affected living conditions. Cities became crowded because many families came from the countryside to find work. Factory chimneys filled the air with smoke, and city streets became filthy. People had to cram together to live in poorly built houses. Unhealthy living conditions led to the spread of diseases. Illnesses claimed the lives of many, especially young children.

People had to endure difficult working conditions. Most men worked at least 12 hours a day, 6 days a week, for very low pay.

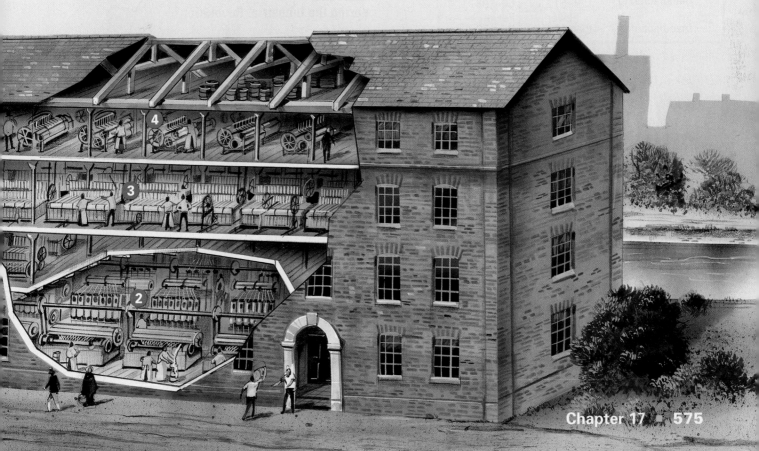

Industrial Revolution in Britain

ATLANTIC OCEAN

North Sea

IRELAND

Aberdeen

Glasgow • Edinburgh

Newcastle upon Tyne

Manchester • Leeds
Liverpool

London

Portsmouth

English Channel

0   75   150 Miles
0   75   150 Kilometers
Lambert Conformal Conic Projection

Major industries

◢ Cotton textiles
🔥 Wool textiles
⚓ Shipbuilding
🔔 Copper manufacturing
🔩 Iron manufacturing
🦅 Lead manufacturing
📄 Food processing

People per square mile		People per square kilometer
More than 512		More than 198
129–512		50–198
Fewer than 129		Fewer than 50

GEOGRAPHY THEME

Human-Environment Interactions
During the Industrial Revolution, many cities in Britain, such as London (above, right), became busy industrial centers.

❓ What were the main industries in and around London?

Women and children worked just as long and hard but for even less pay. As one textile worker said in 1832,

❝Whilst the engine runs, the people must work—men, women, and children are yoked together with iron and steam.❞

Children often had the most dangerous jobs. Some children were made to climb onto the spinning machines to repair broken threads—while the machines were running! Many were injured or killed.

Over time, the lives of workers did improve. Machines instead of people were used for most hard physical labor. Although workers' wages were low, they were steady. People could buy meat and vegetables once in a while to go with their bread and cheese.

REVIEW **What was life like for working people during the Industrial Revolution?**

World Leadership

In 1851 Britain hosted the Great Exhibition in the Crystal Palace in London. People came from all over Europe and the United States to see new inventions from Britain and other countries. There were steam engines, power looms, farm machinery, and more on display. Most of the inventions were British.

The Industrial Revolution, the visitors agreed, had made Britain the "workshop of the world." By 1851 Britain had more miles of railroad and more factories than any other country. The United States, Germany, Belgium, and France used Britain as a model for their own industrial revolutions.

The Crystal Palace in London was the site of the Great Exhibition in 1851. Its glass-and-iron frame housed about 14,000 exhibits on 8 miles (12.8 km) of display tables.

Economic success gave Britain and the other industrial nations new strength in dealing with other nations and peoples. In search of new markets—places to sell their goods—they expanded their colonies in Asia. They also forced China and Japan to sign new trade agreements. Next, the European industrial countries turned to Africa. This huge continent had plenty of inexpensive raw materials for Europe's factories and possible markets for its goods.

The strength of the industrial nations sent a clear message to the world that industrial nations would be the winners. In Asia the country of Japan listened to this message. The Japanese government quickly passed laws that helped make it easier to build new industries. By 1900 Japan, too, was having an industrial revolution.

REVIEW What steps did the industrial countries take to find new markets and new sources of raw materials?

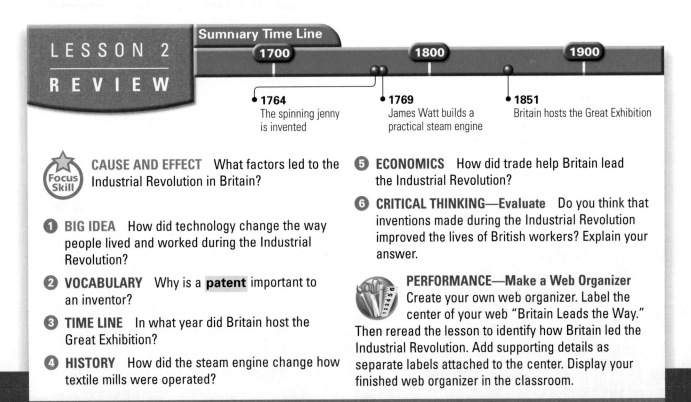

LESSON 2
REVIEW

Summary Time Line

1700 — 1800 — 1900

1764
The spinning jenny is invented

1769
James Watt builds a practical steam engine

1851
Britain hosts the Great Exhibition

Focus Skill **CAUSE AND EFFECT** What factors led to the Industrial Revolution in Britain?

1 BIG IDEA How did technology change the way people lived and worked during the Industrial Revolution?

2 VOCABULARY Why is a **patent** important to an inventor?

3 TIME LINE In what year did Britain host the Great Exhibition?

4 HISTORY How did the steam engine change how textile mills were operated?

5 ECONOMICS How did trade help Britain lead the Industrial Revolution?

6 CRITICAL THINKING—Evaluate Do you think that inventions made during the Industrial Revolution improved the lives of British workers? Explain your answer.

PERFORMANCE—Make a Web Organizer
Create your own web organizer. Label the center of your web "Britain Leads the Way." Then reread the lesson to identify how Britain led the Industrial Revolution. Add supporting details as separate labels attached to the center. Display your finished web organizer in the classroom.

LESSON

3 Capitalism and Classes

CAUSE AND EFFECT
As you read, identify the causes and effects of different economic systems.

BIG IDEA
Capitalism created much wealth for countries and for some individuals.

VOCABULARY
- economic system
- traditional economy
- command economy
- market economy
- demand
- supply
- capitalism
- laissez-faire
- free enterprise
- strike
- labor union
- socialism

1700 — 1800 — 1900 — PRESENT

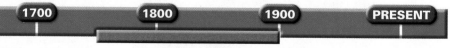

1750–1900

The European industrial countries grew rich in the 1800s, but their wealth was not shared equally. Some people became very rich while others stayed poor. In many countries the gap between rich and poor grew wider, leading to social conflict.

Kinds of Economies

One of the reasons that Britain led the way in the Industrial Revolution was its economic system. An **economic system** is the way a country produces and uses goods and services. A **traditional economy** is one that does not see much change over time. In a traditional economy people spend most of their time raising food for themselves. Without a surplus of food to sell, they are not able to buy better tools to improve their ways of farming. They continue working as they always have.

Built in 1411 at the center of London, Guildhall provided a place for the city's craftworkers to meet and organize.

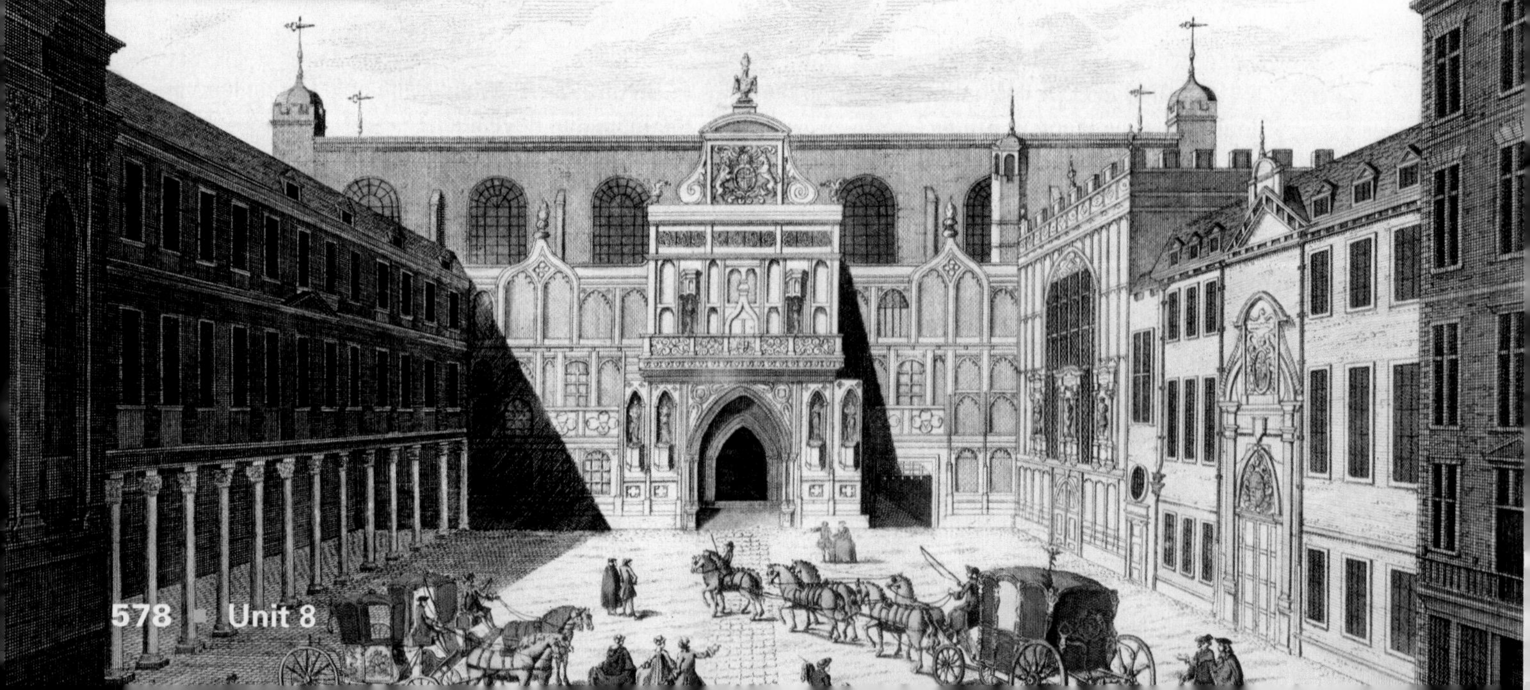

Teapot

Shoes

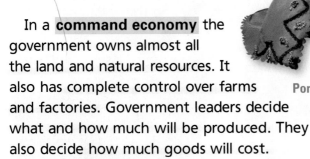

Porcelain doll

In a **command economy** the government owns almost all the land and natural resources. It also has complete control over farms and factories. Government leaders decide what and how much will be produced. They also decide how much goods will cost.

In a **market economy** the people decide which goods and services to buy. The people also decide how they will earn their living. A market economy is based on the system of supply and demand. When a person buys a product or service, he or she is showing a **demand** for that product or service. If there is a high demand, the producer will increase the **supply**, or amount offered for sale. The producer will do this to make a greater profit.

During the Middle Ages, Britain had a traditional economy. Most people farmed and grew just enough to survive.

In the 1700s Britain adopted a kind of market economy known as **capitalism**. Entrepreneurs spent money, or capital, to start businesses. They hoped that the business would grow and earn money for them.

REVIEW What are the three main kinds of economic systems?

Scottish economist Adam Smith

Adam Smith's Ideas

In 1776 the Scottish economist Adam Smith explained in a book called *The Wealth of Nations* how capitalism works. In his book Smith wrote about "the natural effort of every individual to better his own condition." He explained that business owners do not make and sell goods because they are kind people. They do it to make a profit. Yet by helping themselves, the business owners help everyone. They provide jobs for workers. They also supply needed goods and services.

Smith felt that governments should not become involved in their country's economy. He encouraged the idea of **laissez-faire** (leh•say-FAIR), a French term meaning to allow people to do as they wish without interference. Smith believed that the principles of supply and demand would keep the economy going. Business would boom, there would be more jobs, and the country would gain much wealth.

Smith's ideas, which became known as **free enterprise**, benefited both business owners and workers. As Smith had predicted, the countries with free enterprise systems grew rich and powerful.

REVIEW What did Adam Smith predict would be the effects of a free enterprise system?
🔵 **CAUSE AND EFFECT**

Many Europeans were among the growing middle class during the late 1800s. Only the wealthy could afford jewels like this sapphire-and-diamond pin (left).

Economic Classes in Europe

The spread of capitalism in Europe changed the economic classes. Before capitalism the aristocracy, or upper class, was made up mainly of wealthy landowners. These people inherited much of their wealth and property. Rather than farm their land themselves, landowners rented it to tenant farmers. During the Industrial Revolution, wealthy factory and business owners began to join the aristocracy. These people were a part of the upper class because of the money that they earned, not because of the family into which they were born.

One of the greatest changes during this period was the growth of the middle class. This class included bankers, shopkeepers, and professional people, such as doctors and lawyers. At the bottom were the factory workers and farmworkers. These people worked long hours for low wages. They were called the working class.

For centuries the upper class had been closed to most people. The Industrial Revolution made it possible for wealthy entrepreneurs to join the upper class. At the same time, differences grew between middle-class and working-class people.

REVIEW Who made up the middle class in Europe?

The lives of working-class people were difficult.

580

Conflict Among Classes

Tensions soon arose among the economic classes. Aristocrats, or upper-class people, looked down on wealthy members of the middle class. They did not respect people who had only recently become wealthy.

In turn, the middle class claimed that the upper class did nothing to earn its wealth. The landlords simply waited for the rents to come in. The economist John Stuart Mill agreed. "They grow richer . . . in their sleep," he wrote, "without working, risking, or economizing."

Working-class people were angry with the middle class. They did not like having to work long hours for low pay in poor working conditions. They wanted a fair share of the profits from their work.

Over time, the working people's anger grew. They realized that without their labor there would be no wealth. To back up their demands for better wages, some workers went on **strike**—they stopped working. Many of these strikes failed because they were poorly planned. Besides, there were many new workers ready to take strikers' jobs.

Some workers thought they could get better results if they formed workers' groups called **labor unions**. At first, most people did not want to join labor unions. Some European governments even passed laws against unions. By the end of the 1800s, however, workers had recognized the value of unions. Unions spoke for the workers and organized strikes that won them better working conditions and higher pay.

For some people, unions and strikes did not change the economic system enough. They said that capitalism should be replaced with a new system called socialism. Under **socialism** the government owns and runs all the industries. Socialists said that capitalism made life hard for working people.

Analyze Tables The table shows the average earnings for British citizens in the mid-1800s. The painting shows British union members demanding the release of workers who were jailed for striking.

◈ What occupations made up the working class?

Average Yearly Earnings for British Citizens, mid–1800s

ECONOMIC CLASS	OCCUPATION	EARNINGS (in British pounds)
Upper Class	aristocrats	30,000
Middle Class	doctors, lawyers	300–800
	teachers, journalists, shopkeepers	150–300
Working Class	carpenters	75–100
	sailors, servants	40–75
	soldiers, factory workers, farmworkers	25

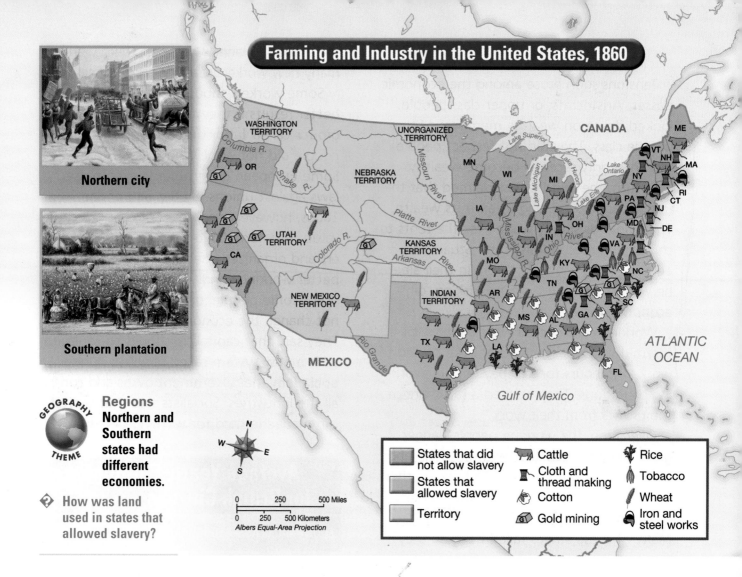

Farming and Industry in the United States, 1860

Northern city

Southern plantation

GEOGRAPHY THEME

Regions
Northern and Southern states had different economies.

❓ How was land used in states that allowed slavery?

N W E S

0   250   500 Miles
0   250   500 Kilometers
Albers Equal-Area Projection

States that did not allow slavery	Cattle	Rice
States that allowed slavery	Cloth and thread making	Tobacco
Territory	Cotton	Wheat
	Gold mining	Iron and steel works

To have a better life, they said, all people should work together and share equally the results of their labor.

In 1848 a German writer named Karl Marx published his ideas about socialism. He called for workers to revolt against the ruling classes. Marx believed that the workers would win this revolution and establish a society without social classes. Workers did not do what Marx said. Even so, his ideas worried many government and business leaders.

REVIEW Why did conflicts arise between the working class and other social classes?

Life in the United States

The United States also faced economic and social division during the 1800s. Two different economic systems divided the new nation. The Southern states continued an economic and social system based on agriculture. Plantation owners made up the upper class. The middle class included owners of smaller farms, merchants, and businesspeople. Next came workers and poor farmers.

Below this class were the people who helped make it possible for the upper class to have its wealth—enslaved Africans.

An 1850s sewing machine

The Northern states developed a three-class economic and social system as they accepted capitalism and the Industrial Revolution. In the upper class were wealthy landowners and factory owners. The middle class included less-wealthy business owners as well as merchants. Below them was the working class. As in Europe many workers faced low wages, long hours, and poor working conditions.

Leaders in the United States did not have the same fears of revolution as those in Europe. In the democratic United States, many workers were able to help themselves by voting. Also, social classes in the United States were not as strictly separated.

Most Americans felt that any citizen of the United States could start with nothing and become wealthy through hard work. American workers also formed unions to work for better working conditions.

REVIEW Why did the United States have less class conflict than Europe?

(Handwritten notes overlaid on page:)

1. The Poor people (Working class) got mad about their low wages, long hours, and poor working conditions. So there was a revolution. middle class start to grow. Some join the upper class.

1. There became more jobs and the country will get wealthier.

2. Capitalism is a market economy but socialism are industries that government runs and owns.

a heartbreaking story

3. 1848
4. It explained how capitalism works.
5. In the notebook. All organized neatly.

6. Ya-Ha8 Enterprise system made country wealthy.

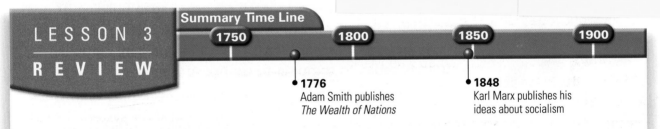

LESSON 3
REVIEW

Summary Time Line

1750   1800   1850   1900

• **1776**
Adam Smith publishes
The Wealth of Nations

• **1848**
Karl Marx publishes his
ideas about socialism

CAUSE AND EFFECT How did the economic system of capitalism affect classes in Europe?

① **BIG IDEA** How might capitalism benefit both business owners and workers?

② **VOCABULARY** Explain the difference between **capitalism** and **socialism**.

③ **TIME LINE** In what year did Karl Marx publish his ideas about socialism?

④ **HISTORY** What did Adam Smith write about in his book *The Wealth of Nations*?

⑤ **ECONOMICS** How were the economies of the northern and the southern United States different in the 1800s?

⑥ **CRITICAL THINKING—Apply** Which economic system did Adam Smith say would create the most wealth for the citizens of a country? Why?

PERFORMANCE—Write a Newspaper Article Imagine that you are a newspaper reporter. Your assignment is to cover a meeting between labor union leaders and business owners about working conditions in a factory. In your article, report what each side wanted and how they were able to reach a compromise.

· LESSON ·

4

CAUSE AND EFFECT

As you read, identify the causes and effects of imperialism.

BIG IDEA

Industrialized countries built new colonial empires during the 1800s.

VOCABULARY

imperialism
cash crop
sepoy
Raj
mutiny
Open Door policy
Monroe Doctrine

The Age of Imperialism

1700 | 1800 | 1900 | PRESENT

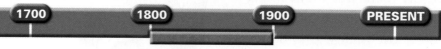

1800 – 1900

To keep their factories operating, industrialized countries needed many kinds of raw materials. They also needed new customers for their manufactured goods. In the 1800s they found both in Africa and Asia.

The Scramble for Africa

Europeans had been increasing their contact with Africans since the 1400s, though mostly just along the African coasts. Europeans knew little about what lay inland. Then, in the 1800s, Europeans began to explore the central parts of Africa.

Reports of beautiful landscapes, exotic animals, and plentiful natural resources soon reached Europe. Tens of thousands of Europeans headed for Africa. European countries started colonies on African land. In doing so, each country began building its own empire. Building an empire by claiming lands, setting up colonies, and controlling those colonies is called **imperialism**. European countries began to compete to control African land.

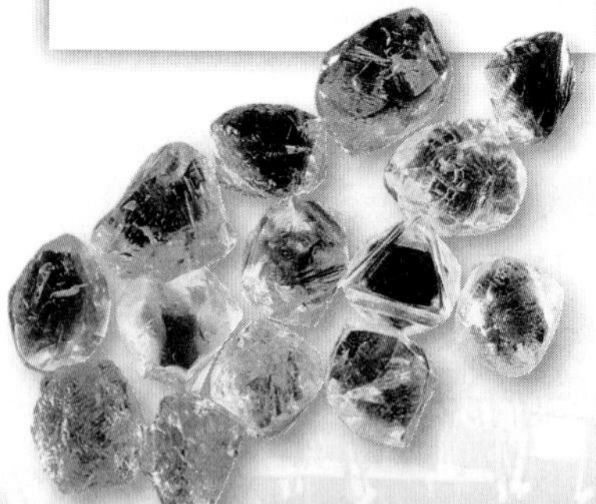

Natural resources in Africa, such as diamonds (above left) mined in South Africa (below), provided much wealth to European countries.

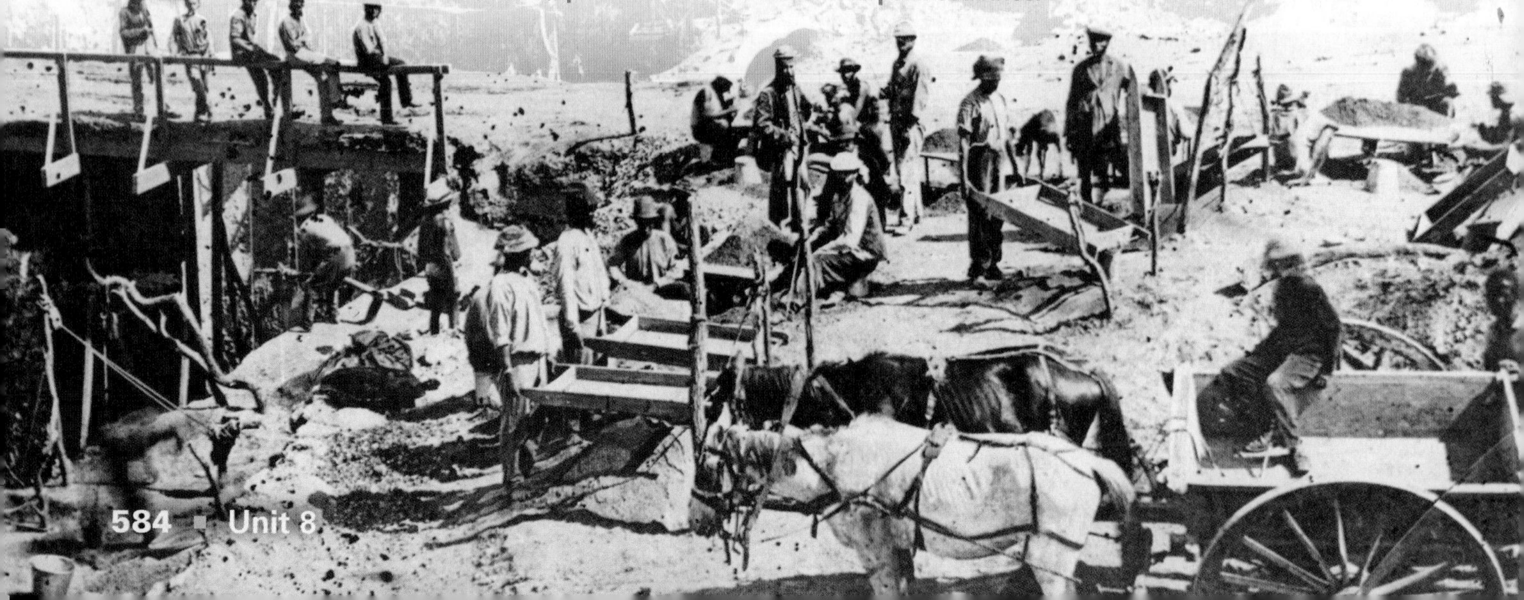

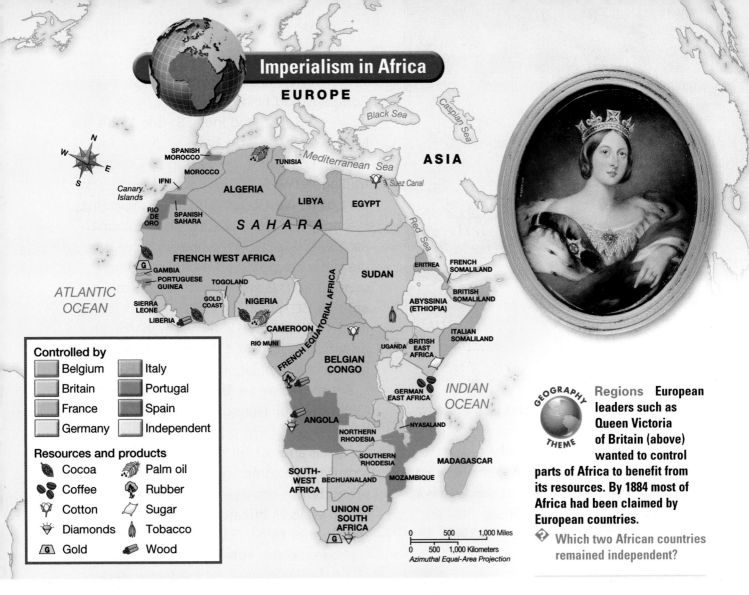

Imperialism in Africa

EUROPE

ASIA

Black Sea

Caspian Sea

SPANISH MOROCCO

Mediterranean Sea

TUNISIA

MOROCCO

IFNI

Canary Islands

Suez Canal

ALGERIA

LIBYA

EGYPT

RIO DE ORO

SPANISH SAHARA

S A H A R A

Red Sea

FRENCH WEST AFRICA

GAMBIA

ATLANTIC OCEAN

PORTUGUESE GUINEA

TOGOLAND

GOLD COAST

SIERRA LEONE

LIBERIA

NIGERIA

CAMEROON

RIO MUNI

FRENCH EQUATORIAL AFRICA

SUDAN

ERITREA

FRENCH SOMALILAND

ABYSSINIA (ETHIOPIA)

BRITISH SOMALILAND

ITALIAN SOMALILAND

UGANDA

BRITISH EAST AFRICA

BELGIAN CONGO

INDIAN OCEAN

GERMAN EAST AFRICA

ANGOLA

NYASALAND

NORTHERN RHODESIA

SOUTH-WEST AFRICA

BECHUANALAND

SOUTHERN RHODESIA

MADAGASCAR

MOZAMBIQUE

UNION OF SOUTH AFRICA

Controlled by

Belgium

Britain

France

Germany

Italy

Portugal

Spain

Independent

Resources and products

Cocoa — Palm oil

Coffee — Rubber

Cotton — Sugar

Diamonds — Tobacco

Gold — Wood

0   500   1,000 Miles
0   500   1,000 Kilometers
Azimuthal Equal-Area Projection

GEOGRAPHY THEME

Regions European leaders such as Queen Victoria of Britain (above) wanted to control parts of Africa to benefit from its resources. By 1884 most of Africa had been claimed by European countries.

Which two African countries remained independent?

Europeans raced to control parts of Africa until 1884. In that year European leaders met to divide Africa among themselves. African leaders were not invited to the meeting. Each European country took over the regions in Africa where it had the most settlements. Little attention was paid to the similarities and differences in religions, languages, and ways of life of the native Africans.

Most European countries used Africa's natural and human resources for their own advantage. African farmers could no longer keep all the crops they raised. European landowners made them grow cash crops instead. **Cash crops** are crops raised to sell rather than to use at home. The African cash crops were then exported to markets in Europe, where they were sold for profit.

African farmers now had less time and land to grow food. Cheap European goods replaced goods made locally. This made Africans more dependent on European merchants. The merchants profited by selling European goods to Africans.

Europeans improved transportation and communication in their African colonies. These improvements, however, were mostly for their own use. In 1869 French engineers and Egyptian workers completed the Suez Canal. This waterway connected the Red Sea to the Mediterranean Sea, saving weeks of travel time between Europe and Asia. In 1875 the British bought the canal. It shortened the trip to India, their richest colony.

REVIEW What effects did imperialism have on the lives of Africans? **CAUSE AND EFFECT**

The Suez Canal shortened the sea route between Britain and India by about 5,000 miles (8,047 km).

African Reaction

Some Europeans believed it was their duty to bring their own culture to the people of Africa. Christian missionaries started schools, and some African students learned to read and write the colonists' languages. The schools did not teach African children about their native languages, religions, and cultures. This concerned some African leaders.

Africans in every part of the continent resisted the European settlers. In western Africa, the Muslim leader Samori Touré fought against French control for 15 years. In eastern Africa nearly 100,000 Africans died in a war with German colonists. In the north the British battled the Sudanese. In the south they fought against the Zulus.

REVIEW How did Africans respond to European settlers?

Muslim leader Samori Touré

The British Raj

Ever since the 1600s, Britain's East India Company had held control over trade between Britain and India. By the 1700s the Mogul rulers of India had lost power in the region. Over time, the East India Company's trading network included India's east coast, part of its west coast, and the Ganges River.

Some Hindu and Muslim princes cooperated with the British company. Those who did not were defeated by the company's own army. This army was made up of **sepoys** (SEE•poyz), or Indian soldiers led by British officers. By 1850 the company controlled almost half of the Indian subcontinent and a population larger than Europe's.

British rule of the Indian subcontinent was called the **Raj**. During the Raj, the East India Company paid low prices for India's raw materials and cotton cloth and sold them for a profit. The company also prospered by selling British goods in India. Through trade, British ways of life arrived in India.

Control by the East India Company angered many Indians. In 1857 thousands of sepoys, backed by the Indian people, started to **mutiny**, or turn against, the company. This rebellion, called the Great Mutiny, lasted more than a year. When it was over, the East India Company turned over control of Indian lands to the British government.

The British government put a new system of rule in place and promised to respect Indian culture. Indian schools and universities were established. Some Indian leaders were invited to serve in the government.

REVIEW What event caused the British Raj to change its policies in India?

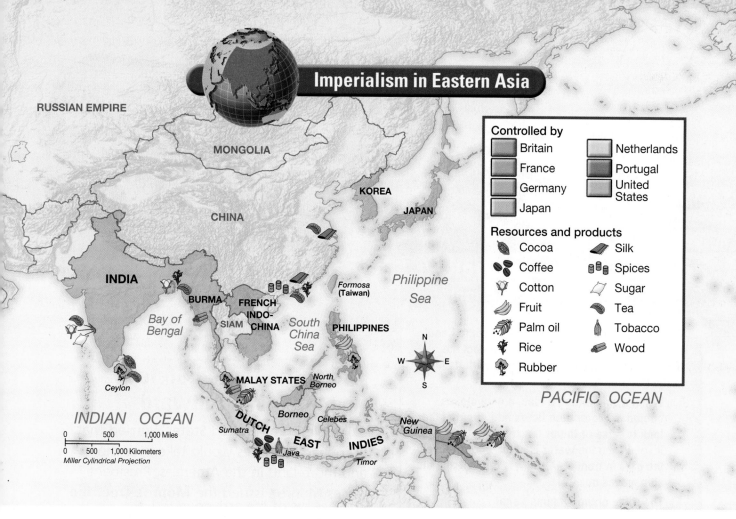

Imperialism in Eastern Asia

RUSSIAN EMPIRE

MONGOLIA

CHINA

KOREA

JAPAN

INDIA

BURMA

FRENCH INDO-CHINA

SIAM

Bay of Bengal

Formosa (Taiwan)

Philippine Sea

South China Sea

PHILIPPINES

Ceylon

MALAY STATES

North Borneo

INDIAN OCEAN

DUTCH

Borneo

Celebes

New Guinea

Sumatra

EAST

INDIES

Java

Timor

PACIFIC OCEAN

0   500   1,000 Miles
0   500   1,000 Kilometers
Miller Cylindrical Projection

Controlled by

Britain		Netherlands	
France		Portugal	
Germany		United States	
Japan			

Resources and products

Cocoa		Silk	
Coffee		Spices	
Cotton		Sugar	
Fruit		Tea	
Palm oil		Tobacco	
Rice		Wood	
Rubber			

GEOGRAPHY THEME

Regions In the 1700s and 1800s, European countries claimed much of eastern Asia.

◆ What resources and products were available in the Dutch East Indies?

Imperialism in China

As in Africa and India, opportunities for trade and profit brought European countries to China. European traders wanted Chinese goods. However, the Chinese seemed happy to live without goods made in Europe.

To open up trade, traders felt they needed to find something the Chinese wanted. The product that the East India Company found a demand for was opium— a dangerous, habit-forming drug.

When China tried to stop the trade of opium by destroying British supplies at a Chinese port, the Opium War began. China fought two Opium Wars against Britain— one from 1839 to 1842 and another in 1856.

The Chinese could not match the advanced weapons of the British military. The treaties ending the wars opened trade in China to Britain as well as to other European countries.

In 1850 the Chinese government was further weakened by a rebellion in southeastern China. During the rebellion the British and French took the opportunity to capture Beijing, China's capital city. Then they helped the Chinese government stop the rebellion. By the rebellion's end in the 1860s, more than 20 million Chinese had died, many of starvation or disease.

Nations from all parts of the world took advantage of China's weakened state.

> ## A CLOSER LOOK
> ### The Panama Canal
>
> The United States completed the Panama Canal in 1914. The canal helped better connect the United States' lands in the Atlantic with its lands in the Pacific.
>
> **1** When a ship enters a lock, a gate closes behind it. Water then flows into or out of the lock to raise or lower the ship to the next level. When the water is at the correct level, the gate in front of the ship is opened and the ship moves on.
>
> **2** The route of the Panama Canal
>
> **3** Side view of the canal locks
>
> **4** The sailing distance between the Atlantic and the Pacific was greatly shortened.
>
> ❖ Why would ship owners be willing to pay high tolls to use the canal?

The United States Looks Outward

People in the United States worried that European countries would take over more and more land in the Americas. President James Monroe issued the **Monroe Doctrine** in 1823. This doctrine, or government plan of action, declared that the United States would go to war to stop European countries from expanding their colonial empires in the Americas.

In 1895 the people of Cuba began a revolution to gain freedom from Spain. When the Spanish used harsh methods to stop the revolution, the people of the United States became angry. They sided with the Cubans, whose island lies only 90 miles (145 km) from the southern tip of Florida in the United States.

In 1898 the United States sent a battleship called the *Maine* to Havana,

Spanish-American War hero Theodore Roosevelt

By 1900 Britain, France, Germany, and other nations controlled many of China's largest cities. Some Chinese reacted angrily to outside control. A secret society, the Boxers, began attacking missionaries and foreign officals. Many nations sent soldiers to stop the Boxer Rebellion. These leaders agreed that an Open Door policy was needed to keep control of China. An **Open Door policy** means that all nations have an equal opportunity to trade freely in a certain place.

REVIEW What nations took control of parts of China?

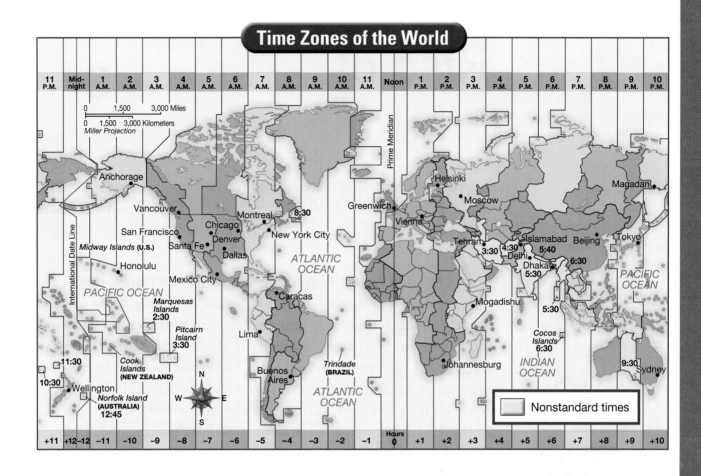

Time Zones of the World

11 P.M.	Mid-night	1 A.M.	2 A.M.	3 A.M.	4 A.M.	5 A.M.	6 A.M.	7 A.M.	8 A.M.	9 A.M.	10 A.M.	11 A.M.	Noon	1 P.M.	2 P.M.	3 P.M.	4 P.M.	5 P.M.	6 P.M.	7 P.M.	8 P.M.	9 P.M.	10 P.M.

0   1,500   3,000 Miles
0   1,500   3,000 Kilometers
Miller Projection

Prime Meridian

Anchorage

Vancouver
Montreal
Greenwich   Helsinki
Moscow   Magadan

Chicago   New York City
San Francisco   Vienna
Denver   8:30   Tehran   Islamabad Beijing Tokyo
Midway Islands (U.S.)   Santa Fe   3:30 4:30 5:40
Dallas   Delhi   6:30
Honolulu   Dhaka
ATLANTIC   5:30   PACIFIC
Mexico City   OCEAN   OCEAN
PACIFIC OCEAN
Caracas   Mogadishu
Marquesas Islands 2:30   5:30

Pitcairn Island 3:30   Lima   *Cocos Islands* 6:30

11:30   *Trindade (BRAZIL)*   INDIAN   9:30   Sydney
Cook Islands   Buenos Aires   OCEAN
10:30   (NEW ZEALAND)   Johannesburg
Wellington   ATLANTIC
Norfolk Island (AUSTRALIA) 12:45   OCEAN

International Date Line

N W E S

Nonstandard times

+11	+12–12	–11	–10	–9	–8	–7	–6	–5	–4	–3	–2	–1	Hours 0	+1	+2	+3	+4	+5	+6	+7	+8	+9	+10

▶ PRACTICE THE SKILL

Study the map above, and answer the following questions.

1. If it is noon in Greenwich, what time is it in Mexico City, Mexico?

2. If it is noon in Greenwich, what time is it in Helsinki, Finland?

3. How many hours behind Sydney, Australia, is Johannesburg, South Africa?

4. How many hours ahead of Beijing, China, is Tokyo, Japan?

▶ APPLY WHAT YOU LEARNED

Write five word problems about time zones, and give them to a classmate to solve. Here is an example: "At 9 P.M., Victor, who lives in Moscow, Russia, telephones his sister in New York City in the United States. What time is it in New York City?"

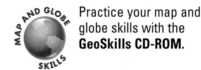

Practice your map and globe skills with the **GeoSkills CD-ROM.**

MAP AND GLOBE SKILLS

5

CAUSE AND EFFECT

As you read, identify the effects that nationalism has had on the creation of countries around the world.

BIG IDEA

Feelings of nationalism led people to create many of the countries that exist today.

VOCABULARY

nationalism
chancellor
kaiser
Manifest Destiny

Rise of Nationalism

| 1700 | 1800 | 1900 | PRESENT |

1825 – 1925

After the French Revolution the people of France felt united because they had fought together to change their government. Political revolutions and competition between countries increased feelings of **nationalism**, or loyalty to a nation, throughout the world. By the early 1800s people viewed one another as citizens of a country. In many countries citizens felt connected by the land, culture, and language they shared. Nationalist movements were begun to unite groups of people into nation-states.

Italian Nationalism

In the 1830s Italy was made up of independent states and kingdoms. The Catholic Church ruled Rome and its surrounding states. Italian nobles controlled a few other states. A number of Italian states, however, were ruled by members of the Austrian and French royal families.

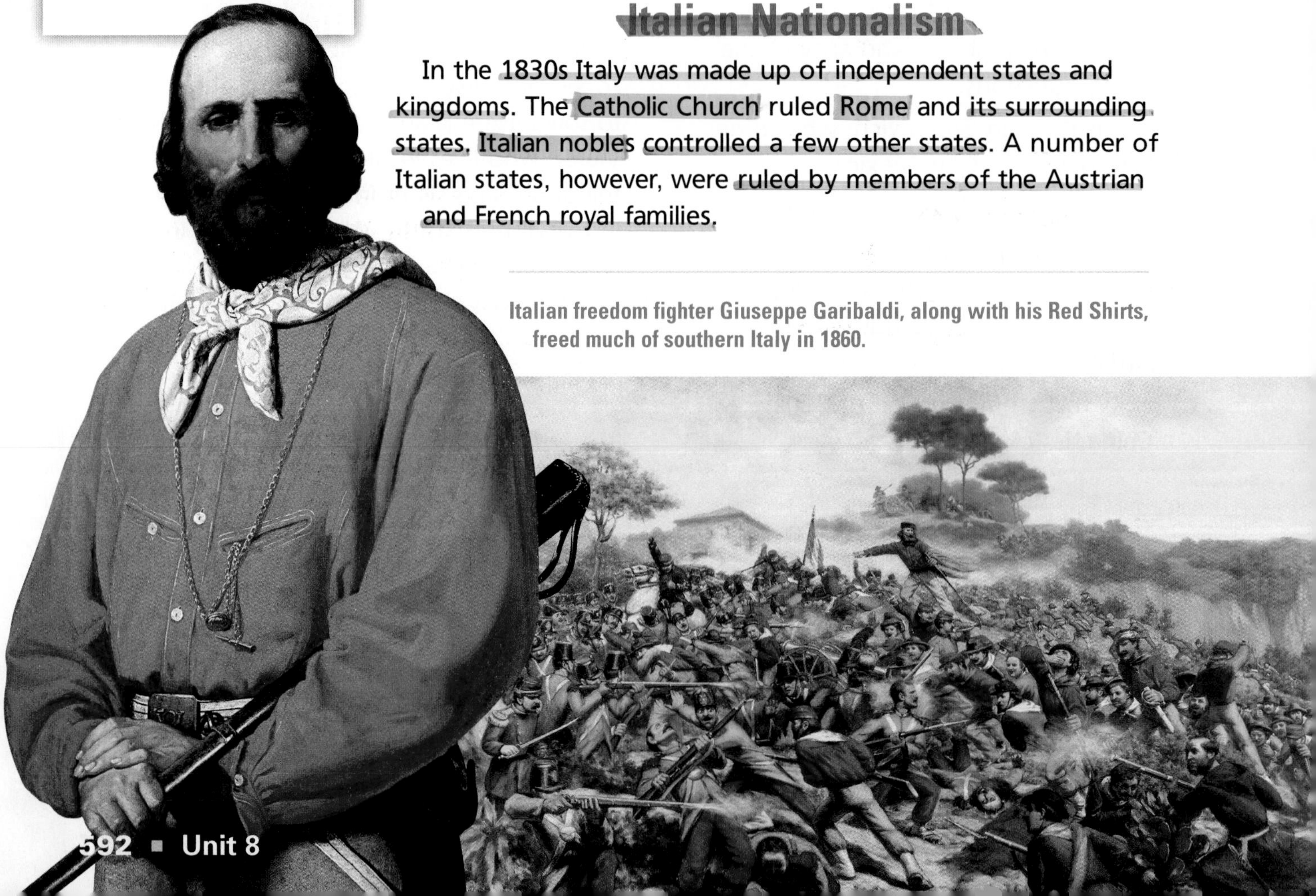

Italian freedom fighter Giuseppe Garibaldi, along with his Red Shirts, freed much of southern Italy in 1860.

Unification of Italy, 1870

ALPS

LOMBARDY 1859 • Milan
VENETIA 1866
PARMA 1860
MODENA 1860
SAN MARINO
Florence •
TUSCANY 1860
PAPAL STATES 1870
KINGDOM OF SARDINIA 1859
Corsica (FRANCE)
Rome •
• Naples
Sardinia
Tyrrhenian Sea
KINGDOM OF THE TWO SICILIES 1860
Sicily

EUROPE

N W E S

Adriatic Sea

0   75   150 Miles
0   75   150 Kilometers
Lambert Conformal Conic Projection

1860 Date joined with kingdom of Italy

Mediterranean Sea

Regions By 1870 the many kingdoms of the Italian Peninsula had become one nation. In this nineteenth-century painting, Italians gather in Turin, Italy, to celebrate the country's unification.

◆ In what year did most states join with the Kingdom of Italy?

Many Italians longed to unite these states and kingdoms into a single nation. In 1831 Giuseppe Mazzini (joo•SEP•ay maht•SEE•nee) formed Young Italy, a nationalist group. Its goal was to unite Italy into one democratic republic governed by the Italian people.

One member of Young Italy, Giuseppe Garibaldi (gar•uh•BAWL•dee), fought for Italy's freedom for many years. In 1860 he and 1,000 followers, all wearing red shirts, captured the island of Sicily. Garibaldi and his Red Shirts then sailed to the mainland, taking Naples. Soon, they had freed much of southern Italy from French rule.

Meanwhile, Count Camillo di Cavour (kah•VUR), chief minister of the Kingdom of Sardinia, had united much of the north. Cavour convinced Garibaldi to set up a kingdom of Italy. King Victor Emmanuel of Sardinia became the first ruler of this new country. Italy became fully united in 1870, when Rome was finally captured.

REVIEW How did Mazzini help organize the Italian nationalist movement?

Unification and Division in Europe

In the early 1800s Germany, like Italy, was a collection of separate states. In 1861 King Wilhelm I became the ruler of Prussia, a German state and one of the most powerful states in Europe. He believed that Germany was meant to be united under Prussian rule. On his side was Otto von Bismarck, the **chancellor**, or prime minister, of Prussia.

Bismarck took violent action to unite the German states under Prussian rule. He stirred feelings of nationalism among Germans by declaring war on other countries. After the Prussian army defeated both Denmark and Austria, northern Germany was unified under Prussia.

Coin showing King Wilhelm I (at left)

Unification of Germany, 1862–1871

North Sea

SWEDEN

DENMARK

Baltic Sea

0   100   200 Miles
0   100   200 Kilometers
Azimuthal Equal-Area Projection

SCHLESWIG 1866
HOLSTEIN 1866
OLDENBURG 1867
MECKLENBURG-SCHWERIN 1867
HANOVER 1866
NETHERLANDS
PRUSSIA 1866
★ Berlin
Vistula River
RUSSIAN EMPIRE

PRUSSIA
BRUNSWICK
ANHALT

BELGIUM
HESSE-CASSEL 1866
NASSAU 1866
THURINGIA 1867
SAXONY 1867
DARMSTADT 1871
BAVARIA 1871
ALSACE-LORRAINE From France 1871
WÜRTTEMBERG 1871
FRANCE
BADEN 1871

SWITZERLAND

AUSTRO-HUNGARIAN EMPIRE

Danube River

BOSNIA   SERBIA

1867 Year state became part of Germany
★ Capital

Regions The Franco-Prussian War led to a new German Empire. This painting shows Prussian Otto von Bismarck (seated at right) meeting with the French emperor after France's surrender.

❖ In which German state was the capital located?

In the south four separate German states remained.

When Germany went to war with France in the Franco-Prussian War, the four states in southern Germany joined with Prussia to form a new German Empire. The German army defeated the French in January 1871. During that same month King Wilhelm I was named **kaiser** (KY•zer), or emperor, of Germany. Bismarck became chancellor of the empire.

While nationalism helped unify countries, it sometimes divided groups within nation-states. Many Irish people were angry that Britain had control of their island. Irish nationalists wanted independence from Britain

In this 1916 document, Irish nationalist leaders declare the Irish Republic.

because of cultural and political differences. Irish nationalists unsuccessfully rebelled against British rule in 1848, 1867, and 1916. It was not until 1921 that the Irish won their independence. However, Northern Ireland, in the northeastern corner of the island, today still remains under British control.

Conflicts also arose in eastern Europe. Throughout the Balkan Peninsula nationalist feelings were strong. Many different peoples lived in this region, including Slavic groups, such as Serbs, Croats, Bulgarians, and Slovenes. Some of these groups were ruled by Austria-Hungary but wanted to build independent nations. Other groups, such as the Bulgarians and the Serbs, already had independence by the 1880s. They wanted others who shared their culture to gain their freedom from Austria-Hungary and join them.

REVIEW What caused conflicts on the Balkan Peninsula?

 CAUSE AND EFFECT

Nationalism in the United States

The rise of nationalism in Europe had been influenced partly by the American Revolution. People everywhere felt inspired by the Americans' fight for independence. The Americans had stood up to Britain and built a new nation. From the beginning, the people of the United States have felt pride in their country.

In the 1800s Americans continued to come together as a nation. At this time many immigrants arrived in the United States. They came from all over the world, spoke many different languages, and had different customs. Still, these new citizens had a sense of belonging to their country.

National pride could also be seen in the ideas that led to the rapid expansion of the United States. In 1845 the words **Manifest Destiny** were first spoken. These words described the belief that the United States was destined, or meant, to have its western border reach the Pacific Ocean.

In the 1840s a war with Mexico resulted in new territory for the United States. As the nation's borders expanded, new states were added to the original 13. By the century's end, Manifest Destiny was complete.

REVIEW What was **Manifest Destiny**?

 GEOGRAPHY THEME

Movement Throughout the 1800s, the United States grew to include more land as its borders moved farther to the south and to the west.

❖ When did the borders of the United States first reach the Pacific Coast?

The Growth of the United States

RUSSIA

ALASKA PURCHASE 1867

CANADA

0 200 400 Miles
0 400 Kilometers

PACIFIC OCEAN

Present-day border

CANADA

TREATY WITH BRITAIN 1842

0 200 400 Miles
0 200 400 Kilometers
Albers Equal-Area Projection

OREGON TERRITORY 1846

TREATY WITH BRITAIN 1818

Lake Superior

Lake Michigan

Lake Huron

Lake Ontario

Lake Erie

130°W

40°N

40°N

LOUISIANA PURCHASE 1803

MEXICAN CESSION 1848

UNITED STATES 1783

PACIFIC OCEAN

ATLANTIC OCEAN

70°W

30°N

30°N

GADSDEN PURCHASE 1853

TEXAS ANNEXATION 1845

1810

1812

1813

FLORIDA 1819

120°W

PACIFIC OCEAN

HAWAII ANNEXATION 1898

0 100 Miles
0 100 Kilometers

MEXICO

Gulf of Mexico

110°W

90°W

80°W

595

After arriving in Japan in 1853, Commodore Matthew Perry met with Japanese officials to discuss trade.

The Rise of Japan

Japanese national pride grew out of a concern over an outside threat. In 1853 two American warships sailed into the harbor of Edo, now Tokyo, Japan. The commander of the ships, Commodore Matthew Perry, insisted that the Japanese open their ports to American traders. The Japanese shogun, or leader, refused.

Perry returned the following year with seven heavily armed ships. The Japanese gave in to the pressure and signed a treaty with the United States. This opened five ports to American merchants.

Soon after that, the Japanese government signed treaties with European countries.

Many Japanese did not think that the treaties were fair. As a result, samurai warriors attacked and killed many outsiders. Then, in 1868, these samurai overthrew the shogun and restored the emperor to power. The emperor called himself and his reign *Meiji* (MAY•jee), or "Enlightened Rule." The time of his reign is called the Meiji Restoration.

The emperor and his advisers took advantage of

Emperor Meiji ruled Japan from 1867 to 1912.

the new nationalist feelings and challenged the West. To compete with the new industrial nations, Meiji officials looked to the West for the technology that would allow Japan to modernize. However, they did not want to change the "spirit of old Japan."

In just 30 years, the Meiji government's program turned Japan into a world power. Japan became a modern, industrialized nation. Railroads connected cities and towns across the island nation, and factories produced goods for export.

To sell their goods, Japanese capitalists began to seek colonial markets. They also needed to obtain raw materials to keep their factories running. Japan built up a strong navy and an army to gain a share of the colonial trade. Japan took the island of Taiwan from China in 1895. Ten years later, Japan surprised nations in Europe and North America when it easily defeated Russia in a war, taking some of its land. Later, Japan captured the Chinese province of Manchuria, which was rich in minerals. By this time, Japan had become the first modern nation-state in Asia.

REVIEW Why did Japan want to become a modern nation-state?

Building railroads was an important part of Japan's modernization during the Meiji Restoration.

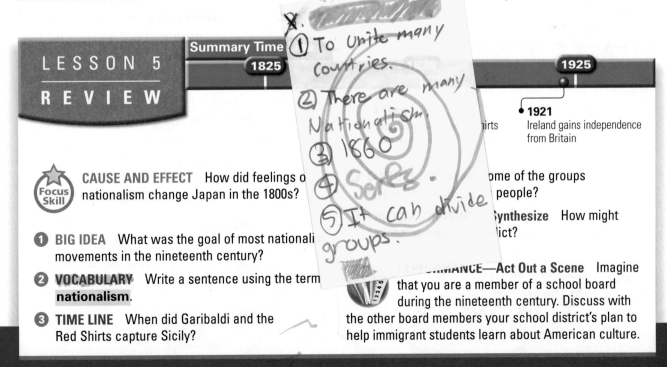

LESSON 5 REVIEW

Summary Time 1825 ... 1925

1921 Ireland gains independence from Britain

CAUSE AND EFFECT How did feelings of nationalism change Japan in the 1800s?

some of the groups ... people?

... Synthesize How might ... lict?

1 BIG IDEA What was the goal of most nationalist movements in the nineteenth century?

2 VOCABULARY Write a sentence using the term **nationalism**.

3 TIME LINE When did Garibaldi and the Red Shirts capture Sicily?

PERFORMANCE—Act Out a Scene Imagine that you are a member of a school board during the nineteenth century. Discuss with the other board members your school district's plan to help immigrant students learn about American culture.

Identify National Symbols

■ WHY IT MATTERS

National symbols are an important way of expressing national identity and pride. Since the formation of the first countries, flags have been important symbols of national identity. A flag stands for a nation's land, its people, and its government. It also expresses ideas or qualities valued by the people of a nation. Knowing the kinds of things that flags represent can help you better understand today's nations and their history and culture.

■ WHAT YOU NEED TO KNOW

Most national flags today use one or more of seven colors—black, blue, green, orange, red, white, and yellow. Traditionally these colors have stood for different qualities. For example, blue stands for loyalty, red for courage, and white for freedom. To Arab nations, the colors black, green, red, and white symbolize Arab unity. The Arab nations use these colors in their national flags to indicate their unity as an ethnic group.

Patterns on many present-day national flags are also traditional. In the Middle Ages some knights used a stripe of white or yellow to separate two colors. The flag of Italy, for example, has a white stripe between stripes of green and red.

The picture symbols used on some flags have a religious meaning. Some flags have a cross, a symbol for Christianity. On other flags the star and crescent, a symbol of Islam, appears. The flag of Israel has the Star of David, a Jewish symbol.

On some flags, stars stand for unity. The number of stars in a flag is sometimes equal to the number of states or provinces united to form a country.

Picture symbols sometimes show an important event in a nation's history. The Mexican flag has an eagle on a cactus holding a snake in its mouth. This represents the history of the Aztec Empire in Mexico.

The Great Seal of the United States

The coat of arms for the former Kingdom of Italy

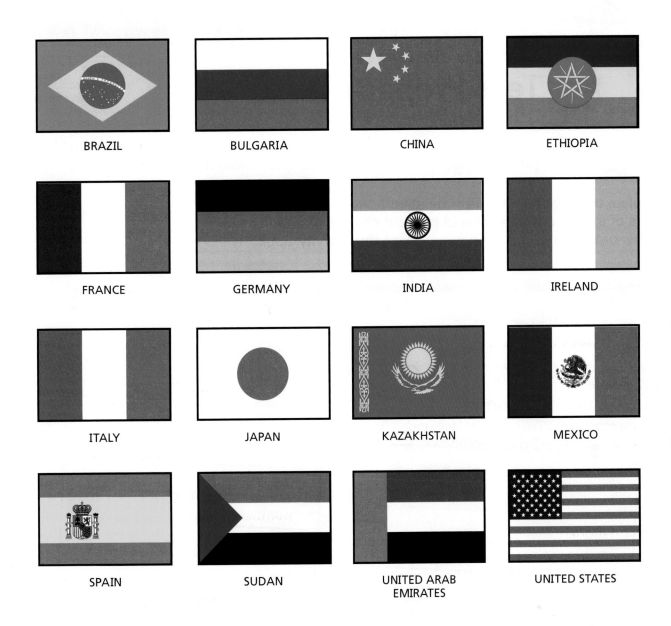

BRAZIL   BULGARIA   CHINA   ETHIOPIA

FRANCE   GERMANY   INDIA   IRELAND

ITALY   JAPAN   KAZAKHSTAN   MEXICO

SPAIN   SUDAN   UNITED ARAB EMIRATES   UNITED STATES

▶ PRACTICE THE SKILL

Study the national flags above. Then use what you have learned about flags and their meaning to answer the following questions.

❶ Which flags have picture symbols?

❷ Which flags are those of Arab nations? How do you know this?

❸ Why do you think the color white is included in the United States flag?

▶ APPLY WHAT YOU LEARNED

Choose a flag from this page or from the Almanac on pages R2–R21 of this book. Research its importance as a national symbol. Then make a bookmark by drawing the flag on a strip of paper or cardboard. Include on the bookmark at least three facts about the flag's importance to the nation's history and culture.

 **Cause and Effect**

Complete this graphic organizer by identifying the causes and effects of events during a time of political change. A copy of this graphic organizer appears on page 158 of the Activity Book.

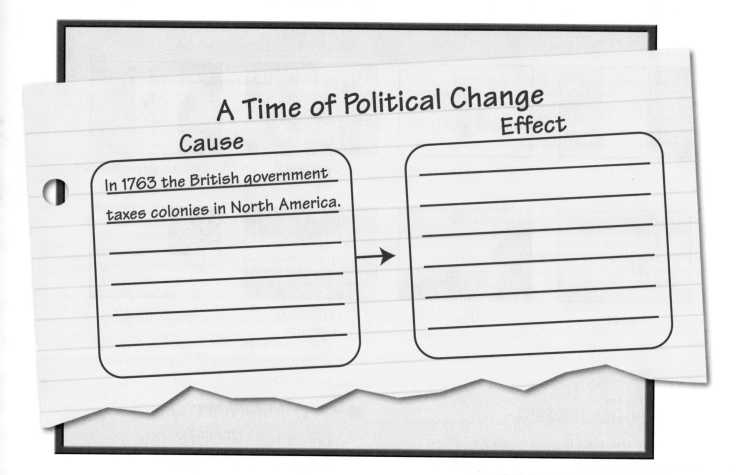

A Time of Political Change

Cause

In 1763 the British government taxes colonies in North America.

Effect

THINK & WRITE

Write a Speech   What is a revolution? Why do revolutions happen? Why are some people willing to risk their freedom or even their lives to participate in a revolution? In your speech, use examples from three revolutions to support your opinions.

Make a Case   Think about what you read about life in Britain before and after the Industrial Revolution. Would you rather have lived in Britain before the Industrial Revolution or after it? Write a paragraph that gives specific evidence to support your case.

1789
The French Revolution begins

1850
A rebellion weakens
the Chinese government

1870
The kingdom of Italy
unites Italians

1871
Germans unite under
the German Empire

1898
The Spanish-American
War is fought

USE THE TIME LINE

Use the chapter summary time line to answer these questions.

1 Which came together first, the German Empire or the kingdom of Italy?

2 In what year was the Spanish-American War fought?

USE VOCABULARY

Explain what each term means and how the terms in each pair are related.

3 **Industrial Revolution** (p. 572), **innovator** (p. 572)

4 **textile** (p. 573), **factory** (p. 574)

5 **strike** (p. 581), **labor union** (p. 581)

RECALL FACTS

Answer these questions.

6 What happened at the 1776 Continental Congress in Philadelphia, Pennsylvania?

7 Who was Jethro Tull?

Write the letter of the best choice.

8 **TEST PREP**   In which country did the storming of the Bastille begin a revolution?
A France
B Ireland
C China
D Brazil

9 **TEST PREP**   François Toussaint-Louverture fought for independence for the colony that became what nation?
F Brazil
G Argentina
H Haiti
J Cuba

10 **TEST PREP**   In what nation did the Boxer Rebellion take place?
A France
B Ireland
C China
D Brazil

THINK CRITICALLY

11 How does the protection inventors receive through patents encourage people to keep inventing new things?

12 How do you think capitalism got its name?

13 Why did Britain and other European nations start colonies in Africa and India?

APPLY SKILLS

Read an Editorial Cartoon

14 Find an editorial cartoon in a recent newspaper or magazine. Does it focus on a political, a cultural, or an economic issue? What point do you think the artist is trying to make? Share your cartoon with the class.

Read a Time Zone Map

15 Find your time zone on the map on page 591. How many hours ahead or behind is your time zone compared to Wellington, New Zealand; Moscow, Russia; and Caracas, Venezuela?

Identify National Symbols

16 Use this book's Almanac, pages R2–R21, to identify ten countries whose flags have stars.

VIMY RIDGE MEMORIAL, VIMY RIDGE, FRANCE

In World War I, soldiers fighting in the open dug trenches for shelter. There was great loss of life. German forces held the Vimy Ridge until Canadian forces pushed them back in April 1917. This was an important victory for the Allied Powers, even though many Canadian and British soldiers were killed. This preserved trench is part of a memorial to the Allies who died in the fighting.

LOCATE IT

Vimy Ridge

FRANCE

Times of War and Times of Peace

> **"The world must be made safe for democracy."**
>
> —Woodrow Wilson,
> United States President, 1917

Make Inferences

To make an **inference,** use what you already know about a subject and what you read to come to a conclusion.

As you read this chapter, make inferences.

- Write what you already know about the chapter's topics. Then list details you read about the people, places, and events.

- Make inferences about how the world has changed since 1900.

What You Know   What You Read   Inferences

World War I

1700   1800   1900   PRESENT

1880 – 1930

MAKE INFERENCES

As you read, make inferences about the effects of World War I on Europe and the rest of the world.

BIG IDEA

World War I caused destruction in much of Europe and spread conflict around the world.

VOCABULARY

alliance
militarism
arms race
assassination
armistice
Great Depression

FAST FACT

Europe and its people suffered greatly during World War I. During one battle, at the Somme River, more than a million soldiers were killed.

The beginning of the twentieth century was a time of discovery and innovation. Advances in science and medicine helped people live longer, healthier lives. The invention of the automobile and the airplane improved transportation. Towering skyscrapers of steel and glass changed the skylines of cities. For many countries this was a period of economic growth. At the same time, many countries began to compete for power.

Tensions Grow

The spirit of nationalism, which grew in Europe in the late 1800s, created conflicts. By 1914 many European countries did not trust one another. European leaders looked for ways to protect their countries from attack. Some nations formed **alliances**, or agreements among nations, groups, or individuals to help one another.

One alliance, known as the Triple Alliance, linked Germany, Austria-Hungary, and Italy. Fearing the strength of this alliance, France and Russia became allies in 1893. Later, Britain joined with France and Russia to form an alliance known as the Triple Entente (ahn•TAHNT).

Citizens show their support as German troops leave Berlin for the war front in 1914.

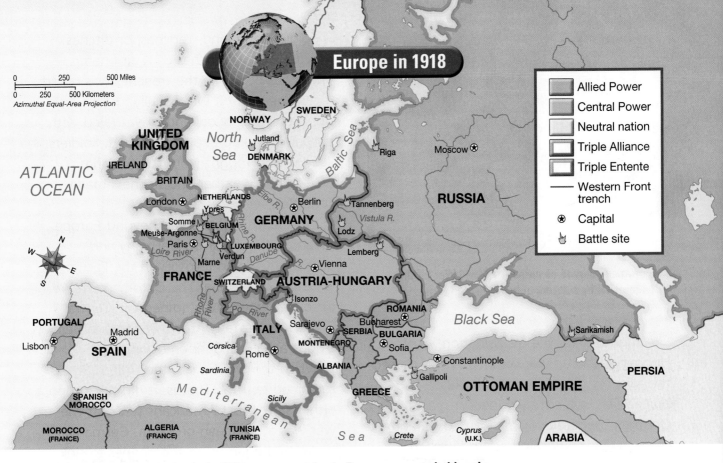

Europe in 1918

Legend:
- Allied Power
- Central Power
- Neutral nation
- Triple Alliance
- Triple Entente
- Western Front trench
- ✪ Capital
- Battle site

GEOGRAPHY THEME

Regions In the early 1900s most countries in Europe supported either the Triple Entente or the Triple Alliance.

❖ Which three world powers made up the Triple Entente? Which three made up the Triple Alliance?

European nations began to build huge armies and navies. This interest in armed power is called **militarism**. Each country wanted to have the largest and most powerful military. Many European leaders believed that they could use force to get whatever they wanted.

Soon all Europe was in an arms race. An **arms race** is a competition among nations to have the most weapons. As the number of weapons in Europe grew, so did people's fear of war. The alliances created a balance of power, but they also divided Europe into two sides. Even a minor event could lead to the start of a war. Such an event soon came to be, on the Balkan Peninsula in southeastern Europe.

REVIEW Why did many European nations form alliances?

The World at War

In 1908 the empire of Austria-Hungary seized the Balkan provinces of Bosnia (BAHZ•nee•uh) and Herzegovina (hairt•suh•goh•VEE•nuh). This angered the Serbs who lived there. They felt that the provinces should be a part of Serbia. On June 28, 1914, Archduke Francis Ferdinand, who was to be the future ruler of Austria-Hungary, arrived in the Bosnian capital, Sarajevo (sair•uh•YAY•voh).

As the archduke and Sophie, his wife, rode through the streets in an open car, they were assassinated by a young Serbian. **Assassination** is murder for a political reason. The leaders of Austria-Hungary believed that the Serbian government had something to do with the assassination.

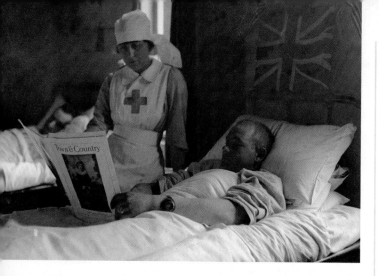

Many women served as nurses in World War I. Others filled jobs left by soldiers at home.

A month after the assassination, Austria-Hungary declared war on Serbia. This caused the alliances to go into action. Russia supported Serbia. Austria-Hungary's main ally, Germany, declared war first on Russia and then on France. Britain declared war on Germany. By the end of August 1914, most of Europe was at war. Britain, France, Russia, and their allies became known as the Allied Powers, or Allies. Germany, Austria-Hungary, and their allies were called the Central Powers.

When the war began, most people thought it would end quickly. Instead the war raged for years. New weapons such as tanks, machine guns, and poison gas made the war especially deadly.

Soldiers dug long trenches, or ditches, that faced the trenches of their enemy. The space between the trenches was called "no-man's land." It was usually just a few hundred yards wide, and it was filled with barbed wire and exploding mines. Soldiers lived in and fought from the trenches for weeks. Bad weather and sickness made conditions even worse.

In time, the war spread beyond Europe. Japan declared war on Germany and attacked German territory in the Pacific Ocean and in China. The Ottoman Empire, in southwestern Asia, joined the Central Powers. In eastern Africa, British and Belgian troops attacked German colonies.

When the war began, the United States remained neutral. That is, it did not support either side. Most Americans felt that the war was a European problem. Germany, however, began using submarines to sink American trading ships headed to Europe.

The British also discovered a German plan that tried to draw Mexico into the war. The United States government and its citizens were outraged by these events. On April 2, 1917, President Woodrow Wilson asked Congress to declare war. Soon, the United States joined the Allies.

REVIEW Why did the United States enter World War I?

British soldiers in trenches during World War I

Europe After the Treaty of Versailles

Capital ⊛

Regions The Treaty of Versailles caused borders in Europe to change. Compare this map with the map on page 605.

❷ What new countries were formed in Europe because of the treaty?

The War Ends

The addition of American forces made a difference to the Allies. By late October 1918, Germany was ready to end the war. On November 11, 1918, German leaders signed an **armistice**, an agreement to stop fighting. Two months later, Allied leaders met in Paris to decide peace terms.

President Wilson wanted a treaty that would create lasting world peace. In a speech to Congress, he made fourteen suggestions for the treaty that became known as the Fourteen Points. One of the Fourteen Points was particularly important to Wilson.

Analyze Graphs This pictograph shows the number of soldiers killed on both sides.

❷ Which side lost more soldiers, the Allied Powers or the Central Powers?

Soldiers Killed in WWI

MAJOR ALLIED POWERS

Russia	
France	
Britain	
Italy	
United States	

MAJOR CENTRAL POWERS

Germany	
Austria-Hungary	
Ottoman Empire	

= 100,000 people

Ticker tape machines printed out the latest prices of stocks.

It would form an organization made up of all nations. This organization would settle disputes and keep the peace.

On June 28, 1919, the Treaty of Versailles (vair•SY) was signed by the Allied nations and by Germany. The treaty called for the creation of the League of Nations, an international organization that would work to keep the peace. The United States, however, did not join. Many Americans wanted to stay out of world politics.

The Treaty of Versailles was very different from what Wilson wanted. The treaty dealt harshly with Germany. The Germans had to give up land, pay money, reduce their army, and take responsibility for the war. Other Central Power nations were also affected. Austria-Hungary was split into several countries. The Ottoman Empire was divided by France and Britain into new nations. The Treaty of Versailles left many people angry.

REVIEW What inferences can you make about the success of the Treaty of Versailles?

🎯 **MAKE INFERENCES**

The Great Depression

After World War I the United States and many other nations made economic progress. By 1930, however, the United States had suffered an economic collapse. Known as the **Great Depression**, it was the worst economic decline in world history.

Just after World War I, Americans spent money freely on goods and services. Factories increased production to meet this new demand. Over time, people could not afford to keep buying more goods. As demand fell, warehouses and stores soon overflowed with unsold goods. Even so, many factories continued to make more and more products with the idea that they would be sold.

At the same time, many Americans began to invest in the stock market. They hoped to make profits by buying and selling shares of stock quickly. Stockbrokers, people who buy and sell stocks for others, allowed buying on credit. This meant that buyers had to pay only a small amount to the stockbrokers at first. Buyers agreed to pay the rest of what they owed at a later date.

This newspaper from the times (below) describes the stock market crash that led to the Great Depression. Soup kitchens, such as this one in Chicago (right), fed the hungry.

In October 1929 some investors became worried about the economy and began selling large amounts of stock. Soon after, panic set in. People tried to sell their stocks, but there were few buyers. The stock market crashed as prices fell rapidly. Investors could not pay stockbrokers what they owed them, and many people lost all their money.

Government policies also helped weaken the United States economy. To protect American farms and industries, the government placed high taxes on imported goods. This made it harder for other countries to sell their goods in the United States. In turn, these countries could not afford American goods.

The economic problems spread quickly. Factories cut production and many workers lost their jobs. Worried about the failing economy, people tried to withdraw their savings from banks. Many banks failed because they could not pay so many people at once. As sources of money became scarce, more businesses closed and even more people lost their jobs.

As the Great Depression spread, it ruined the economies of nations around the world. European economies, already weak from the war, suffered even more than the United States. With unrest growing, people looked for political leaders who might offer them hope.

REVIEW **What led to the Great Depression?**

During the Great Depression, parts of the southwestern United States suffered many bad droughts. Because of the dust storms that developed in the region, it became known as the Dust Bowl.

LESSON 1
———
R E V I E W

Summary Time Line

1880 1905 1930

• **1914**
World War I begins

• **1918**
World War I ends

• **1929**
The stock market crashes in the United States

 MAKE INFERENCES Do you think that conditions in Europe after World War I led to more conflicts? Explain.

1 BIG IDEA Which countries fought against each other in World War I?

2 VOCABULARY Write a sentence that explains how the terms **militarism** and **arms race** are related.

3 TIME LINE In which year did World War I begin?

4 HISTORY Which countries formed the Triple Alliance?

5 CRITICAL THINKING—Analyze Why do you think stockbrokers sold stocks on credit?

 PERFORMANCE—Hold a Debate Learn more about Germany's role in World War I, using library resources or the Internet. In a class debate, groups should argue for or against treating Germany harshly after the war. Be sure that arguments are supported with facts and details.

Identify Changing Borders

WHY IT MATTERS

At one time the empire of Austria-Hungary controlled a large part of eastern Europe. After World War I, Austria-Hungary was divided up, changing the borders in eastern Europe. By comparing maps from different time periods, you can learn how the borders of countries have changed and how different parts of the world looked in the past.

WHAT YOU NEED TO KNOW

Maps of different time periods can be found in historical atlases and history books. The title or map key usually tells which time period is shown on a map. Color is often used to show the lands controlled or claimed by different countries.

Look at the map on this page. It shows Austria-Hungary before the beginning of World War I. The pink area on the map

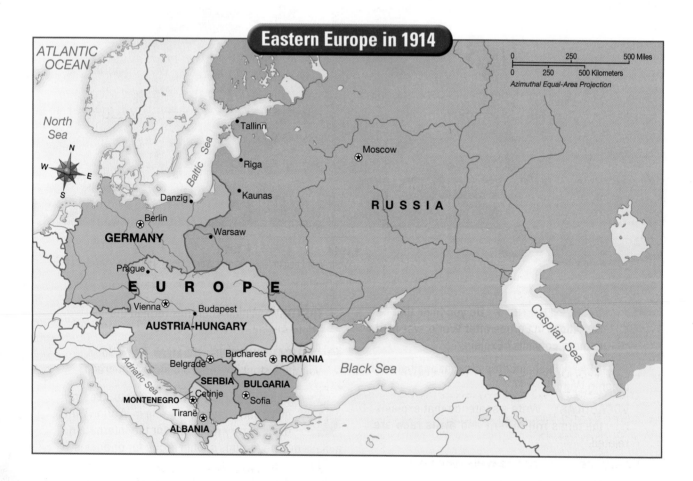

Eastern Europe in 1914

ATLANTIC OCEAN

250   500 Miles
250   500 Kilometers
Azimuthal Equal-Area Projection

North Sea

Baltic Sea

Tallinn

Moscow

Riga

Kaunas

R U S S I A

Danzig

Berlin

GERMANY

Warsaw

Prague

E U R O P E

Vienna   Budapest

AUSTRIA-HUNGARY

Bucharest   **ROMANIA**

Belgrade

SERBIA   **BULGARIA**

Black Sea

Caspian Sea

MONTENEGRO   Cetinje

Sofia

Adriatic Sea

Tiranë

ALBANIA

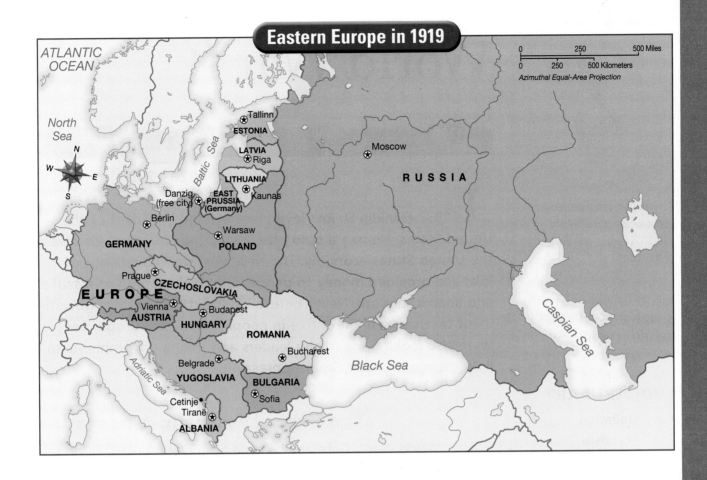

Eastern Europe in 1919

ATLANTIC OCEAN

North Sea

Baltic Sea

ESTONIA — Tallinn

LATVIA — Riga

LITHUANIA — Kaunas

Danzig (free city)

EAST PRUSSIA (Germany)

Berlin

GERMANY

Warsaw

POLAND

Prague

CZECHOSLOVAKIA

E U R O P E

Vienna

AUSTRIA

Budapest

HUNGARY

ROMANIA

Bucharest

Belgrade

YUGOSLAVIA

BULGARIA

Sofia

Adriatic Sea

Cetinje

Tiranë

ALBANIA

Moscow

R U S S I A

Caspian Sea

Black Sea

0   250   500 Miles
0   250   500 Kilometers
Azimuthal Equal-Area Projection

---

shows all the land controlled by Austria-Hungary in 1914. The lands controlled by neighboring countries are represented by different colors.

Now look at the map above. It shows how the same area looked after World War I. Notice that many new countries were formed by the treaties that ended the war.

▶ PRACTICE THE SKILL

Study the maps to answer these questions.

1 After World War I, which new countries were formed in eastern Europe?

2 After World War I, which countries no longer existed?

3 Which new countries were formed completely from land that was once part of Austria-Hungary?

4 Which other countries gained some land that was once part of Austria-Hungary?

▶ APPLY WHAT YOU LEARNED

Use a historical atlas or history book to find maps that show the growth of the United States. Then write a paragraph that describes how the size of the United States changed over time. Draw your own map to illustrate your paragraph. Use different colors to show how the United States looked during different periods of its history. Share your paragraph and map with your classmates.

Practice your map and globe skills with the **GeoSkills CD-ROM.**

MAKE INFERENCES

As you read, make inferences about the effects of World War II on Europe and the rest of the world.

BIG IDEA

Both economic and social problems in Europe following World War I led to another world war.

VOCABULARY

inflation
fascism
propaganda
liberate
concentration camp
genocide
Holocaust

World War II

1700	1800	1900	PRESENT

1920 – 1950

In 1932 Franklin D. Roosevelt was elected President of the United States. He had a bold plan, called the New Deal, to save the United States economy. The New Deal created millions of jobs and provided money to people who were retired or disabled and unable to work. Never before had the United States government taken such a direct role in people's lives. In Europe, people were also looking for strong leaders and strong governments to help them out of the Great Depression.

The Rise of Fascism

After World War I, Germany became a federal republic. During the 1920s and 1930s, Germany faced terrible problems. There were few jobs. High **inflation**—a continuing increase in prices—made German money almost worthless.

Many Germans lost faith in their government. They believed that signing the Treaty of Versailles had turned Germany into a poor, weak country. The German people looked for a strong leader who would make Germany powerful again. Some thought that leader was Adolf Hitler.

German soldiers gather to hear Adolf Hitler at a Nazi party rally in Nuremberg, Germany, in 1936.

Hitler believed that the best way to solve Germany's problems was by adopting the ideas of fascism (FA•shih•zuhm). **Fascism** is a set of political ideas that values strong government control, military strength, and extreme nationalism. To promote these ideas, Hitler helped form the National Socialist, or Nazi (NAHT•see), party in 1920.

By 1933 members of the Nazi party had been elected to important positions in the German government. That same year, Hitler forced Germany's president to make him chancellor. Then, he took the title of *führer* (FYOOR•er), or leader of the German people.

As führer, Hitler banned all political parties except the Nazi party and ended all elections. He formed a secret police force called the Gestapo (guh•STAH•poh), which arrested anyone who disagreed with the government.

To keep the support of the German people, Hitler used propaganda. **Propaganda** is information or rumors used to help or hurt a cause. A key part of Hitler's propaganda blamed Germany's troubles on the Jewish people. Many Germans believed the propaganda and did not object when the rights and property of Jews were taken away.

Around this time, other countries also changed governments in hopes of gaining power. In Italy the Fascist party came to power in 1922, led by Benito Mussolini (moo•suh•LEE•nee). In Japan a group of army officers, rather than a political party, took control of the government. They promised to build a great empire.

Germany, Italy, and Japan formed an alliance known as the Axis Powers. Each country hoped to create an empire by taking over the land of other countries.

REVIEW Why did fascism take hold in Germany?

Severe bombings by the Germans left much of London in ruins during World War II.

A Second World War

At first, little was done to stop the Axis Powers. European leaders did not want to risk another war. They felt that the fascists' desire for glory and power would soon be met.

In 1939 Germany attacked Poland. The Allied Powers—Britain and France—felt that Hitler had finally gone too far. They declared war on Germany.

By 1940, Germany controlled France, Poland, Norway, Belgium, Denmark, and the Netherlands. Britain, led by Winston Churchill, remained undefeated. He stated,

Winston Churchill

❝We shall fight on the beaches, we shall fight on the landing grounds, we shall fight in the fields and in the streets, we shall fight in the hills; we shall never surrender.❞

After facing strong resistance from the British, Hitler turned his attention elsewhere. With Mussolini, he planned to conquer the Mediterranean region. Also, even though Hitler had made a peace agreement with the Soviet Union—made up of Russia and other republics—he attacked it in 1941.

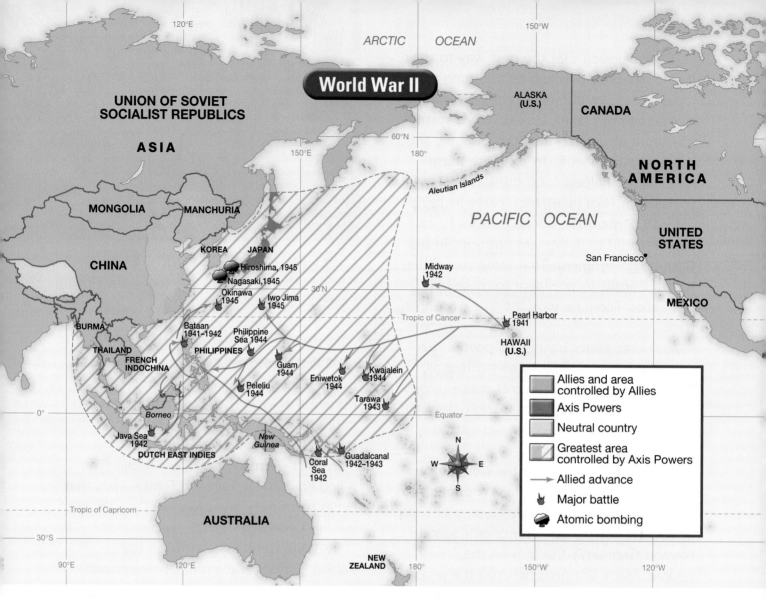

World War II

Allies and area controlled by Allies

Axis Powers

Neutral country

Greatest area controlled by Axis Powers

→ Allied advance

Major battle

Atomic bombing

GEOGRAPHY THEME

Location   People in all parts of the world felt the effects of World War II.

◈ Between which lines of latitude did most of the battles in the Pacific take place?

In the Pacific the Japanese captured much of China along with several Pacific islands. For a time, the Axis Powers seemed unstoppable.

Then, in December 1941, the Japanese attacked the United States naval base at Pearl Harbor, Hawaii. The United States joined the war against the Axis Powers. As in World War I, the support of American forces helped the Allies. The Axis Powers soon faced a number of setbacks.

The German army found itself caught in a long and bitter struggle against the Soviet Union. Although the German soldiers had better equipment, they were not prepared for the harsh climate of the Soviet winter. Allied forces began to win important battles in North Africa and on the Italian Peninsula.

Many women served as Army volunteers in World War II (left). The Allies invaded Normandy on D day (opposite).

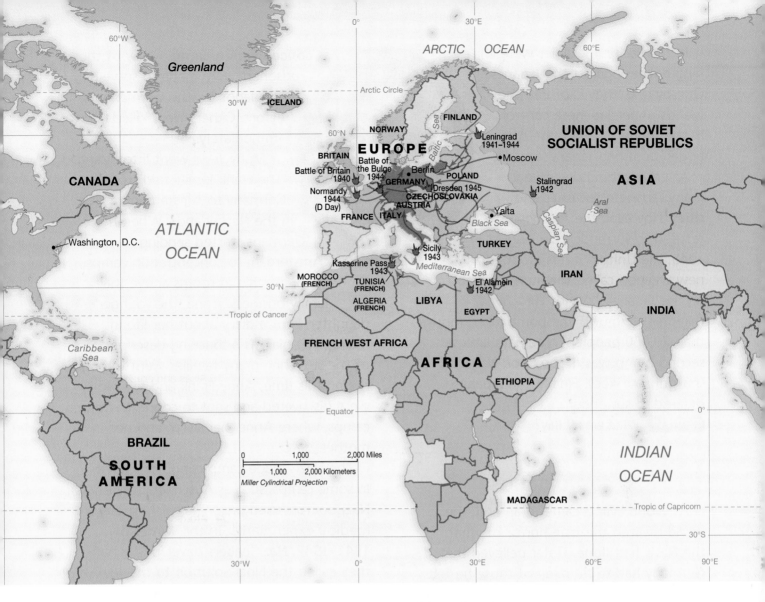

Italy surrendered to the Allies in September 1943. The Axis Powers had begun to crumble. Then, on June 6, 1944, Allied forces landed on the beaches of Normandy, in northern France.

The Allied invasion of France—known as D day—cost thousands of lives. Even so, the Allies held the beaches and pushed toward Germany.

Within a month, the Allies had moved far into France. By September they had **liberated**, or freed, Paris, the French capital. Less than a year later, on May 7, 1945, Germany surrendered.

In the Pacific the Allies were winning battles against the Japanese. One by one, they captured the islands under Japanese control. In the spring of 1945, the Allies began bombing Japanese cities.

Allied bombing destroyed many Japanese factories and cities. However, the Japanese refused to surrender. On August 6, 1945, the United States dropped a new weapon called the atomic bomb on the Japanese city of Hiroshima (hir•uh•SHEE•muh). The bomb killed more than 70,000 people. Three days later, a second bomb was dropped on Nagasaki (na•guh•SAH•kee). Finally, the Japanese offered to surrender.

REVIEW What was D day?

The Holocaust

As World War II came to an end, the world realized the true horror of what the Nazis had done. Hitler believed that Germany had to rid itself of those he felt were "undesirable" people. Jews, Gypsies, persons with disabilities, and opponents of the Nazi party were all targets of Hitler's hatred. Hitler put a plan into action to get rid of all the people he felt were inferior.

The first arrests of Jews took place during the early 1940s. They were sent to a kind of prison called a

Anne Frank

concentration camp. Many of the prisoners were made to serve as slave labor for the German war effort. Others were killed immediately.

Many Jews went into hiding. The Frank family fled from Germany to Amsterdam, a city in the Netherlands. When the Germans started sending Jews in Amsterdam to concentration camps, the Franks hid in rooms above their family business. Anne, the younger daughter, kept a diary about her life in hiding. Her diary is a touching description of the suffering many families went through during this time. Anne Frank and her family were discovered and sent to concentration camps, where Anne, her sister, and her mother died.

The Nazis made camp conditions terrible. In some camps, such as Auschwitz (OWSH•vits), Nazi doctors used prisoners for horrible medical experiments. In the winter of 1941–1942, Nazi leaders developed what they called the Final Solution to the Jewish Problem. This solution was **genocide**, the killing of an entire group of people.

By the end of the war, the Nazis had killed 6 million Jews. Another 6 million non-Jews were also killed. The mass killing of the Jewish people is now known as the **Holocaust**.

REVIEW What was the Holocaust?

The Nazis forced Jewish people to wear a yellow star of David (left) to make them easily identifiable. Prisoners in concentration camps (below) suffered horribly.

After the War

As many as 50 million people, including both soldiers and citizens, may have died during World War II. The fighting and bombing left many cities and towns across Europe and Asia in ruins. Large numbers of people had to leave their homes to seek shelter and safety.

The war-torn world needed repair. Allied leaders met to decide how to rebuild. The Soviet Union and the other Allies disagreed about rebuilding Germany. As a result, they divided Germany into two parts. One part, West Germany, was further divided among Britain, France, and the United States. The other part, East Germany, came under Soviet control. Berlin, Germany's capital, was also divided into West Berlin and East Berlin.

Together, the Allies created a new international organization, the United Nations, to keep world peace. In addition, the United States Congress approved the Marshall Plan. The plan provided about $13 billion to help rebuild Europe.

Members of the United Nations take part in a meeting in 1946 (above). The United Nations logo (left) shows all populated continents of the world.

To help the rebuilding, Britain, France, and the United States united West Germany. The Soviet Union felt that this challenged its control of East Germany. As World War II faded, new tensions between the United States and the Soviet Union emerged.

REVIEW **What inferences can you make about relations between the United States and the Soviet Union after World War II?**
Ⓢ **MAKE INFERENCES**

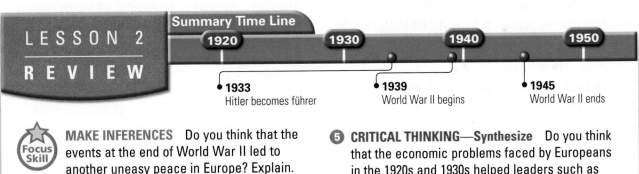

LESSON 2 REVIEW

Summary Time Line

1920	1930	1940	1950

● **1933** Hitler becomes führer

● **1939** World War II begins

● **1945** World War II ends

MAKE INFERENCES Do you think that the events at the end of World War II led to another uneasy peace in Europe? Explain.

1 **BIG IDEA** What are some of the events that led to World War II?

2 **VOCABULARY** How were **concentration camps** part of Hitler's plan of **genocide**?

3 **TIME LINE** How many years after World War II began did World War II end?

4 **ECONOMICS** How did President Roosevelt's New Deal help improve the economy of the United States?

5 **CRITICAL THINKING—Synthesize** Do you think that the economic problems faced by Europeans in the 1920s and 1930s helped leaders such as Adolf Hitler and Benito Mussolini come to power? Why or why not?

PERFORMANCE—Write a Report Learn more about D day, the Allied invasion of Normandy in France. Use the Internet and library resources to conduct your research. Find out details about events leading up to the invasion, the Allied attack, and the historical importance of D day. Using this information, write a report on D day.

Compare Different Kinds of Graphs

VOCABULARY

trend

▶ WHY IT MATTERS

During World War II, many workers in the United States left their jobs to join the military. This meant that hundreds of thousands of new workers would be needed to fill these jobs. Many of these workers were women. As they had done in World War I, women took over jobs that previously had been held only by men.

Suppose you want to prepare a report on production and the labor force during World War II. One way you might do this is by making graphs. Knowing how to read and make different kinds of graphs can help you compare large amounts of information.

▶ WHAT YOU NEED TO KNOW

Different kinds of graphs show different information in different ways. A line graph shows change. It is particularly useful in showing a **trend**, or the way something changes over time. The line graphs on this page show the changes in United States military personnel from 1940 to 1946 and the changes in United States aircraft production from 1941 to 1945.

A bar graph shows data using bars and is especially useful for quick comparisons. The bar graph on page 619 shows the number of female workers in the United States from 1900 to 1950.

▶ PRACTICE THE SKILL

Compare the values in the graphs by answering the following questions.

1 Did the number of women in the labor force increase or decrease between 1900 and 1950? By how much?

2 In which year were the most aircraft built? How many people served in the military in this year?

3 In which year did the number of people serving in the military decrease? Did the number of women in the labor force decrease during this period?

▶ APPLY WHAT YOU LEARNED

Write a paragraph about the information shown in the graphs on these pages. Do you think the graphs make it easier to understand and compare this information? Why or why not? Share your paragraph with a partner.

Women in the Labor Force, 1900–1950

Number of Employed Women (in millions)

Year

Women in World War II took over many jobs once held by men who went off to war.

3

The Rise of Communism

 MAKE INFERENCES

As you read, make inferences about the rise of communism in Russia and other parts of the world.

MAIN IDEA

A revolution in Russia led to a new system of government called communism that spread to other parts of the world.

VOCABULARY

communism
czar
soviet
collective
totalitarian
purge
cold war
warlord
Long March

In the early 1900s a new government based on the ideas of Karl Marx came to power in Russia. **Communism** is a system in which all property and all means of production—such as factories and farms—belong to the people as a group. Later, communism would spread from Russia to other parts of the world.

The Czars and the Russian Revolution

Since about 1480, Russia had been ruled by a czar. **Czar** (ZAHR) is the Russian word for *Caesar*, or ruler. The Russian czars expanded the country's borders and built Russia into a powerful nation. By the 1600s, however, Russia was suffering from political and economic problems. This difficult period became known as the Time of Troubles. While much of western Europe was becoming modern, Russia's growth slowed.

A new leader, Peter the Great, became czar in the late 1600s. His goal was to modernize Russia. He introduced European ideas, art, and architecture into Russian culture. Yet the lives of Russian peasants, or serfs, improved little.

The Winter Palace in St. Petersburg, Russia (below). Peter the Great (left) ruled Russia until 1725.

• BIOGRAPHY •

Catherine the Great 1729–1796

Character Trait: Responsibility

Educating people was important to Catherine the Great. During Catherine's time most people in Russia had never been to school. Catherine had schools built in every Russian town. These schools offered free education for the boys and girls of Russia's noble class. In time, there were more than 300 schools and 20,000 students in Russia.

GO ONLINE

MULTIMEDIA BIOGRAPHIES
Visit The Learning Site at **www.harcourtschool.com** to learn about other famous people.

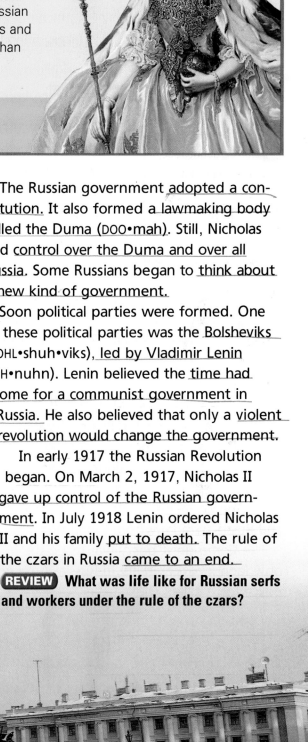

Catherine the Great, who came to power in 1762, also worked to make Russia more modern. She supported education and the arts. By the end of Catherine's rule, however, most Russians had seen little change.

By the late 1800s the czar and nobles held all of the wealth and power. Peasants and factory workers owned almost nothing. Czar Nicholas II, who took power in 1894, wanted to keep things as they were.

In January 1905 thousands of angry people gathered at the czar's Winter Palace in St. Petersburg. They demanded that Nicholas improve their living conditions. Soldiers fired at the crowd, killing and wounding hundreds. This event, known as Bloody Sunday, caused the Russian workers to go on strike. To end the strike, Nicholas met the demands of the workers.

The Russian government adopted a constitution. It also formed a lawmaking body called the Duma (DOO•mah). Still, Nicholas had control over the Duma and over all Russia. Some Russians began to think about a new kind of government.

Soon political parties were formed. One of these political parties was the Bolsheviks (BOHL•shuh•viks), led by Vladimir Lenin (LEH•nuhn). Lenin believed the time had come for a communist government in Russia. He also believed that only a violent revolution would change the government.

In early 1917 the Russian Revolution began. On March 2, 1917, Nicholas II gave up control of the Russian government. In July 1918 Lenin ordered Nicholas II and his family put to death. The rule of the czars in Russia came to an end.

REVIEW What was life like for Russian serfs and workers under the rule of the czars?

Russian Expansion, 1500–1922

ARCTIC OCEAN

Baltic Sea
Warsaw
Tallinn
Riga
Barents Sea
St. Petersburg
Novgorod
Archangel'sk
Kiev
Moscow
Odessa
Black Sea
Volga River
Tiflis (Tbilisi)
Caspian Sea
Omsk
Aral Sea
Bukhara
Irkutsk
Lake Baikal
Okhotsk
Kamchatka Peninsula
Sea of Okhotsk
Amur River
Vladivostok
Sea of Japan

Legend:

- Border of the Soviet Union, 1922
- Present-day borders

Growth of Russia under:
- Ivan III, about 1500
- Peter the Great, about 1725
- Catherine the Great, about 1796
- Nicholas I, about 1855

N W E S

0 500 1,000 Miles
0 500 1,000 Kilometers
Two-Point Equidistant Projection

GEOGRAPHY THEME

Movement **Over the centuries Russia grew to include much of northern Asia.**

❖ Under whose rule did Russia grow most in size?

The Soviet Union

One of the reasons the Russian Revolution succeeded was that most Russians no longer wanted their country to fight in World War I. In March 1918, the Russian government signed peace treaties with the Central Powers, and Russia withdrew from World War I.

The Communist party was made the only legal political party in Russia. A secret police force called the

Cheka (CHAY•kah) was formed. Lenin ordered the Cheka to find anyone opposed to the communist government. The Cheka killed or put in prison thousands of Russians.

In 1922 Russia became the Union of Soviet Socialist Republics (USSR), or Soviet Union. A **soviet** is an elected government council in a communist country. In 1924 Lenin died. Joseph Stalin (STAH•luhn) replaced Lenin as the leader of the Soviet Union.

Stalin wanted to make the Soviet Union one of the strongest nations in the world. To produce more food, he began to form **collectives**. These were large farms, run by the government, on which people worked together as a group. He also built hundreds of factories and forced thousands of Russians to work in them.

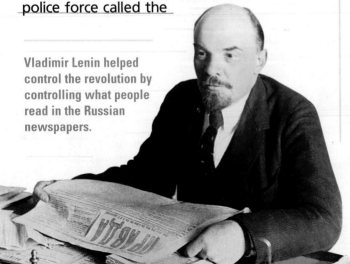

Vladimir Lenin helped control the revolution by controlling what people read in the Russian newspapers.

Under Stalin, the Soviet Union became a **totalitarian** (toh•ta•luh•TAIR•ee•uhn) state—a state in which the government has total control over people's lives. When citizens protested and called for change, Stalin ordered **purges**. Those who opposed Stalin's ideas were killed or imprisoned by the secret police. Millions of prisoners were sent to forced-labor camps in Siberia, a very cold region of the Soviet Union.

Joseph Stalin

Shortly before World War II, the Soviet Union formed an alliance with Nazi Germany. Stalin and Hitler agreed to divide Poland between them. Then Hitler went against the agreement, and his army invaded Russia. After this attack the Soviet Union joined the Allies. About 20 million Soviets lost their lives during World War II.

Before the end of the war, the Soviets and the other Allies began to disagree. The other Allied Powers did not want the Soviet Union to spread communism.

At the end of World War II, the Soviet Union took control of eastern Europe. Stalin did not let these countries rule themselves. He put in power communist governments that obeyed him.

The Soviet Union was also taking bold steps in Germany. The Soviets controlled the eastern half of Germany and East Berlin. The other Allies controlled the western half and West Berlin. In 1948 the Soviet army blocked all land and water routes between West Germany and Berlin, which was located in East Germany. The United States and Britain responded by sending supplies to West Berlin by air. This event became known as the Berlin Airlift. In May 1949 the Soviets ended the blockade.

The Berlin Airlift was one of the first encounters between the United States and the Soviet Union in the Cold War. A **cold war** is fought mostly with words and ideas rather than with soldiers and weapons.

REVIEW What inferences can you make about life in the Soviet Union under communism?
(Focus Skill) **MAKE INFERENCES**

Propaganda Posters

Analyze Primary Sources

Posters such as these were used in the Soviet Union to express political messages.

❶ The poster on the left urges Soviet citizens to teach their children by using government-published textbooks.

❷ The poster on the right honors the seventh anniversary of the Russian Revolution in 1924.

❔ Without knowing the Russian language, how can you tell the message of each poster?

Spread of Communism in China

Route of Long March
⊛ National capital (after Communist takeover)

Areas occupied by Communists, 1934–1949

1934–1945
1945–June 1946
July 1946–June 1947
July 1947–June 1948
July 1948–June 1949
July–September 1949
After October 1949

Movement   In 1934 the Long March took Chinese Communists to safety in the northwest. Just 15 years later the Communists had taken control of all of China.

❷ Why do you think the Long March did not follow a more direct route?

Communism Spreads to China

By the early 1900s, China was a weak and disorganized country. Parts of China were controlled by other nations. The emperor seemed unable to stop this foreign control, but many young Chinese demanded change. They began to form political parties to fight against foreign control.

The Guomindang (GWOH•min•dahng), or People's Nationalist party, grew out of calls for change. Its leader, Sun Yatsen (SUN YAHT•SEN), wanted China to become a republic. He believed that as a republic, China could gain power and get rid of foreign control.

In 1911 the Nationalists rebelled against the emperor and forced him to step down. Sun Yatsen became the leader of the new Chinese republic. The new government failed to unite the country, however. **Warlords**, leaders with their own small armies, had taken over much of China.

Chiang Kaishek (jee•AHNG KY•SHEK) became the leader of the Nationalists in 1925. He began to build up the army and to unite China. At the same time, some people left the Nationalist party to form the Communist party. These people wanted the peasants to have more say in government. Nationalists and Communists soon clashed.

By 1934 the Nationalists had trapped the Communists in southeastern China. About

100,000 Communists began what came to be known as the **Long March**, a walk of 6,000 miles (9,656 km) to northwestern China. During the march, Mao Zedong (MOW ZUH•DUNG) became their leader.

In northwestern China the strength of the Communists grew. After a long and violent civil war, the Communists drove out the Nationalists. In 1949 Mao helped establish the world's most populous communist country, the People's Republic of China.

Mao's government faced many challenges. Mao wanted to modernize China's economy. His first plan succeeded. A second plan, called the Great Leap Forward, failed, however. Mao blamed the failure on people who he felt were not accepting his ways.

In response, Mao ordered a Cultural Revolution in China to cut people's ties to the past. During this time Mao appointed young people—who became known as the Red Guard—to destroy anything that showed the past. Many books, works of art, and buildings were destroyed. Some people were jailed, sent to work camps, or even killed.

Followers of Communist leader Mao Zedong (above) carried the "Little Red Book" (left) filled with his teachings.

By 1968 Mao felt that the Red Guard was out of control. He called an end to the Cultural Revolution. Because of the disorder, farm and factory production in China had slowed. The Cultural Revolution had nearly destroyed the Chinese economy.

REVIEW Why did the Nationalists rebel against the emperor?

LESSON 3 REVIEW

Summary Time Line

1900 — 1935 — 1970

1917 The Communist party takes control of Russia

1949 China becomes a communist nation

1968 Mao ends the Cultural Revolution

Focus Skill **MAKE INFERENCES** Why do you think the Russian and Chinese people wanted a change of government?

1 BIG IDEA Why do you think the ideas of communism were popular with peasants and workers in Russia and China?

2 VOCABULARY Explain how Joseph Stalin used **purges** to make the Soviet Union a **totalitarian** state.

3 TIME LINE Did China become a communist country before or after Russia did?

4 GEOGRAPHY Who controlled East Germany and East Berlin after World War II?

5 CRITICAL THINKING—Analyze Do you think life for most Russians was better under the czars or during the Soviet Union? Explain.

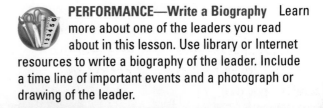

PERFORMANCE—Write a Biography Learn more about one of the leaders you read about in this lesson. Use library or Internet resources to write a biography of the leader. Include a time line of important events and a photograph or drawing of the leader.

4

A Changing World

★ Focus Skill

MAKE INFERENCES

As you read, make inferences about the Cold War tensions and their effects on the world.

BIG IDEA

As the United States and the Soviet Union competed in the Cold War, new conflicts broke out around the world.

VOCABULARY

superpower
containment
détente

President Harry Truman (below, right) signs the treaty (below, left) that created NATO in 1949.

1945 – 1995

In 1946 Winston Churchill, the former prime minister of Britain, visited the United States. During the visit Churchill gave a famous speech. In this speech he warned that an "iron curtain" had fallen across Europe. The term *Iron Curtain* meant that the eastern European countries controlled by the Soviet Union were closed off from contact and trade with noncommunist countries.

Cold War Tensions

After World War II the Soviet Union and the United States emerged as **superpowers**, the world's most powerful nations. Leaders in the United States feared that the Soviets would spread communism, by force if necessary, to other nations. The Soviets feared that the United States would try to spread its culture and ideas about democracy to countries under Soviet control.

Many Americans supported a policy of **containment**. That is, they wanted to develop ways to keep the Soviet Union and China from spreading communism. Although this policy focused on non-military actions, both the United States and the Soviet Union prepared for war. Soon an arms race began between the two nations.

I CERTIFY THAT the foregoing is a true copy of the North Atlantic Treaty signed at Washington on April 4, 1949 in the English and French languages, the signed original of which is deposited in the archives of the Government of the United States of America.

IN TESTIMONY WHEREOF, I, DEAN ACHESON, Secretary of State of the United States of America, have hereunto caused the seal of the Department of State to be affixed and my name subscribed by the Authentication Officer of the said Department, at the city of Washington, in the District of Columbia, this fourth day of April, 1949.

European Alliances in 1955

Legend:
- NATO country
- Noncommunist country not in NATO
- Warsaw Pact country
- Communist country not in Warsaw Pact

Canada and the United States are also NATO members.

Map labels: ICELAND, Arctic Circle, NORWAY, SWEDEN, FINLAND, North Sea, Baltic Sea, IRELAND, GREAT BRITAIN, DENMARK, NETHERLANDS, EAST GERMANY, POLAND, SOVIET UNION, BELGIUM, WEST GERMANY, CZECHOSLOVAKIA, LUXEMBOURG, FRANCE, AUSTRIA, HUNGARY, SWITZERLAND, ROMANIA, ATLANTIC OCEAN, PORTUGAL, SPAIN, Corsica, ITALY, YUGOSLAVIA, BULGARIA, Sardinia, ALBANIA, Black Sea, Caspian Sea, Mediterranean Sea, Sicily, GREECE, TURKEY, ASIA

Scale: 0 250 500 Miles / 0 250 500 Kilometers
Azimuthal Equal-Area Projection

GEOGRAPHY THEME

Regions By 1955 most European nations had joined an alliance.

❓ In what part of Europe were most of the Warsaw Pact members located? Where in Europe were most of the NATO members located?

The United Nations was unable to bring the United States and the Soviet Union together. Both sides began to make alliances with other countries to defend themselves in case of an attack.

In 1949 the United States joined European nations, such as Britain, Italy, and France, in the North Atlantic Treaty Organization (NATO). In 1955 the Soviet Union organized its eastern European allies, such as Hungary, Poland, and Romania, to form the Warsaw Pact. As the superpowers competed against each other in Europe, the Cold War spread to other regions of the world.

REVIEW What fueled tensions between the United States and the Soviet Union?

Korea and Cuba

Tensions during the Cold War sometimes led to armed conflicts. In these conflicts, the United States and the Soviet Union did not fight each other directly. Instead, each country supported opposing armies in other countries.

After World War II the country of Korea was divided into two parts. With the Soviet Union's help, a communist government came to power in North Korea. In 1950 North Korea invaded noncommunist South Korea to try to unite all of Korea under a communist government.

Many United States soldiers who fought in the Korean War received the Korean Service Medal.

A United States patrol plane flies over a Soviet ship (above) during the Cuban Missile Crisis. On television, President Kennedy (left) addresses the nation about the crisis as concerned citizens watch.

The United States and the United Nations sent troops to protect South Korea. The Soviet Union and China helped North Korea.

The Korean War ended in 1953 with neither side able to claim victory. A border was set between North Korea and South Korea at the 38th parallel—or 38 degrees north latitude. This remains the border today.

In the 1960s the tension between the Soviet Union and the United States once again reached dangerous levels. In 1962 the United States discovered Soviet missiles in Cuba, a communist country located 90 miles (145 km) southeast of Florida. United States President John F. Kennedy demanded that Soviet leader Nikita Khrushchev (nuh•KEE•tuh KRUSH•chawf) have the missiles removed.

President Kennedy ordered a blockade to stop the Soviet shipment of supplies to Cuba. Soviet cargo ships continued to sail toward the blockade. This situation, known as the Cuban Missile Crisis, brought the countries of the United States and the Soviet Union very close to war.

At the last minute the Soviet ships turned around. Khrushchev agreed to remove the missiles from Cuba, and Kennedy agreed not to attack Cuba.

In 1963 the United States and the Soviet Union signed a treaty limiting the testing of nuclear weapons. Despite this move toward peace, another Cold War conflict was already forming.

REVIEW Why did President Kennedy order a blockade against Cuba?

Vietnam

The next military conflict of the Cold War broke out in Vietnam, a country in southeastern Asia. Vietnam had won its independence from France in 1954. The country, however, was divided into northern and southern regions.

North Vietnam had a communist government supported by China and the Soviet Union. Vietnamese Communists, or Vietcong, sought to overthrow the government of South Vietnam. South Vietnam was supported by the United States. When Vietnam failed to reunite through elections in 1956, North Vietnam and South Vietnam went to war.

The United States government wanted to stop the spread of communism in Asia. At first, the United States government sent military advisers to help the army of South Vietnam win the war. When a victory by South Vietnam seemed unlikely, President Lyndon Johnson ordered United States soldiers into Vietnam.

By 1965 more than 180,000 soldiers from the United States were fighting in Vietnam. By 1967 the number of American soldiers had increased to more than 390,000. By 1969 there were 550,000 American soldiers in Vietnam.

Many Americans opposed United States participation in the war. Lack of military success led President Richard Nixon to order an increase in bombing. Protests, however, caused him to withdraw troops. In 1973 the United States, North Vietnam, and South Vietnam agreed to a cease-fire, or a stop in fighting. The United States withdrew from the war. About 58,000 Americans had died in the war, and 360,000 had been wounded.

Fighting between the armies of North and South Vietnam soon began again. In April 1975 North Vietnam's army captured Saigon, the capital of South Vietnam. North Vietnam had won the war. The two countries were reunited under the communist government of North Vietnam.

Since Vietnam was now completely under the control of a communist government, the United States stopped communicating and trading with the country. Trade and communication with Vietnam did not begin again until 1994.

REVIEW **What inferences can you make about the increase in the number of soldiers sent to Vietnam?** **MAKE INFERENCES**

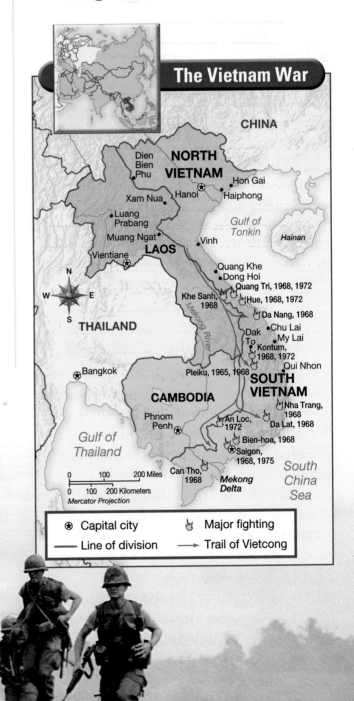

The Vietnam War

Location **Vietnam was once divided into two warring parts. American soldiers (below) defended South Vietnam.**

◈ **In which part of Vietnam did most of the fighting take place?**

⊗ Capital city   ♨ Major fighting
—— Line of division   ⟶ Trail of Vietcong

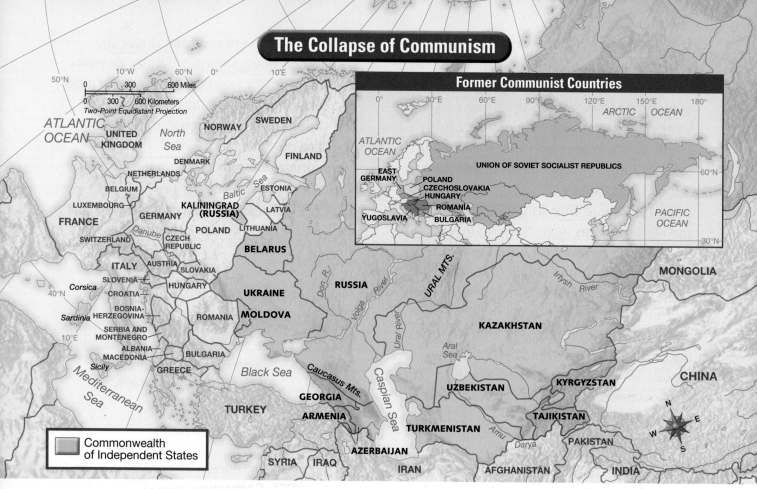

The Collapse of Communism

Former Communist Countries

Regions The Soviet Union broke apart into 15 independent nations.

❖ What new nations were formed from the Soviet Union?

The End of the Cold War

In the 1970s the United States government began a new policy toward communist governments. Known as **détente** (day•TAHNT), the policy's goal was to relax the tensions between communist nations and democratic nations.

In 1972 United States President Richard Nixon met with communist leader Mao Zedong in China. The United States and China agreed to allow trade and some travel between the two nations.

In Europe, Cold War tensions began to fade. By the 1980s, after years of Cold War spending, the Soviet economy was weak. In contrast the United States was gaining economic strength.

President Ronald Reagan believed in a policy of "peace through strength." As President he increased defense spending. He said that the Cold War was a "struggle between right and wrong, good and evil."

Mikhail Gorbachev (gawr•buh•CHAWV) became the Soviet leader in 1985. He knew that the Soviet Union could not continue the arms race with the United States. The once-powerful Soviet economy was near collapse. The Soviet people suffered from shortages of food and other needs.

Gorbachev introduced new policies to help the Soviet economy and people. One of the policies was *perestroika* (pair•uh•STROY•kuh), or "restructuring," to rebuild the Soviet economy and political system. Another policy was *glasnost* (GLAZ•nohst), or "openness," which

Built in 1961, the Berlin Wall seemed to go up almost overnight (inset). When East Germany opened its borders in 1989, thousands of people fled the country. Soon after, East and West Berliners armed with hammers and other tools tore down the Berlin Wall.

gave Soviet citizens new freedom to speak out without fear of being punished.

With the introduction of *glasnost*, some people began to speak out very strongly. In fact, people living in the Soviet republics along the Baltic Sea—Lithuania, Latvia, and Estonia—called for total independence. The countries in eastern Europe under Soviet control also called for more freedom. By the late 1980s Gorbachev realized that it was not possible to stop the tide of change.

In 1989 Poland became the first country in eastern Europe to gain independence from the Soviet Union. The next year East and West Germany reunited. One by one, elections were held in eastern European countries, and new independent governments came to power. The Soviet Union itself was on the verge of collapse.

In 1991 the Soviet Union broke up into 15 independent republics, 12 of which joined the Commonwealth of Independent States (CIS). Gorbachev soon stepped down as leader of the Soviet Union, a country that no longer existed. The Cold War had come to an end.

REVIEW What policies helped lead to the collapse of the Soviet Union?

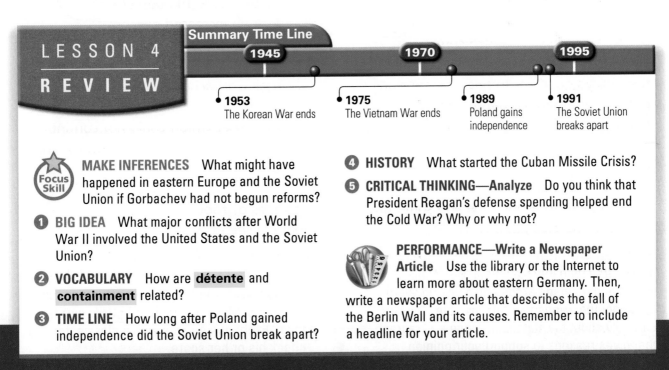

LESSON 4 REVIEW

Summary Time Line

| 1945 | 1970 | 1995 |

1953 The Korean War ends

1975 The Vietnam War ends

1989 Poland gains independence

1991 The Soviet Union breaks apart

Focus Skill **MAKE INFERENCES** What might have happened in eastern Europe and the Soviet Union if Gorbachev had not begun reforms?

1 **BIG IDEA** What major conflicts after World War II involved the United States and the Soviet Union?

2 **VOCABULARY** How are **détente** and **containment** related?

3 **TIME LINE** How long after Poland gained independence did the Soviet Union break apart?

4 **HISTORY** What started the Cuban Missile Crisis?

5 **CRITICAL THINKING—Analyze** Do you think that President Reagan's defense spending helped end the Cold War? Why or why not?

PERFORMANCE—Write a Newspaper Article Use the library or the Internet to learn more about eastern Germany. Then, write a newspaper article that describes the fall of the Berlin Wall and its causes. Remember to include a headline for your article.

· CHAPTER ·

18 Review and Test Preparation

Summary Time Line
1880   1903
• 1914
World War I begins

 **Make Inferences**

Use this graphic organizer to show that you understand how to make inferences about World War I by combining facts you already know with details from what you have read. A copy of this graphic organizer appears on page 169 of the Activity Book.

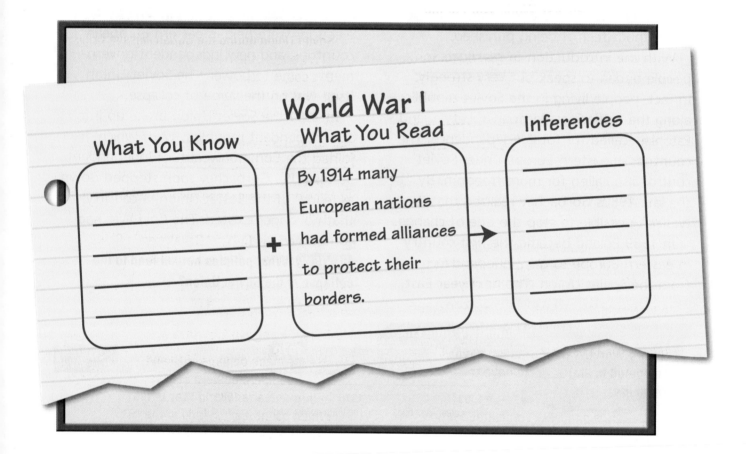

World War I

What You Know

+

What You Read

By 1914 many European nations had formed alliances to protect their borders.

→

Inferences

THINK & WRITE

Write an Opinion Tell whether you agree or disagree with this statement: Decisions world leaders made at the end of World War I made another world war unavoidable. Think carefully about the statement. Write a paragraph that gives reasons to support your opinion.

Write Questions Write 10 questions about people, places, events, and ideas related to the Cold War. Then write the answers to those questions. Make a pencil-and-paper quiz from them. Exchange quizzes with a classmate, and check his or her score.

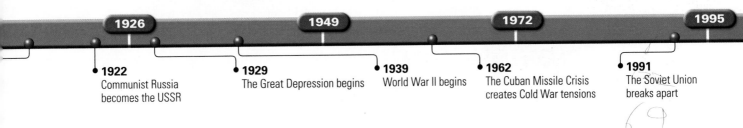

| 1926 | 1949 | 1972 | 1995 |

1922
Communist Russia
becomes the USSR

1929
The Great Depression begins

1939
World War II begins

1962
The Cuban Missile Crisis
creates Cold War tensions

1991
The Soviet Union
breaks apart

USE THE TIME LINE

Use the chapter summary time line to answer these questions.

1 How much time passed between the beginning of the USSR and its collapse?

2 Which happened first, World War I or the Great Depression?

USE VOCABULARY

Use one of the terms in the box to complete each sentence.

> arms race (p. 605)
>
> assassination (p. 605)
>
> inflation (p. 612)
>
> propaganda (p. 613)
>
> totalitarian (p. 623)

3 Hitler used _____ to gain the German people's support for the Nazi Party.

4 In a(n) _____ society—such as the Soviet Union under Stalin—the government has complete control over people's lives.

5 After World War I, high _____ made German money almost worthless.

6 Before World War I, European nations competed in a(n) _____ to have the most weapons.

7 A(n) _____ is a murder committed for political reasons.

RECALL FACTS

Answer these questions.

8 What event led the United States to become involved in World War II?

9 What world leader made the phrase "iron curtain" famous?

Write the letter of the best choice.

10 **TEST PREP** Who was the last czar of Russia?
  A Nicholas I
  B Peter the Great
  C Catherine the Great
  D Nicholas II

11 **TEST PREP** Who was the leader of the Soviet Union during the Cuban Missile Crisis?
  F Vladimir Lenin
  G Joseph Stalin
  H Nikita Krushchev
  J Mikhail Gorbachev

THINK CRITICALLY

12 Why do you think the Cold War was called "cold"?

13 How was the Cultural Revolution in China different from other revolutions?

APPLY SKILLS

Identify Changing Borders

14 Use the maps on pages 610 and 611 to compare eastern Europe before and after World War I. Which countries lost land to the new countries that were formed?

Compare Different Kinds of Graphs

15 Which would be the better kind of graph to show a student's social studies test scores over time, a bar graph or a line graph? Why?

Chapter 18 ▪ 633

SÃO PAULO, BRAZIL

São Paulo is one of the fastest-growing cities in the world. Located in southeastern Brazil at an altitude of 2,690 feet (820 m), São Paulo spreads across the foothills of Serra do Mar, or "Mountains of the Sea." Already the largest city in Brazil, São Paulo has the fifth-largest metropolitan area in the world.

LOCATE IT

BRAZIL

São Paulo

19

Global Challenges

"Your world is as big as you make it."

—Georgia Douglas Johnson,
American poet, 1880–1966

Summarize

When you **summarize,** you retell briefly what you have read, using your own words.

After you read this chapter, summarize what you have learned.

• **Identify the main topic of each lesson.**

• **List the key facts of the events you read about.**

• **Summarize what you read.**

Topic   Key Facts   Summary

1

Economic Challenges

 SUMMARIZE
As you read, summarize both past and present economic challenges of the world.

BIG IDEA
The global economy has presented opportunities and challenges for countries around the world.

VOCABULARY

global economy
recession
mixed economy
trade agreement
developed country
developing country
GDP
telecommunication
Internet

FAST FACT

In the United States in 1945, a loaf of bread cost 9 cents, a gallon of milk cost 62 cents, and a postage stamp cost 3 cents.

| 1700 | 1800 | 1900 | PRESENT |

1945 – Present

After World War II, most economies around the world were weak. The war had caused damage to cities and businesses all over Europe and Asia. On a visit to Europe, United States President Harry S. Truman exclaimed, "I never saw such destruction!" World leaders wanted to avoid a depression like the one that had followed World War I. They looked for ways to rebuild the **global economy**, or the trade of goods and services around the world.

Rebuilding the Global Economy

To rebuild the global economy, world leaders created the World Bank and the International Monetary Fund (IMF). By 1947 these organizations were providing money to help countries that had been damaged by the war. The United States also gave large amounts of money to Japan and to countries in western Europe.

In eastern Asia, workers in Japan, South Korea, and Taiwan were soon manufacturing radios, televisions, and other electronic products. Millions of consumers in the United States and Europe bought these goods. Because of this, Japan's economy grew during the early 1950s and through the late 1980s.

In contrast, countries in southeastern Asia, such as Vietnam and Indonesia, struggled. Newly independent from rule by European countries, they lacked strong governments and the money to build new economies. Over time, however, money from the World Bank, the IMF, and individual countries flowed into the region. By the

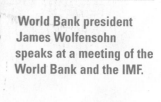

World Bank president James Wolfensohn speaks at a meeting of the World Bank and the IMF.

J. WOLFENSOHN

Rows of nearly identical houses (right) filled new communities like Levittown in New York (above) after World War II.

1980s Indonesia, Malaysia, Singapore, and Thailand began exporting electronic products. As a result, their economies improved.

Countries in Africa south of the Sahara also struggled with their independence. Many of them depended on a small number of exports for income. When demand or prices for these products dropped, the economies of these countries suffered.

Some economies in southwestern Asia and northern Africa grew after World War II. World demand for petroleum brought much wealth to the oil-rich countries there. Saudi Arabia, Iraq, and Kuwait have the largest oil deposits in those regions.

Some Latin American countries focused on regional or national trade. Others depended on a few exports such as coffee or bananas. They needed to borrow money to develop their economies. By the 1980s these nations faced huge debts.

With money provided by the United States in its Marshall Plan, countries in western Europe rebuilt their cities and economies. By the early 1950s their economies were stronger than they had been before the war. Into the 1980s these countries developed many new industries in agriculture, banking, and manufacturing.

After the war the United States economy grew faster than it ever had before. The demand for housing and automobiles created many new jobs. People bought new televisions and other appliances. The demand for American products around the world helped make the economy strong. Recessions, however, affected the economy during the 1970s and early 1980s. A **recession** is a period during which an economy stops growing. In 1983 the economy of the United States entered a new period of growth. For many years the United States has had the largest and strongest economy in the world.

REVIEW Why did the United States economy grow so fast after World War II?

 SUMMARIZE

A television from the 1950s

Command Economies in Communist Countries

After the war most nations around the world had either market economies or mixed economies. A **mixed economy** is one that combines free enterprise and government control.

China, North Korea, and communist countries in eastern Europe had no free enterprise. They had command economies like the Soviet Union's. Their communist governments made all economic decisions.

The economy of the Soviet Union continued to grow well into the 1970s. When it stopped growing in the 1980s, the Soviet government began reforms. These changes introduced ideas of a market economy to the Soviet economy.

After some successes and many failures, China's economy expanded greatly in the late 1970s. At that time, China began to take part in the global economy, opening its markets to trade with other countries. Like the Soviet Union, it began to adopt ideas of a market economy. By the mid-1980s communist China had one of the world's fastest-growing economies.

REVIEW What reforms helped China's economy grow in the late 1970s?

The government of China built modern manufacturing centers to improve its economy. The city of Pudong was built on land that was formerly a swamp.

New Challenges

In the 1990s many more countries became connected economically in a process called globalization. Former Soviet republics and eastern European countries returned to market economies after the collapse of Soviet control over their governments. In Asia many countries began exporting high-tech products. The United States entered its strongest period of economic growth.

Even with these successes, problems developed in the global economy. In the early 1990s Japan's economy weakened as sales of many Japanese products decreased. In 1994 Mexico's currency, the *peso*, lost much of its value. In 1997 an economic decline spread through much of southeastern Asia.

After almost 10 years of growth, the economy of the United States began to weaken in 2000. Sales of high-tech products and services declined. Because of this, United States stock markets dropped sharply. Also, several large corporations in the United States were found to have reported higher profits than they actually had. As a result of these events, many people lost confidence in the economy. The United States government has been working to strengthen its economy. Most experts expect the United States economy to recover and slowly grow.

REVIEW What event created new market economies in eastern Europe?

Major NAFTA Highway Routes

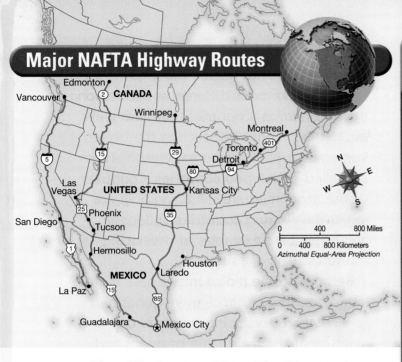

Movement Highways provide routes for goods traded among NAFTA's members.

❓ Which highways connect Mexico City, Mexico, to Winnipeg, Canada?

Trade Agreements

A **trade agreement** is an agreement between countries to lower tariffs, or taxes, on goods traded between them. Lower taxes encourage more trade. Increased trade helps economies grow.

Six European countries agreed to make their economies stronger by signing a trade agreement in 1951. By 1993 the group had 15 members and was called the European Union (EU). In 1999 most EU countries began to use a common form of money called the euro to make trade easier. In the next few years, the EU plans to expand its membership to include former communist countries in eastern Europe.

The United States, Canada, and Mexico signed NAFTA, the North American Free Trade Agreement, in 1992. Like the EU's trade agreement, NAFTA aims to increase trade in its own region.

A euro coin

POINTS OF VIEW
NAFTA

While trade agreements such as NAFTA are becoming more common, not everyone thinks that these agreements are good.

GEORGE W. BUSH, U.S. President

❝NAFTA has created more choices at lower prices for consumers in all three nations, and it has created good jobs for our workers.❞

JOSÉ MIGUEL VIVANCO, Executive Director of Human Rights Watch

❝NAFTA . . . represents a very serious blow to labor rights in the region.❞

VICENTE FOX, President of Mexico

❝NAFTA has created jobs in Mexico. It has created jobs in the United States.❞

THEA LEE, Assistant Director for International Economics at the AFL–CIO

❝NAFTA . . . is not a fair set of rules.❞

Analyze the Viewpoints

❶ What view about NAFTA does each person hold?

❷ **Make It Relevant** Learn more about the debate over NAFTA's success. Write a paragraph expressing your opinion about whether NAFTA has been successful.

The United States has recently discussed trade agreements with other countries in Latin America.

Other trade partnerships exist around the world. ASEAN stands for the Association of Southeast Asian Nations. It is made up of ten countries in southeastern Asia, including Indonesia, Malaysia, Singapore, and Vietnam.

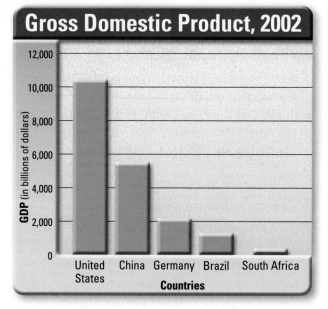

Gross Domestic Product, 2002

GDP (in billions of dollars)

12,000
10,000
8,000
6,000
4,000
2,000
0

United States | China | Germany | Brazil | South Africa

Countries

Analyze Graphs Gross domestic product is used to measure the size of a country's economy.

◈ Which country on the graph has a GDP that is about twice the size of Brazil's GDP?

Argentina, Paraguay, Uruguay, and Brazil formed a group called Mercosur (MAIR•koh•soor) to encourage economic cooperation in South America. Chile and Bolivia are also part of Mercosur.

The members of the Organization of Petroleum Exporting Countries, or OPEC, are 11 countries with economies that rely on oil exports. Saudi Arabia, Kuwait, and Venezuela are among OPEC's members. OPEC tries to control the production and price of oil around the world.

To help meet the challenges of global trade, the World Trade Organization (WTO) was formed in 1995. More than 140 nations have joined the WTO. The WTO's goal is to set trade rules. The WTO believes that such rules will create more trade. Others believe that strong nations still have advantages over weak ones.

REVIEW How do trade agreements help economies grow?

Measuring Economies

Global trade has helped many countries. However, enormous differences exist among their economies. Countries that have well-established economies, such as the United States and Japan, have great wealth. These are called **developed countries**. Countries whose economies are still being built are called **developing countries**. Indonesia and Nigeria are examples of developing countries.

Because developed countries have more industries, they produce more goods and services than developing countries do. One measure of the total value of goods and services a country produces is its **GDP**, or gross domestic product. The GDPs of developed countries are higher than the GDPs of developing ones. In 2003 the GDP of the United States reached about $10 trillion. A trillion is a thousand billions.

REVIEW Why do developed countries have higher GDPs than developing ones?

The Technology Age

In the 1980s new kinds of technology began affecting the lives of people and businesses around the world. Electronic communication made it possible for people and companies to keep in touch quickly and almost anywhere.

The word **telecommunication** describes all the ways of sending and receiving information at a distance. Telephones, cell phones, fax machines, e-mail, and computer networks are all used in telecommunication.

Travelers can use a Global Positioning System (GPS) receiver to find out their location from anywhere in the world.

• SCIENCE AND TECHNOLOGY •

History of the Internet

Most people think of the Internet as a new technology. However, the Internet had its beginnings in the 1960s. At that time, the United States government wanted to find a way for its computers to communicate with one another in case of war. Researchers created a way of linking computers into a network. By 1981 the network connected about 200 computers. Soon, it was called the Internet. When Internet search engines became available in 1993, the Internet grew. Today the Internet connects millions of computers.

In the 1990s the Internet became important in telecommunication. The **Internet** is a large computer network made up of thousands of smaller networks that are linked with one another. People use the Internet to communicate, to buy things, to conduct business, and to gather information.

The Internet is also important to the global economy. Many companies now sell their products or services on the Internet.

In the late 1990s the Internet became so widely used that many people thought stores might become a thing of the past. However, by 2001 many businesses that sold products only on the Internet had gone out of business. Even so, the Internet is still growing and will likely continue to be important in our lives.

REVIEW What are some forms of telecommunication?

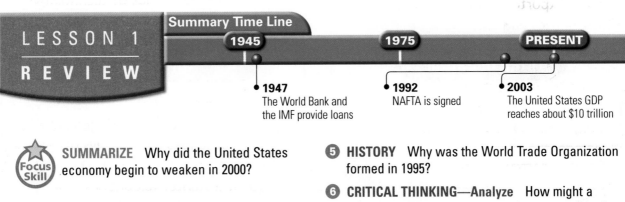

LESSON 1 REVIEW

Summary Time Line

1945 — 1975 — PRESENT

1947 The World Bank and the IMF provide loans

1992 NAFTA is signed

2003 The United States GDP reaches about $10 trillion

SUMMARIZE Why did the United States economy begin to weaken in 2000?

1 **BIG IDEA** How did world leaders help rebuild the global economy after World War II?

2 **VOCABULARY** Use the word **Internet** in a sentence about **telecommunication**.

3 **TIME LINE** When was NAFTA signed?

4 **ECONOMICS** After the war, how were the economies of communist countries different from the economies of other countries?

5 **HISTORY** Why was the World Trade Organization formed in 1995?

6 **CRITICAL THINKING—Analyze** How might a trade agreement help improve the economies of countries that do not produce many goods?

PERFORMANCE—Write a Letter Write a letter that you might send to a newspaper, expressing your point of view on an issue related to the global economy. Your issue might deal with topics such as trade agreements, workers, or kinds of economies.

·SKILLS·

MAP AND GLOBE

Compare Different Kinds of Maps

WHY IT MATTERS

There are many kinds of maps, and each kind shows different information. For example, political maps mark present-day cities, countries, and borders. Physical maps show physical features. Maps can also show economic and cultural information.

If you look at Map A below, a political map, you will see that Japan is an island nation located east of China. At 143,619 square miles (371,944 sq km), the country of Japan is slightly smaller than the state of California. It includes four large islands and many smaller islands. From the physical map, Map B, you may be able to see that Japan is mostly covered by mountains. By studying

Map C, a mineral resources map, you can learn about some of the resources of Japan. Map D, a population map, shows where the people of Japan live.

Using different maps together is helpful. It allows you to make connections between the history, geography, economics, government, and culture of a country or region.

WHAT YOU NEED TO KNOW

Study the maps and compare them. When comparing maps, you can follow these steps:

1. Look at each map's title to find out what kind of map it is.

2. Read each map and map key to find out what information is being presented.

3. Think about how the maps can be used together to learn more information.

Map A: Political Map of Japan

Map B: Physical Map of Japan

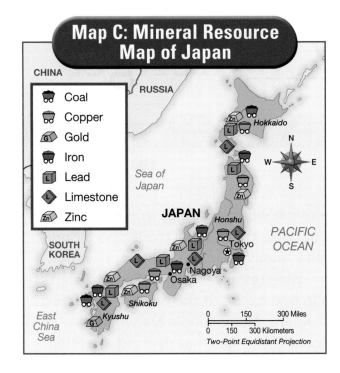

Map C: Mineral Resource Map of Japan

CHINA

RUSSIA

Legend:
- Coal
- Copper
- Gold
- Iron
- Lead
- Limestone
- Zinc

Sea of Japan

JAPAN

Hokkaido

Honshu

PACIFIC OCEAN

Tokyo

SOUTH KOREA

Nagoya

Osaka

Shikoku

Kyushu

East China Sea

0   150   300 Miles
0   150   300 Kilometers
Two-Point Equidistant Projection

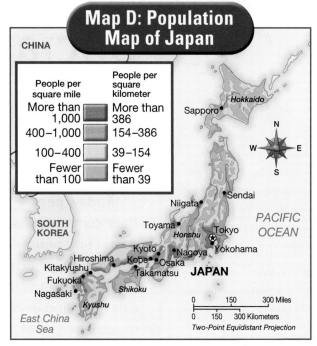

Map D: Population Map of Japan

CHINA

People per square mile
- More than 1,000
- 400–1,000
- 100–400
- Fewer than 100

People per square kilometer
- More than 386
- 154–386
- 39–154
- Fewer than 39

Hokkaido

Sapporo

SOUTH KOREA

Niigata

Sendai

Toyama

Honshu

Tokyo

PACIFIC OCEAN

Hiroshima

Kyoto

Nagoya

Yokohama

Kitakyushu

Kobe

Osaka

Fukuoka

Takamatsu

JAPAN

Nagasaki

Shikoku

Kyushu

East China Sea

0   150   300 Miles
0   150   300 Kilometers
Two-Point Equidistant Projection

▶ PRACTICE THE SKILL

Use the information on the maps to answer the following questions:

1 On which Japanese island are the Chugoku Mountains located?

2 On which Japanese island can gold be found?

3 How many people per square mile live in Japan's capital?

4 What major cities are found on the Japanese island of Kyushu?

Mount Fuji is Japan's highest mountain at 12,388 feet (3,776 m).

▶ APPLY WHAT YOU LEARNED

Use library resources to find a population map and a physical map of your state. On the population map, find a large city and a small town. Then use the maps together to answer these questions:

1 What physical features surround the large city? Do you think these features affected the city's growth? Explain.

2 From the physical map, can you tell why the small town is not larger? What physical features may have limited its growth? Explain.

Practice your map and globe skills with the **GeoSkills CD-ROM**.

MAP AND GLOBE SKILLS

2

SUMMARIZE

Use the information you read to summarize the challenges of the world's growing population.

BIG IDEA

People around the world face many social challenges.

VOCABULARY

human rights

apartheid

demographer

Social Challenges

1700	1800	1900	PRESENT

1945 – Present

Today, people around the world face problems that affect their communities and nations. These social challenges include protecting people's rights, ending religious conflict, slowing population growth, and using resources wisely. The challenges faced by citizens living in one region of the world often affect citizens living in other regions. Many people are working together to meet the social challenges that demand attention.

The Challenge of Human Rights

In 1948, world leaders met at the United Nations to identify the most important social challenges facing the world's people. One important challenge they found was the need to protect human rights. **Human rights** are the freedoms that all people should have, such as freedom of speech and freedom of religion.

Rosa Parks (left) and Martin Luther King, Jr. (below), used peaceful ways to work for civil rights for African Americans during the 1950s and 1960s.

In 2002 Mary Robinson, the United Nations High Commissioner for Human Rights, planted red hands with another human-rights worker. The red hands were planted to mark the beginning of a treaty that banned the use of child soldiers.

To help meet the challenge, the United Nations adopted the Universal Declaration of Human Rights. In its 30 articles, the Declaration denounces slavery and cruel punishments. It also calls for freedom of assembly and freedom of thought for all the world's people. In addition, the Declaration states that all people should be treated equally. Since 1948 many countries have supported the Declaration.

These countries try to persuade governments that do not protect their citizens' human rights to change their policies. To do this, they may place an embargo against such a country.

In the 1980s many countries joined in an embargo against South Africa because of its policy of **apartheid** (uh•PAR•tayt), or separation. This policy separated all nonwhite South Africans from white South Africans. As a result of the embargo, South Africa changed its policies. By 2000, South Africans had elected two black South Africans to the presidency—

Nelson Mandela was South Africa's first black president.

first Nelson Mandela and then Thabo Mbeki (TAH•boh em•BEK•ee).

Women's rights are an important part of human rights. Even so, women's goals for achieving or protecting their rights vary from region to region. Some women work to protect their rights as wives and mothers. Other women struggle to have the same opportunities that are available to men.

Until 2001 the former Taliban government in Afghanistan placed harsh rules on the lives of women there. This strict Islamic government would not allow girls and women to attend school or go to work. Many nations spoke out against this policy.

Human rights also include the rights of children. A recent study estimates that 120 million children between the ages of 5 and 14 work full time in developing countries such as India and Ecuador. Incomes in these countries are so low that many children must work to help their families survive. Human rights supporters are against the use of child workers. They declare that every child has the right to an education. At present, millions of children around the world never learn to read and write.

REVIEW What did the United Nations do to promote human rights in 1948?

Israel: 1947 to Present

LEBANON

SYRIA

Land gained after Six-Day War, 1967, and still occupied

GOLAN HEIGHTS

Acre

Haifa

Land gained after Six-Day War, 1967; some Palestinian self-rule

Nazareth

Lake Tiberias (Sea of Galilee)

Mediterranean Sea

Jordan River

Tel Aviv

WEST BANK

Land gained after Six-Day War, 1967

Jericho

Jerusalem
Bethlehem

Land gained after Six-Day War, 1967, and returned to Egypt

Gaza

Hebron

Dead Sea

GAZA STRIP

Beersheba

Land gained after 1948 War

ISRAEL

JORDAN

EGYPT

Negev

Jewish state under 1947 partition plan

Sinai Peninsula

Status to be determined

----- Disputed

0   25   50 Miles

0   25   50 Kilometers

Transverse Cylindrical Projection

GEOGRAPHY THEME

Regions Palestinians and Israelis have long had conflicts over land claims. To build understanding, Palestinian and Israeli children (below) attend a camp together.

❖ Which countries share a border with Israel?

Religion in Today's World

Religion is important in the lives of many people today, just as it has been for centuries. Besides teaching beliefs, religion plays an active role in meeting social challenges. Many religious groups provide meals for the homeless in their communities. Religious groups also supply food and medical care to people in countries where there is poverty or famine.

Religion has its own challenges. In 2000 the United States government reported on a study of religious freedom around the world. The report stated that many people live in countries where religion is controlled or religious freedom is not allowed.

China, for example, requires all religious groups to be approved by the government. Members of groups that are not approved are treated badly. Saudi Arabia provides no religious freedom to people who are not Muslims. Myanmar (formerly Burma) mistreats followers of Buddhism there.

Different religious beliefs can add to the political conflicts that exist among neighboring countries. In southwestern Asia, for example, different religious beliefs have stirred strong feelings over land claims. In 1947 the United Nations decided to divide the land known as Palestine. One part would be a Jewish state with mostly Jewish citizens. The other part would be an Arab state with mostly Muslim citizens.

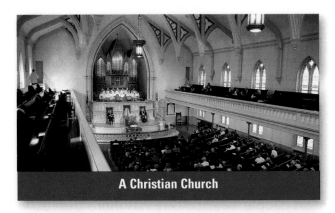

A Christian Church

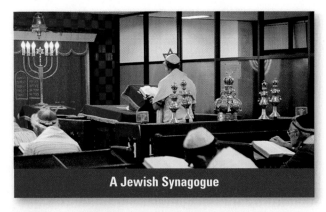

A Jewish Synagogue

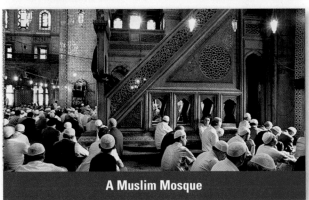

A Muslim Mosque

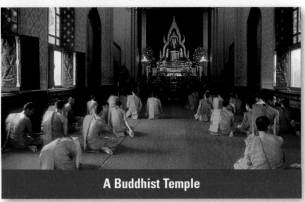

A Buddhist Temple

The next year, Jewish leaders announced the creation of Israel as an independent country. In an effort to destroy the new nation, Arab armies from neighboring countries attacked it. However, by 1949 Israel had defeated the Arabs and gained control of about half of the land planned for the new Arab state of Palestine. Over the years Israel and the Arab nations have fought wars over this land. During the 1990s and into the new century, United States Presidents have worked with Arab and Israeli leaders to try to find a peaceful end to the conflict.

Religious conflicts can also occur among different groups within the same religion. In the 1980s conflicts over land claims arose between Shi'i Muslims and Sunni Muslims in Iran and Iraq. Long ago, Protestants broke away from the Catholic Church during the Reformation in Europe. Today most Protestants and Catholics respect each other's beliefs. However, they still have conflicts in Northern Ireland.

Religions continue to spread throughout the world. There are about 2 billion Christians in the world, 1 billion Muslims, 800 million Hindus, 350 million Buddhists, and 14 million Jews. The world also has many followers of other religions. In the United States and in many other countries, people with different religious beliefs live side by side in peace.

REVIEW In 2000, what did a United States government study on religious freedoms around the world reveal?

Population Growth

In the years between 1800 and 1960, the world's population increased from 1 billion to 3 billion people. Between 1960 and 2000 it grew from 3 billion to 6 billion, doubling in just 40 years. **Demographers** (dih•MAH•gruh•ferz), or geographers who study population, have identified two changes as causes for this rapid increase. First, many children now survive illnesses that often caused death in the past.

World Population, 2003

Asia 60.6%

Europe 11.6%

Oceania 0.5%

Africa 13.6%

South America 5.8%

North America 7.9%

Analyze Graphs Asia has the highest percent of the world's total population.

❖ How does Europe's population percent compare with North America's?

Second, adults now live longer. These changes are the result of improvements in diet, new medicines, and better health care.

Studies by demographers provide many important findings. For example, population growth is now greatest in the world's poorest regions. During the twentieth century, Asia's population increased by 400 percent, Africa's by 550 percent, and Latin America's by 700 percent. In North America and Europe, population increased much more slowly because many people chose to have smaller families.

A result of population increase is the growth of cities, especially in Asia, Africa, and Latin America. Together, the twin cities of Tokyo and Yokohama have about 30 million people. Mexico City has more than 20 million. As more people move into urban areas, fewer people are left in rural areas.

In 2003 the world's population was more than 6.3 billion people. At present growth rates, the world's population will reach 9 billion people by 2035. Some experts fear that the world will not be able to produce enough food for so many people. Some countries with high population growth rates are encouraging their citizens to have fewer children. China has slowed its population growth by encouraging each family to have one child only. Many Chinese citizens believe this is too much government control.

REVIEW Why did the population of the world increase rapidly between 1960 and 2000?

SUMMARIZE

The country of Monaco (left) has the highest population density in the world, while Mongolia (below) has the lowest.

Natural Resources

As the world's population continues to grow, so does the demand for natural resources. Natural resources include animals, plants, minerals, and water. People use natural resources to make food, energy, and raw materials for products.

These uses of natural resources create many jobs. People work in many kinds of industries that rely on natural resources. These industries include manufacturing, mining, farming, and forestry. Without natural resources, factory workers, farmers, and many others would not have jobs.

Because natural resources are so important, people have a responsibility to use them wisely. Over the years, people in both developed and developing countries have damaged the world's natural resources.

In recent years some governments have passed laws to protect natural resources. For example, many countries have laws that control the use and the cleanliness of water.

Wind turbines such as these in California produce electricity for use in homes and businesses.

Manufacturers have designed products that use less energy and fewer raw materials. Individuals have learned to conserve natural resources, or keep them from being wasted. Today many people understand the need to protect the world's natural resources.

REVIEW How does population growth affect natural resources?

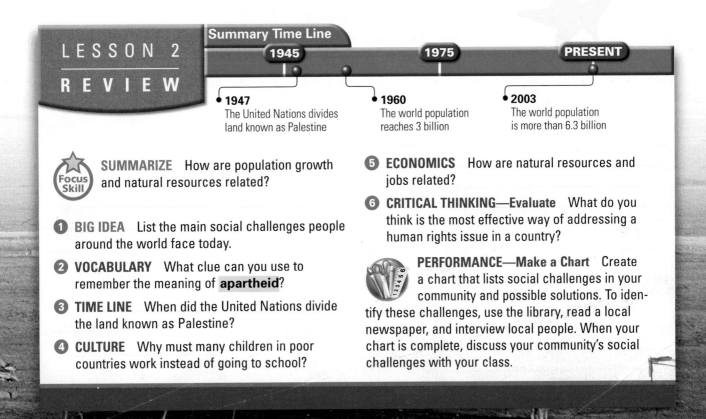

LESSON 2 REVIEW

Summary Time Line

| 1945 | | 1975 | PRESENT |

1947
The United Nations divides land known as Palestine

1960
The world population reaches 3 billion

2003
The world population is more than 6.3 billion

Focus Skill

SUMMARIZE How are population growth and natural resources related?

1 BIG IDEA List the main social challenges people around the world face today.

2 VOCABULARY What clue can you use to remember the meaning of **apartheid**?

3 TIME LINE When did the United Nations divide the land known as Palestine?

4 CULTURE Why must many children in poor countries work instead of going to school?

5 ECONOMICS How are natural resources and jobs related?

6 CRITICAL THINKING—Evaluate What do you think is the most effective way of addressing a human rights issue in a country?

PERFORMANCE—Make a Chart Create a chart that lists social challenges in your community and possible solutions. To identify these challenges, use the library, read a local newspaper, and interview local people. When your chart is complete, discuss your community's social challenges with your class.

·SKILLS·

CHART AND GRAPH

Read a Cartogram

VOCABULARY

cartogram
population cartogram

▶ WHY IT MATTERS

With the exception of China, the countries of eastern Asia are not very large in size. The populations of most of these small countries, however, are greater than those of some countries that are large in size. Population is not spread evenly around the world. Some areas are almost empty, while other areas are very crowded. Factors such as resources, elevation, climate, historical events, and ways of life affect an area's population.

One way to show population is to use a cartogram. A **cartogram** is a diagram that gives information about places by the size shown for each place. A **population cartogram** shows which countries have many people and which have few people.

▶ WHAT YOU NEED TO KNOW

On most maps, the size of each country or continent is based on the size of its land area. On a cartogram,

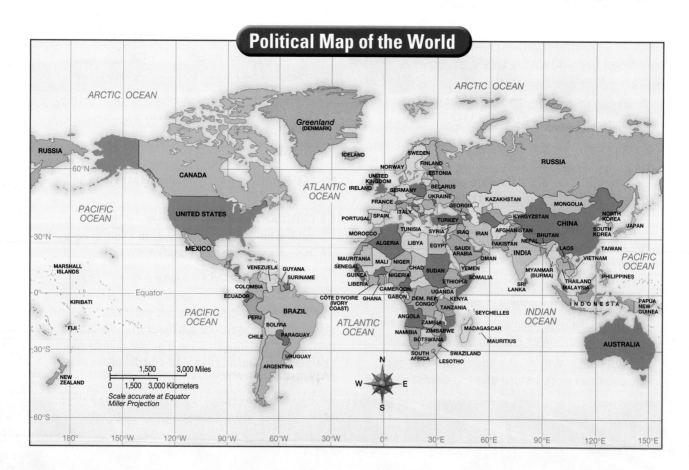

Political Map of the World

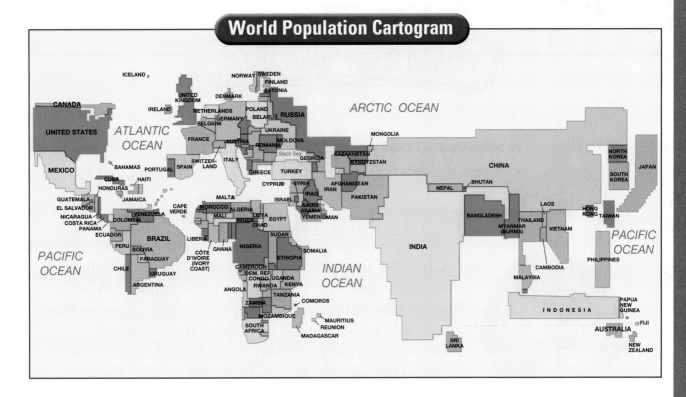

World Population Cartogram

the size of the country or continent is based on a statistic, such as population. A population cartogram shows the size of each country according to the size of its population. A country with a large population would be shown much larger than a country with a small population. When countries are shown in this way, you can quickly compare populations.

The map on page 650 is a political map of the world. The size of each country is based on the size of its land area. Compare the sizes of China and Russia. Which is larger?

The cartogram on this page is a population cartogram. The size of each country is based on the size of its population. Compare the sizes of China and Russia again. Although China has a smaller land area than Russia, it is shown larger than Russia on the cartogram because it has more people.

▶ PRACTICE THE SKILL

Answer these questions. Use the map and the cartogram to compare land areas and populations.

1 Compare Japan and Australia. Which country has the larger land area? Which country has the larger population?

2 Which continent on the cartogram has the largest population? the smallest population? Explain.

▶ APPLY WHAT YOU LEARNED

With a partner, brainstorm other statistics that could be shown on a cartogram. Decide on one kind of statistic, and choose one continent, such as Asia. Use reference sources or the Internet to locate the statistics, and make a cartogram for the countries of your continent.

Next, write questions that can be answered by looking at your cartogram. Exchange cartograms and questions with another pair of students, and answer each other's questions.

Inventions in Communication

Until the mid-1800s, people communicated mostly through written messages. The invention of the telegraph in 1844 and the telephone in 1876 allowed people to send messages instantly over wires. In 1895 Guglielmo Marconi (gool•YEL•moh mahr•KOH•nee) invented a way to send signals through the air without wires. This was the beginning of radio. In 1927 Philo T. Farnsworth's television added pictures to sound. In the 1980s computers allowed people to send and receive messages electronically. Cellular phones allowed instant communication almost anywhere. Today advances in communication technology continue at a rapid rate.

Person using an early telephone

FROM THE SMITHSONIAN INSTITUTION IN WASHINGTON, D.C.

Telegraph key used by Samuel F. B. Morse on his first telegraph line in 1844

First model of the telephone, invented by Alexander Graham Bell in 1876

Wooden cabinet radio from the late 1920s

Analyze the Primary Source

1. Which early communication devices pictured resemble communication devices of today?

2. Compare the cellular phone with Bell's telephone. How are they alike, and how are they different?

3. How does the cellular phone use technology from both the radio and the telephone?

In 1976 people could buy a kit for this early Apple computer and build it at home.

ACTIVITY

Research and Explain Use library or Internet resources to research one item on these pages. Then, write a paragraph that identifies the inventor of the item, describes how it was invented, and how it changed people's lives.

RESEARCH

Visit The Learning Site at **www.harcourtschool.com** to research other primary sources.

Early cellular phone, 1980s

3

SUMMARIZE

As you read, summarize how the United States fulfills its leadership role in the world.

BIG IDEA

Today's political challenges include keeping the peace around the world.

VOCABULARY

peacekeeping force
ethnic cleansing
terrorism

Political Challenges

| 1700 | 1800 | 1900 | PRESENT |

1990–Present

The 1990s began with both successes and challenges for governments around the world. The breakup of the Soviet Union created strong democracies in some nations but weak ones in others. With the end of the Cold War, people everywhere hoped that the world would be a safer place. Unfortunately, the world still has many dangers and faces many challenges.

One Superpower

After the Cold War the United States was the world's only super-power. The country has a stable government, a strong economy, and a powerful military. Many of the world's nations look to the United States for leadership in meeting global political challenges.

The Persian Gulf War of 1990–1991 showed one way that the United States fulfills its leadership role. In 1990 Iraq's dictator, Saddam Hussein (suh•DAHM hoo•SAYN), invaded Kuwait, a small

Southeastern Europeans (below) showed their unity by forming a human chain. A United States soldier (left) gives money to Serbian schoolchildren.

An American soldier stands on a destroyed Iraqi tank during the Persian Gulf War of 1990–1991. In the distance Kuwaiti oil wells burn after Iraqi troops set them on fire.

neighboring country. In 1991 an international military force, led by the United States, freed Kuwait from Iraq.

Sometimes the United States works as a partner with the United Nations or the North Atlantic Treaty Organization (NATO) in peacekeeping missions. Together, they send peacekeeping forces to troubled countries. **Peacekeeping forces** are troops who work to keep the peace. They act when groups in conflict cannot reach an agreement. Because the United States has the strongest military forces, it often takes the lead in these missions.

In the 1990s United States troops took part in NATO peacekeeping forces in southeastern Europe. Civil wars had broken out in what was then Yugoslavia. In 1991 and 1992, four of the six republics that made up Yugoslavia declared independence. The four republics were Croatia, Slovenia, Macedonia, and Bosnia and Herzegovina. The two remaining republics, Serbia and Montenegro, formed a new Yugoslavia. The Serbs,

an ethnic group living in Yugoslavia, were against the country's division. They fought against other ethnic groups living there who wanted self-rule.

The world heard shocking reports that the Serbs were carrying out ethnic cleansing. **Ethnic cleansing** is the forcing out or killing of certain ethnic groups from a country or region. The NATO peacekeeping forces, which included 20,000 American soldiers, worked to prevent these acts and to keep the peace.

In 1998 the president of Yugoslavia, Slobodan Milosevic (SLOH•buh•dahn mee•LOH•shuh•vich), sent troops to Kosovo (KAW•suh•voh), a province in Serbia. Like the former republics of Yugoslavia, Kosovo wanted independence. Milosevic's troops killed thousands of citizens in Kosovo. Again the United States and other NATO countries sent peacekeeping forces. Milosevic was removed from power in 2000. Three years later Yugoslavia became the country of Serbia and Montenegro.

A United States B-2 stealth bomber

REVIEW What happened in Yugoslavia in the early 1990s?

The War on Terrorism

On September 11, 2001, the United States was the target of a horrible act of **terrorism**, or violence to further a cause. Terrorists hijacked, or illegally took control of, four airplanes. They crashed two planes into the twin towers of the World Trade Center in New York City. A third plane crashed into the Pentagon, the nation's military headquarters, near Washington, D.C. The fourth plane crashed in a field in rural Pennsylvania. Thousands of Americans and others died on that tragic day, which became known as 9/11.

The people of the United States were shocked at the hatred shown by the attacks. President George W. Bush declared that the United States would launch a war against terrorism. In a speech on fighting terrorism, he stated:

> 66 We will not tire, we will not falter, and we will not fail. 99

The United States soon found out that the 9/11 terrorists had links to the Taliban government of Afghanistan. The Taliban had allowed the terrorists to plan and train for the 9/11 attacks in Afghanistan. The United States demanded that the terrorist leaders be arrested, but the Taliban refused. Because of this, the United States and allies overthrew the Taliban government in late 2001.

In addition to fighting terrorism, the United States became determined to prevent any future threats to the country. In 2002 President Bush declared that Iraqi leader Saddam Hussein was a danger to the United States. Along with some of its allies, the United States invaded Iraq and toppled Hussein's government in 2003. Afterward, the United States began to lead efforts to rebuild Iraq, which for many years had been under Hussein's harsh rule.

REVIEW Why did the United States and its allies overthrow the Taliban government in Afghanistan? SUMMARIZE

The World Trade Center towers (below) burn after the 9/11 attacks. Firefighters (right) walk through the ruins.

A Demilitarized Zone (DMZ) forms the border between North Korea and South Korea.

Nuclear Weapons

The threat of a global nuclear war decreased with the end of the Cold War. The United States and Russia agreed to reduce the numbers of their nuclear weapons dramatically. The threat of regional nuclear conflicts, however, still exists.

In southern Asia both India and Pakistan have nuclear weapons. Other countries worry that they will use them because the two countries have a border conflict. Each country claims an area of land called Kashmir, which lies between the two borders. To show its military power, India tested several nuclear weapons in 1998. In response, Pakistan tested several of its own.

Similar tensions exist between North Korea and South Korea, in eastern Asia. The division of the Korean Peninsula after World War II was meant to be temporary. However, each part went on to form its own government. While reuniting the two Koreas seemed possible in the past, it now appears unlikely. In 2002 North Korea's government revealed that it had a nuclear weapons program, increasing tensions further.

REVIEW In which regions do threats of nuclear conflicts exist today?

Challenges for Democracy

Some countries around the world still do not have democratic freedoms. When the citizens of those countries ask for more freedoms, their governments often refuse.

In 1989 Chinese students and other citizens held a protest in Beijing's Tiananmen Square for greater democracy in China. The Chinese military fired on the crowd, killing hundreds of the protesters. Even so, many Chinese citizens are not afraid to protest against their government. In 2003 tens of thousands of citizens in Hong Kong protested new Chinese laws that would reduce their freedoms.

The citizens of Myanmar are working for democracy, too. Led by Aung San Suu Kyi (AWNG SAHN SOO CHEE), they protest against the harsh rule of the country's military dictatorship. In 1991 Aung San Suu Kyi won the Nobel Peace Prize for her leadership in favor of democracy.

Pro-democracy leader Aung San Suu Kyi

Chapter 19 ■ 657

Citizens of Haiti wait for representatives from the Organization of American States, a group that helps North and South American countries resolve problems.

The Myanmar government has arrested Aung San Suu Kyi many times for her views.

While some governments fight against democracy, others struggle to achieve it. Since the Soviet Union broke apart in 1991, Russia has worked to establish democracy. Wanting a strong democratic leader, voters elected Vladimir Putin as president in 2000. Russia's relations with the United States and Europe improved under Putin's leadership. In 2002 Russia became a special partner of NATO.

After decades under dictatorships, most countries in Latin America have formed democratic governments since the 1990s. They still face many problems, however. Much of Central America is still recovering from years of civil

A soldier holds equipment used to detect land mines. After years of war, land mines are being removed across Central America.

wars. In the early 1990s fighting ended in El Salvador and Nicaragua. The two sides in Guatemala's 35-year conflict signed a peace treaty in 1996.

Not all democracies in South America are stable. Beginning in the 1990s, severe economic problems led to political unrest in Argentina. As its economy worsened in the early 2000s, Argentina's leadership weakened. From 2001 to 2003, the country had five different presidents.

Many experts worry that Argentina's crisis might affect Brazil, South America's largest democracy. Brazil already faces huge debts and inflation. Because of these problems, many Brazilians are looking for strong leadership. Brazil's president Lula da Silva, who took office in 2003, promised to reform the country's government and economy.

In Mexico's democracy, much political change is taking place. The

President George W. Bush meets with leaders of democracies in western Africa.

Institutional Revolutionary party (PRI) ruled Mexico for 71 years. In 2000, however, the Mexican people elected Vicente Fox of the National Action party to the presidency.

Fox has moved quickly on many difficult issues. For example, he is trying to reduce tensions between the Mexican government and Indians living in the state of Chiapas. Mayan people there have rebelled against their poor living conditions. Also, Fox is working with the United States on the problem of illegal immigration of Mexicans into the United States.

No continent presents more challenges than Africa. Many of its democracies struggle with crop failures, disease, poverty, and war. The future of democracy in Africa may lie in its leaders working together. Today more than 50 African nations are members of the African Union (AU). This organization works for greater unity among African nations and the peoples of Africa.

REVIEW **What happened at Tiananmen Square?**

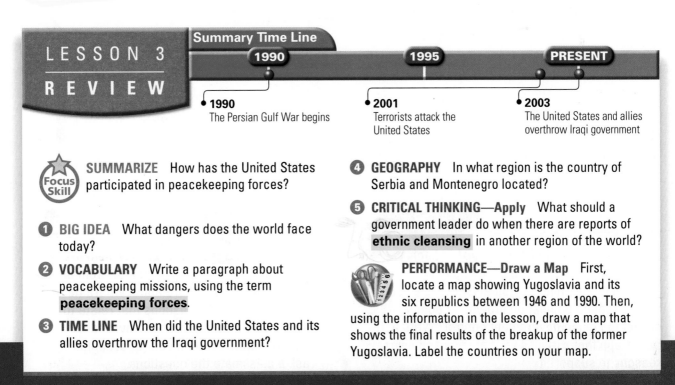

LESSON 3 REVIEW

Summary Time Line

1990	1995	PRESENT

1990
The Persian Gulf War begins

2001
Terrorists attack the United States

2003
The United States and allies overthrow Iraqi government

Focus Skill **SUMMARIZE** How has the United States participated in peacekeeping forces?

1. **BIG IDEA** What dangers does the world face today?

2. **VOCABULARY** Write a paragraph about peacekeeping missions, using the term **peacekeeping forces**.

3. **TIME LINE** When did the United States and its allies overthrow the Iraqi government?

4. **GEOGRAPHY** In what region is the country of Serbia and Montenegro located?

5. **CRITICAL THINKING—Apply** What should a government leader do when there are reports of **ethnic cleansing** in another region of the world?

PERFORMANCE—Draw a Map First, locate a map showing Yugoslavia and its six republics between 1946 and 1990. Then, using the information in the lesson, draw a map that shows the final results of the breakup of the former Yugoslavia. Label the countries on your map.

Review and Test Preparation

Summary Time Line

1945   1955

1948
The United Nations adopts
the Universal Declaration
of Human Rights

Focus Skill ☆ Summarize

Use this graphic organizer to show that you understand how to
summarize the economic challenges the world has faced since
World War II. A copy of this graphic organizer appears on page
178 of the Activity Book.

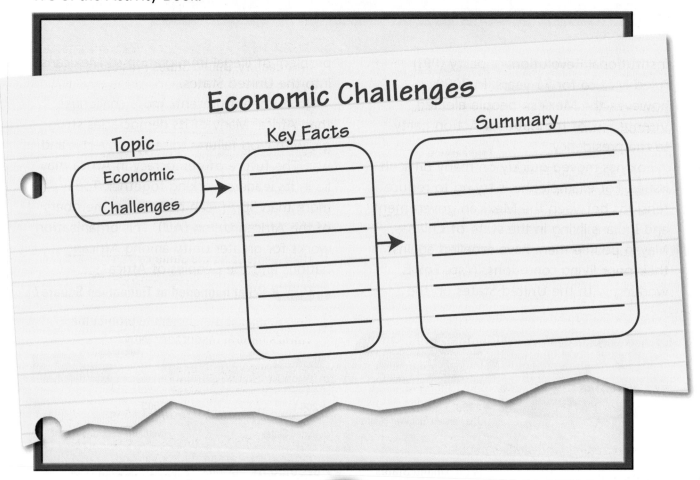

THINK & WRITE

Write a Persuasive Paragraph Each
family in China is allowed by law to have no
more than one child. Do you think this is a good
way to reduce population growth, or does it
reflect too much government control? Write a
paragraph that explains your opinion and gives
reasons to support it.

Create a Questionnaire Write a list of
questions you might ask a person from another
country to find out more about where he or
she lives. Include questions that relate to
a country's culture, its economy, and its
government. To try out your questionnaire,
ask a classmate the questions.

1970s
China begins to reform its economy

1990s
The Internet becomes important in telecommunication

2001
Terrorists attack the United States

2003
The Iraqi government is overthrown

USE THE TIME LINE

Use the chapter summary time line to answer these questions.

1 What did the United Nations adopt in 1948?

2 In which year was Iraq's government overthrown?

USE VOCABULARY

Identify the term that correctly matches each description.

global economy (p. 636)
recession (p. 637)
trade agreement (p. 639)
human rights (p. 644)
demographer (p. 647)
terrorism (p. 656)

3 the trade of goods and services around the world

4 acts of violence committed to further a cause

5 a period during which an economy stops growing

6 a promise between countries to lower tariffs on each other's goods

7 the freedoms that all people should have, including freedom of speech and freedom of religion

8 a geographer who studies population

RECALL FACTS

Answer these questions.

9 What is GDP? What does it mean for a country to have a high GDP?

10 Why did the world's population increase rapidly between 1960 and 2000?

11 What nations now make up what used to be Yugoslavia?

Write the letter of the best choice.

12 **TEST PREP** All of the following are forms of telecommunication *except*—
A cell phones.
B the Internet.
C the United States mail.
D fax machines.

13 **TEST PREP** During the 1990s and into the new century, United States Presidents have worked to solve conflicts between what two groups in southwestern Asia?
F Israelis and Palestinians
G Protestants and Catholics
H Shi'i Muslims and Sunni Muslims
J Hindus and Buddhists

THINK CRITICALLY

14 How might using the same currency—the euro—make trade easier between members of the European Union?

15 Do you think it is important to protect the world's natural resources? Why?

APPLY SKILLS

Compare Different Kinds of Maps

16 Study the maps on pages 642–643. Write a paragraph that describes the maps and tells how each can be used to find out information about Japan.

MAP AND GLOBE SKILLS

Read a Cartogram

17 Look at the World Population Cartogram on page 651. Which country in Asia has the largest population?

CHART AND GRAPH SKILLS

VISIT

Anne Frank House

GET READY

Today the Anne Frank House in Amsterdam, the Netherlands, is open to visitors. It was in this house that a 13-year-old German-Jewish girl began to keep a diary of her life.

During World War II, Anne Frank, her family, and several friends went into hiding. They lived very quietly in a secret apartment when the Nazis occupied the Netherlands. In the end, however, the Franks and their friends were discovered and arrested by the Nazis. Anne Frank died in a German concentration camp.

Visitors to the house can get an idea of what life there must have been like. They can also see Anne Frank's diary on display.

WHAT TO SEE

Today, visitors to the Anne Frank House can see how the young girl and her family lived during their time of terror.

LOCATE IT

North Sea

Amsterdam

NETHERLANDS

During her time of hiding, Anne Frank kept a detailed diary of her experiences. She wrote about her day-to-day life, her relationships with those who shared the apartment, and her thoughts about the world.

Anne Frank, with her family (above left) and alone (above right).

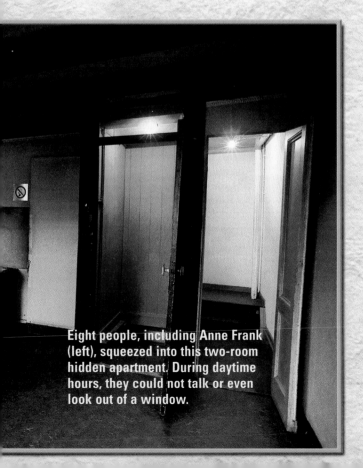

Eight people, including Anne Frank (left), squeezed into this two-room hidden apartment. During daytime hours, they could not talk or even look out of a window.

TAKE A FIELD TRIP

GO ONLINE

A VIRTUAL TOUR
Visit The Learning Site at **www.harcourtschool.com** to take virtual tours of other historic homes.

CNN Turner Le@rning®

A VIDEO TOUR
Check your media center or classroom library for a videotape of students reflecting on Anne Frank's diary.

8 Review and Test Preparation

VISUAL SUMMARY

Write a Paragraph Write a paragraph that explains how any two scenes shown on the time line are related.

USE VOCABULARY

Identify the term that correctly matches each definition.

imperialism (p. 584), **superpower** (p. 626)

alliance (p. 604), **terrorism** (p. 656)

1 The attacks of September 11, 2001, were an example of ——.

2 Building an empire by claiming lands, setting up colonies, and controlling those colonies from far away is called ——.

3 Since the breakup of the Soviet Union in 1991, the United States has been the world's only ——.

4 A(n) —— is an agreement among nations, groups, or individuals to help one another in times of need.

RECALL FACTS

Answer these questions.

5 What is the opening section of the Declaration of Independence called?

6 Which continent now faces more challenges than any other, including hunger, disease, poverty, and war?

Write the letter of the best choice.

7 **TEST PREP** All of these statements are true about Britain *except*—
   A Its Parliament includes the House of Commons and the House of Lords.
   B It once ruled India.
   C Catherine the Great was one of its leaders.
   D The Industrial Revolution began there.

8 **TEST PREP** Which of these is *not* associated with China?
   F the Opium Wars
   G leaders called czars
   H Mao Zedong and the Red Guard
   J the 1989 protest in Tiananmen Square

Visual Summary

1700   **1800**

1775 The American Revolution begins p. 566

1830 Most of Latin America is independent p. 569

1850 The Industrial Revolution continues p. 575

9 TEST PREP The United States is part of each of these groups *except*—

A NAFTA.

B OPEC.

C WTO.

D the United Nations.

THINK CRITICALLY

10 How did the American Revolution—and the feelings of nationalism it inspired—change the rest of the world?

11 Do you think a trade embargo is a good way to get a nation's government to change its policies? Why or why not?

APPLY SKILLS

Identify Changing Borders
Use the maps on this page to answer these questions.

12 Which country is united today that was not united in 1980?

13 Of what country were present-day Slovenia, Croatia, Bosnia and Herzegovina, and Serbia and Montenegro once part?

14 Which countries in Europe were once part of the Soviet Union?

15 What countries were once part of Czechoslovakia?

Europe, 1980

Present-Day Europe

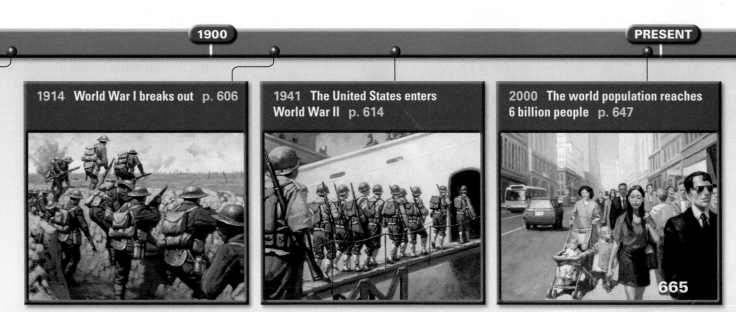

1900   PRESENT

1914 World War I breaks out p. 606

1941 The United States enters World War II p. 614

2000 The world population reaches 6 billion people p. 647

Unit Activities

GO ONLINE Visit The Learning Site at www.harcourtschool.com for additional activities.

Create a Guidebook

Use library or online resources to find out more about the United Nations. Create a guidebook for tourists who visit the United Nations headquarters in New York City. First, brainstorm a list of questions you think a visitor might want answered about the United Nations. Organize those questions into categories that will become chapters of your guidebook. Use library or online resources to write and illustrate one of those chapters.

Create an Agricultural Innovations Magazine

Contribute to a class magazine on agricultural innovations of the past, present, and future. What topics should your magazine include from the past? What innovations in use today should be included? How has agriculture changed since the 1700s? How might it continue to change in the future? Use library and online resources to find out more about your topic. Then write an article and share it with other students.

VISIT YOUR LIBRARY

■ *Kids During the Great Depression* by Lisa A. Wroble. PowerKids Press.

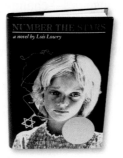

■ *Number the Stars* by Lois Lowry. HarperTrophy.

■ *Zlata's Diary: A Child's Life in Sarajevo* by Zlata Filipović. Penguin USA.

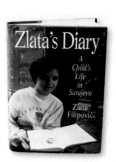

COMPLETE THE UNIT PROJECT

Hall of Fame Work with a group of your classmates to finish the unit project—a hall of fame honoring individuals you read about in the unit. Your group should choose five people from the unit to include in your hall of fame. Then design a poster that includes short biographies as well as drawings or pictures of the people you have chosen. Display your group's finished posters together with those of the other groups.

For Your Reference

Almanac

Facts About the World

Country Flag	Country	Capital	Population*	Area (sq. mi.)	Economy
Africa					
	Algeria	Algiers	32,818,500	919,590	oil, natural gas, light industry, food processing, grains, iron, mining, petrochemical
	Angola	Luanda	10,766,471	481,351	textiles, coffee, sugarcane, bananas, iron, diamonds, cement, fish processing, phosphates
	Benin	Porto-Novo	7,041,490	43,483	palm products, peanuts, cotton, corn, oil, construction materials, petroleum
	Botswana	Gaborone	1,573,267	231,803	livestock processing, corn, coal, copper, tourism, diamonds, salt, silver
	Burkina Faso	Ouagadougou	13,228,460	105,869	agricultural processing, textiles, millet, sorghum, manganese, soap, gold, beverages
	Burundi	Bujumbura	6,096,156	10,745	food processing, coffee, cotton, tea, nickel, soap, shoes
	Cameroon	Yaoundé	15,746,179	183,567	oil products, food processing, cocoa, coffee, lumber, textiles
	Cape Verde	Praia	412,137	1,557	bananas, coffee, sweet potatoes, salt, fish processing, ship repair
	Central African Republic	Bangui	3,683,538	240,534	textiles, cotton, coffee, diamonds, sawmills, footwear, assembly of bicycles and motorcycles

Country Flag	Country	Capital	Population*	Area (sq. mi.)	Economy
	Chad	N'Djamena	9,253,493	495,752	cotton, sorghum, millet, uranium, meat packing, soap, construction materials
	Comoros	Moroni	632,948	838	perfume, textiles, vanilla, coconut oil, plants, fruits, furniture, jewelry, construction materials
	Republic of the Congo	Brazzaville	2,954,258	132,046	oil, wood products, cocoa, coffee, potash, soap, sugar milling
	Côte d'Ivoire (Ivory Coast)	Yamoussoukro	16,962,491	124,502	food processing, coffee, cocoa, oil, diamonds, textiles, fertilizer, construction materials
	Democratic Republic of the Congo	Kinshasa	56,625,039	905,563	mining, food processing, sugar, rice, cobalt, cement, diamonds, textiles
	Djibouti	Djibouti	457,130	8,880	mainly service activities, dairy products, mineral water bottling
	Egypt	Cairo	74,718,797	386,660	textiles, tourism, chemicals, cotton, rice, beans, oil, gas, construction, cement, metals
	Equatorial Guinea	Malabo	510,473	10,830	fish, cocoa, coffee, bananas, oil, saw milling, natural gas
	Eritrea	Asmara	4,362,254	46,842	food processing, cotton, coffee, tobacco, gold, potash, textiles
	Ethiopia	Addis Ababa	66,557,553	435,184	food processing, textiles, coffee, grains, platinum, gold

* These population figures are from the most recent available statistics.

Country Flag	Country	Capital	Population*	Area (sq. mi.)	Economy
	Gabon	Libreville	1,321,560	103,346	textiles, cocoa, coffee, oil, manganese, uranium, cement
	Gambia	Banjul	1,501,050	4,363	tourism, peanuts, rice, fish, woodworking, metalworking
	Ghana	Accra	20,467,747	92,456	aluminum, cocoa, gold, manganese, food processing, lumbering
	Guinea	Conakry	9,030,220	94,925	mining, bananas, pineapples, iron, bauxite, diamonds
	Guinea-Bissau	Bissau	1,360,827	13,946	peanuts, cashews, cotton, rice, bauxite, agricultural processing
	Kenya	Nairobi	31,639,091	224,961	tourism, oil refining, coffee, corn, gold, limestone, cement, soap, textiles
	Lesotho	Maseru	1,861,959	11,720	food processing, textiles, corn, grains, diamonds, construction, tourism
	Liberia	Monrovia	3,317,176	43,000	mining, rice, cassava, coffee, iron, diamonds, gold, rubber, timber
	Libya	Tripoli	5,499,074	679,358	oil, food processing, dates, olives, gypsum, handicrafts, textiles, cement
	Madagascar	Antananarivo	16,979,744	226,656	textiles, meat processing, coffee, cloves, vanilla, chromite, graphite, soap, paper, petroleum, tourism
	Malawi	Lilongwe	11,651,239	45,745	agricultural processing, sugar, tea, tobacco, coffee

Country Flag	Country	Capital	Population*	Area (sq. mi.)	Economy
	Mali	Bamako	11,626,219	478,764	millet, rice, peanuts, cotton, gold, phosphates, construction
	Mauritania	Nouakchott	2,912,584	397,953	fish processing, dates, grains, iron ore, gypsum
	Mauritius	Port Louis	1,210,447	788	tourism, textiles, sugarcane, tea, metal products
	Morocco	Rabat	31,689,265	172,413	carpets, clothing, leather goods, grains, fruits, phosphates, iron ore, tourism
	Mozambique	Maputo	17,479,266	309,494	chemicals, petroleum products, cashews, cotton, sugar, coal, titanium, textiles, glass, cement
	Namibia	Windhoek	1,927,447	318,694	diamonds, copper, gold, fish, meat packing, dairy products
	Niger	Niamey	11,058,590	489,189	peanuts, cotton, uranium, coal, iron, gold, petroleum
	Nigeria	Abuja	133,881,703	356,667	oil, gas, textiles, cocoa, palm products, construction materials, chemicals, ceramics, steel
	Rwanda	Kigali	7,810,056	10,169	coffee, tea, tin, cement, soap, furniture, shoes, textiles
	São Tomé and Príncipe	São Tomé	175,883	386	cocoa, coconuts, textiles, soap, fish processing, timber
	Senegal	Dakar	10,580,307	75,749	food processing, fishing, peanuts, millet, phosphates, construction materials, fertilizer production

* These population figures are from the most recent available statistics.

Country Flag	Country	Capital	Population*	Area (sq. mi.)	Economy
	Seychelles	Victoria	80,469	176	food processing, tourism, coconut products, cinnamon, vanilla, fishing, boat building, printing
	Sierra Leone	Freetown	5,732,681	27,699	mining, cocoa, coffee, diamonds, titanium, textiles, footwear
	Somalia	Mogadishu	8,025,190	246,199	sugar, bananas, iron, tin, textiles
	South Africa	Cape Town/ Pretoria	42,768,678	471,008	steel, automobiles, corn, other grains, gold, diamonds, platinum, metalworking, textiles, chemicals
	Sudan	Khartoum	38,114,160	967,493	textiles, gum arabic, cotton, chromium, copper, cement, sugar, shoes, petroleum refining
	Swaziland	Mbabane	1,161,219	6,704	wood pulp, sugar, corn, cotton, asbestos, clay, coal
	Tanzania	Dar es Salaam	35,922,454	364,898	agricultural processing, cotton, tin, diamonds, textiles, fertilizer, salt
	Togo	Lomé	5,429,299	21,925	textiles, coffee, cocoa, yams, phosphates, handicrafts
	Tunisia	Tunis	9,924,742	63,170	food processing, textiles, oil products, grains, olives, dates, phosphates, tourism
	Uganda	Kampala	25,632,794	91,135	textiles, cement, coffee, cotton, tea, copper, cobalt, sugar

Country Flag	Country	Capital	Population*	Area (sq. mi.)	Economy
	Zambia	Lusaka	10,307,333	290,584	corn, cassava, sugar, cobalt, copper, zinc, emeralds, gold, silver, construction, chemicals
	Zimbabwe	Harare	12,576,742	150,803	clothing, steel, chemicals, tobacco, sugar, chromium, gold, nickel, wood products, steel

Asia

Country Flag	Country	Capital	Population*	Area (sq. mi.)	Economy
	Afghanistan	Kabul	28,717,213	250,000	textiles, furniture, wheat, fruits, copper, coal, wool, natural gas, oil, soap
	Armenia	Yerevan	3,326,448	11,506	vegetables, grapes, copper, gold, electric motors, tires, chemicals, trucks, watches, microelectronics
	Azerbaijan	Baku	7,830,764	33,436	oil, grains, cotton, iron, cattle, cement, textiles
	Bahrain	Manama	667,238	257	oil, gas, fruits, vegetables, ship repairing, tourism
	Bangladesh	Dhaka	138,448,210	55,598	jute, textiles, fertilizers, rice, tea, cement, chemical fertilizer
	Bhutan	Thimphu	2,139,549	18,147	rice, corn, timber, cement, processed fruits
	Brunei	Bandar Seri Begawan	358,098	2,228	petroleum, rice, bananas, cassava, construction

* These population figures are from the most recent available statistics.

Country Flag	Country	Capital	Population*	Area (sq. mi.)	Economy
	Cambodia	Phnom Penh	13,124,764	69,900	rice, wood, rubber, corn, gemstones, garments, wood and wood products, cement
	China	Beijing	1,286,975,468	3,705,386	iron, steel, textiles, tea, rice and other grains, cotton, coal, petroleum, cement, food processing, toys, footwear
	Cyprus	Nicosia	771,657	3,571	barley, grapes, olives, copper, tourism, metal products, wood products
	East Timor	Dili	997,853	5,814	coffee, mining, marble, fishing, tourism
	Georgia	Tbilisi	4,934,413	26,911	manganese, citrus fruits, potatoes, corn, steel, aircraft, machine tools, textiles
	India	New Delhi	1,049,700,118	1,269,338	textiles, steel, rice and other grains, tea, spices, coal, iron, chemicals, cement, mining, petroleum
	Indonesia	Jakarta	234,893,453	741,096	textiles, rice, cocoa, peanuts, nickel, tin, oil, petroleum, plywood, chemical fertilizers, rubber, tourism
	Iran	Tehran	68,278,826	636,293	sugar refining, carpets, rice and other grains, oil, gas, textiles, cement, construction materials
	Iraq	Baghdad	24,683,313	168,753	textiles, grains, dates, oil, chemicals, construction materials
	Israel	Jerusalem	6,116,533	8,019	diamond cutting, textiles, electronics, citrus fruits, copper, phosphates, tourism, chemicals, metal products
	Japan	Tokyo	127,214,499	145,882	electronics, automobiles, fishing, rice, potatoes, machine tools, ships, textiles

Country Flag	Country	Capital	Population*	Area (sq. mi.)	Economy
	Jordan	Amman	5,460,265	35,687	oil refining, cement, grains, olives, phosphates, tourism, potash
	Kazakhstan	Astana	16,763,795	1,049,150	steel, grains, cotton, oil, coal, phosphates, electric motors, construction materials
	Kuwait	Kuwait	2,183,161	6,880	oil, oil products, gas, food processing, construction materials
	Kyrgyzstan	Bishkek	4,892,808	76,641	textiles, mining, tobacco, cotton, sugar beets, gold, refrigerators, furniture, electric motors
	Laos	Vientiane	5,921,545	91,428	wood products, mining, sweet potatoes, corn, cotton, gypsum, construction
	Lebanon	Beirut	3,727,703	4,015	banking, textiles, oil refining, fruits, olives, vegetables, jewelry, wood and furniture products, metal fabricating
	Malaysia	Kuala Lumpur	23,092,940	127,316	rubber goods, logging, steel, electronics, palm oil, tin, iron, petroleum production
	Maldives	Male	329,684	116	fish processing, tourism, coconuts, sweet potatoes, corn, shipping, boat building, garments, handicrafts
	Mongolia	Ulaanbaatar	2,712,315	604,247	food processing, mining, grains, coal, oil, construction materials, copper
	Myanmar (Burma)	Yangon (Rangoon)	42,510,537	261,969	textiles, petroleum, rice, sugarcane, lead, gemstones, pharmaceuticals, copper, tin, fertilizer, construction materials

* These population figures are from the most recent available statistics.

Country Flag	Country	Capital	Population*	Area (sq. mi.)	Economy
	Nepal	Kathmandu	26,469,569	54,363	sugar, jute, tourism, rice and other grains, quartz, carpet, textiles, cement and brick production
	North Korea	P'yongyang	22,466,481	46,540	textiles, corn, potatoes, coal, lead, machine building, chemicals, mining, tourism
	Oman	Muscat	2,807,125	82,031	dates, vegetables, limes, oil, gas, construction, cement, copper
	Pakistan	Islamabad	150,694,740	310,401	textiles, petroleum products, rice, wheat, natural gas, iron ore, paper products, clothing
	Palau	Koror	19,717	177	tourism, fish, coconuts, copra, cassava, sweet potatoes, garment making
	Philippines	Manila	84,619,974	115,830	textiles, clothing, wood products, sugar, cobalt, copper, food processing, electronics, fishing
	Qatar	Doha	817,052	4,416	oil, petroleum products, fertilizers, cement
	Saudi Arabia	Riyadh	24,293,844	756,981	oil, oil products, gas, dates, wheat, cement, construction, fertilizer
	Singapore	Singapore	4,608,595	267	shipbuilding, oil refining, electronics, banking, tourism, rubber processing, biotechnology
	South Korea	Seoul	48,289,037	38,023	electronics, automobiles, textiles, clothing, rice, barley, tungsten, shipbuilding, footwear
	Sri Lanka	Colombo	19,742,439	25,332	clothing, textiles, tea, coconuts, rice, graphite, limestone, processing of rubber, cement, petroleum refining

Country Flag	Country	Capital	Population*	Area (sq. mi.)	Economy
	Syria	Damascus	17,585,540	71,498	oil products, textiles, cotton, grains, olives, phosphate, rock mining
	Taiwan	Taipei	22,603,000	13,892	textiles, clothing, electronics, rice, fruits, coal, marble, iron, steel, cement, machinery
	Tajikistan	Dushanbe	6,863,752	55,251	aluminum, cement, barley, coal, lead, chemicals and fertilizers, machine tools
	Thailand	Bangkok	64,265,276	198,455	textiles, tourism, rice, corn, tapioca, sugarcane, cement, furniture, plastics, tungsten, tin
	Turkey**	Ankara	68,109,469	301,382	steel, textiles, grains, mercury, food processing, mining, petroleum, lumber, paper
	Turkmenistan	Ashgabat	4,775,544	188,455	oil, mining, textiles, grains, cotton, coal, sulfur, salt, natural gas
	United Arab Emirates	Abu Dhabi	2,484,818	32,000	oil, vegetables, dates, fishing, construction materials, handicrafts
	Uzbekistan	Tashkent	25,981,647	172,741	machinery, natural gas, vegetables, cotton, textiles, food processing
	Vietnam	Hanoi	81,624,716	127,243	food processing, textiles, rice, sugar, phosphates, cement, fertilizer, steel, paper, oil, coal
	Yemen	Sanaa	19,349,881	203,849	oil, grains, fruits, salt, food processing, handicrafts

** in both Asia and Europe

* These population figures are from the most recent available statistics.

Country Flag	Country	Capital	Population*	Area (sq. mi.)	Economy

Australia and Oceania

Country Flag	Country	Capital	Population*	Area (sq. mi.)	Economy
	Australia	Canberra	19,731,894	2,967,893	iron, steel, textiles, electrical equipment, wheat, cotton, fruits, bauxite, coal, mining, food processing
	Fiji	Suva	868,531	7,054	tourism, sugar, bananas, gold, timber, clothing, silver
	Kiribati	Tarawa	98,549	313	fishing, coconut oil, breadfruit, sweet potatoes, handicrafts
	Marshall Islands	Majuro	56,429	70	agriculture, tourism, fish, crafts from shells, wood and pearls
	Federated States of Micronesia	Palikir	136,973	271	tourism, tropical fruits, vegetables, pepper, construction, fish processing
	Nauru	Yaren	12,570	8.11	phosphates, coconut products
	New Zealand	Wellington	3,951,307	103,737	food processing, textiles, machinery, fish, forest products, grains, potatoes, gold, gas, iron, coal, tourism
	Papua New Guinea	Port Moresby	5,295,816	178,703	coffee, coconuts, cocoa, gold, copper, silver, plywood production, construction, tourism
	Samoa	Apia	178,173	1,104	timber, tourism, coconuts, yams, hardwoods, fish

Country Flag	Country	Capital	Population*	Area (sq. mi.)	Economy
	Solomon Islands	Honiara	509,190	10,985	fishing, coconuts, rice, gold, bauxite, mining, timber
	Tonga	Nuku'alofa	108,141	289	tourism, fishing, coconut products, bananas
	Tuvalu	Funafuti	11,305	10	coconut products, coconuts, fishing, tourism
	Vanuatu	Port-Vila	199,414	5,700	fish processing, meat canneries, tourism, coconut products, manganese, wood processing

Europe

Country Flag	Country	Capital	Population*	Area (sq. mi.)	Economy
	Albania	Tiranë	3,582,205	11,100	cement, textiles, food processing, corn, wheat, chromium, coal, lumber, chemicals, mining
	Andorra	Andorra la Vella	69,150	181	tourism, sheep, tobacco products, iron, lead, timber
	Austria	Vienna	8,188,207	32,378	steel, machinery, automobiles, grains, iron ore, construction, lumber and wood processing, tourism
	Belarus	Minsk	10,322,151	80,154	manufacturing, chemicals, grains, vegetables, tractors, fertilizer, textiles
	Belgium	Brussels	10,289,088	11,780	steel, glassware, diamond cutting, automobiles, wheat, coal, engineering, textiles, petroleum
	Bosnia and Herzegovina	Sarajevo	3,989,018	19,741	steel, mining, textiles, timber, corn, wheat, berries, bauxite, iron, coal, vehicle assembly

* These population figures are from the most recent available statistics.

Country Flag	Country	Capital	Population*	Area (sq. mi.)	Economy
	Bulgaria	Sofia	7,537,929	42,822	chemicals, machinery, metals, textiles, grains, fruits, bauxite, copper, zinc, construction materials
	Croatia	Zagreb	4,422,248	21,831	chemicals, plastics, steel, paper, olives, wheat, oil, bauxite, electronics, aluminum, textiles, petroleum, shipbuilding
	Czech Republic	Prague	10,249,216	30,450	machinery, oil products, glass, wheat, sugar beets, rye, coal, kaolin, motor vehicles, metal crafting
	Denmark	Copenhagen	5,384,384	16,639	food processing, machinery, textiles, furniture, grains, potatoes, dairy products, oil, salt, electronics, construction
	Estonia	Tallinn	1,408,556	17,462	shipbuilding, electric motors, potatoes, oil, phosphates, cement, furniture, paper, shoes
	Finland	Helsinki	5,190,785	130,127	metal, wood products, grains, copper, iron, paper, food stuffs, chemicals
	France	Paris	60,180,529	211,208	steel, textiles, tourism, wine, perfume, grains, fruits, vegetables, bauxite, iron, automobiles, electronics, mining
	Germany	Berlin	82,398,326	137,846	shipbuilding, automobiles, grains, potatoes, coal, potash, steel, iron, cement, machinery, electronics, food and beverages, textiles
	Greece	Athens	10,665,989	50,942	textiles, tourism, chemicals, wine, grains, olives, grapes, citrus fruits, bauxite, mining, petroleum
	Hungary	Budapest	10,045,407	35,919	iron, steel, wheat, corn, sunflowers, bauxite, coal, mining, construction materials, motor vehicles

Country Flag	Country	Capital	Population*	Area (sq. mi.)	Economy
	Iceland	Reykjavik	280,798	39,768	fish, aluminum, potatoes, tourism
	Ireland	Dublin	3,924,140	27,135	food processing, textiles, chemicals, tourism, potatoes, grains, zinc, lead, pharmaceuticals, machinery
	Italy	Rome	57,998,353	116,305	tourism, steel, machinery, automobiles, textiles, shoes, grapes, olives and olive oil, mercury, potash, sulfur, iron, food processing
	Latvia	Riga	2,348,784	24,938	machinery, train cars, grains, sugar beets, fertilizer, electronics, pharmaceuticals, processed foods
	Liechtenstein	Vaduz	33,145	62	electronics, textiles, ceramics, vegetables, wheat, metal manufacturing, tourism
	Lithuania	Vilnius	3,592,561	25,174	machinery, shipbuilding, grains, potatoes, vegetables, electric motors, petroleum refining, fertilizer
	Luxembourg	Luxembourg	454,157	998	steel, chemicals, food processing, grains, potatoes, grapes, metal products, tires, glass, aluminum
	Macedonia	Skopje	2,063,122	9,781	mining, textiles, wheat, rice, chromium, lead, coal, wood products
	Malta	Valletta	400,420	122	textiles, tourism, potatoes, tomatoes, electronics, shipbuilding and repair, construction
	Moldova	Chisinau	4,439,502	13,067	canning, wine, textiles, grains, lignite, gypsum, sugar, shoes, refrigerators and freezers

* These population figures are from the most recent available statistics.

Country Flag	Country	Capital	Population*	Area (sq. mi.)	Economy
	Monaco	Monaco	32,130	465 acres	tourism, chemicals, plastics
	Montenegro	Podgorica	620,145	5,333	steel, aluminum, coal-mining, forestry, textiles, tourism
	Netherlands	Amsterdam/ The Hague	16,150,511	16,033	metals, machinery, chemicals, grains, potatoes, flowers, oil, gas, fishing
	Norway	Oslo	4,546,123	125,181	paper, shipbuilding, grains, potatoes, copper, petroleum, chemicals, timber, mining, textiles
	Poland	Warsaw	38,622,660	120,728	shipbuilding, chemicals, grains, potatoes, sugar beets, coal, copper, silver, iron, steel, food processing, glass
	Portugal	Lisbon	10,102,022	35,672	textiles, footwear, cork, fish, grains, potatoes, tungsten, uranium, iron, metal working, oil refining, chemicals, tourism
	Romania	Bucharest	22,271,839	91,699	mining, machinery, oil, oil products, grains, grapes, gas, coal, timber, chemicals, food processing
	Russia**	Moscow	144,526,278	6,592,735	steel, machinery, motor vehicles, chemicals, textiles, grains, sugar beets, mercury, cobalt, shipbuilding, handicrafts
	San Marino	San Marino	28,119	24	tourism, postage stamps, woolen goods, wheat, grapes, ceramics, cement, wine
	Serbia	Belgrade	9,975,991	34,116	steel, machinery, corn and other grains, oil, gas, coal, mining, footwear, chemicals, pharmaceuticals
	Slovakia	Bratislava	5,430,033	18,859	iron, steel, glass, grains, potatoes, chemicals, textiles, rubber products

** in both Asia and Europe

Country Flag	Country	Capital	Population*	Area (sq. mi.)	Economy
	Slovenia	Ljubljana	1,935,677	7,827	electronics, vehicles, coal, lead, zinc, wood products, chemicals, machine tools
	Spain	Madrid	40,217,413	194,896	machinery, textiles, grains, olives, grapes, lignite, uranium, lead, chemicals, shipbuilding, tourism
	Sweden	Stockholm	8,878,085	173,731	steel, machinery, vehicles, grains, potatoes, zinc, iron, lead, paper products, processed foods, motor vehicles
	Switzerland	Bern	7,318,638	15,943	machinery, chemicals, watches, cheese, chocolate products, tourism, salt
	Ukraine	Kiev	48,055,439	233,089	chemicals, machinery, grains, sugar beets, potatoes, iron, manganese, coal, food processing
	United Kingdom	London	60,094,648	94,525	steel, vehicles, shipbuilding, banking, textiles, grains, sugar beets, coal, tin, oil, gas, limestone, chemicals, petroleum, paper and paper products
	Vatican City	—	900	109 acres	tourism, postage stamps

North America

Country Flag	Country	Capital	Population*	Area (sq. mi.)	Economy
	Antigua and Barbuda	St. John's	67,897	171	manufacturing, tourism, construction
	Bahamas	Nassau	297,477	5,382	tourism, rum, banking, pharmaceuticals, fishing
	Barbados	Bridgetown	277,264	166	sugar, tourism, manufacturing

* These population figures are from the most recent available statistics.

Country Flag	Country	Capital	Population*	Area (sq. mi.)	Economy
	Belize	Belmopan	266,440	8,867	sugar, garment production, food processing, tourism
	Canada	Ottawa	32,207,113	3,851,788	nickel, zinc, copper, gold, livestock, fish, chemicals, wood and paper products, petroleum
	Costa Rica	San José	3,896,092	19,730	furniture, aluminum, textiles, fertilizers, coffee, gold, construction materials, plastic products
	Cuba	Havana	11,263,429	42,803	food processing, tobacco, sugar, rice, coffee, cobalt, nickel, iron, copper, salt, textiles, chemicals, petroleum
	Dominica	Roseau	69,655	291	tourism, bananas, citrus fruits, pumice, soap, furniture, cement blocks
	Dominican Republic	Santo Domingo	8,715,602	18,815	cement, tourism, sugar, cocoa, coffee, nickel, bauxite, gold
	El Salvador	San Salvador	6,470,379	8,124	food products, tobacco, coffee, corn, sugar, chemicals, fertilizer, textiles
	Grenada	St. George's	89,258	133	textiles, spices, bananas, cocoa, tourism, construction
	Guatemala	Guatemala City	13,909,384	42,042	furniture, rubber, textiles, coffee, sugar, bananas, oil, chemicals, petroleum, metals
	Haiti	Port-au-Prince	7,527,817	10,714	textiles, coffee, sugar, bananas, bauxite, tourism, cement

Country Flag	Country	Capital	Population*	Area (sq. mi.)	Economy
	Honduras	Tegucigalpa	6,669,789	43,278	textiles, wood products, bananas, sugar, gold, silver, copper, lead
	Jamaica	Kingston	2,695,867	4,244	tourism, sugar, coffee, bananas, potatoes, bauxite, limestone, textiles, rum, food processing
	Mexico	Mexico City	104,907,991	761,602	steel, chemicals, textiles, rubber, petroleum, tourism, cotton, coffee, wheat, silver, lead, zinc, gold, oil, gas, mining, motor vehicles
	Nicaragua	Managua	5,128,517	49,998	food processing, chemicals, textiles, cotton, fruits, coffee, gold, silver, copper, petroleum refining, beverages, footwear
	Panama	Panama City	2,960,784	30,193	oil refining, international banking, bananas, rice, copper, mahogany, shrimp, cement, sugar milling
	Saint Kitts and Nevis	Basseterre	38,763	101	sugar, tourism, cotton, salt, clothing, footwear
	Saint Lucia	Castries	162,157	239	clothing, tourism, bananas, coconuts, forests, beverages, cardboard boxes
	Saint Vincent and the Grenadines	Kingstown	116,812	150	tourism, bananas, arrowroot, coconuts, food processing, clothing, furniture
	Trinidad and Tobago	Port-of-Spain	1,104,209	1,980	oil products, chemicals, tourism, sugar, cocoa, asphalt, oil, gas, cotton textiles
	United States of America	Washington, D.C.	290,342,554	3,794,083	wheat, corn, coal, lead, uranium, iron, copper, gold, computers, electronics, machinery, motor vehicles, chemicals, lumber, mining

* These population figures are from the most recent available statistics.

Country Flag	Country	Capital	Population*	Area (sq. mi.)	Economy

South America

Country Flag	Country	Capital	Population*	Area (sq. mi.)	Economy
	Argentina	Buenos Aires	38,740,807	1,068,296	food processing, automobiles, chemicals, grains, oil, lead, textiles, printing, steel
	Bolivia	La Paz/Sucre	8,586,443	424,162	mining, tobacco, coffee, sugar, potatoes, soybeans, tin, tungsten, handicrafts, clothing
	Brazil	Brasília	182,032,604	3,286,470	steel, automobiles, textiles, coffee, soybeans, sugar, iron, manganese, shoes, chemicals, cement, lumber, aircraft
	Chile	Santiago	15,665,216	292,258	fish, wood, grains, grapes, beans, copper, cement, textiles
	Colombia	Bogotá	41,662,073	439,733	textiles, food processing, coffee, rice, bananas, emeralds, oil, gas, cement, gold
	Ecuador	Quito	13,710,234	109,483	food processing, bananas, coffee, oil, gas, copper, zinc, silver, gold, textiles, metal work, fishing
	Guyana	Georgetown	702,100	83,000	mining, textiles, sugar, bauxite, diamonds, gold, rice, fishing
	Paraguay	Asunción	6,036,900	157,046	food processing, textiles, cement, corn, cotton, iron, manganese, limestone, sugar, wood products
	Peru	Lima	28,409,897	496,223	fishing, mining, textiles, cotton, sugar, coffee, rice, copper, silver, gold, oil, auto assembly, cement, shipbuilding

Country Flag	Country	Capital	Population*	Area (sq. mi.)	Economy
	Suriname	Paramaribo	435,449	63,039	aluminum, food processing, rice, sugar, fruits, bauxite, iron, lumbering, fishing
	Uruguay	Montevideo	3,413,329	68,039	meat packing, textiles, wine, corn, wheat, oil refining, food processing, chemicals
	Venezuela	Caracas	24,654,694	352,143	steel, textiles, coffee, rice, corn, oil, gas, iron, petroleum, mining, motor vehicle assembly

* These population figures are from the most recent available statistics.

Biographical Dictionary

The Biographical Dictionary lists many of the important people introduced in this book. The page number tells where the main discussion of each person starts. See the Index for other page references.

A

Abraham *2000s B.C.* Earliest ancestor of the Israelites, according to the Bible. p. 72

Akbar (AK•ber) *1542–1605* Considered the greatest of Mogul emperors, he united nearly all of India and was responsible for many reforms. p. 538

Akhenaton (ahk•NAH•tuhn) *c. 1300s B.C.* Egyptian ruler who changed his name from Amenhotep IV. He and Nefertiti, his wife, urged the Egyptians to worship only one god, the Aton. p. 127

Alaric (A•luh•rik) *c. 370–410* King of the Visigoths, who crossed the Alps and attacked the city of Rome in 410. p. 331

al-Bakri (al•BAHK•ree) *c. 1000s* Muslim geographer. p. 442

Alexander the Great *356 B.C.–323 B.C.* Son of Philip II. He was tutored by Aristotle and after Philip's death became king of Macedonia in 336 B.C. As ruler, Alexander built a huge empire. p. 264

al-Mansur (al•man•SOOR) Founder of the city of Baghdad. p. 456

Amenemhet (ahm•uhn•em•HET) *1900s B.C.* Vizier who made Egypt an empire. Started the period called the Middle Kingdom, which lasted for 200 years. p. 125

Archimedes (ar•kuh•MEE•deez) *c. 287 B.C.–212 B.C.* Greek teacher and inventor who used mathematics to build many useful machines. p. 269

Aristarchus (air•uh•STAR•kuhs) *c. 200s B.C.* Greek teacher who used mathematics to discover that Earth moves in a path around the sun. p. 269

Aristophanes (air•uh•STAH•fuh•neez) *c. 450 B.C.–c. 388 B.C.* Ancient Greek writer of comedies, or humorous plays. p. 259

Aristotle (AIR•uh•stah•tuhl) *384 B.C.–322 B.C.* Greek philosopher and tutor of Alexander the Great. He is considered one of the greatest thinkers of all time. p. 261

Ashoka (uh•SHOH•kuh) *c. 200s B.C.* Maurya emperor, remembered as "the greatest and noblest ruler India has known." p. 214

Ashurbanipal (ah•suhr•BAH•nuh•pahl) Grandson of Sennacherib. Ruled Assyria from 688 B.C. to 626 B.C. He established one of the largest libraries in the city of Nineveh. The library contained many Sumerian cuneiform tablets. p. 108

Atahuallpa (ah•tah•WAHL•pah) *c. 1502?–1533* Last Inca king to rule what is now Peru. He was killed in the Spanish conquest of the Incas. p. 512

Attila (uh•TIH•luh) *c. 406–453* King of the Huns. p. 331

Augustus Caesar (ah•GUS•tes SEE•zer) *63 B.C.–A.D. 14* First Roman emperor, a great nephew of Julius Caesar; originally known as Octavian. p. 289

Aung San Suu Kyi (AWNG SAHN SOO CHEE) *1945–* Myanmar political leader and the daughter of assassinated nationalist general U Aung San. She won the Nobel Peace Prize for her leadership in favor of democracy. p. 657

Aurangzeb (ow•ruhng•ZEB) *1618–1707* The son and successor of Shah Jahan of the Mogul Empire. p. 539

Awil-Marduk (MAHR•dook) Son of Nebuchadnezzar. p. 111

B

Babur (BAH•ber) *1483–1530* Muslim king who founded the Mogul Empire in India. p. 538

Batu *c. 1200s* Grandson of Genghis Khan and conqueror of what are now Russia, Poland, and Hungary in Europe and parts of Asia. p. 431

Belisarius (beh•luh•SAR•ee•uhs) *c. 505–c. 565* Byzantine general during the reign of Justinian I. He reclaimed much of the old Roman Empire. p. 413

Bindusara (bin•doo•SAR•uh) Son of Chandragupta Maurya. Together with his grandson Ashoka, he brought nearly all India under one rule. p. 213

Bismark, Otto von *1815–1898* Prussian statesperson and first chancellor, or prime minister, of Prussia. p. 593

Bolívar, Simón (boh•LEE•var, see•MOHN) *1783–1830* South American soldier, statesperson, and revolutionary leader. He freed Colombia, Venezuela, Ecuador, and Peru from Spanish rule. p. 569

Bonaparte, Napoleon (BOH•nuh•part, nuh•POH•lee•uhn) *1769–1821* French military leader and emperor of France. p. 568

Brueghel, Pieter (BROO•guhl, PEE•ter) *c. 1525–1569* A Dutch artist known for his religious paintings and scenes of everyday life. p. 495

Bush, George W. *1946–* Forty-third President of the United States. p. 656

C

Caboto, Giovanni (kah•BOH•toh) *c. 1450–c. 1499* Italian navigator and explorer; also known as John Cabot. While seeking a western route to Asia, he reached the northeast coast of America and claimed it for England. p. 506

Cabral, Pedro (kah•BRAHL) *c. 1467–1520* Portuguese navigator who claimed Brazil for Portugal. p. 512

Caesar, Julius (SEE•zer, JOO•lee•uhs) *100 B.C.–44 B.C.* Roman statesperson and general. He was dictator of Rome until he was murdered by a group of senators. p. 286

Cambyses (kam•BY•seez) *c. 500s B.C.* Persian king who made Egypt a part of his empire in 525 B.C. p. 197

Cartier, Jacques (kar•TYAY, ZHAHK) *1491–1557* French sailor and explorer. His explorations gave France its claim to Canada. p. 514

Castiglione, Baldassare (kahs•teel•YOH•nay, bahl•das•SAR•ay) *1478–1529* An Italian soldier, author, and statesperson. He wrote the book *The Courtier,* which gives a vivid and elegant picture of 15th- and 16th-century court life. p. 492

Catherine the Great *1729–1796* Russian empress who supported learning and the arts but neglected the Russian peasant class. p. 621

Cavour, Camillo di (kah•VUR) *1810–1861* Italian statesperson who united much of northern Italy and encouraged Guiseppe Garibaldi to set up a kingdom of Italy. p. 593

Chandragupta Maurya (chuhn•druh•GOOP•tuh MOW•ree•uh) *c. 300s B.C.* Founder of the Maurya Empire in India. p. 212

Chandragupta I (chuhn•druh•GOOP•tuh) *c. 300s* Gupta emperor of India. He gave up his throne to his son Samudragupta. p. 215

Chandragupta II *c. 400s* Son of Samudragupta. He encouraged learning during his reign, which lasted from about 380 to 415. p. 215

Charlemagne (SHAR•luh•mayn) *742–814* King of the Franks and emperor of the Romans, also known as Charles the Great. He strengthened Christianity, resulting in the start of the Holy Roman Empire. p. 339

Charles V *1500–1558* King of Germany from 1516 to 1556. p. 500

Chiang Kai-shek (jee•AHNG ky•SHEK) *1887–1975* Chinese general and politician. He followed Sun Yatsen as president of the Chinese Nationalist government. p. 624

Churchill, Winston *1874–1965* British statesperson, author, and prime minister of Britain from 1940 to 1945. p. 613

Cicero (SIH•suh•roh) *106 B.C.–43 B.C.* Roman orator, statesperson, and philosopher. He served as a consul of Rome. p. 286

Cleisthenes (KLYS•thuh•neez) *c. 570 B.C.–508 B.C.* Athenian leader who is regarded as the founder of democracy. p. 253

Cleopatra *69 B.C.–30 B.C.* Egyptian queen who, with Mark Antony, planned to set up an independent empire until the Roman leader Octavian defeated them. p. 289

Clovis (KLOH•vuhs) *c. 466–511* Leader of the Franks, who captured the last Roman territory in Gaul. p. 333

Columbus, Christopher *1451–1506* Italian-born explorer for Spain who in 1492 sailed west from Spain and thought he had reached Asia but had actually reached islands near the Americas, lands that were unknown to Europeans. p. 504

Commodus (KAH•muh•duhs) *161–192* Roman emperor, son and successor of Marcus Aurelius. p. 325

Confucius (kuhn•FYOO•shuhs) *551 B.C.–479 B.C.* Philosopher considered to be the most revered person in Chinese history. His philosophy, known as Confucianism, became a guide for the way people lived. p. 219

Constantine (KAHN•stuhn•teen) *c. 280–337* Roman general and emperor. The Edict of Milan, which was issued in 313 (during his reign), made Christianity an accepted religion within the Roman Empire. p. 304

Copernicus, Nicolaus (koh•PER•nih•kuhs, nik•uh•LAY•uhs) *1473–1543* Polish astronomer and philosopher. Against popular belief, he formed the theory that Earth rotates on its axis and revolves around the sun. p. 493

Cortés, Hernando (kawr•TEZ, air•NAHN•doh) *1485–1547* Spanish conquistador who conquered the Aztec Empire. p. 510

Cyrus the Great *c. 585 B.C.–529 B.C.* Leader who built the Persian Empire and conquered Babylon. p. 196

D

Daji *c. 200s B.C.* Wife of King Zhouxin. p. 152

Darius I (duh•RY•uhs) *550 B.C.–486 B.C.* Persian ruler who brought order to the Persian Empire. He also built roads; established a postal system; and standardized weights, measures, and coinage. p. 198

David *c. 1010 B.C.–962 B.C.* Second king of Israel; led the defeat of the Philistines. p. 183

Democritus of Abdera (dih•MAH•kruh•tuhs) *c. 460–about c. 370 B.C.* Greek philosopher upon whose ideas much of the modern science of physics is based. p. 262

Dias, Bartholomeu (DEE•ahsh, bar•too•loo•MAY•oo) *1450–1500* Portuguese navigator who sailed around the tip of Africa and into the Indian Ocean. p. 504

Dido (DY•doh) In Roman mythology, said to be the founder and queen of Carthage. p. 190

Dio Cassius (DEE•oh KA•shuhs) *c. 155–235?* Roman historian and administrator. p. 325

Diocletian (dy•uh•KLEE•shuhn) *c. 245–c. 313* As emperor he tried to strengthen the struggling Roman Empire. p. 326

Drake, Francis *c. 1540–1596* Admiral who was the first English navigator to circumnavigate the globe. p. 506

E

Einhard (YN•hart) *c. 770–840* Frankish historian who wrote the *Life of Charlemagne.* p. 340

Elizabeth I *1533–1603* Daughter of Henry VIII and Anne Boleyn. Known as Good Queen Bess, she made England a world power during her 45-year reign; gave the East India Company the right to control trade between India and England. p. 506

Erasmus, Desiderius (ih•RAZ•muhs, day•see•DAIR•yuhs) *1466?–1536* Dutch humanist and scholar. p. 495

Eratosthenes (air•uh•TAHS•thuh•neez) *c. 275 B.C.–c. 195 B.C.* Greek scholar. Especially noted as an astronomer, he is credited with measuring the circumference and tilt of Earth, the size of Earth, and the distance from Earth to the sun and the moon. p. 269

Euclid (YOO•kluhd) *c. 300s B.C.* Greek teacher who began the study of geometry. p. 269

Ezana (AY•zah•nah) Fourth-century A.D. king of Aksum. He declared Aksum a Christian city. p. 353

F

Fatima *c. 616–633* Daughter of Muhammad and Khadija. p. 423

Faxian (FAH•SHYUHN) *c. 400s* Buddhist missionary from China who traveled in India and wrote about the scenes he observed. p. 215

Ferdinand *1452–1516* Spanish king who, with Queen Isabella, led the Reconquista, or Reconquest, to drive the Moors from Spain. He and Isabella paid for Columbus's expeditions to the Americas. p. 486

Fox, Vicente *1942–* President of Mexico. p. 659

Francis Ferdinand *1863–1914* Archduke of Austria-Hungary whose assassination in 1914 is considered the direct cause of World War I. p. 605

Frank, Anne *1929–1945* Young Jewish girl who hid with her family to escape the Nazi terror during the Holocaust. She is most remembered for the diary she kept while in hiding. She died in a German concentration camp. p. 616

Franklin, Benjamin *1706–1790* American leader who was sent to Britain to ask Parliament for representation. He was a writer of the Declaration of Independence, a delegate to the Constitutional Convention, and a respected scientist and business leader. p. 570

Frederick the Wise *1463–1525* German prince also known as Frederick III, who gave protection to Martin Luther. p. 500

G

Galilei, Galileo (ga•luh•LAY, ga•luh•LAY•oh) *1564–1642* Italian mathematician, astronomer, and physicist. He improved the telescope and used it to prove Nicolaus Copernicus's theory that Earth revolves around the sun. p. 494

Gama, Vasco da *c. 1460–1524* Portuguese navigator who completed the first voyage from western Europe around Africa to the East. p. 504

Gao Zong (GOW ZAWNG) *1100s* Chinese emperor who encouraged sea trade to improve China's economy. p. 458

Garibaldi, Giuseppe (GAR•uh•BAWL•dee, joo•SEP•ay) *1807–1882* Italian military and nationalist leader who fought for freedom in southern Italy. p. 593

Gautama, Siddhartha (GOW•tuh•muh, sih•DAR•tuh) *563 B.C.–c. 483 B.C.* Philosopher known as Buddha, or the "Enlightened One," who gave up worldly goods to search for enlightenment and truth. He founded the religion of Buddhism in India. p. 209

Genghis Khan (JENG•guhs KAHN) *c. 1162–1227* Mongol leader who began the Mongol Empire. p. 431

Genseric (GEN•suh•rik) *c. 390–477* King of the Vandals. p. 332

George III *1738–1820* King of Britain during the Revolutionary War. p. 532

Gilgamesh *c. 2700s B.C.* King of the ancient Sumerian city-state of Uruk. He is the subject of one of the world's oldest stories. p. 95

Gorbachev, Mikhail (gawr•buh•CHAWV, mee•kah•EEL) *1931–* Secretary general of the Communist party of the Soviet Union from 1985 to 1991. He supported new ideas that included restructuring the government and making it more open to Soviet citizens. p. 630

Gregory I *c. 540–604* Pope instrumental in developing important church teachings, setting up monasteries, and creating rules of behavior for priests. p. 339

Gregory VII *1020–1085* Pope who fought to establish the supremacy of the pope over the Church and the supremacy of the Church over the state. p. 484

Gutenberg, Johannes (GOO•tuhn•berg, yoh•HAHN•uhs) *1390–1468* German inventor who was the first to use movable type in Europe. p. 494

H

Hammurabi (ha•muh•RAH•bee) *c. 1792 B.C.–1750 B.C.* King of the city-state of Babylon. He compiled the set of laws known as the Code of Hammurabi. p. 101

Hannibal *247 B.C.–183 B.C.* Carthaginian general who attacked Rome during the Second Punic War. p. 285

Hargreaves, James *1720?–1778* English weaver who invented the spinning jenny. p. 574

Hatshepsut (hat•SHEP•soot) *c. 1503 B.C.–1482 B.C.* Female Egyptian pharaoh who expanded Egyptian trade routes. p. 126

Henry the Navigator *1394–1460* Portuguese prince and founder of a school of navigation. He made Portugal a world sea power. p. 504

Henry VIII *1491–1547* King of England who began the English Reformation by separating from the Roman Catholic Church and becoming supreme head of the Church of England. p. 506

Herodotus (hih•RAH•duh•tuhs) *c. 484 B.C.–c. 430 B.C.* Greek historian who traveled through most of the world known to the Greeks during his time. p. 118

Hippocrates (hih•PAH•kruh•teez) *c. 460 B.C.–c. 377 B.C.* Greek physician known as the Father of Medicine. p. 259

Hitler, Adolf *1889–1945* German politician and führer. As Nazi dictator of Germany, he planned to conquer the world, believing that the German race was superior to others. During his time in power, he ordered 12 million people killed. p. 612

Homer *c. 700s B.C.* Greek poet and author of the epic poems the *Iliad* and the *Odyssey*. Much of what we know of the Mycenaeans comes from his stories. p. 248

Hong Wu *1328–1398* Ruler who founded China's Ming dynasty. He drove out the Mongols, ending the Yuan dynasty. Although he unified all of China, he proved to be a cruel leader. p. 528

Horace *8 B.C.–A.D. 65* Roman poet. p. 297

Hudson, Henry *?–1611* Explorer who sailed up the Hudson River, giving the Dutch a claim to the area. p. 515

Hussein, Saddam (hoo•SAYN, suh•DAHM) *1935–* Military ruler of Iraq from 1979 until the Second Gulf War. p. 654

Ibn Battuta (IB•uhn bat•TOO•tah) *1304–?* Moroccan geographer and traveler. p. 523

Ibrahim Pasha (ih•brah•HEEM PAH•shah) *1789–1848* The grand vizier, or adviser, to Süleyman of the Ottoman Empire. p. 538

Imhotep (im•HOH•tep) *c. 2600s B.C.* Royal architect of Egypt who built Pharaoh Zoser's step pyramid in about 2650 B.C. p. 123

Isaac *c. 2000s B.C.* Son of Abraham, according to the Bible. p. 181

Isabella *1451–1504* Spanish queen who, along with King Ferdinand, led the Reconquista, or Reconquest, to drive the Moors from Spain. She and King Ferdinand paid for Columbus's expeditions to the Americas. p. 486

Ishmael *c. 2000s B.C.* Son of Abraham, according to the Bible. p. 181

Jacob *c. 2000s B.C.* Early leader of the descendants of the Israelites, according to the Bible. Later called Israel, he was the son of Isaac and grandson of Abraham. p. 181

Jahangir (juh•HAHN•gir) *1569–1627* The son of Akbar, who continued his father's policy of expansion for the Mogul Empire. p. 539

Jefferson, Thomas *1743–1826* Third President of the United States and the main writer of the Declaration of Independence. p. 566

Jesus *c. 4 B.C.–c. A.D. 30* The person whose life and teachings are the basis of Christianity. Believing him to be the Son of God, his disciples proclaimed him the Messiah and savior of humankind. p. 301

John *1167–1216* King of England who was made to sign the Magna Carta. p. 488

Johnson, Lyndon *1908–1973* Thirty-sixth President of the United States. p. 629

Jonson, Ben *1572–1637* English playwright and poet. p. 495

Justinian I *483–565* Byzantine emperor. His set of laws, known as the Justinian Code, is the basis of law in Europe today. p. 412

K

Kalidasa (kah•lih•DAH•suh) *c. 400s* An author, poet, and playwright during India's classical age, he is considered to be among India's greatest writers. p. 216

Kangxi (KAHNG•SHEE) The second emperor of the Qing dynasty in China. He ordered the creation of a dictionary of Chinese characters. p. 531

Kashta (KASH•tuh) *700s B.C.* King of ancient Kush in Nubia; father of Piye. p. 135

Kennedy, John F. *1917–1963* Thirty-fifth President of the United States. p. 628

Khadija (kah•DEE•juh) *c. 595–619* Wife of the prophet Muhammad. She provided encouragement to him and support for his mission. p. 421

Khrushchev, Nikita (KRUSH•chawf, nuh•KEE•tuh) *1894–1971* Soviet politician and premier. p. 628

Khufu (KOO•foo) *c. 2500s B.C.* Egyptian king who built the Great Pyramid at Giza, the most famous of Egypt's pyramids. p. 124

Kublai Khan (KOO•bluh KAHN) *1215–1294* Grandson of Genghis Khan and founder of the Mongol dynasty in China. p. 432

L

Lenin, Vladimir (LEH•nuhn) *1870–1924* Russian leader of the Communist revolution of 1917 and first premier of the Soviet Union. p. 621

Leo Africanus (LEE•oh af•rih•KAY•nuhs) *c. 1485–c. 1554* Arab traveler and geographer. For a long time his writings were the only source of information about the geography of Sudan. p. 444

Leo III *795–816* Pope who crowned Charlemagne emperor of Rome. p. 340

Leo X *1475–1521* Pope from 1513 to 1521. He was a patron of the arts but drained the papal treasury by his rich living. p. 498

Leonardo da Vinci (lee•uh•NAR•doh duh VIN•chee) *1452–1519* Italian Renaissance painter, sculptor, architect, engineer, and scientist. The *Mona Lisa* is one of his best-known works. p. 493

Li Si (LEE SUH) Adviser to Emperor Shi Huangdi of the ancient Qin dynasty in China. p. 222

Livy (LIH•vee) *59 B.C.–A.D. 17* Roman historian. p. 277

Locke, John *1632–1704* English writer and philosopher who was an important thinker during the period of the Enlightenment. p. 565

Louis (LOO•ee) **XVI** *1754–1793* King of France. His efforts to raise taxes led to the French Revolution. p. 567

Lula da Silva *1945–* Brazilian president who promised government and economic reform. p. 658

Luther, Martin *1483–1546* German religious reformer whose ideas led to the Protestant Reformation. p. 499

M

Macartney, George, Lord A British ambassador to China. p. 532

Machiavelli, Niccolò (ma•kee•uh•VEH•lee, NEE•koh•loh) *1469–1527* Italian statesperson and author whose book *The Prince* encouraged leaders to use whatever means necessary to keep control. p. 492

Magellan, Ferdinand (mah•JEH•luhn) *c. 1480–1521* Portuguese navigator who sailed through what is now known as the Strait of Magellan. One of his ships completed a circumnavigation of the globe. p. 506

Mahavira *c. 599 B.C.–490 B.C.* An Indian prince who founded Jainism. p. 209

Malakaye *c. 500s B.C.* Queen of Kush in about 500 B.C. p. 137

Manco Capac (MAHNG•koh KAH•pahk) *c. 2000s B.C.* According to legend, the founder of the Inca city of Cuzco. p. 385

BIOGRAPHICAL DICTIONARY

Mandela, Nelson *1918–* South African leader of the African National Congress. He was imprisoned for 25 years for conspiracy to overthrow the South African government. Served as president of South Africa. p. 645

Mansa Musa *?–c. 1332* Emperor of Mali who is remembered for his pilgrimage to Mecca. During his rule Mali became known as a wealthy state and a center of learning. p. 443

Mao Zedong (MOW ZUH•DUNG) *1893–1976* Chinese soldier and statesperson. He was chairman of the Communist party and of the People's Republic of China. p. 625

Marcus Aurelius (MAHR•kus oh•REE•lee•uhs) *121–180* The last Roman emperor during the *Pax Romana*, or Rome's time of peace. p. 324

Mark Antony *c. 82 B.C.–30 B.C.* Roman orator and general. He lost control of Roman lands when he was defeated by Octavian in 31 B.C. p. 288

Marquette, Jacques *1637–1675* French Jesuit missionary and explorer in North America. p. 515

Marx, Karl *1818–1883* German political philosopher. With Friedrich Engels, he wrote *The Communist Manifesto* and *Das Kapital*—books on social and political reform. p. 582

Mary Along with her husband, William of Orange, agreed to the English Bill of Rights in order to rule England. p. 565

Matope (mah•TOH•pay) Builder of the Mutapa Empire in Africa. p. 524

Maximian (mak•SIM•ee•uhn) Ruled the Roman Empire along with Diocletian. He ruled the western part of the Roman Empire, and Diocletian ruled the eastern part. p. 326

Mazzini, Giuseppe (maht•SEE•nee, joo•SEP•ay) *1805–1872* Italian patriot and founder of Young Italy, a group that worked to unite Italy under a republican form of government. p. 593

Medici, Cosimo de' (MED•ee•chee) *1519–1574* Duke of Florence and a supporter of the arts. p. 491

Mehmed II (meh•MET) *1432–1481* Sultan of the Ottoman Empire who organized a well-run government and encouraged education. p. 536

Menes (MEE•neez) *c. 3000 B.C.* According to legend, the king who united ancient Egypt. p. 120

Mentuhotep II (men•too•HOH•tep) *c. 2005 B.C.* First ruler of the Middle Kingdom. He restored unity to Egypt. p. 124

Mentuhotep III *c. 1900s B.C.* The son of Mentuhotep II. He reopened the desert trade route through the Wadi Hammamat to the Red Sea and resumed trade with Punt. p. 124

Mentuhotep IV *c. 1900s B.C.* The last king of the eleventh dynasty of Egypt. p. 125

Michelangelo Buonarroti (my•kuh•LAN•juh•loh bwaw•naw•RAW•tee) *1475–1564* Italian Renaissance sculptor, painter, architect, and poet. He is perhaps best remembered for his Sistine Chapel frescoes. p. 493

Mill, John Stuart *1806–1873* English philosopher and economist. He studied the conflict among social classes in Europe. p. 581

Milosevic, Slobodan (mee•LOH•shuh•vich, SLOH•buh•dahn) Former president of Yugoslavia known for his harsh rule. p. 655

Minamoto Yoritomo (MEE•nah•moh•toh yoh•REE•toh•moh) *1147–1199* As shogun he created a system that ended in Japan's being torn by civil war. p. 369

Minos (MY•nuhs) *c. 2000s B.C.* According to legend, the ruler of ancient Crete during the years of its greatest success. p. 245

More, Thomas *1478–1535* English statesperson and author. p. 495

Morse, Edward S. *1838–1925* An American scientist who made an important archaeological find, the discovery of pottery from an ancient people in Japan known as the Jomon. p. 364

Moses *c. 1200s B.C.* Prophet and lawgiver who, according to the Bible, led the Israelites out of Egyptian captivity and received the Ten Commandments from God. p. 182

Motecuhzoma I (maw•tay•kwah•SOH•mah) *1466–1520* Ruler of the Aztecs, responsible for much of the growth of the Aztec Empire; also known as Montezuma. p. 379

Motecuhzoma II *c. 1480–1520* Aztec emperor defeated by Hernando Cortés in 1520. p. 380

Muhammad *c. 570–632* Prophet who brought the message of Islam to the world. p. 421

Murasaki Shikibu, Lady (MUR•ah•SAHK•ee SHEE•kee•BOO) *c. 978–1026* Japanese writer of *The Tale of Genji*. Her work is considered the first real novel in the world and is a classic of Japanese literature. p. 368

Mussolini, Benito (moo•suh•LEE•nee) *1883–1945* Italian dictator and Fascist prime minister of Italy. p. 613

Mutota (moo•TOH•tah) Began the campaign to unite Africa. p. 524

N

Nabonidus (nah•ben•EYE•dahs) *c. 500s B.C.* The last king of the New Babylonian Empire. p. 111

Narmer *c. 2900s B.C.* King who may have united Upper Egypt and Lower Egypt of ancient Egypt. p. 121

Nebuchadnezzar (neh•buh•kuhd•NEH•zer) *c. 630–561 B.C.* King of the New Babylonian Empire. He is remembered for such building projects as the Tower of Babel and the Hanging Gardens of Babylon. p. 110

Nerfertiti (nef•er•TEET•ee) *c. 1300s B.C.* Wife of Akhenaton. p. 127

Nicholas II *1868–1918* Russian czar when the Russian Revolution began. p. 621

Nixon, Richard *1913–1994* Thirty-seventh President of the United States. p. 630

Nur Jahan (NOOR juh•HAHN) *?–c. 1645* Empress during the rule of Jahangir, she ruled the Mogul Empire on her husband's behalf. p. 539

O

Odoacer (OH•duh•way•ser) *433–493* Germanic chief who overthrew the Roman emperor in the west. p. 332

Olympias (oh•LIM•pee•uhs) *c. 375 B.C.–316 B.C.* Macedonian queen who was mother of Alexander the Great. p. 264

Ovid (AH•vuhd) *43 B.C.–A.D. 18* Roman poet. p. 297

P

Pachacuti (pah•chah•KOO•tee) *?–1471* Inca ruler whose empire extended from Peru to Ecuador. p. 385

Paul *c. 5 B.C.–c. A.D. 62* A Jew who converted to Christianity and became an apostle. He founded new churches and wrote many epistles, or letters, about Jesus to church members. p. 303

Pepin III *c. 714–768* King of the Franks and father of Charlemagne. p. 340

Pericles (PAIR•uh•kleez) *c. 495 B.C.–429 B.C.* Leader who ruled Athens during its Golden Age. p. 258

Perry, Matthew *1794–1858* American naval officer who pressured Japan to open its ports for trade with the United States and other countries. p. 596

Peter the Great *1672–1725* Russian czar from 1682 to 1725 who helped place Russia among the great European powers. p. 620

Philip II *382 B.C.–336 B.C.* King of Macedonia and father of Alexander the Great. p. 264

Philip II *1527–1598* King of Spain who sent the Spanish Armada to attack England. p. 507

Pilate, Pontius *?B.C.–c. A.D. 36* Roman governor of Judaea. He was the judge at Jesus's trial and sentenced him to death by crucifixion. p. 302

Piye (PEE•yeh) *c. 751 B.C.–716 B.C.* King of Kush and son of Kashta; he conquered Lower Egypt. He is also known as Piankhi. p. 135

Pizarro, Francisco (pee•SAR•oh, frahn•SEES•koh) *1475?–1541* Spanish conquistador who conquered the Inca Empire. p. 511

Plato (PLAY•toh) *c. 428 B.C.–c. 348 B.C.* Greek philosopher, student of Socrates, and teacher of Aristotle. p. 260

Pliny the Younger (PLIH•nee) *c. 61–c. 113* Roman government official in Asia Minor. He is perhaps best remembered for his account of the volcanic eruption of Vesuvius. p. 298

Polo, Maffeo Trader from Venice; uncle of Marco Polo. p. 434

Polo, Marco *1254–1324* Italian traveler who was among the first European traders to visit China and record his experiences. p. 434

Polo, Niccolò Trader from Venice; father of Marco Polo. p. 434

Polycarp *69–155* Bishop who was killed for refusing to give up his belief in Christianity. p. 303

Pompey (PAHM•pee) *106 B.C.–48 B.C.* Roman general and statesperson who became consul after Lucius Sulla. p. 286

Putin, Vladimir (POO•tin, VLAD•ih•mihr) *1952–* Russian government official and political leader; second elected president of Russia. p. 658

Puyi (POO•EE) *1906–1967* The last emperor of China. p. 533

Pythagoras of Samos (pah•THAG•or•ahs) *c. 580 B.C.–500 B.C.* Greek philosopher and mathematician; the inventor of geometry. p. 262

Q

Qianlong (CHYAHN•LUHNG) *1711–1799* The grandson of Kangxi; he expanded China's control and supported the arts. p. 531

R

Raleigh, Walter (RAH•lee) *1554–1618* English explorer who used his own money to set up England's first colony in North America, on Roanoke Island near what is now North Carolina. p. 506

Reagan, Ronald *1911–2004* Fortieth President of the United States. p. 630

Romulus Augustulus (RAHM•yoo•luhs ah•GUS•tyoo•luhs) The last emperor of the Western Roman Empire. p. 332

Roosevelt, Franklin D. *1882–1945* Thirty-second President of the United States. p. 612

Roxelana (rahk•suh•LAHN•uh) *c. 1600s* Wife and adviser of Süleyman, who led the Ottoman Empire. p. 538

S

Saint Patrick *c. 385–461* Christian missionary, also known as the Apostle of Ireland. p. 339

San Martín, José de (san mar•TEEN) *1778–1850* Argentinian soldier and statesperson; led the fight for independence from Spanish rule in southern South America. p. 569

Sargon (SAR•gon) *c. 2334 B.C.–2279 B.C.* Warrior who founded the Akkadian Empire and so became the first ruler of an empire. p. 98

Saul *c. 1000s B.C.* First king of Israel. p. 183

Scipio (SIH•pee•oh) *c. 237 B.C.–183 B.C.* Roman general who defeated Hannibal of Carthage. p. 285

Sennacherib (suh•NA•kuh•ruhb) *c. 700s B.C.–681 B.C.* King of Assyria from 704 B.C. to 681 B.C. p. 107

Shabaka (SHA•bah•kah) *?–695 B.C.* Piye's brother and the pharaoh who established the Kushite dynasty. p. 135

Shah Jahan (SHAH juh•HAHN) *1592–1666* During his rule Mogul power reached its highest point. He constructed the Taj Mahal. p. 539

Shakespeare, William *1564–1616* English dramatist and poet. He is considered to be among the greatest writers of all time. p. 495

Shanakdakhete *c. 100s B.C.* Queen of Meroë. p. 137

Shi Huangdi (SHIR HWAHNG•DEE) *c. 259 B.C.–210 B.C.* Ruler of the Qin dynasty and unifier of China. p. 221

Shun Chinese ruler before Yu the Great. p. 148

Sinan (suh•NAHN) *1489–1588* Considered the greatest Ottoman architect, his ideas influenced nearly all later Turkish architecture. p. 538

Smith, Adam *1723–1790* A Scottish economist and author who wrote *The Wealth of Nations*, a book on the workings of capitalism. p. 579

Smith, John *1580–1631* English explorer who, as leader of the Jamestown settlement, saved its people from starvation. p. 515

Socrates (SAH•kruh•teez) *c. 470 B.C.–c. 399 B.C.* Greek philosopher who taught by asking questions. p. 260

Solomon *c. 900s B.C.* David's son and king of Israel under whose rule Israel rose to the height of its greatness. p. 183

Solon *c. 630 B.C.–c. 560 B.C.* Poet and statesperson who helped bring democracy to the Greek city-state of Athens. p. 253

Sophocles (SAH•fuh•kleez) *c. 496 B.C.–c. 406 B.C.* Ancient Greek writer of tragedies, or serious plays. p. 259

Stalin , Joseph (STAH•luhn) *1879–1953* Soviet dictator after Lenin's death. During his rule the Soviet Union became a totalitarian state and a world power. p. 622

Stowe, Harriet Beecher *1811–1896* American abolitionist who in 1852 wrote the book *Uncle Tom's Cabin*. p. 583

Strabo *?64 B.C.–A.D. 23?* Greek geographer. p. 185

Süleyman I (SOO•lay•mahn) *c. 1494–1566* Sultan whose reign was considered a high point of the Ottoman Empire. He made Istanbul into a great capital and encouraged arts and sciences. p. 537

Sulla, Lucius *138 B.C.–78 B.C.* Roman general, politician, and dictator of Rome for three years. p. 286

Sun Yat-sen (SUN YAHT•SEN) *1866–1925* Chinese statesperson and revolutionary leader of the Guomindang, or People's Nationalist party. p. 624

Tacitus (TA•suh•tuhs) *c. 55–c. 117* Roman historian. p. 297

Thabo Mbeki (TAH•boh em•BEK•ee) *1942–* South African president. p. 645

Theodora *c. 500–548* Empress and wife of Justinian I of the Byzantine Empire. Her influence helped women gain rights. p. 413

Theodosius I (thee•uh•DOH•shuhs) *c. 347–395* Roman emperor who in 392 made Christianity the official religion of the Roman Empire. p. 305

Thucydides (thoo•SIH•duh•deez) A Greek historian. p. 260

Thutmose I (thoot•MUH•suh) *c. 1500s B.C.* Pharaoh who expanded Egypt's rule far into Nubia. Father of Hatshepsut. p. 126

Tomyris (tuh•MY•ruhs) *c. 600s B.C.* Queen whose land was invaded by Cyrus the Great of Persia. Cyrus was killed during the battle with her armies. p. 197

Touré, Samori *c. 1830–1900* Led 30,000 soldiers in a 15-year campaign to keep the French from controlling lands in Africa. p. 586

Toussaint-Louverture, François (too•SAN loo•vair•TYOOR, fran•SWAH) *c. 1743–1803* Haitian general and liberator who established the free and independent country of Haiti. p. 569

Truman, Harry S. *1884–1972* Thirty-third President of the United States. p. 636

Tutankhamen (too•tang•KAH•muhn) *c. 1370 B.C.–1352 B.C.* During his brief rule as pharaoh, his ministers restored the old religion of Egypt. He was buried in a solid-gold coffin. p. 128

Urban II (ER•ben) *1042–1099* Pope who called on all Christians to fight in the First Crusade to retake Jerusalem from the Muslims. p. 485

Vespasian (ve•SPAY•zhuhn) Roman emperor who ordered the building of the Colosseum. p. 296

Vespucci, Amerigo (veh•SPOO•chee, uh•MAIR•ih•goh) *1454–1512* Italian navigator who explored the coast of what is now Brazil. North and South America are named after him. p. 506

Victor Emmanuel *1820–1878* The king of Sardinia and first king of a united Italy. p. 593

Virgil (VER•juhl) *70 B.C.–19 B.C.* Roman poet who wrote the epic the *Aeneid,* about Rome's heroic past. p. 297

Vortigern (VAWR•tuh•gern) According to legend, British king who helped create the kingdom that became known as England. p. 333

Washington, George *1732–1799* First United States President, leader of the Continental army during the Revolutionary War, and president of the Constitutional Convention. p. 566

Watt, James *1736–1819* Scottish engineer and inventor who made many improvements to the steam engine. p. 574

Wilhelm I *1797–1888* King of Prussia and German emperor. p. 593

William of Orange *1626–1650* The prince of Orange and husband of Mary; to become king and queen of England, they had to agree to the English Bill of Rights. p. 565

Wilson, Woodrow *1856–1924* Twenty-eighth President of the United States, who held office during World War I. p. 606

X

Xerxes (ZERK•seez) *c. 519 B.C.–c. 465 B.C.* King of Persia and son of Darius I. p. 199

Xilingshi (SEE•LING•SHIR) *c. 2700s B.C.* Chinese ruler's wife who, according to a legend, discovered silk in 2700 B.C. p. 150

Yi First ruler of the Choson kingdom of early Korea, which introduced paper money and coins into the kingdom in the 1400s. p. 363

Yong Le (YUHNG LEH) *1360–1424* The power of China's Ming dynasty reached its highest point during his reign. p. 529

Yu the Great *c. 2000s B.C.* Believed by some to have been king of the Huang He valley in about 2000 B.C. According to legend, his family started the Xia dynasty. p. 148

Zarathustra (zar•uh•THOOS•truh) *c. 600s B.C.–c. 500s B.C.* Persian religious leader who founded a religion now known as Zoroastrianism. p. 200

Zheng He (JUHNG HUH) *1400s* Chinese admiral whose explorations strengthened China's power in sea trade. p. 458

Zhouxin (JOH•SHIN) *c. 200s B.C.* Last king of the Shang dynasty. p. 152

Zoscales (zohs•KAL•eez) King of Aksum during the first century A.D. p. 353

Zoser *c. 2600s B.C.* King of Egypt in the twenty-seventh century B.C. p. 123

BIOGRAPHICAL
DICTIONARY

Gazetteer

The Gazetteer is a geographical dictionary that will help you locate places discussed in this book. The page number tells where each place appears on a map.

A

Accra (AH•kruh) The capital of Ghana. (5°N, 0°W) p. 527

Acre A city located on the west coast of Israel. (33°N, 35°E) p. 646

Addis Ababa The capital of Ethiopia. (9°N, 38°E) p. 43

Adriatic Sea An arm of the Mediterranean Sea; located east of Italy and west of the Balkan Peninsula. p. 278

Adulis (AH•joo•luhs) A port city in the ancient kingdom of Aksum, located on the Red Sea. p. 349

Aegean Sea (ih•JEE•uhn) An arm of the Mediterranean Sea between Asia Minor and Greece. p. 246

Afghanistan A country in central Asia; located between Pakistan and Iran. p. 47

Africa One of the world's seven continents. p. 21

Agade *See* Akkad. p. 100

Agra The capital of the historic Mogul Empire; located in north-central India on the Yamuna River. (27°N, 78°E) p. 539

Akkad (AH•kahd) The capital of the historic Akkadian Empire; located in southwestern Asia. p. 100

Aksum (AHK•soom) The capital of the ancient kingdom of Aksum. p. 349

Al Mahalla al Kubra A city in northern Egypt, in the Nile Delta. (31°N, 31°E) p. 33

Al Minya A city in northern Egypt, on the Nile River. (28°N, 31°E) p. 33

Albania A European country located on the Balkan Peninsula, on the Adriatic Sea. p. 605

Alexandria (a•lig•ZAN•dree•uh) A port on the Mediterranean Sea; located on the northern coast of Egypt on the Nile Delta; also the name of many other cities founded by Alexander the Great. (31°N, 30°E) p. 287

Algeria A country in northern Africa; located on the coast of the Mediterranean Sea. p. 585

Algiers The capital of Algeria; located in north-central Algeria on the Bay of Algiers. (37°N, 3°E) p. 537

Alps The largest group of mountains in south-central Europe; located in France, Switzerland, Italy, Austria, Slovenia, Bosnia and Herzegovina, Serbia and Montenegro, Albania, and Croatia. p. 194

Al-Ubaid (oo•BAYD) An ancient settlement; located in present-day southeastern Iraq. (31°N, 46°E) p. 69

Amazon River The largest river in the world; flows across northern Brazil in South America and into the Atlantic Ocean. p. 37

Amri An early city in the Indus Valley, on the Indus River. p. 143

Amur River A river in northeastern Asia; forms part of the border between Russia and China. p. 27

Anatolia (a•nuh•TOH•lee•uh) A peninsula in southwestern Asia, which forms the Asian part of present-day Turkey; also known as Asia Minor. p. 191

Andes A mountain system in South America, extending along the western coast from Panama to Tierra del Fuego. p. 385

Andorra A country in western Europe located in the Pyrenees mountains between Spain and France. p. 332

Andorra la Vella The capital of Andorra. (42°N, 2°E) p. 332

Angola A former part of the historic African kingdom of Kongo and a colony of Portugal; present-day country in southern Africa on the Atlantic coast. p. 585

Ankara The capital of Turkey. (40°N, 33°E) p. 43

Antananarivo The capital of Madagascar. (19°S, 47°E) p. 43

Antarctica One of the world's seven continents. p. 55

Antioch A center of early Christianity; located in western Asia Minor near the town of Yalvac, Turkey. (36°N, 36°E) p. 303

Anyang (AHN•YAHNG) The last capital of the Shang dynasty of ancient China; city located in present-day east-central China. (36°N, 114°E) p. 149

Apennines (A•puh•nynz) A mountain range that runs north and south through the center of Italy. p. 278

Apia The capital of Samoa. (13°S, 171°W) p. 546

Arabia The historic name for the lands now known as the Arabian Peninsula, the Sinai Peninsula, Syria, and Mesopotamia. p. 423

Arabian Peninsula A peninsula bordered by the Red Sea, the Persian Gulf, and the Arabian Sea in southwestern Asia; location of the countries of Saudi Arabia, Yemen, Oman, the United Arab Emirates, Qatar, and Kuwait. p. 182

Arabian Sea The sea located west of India and east of the Arabian Peninsula; forms the southern border of southwestern Asia. p. 27

Aral Sea (AIR•uhl) A large inland body of water that flows through the countries of Kazakhstan and Uzbekistan in central Asia. p. 622

Archangel'sk A Russian port city in Europe. (65°N, 41°E) p. 622

Arctic Ocean One of the world's four oceans. p. 27

Argentina A country in South America, on the Atlantic coast. p. 385

Armenia A country in western Asia. p. 452

Asia One of the world's seven continents. p. 21

Asia Minor A peninsula at the western end of Asia; located between the Black Sea and the Mediterranean Sea; now occupied by part of Turkey. p. 191

Assisi A town in central Italy; home of St. Francis of Assisi during the Middle Ages. (43°N, 13°E) p. 491

Assur (AH•sur) (also called Assyria) An ancient Mesopotamian city on the Tigris River. (36°N, 43°E) p. 108

Assyria (uh•SIR•ee•uh) An ancient empire in southwestern Asia. p. 182

Asunción The capital of Paraguay. (25°S, 57°W) p. 43

Aswan An ancient trade center and present-day city located in southeastern Egypt, on the Nile River near Lake Nasser and the Aswan High Dam. (24°N, 33°E) p. 33

Asyut A city in central Egypt, located on the Nile River. (27°N, 31°E) p. 33

Atacama Desert A desert in northern Chile. p. 385

Athens An ancient Greek city-state and the capital of present-day Greece; located near the southeastern coast of Greece. (38°N, 24°E) p. 251

Atlantic Ocean One of the world's four oceans. p. 27

Atlas Mountains A mountain system in northern Africa. p. 194

Attica (A•tih•kuh) An ancient region in the southeastern part of the Greek mainland; home of the ancient Greek city-state of Athens. p. 251

Australia One of the world's seven continents; a present-day country filling the continent of Australia. p. 21

Austria A country in central Europe. p. 607

Austria-Hungary A former empire in east-central Europe. p. 605

Azerbaijan (a•zer•by•JAHN) A country in southeastern Europe, located west of the Caspian Sea; formerly part of the Soviet Union. p. 630

B

Babylon The capital of the ancient Babylonian Empire; located on the Euphrates River in central Iraq. (33°N, 44°E) p. 110

Babylonia (ba•buh•LOH•nyuh) An ancient kingdom in the lower Tigris-Euphrates river valley in southwestern Asia. p. 198

Bactria An ancient country of southwestern Asia. p. 198

Baghdad The capital of Iraq; located on both sides of the Tigris River in the eastern part of the country. (33°N, 44°E) p. 452

Bahamas An archipelago of about 700 islands off the east coast of Florida. p. 46

Balearic Islands (ba•lee•AIR•ik) An island group in the western Mediterranean Sea, off the eastern coast of Spain; forms the Spanish province of Baleares. p. 194

Balkan Peninsula A peninsula extending from mainland Europe into the Mediterranean Sea; occupied by Greece, Albania, Slovenia, Croatia, Bosnia and Herzegovina, Serbia and Montenegro, Romania, Bulgaria, and Turkey. p. 414

Baltic Sea The sea located on the southeastern side of the Scandinavian Peninsula. p. 464

Bamako The capital of Mali. (12°N, 8°W) p. 43

Bangkok The capital of Thailand; located on the southern end of the Chao Phraya River on the Gulf of Thailand. (14°N, 100°E) p. 43

Bangladesh (bahn•gluh•DESH) A country in southern Asia on the coast of the Bay of Bengal. p. 143

Bangui The capital of the Central African Republic. (4°N, 18°E) p. 43

Barcelona A province and city of Spain; located northeast of Madrid. (41°N, 2°E) p. 332

Barents Sea A part of the Arctic Ocean; located between Spitsbergen and Novaya Zemlya. p. 27

Batavia A former trade center; located on the island of Java. p. 540

Bay of Bengal An inlet of the Indian Ocean that runs alongside eastern India. p. 143

Beaufort Sea Part of the Arctic Ocean northeast of Alaska. p. 27

Beersheba (bir•SHEE•buh) An ancient city in southern Israel. (31°N, 35°E) p. 182

Beidha An ancient settlement in southwestern Asia. p. 69

Beijing (bay•JING) The capital of China; located in northeastern China; present-day name for Kublai Khan's historic capital of Khanbalik. (40°N, 116°E) p. 43

Belarus (byay•luh•ROOS) A country in Asia; located north of Ukraine, west of Russia, and east of Poland; formerly part of the Soviet Union. p. 47

Belém A city on the eastern coast of Brazil. p. 37

Belgium A country in western Europe; located on the coast of the North Sea. p. 605

Belgrade The capital of Serbia; located at the junction of the Sava and Danube Rivers. (45°N, 21°E) p. 607

Belize (buh•LEEZ) A country in Central America, located on the Yucatán Peninsula. p. 158

Belmopan The capital of Belize. (17°N, 88°W) p. 160

Bering Sea A part of the northern Pacific Ocean between northeastern Siberia and Alaska. p. 27

Berlin The capital of Germany; located in northeastern Germany. (53°N, 12°E) p. 605

Bethel A city in the ancient kingdom of Israel. p. 184

Bethlehem An ancient and present-day city in southwestern Asia; birthplace of Jesus, according to the Bible. (32°N, 35°E) p. 646

Black Sea A sea between Europe and Asia; surrounded by Bulgaria, Romania, Moldova, Ukraine, Russia, Georgia, and Turkey. p. 100

Blue Nile River A part of the Nile River in Africa. p. 117

Bogotá The capital of Colombia. (4°S, 74°W) p. 515

Bolivia A country in South America. p. 46

Bologna A historic and present-day city in north-central Italy. (45°N, 11°E) p. 491

Bombay *See* Mumbai.

Borneo An island on the Malay Archipelago. (1°N, 115°E) p. 540

Bosnia and Herzegovina (BAHZ•nee•uh hairt•suh•goh•VEE•nuh) A country in eastern Europe; part of the former Yugoslavia. p. 630

Boston An early English settlement and capital of present-day Massachusetts. (42°N, 71°W) p. 515

Botswana A country in southern Africa. p. 47

Brahmaputra River A river in southern Asia; flows through China, India, and Bangladesh into the Bay of Bengal. p. 539

Brazil A country in eastern South America. p. 385

Bristol A city on the Avon River, in southwestern England. (51°N, 3°W) p. 527

Britain *See* United Kingdom. p. 605

British Honduras The colonial name of Belize, a Central American country on the Caribbean Sea. p. 568

British Somaliland Former name of the now independent country of Somalia in northeastern Africa; once controlled by Italy and the British Empire. p. 585

Bruges (BROOZH) A historic city near the North Sea, in northwestern Belgium. (51°N, 3°E) p. 467

Brussels The capital of Belgium, in Europe. (51°N, 4°E) p. 607

Bucharest The capital of Romania. (44°N, 26°E) p. 605

Budapest The capital of Hungary; includes the former towns of Buda and Pest. (47°N, 19°E) p. 607

Buenos Aires (BWAY•nohs EYE•rays) A port city and capital of Argentina, in South America. (34°S, 58°W) p. 515

Buhen A city in ancient Egypt on the Nile River. p. 117

Bulgaria A country in southeastern Europe; located on the Balkan Peninsula. p. 47

Burkina Faso A country in western Africa. p. 47

Burma *See* Myanmar.

Byblos A city on the Mediterranean Sea in ancient Phoenicia. p. 191

Byzantium (buh•ZAN•tee•uhm) *See* Constantinople. p. 326

C

Cadiz (kah•DIZ) A port in southwestern Spain on the Gulf of Cádiz, an inlet of the Atlantic Ocean. p. 527

Cairo The capital of Egypt; located in northeastern Egypt on the Nile River. (30°N, 31°E) p. 125

Cajamarca A city in western Peru, in South America. (7°S, 76°W) p. 511

Calcutta *See* Kolkata.

Calicut A city in southwestern India, on the coast of the Arabian Sea. (11°N, 75°E) p. 540

Cambodia A country in southeastern Asia; located on the Indochina Peninsula. p. 629

Cameroon (ka•muh•ROON) A former French and British colony; now an independent country in western Africa. p. 585

Canaan An ancient region in southwestern Asia; located between the Jordan River and the Mediterranean Sea. p. 182

Canada A country in the northern part of North America. p. 46

Canary Islands An island group in the Atlantic Ocean; located off the northwestern coast of Africa. p. 585

Cape Town A seaport city and the capital of the country of South Africa. (34°S, 18°E) p. 43

Capri An island off the western coast of Italy in the Tyrrhenian Sea. p. 297

Caracas (kah•RAH•kahs) The capital of Venezuela, in South America; located near the coast of the Caribbean Sea. (11°N, 67°W) p. 515

Caribbean Sea The sea bordered by Central America, South America, and the West Indies. p. 27

Cartagena (kar•tah•HAY•nah) An ancient and present-day city in southeastern Spain; also called New Carthage. (38°N, 1°W) p. 287

Carthage (KAR•thij) An ancient Phoenician city-state; located on the northern coast of present-day Tunisia. (37°N, 10°E) p. 287

Caspian Sea A large salt lake between Europe and Asia, east of the Black Sea. p. 27

Çatal Hüyük (chah•TAHL hoo•YOOK) One of the earliest human agricultural settlements discovered, dating from c. 7000 B.C. to 5600 B.C.; located in central Turkey. (38°N, 33°E) p. 69

Caucasus Mountains (KAW•kuh•suhs) A mountain range between the Black and Caspian Seas; borders Russia, Georgia, and Azerbaijan. p. 198

Celebes (SEL•uh•beez) An Indonesian island; located in southeastern Asia in the Malay Archipelago. p. 540

Central African Republic A country in central Africa. p. 47

Cetinje The capital of the republic of Montenegro in the country of Serbia and Montenegro. p. 610

Ceylon *See* Sri Lanka. p. 587

Chad A country in northern Africa. p. 47

Chang Jiang (CHAHNG JYAHNG) A river in eastern China; flows from the Plateau of Tibet to the East China Sea. p. 27

Chang'an (CHAHNG•AHN) An ancient capital of the Han dynasty of China; now known as Xi'an, or Sian; located in central China on the Wei River. (34°N, 109°E) p. 222

Chanhu-Daro An early city in the Indus Valley, on the Indus River. p. 143

Chaoge An ancient city of the Shang dynasty. (35°N, 115°E) p. 149

Charles Town An early English settlement in North America. p. 515

Chatham Islands An island group located in the southern Pacific Ocean, east of New Zealand. p. 460

Chile (CHEE•lay) A country on the southwestern coast of South America. p. 385

China An ancient empire and present-day country in eastern Asia; currently the world's most heavily populated country. p. 149

Cologne (kuh•LOHN) A city in northwestern Germany on the Rhine River. (51°N, 7°E) p. 467

Colombia A country in northwestern South America. p. 385

Colombo The capital of Sri Lanka. (7°N, 80°E) p. 43

Congo River A river in central Africa; flows through the Democratic Republic of the Congo to the Atlantic Ocean. p. 349

Constantinople (kahn•stan•tuhn•OH•puhl) Formerly the ancient city of Byzantium; rebuilt, renamed, and made the capital of the Byzantine Empire by Constantine I in A.D. 330; now known as Istanbul, Turkey. (41°N, 28°E) p. 326

Copenhagen The capital and a port of Denmark. (56°N, 13°E) p. 607

Coral Sea A sea located north of Queensland, Australia, and south of Papua New Guinea. p. 546

Córdoba The historic capital of Andalusia; located in southern Spain on the Guadalquivir River. (38°N, 5°W) p. 424

Corinth An ancient city-state and a present-day city; located on the isthmus between the Peloponnesus and the Greek mainland. (38°N, 23°E) p. 246

Corsica A French island in the Mediterranean Sea; located west of Italy. (42°N, 9°E) p. 194

Costa Rica A country in Central America; located west of Panama; bordered by the Caribbean Sea and Pacific Ocean. p. 46

Côte d'Ivoire (koht dee•VWAHR) A country in western Africa; the Ivory Coast. p. 650

Crete A large Greek island located southeast of the Balkan Peninsula; separates the Mediterranean and Aegean Seas. p. 194

Croatia (kroh•AY•shuh) A country in southeastern Europe; part of the former Yugoslavia. p. 630

Cuba An island country located south of the United States in the Greater Antilles of the West Indies. p. 46

Cuzco (KOOS•koh) The capital of the ancient Inca Empire and a present-day city in southern Peru. (14°S, 72°W) p. 385

Cydonia An ancient Greek city-state, located on the island of Crete. p. 251

Cyprus An island country in the eastern Mediterranean Sea. p. 191

Cyrene (sy•REE•nee) An ancient city in northern Africa; located in present-day Libya on the Mediterranean Sea. (33°N, 22°E) p. 287

Czechoslovakia (che•kuh•sloh•VAH•kee•uh) A former country in central Europe; where the Czech Republic and Slovakia are today. p. 607

D

Damascus (duh•MAS•kuhs) The capital of Syria, in southwestern Asia. (33°N, 36°E) p. 191

Danube River (DAN•yoob) A river in central Europe; flows from southwestern Germany to the Black Sea. p. 27

Danzig A port in central northern Poland on the Gulf of Gdansk, an inlet of the Baltic Sea; now known as Gdansk. (54°N, 19°E) p. 464

Dead Sea A salt lake in Israel and Jordan; the world's lowest place at about 1,310 feet (400 m) below sea level. p. 646

Deccan Plateau (DEH•kuhn) A triangle-shaped plateau in central India, between the Western and Eastern Ghats. p. 207

Delhi (DEH•lee) A city in northern India. (29°N, 77°E) p. 539

Delphi (DEL•fy) A sacred place to the ancient Greeks; located in central Greece, near the Gulf of Corinth. (38°N, 23°E) p. 246

Democratic Republic of the Congo A country in central Africa. p. 47

Denmark A country in central Europe; occupies the northern part of the Jutland Peninsula. p. 605

Dominican Republic A country on the island of Hispaniola in the Caribbean Sea. p. 46

Dresden A German industrial city and the capital of Dresden district; located southeast of Leipzig. (51°N, 14°E) p. 615

Dutch East Indies Former name of Indonesia in southeastern Asia; consists of an archipelago extending from 95°E to 141°E. p. 540

E

East China Sea The part of the China Sea north of Taiwan. p. 149

Easter Island An island off the western coast of South America, in the Pacific Ocean. p. 460

Eastern Ghats (GAWTS) A chain of mountains in southeastern India. p. 143

Ecuador (EH•kwah•dohr) A country in northwestern South America; located on the Pacific coast. p. 385

Edessa (ih•DEH•suh) An ancient city in Asia Minor. (37°N, 38°E). p. 303

Edinburgh The capital of Scotland; located in southeastern Scotland, on the North Sea coast. (56°N, 3°W) p. 576

Egypt An ancient land and present-day country in northern Africa, on the coast of the Mediterranean and Red Seas. p. 125

Elba An Italian island in the Tyrrhenian Sea, off the northwestern coast of Italy. p. 491

Elbe River A river in northern Europe; flows from the Czech Republic across Germany and into the North Sea. p. 467

Elephantine A city in ancient Egypt, on an island in the Nile River. p. 117

Elis An ancient Greek city-state, located on the Peloponnesus. p. 251

England One of the four divisions of the United Kingdom; occupies most of the southern part of the United Kingdom. p. 467

English Channel An extension and connection of the Atlantic Ocean and the North Sea; south of the British Isles and north of France. p. 576

Ephesus An ancient Greek city-state in eastern Asia Minor near the coast of the Aegean Sea. p. 251

Eridu (ER•ih•doo) The earliest known Sumerian city; located in Mesopotamia near the Euphrates River in present-day southeastern Iraq. (31°N, 46°E) p. 69

Eritrea (air•ih•TREE•uh) A country on the Red Sea in northern Africa; located north of Ethiopia. p. 585

Erlitou An ancient city of the Shang dynasty. (35°N, 115°E) p. 149

Estonia A country in northeastern Europe; formerly part of the Soviet Union. p. 607

Ethiopia A country in eastern Africa. p. 47

Euphrates River (yoo•FRAY•teez) A river that begins in Turkey, flows through Syria and Iraq, and empties into the Persian Gulf. p. 69

Europe One of the world's seven continents. p. 21

Ezion-geber (ee•zee•uhn•GEE•ber) An ancient town and present-day archaeological site; located near Aqaba, in southwestern Jordan. (29°N, 35°E) p. 182

F

Fertile Crescent An area of land in southwestern Asia; extends from present-day Israel through Lebanon, Syria, Turkey, and Iraq to the Persian Gulf. p. 69

Fiji (FEE•jee) An island country in Melanesia, Oceania, in the southern Pacific Ocean. p. 546

Finland A country in northern Europe; located north of Estonia and east of Sweden on the Gulf of Bothnia. p. 607

Florence A city on the Arno River in central Italy. (44°N, 11°E) p. 491

Formosa *See* Taiwan. p. 587

France A country in western Europe. p. 605

French Equatorial Africa The colonial name of the former French territories in northern Africa—Chad, Ubangi-Shari, Gabon, and Middle Congo. p. 585

French Guiana An overseas department of France; located on the northern Atlantic coast of South America. p. 568

French Indochina The colonial name of former French territories in southeastern Asia; located where Cambodia, Laos, and Vietnam are now. p. 587

Funafuti The capital of Tuvalu. (8°S, 179°E) p. 546

Gabon A country in western Africa. p. 47

Ganges River (GAN•jeez) A holy river in India that flows from the Himalaya Mountains into the Bay of Bengal. p. 143

Gao (GOW) A trading center of the ancient Songhai Empire of western Africa; located on the Niger River in central Mali. (15°N, 4°W) p. 444

Gaul An ancient land that included most of the present-day countries of France and Belgium; once part of the Roman Empire. p. 331

Gaza (GAH•zuh) A city in southwestern Asia; located near the Mediterranean Sea. (32°N, 34°E) p. 646

Gaza Strip (GAH•zuh) An area of land around the city of Gaza, on the coast of the Mediterranean Sea. p. 646

Genoa A historic city-state trading center and present-day seaport on the Ligurian Sea, on the coast of northwestern Italy. (44°N, 9°E) p. 452

Georgia A country on the Black Sea in southeastern Europe; formerly part of the Soviet Union. p. 630

Germany A country in north-central Europe. p. 47

Ghana (GAH•nuh) A country on the western coast of Africa; called the Gold Coast by Portuguese and Dutch colonizers. p. 47

Giza (GEE•zuh) An ancient and present-day city in northeastern Egypt; located on the Nile River, across from Cairo; site of ancient pyramids. (30°N, 31°E) p. 125

Glasgow A port city near the Atlantic coast of southwestern Scotland. (56°N, 4°W) p. 576

Goa A state and city in India; located on the Malabar Coast. (16°N, 74°E) p. 540

Gobi A desert in eastern Asia; located in Mongolia and China. p. 452

Godavari River A river in central India. p. 143

Golan Heights A region in southwestern Asia under the control of Israel. (33°N, 36°E) p. 646

Gold Coast *See* Ghana. p. 585

Granada A province in the Sierra Nevada, in southern Spain. (37°N, 4°W) p. 303

Grand Canal A canal that flows through the city of Venice, in Italy. p. 42

Great Lakes A group of five freshwater lakes on the border between Canada and the United States; includes Lake Huron, Lake Ontario, Lake Erie, Lake Michigan, and Lake Superior. p. 27

Great Rift Valley An area in eastern Africa. p. 352

Great Zimbabwe An ancient African settlement; located in what is present-day Zimbabwe. p. 523

Greece Present-day country in Europe; located on the southern end of the Balkan Peninsula; site of the ancient Greek civilization. p. 287

Greenland The largest island in the world; located off northeastern North America; a territory of Denmark. p. 650

Guadalajara (gwah•duh•luh•HAR•uh) The capital of Jalisco state in central Mexico. (21°N, 103°W) p. 639

Guadalcanal An island of the Solomon Islands in the western Pacific Ocean. p. 546

Guadalquivir River A river in southern Spain. p. 424

Guam An unincorporated United States territory; largest and southernmost of the Mariana Islands; located in the western Pacific Ocean. p. 614

Guangzhou (GWAHNG•JOH) A Chinese port city located on the Zhu River in southeastern China; formerly called Canton. (23°N, 113°E) p. 540

Guatemala A country in Central America; former part of the region controlled by the Maya and later a colony of Spain. p. 158

Guilin (GWEE•LIN) A city in southern China. (25°N, 110°E). p. 24

Guinea (GIH•nee) A country in western Africa on the Atlantic coast. p. 47

Gulf of Aqaba (AH•kah•buh) An inlet of the Red Sea; located between Saudi Arabia and the Sinai Peninsula. p. 182

Gulf of Bothnia An inlet of the Baltic Sea, between Sweden and Finland. p. 467

Gulf of Mexico A gulf located south of the United States, east of Mexico, and west of Cuba. p. 27

Gulf of Suez An inlet of the Red Sea, between Egypt and the Sinai Peninsula. p. 182

Gulf of Tehuantepec An inlet of the Pacific Ocean, off the coast of southeastern Mexico. p. 158

Gulf of Thailand An inlet of the South China Sea; located between Malaysia and Thailand. p. 357

Gulf of Tonkin An inlet of the South China Sea; located between Vietnam and China. p. 357

Guyana (gee•AH•nuh) A country in the northern part of South America. p. 385

H

Hadrumetum (HA•druh•meh•tuhm) An ancient Phoenician colony in Africa, on the Mediterranean Sea. p. 194

Hainan An island in the South China Sea; located off the coast of southeastern China. (19°N, 110°E) p. 357

Haiti A country on the island of Hispaniola in the Caribbean Sea; located southeast of Cuba. p. 568

GAZETTEER

Hamburg A city in northern Germany; located near the Elbe River and the North Sea. (54°N, 10°E) p. 467

Hangzhou (HAHNG•JOH) An ancient and present-day city located on the eastern coast of central China. (30°N, 120°E) p. 452

Hanoi (ha•NOY) The capital of Vietnam; located on the northern Red River. (21°N, 106°E) p. 629

Haran A city on the Euphrates River in present-day Iraq. p. 182

Harappa (huh•RA•puh) An ancient center of Indus civilization; located in the Indus Valley, in present-day Pakistan. (31°N, 71°E) p. 143

Harbin The capital of Heilungkiang province, in northeastern China. (45°N, 126°E) p. 155

Havana The capital of Cuba. p. 515

Hebron (HEE•bruhn) An ancient city of Judaea; located southwest of Jerusalem on the West Bank. (32°N, 35°E) p. 184

Helsinki The capital and a port city of Finland, in Europe. (60°N, 25°E) p. 607

Himalayas (hih•muh•LAY•uhz) A mountain system on the northern edge of southern Asia; runs through Nepal, Bhutan, southern Tibet, and northern India. p. 149

Hindu Kush A mountain system that extends southwest from the Pamirs in eastern Tajikistan, through northwestern Afghanistan. p. 207

Hippo Regius An ancient Phoenician colony in northern Africa on the Mediterranean Sea. p. 194

Hiroshima (hir•uh•SHEE•muh) An industrial city located on the island of Honshu, Japan; a key city in World War II. (34°N, 133°E) p. 614

Hispaniola An island in the Greater Antilles of the West Indies in the Caribbean Sea; occupied by the countries of Haiti and the Dominican Republic. p. 511

Ho Chi Minh City A city in Vietnam. (11°N, 107°E) p. 43

Hoa Lu The capital of Vietnam from A.D. 968 to 1010. p. 359

Honduras A country in Central America. p. 46

Hong Kong A large city in southeastern China; formerly a British colony. (22°N, 114°E) p. 43

Hongshui River A river that flows through China to the South China Sea. p. 357

Honiara The capital of the Solomon Islands; located on Guadalcanal. (9°S, 160°E) p. 546

Honshu The largest of the four main islands of Japan. p. 365

Huang He (HWAHNG HUH) A river in China that flows east from the Plateau of Tibet; also known as the Yellow River. p. 149

Huixian An ancient city of the Shang dynasty. (35°N, 115°E) p. 149

Hungary A country in central Europe. p. 607

Iceland A European island country in the northern Atlantic Ocean; located southeast of Greenland. p. 627

India A country in southern Asia; occupies much of a large peninsula extending from central Asia into the Indian Ocean; the name given to the ancient land that is present-day Pakistan and India. p. 143

Indian Ocean One of the world's four oceans. p. 27

Indochina A peninsula in southeastern Asia that contains the present-day countries of Vietnam, Laos, Cambodia, Thailand, Myanmar (formerly Burma), and part of Malaysia. p. 540

Indonesia A country of islands in southeastern Asia. p. 460

Indus River A river in southern Asia; flows from Tibet through northern India and Pakistan and into the Arabian Sea. p. 143

Ionian Sea A sea located east of Italy and west of Greece. p. 246

Iquitos A city in northeastern Peru. (3°S, 73°W) p. 37

Iran A country in southwestern Asia; formerly known as Persia; located on the Persian Gulf. p. 196

Iraq A country in southwestern Asia; includes former lands of the Sumerians, Mesopotamians, Babylonians, and Assyrians. p. 92

Ireland A country in western Europe, often called the Republic of Ireland; located in the British Isles. p. 605

Isonzo River A river in Slovenia and northeastern Italy; area of heavy fighting during World War I. p. 605

Israel An ancient kingdom and present-day country; a holy land for Jews, Christians, and Muslims; located on the eastern coast of the Mediterranean Sea. p. 646

Istanbul (is•tuhn•BOOL) The largest city in Turkey; formerly Constantinople. (41°N, 28°E) p. 192

Isthmus of Panama (IS•muhs) A narrow land bridge containing the country of Panama; located between the Caribbean Sea and the Pacific Ocean; connects Central America and South America. p. 568

Isthmus of Tehuantepec A narrow land bridge between the Gulf of Mexico and the Pacific Ocean that connects North America and South America. p. 379

Italian Peninsula A boot-shaped peninsula that extends from south-central Europe into the Mediterranean Sea. p. 278

Italy An ancient land and present-day European country; located on the Italian Peninsula. p. 605

Iwo Jima (EE•woh JEE•muh) A center island of the Volcano Islands, Japan, located south of Tokyo; scene of heavy fighting during World War II. (27°N, 140°E) p. 614

Jakarta (Djakarta) The capital of Indonesia. (6°S, 106°E) p. 43

Jamaica An island country in the Greater Antilles in the Caribbean Sea. p. 511

Jamestown An early English settlement in North America. p. 515

Japan An island country in eastern Asia, off the Pacific coasts of China and Russia. p. 365

Jarmo The site of the ancient Kurdish village of Qallat Jarmo; located in northern Iraq. (36°N, 45°E) p. 69

Java The most populated island of Indonesia; located in southern Indonesia. p. 540

Java Sea A part of the Pacific Ocean north of Java, south of Borneo, and east of Sumatra. p. 614

Jenné (jeh•NAY) A city of the ancient Songhai Empire of western Africa; located on the Niger River in central Mali. (14°N, 4°W) p. 444

Jenne-Jeno (jeh•NAY juh•NOH) The first known city south of the Sahara; located on the Niger River in present-day Mali. (14°N, 4°W) p. 349

Jericho (JAIR•ih•koh) The oldest known city in the world; located north of the Dead Sea, in present-day Jordan. (32°N, 35°E) p. 69

Jerusalem The capital of Israel; a holy city for Jews, Christians, and Muslims. (32°N, 35°E) p. 487

Johannesburg A city located in the country of South Africa. (26°S, 28°E) p. 43

Joppa An ancient city in Israel, now known as Jaffa; located northwest of Jerusalem. (32°N, 35°E) p. 184

Jordan A country in southwestern Asia. p. 33

Jordan River A river that flows from the mountains of Syria in southwestern Asia into the Dead Sea. p. 646

Jutland A peninsula occupied by the mainland of Denmark and part of Germany. p. 605

K

Kalahari Desert A desert in southern Africa. p. 352

Kamchatka Peninsula (kuhm•CHAHT•kuh) A peninsula in northeastern Russia; surrounded by the Sea of Okhotsk and the Bering Sea. p. 622

Kampala The capital of Uganda. (0°N, 32°E) p. 43

Kanem (KAH•nem) An ancient kingdom of western Africa, located on the shores of Lake Chad. p. 444

Karakorum (kar•uh•KOHR•uhm) The capital of Mongolia under Genghis Khan; located in the Gobi on the southern end of the Orhon River. (47°N, 103°E) p. 434

Kathmandu The capital of Nepal, on the Indian subcontinent; located in a valley of the Himalayas. (27°N, 85°E) p. 43

Kaunas The former capital of Lithuania. (55°N, 24°E) p. 607

Kazakhstan (ka•zak•STAHN) A country in central Asia; formerly part of the Soviet Union. p. 630

Kenya A country in eastern Africa. p. 47

Kerma A capital of the ancient kingdom of Kush; located on the Nile River in Sudan. (20°N, 30°E) p. 133

Khanbalik (kahn•buh•LEEK) See Beijing. p. 434

Khartoum (kar•TOOM) The capital of present-day Sudan. (15°N, 32°E) p. 43

Khyber Pass (KY•ber) A narrow pass through the Hindu Kush mountains on the border between Afghanistan and Pakistan in Asia. p. 539

Kiev (KEE•ef) The capital of Ukraine; located on the Dnieper River, in central Ukraine. (50°S, 31°E) p. 464

Kilwa (KIL•wah) An ancient Swahili trading city on a small island near present-day Tanzania in eastern Africa. (9°S, 40°E) p. 523

King's Lynn A town in England located in Norfolk on the Ouse River. (53°N, 0°) p. 467

Kinshasa The capital of the Democratic Republic of the Congo. (4°S, 15°E) p. 43

Kiribati A country of 33 islands in the Pacific Ocean near the equator. p. 546

Kish An ancient Sumerian city-state on the Euphrates River; located in present-day Iraq. (33°N, 45°E) p. 94

Knossos (NAHS•uhs) The capital of the ancient Minoan civilization; located on the island of Crete off the coast of present-day Greece. (35°N, 25°E) p. 246

Koguryo (koh•gur•YOH) One of the Three Kingdoms of ancient Korea; it occupied the northern part of the peninsula. p. 360

Kolkata (Calcutta) A large city and port in northeastern India; located on the Hugli River. (22°N, 88°E) p. 43

Kongju The capital of the kingdom of Paekche, in ancient Korea. (36°N, 127°E) p. 360

Korea A peninsula off the coast of China; now divided between two countries—North Korea and South Korea. p. 587

Koror The capital of Palau in the western Pacific Ocean. (7°N, 134°E) p. 546

Krishna River A river in southern India. p. 143

Kumbi-Saleh (KOOM•bee SAH•lay) The ancient capital of the empire of Ghana in western Africa; located in the southwestern corner of present-day Mauritania. (16°N, 15°W) p. 444

Kunlun Shan (KOON•LOON SHAN) A mountain range in western China. p. 149

Kush An ancient Nubian kingdom; located in the Nile Valley in the northern part of present-day Sudan. p. 133

Kyongju The capital of the kingdom of Silla, in ancient Korea. (35°N, 129°E) p. 360

Kyrgyzstan (kir•gih•STAN) A country in central Asia; formerly part of the Soviet Union. p. 630

Kyushu (kee•OO•shoo) The southernmost of the four main islands of Japan. p. 365

L

Lagash (LAY•gash) A city of ancient Sumer and a city-state in ancient Babylonia; located near the coast of the Persian Gulf, in southeastern Iraq. (32°N, 47°E) p. 94

Lagos A seaport in Nigeria. (6°N, 3°E) p. 43

Lake Chad A lake in northern Africa on the border of Chad, Cameroon, Nigeria, and Niger. p. 444

Lake Izabal A lake in eastern Guatemala. p. 160

Lake Malawi A large lake along the eastern border of Malawi in southern Africa; also called Lake Nyasa. p. 523

Lake Nasser A lake in southern Egypt and northern Sudan. p. 33

Lake Petén-Itzá (peh•TEN•eet•sah) A lake in northern Guatemala. p. 160

Lake Tanganyika (tan•guhn•YEE•kuh) A lake in Tanzania and the Democratic Republic of the Congo, in the Great Rift Valley of southern Africa. p. 523

Lake Texcoco (tes•KOH•koh) A dry lake near Mexico City; an island in the lake was the site of the Aztec capital Tenochtitlán. p. 377

Lake Tiberias See Sea of Galilee p. 646

M

Lake Titicaca (tee•tee•KAH•kah) A lake on the Peru-Bolivia border in South America; the highest navigable lake in the world at 12,507 feet (3,812 m) above sea level. p. 31

Lake Victoria A lake in Tanzania, Kenya, and Uganda in southeastern Africa. p. 523

Laos A country located on the Indochina Peninsula in southeastern Asia; once part of former French Indochina. p. 47

Larsa A city in ancient Babylonia, near the Euphrates River, in present-day southeastern Iraq. (31°N, 46°E) p. 94

Latvia A country in eastern Europe; formerly part of the Soviet Union. p. 607

Leeds An inland port city in central England, on the River Aire. (54°N, 2°W) p. 576

Lena River A river in Russia; flows into the Laptev Sea. p. 27

Leningrad *See* St. Petersburg. p. 615

Lepanto A city in Greece; a battle site for the Ottoman Empire. p. 537

Lesotho An independent country located within the borders of the country of South Africa in Africa. p. 650

Liberia A country in western Africa; originally a republic for freed slaves from the United States; located on the Atlantic coast of western Africa. p. 585

Libya A country in northern Africa; located on the Mediterranean Sea. p. 585

Libyan Desert A desert in northern Africa; located in Libya, Egypt, and Sudan. p. 133

Lima The capital of Peru. (12°S, 77°W) p. 385

Lisbon The capital of Portugal; located on the Atlantic coast of Europe. (39°N, 9°W) p. 605

Lithuania A country in eastern Europe; formerly part of the Soviet Union. p. 607

Liverpool A port city on the English coast of the northwestern British Isles. (53°N, 3°W) p. 576

Lodz A province of central Poland. p. 605

Loire River (luh•WAR) The longest river in France; located in southeastern France. p. 605

Lombardy A region in northern Italy. p. 593

London The capital of the United Kingdom; located on the Thames River, in southeastern England. (51°N, 0°) p. 605

Lothal An ancient settlement in western India. (22°N, 72°E) p. 143

Luanda The capital of Angola. (8°S, 13°E) p. 43

Lübeck A German port city on the Baltic Sea. (44°N, 10°E) p. 467

Lucca A city on the western coast of Italy. (54°N, 10°E) p. 491

Luoyang (luh•WOH•YAHNG) The former capital of the Zhou dynasty in ancient China; located in what is present-day central China, on the Huang He. (35°N, 113°E) p. 149

Lusaka The capital of Zambia. (15°S, 28°E) p. 43

Luxembourg A country in western Europe. p. 605

Luxor A city in Egypt on the Nile River. (26°N, 33°E) p. 33

Lydia An ancient land located on the western end of Asia Minor, in present-day Turkey in southwestern Asia. p. 198

Macao (muh•KOW) A former Portuguese colony in southern China, on the South China Sea. p. 530

Macedonia A present-day country in southeastern Europe; an ancient kingdom near the Aegean Sea, located on lands that are part of present-day Greece and Turkey. p. 198

Machu Picchu (MAH•choo PEE•choo) The ruins of an ancient Inca city; located in the Andes Mountains in what is now central Peru in South America. (13°S, 73°W) p. 385

Mackenzie River A river in Canada; the second-largest river in North America; flows into the Beaufort Sea. p. 27

Madagascar An island country located in the Indian Ocean, off the eastern coast of southern Africa. p. 585

Madras The capital of Tamil Nadu state, India. (13°N, 80°E) p. 540

Madrid A city located in central Spain, in Europe, on the Manzanares River. (40°N, 4°W) p. 605

Majuro The capital of the Marshall Islands. (7°N, 171°E) p. 546

Malacca (muh•LAH•kuh) A trade center on the Strait of Malacca. p. 540

Malaysia (muh•LAY•zhuh) An independent federation; located in southeastern Asia. p. 460

Mali A former western African empire and a present-day country. p. 444

Mallia An ancient Minoan city in Crete. p. 246

Manchester A manufacturing port city on the Irwell River in England. (54°N, 2°W) p. 576

Manchuria A large region on the northeastern end of China. p. 624

Manila The capital of the Philippines. (14°N, 121°E) p. 540

Marathon An ancient Greek town in eastern Attica; the site of an ancient Greek victory during the Persian Wars. (38°N, 24°E) p. 246

Mari A city on the Euphrates River, in ancient Mesopotamia. p. 94

Mariana Islands An island group in Micronesia, Oceania; includes the unincorporated United States territory of Guam. p. 460

Marne River A river in northeastern France; flows west into the Seine River. p. 605

Marshall Islands A group of 32 islands and more than 867 reefs located in the western Pacific Ocean. p. 460

Mauritania (maw•ruh•TAY•nee•uh) A country in western Africa. p. 47

Mecca (MEH•kuh) A city in Saudi Arabia near the Red Sea; a holy city for Muslims; also known as Makkah. (22°N, 40°E) p. 423

Media The ancient country of the Medes; located in present-day northwestern Iran. p. 198

Medina A city in western Saudi Arabia; an early Muslim capital. (25°N, 40°E) p. 423

Mediterranean Sea The sea south of Europe, north of Africa, and west of Asia; connects to the Atlantic Ocean, the Red Sea, and the Black Sea. p. 69

Mekong Delta The fertile region across which flow the several mouths of the Mekong River, near Ho Chi Minh City, Vietnam. p. 30

Mekong River A river in southeastern Asia; flows from the mountains of Tibet into the South China Sea. p. 357

Melanesia (meh•luh•NEE•zhuh) The name given to a group of the southwestern Pacific Islands; located northeast of Australia and south of the equator. p. 460

Memphis An ancient Egyptian capital; located along the Nile River in northern Egypt. (30°N, 31°E) p. 117

Meroë (MAIR•oh•wee) A capital of the ancient kingdom of Kush; located on the eastern bank of the Nile River in northern Sudan. (17°N, 34°E) p. 133

Mesopotamia (meh•suh•puh•TAY•mee•uh) An ancient land in southwestern Asia; located between the Tigris and Euphrates Rivers. p. 94

Mexico A country in southern North America; located between the United States and Central America. p. 568

Mexico City The capital of Mexico; located in central Mexico. (19°N, 99°W) p. 515

Micronesia (my•kruh•NEE•zhuh) The name of a group of western Pacific Islands located east of the Philippines and north of the equator. p. 460

Middle America A world region; includes Mexico, the countries of Central America, and sometimes the islands of the Caribbean Sea. p. 64

Midway Comprised of Eastern and Sand Islands, parts of a coral atoll; located in the central Pacific Ocean. p. 614

Milan A city in northern Italy. (45°N, 9°E) p. 491

Mississippi River The largest river in the United States; flows from Minnesota to the Gulf of Mexico. p. 27

Missouri River A tributary of the Mississippi River; flows from Montana to St. Louis, Missouri. p. 27

Mogadishu (mah•guh•DIH•shoo) A port city on the Indian Ocean in southern Somalia, in Africa. (2°N, 45°E) p. 523

Mohács A city in Hungary; a battle site of the Ottoman Empire. (46°N, 18°E) p. 537

Mohenjo-Daro (moh•HEN•joh DAR•oh) An ancient city in the Indus Valley; located in present-day Pakistan. p. 143

Moldova A country in eastern Europe; formerly part of the Soviet Union. p. 630

Mombasa An island port on the coast of the Indian Ocean in southern Kenya, in Africa. (4°S, 40°E) p. 523

Mongolia A country in eastern Asia. p. 430

Monrovia The capital of Liberia. (6°N, 10°W) p. 43

Montenegro A republic in Serbia and Montenegro, which was once part of the former Yugoslavia. p. 605

Montreal Canada's largest city and chief port of entry. (46°N, 74°W) p. 43

Morocco (muh•RAH•koh) A country in northern Africa; bordered by the Mediterranean Sea and the Atlantic Ocean. p. 585

Moscow The capital of Russia; located on the Moscow River. (56°N, 38°E) p. 605

Mount Fuji A mountain on the island of Honshu, Japan. p. 365

Mount Olympus A mountain believed to be the home of the gods and goddesses of ancient Greek mythology; located on the eastern coast of Greece. p. 246

Mount Sinai A mountain peak located on the Sinai Peninsula. p. 182

Mount Vesuvius A volcano near the city of Pompeii, Italy; erupted in A.D. 79, burying the city for 17 centuries. p. 297

Mozambique (moh•zuhm•BEEK) A country in southern Africa; formerly Portuguese East Africa. p. 585

Mumbai (Bombay) A city on the western coast of central India. (19°N, 73°E) p. 43

Mureybit A village in ancient Mesopotamia; located in present-day Syria. (37°N, 38°E) p. 69

My Lai A Vietnamese village located south of Chu Lai. (15°N, 109°E) p. 629

Myanmar (Burma) A country on the Indochina Peninsula in southeastern Asia. p. 47

Mycenae (my•SEE•nee) An ancient city-state and empire in ancient Greece; located on the eastern side of the Peloponnesus. (38°N, 23°E) p. 246

Mytilene An ancient Greek city-state in western Asia Minor on the Aegean Sea. p. 251

N

Nagasaki (nah•guh•SAH•kee) A city on the coast of the island of Kyushu in southern Japan; a key city in World War II. (33°N, 130°E) p. 614

Nairobi The capital of Kenya. (1°S, 36°E) p. 43

Namib Desert A desert in southwestern Africa. p. 349

Namibia A country in southwestern Africa. p. 47

Napata (NA•puh•tuh) A capital of the ancient kingdom of Kush; located on the Nile River in northern Sudan, in Africa. (19°N, 32°E) p. 133

Naples (NAY•puhlz) An Italian port city on the Tyrrhenian Sea; located on the western coast of southern Italy. (41°N, 14°E) p. 491

Narmada River (ner•MAH•duh) A sacred Hindu river; it begins in eastern India and empties into the Gulf of Cambay. p. 143

Nasiriya A small farming village in southeastern Iraq on the Euphrates River. (31°N, 46°E). p. 92

Nazareth (NA•zuh•ruhth) A city in northern Israel. (33°N, 35°E) p. 184

Negev (NEH•gev) A desert located in southern Israel. p. 646

Nepal (nuh•PAWL) A country located in southern Asia, north of India. p. 47

Netherlands A country on the northern coast of central Europe, on the North Sea. p. 605

New Carthage *See* Cartagena. p. 287

New Guinea An island in the Malay Archipelago; located north of eastern Australia; occupied by Papua New Guinea and part of Indonesia. p. 587

New York The largest city in New York State, on the east coast of the United States. (41°N, 74°W) p. 43

New Zealand An island-group country in the southwestern Pacific Ocean, southeast of Australia. p. 460

Newcastle upon Tyne A city in northern England on the Tyne River. (55°N, 2°W) p. 576

Nicaragua A country in Central America. p. 46

Niger (NY•jer) A country in western Africa. p. 347

Niger River A river in western Africa; flows from Guinea through Mali, Niger, and Nigeria, into the Gulf of Guinea. p. 349

Nigeria (ny•JIR•ee•uh) A country on the Gulf of Guinea, in western Africa. p. 585

GAZETTEER

Nile Delta An area of low-lying land in northeastern Egypt where the Nile River divides into branches that spread out to the Mediterranean Sea. p. 133

Nile River A river in northeastern Africa; flows from Lake Victoria and empties into the Mediterranean Sea at the northeastern coast of Egypt. p. 117

Nineveh (NIH•nuh•vuh) The capital of the ancient Assyrian Empire; the ruins are located on the Tigris River, in northern Iraq. (36°N, 43°E) p. 108

Nippur (ni•PUR) An ancient Sumerian and Babylonian city in southwestern Asia, in present-day central Iraq. (32°N, 45°E) p. 94

Nok A ancient village in present-day Nigeria. p. 349

Normandy A historical region of northwestern France; site of Allied D day invasion during World War II. p. 615

North America One of the world's seven continents. p. 21

North Borneo The British colonial name of Sabah; a state of Malaysia; located in northeastern Borneo. p. 587

North Korea A country that lies north of the 38th parallel on the Korean Peninsula, off the coast of China. p. 47

North Sea The sea located east of Britain and west of Denmark. p. 467

North Vietnam A former country located in southeastern Asia; now part of Vietnam. p. 629

Norway A European country; located on the northwestern Scandinavian Peninsula. p. 467

Nouakchott The capital of Mauritania, in western Africa. (18°N, 16°W) p. 43

Novgorod (NAHV•guh•rahd) A medieval principality in eastern Europe in what is present-day Russia. p. 622

Nubia (NOO•bee•uh) An ancient land in Africa that extended along the Nile River from Egypt's southern border to close to present-day Khartoum, Sudan. p. 133

Nubian Desert A desert region in Sudan, Africa, east of the Nile River. p. 133

Nuku'alofa The capital of Tonga, in the southwestern Pacific Ocean. (21°S, 175°W) p. 546

O

Ob River A river in western Russia, in Asia. p. 27

Oder River A large river in central Europe; flows from northeastern Czech Republic to the Baltic Sea. p. 467

Ohio River A tributary of the Mississippi River; this river begins in Pittsburgh, Pennsylvania, and ends in Cairo, Illinois. p. 27

Okinawa (oh•kee•NAH•wah) An island group; located in the center of the Ryukyu Islands between the East China Sea and the Pacific Ocean. p. 614

Olympia A plain in the northwestern Peloponnesus; an ancient Greek religious center and site of the early Olympic Games. (40°N, 22°E) p. 246

Oman A country in southwestern Asia; located on the Arabian Peninsula. p. 47

Orinoco River A river in northeastern South America. p. 27

Oslo The capital of Norway; located in southeastern Norway at the northern end of the Oslo Fjord. (60°N, 11°E) p. 607

P

Pacific Ocean The largest of the world's four oceans. p. 55

Paekche (PAK•chuh) One of the Three Kingdoms of ancient Korea; occupied the southwestern part of the peninsula. p. 360

Pakistan A country in southern Asia. p. 143

Palau An archipelago in the western Pacific Ocean near the Philippines. p. 546

Palikir The capital of Micronesia. (7°N, 158°E) p. 546

Pamplona (pam•PLOH•nah) A city in northern Spain. (43°N, 25°W) p. 332

Panama A country in Central America. p. 46

Pangaea (pan•JEE•uh) The name given to the world's ancient supercontinent. p. 21

Panlongcheng An ancient city of the Shang dynasty. (30°N, 115°E) p. 149

Papal States The home and kingdom of the Roman Catholic Church from 754–1870; located in central Italy. p. 593

Papua New Guinea A country in Melanesia; occupies half of the island of New Guinea and about 600 smaller islands. p. 546

Paraguay (PAH•rah•gwy) A country in central South America. p. 568

Paraná River A river in southeastern South America. p. 27

Paris The capital of France; located on the Seine River. (49°N, 2°E) p. 605

Parthia (PAR•thee•uh) A historic land that was part of the ancient Assyrian and Persian Empires; located in southwestern Asia. p. 198

Pasargadae (puh•SAR•guh•dee) A city in ancient Persia, located in present-day Iran. p. 196

Pearl Harbor An inlet on the southern coast of Oahu Island, Hawaii; site of the Japanese bombing attack that brought the United States into World War II. (21°N, 158°W) p. 614

Peloponnesus (peh•luh•puh•NEE•suhs) A wide peninsula on the southern end of Greece; home of the ancient city-states of Sparta and Corinth. p. 246

Persepolis (per•SEH•puh•luhs) The capital of the ancient Persian Empire; located near Shiraz in present-day Iran. p. 198

Persia An ancient empire that included the ancient lands of Persia, Egypt, Syria, Assyria, Mesopotamia, and Babylonia. p. 198

Persian Gulf A gulf in southwestern Asia; connects the Gulf of Oman and the Arabian Sea. p. 100

Peru A country on the Pacific coast of South America. p. 568

Perugia An ancient city of the Etruscans and a city in central Italy on the Tiber River. (43°N, 12°E) p. 278

Phaistos (FES•tuhs) One of the largest Minoan cities; located on Crete. (35°N, 25°E) p. 246

Philippine Sea The part of the western Pacific Ocean east of the Philippines. p. 540

Philippines An archipelago and country in southeastern Asia; located east of the Indochina Peninsula. p. 540

Philistia (fuh•LIS•tee•uh) An ancient land in southwestern Asia. p. 184

Phnom Penh (NAHM PEN) The capital of Cambodia. (12°N, 105°E) p. 541

Phocaea (foh•SEE•uh) An ancient Greek city-state in western Asia Minor on the Aegean Sea. p. 251

Phoenicia (fih•NEE•shuh) An ancient land; located in present-day Lebanon and northern Israel. p. 191

Pindus Mountains A mountain range in northwestern Greece. p. 246

Plataea (pluh•TEE•uh) An ancient city in present-day east-central Greece. (39°N, 23°E) p. 257

Po River A river in northern Italy; flows from Mount Viso into the northern Adriatic Sea. p. 278

Poland A country in eastern Europe, bordering on the Baltic Sea. p. 607

Polynesia (pah•luh•NEE•zhuh) The name of a group of central Pacific Islands; includes New Zealand, Samoa, Tahiti, and the Hawaiian Islands. p. 460

Pompeii (pahm•PAY) An ancient Roman city; site of Mt. Vesuvius's volcanic eruption in A.D. 79 that buried the city for 17 centuries. p. 297

Popocatépetl (poh•puh•KAT•uh•peh•tuhl) A volcano in southern Mexico. p. 379

Port Moresby The capital of Papua New Guinea. (9°S, 147°E) p. 546

Port Said A port city on the Mediterranean Sea at the northern end of the Suez Canal. (31°N, 32°E) p. 33

Port-au-Prince The capital of Haiti. (18°N, 72°W) p. 43

Portsmouth A city in southern England, on the English Channel. p. 576

Portugal A country in western Europe; located on the Iberian Peninsula. p. 505

Portuguese Guinea A former Portuguese colony on the western African coast; the present-day country of Guinea-Bissau. p. 585

Port-Vila The capital of Vanuatu. (17°S, 168°E) p. 546

Prague The capital of the Czech Republic; located on both sides of the Vltava River. (50°N, 14°E) p. 607

Prussia A former kingdom in northern Europe; located in what is present-day Germany. p. 594

Puerto Rico An island and a self-governing commonwealth of the United States; located in the Greater Antilles of the West Indies in the Caribbean Sea. p. 568

Pylos An ancient Mycenaean city. p. 246

P'yongyang (pyawng•YAHNG) The capital of the ancient Old Choson kingdom and present-day North Korea. (39°N, 126°E) p. 360

Pyrenees (PIR•uh•neez) The mountain range that separates the Iberian Peninsula from the rest of Europe; forms the border between present-day Spain and France. p. 332

Q

Quebec A city in eastern Canada. p. 515

Quito The capital of Ecuador. (0°S, 78°W) p. 385

R

Rabat The capital of Morocco. (34°N, 7°W) p. 43

Ramses An ancient Egyptian city; located in Goshen, near Tanis. p. 182

Red River A river that flows through northern Vietnam to the Gulf of Tonkin. p. 357

Red Sea The sea between northeastern Africa and the Arabian Peninsula; connected to the Mediterranean Sea by the Suez Canal and to the Arabian Sea by the Gulf of Aden. p. 69

Reval The former name of the capital of Estonia; now known as Tallinn. (60°N, 25°E) p. 464

Reykjavik The capital of Iceland. (64°N, 22°E) p. 43

Rhine River A river in western Europe; flows across Switzerland, western Germany, and the Netherlands to the North Sea. p. 27

Rhodes A Greek island in the southeastern Aegean Sea. p. 194

Rhone River A river in Switzerland and France, rising in the Alps and flowing into the Gulf of Lions. p. 605

Riga The capital of Latvia, in northern Europe. (57°N, 24°E) p. 605

Rio Grande A river in central North America that forms part of the border of the United States and Mexico. p. 27

Romania A country in southeastern Europe, bordering the Black Sea. p. 605

Rome The capital of the ancient Roman Empire and of present-day Italy; located on the Tiber River. (42°N, 13°E) p. 278

Russia A historic empire and the largest republic of the former Soviet Union; a country in northeastern Europe and northwestern Asia. p. 607

S

Sahara A desert covering the northern third of Africa. p. 117

Sahel The semiarid region next to the Sahara. p. 349

Saigon A city that was the capital of South Vietnam; renamed Ho Chi Minh City; now part of Vietnam. (11°N, 107°E) p. 629

Salamis (SA•luh•muhs) An island off the coast of the Balkan Peninsula. p. 257

Samaria An ancient city in southwestern Asia; the capital of the ancient kingdom of Israel. p. 184

Samarkand A city in eastern Uzbekistan. (40°N, 67°E) p. 452

Samoa A group of Pacific Islands in southwestern Polynesia. p. 460

San Marino A small country on Mount Titano, in northern Italy. p. 593

San Salvador One of the Bahama Islands; where Christopher Columbus first landed in the Americas on October 12, 1492. p. 505

Santiago The capital of Chile. (33°S, 70°W) p. 515

Santo Domingo The capital of the Dominican Republic. (18°N, 70°W) p. 515

São Paulo The largest city in Brazil; located on the Tietê River. (23°S, 46°W) p. 43

Sarajevo (sair•uh•YAY•voh) A city in central Bosnia and Herzegovina. (44°N, 18°E) p. 605

Sardinia An island in the Mediterranean Sea; located west of mainland Italy. p. 593

Sardis The capital of ancient Lydia; located in west-central Turkey. (38°N, 28°E) p. 191

Saudi Arabia A country that occupies most of the Arabian Peninsula in southwestern Asia. p. 33

Sea of Galilee A freshwater lake in northern Israel; also known as Lake Tiberias. p. 184

Sea of Japan A sea located west of Japan and east of Russia, North Korea, and South Korea; also called the East Sea. p. 27

Sea of Marmara (MAR•muh•ruh) A small sea in northwestern Turkey; connects the Black and Aegean Seas. p. 246

Sea of Okhotsk (oh•KAHTSK) A sea off the eastern coast of Russia. p. 622

Senegal A country in western Africa. p. 47

Serbia A republic of the country of Serbia and Montenegro, which was once part of the former Yugoslavia. p. 605

Seychelles An island group and republic; located in the Indian Ocean, p. 650

Shanghai (SHANG•HY) A Chinese port on the East China Sea; located near the mouth of the Chang Jiang. (31°N, 121°E) p. 43

Shechem (SHEH•kuhm) An ancient town located north of Jerusalem, Israel. (32°N, 35°E) p. 182

Shikoku The smallest of the four main islands of Japan; located south of Honshu. p. 365

Sicily An Italian island off the southwestern tip of the Italian Peninsula. p. 605

Sidon A city in ancient Phoenicia on the Mediterranean Sea. p. 191

Siena An Italian city-state and stop on the Silk Road. p. 452

Sierra Leone A country on the Atlantic coast of western Africa; a former slave colony. p. 585

Sierra Madre del Sur A mountain range in southern Mexico that runs along the Pacific coast. p. 379

Sierra Madre Occidental A mountain range in northwestern Mexico that runs along the Pacific coast. p. 158

Sierra Madre Oriental A mountain range in eastern Mexico that runs along the coast of the Gulf of Mexico. p. 158

Silla (SIH•luh) One of the Three Kingdoms of ancient Korea; occupied the southeastern part of the peninsula. p. 360

Sinai Peninsula The peninsula between northeastern Africa and southwestern Asia; part of the country of Egypt. p. 191

Singapore A small island country off the southern tip of the Malay Peninsula, in southeastern Asia; also the name of the capital. (1°N, 103°E) p. 43

Slovakia A country in eastern Europe, south of Poland. p. 630

Slovenia (sloh•VEE•nee•uh) A country in eastern Europe. p. 630

Sofala (soh•FAH•lah) A trading port on the southeastern coast of Africa. (20°S, 34°E) p. 523

Sofia The capital of Bulgaria. (43°N, 23°E) p. 605

Sohag A city in Egypt on the Nile River. (26°N, 32°E) p. 33

Somalia A country in eastern Africa. p. 47

South Africa A country located on the southern tip of Africa, between the Atlantic and Indian Oceans. p. 47

South America One of the world's seven continents. p. 21

South China Sea A part of the China Sea south of Taiwan. p. 357

South Korea A country that lies south of the 38th parallel on the Korean Peninsula, off the coast of China. p. 47

South Vietnam A former independent country; located west of the South China Sea; now part of Vietnam. p. 629

Spain A country in southwestern Europe; on the Iberian Peninsula. p. 605

Sparta An ancient Greek city-state in the southern Peloponnesus. p. 251

Sri Lanka An island country in southern Asia; formerly Ceylon; located off the eastern coast of India. p. 143

St. Petersburg A city located on the Gulf of Finland that once served as capital of the Russian Empire; it was renamed Leningrad under Soviet rule, but regained its original name in 1991. (60°N, 30°E) p. 622

Stalingrad The former name of Volgograd; located on the Volga River. (49°N, 44°E) p. 615

Stockholm The largest city and capital of Sweden; located on the Baltic Sea. (59°N, 18°E) p. 467

Strait of Gibraltar A narrow passage of water between Europe and Africa. p. 194

Strait of Malacca (muh•LAH•kuh) A body of water that connects the Indian Ocean to the South China Sea. p. 540

Sudan A country on the eastern coast of northern Africa. p. 47

Suez Canal A canal linking the Mediterranean Sea and the Gulf of Suez; located in northeastern Egypt. p. 33

Sumatra (su•MAH•truh) The westernmost island of Indonesia; located off the Malay Peninsula in southeastern Asia. p. 540

Sumer (SOO•mer) An ancient region in southern Mesopotamia; located on the Persian Gulf, in present-day southeastern Iraq. p. 94

Suriname A country in South America. p. 37

Susa A capital of the Persian Empire; connected to Sardis, in Asia Minor, by the Royal Road. p. 198

Suva The capital of Fiji. (18°S, 178°E) p. 546

Swaziland A country in southern Africa. p. 650

Sweden A European country on the southeastern part of the Scandinavian Peninsula. p. 47

Switzerland A country in central Europe. p. 605

Syracuse A seaport city in Sicily, Italy; located on the Ionian Sea. (37°N, 15°E) p. 464

Syria A country located on the eastern end of the Mediterranean Sea. p. 423

Syrian Desert A desert covering southern Syria, northeastern Jordan, western Iraq, and northern Saudi Arabia, in southwestern Asia. p. 94

T

Tabriz (tuh•BREEZ) A city in northwestern Iran, on a small river near Lake Urmia. (38°N, 46°E) p. 434

Taiwan (TY•WAHN) An island country; located off the southeastern coast of China. p. 149

Taixicun An ancient city of the Shang dynasty. (39°N, 115°E) p. 149

Tajikistan (tah•jih•kih•STAN) A country in western Asia; formerly part of the Soviet Union. p. 630

Takla Makan A desert in northwestern China. p. 149

Tanzania (tan•zuh•NEE•uh) A country in eastern Africa. p. 47

Tarawa (tuh•RAH•wuh) The capital of Kiribati. (1°N, 173°E) p. 546

Tashkent The capital of Uzbekistan; located in western Asia. (41°N, 69°E) p. 43

Taurus Mountains A mountain range in southern Turkey; runs parallel to the southern Mediterranean coast and forms the border between Turkey and Syria. p. 69

Tegucigalpa (tuh•goo•suh•GAL•puh) The capital of Honduras. (14°N, 87°W) p. 43

Tehran The capital of Iran. (35°N, 51°E) p. 43

Tel Aviv A city in and former capital of Israel. (32°N, 35°E) p. 646

Tenochtitlán (tay•nohch•teet•LAHN) The capital of the ancient Aztec Empire; present-day Mexico City has been built on the ruins. (19°N, 99°W) p. 379

Teotihuacán (tay•oh•tee•wah•KAHN) A city in central Mexico. (20°N, 99°W) p. 379

Teotitlán An independent city-state in the ancient Aztec Empire. p. 379

Texcoco (tes•KOH•koh) A city in central Mexico; east of Lake Texcoco. (19°N, 99°W) p. 379

Thailand A country formerly known as Siam; located in southeastern Asia on the Indochina and Malay Peninsulas. p. 47

Thar Desert Also called the Great Indian Desert; located in India and Pakistan. p. 143

Thebes The capital of ancient Egypt during the Middle Kingdom; located in southern Egypt. (26°N, 33°E) p. 117

Thermopylae (ther•MAH•puh•lee) The site of an ancient Greek defeat during the Persian Wars; a mountain pass in southern Greece. (39°N, 23°E) p. 257

Thessaly (THEH•suh•lee) An ancient and present-day region in Greece; located on the eastern Balkan Peninsula. p. 257

Thrace An ancient land; located in present-day Turkey, Bulgaria, Macedonia, and part of northwestern Greece. p. 198

Tian Shan A mountain system in central Asia; extends northeast from the Pamirs into Xinjiang Uygur. p. 149

Tiber River A river in central Italy; flows from the Apennines, through Rome, and into the Tyrrhenian Sea. p. 278

Tibet A region covering most of southwestern China. p. 452

Tigris River A river in southwestern Asia; begins in eastern Turkey and joins the Euphrates River in Iraq. p. 69

Tigris-Euphrates Valley A valley of fertile land located between the Tigris and Euphrates Rivers. p. 64

Tikal (tih•KAHL) The largest ancient Mayan city; located in present-day Guatemala. p. 160

Timbuktu (tim•buhk•TOO) An ancient Songhai trading center and present-day city; located in Mali in the Sahara, north of the Niger River. (17°N, 3°W) p. 444

Timor An island in eastern Indonesia. p. 587

Tiranë The capital of Albania. (41°N, 20°E) p. 607

Tiryns (TIR•uhnz) An ancient Mycenaean city. p. 246

Tlacopán (tlah•koh•PAHN) An ancient Aztec city. (20°N, 100°W) p. 379

Tlaxcala An ancient city in the city-state of Tlaxcalan in the Aztec Empire. p. 379

Tlaxcalan An independent city-state in the ancient Aztec Empire. p. 379

Tokyo The capital of Japan. (36°N, 140°E) p. 43

Tonga A country comprised of about 150 small islands in the southwestern Pacific Ocean. p. 546

Toronto The capital of Ontario, Canada. (44°N, 79°W) p. 639

Tripoli The ancient Phoenician city of Oea and present-day capital of Libya. (33°N, 13°E) p. 464

Trondheim A port city in Norway. (63°N, 10°E) p. 467

Troy An ancient city in northwestern Asia Minor. (40°N, 26°E) p. 246

Tula An ancient city of the Aztec Empire. p. 379

Tumbes A city on the northwestern coast of Peru, in South America. (3°S, 80°W) p. 511

Tunis The capital of Tunisia. (37°N, 10°E) p. 464

Tunisia A country in northern Africa. p. 585

Turkey A country located in southeastern Europe and southwestern Asia. p. 607

Turkmenistan (terk•meh•nuh•STAN) A country in western Asia; formerly part of the Soviet Union. p. 630

Tuscany A region on the western coast of Italy. p. 593

Tuvalu A country made up of nine islands in the western Pacific Ocean. p. 546

Tuxtla Mountains A mountain range between the Isthmus of Tehuantepec and the Yucatán Peninsula, in Mexico. p. 379

Tyre (TYR) The capital of ancient Phoenicia and present-day town in southern Lebanon. (33°N, 35°E) p. 191

Tyrrhenian Sea (tuh•REE•nee•uhn) The sea located west of the Italian Peninsula, north of Sicily, and east of Sardinia and Corsica. p. 278

U

Uganda A country in eastern Africa. p. 585

Ukraine (yoo•KRAYN) A country in eastern Europe; formerly part of the Soviet Union. p. 47

Ulaanbaatar (Ulan Bator) The capital of Mongolia. (48°N, 107°E) p. 43

United Kingdom A European country made up of four kingdoms in the British Isles: England, Scotland, Wales, and Northern Ireland. p. 47

United States A country in North America; a federal republic of 50 states. p. 46

Ur (UR) A city in ancient Sumer; located on the Euphrates River, in what is now southeastern Iraq. (31°N, 46°E) p. 69

Uruguay (YUR•uh•gway) A country on the Atlantic coast of South America. p. 46

Uruk An ancient Sumerian city in southwestern Asia; located near the eastern bank of the Euphrates River, in present-day southeastern Iraq. (31°N, 46°E) p. 94

Uzbekistan (uz•beh•kih•STAN) A country in western Asia; formerly part of the Soviet Union. p. 47

GAZETTEER

Valley of Mexico A large valley in central Mexico; site of the ancient Aztec Empire capital, Tenochtitlán; location of present-day Mexico City. p. 158

Vancouver A city in southwestern Canada; located in British Columbia. (49°N, 123°W) p. 639

Vanuatu An island country; located in the southwestern Pacific Ocean, p. 546

Venezuela A country in northern South America. p. 568

Venice A city of 118 islands in northeastern Italy on the Adriatic Sea. (45°N, 12°E) p. 42

Veracruz A seaport in eastern Mexico, on the Gulf of Mexico. (19°N, 96°W) p. 511

Verona A city in northeastern Italy. (45°N, 11°E) p. 491

Vienna The capital city of Austria, in Europe; located in northeastern Austria on the Danube River. (48°N, 16°E) p. 605

Vientiane (vyen•TYAHN) The capital of Laos. (18°N, 103°E) p. 629

Vietnam A country in southeastern Asia; located on the Indochina Peninsula. p. 357

Vindhya Range (VIN•dyuh) A mountain range in central India. p. 143

Vistula River A river in Poland in eastern Europe; it flows from the Carpathian Mountains into the Baltic Sea. p. 605

Volga River The longest river in Europe; it runs from Russia to the Caspian Sea. p. 27

Wangara An ancient kingdom of western Africa. p. 444

Warsaw The capital of Poland. (52°N, 21°E) p. 607

Wellington The capital of New Zealand. (41°S, 174°E) p. 43

Western Ghats (GAWTS) A chain of mountains in southwestern India. p. 143

White Nile River A part of the Nile River in Africa. p. 117

Wucheng An ancient city of the Shang dynasty. (29°N, 115°E) p. 149

X

Xi Jiang A river in southeastern China; it flows into the South China Sea. p. 149

Xi'an (SHEE•AHN) A city in east-central China; also known as Sian; formerly Chang'an. (34°N, 109°E) p. 155

Xiang An ancient city of the Shang dynasty. (35°N, 115°E) p. 149

Xingtai An ancient city of the Shang dynasty. (35°N, 115°E) p. 149

Yalta A city in Ukraine. (45°N, 34°E) p. 615

Yaren A district of Nauru. (0°S, 166°E) p. 546

Yellow Sea The sea west of the Korean Peninsula and east of China. p. 149

Yemen A country on the southern coast of the Arabian Peninsula. p. 47

Yopotzingo An independent city-state in the ancient Aztec Empire. p. 379

Yucatán Peninsula A peninsula extending from the eastern coast of Central America; occupied by the countries of Mexico, Belize, and Guatemala. p. 158

Yugoslavia (yoo•goh•SLAH•vee•uh) A former country in Europe, which broke up into several independent republics. p. 607

Yukon River A river in northwestern North America. p. 27

Z

Zagros Mountains (ZAH•gruhs) A mountain range located in western and southern Iran. p. 100

Zama The site of Hannibal's and Carthage's final defeat in the Second Punic War; located in northern Tunisia. (35°N, 9°E) p. 287

Zambezi River A river in southern Africa; flows from northwestern Zambia to the Indian Ocean. p. 523

Zambia A country in southern Africa. p. 47

Zaragoza (za•ruh•GOH•zuh) A city along the Ebro River in northeastern Spain. (42°N, 1°W) p. 332

Zhengzhou (JUHNG•JOH) An ancient city of the Shang dynasty. (34°N, 114°E) p. 149

Zimbabwe (zim•BAH•bway) A country in southern Africa. p. 47

GAZETTEER

Glossary

The Glossary contains important social studies words and their definitions. Each word is respelled as it would be in a dictionary. When you see this mark ´ after a syllable, pronounce that syllable with more force than the other syllables. The page number at the end of the definition tells where to find the word in your book.

add, āce, câre, pälm; end, ēqual; it, īce; odd, ōpen, ôrder; took, pool; up, bûrn; yoo as *u* in *fuse*; oil; pout; ə as *a* in *above*, *e* in *sicken*, *i* in *possible*, *o* in *melon*, *u* in *circus*; check; ring; thin; this; zh as in *vision*

A

Aborigine (a•bə•ri´jə•nē) The name given to the original inhabitants of Australia. p. 544

absolute authority (ab´sə•loot ə•thôr´ə•tē) A system of government in which one person has complete control. p. 94

absolute location (ab´sə•loot lō•kā´shən) Exact location on Earth. p. 6

academy (ə•ka´də•mē) A school offering instruction or training in a special field. p. 261

acropolis (ə•krä´pə•ləs) A fort built on a hill. p. 250

A.D. (ā•dē) Stands for *anno Domini*, a Latin phrase meaning "in the year of the Lord." This abbreviation identifies approximately how many years have passed since the birth of Jesus Christ. p. 66

adapt (ə•dapt´) To change in order to make more useful. p. 6

afterlife (af´tər•līf) A life after death. p. 119

agora (a´gə•rə) An open-air market and gathering place in many ancient Greek city-states. p. 251

agriculture (a´gri•kul•chər) The raising of domesticated plants and animals; farming. p. 63

alliance (ə•lī´əns) An agreement to cooperate. p. 604

ally (a´lī) A supporter. p. 134

altitude (al´tə•tood) Elevation. p. 36

ambassador (am•ba´sə•dər) A representative of a government. p. 532

analyze (a´nəl•īz) To break something down into its parts to see how those parts connect. p. 3

ancestor (an´ses•tər) A deceased relative who lived longer ago than a grandparent. p. 151

animism (a´nə•mi•zəm) A religious belief that natural objects or physical features have spirits. p. 356

annex (ə•neks´) To add on. p. 125

apartheid (ə•pär´tāt) The former government policy of South Africa that stressed the separation, or "apartness," of races. p. 645

apostle (ə•pä´səl) A person sent out to teach others. p. 302

aqueduct (a´kwə•dəkt) A system of bridges and canals used to carry water to a city. p. 296

archaeologist (är•kē•ä´lə•jist) A scientist who locates and studies the things left behind by people long ago. p. 58

archipelago (är•kə•pe´lə•gō) A chain of islands. p. 461

arid (ar´əd) Very dry, with little rainfall. p. 38

aristocracy (ar•ə•stä´krə•sē) A wealthy ruling class. p. 253

armada (är•mä´də) A fleet of warships. p. 507

armistice (är´mə•stəs) An agreement to stop fighting. p. 607

arms race (ärmz rās) A competition among nations to have the most weapons. p. 605

artifact (är´tə•fakt) A human-made object, especially from long ago. p. 56

artisan (är´tə•zən) A person skilled in a craft, such as carving. p. 144

Asia Minor (ā´zhə mī´nər) The peninsula in southwestern Turkey that forms the Asian part of Turkey. p. 191

assassination (ə•sas•ən•ā´shən) Murder for a political reason. p. 605

assimilate (ə•si´mə•lāt) The process in which the cultural traits of newcomers to a country become similar to those of the people already in the new country. p. 147

astrolabe (as´trə•lāb) An instrument that helped sailors navigate by using the positions of the stars. p. 503

B

band (band) A small group of people made up of related families. p. 52

barbarian (bär•bâr´ē•ən) The name given to outsiders by the ancient Greeks and later by the ancient Romans. p. 255

barter (bär´tər) The exchange of one good or service for another. p. 192

basilica (bə•si´li•kə) A huge marble government building in ancient Rome. p. 294

B.C. (bē•sē´) Stands for "before Christ." p. 66

B.C.E. (bē•sē•ē) Stands for "before the Common Era," and refers to the same years as B.C. p. 66

Buddhism (boo´di•zəm) An ancient religion based on the teachings of Siddhartha Gautama, who became known as the Buddha. p. 211

bureaucracy (byŏŏ•rok´rə•sē) A network of nonelected government officials. p. 95

burgher (bûr´gər) A social class made up of middle class workers such as merchants and craftworkers. p. 487

C

caliph (kā•ləf´) A successor to Muhammad. p. 422

capitalism (kap´ə•təl•iz•əm) An economic system in which individuals invest money, or capital, in businesses. p. 579

caravansary (kar•ə•van´sə•rē) An inn where desert travelers found food and shelter. p. 449

caravel (kar´ə•vəl) A kind of ship that used either square or lateen sails to travel long distances swiftly. p. 503

cardinal directions (kär´də•nəl də•rek´shənz) The main directions—north, south, east, and west. p.A3

cartogram (kär´tə•gram) A diagram that gives information about places by the size shown for each place. p. 650

cartographer (kär•tä´grə•fər) A mapmaker. p. 450

cash crop (kash krop) A crop that is raised to sell to others rather than to use at home. p. 585

caste (kast) A system in which a person's position in society is determined by his or her birth into a particular social class. p. 208

cataract (ka´tə•rakt) A waterfall or a place in a river where water runs rapidly over rocks. p. 120

cathedral (kə•thē´drəl) A large Christian church. p. 484

Catholic (kath´lik) A form of Christianity. p. 415

cause (kôz) An event or an action that makes something else happen. p. 6

causeway (kôz´wā) A human-made land bridge. p. 378

cavalry (ka´vəl•rē) A group of soldiers who ride horses or other animals to make swift attacks. p. 197

C.E. (sē•ē´) Stands for "Common Era" and refers to the same years as A.D. p. 66

census (sen´səs) A count of a country's people. p. 293

centralized government (sen´trə•līzd gu´vərn•mənt) A form of government in which the national government maintains the power. p. 101

ceramic (sə•ra´mik) A product such as pottery that is made from baked clay. p. 132

ceremonial center (ser•ə•mō´nē•əl sen´tər) An area used for religious ceremonies by the ancient people of the Americas. p. 157

chancellor (chan´sə•lər) A prime minister of a country. p. 593

character (kar´ik•tər) A symbol used in writing. p. 151

chariot (char´ē•ət) A two-wheeled, horse-drawn cart used in ancient times to carry soldiers into battle. p. 103

chinampa (chē•näm´pä) A human-made island created from a platform of woven reeds. Aztec farmers grew vegetables on these "floating gardens." p. 378

Christendom (kri´sən•dəm) The community of Christians from all kingdoms and nations. p. 339

Christianity (kris•chē•an´ə•tē) The religion based on the life and teachings of Jesus Christ. p. 299

chronology (krə•nä´lə•jē) A record of events in the order in which they happened. p. 2

circle graph (sûr´kəl graf) A graph that shows information by means of a circle divided into parts; also called a pie chart. p. 426

circumnavigation (sûr•kəm•nav•ə•gā´shən) A journey around the world by ship. p. 506

citadel (si´tə•dəl) A large, fortlike structure. p. 145

city-state (sit´ē•stāt) A city and its surrounding farmlands, with its own government and leaders. p. 73

civic participation (si´vik pär•ti•sə•pā´shən) Concern with and involvement in one's community, state, nation, or world. p. 9

civics (si´viks) The study of the rights and duties of citizens. p. 9

civil service (siv´əl sûr´vəs) The part of a bureaucracy that oversees the day-to-day business of running a government. p. 222

civilization (siv•ə•lə•zā´shən) A society with developed forms of religion, ways of governing, and centers of learning. p. 73

clan (klan) A group of related families. p. 360

classify (kla´sə•fī) To sort or group. p. 162

climate (klī´mət) The kind of weather a place has over a long period of time. p. 34

climograph (klī´mə•graf) A kind of graph that shows both the average monthly temperature and the average monthly precipitation for a place. p. 354

code (kōd) A set of laws written down in a clear and orderly way. p. 101

codex (kō´deks) A hand-lettered book of glyphs, such as those used by the Maya, that contains a record of such subjects as religion and learning. p. 161

cold war (kōld wôr) A conflict between nations fought with words and ideas rather than with soldiers and weapons. p. 623

collective (kə•lek´tiv) A large farm, sometimes owned by the government, on which people work together as a group. p. 622

colonization (kä•lə•nə•zā´shən) The settlement of a colony. p. 510

colony (kä´lə•nē) An area of land ruled by a government in another land. p. 190

Columbian exchange (kə•lum´bē•ən iks•chānj´) The movement of people, animals, plants, diseases, and ideas between Europe and the Americas in the 1400s and 1500s. p. 513

comedy (kom´ə•dē) A play written to make an audience laugh. p. 259

command economy (kə•mand´ i•kä´nə•mē) An economy in which the government owns almost all of the land and natural resources and makes most of the decisions. p. 579

commerce (kä´mûrs) The buying and selling of goods. p. 188

commercial (kə•mər´shəl) Related to a trade center. p. 143

communism (käm´yə•ni•zəm) A governing and economic system in which all property and all means of production belong to the people as a group. p. 620

compass rose (kum´pəs rōz) A direction marker on a map. p. A3

complex society (käm´pleks sə•sī´ə•tē) A social system with a reliable food source and with established laws, customs, and job specialization. p. 71

compromise (käm´prə•mīz) To give up some of what you want in order to reach an agreement. p. 104

concentration camp (kän•sən•trā´shən kamp) A guarded camp where prisoners are held. p. 616

confederation (kən•fe•də•rā´shən) A loose group of governments working together. p. 278

conflict (kän´flikt) A disagreement between two or more people or groups. p. 104

conformal projection (kən•fôr´məl prə•jek´shən) A map projection that shows shapes correctly but distorts sizes of places, especially near the poles. p. 542

Confucianism (kən•fyōō´shə•ni•zəm) The ideas of the Chinese philosopher Confucius, which became a guide for the way people should live. p. 220

conquer (käng´kər) To take over. p. 98

conquistador (kän•kēs´tə•dôr) A Spanish conqueror who came to the Americas in search of gold. p. 510

consequence (kän´sə•kwens) A result. p. 52

constitution (kon•stə•tōō´shən) A written plan of government. p. 566

constitutional monarchy (kon•stə•tōō´shə•nəl mä´nər•kē) A government with a written plan, or constitution, that includes a monarch as a ceremonial leader and a parliament or other legislature to make the laws. p. 565

consul (kän´səl) One of two chief officials who held office in the ancient Roman Republic. p. 279

containment (kən•tān´mənt) The policy of preventing a country from gaining control of another country. p. 626

continental drift (kän•tən•en´təl drift´) The continuing movement of continental plates. p. 21

contour line (kän´tōōr līn) On an elevation map, a line that connects all points of equal elevation. p. 154

coureurs de bois (kōō•rûrz´də bwä´) A term that means "runners of the woods," referring to French trappers who traded with the Native Americans. p. 514

courier (kōōr´ē•ər) A person who delivers messages. p. 199

covenant (kuv´ə•nənt) An agreement. p. 181

crop rotation (krop rō•tā´shən) A farming method in which the kinds of crops planted in a field are alternated every year to help keep the soil fertile. p. 573

Crusade (krōō•sād´) One of a series of wars fought between Christians and Muslims in the Middle Ages over control of the Holy Land. p. 485

crusader (krōō•sā´dər) A Christian soldier who fought to free the Holy Land from Muslim Turks in the Middle Ages. p. 485

cultivate (kul´tə•vāt) To prepare and use soil for the growing of crops. p. 62

cultural borrowing (kulch´rəl bär´ə•wing) The taking of culture traits from one culture for use in another. p. 158

culture (kul´chər) A unique way of life that sets a group of people apart from others. p. 8

culture trait (kul´chər trāt´) A characteristic of a culture. p. 160

cuneiform (kyōō•nē´ə•fôrm) A form of ancient writing used in southwestern Asia. p. 95

current (kur´ənt) A giant stream of ocean water. p. 27

czar (zär) A Russian title meaning "Caesar," or ruler. p. 620

D

daimyo (dī´mē•ō) A local noble in feudal Japan. p. 368

Daoism (dou´i•zəm) A philosophy that teaches that the key to long life and happiness is to accept life as it is. p. 223

decimal system (de´sə•məl sis´təm) A counting system based on the number 10. p. 246

decipher (dē•sī´fər) To interpret the meaning of something. p. 137

decree (di•krē´) An official order or decision made by a ruler. p. 108

deity (dē´ə•tē) A god. p. 119

delta (del´tə) A triangle-shaped piece of land built from soil deposited at the mouth of a river. p. 24

demagogue (de´mə•gäg) A leader who stirs up feelings and fears to gain power. p. 260

demand (di•mand´) The amount of a good or a service that people are willing to buy at a given price. p. 579

democracy (di•mä´krə•sē) A governing system in which a country's people elect their leaders and rule by majority. p. 253

demographer (di•mä´grə•fer) A geographer who studies human populations. p. 647

deposition (de•pə•zi´shən) The process of dropping, or depositing, sediment in a new location. p. 24

descendant (di•sen´dənt) A person who is descended from a certain ancestor. p. 52

desertification (di•zûr•tə•fə•kā´shən) The long-term process in which fertile land is changed into desert. p. 41

détente (dā•tänt´) A relaxing of tensions. p. 630

developed country (di•ve´ləpt kun´trē) A country with a well-established economy and, generally, containing all four forms of industry. p. 640

developing country (di•ve´lə•ping kun´trē) A country whose economy is still being built. p. 640

dhow (dou) An Arab sailboat. p. 457

Diaspora (dī•as´pə•rə) The settling of Jews outside of ancient Israel. p. 184

dictator (dik´tā•tər) A ruler with absolute authority. p. 279

diffuse (di•fyo͞oz) To spread or scatter widely. p. 264

diplomat (di´plə•mat) A person skilled in developing treaties between nations. p. 458

disciple (di•sī´pəl) A follower of a religion. p. 301

distortion (di•stôr´shən) An area that is not accurate on a map projection. p. 542

division of labor (də•vi´zhən əv lā´bər) The sharing of large jobs so that each worker does only part of the work. p. 93

doge (dōj) A leader in an Italian city-state. p. 466

domesticate (də•mes´tə•kāt) To tame plants or animals for human use. p. 60

dominant (dä´mə•nənt) More powerful. p. 245

drainage basin (drā´nij bā´sən) The land drained by a river system. p. 30

dreamtime (drēm´tīm) An ancient time, according to Australian Aborigines, when spirits created the land and gave all things in it to the people. p. 544

drought (drout) A long period of time in which little or no rain falls. p. 42

dynasty (dī´nəs•tē) A series of rulers from the same family. p. 121

E

earth lodge (urth läj) A round log home covered with packed earth. p. 392

economic system (ek•ə•nä´mik sis´təm) The way a country produces and uses goods and services. p. 578

economics (ek•ə•nä´miks) The study of the way that goods and wealth are produced, distributed, and used. p. 10

economy (i•kä´nə•mē) The way people use resources to meet their needs. p. 10

edict (ē´dikt) A command or decree. p. 214

editorial cartoon (e•də•tōr´ē•əl kär•to͞on´) A cartoon that represents the artist's point of view about people, current events, or politics. p. 570

effect (i•fekt´) The result of an event or action. p. 6

embargo (im•bär´gō) A limit or ban on trade. p. 467

emissary (e´mə•ser•ē) A person sent to represent another person or country. p. 367

empire (em´pīr) Vast lands and varied people that come under control of a single government. p. 99

encomienda (en•kō•mē•en´dä) A system in which Native Americans had to work for Spanish colonists and accept their religion. p. 514

enlightenment (in•lī´tən•mənt) A complete understanding of truth. p. 210

Enlightenment (in•lī´tən•mənt) A movement that began in France in the 1700s and focused on ways to create a government that protected the rights of individuals. p. 564

entrepreneur (än•trə•prə•nûr´) A person who starts and runs a business. p. 575

environment (en•vī´rən•mənt) Surroundings. p. 40

envoy (en´voi) An official or messenger sent by a government to do business with another. p. 413

epic (e´pik) A long story-poem. p. 248

equal-area projection (ē´kwəl âr´ē•ə prə•jek´shən) A map projection that shows the sizes of regions in correct relation to one another but distorts shapes. p. 542

equator (i•kwā´tər) An imaginary line that circles Earth halfway between the North Pole and the South Pole. The line divides Earth into the Northern Hemisphere and the Southern Hemisphere. p. 32

erosion (i•rō´zhən) The carrying away of land by forces of nature. p. 24

ethnic cleansing (eth´nik klen´zing) The forcing out or killing of certain ethnic groups. p. 655

evidence (e´və•dəns) Proof. pp. 2, 58

exile (eg´zīl) To force a person or group to live in another place. p. 184

Exodus (ek´sə•dəs) The journey of Moses and the Israelites from Egypt, through the desert, and back toward Canaan, as described in the Bible. p. 182

expedition (ek´spə•di´shən) A journey or an exploration. p. 268

export (ek´spōrt) A good sent to another place for sale. p. 70

extinct (ik•sting(k)t´) No longer living; died out. p. 52

F

fact (fakt) A statement that can be proved true. p. 336

factory (fak´tə•rē) A large building where goods are made. p. 574

fascism (fa´shi•zəm) Political ideas that stress strong government control, military strength, and extreme nationalism. p. 613

fault (fôlt) A crack in Earth's crust along which movement occurs. p. 22

federal republic (fe´də•rəl ri•pu´blik) A form of government consisting of three branches—one to make the laws, one to interpret them, and one to enforce them. p. 567

federation (fe•də•rā´shən) A union of groups or states under a central authority. p. 360

feudalism (fyoo´dəl•i•zəm) A political system of exchanging land for loyalty and protection. p. 219

filial piety (fi´lē•əl pī´ə•tē) Fulfilling one's duty to one's parents by being respectful to them. p. 220

flow chart (flō chart) A drawing that shows the order in which things happen. p. 282

forum (fōr´əm) A public square in ancient Rome. p. 294

frame of reference (frām əv re´fə•rens) A general viewpoint that shapes a person's opinions and feelings about issues. p. 186

free enterprise (frē en´tər•prīz) An economic system in which people choose what to make, sell, and buy, without government control. p. 579

fresco (fres´kō) A picture painted on wet plaster. p. 216

G

GDP (jē dē pē) Gross domestic product, or the total value of the goods and services produced in a country. p. 640

genocide (je´nə•sīd) The killing of an entire group of people. p. 616

geography (jē•ä´grə•fē) The study of Earth's physical and human features. p. 6

glacier (glā´shər) A thick mass of slow-moving ice. p. 23

gladiator (gla´dē•ā•tər) In ancient Rome, a slave or prisoner who fought, often to the death, for the entertainment of others. p. 296

global economy (glō´bəl i•kä´nə•mē) The trade of goods and services around the world. p. 636

glyph (glif) A picture-symbol that represents an object, an idea, or a sound. p. 160

Gospels (gäs´pəlz) The first four books of the New Testament, which describe Jesus Christ's life and teachings. p. 304

government (gu´vərn•mənt) An organized system that groups of people use to make laws and decisions. p. 9

granary (grā´nə•rē) A building in which grain is stored. p. 145

Great Depression (grāt di•pre´shən) The economic decline during the 1930s that was the worst in the world's history. p. 608

Greek fire (grēk fīr) A chemical mixture, used by the Byzantine navy, that caught fire when it was ignited. p. 463

grid system (grid sis´təm) The north-south and east-west lines on a map that cross each other to form a rectangular pattern. p. A2

guild (gild) A trade association that sets standards for the quality of goods and fair labor practices. p. 487

H

Hansa (han´sə *or* hän´zä) A group of northern European merchants who worked together to protect themselves. p. 466

heir (âr) A person who has the right to another person's property or title. p. 125

heresy (her´ə•sē) The denial of the beliefs of a church. p. 499

heritage (hâr´ə•tij) The elements of culture that have been passed down from one generation to another. p. 8

hieroglyphics (hī•rə•gli´fiks) A writing system in which pictures or symbols stand for sounds, words, or ideas. p. 122

Hinduism (hin´doo•i•zəm) A religion native to India, featuring belief in many gods and reincarnation. p. 208

historical empathy (hi•stôr´i•kəl em´pə•thē) The understanding of the actions and feelings of people from past times and other places. p. 3

history (his´tə•rē) The study of people and events of the past. p. 2

Holocaust (hō´lə•kôst) The mass killing of millions of Jews and other people by the Nazis during World War II. p. 616

human feature (hyoo´mən fē´chər) A building, a bridge, a farm, a road, or people themselves. p. 6

human rights (hyoo´mən rīts) Freedoms that most societies believe all people should have. p. 644

humanism (hyoo´mən•i•zəm) A way of thinking that focuses on the ideas and actions of individuals. p. 491

I

icon (ī´kän) A holy picture of Jesus Christ or of a saint. p. 415

immunity (i•myoo´nə•tē) Resistance to disease. p. 513

imperialism (im•pir´ē•əl•i•zəm) The practice by a country of acquiring more lands, establishing colonies, and controlling the colonies. p. 584

import (im´pōrt) A good brought in for sale from another place. p. 70

independence (in•də•pen´dəns) The freedom to govern oneself. p. 134

indigenous (in•di´jə•nəs) Native to a place. p. 512

GLOSSARY

Indochina (in•dō•chī´nə) A peninsula in Asia that includes the present-day countries of Vietnam, Laos, Cambodia, Thailand, Myanmar, and part of Malaysia. p. 541

indulgence (in•dul´jəns) A purchased pardon for sins. p. 498

Industrial Revolution (in•dus´trē•əl re•və•lōō´shən) The period of technological advances, beginning in the 1700s, that forever changed the way people live and work. p. 572

infantry (in´fən•trē) Soldiers trained to fight mainly on foot. p. 197

inflation (in•flā´shən) A continuing increase in the price of goods and services. p. 612

innovation (i•nə•vā´shən) A new way of doing things. p. 92

innovator (i´nə•vā•tər) A person who thinks of new ideas and invents new technologies. p. 572

inscription (in•skrip´shən) A written message etched into a long-lasting surface. p. 144

inset map (in´set map) A small map inside a larger map. p. A2

intermediate direction (in•tər•mē´dē•ət də•rek´shən) A direction that is between two cardinal directions—northeast, northwest, southeast, and southwest. p. A3

Internet (in´tər•net) The system that joins computers around the world for the exchange of information. p. 641

inundation (i´nən•dā•shən) The yearly time of flooding in ancient Egypt. p. 118

irrigation (ir•ə•gā´shən) The use of connected ditches, canals, or pipes to move water to dry areas. p. 41

Islam (is•läm´) The religion of Muslims, based on belief in one God, or Allah. p. 421

isolation (ī•sə•lā´shən) Separation from others. p. 529

Jainism (jī´ni•zəm) A religion based on the belief that every living being has a soul and a temporary physical body. p. 210

Janissary (ja´nə•ser•ē) A member of a well-trained group of soldiers who served in the Ottoman army. p. 537

jizya (jiz´yä) A special tax paid to the Ottoman government by non-Muslims so that they could follow their own religions and religious leaders. p. 536

Judaism (jōō´də•i•zəm) The religion of the Jewish people. p. 182

junk (jungk) A large wooden ship of Chinese origin with four-sided sails. p. 458

Justinian Code (jə•sti´nē•ən kōd) A set of laws, written by the Byzantine emperor Justinian, that served the Byzantine Empire for hundreds of years. p. 413

kaiser (kī´zər) The German word for *emperor*. p. 594

kami (kä´mē) Spirits, in the Shinto religion, that live in all natural things. p. 366

kastom (käs´təm) A system of behavior in the Pacific Islands, based on customs and traditional beliefs. p. 547

khan (kän) The title given to strong Mongol leaders who sometimes brought rival clans together and created almost unstoppable fighting forces. p. 430

khanate (kä´nāt) A region in the Mongol Empire having its own leader, or khan, and government. p. 432

knight (nīt) An armed soldier on horseback, who provided protection for a feudal lord. p. 485

labor union (lā´bər yōōn´yən) A group of organized workers whose goal is to ensure good working conditions and fair treatment by employers. p. 581

laissez-faire (le•sā•fâr´) A government policy of letting an economy continue without interference. p. 579

land use (land yōōs) The way most of the land in a place is used. p. 446

lateen sail (lə•tēn´ sāl) A triangle-shaped sail that enables a ship to travel into the wind. p. 457

latitude (la´tə•tōōd) Distance north or south of the equator. p. 32

lava (lä´və) Magma that has broken through Earth's crust and is on the surface. p. 23

league (lēg) A group of allies. p. 257

legacy (le´gə•sē) Anything handed down from an ancestor. p. 268

Legalism (lē´gə•li•zəm) Chinese teachings that say that people obey their rulers out of fear, not out of respect. p. 221

legend (le´jənd) A story handed down from earlier times. p. 148

liberate (li´bə•rāt) To set free. p. 615

livestock (līv´stäk) Domesticated animals, such as cattle, sheep, and pigs, that provide a resource. p. 61

locator (lō´kā•tər) A small map or a picture of a globe that shows where the area represented on a larger map is located in a state, in a country, on a continent, or in the world. p. A2

loess (les) Sandy, yellow, fertile soil. p. 148

Long March (lông märch) Mao Zedong and his followers' 6,000-mile (9,656-km) journey across China away from Nationalist forces. p. 625

longhouse (lông´hous) A Native American rectangular house made of wood frames covered with bark and shared by several families. p. 391

GLOSSARY

longitude (län´jə•tōōd) Distance east or west of the prime meridian. p. 32

longship (lông´ship) A narrow, flat-bottomed boat used long ago by the Vikings. p. 341

loyalty (loi´əl•tē) Devotion to or support of someone or something. p. 325

M

magma (mag´mə) Melted rock within Earth. p. 22

Magna Carta (mag´nə kär´tə) The document that English nobles forced King John to agree to in 1215, limiting the king's power. p. 488

mandate (man´dāt) An order for or a right to something. p. 153

Manifest Destiny (ma´nə•fest des´tə•nē) The belief, shared by many Americans in the 1800s, that the United States should one day stretch from the Atlantic Ocean to the Pacific Ocean. p. 595

manor (ma´nər) A large plot of land made up of forests, meadows, farmland, a village, a church, and the house or castle of the noble who owned it all. p. 334

manor system (ma´nər sis´təm) An economic system of exchanging land use and protection for goods and services. p. 334

mansa (män´sə) The title for a ruler in the Mali Empire of western Africa. p. 443

map key (map kē) The part of a map that explains what the symbols on the map stand for; sometimes called a map legend. p. A3

map scale (map skāl) The part of a map that compares distance on the map with distance in the real world. p. A3

map title (map tī´təl) The words on a map that describe the subject of the map. p. A2

market economy (mär´kit i•kä´nə•mē) An economy in which the people, not the government, own and control businesses. p. 579

martyr (mär´tər) A person who willingly suffers or dies for his or her beliefs. p. 303

medieval (mē•dē´vəl) Relating to the period of time from about A.D. 500 to A.D. 1000. p. 338

merchant (mûr´chənt) A person who buys and sells goods to make a living. p. 96

mesa (mā´sə) A flat-topped hill with steep slopes. p. 393

Mesoamerica (me´zō•ə•mer´i•kə) The region that includes Mexico and Central America; also called Middle America. p. 376

messiah (mə•sī´ə) A person sent by God to bring justice to the world. p. 301

metropolitan area (me•trə•pä´lə•tən âr´ē•ə) A city and all the suburbs around it. p. 45

migration (mī•grā´shən) The movement of people from one place to another. p. 44

militarism (mi´lə•tə•ri•zəm) A nation's interest in armed power. p. 605

minaret (mi•nə•ret´) A tower connected to a mosque, from which the faithful are called to prayer five times a day. p. 425

mineral (min´rəl) A natural resource found in rocks. p. 133

miniature (mi´nē•ə•chŏŏr) A very small painting or picture. p. 539

missionary (mi´shə•ner•ē) A person sent somewhere else to teach about his or her religion. p. 214

mitima (mid´ä•mä) The Incan practice of sending conquered people to live in different places, away from their homelands. p. 387

mixed economy (mikst i•kä´nə•mē) An economy that combines free enterprise and government control. p. 638

modify (mä´də•fī) To make a change in. p. 6

monarchy (mä´nər•kē) The system of government in which a king or a queen rules. p. 94

monastery (mä´nə•ster•ē) A place where a religious group resides; a center of Christian life. p. 339

money economy (mu´nē i•kä´nə•mē) An economic system based on the use of money instead of barter. p. 192

monopoly (mə•nä´pə•lē) Complete control or ownership. p. 413

monotheism (mä´nə•thē•i•zəm) A belief in one God. p. 181

Monroe Doctrine (mən•rō´ däk´trən) A government plan of action issued by President James Monroe declaring that the United States would go to war to stop European expansion in the Americas. p. 588

monsoon (män•sōōn´) A strong seasonal wind that brings heavy rains. p. 147

mosque (mosk) An Islamic house of worship. p. 425

movable type (mōō´və•bəl tīp) Letters and numbers made from individual pieces of metal that can be positioned to form rows of words. p. 494

mummy (mu´mē) A preserved body. p. 120

Muslim (mus´ləm) A follower of Islam. p. 421

mutiny (myōō´tə•nē) to rebel against the leader of one's group. p. 586

mythology (mi•thä´lə•jē) A collection of myths, or traditional stories, handed down from generation to generation. p. 245

N

nationalism (nash´ə•nə•li•zəm) A strong feeling of loyalty to a nation or country. p. 592

nation-state (nā´shən•stāt) A region with a united group of people and a single government. p. 120

nirvana (nir•vä´nə) In Buddhism, a state of complete bliss that is free from all passion, desire, and suffering. p. 211

noble (nō´bəl) A person of high rank or title in a society. p. 196

nomad (nō´mad) A person without a permanent home. p. 61

nome (nōm) An ancient Egyptian district. p. 126

nonviolence (nän•vī´ə•ləns) The use of peaceful ways to bring about change. p. 210

O

oasis (ō•ā´səs) A place in the desert that has a dependable source of water. p. 69

obelisk (ō´bə•lisk) An ancient stone monument; a tall, slender stone pillar with four sides and a pointed top. p. 133

obsidian (əb•si´dē•ən) A volcanic black rock often used by ancient people to make tools. p. 69

oligarchy (ä´lə•gär•kē) A system in which a small group controls the government. p. 252

Open Door policy (ō´pən dōr pä´lə•sē) A policy that gives all countries an equal opportunity to trade freely in a certain place. p. 588

opinion (ə•pin´yən) A statement of belief or judgment. p. 336

opportunity cost (ä•pər•tōō´nə•tē kôst) The cost of giving up something when choosing something else instead. p. 454

oracle bone (ôr´ə•kəl bōn) A bone or shell that contains ancient Chinese writing. p. 151

oral history (ōr´əl his´tə•rē) Accounts told by people who did not have a written language or who did not write down what happened. p. 2

orthodox (ôr´thə•däks) In religion, supported and accepted by tradition. p. 414

outrigger (out´ri•gər) A wooden frame placed on the side of a boat or canoe to keep the craft steady in rough seas. p. 460

overpopulation (ō•vər•pop•yə•lā´shən) The condition of having too many people living in one place. p. 351

P

paddy (pa´dē) A walled wet field in which rice is grown. p. 366

palisade (pa•lə•sād´) A wall made of sharpened stakes made from tree trunks, built to protect a village from enemies or wild animals. p. 392

papyrus (pə•pī´rəs) A paperlike material on which ancient Egyptians wrote; made from reeds that grow in the Nile River. p. 122

parallel time line (par´ə•lel tīm līn) A grouping of time lines that display different kinds of information for the same period of time. p. 66

passport (pas´pōrt) A document giving a person permission to travel abroad. p. 451

pastoral society (pas´tə•rəl sə•sī´ə•tē) A group of people whose way of life depends on herding. p. 61

patent (pa´tənt) A legal document stating that only the inventor has the right to make and sell his or her new product. p. 574

patriarch (pā´trē•ärk) A church leader. p. 415

patrician (pə•tri´shən) A descendant of Rome's earliest settlers. p. 279

patriotism (pā´trē•ə•ti•zəm) Love of one's country. p. 297

patron (pā´trən) A wealthy person who pays artists or writers to produce their works. p. 258

peacekeeping force (pēs´kē•ping fôrs) Troops whose job it is to keep the peace. p. 655

peasant (pe´zənt) A poor person who lives on and farms the land. p. 218

penal colony (pē´nəl kä´lə•nē) A settlement for criminals; a prison colony. p. 545

persecute (pûr´si•kyōot) To seek out and punish people. p. 303

perspective (pər•spek´tiv) A certain point of view. p. 3

pharaoh (fer´ō) A ruler of ancient Egypt. p. 126

philosopher (fə•lä´sə•fər) A person who studies the meaning of life; a thinker. p. 219

physical feature (fi´zi•kəl fē´chər) A feature such as a landform, a body of water, or a resource that has been formed by nature. p. 6

pictograph (pik´tə•graf) A drawing or symbol used to represent a word or an idea. p. 95

plague (plāg) A deadly sickness or disease. p. 260

plantation (plan•tā´shən) A huge farm. p. 526

plebeian (pli•bē´ən) A member of the common people of ancient Rome. p. 280

plunder (plun´dər) To take goods by force. p. 431

point of view (point əv vyōo) A person's set of beliefs that have been shaped by factors such as whether that person is old or young, male or female, or rich or poor, or by the person's culture, religion, race, or nationality. p. 418

policy (pä´lə•sē) A plan of action. p. 253

polytheism (pä´lē•thē•i•zəm) A belief in many gods. p. 200

pope (pōp) The leader of the Roman Catholic Church. p. 305

population cartogram (pä•pyə•lā´shən kär´tə•gram) A diagram that shows which countries have many people and which have few people. p. 650

population density (pä•pyə•lā´shən den´sə•tē) The number of people living on a square unit of land. p. 46

population distribution (pä•pyə•lā´shən dis•trə•byōo´shən) The way people are spread out in different places throughout the world. p. 40

population pyramid (pä•pyə•lā′shən pir′ə•mid) A graph that shows how a country's population is divided by age and by gender (male or female). p. 534

portico (pōr′ti•co) A covered walkway. p. 327

preamble (prē′am•bəl) An introduction; the first part. p. 566

predict (pri•dikt′) To tell ahead of time what will happen. p. 118

prediction (pri•dik′shən) A decision about what may happen next, based on the way things are. p. 306

primary source (prī′mer•ē sôrs′) A record made by people who saw or took part in an event. p. 4

prime meridian (prīm mə•ri′dē•ən) The meridian marked 0° longitude. It runs north and south through Greenwich, England. p. 33

principle (prin′sə•pəl) A rule or code of conduct; a belief. p. 101

projection (prə•jek′shən) One of many different views showing round Earth on a flat map. p. 542

propaganda (prä•pə•gan′də) The spreading of information, ideas, or rumors to help or hurt a cause. p. 613

prophet (prä′fət) A person who others believe speaks or writes with a message from God or a god. p. 200

prosperity (prä•sper′ə•tē) Economic success or well-being. p. 124

Protestant (prä′təs•tənt) One who was against efforts by Charles V and other Catholic leaders to end the movement led by Martin Luther. p. 500

province (prä′vəns) A self-governing region. p. 285

purge (pûrj) The killing or imprisonment of citizens who oppose the government. p. 623

pyramid (pir′ə•mid) A stone structure having a square base and triangular sides that come to a point at the top and used as a burial place for a dead ruler. p. 123

Q

Quechua (kech′ə•wə) The Inca language. p. 387

quinoa (kēn′wä) A high-protein grain grown by the ancient Incas. p. 384

quipu (kē′pōō) Colored knotted strings used by the Incas for recording information. p. 388

Qur'an (kə•ran′ or kə•rän′) The holy book of Islam. p. 421

R

rain forest (rān fôr′əst) A forest with thick vegetation and tall trees that block the sunlight. p. 38

rain shadow (rān sha′dō) The drier side of a mountain. p. 37

Raj (räj) British rule of the Indian subcontinent. p. 586

rajah (rä′jə) An Indian prince. p. 212

raw materials (rô mə•tir′ē•əlz) Natural resources that can be made into useful products. p. 446

recession (ri•sesh′ən) A period during which an economy stops growing. p. 637

reclaim (ri•klām′) To take back, as the surrounding environment can do to human-made structures. p. 161

Reconquista (rā•kōn•kēs′tä) The plan to make Spain all Catholic; also called the Reconquest. p. 486

Reformation (re•fər•mā′shən) A Christian movement that began in sixteenth-century Europe as an attempt to reform the Roman Catholic Church; resulted in the founding of Protestantism. p. 501

regent (rē′jənt) A person who governs in place of a ruler. p. 368

region (rē′jən) An area on Earth whose features make it different from other areas. p. 6

regulate (re′gyə•lāt) To control according to a set of rules. p. 143

reincarnation (rē•in•kär•nā′shən) The belief that the soul lives on after death and returns to life in a new body. p. 208

relative location (re′lə•tiv lō•kā′shən) Where a place is in relation to other places. p. 6

relief (ri•lēf′) A wall carving that stands out from the surface of a building. p. 109

relief map (ri•lēf′ map) A map that shows the differences in height or depth of hills, valleys, and other physical features. p. 154

Renaissance (re′nə•säns) The time from about 1400 to 1600 in which Europeans entered a new age of thought, learning, art, and science; a French word meaning "rebirth." p. 490

republic (ri•pu′blik) A form of government in which the citizens elect representatives to make and enforce the laws. p. 279

reservoir (re′zə•vwär) A human-made lake. p. 31

resurrection (re•zə•rek′shən) A rising from the dead. p. 302

revolution (re•və•lōō′shən) A sudden change in the way people think and act. p. 564

rift (rift) A crack in the Earth's crust. p. 30

river system (ri′vər sis′təm) A river and all its tributaries. p. 29

S

saga (sä′gə) An adventure story about the brave deeds of people. p. 341

salvation (sal•vā′shən) The saving of the human soul from evil with a promise of life after death. p. 300

samurai (sa′mə•rī) A Japanese warrior. p. 368

Sanskrit (san′skrit) A language of India, first spoken by the ancient Aryans. p. 209

savanna (sə•va´nə) A grassy plain. p. 349

scale (skāl) The relationship between the distances on a map and the actual distances on Earth. p. 382

scholar (skä´lər) A person seeking knowledge. p. 269

scientific method (sī•ən•ti´fik me´thəd) A system of observing and experimenting to determine whether an idea should be accepted as true. p. 494

scribe (skrīb) A person who writes things for others. p. 109

secondary source (se´kən•dâr•ē sôrs) A record of an event made by someone who was not there at the time. p. 4

self-sufficient (self•sə•fi´shənt) Able to provide for one's own needs without help. p. 335

Senate (se´nət) A council of representatives. p. 279

sepoy (sē´poi) An Indian soldier led by British officers. p. 586

serf (sûrf) A peasant who worked on a manor. p. 335

Shi'i (shē´ə) The second-largest branch of Islam, whose followers stay loyal to the descendants of the fourth caliph, Ali, of the eighth century. p. 423

Shinto (shin´tō) A religion of Japan. The word means "the way of the gods." p. 366

shogun (shō´gən) In Japan, a leading general who held all the authority. p. 369

siege (sēj) A long-lasting attack. p. 432

Silk Road (silk rōd) An overland trade route that linked China with Europe. p. 223

slash and burn (slash and bûrn) To cut and burn forestlands to gain new farmland. p. 65

smelt (smelt) To melt an ore to obtain its metal. p. 350

social class (sō´shəl klas) A group that has a particular level of importance in a society. p. 96

socialism (sō´shə•li•zəm) An economic system in which a government owns and runs all industries. p. 581

society (sə•sī´ə•tē) An organized group of people living and working under a set of rules and traditions. p. 8

soviet (sō´vē•et) An elected government council in a communist country. p. 622

specialize (spe´shə•līz) To work at only one kind of job. p. 57

standardize (stan´dər•dīz) To make all things of a certain kind alike. p. 152

standing army (stan´ding är´mē) An army with paid, full-time soldiers. p. 99

staple (stā´pəl) Any food or other common item that is used regularly. p. 357

star path (stär path) The way stars seem to move because of Earth's rotation. p. 461

steppe (step) A dry plain with grasses and thorny plants. p. 420

strategic (strə•tē´jik) Of great importance. p. 248

strike (strīk) The action of refusing to work until certain requirements are met. p. 581

subcontinent (sub•kän´tən•ənt) A large land area isolated from the rest of a continent. p. 142

sultan (sul´tən) A monarch in a Muslim country long ago. p. 523

Sunni (soo´nē) The largest branch of Islam, whose followers accept the changing dynasties of the Muslim Empire of the eighth century. p. 423

superpower (soo´pər•pou•ər) A nation that is one of the world's most powerful nations. p. 626

supply (sə•plī´) The amount of a good or a service offered for sale. p. 579

surplus (sûr´pləs) An extra supply. p. 93

Swahili (swä•hē´lē) The Bantu-speaking people and the Bantu language of eastern Africa. p. 522

synagogue (si´nə•gäg) A Jewish house of worship. p. 185

T

tabu (tə•boo´) Forbidden. p. 546

tariff (tar´əf) A tax on goods or services. p. 442

taxation (tak•sā´shən) The practice of requiring people to pay for the running of their government. p. 100

technology (tek•nä´lə•jē) The use of skills and knowledge to make the work of everyday life easier. p. 53

telecommunication (te•li•kə•myoo•nə•kā´shən) All the electronic ways of sending and receiving information across distances. p. 640

telescoping time line (te´lə•skōp•ing tīm līn) On a time line, a blown-up section that gives a closer view of one time period. p. 224

temperate (tem´pə•rət) Neither very hot nor very cold. p. 35

Ten Commandments (ten kə•mand´mənts) A set of laws for responsible behavior that, according to the Bible, were given to the Jewish people by God. p. 182

terrain (tə•rān´) The physical features of land. p. 386

territorial expansion (ter•ə•tōr´ē•əl ik•span´shən) The adding of new lands. p. 341

territory (ter´ə•tōr•ē) A large division of a country that may not have the same rights of self-government as the rest of the country. p. 109

terrorism (ter´ər•i•zəm) The deliberate use of violence to further a cause. p. 656

textile (tek´stīl) Cloth. p. 573

thematic map (thi•ma´tik map) A map with a specific theme or topic, such as population, culture, or history. p. 46

theory (thē´ə•rē) A possible explanation or unproved assumption. p. 20

tidal wave (tī´dəl wāv) A giant ocean wave. p. 28

tide (tīd) The regular, rhythmic rise and fall of ocean waters. p. 28

GLOSSARY

time zone (tīm zōn) A division of Earth in which all places have the same time; the time is different from that in other time zones. p. 590

totalitarian (tō•ta•lə•ter´ē•ən) Having to do with a government that has complete control over people's lives. p. 623

totem pole (tō´təm pōl) A tall wooden post carved with shapes of animals and people and representing a family's history and importance. p. 395

trade agreement (trād ə•grē´mənt) An agreement between countries to lower tariffs, or taxes, on goods traded between them. p. 639

trade route (trād rōōt) A path that traders use as they exchange goods. p. 133

trade-off (trād´ôf) Giving up of one thing in order to get another. p. 454

trading network (trād´ing net´wərk) A system in which buyers and sellers from different places can exchange goods. p. 136

traditional economy (trə•dish´nəl i•kä´nə•mē) An economy that does not change much over time and is based mainly on farming. p. 578

tradition (trə´di•shən) A custom or belief handed down from generation to generation. p. 186

tragedy (tra´jə•dē) A serious play with an unhappy ending. p. 259

travelogue (tra´və•lôg) A book about travels. p. 435

treaty (trē´tē) An agreement between nations about peace, trade, or other matters. p. 452

trench (trench) A deep ocean valley. p. 27

trend (trend) The way something changes over time. p. 618

triangular trade (trī•an´gyə•lər trād) A system in which traders exchanged goods for slaves in Africa, sold the slaves for products from plantations in the Americas, and then sold the products in Europe. p. 526

tribune (tri´byōōn) A plebeian official who could attend meetings of the assembly in ancient Rome. p. 280

tributary (tri´byə•ter•ē) A small river that feeds into a larger river. p. 29

tribute (tri´byōōt) Required yearly payments from one ruler or country to another, more powerful ruler or country. p. 198

triumvirate (trī•əm´və•rət) A group of three rulers who share power. p. 288

tropic (trä´pik) An area on Earth at or near the equator, between the Tropic of Cancer and the Tropic of Capricorn. p. 35

tundra (tun´drə) A flat and treeless plain of frozen ground. p. 395

turning point (tûrn´ing point) A single event that causes important or dramatic change. p. 214

typhoon (tī•fōōn´) A huge storm with heavy rains and high winds. p. 434

tyrant (tī´rənt) A cruel ruler. p. 152

urban planning (ûr´bən plan´ing) A plan or thought for the design of a city. p. 145

urbanization (ûr•bə•nə•zā´shən) The movement of people from the countryside to the cities. p. 45

V

vandal (van´dəl) Someone who purposely damages property; the word comes from the Vandals, a Germanic tribe that attacked Rome and stole valuable items. p. 332

vegetation (ve•jə•tā´shən) Plant life. p. 37

vernacular (vər•na´kyə•lər) The everyday language of people. p. 491

veto (vē´tō) To stop or reject the actions of another. p. 279

virtue (vûr´chōō) A right action; a good quality. p. 153

vizier (və•zir´) The chief adviser to an ancient Egyptian pharaoh. p. 125

W

warfare (wôr´fâr) A military activity undertaken by one nation to weaken or destroy another. p. 106

warlord (wôr´lôrd) A person who commands a small army. p. 624

water cycle (wô´tər sī´kəl) The circulation of water from Earth's surface to the atmosphere and back. p. 28

weathering (we´thər•ing) The wearing away of rock through some kind of motion. p. 23

wigwam (wig´wäm) A round, bark-covered Native American shelter. p. 391

Z

ziggurat (zi´gə•rat) A tall stepped tower built by the ancient Sumerians as a temple to a god. p. 71

Index

Page references for illustrations are set in italic type. An italic *m* indicates a map. Page references set in boldface type indicate the pages on which vocabulary terms are defined.

INDEX

INDEX

INDEX

INDEX

INDEX

Christie's Images/Corbis; 128 British Museum, London, Great Britain/Art Resource, NY; 129 Boltin Picture Library; 130 (tr) Boltin Picture Library; 130 (bl-top) Sandro Vannini/Corbis; 130 (bl-bottom) Sandro Vannini/Corbis; 130 (br) Sandro Vannini/Corbis; 131 (cr) Boltin Picture Library; 131 (tl) Boltin Picture Library; 131 (br) Gianni Dagli Orti/Corbis; 132-133 F. Jackson/Bruce Coleman Inc.; 132 (bl) Réunion des Musées Nationaux/Art Resource, NY; 134 Borromeo/Art Resource, NY; 135 (bc) Ram-headed sphinx on a column, Nubian, Napatan Period, reign of Piye, 747-716 B.C. Object Place: Sudan, Nubia, (el-Kurru), Tomb Ku 55, Gilt silver; glass. Height: 9 cm (3 9/16 in.), Museum of Fine Arts, Boston: Harvard University - Museum of Fine Arts Expedition 24.972, Photo copyright 2003 Museum of Fine Arts Boston; 135 (tl) Musée du Louvre Paris/Dagli Orti/The Art Archive; 135 (tr) Werner Forman/Art Resource, NY; 136 (tl) Hinged bracelet of gold with enamel decoration showing a seated figure of the goddess Hathor, Nubian, Meroitic Period, about 100 B.C. Sudan, Nubia, Gold, enamel, Height x length: 1.8 x 12.5 cm (11/16 x 4 15/16 in.) Museum of Fine Arts Boston, Harvard University - Museum of Fine Arts Expedition, 1920. Photograph copyright 2003 Museum of Fine Arts, Boston; 136 (bc) Egyptian Museum Cairo/Dagli Orti (A)/The Art Archive; 136 (tr) James Gurney; 137 Mask of Queen Malakaye. Nubian. Napatan Period, reign of Tanwetamani, 664-653 B.C. Sudan, Nubia, (Nuri) Gilt silver. Height x width x depth: 13 x 11.5 x 1.1 cm (5 1/8 x 4 1/2 x 7/16 in.) Museum of Fine Arts, Boston: Harvard University - Museum of Fine Arts Expedition 20.1059, Photo copyright 2003 Museum of Fine Arts Boston; 140-141 Robert Freck/Odyssey Productions; 142 John Noble/Corbis; 143 The Art Archive; 144 National Museum Karachi/Dagli Orti/The Art Archive; 145 (inset-gold button) National Museum Karachi/Dagli Orti (A)/The Art Archive; 145 (t) Archivo Iconografico, S.A./Corbis; 146-147 P. Koch/Robert Harding Picture Library; 146 (tc) Scala/Art Resource, NY; 147 (tr) Randy Olson/National Geographic Image Collection; 147 (inset) Corbis; 148 G. Corrigan/Robert Harding Picture Library; 150-151 Hanan Isachar/Corbis; 150 (br) The Granger Collection; 150 (tc) Francis G. Mayer/Corbis; 150 (b) Asian Art & Archaeology, Inc/Corbis; 150 (br) Elio Ciol/Corbis; 151 (bc) Wang Lu/ChinaStock; 151 (tr) H. Rogers/Art Directors & TRIP Photo Library; 152 Topham/The Image Works, Inc.; 153 (tr) The British Museum/Topham-HIP/The Image Works, Inc.; 153 (tl) Réunion des Musées Nationaux/Art Resource, NY; 157 (bc) Museum of Mankind London/Eileen Tweedy/The Art Archive; 157 (tr) Werner Forman/Art Resource, NY; 158 (r) National Anthropological Museum Mexico/Dagli Orti/The Art Archive; 158 (tr) Bowers Museum of Cultural Art/Corbis; 158 (bl) Christopher von Nagy; 159 (cr) Dagli Orti/The Art Archive; 159 (tr) SuperStock; 161 (tl) Robert Frerck/Odyssey Productions; 161 (tr) Suzanne Murphy-Larronde Photography; 163 (bl) Boltin Picture Library; 163 (br) Asian Art & Archaeology, Inc./Corbis; 163 (bc) Art Directors & TRIP Photo Library; 166 (b) Sergio Pitamitz/Alamy.com; 166-167 Kenneth Garrett/Woodfin Camp & Associates; 167 (bl) Kenneth Garrett/Woodfin Camp & Associates; 167 (cr) Honduras Institute Tegucigalpa/The Art Archive; 167 (tr-pendant) Werner Forman/Art Resource, NY; 167 (tr-flare) Werner Forman/Art Resource, NY

UNIT 3

Opener (object) Dagli Orti/The Art Archive; Opener (bg) David Allan Brandt/Stone/Getty Images; Opener (spread) David Allan Brandt/Stone/Getty Images; 171 Dagli Orti/The Art Archive; 174-175 O. Louis Mazzatenta/National Geographic Image Collection; 175 (inset) Keren Su/China Span; 176-177 Keren Su/China Span; 176 (tl) Doug Stern/National Geographic Image Collection; 177 (cl) Glen Allison/Stone/Getty Images; 178-179 Wolfgang Kaehler Photography; 180 (bl) R. Sheridan/Ancient Art & Architecture Collection, Ltd.; 181 (tr) National Gallery Budapest/Dagli Orti/The Art Archive; 181 (c) SuperStock; 182 Richard Hutchings/Photo Researchers, Inc.; 183 (tl) Mary Evans Picture Library; 184 (br) The Art Archive; 184 (tl) Erich Lessing/Art Resource, NY; 185 Michael Macioce/Klezmatics; 186 Michael P. Gadomski/SuperStock; 186 (inset-synagogue) Richard Cummins/Corbis; 186 (inset-mosque) Corbis; 189 Archivo Iconografico, S.A./Corbis; 190 The Granger Collection; 190 (bc) Musée des Beaux-Arts, Caen, France/Giraudon/Bridgeman Art Library; 192-193 Michele Burgess/Index Stock Imagery; 192 (tl) The British Museum; 192 (tr) Jan Vinchon Numismatist Paris/Dagli Orti/The Art Archive; 192 (tc) Erich Lessing/Art Resource, NY; 193 (tr) Grant Heilman Photography; 193 (tc) American Numismatic Society; 193 (tl) Fitzwilliam Museum, University of Cambridge, UK/Bridgeman Art Library; 194 Museum of Carthage/Dagli Orti (A)/The Art Archive; 195 (tl) Ancient Art & Architecture Collection, Ltd.; 195 (tr) Private Collection Beirut/Dagli Orti (A)/The Art Archive; 196-197 Chris Lisle/Corbis; 197 The British Museum/Topham/The Image Works, Inc.; 198 Dagli Orti/The Art Archive; 199 (inset) Louvre, Paris, France/Lauros-Giraudon/Bridgeman Art Library; 199 (tc) Giraudon/Art Resource, NY; 199 (b) Robert Harding Picture Library; 201 (tr) The Art Archive; 201 (tl) Bridgeman Art Library; 204-205 Dinodia Picture Agency; 207 Borromeo/Art Resource, NY; 208 Museo Nazionale d'Arte Orientale Rome/Dagli Orti/The Art Archive; 209 (t) Oriental Museum, Durham University, UK/Bridgeman Art Library; 209 (b) National Museum of India, New Delhi, India/Bridgeman Art Library; 210 (b) Marc Bernheim/Woodfin Camp & Associates; 210 (t) British Library/The Art Archive; 211 Sujoy Das/Stock Boston; 212-213 Brian A. Vikander/Corbis; 212 (cl) The British Museum; 214 (b) Dave Sarnoth/Dinodia Picture Agency; 214 (tr) Hulton Archive/Getty Images; 216 (b) Giraudon/Bridgeman Art Library; 216 (t) Charles & Josette Lenars/Corbis; 216 (inset) Lindsay Hebberd/Corbis; 217 (inset) Ancient Art & Architecture Collection, Ltd.; 217 (tr) The British Museum; 218 Burstein Collection/Corbis; 219 (tl) ChinaStock; 219 (b) Gian Berto Vanni/Art Resource, NY; 220-221 Aldo Torelli/Stone/Getty Images; 222 (bc) Dagli Orti/The Art Archive; 222 (br) Nigel Hicks/SuperStock; 223 Science Museum, London/Topham/The Image Works, Inc.; 225 The Granger Collection; 226-227 Asian Art & Archaeology, Inc./Corbis; 226 (tr) Langevin Jacques/Corbis/Sygma; 227 (tc) Cultural Relics Publishing House; 227 (cr) Asian Art & Archaeology, Inc./Corbis; 227 (tl) Asian Art & Archaeology, Inc./Corbis; 230-231 (bg) Keren Su/Corbis; 230 (inset) Li jiangang/Imaginechina.com; 231 (tr) Dennis Cox/ChinaStock; 231 (cr) ChinaStock; 231 (bl) Wu hui/Imaginechina.com

UNIT 4

Opener (object) Erich Lessing/Art Resource, NY; Opener (bg) Steve Vidler/SuperStock; Opener (spread) Steve Vidler/SuperStock; 235 Erich Lessing/Art Resource, NY; 242-243 Yann Arthus-Bertrand/Corbis; 244 (bl) Gianni Dagli Orti/Corbis; 244-245 P. Richards/Art Directors & TRIP Photo Library; 245 (tr) SuperStock; 246 Nimatallah/Art Resource, NY; 247 (tc) Archivo Iconografico, S.A./Corbis; 247 (br-inset) Institute of Nautical Archeology; 247 (bl-inset) Institute of Nautical Archeology; 247 (b) Institute of Nautical Archeology; 249 Erich Lessing/Art Resource, NY; 250 (bl) R. Rainford/Robert Harding Picture Library/Alamy.com; 250 (b) George Grigoriou/Stone/Getty Images; 251 Ancient Art & Architecture Collection, Ltd.; 252 (tc) Boltin Picture Library; 252 (tl) Louvre, Paris, France/Bridgeman Art Library Giraudon/Bridgeman Art Library; 252 (tr) Réunion des Musées Nationaux/Art Resource, NY; 253 (t) The Granger Collection; 253 (b) Nimatallah/AKG Images; 254-255 Andy Lyons/Getty Images Editorial; 254 (t) Ashmolean Museum, Oxford, UK/Bridgeman Art Library; 255 (t) Musée du Louvre Paris/Dagli Orti/The Art Archive; 256 Museo Naval Madrid/Dagli Orti/The Art Archive; 257 C. M. Dixon Colour Photo Library; 258 British Museum, London, UK/Bridgeman Art Library; 259 Mimmo Jodice/Corbis; 260 (c) JFB/The Art Archive; 260 (tl) Museo Capitolino, Rome, Italy/ET Archive, London/SuperStock; 261 Scala/Art Resource, NY; 262 Kunsthistorisches Museum, Vienna, Austria/Bridgeman Art Library; 263 AKG Images; 264 Walter Bibikow/Taxi/Getty Images; 265 (b) Archaeological Museum Salonica/Dagli Orti/The Art Archive; 265 (t) David Lees/Corbis; 266 (b) Jordan Anders Blomqvist/Lonely Planet Images; 266 (t) Museo Archeologico, Florence, Italy/Lauros/Giraudon/Bridgeman Art Library; 268-269 Nik Wheeler/Corbis; 268 (t) Scala/Art Resource, NY; 269 (t) AKG Images; 270 (b) Dagli Orti/The Art Archive; 270 (cl) Archaeological Museum Corinth/Dagli Orti/The Art Archive; 270 (c) Dagli Orti/The Art Archive; 270 (cr) Archaeological Museum Corinth/Dagli Orti/The Art Archive; 271 (tr) H. R. Goette (Neg 2001/1086 F)/DAI, Athens (Deutsches Archäologisches Institut); 271 (br) Michele Burgess/Index Stock Imagery; 271 (tl) Nimatallah/Art Resource, NY; 274-275 David Marshall/Index Stock Imagery; 276-277 Vittoriano Rastelli/Corbis; 277 (t) Leeds Museums and Art Galleries (City Museum) UK/Bridgeman Art Library; 278 Pierre Boulat/COS/Woodfin Camp & Associates; 279 (b) Scala/Art Resource, NY; 279 (c) Araldo de Luca/Corbis; 281 (tc-dog tag) British Museum; 281 (tc) Archaeological Museum Châtillon-sur-Seine/Dagli Orti/The Art Archive; 282 Tim McCarthy/Art Resource, NY; 284 (bl) Museo della Civilta Romana Rome/Dagli Orti/The Art Archive; 284 (bc) Scala/Art Resource, NY; 284 (br) Scala/Art Resource, NY; 285 (t) Museo Capitolino Rome/Dagli Orti/The Art Archive; 285 (b) Scala/Art Resource, NY; 286 (t) Scala/Art Resource, NY; 286 (b) Giraudon/Art Resource, NY; 287 Cameraphoto/Art Resource, NY; 288-289 North Carolina Museum of Art/Corbis; 288 (t) Antiqua, Inc.; 289 (t) Sandro Vannini/Corbis; 290 Ancient Art & Architecture Collection, Ltd; 292-293 Réunion des Musées Nationaux/Art Resource, NY; 292 (bl) SuperStock; 293 (inset) Dagli Orti (A)/The Art Archive; 294-295 Art by William H. Bond/National Geographic Image Collection; 294 (t-inset) Alinari/Art Resource,

NY; 294 (b-inset) Angelo Hornak/Corbis; 295 (br) David Marshall/Index Stock Imagery; 295 (bl) Scala/Art Resource, NY; 295 (t-inset) Scala/Art Resource, NY; 295 (cr) Vittoriano Rastelli/Corbis; 296 (inset) Archaeological Museum Naples/Dagli Orti/The Art Archive; 296 (b) Archaeological Museum Merida Spain/The Art Archive; 297 (tl-inset) Alinari/Art Resource, NY; 297 John and Lisa Merrill/Corbis; 298 (tr) Ancient Art & Architecture Collection, Ltd.; 298 (c) Museo Nazionale Terme Rome/Dagli Orti/The Art Archive; 298 (tl) Musée du Louvre Paris/Dagli Orti/The Art Archive; 299 Archivo Iconografico, S.A./Corbis; 300 (b) Araldo de Luca/Corbis/Sygma; 300 (t) Scala/Art Resource, NY; 301 (c) Musée du Louvre Paris/Dagli Orti/The Art Archive; 301 (br) AKG Images; 302 (inset) Scala/Art Resource, NY; 302 A. Woolfitt/Robert Harding Picture Library; 303 Bardo Museum Tunis/Dagli Orti/The Art Archive; 304 (t) Angel Terry/Alamy.com; 304 (b) Scala/Art Resource, NY; 304 (tl-inset) Araldo de Luca/Corbis; 305 Biblioteca Capitolare Vercelli/Dagli Orti/The Art Archive; 306-307 Dallas and John Heaton/Corbis; 310 (br) Keren Su/Corbis; 310 (cr) Nevada Wier/Corbis; 311 (bl) Keren Su/China Span; 311 (tr) Keren Su/China Span; 311 (tl) Nevada Wier/Corbis; 311 (br) Jin ge/Imaginechina.com

UNIT 5

Opener (object) Werner Forman/Art Resource, NY; Opener (bg) Tom Till Photography; Opener (spread) Tom Till Photography; 315 Werner Forman/Art Resource, NY; 322-323 Charles Tait Photographic Limited; 324-325 Richard T. Nowitz/National Geographic Image Collection; 325 (tr) Musée Luxembourgeois Arlon Belgium/Dagli Orti/The Art Archive; 326 Erich Lessing/Art Resource, NY; 327 (tr) Robert Frerck/Odyssey Productions; 327 (bc) Scala/Art Resource, NY; 327 (tl) Réunion des Musées Nationaux/Art Resource, NY; 328 (cl) Pirozzi/AKG Images; 328-329 Mark Segal/Panoramic Images; 329 (cr) Brian Lawrence/SuperStock; 330 (bl) Bibliothèque des Arts Décoratifs Paris/Dagli Orti/The Art Archive; 330 (c) Giraudon/Art Resource, NY; 332 David Hughes/Stone/Getty Images; 333 (inset) British Museum/Eileen Tweedy/The Art Archive; 333 (t) AKG Images; 336 Bettmann/Corbis; 337 (tr) British Library/The Art Archive; 337 (bc) The Art Archive; 338-339 Patrick Ward/Corbis; 338 (inset) The Bowes Museum, Barnard Castle, County Durham, UK/Bridgeman Art Library; 339 (tr) SuperStock; 340 (t) Erich Lessing/Art Resource, NY; 340 (b) Gianni Dagli Orti/Corbis; 341 (b) Wedigo Ferchland/Bruce Coleman Inc.; 341 (tc) Erich Lessing/Art Resource, NY; 342 Edwin Wallace/Mary Evans Picture Library; 343 (t) World Book Publishing; 343 (inset) The Art Archive; 346-347 Angelo Hornak/Corbis; 348-349 Anthony Ham/Lonely Planet Images; 349 (c) John Elk III Photography; 350 (t) Lauré Communications; 350 (b) Werner Forman/Art Resource, NY; 351 (b) Ian Murphy/Stone/Getty Images; 352 (br) American Numismatic Society; 353 (bc) Kazuyoshi Nomachi/HAGA/The Image Works, Inc.; 353 The British Library/Topham-HIP/The Image Works, Inc.; 354 Anthony Ham/Lonely Planet Images; 356-357 Stock Image/SuperStock; 357 (c) Erich Lessing/Art Resource, NY; 358 (b) Digital Vision; 358 (t) Leonard de Selva/Corbis; 359 (t) Catherine Karnow/Corbis; 359 (b) Dallas and John Heaton/Corbis; 360 Werner Forman/Art Resource, NY; 361 (t) The British Museum/Topham-HIP/The Image Works, Inc.; 361 (b) Janet Wishnetsky/Corbis; 362 (t) Craig Brown/

Index Stock Imagery; 362 (b) The British Museum/Topham-HIP/The Image Works, Inc.; 362 (t-inset) Réunion des Musées Nationaux/Art Resource, NY; 363 Leonard de Selva/Corbis; 366 Jon Burbank/The Image Works, Inc.; 366 (t-Jomon) Sakamoto Photo Research Laboratory/Corbis; 366 (t-Yayoi) Sakamoto Photo Research Laboratory/Corbis; 367 Werner Forman/Art Resource, NY; 368 The British Museum/Topham HIP/The Image Works, Inc.; 369 (tr) Pacific Press Service; 369 (c) Victoria & Albert Museum/Michael Holford Photographs; 370 (r) The National Museum of Japanese History; 370 (bl) The National Museum of Japanese History; 371 (tl) The National Museum of Japanese History; 371 (br) Victoria & Albert Museum, London/Art Resource, NY; 375-376 Galen Rowell/Corbis; 376 (inset) Gianni Dagli Orti/Corbis; 376-377 Schalkwijk/Art Resource, NY; 378 (inset) Robert Frerck/Odyssey Productions; 378 Dagli Orti/The Art Archive; 378 (tc) National Anthropological Museum Mexico/Dagli Orti/The Art Archive; 379 John Bigelow Taylor/Art Resource, NY; 380 (t) National Anthropological Museum Mexico/Dagli Orti/The Art Archive; 380 (b) Werner Forman/Art Resource, NY; 381 (inset) SuperStock; 381 (tr) Giraudon/Art Resource, NY; 384 (inset) Museo Pedro de Osma Lima/Mireille Vautier/The Art Archive; 384 Glen Allison/Alamy.com; 385 Museo de America, Madrid, Spain/Bridgeman Art Library; 386 Werner Forman/Art Resource, NY; 388 (b) Tui De Roy/Minden Pictures; 388 (br-inset) David Tejada/Stone/Getty Images; 388 (tc) Werner Forman/Art Resource, NY; 389 (inset) Archaeological Museum Lima/Mireille Vautier/The Art Archive; 389 Dave G. Houser/Corbis; 390 (b) L. K. Townsend/Cahokia Mounds State Historic Site; 390 (bl) Werner Forman/Art Resource, NY; 392 (t) Marilyn "Angel" Wynn/Nativestock.com; 392 (b) Smithsonian American Art Museum, Gift of Mrs. Joseph Harrison, Jr., 1985.66.383/Art Resource, NY; 393 (t) SuperStock; 393 (t-inset) George H. H. Huey/Corbis; 393 (b) Buddy Mays/Corbis; 395 Werner Forman/Art Resource, NY; 398-399 Steve Raymer/Corbis; 398 (c-inset) Zhang guosheng/Imaginechina.com; 399 (tc) David Alan Harvey/Woodfin Camp & Associates; 399 (tr) PhotoDisc; 399 (tl) Grayce Roessler/Index Stock Imagery; 399 (c-inset) Glen Allison/Stone/Getty Images

UNIT 6

Opener (object) Asian Art & Archaeology, Inc./Corbis; Opener (bg) Ric Ergenbright Photography; Opener (spread) Ric Ergenbright Photography; 403 Asian Art & Archaeology, Inc./Corbis; 410-411 Robert Frerck/Stone/Getty Images; 412 Michele Burgess/Index Stock Imagery; 413 (tr) Dagli Orti/The Art Archive; 413 (b) Dagli Orti/The Art Archive; 414 Réunion des Musées Nationaux/Art Resource, NY; 415 Allison Wright/Corbis; 416 (b) Robert Frerck/Odyssey Productions; 416 (t) Dagli Orti/The Art Archive; 416 (inset) AKG Images; 417 (tl) AKG Images; 417 (tr) Museo Correr, Venice, Italy/Bridgeman Art Library; 418 British Library/The Art Archive; 419 Araldo de Luca/Corbis; 420-421 W. Robert Moore/National Geographic Image Collection; 420 (bl) Victoria and Albert Museum London/Sally Chappell/The Art Archive; 421 (t) Art Directors & TRIP Photo Library; 422 (c) Shepard Sherbell/Corbis/SABA; 422 (br) AKG Images; 423 Bargello Museum Florence/Dagli Orti/The Art Archive; 424 Ken Welsh/Bridgeman Art Library; 425 (tl) AKG Images; 425 (tr) Michael Freeman/Corbis; 426 Christine Osborne/World

Religions/Alamy.com; 428 (b) The British Library; 428 (tr) Gianni Dagli Orti/Corbis; 429 (tl) British Library; 429 (br) British Library; 430-431 Nik Wheeler/Corbis; 430 (inset) M. Barlow/Art Directors & TRIP Photo Library; 431 (c) Ancient Art & Architecture Collection, Ltd.; 432 (t) AKG Images; 433 Victoria & Albert Museum, London/Art Resource, NY; 435 (c) The Art Archive; 435 (c-book page) AKG Images; 438-439 John Elk III Photography; 440 (cl) Musée des Arts Africains et Océaniens/Dagli Orti/The Art Archive; 440-441 David Else/Lonely Planet Images; 442 (t) Musée des Arts Africains et Océaniens/Dagli Orti/The Art Archive; 442 (b) Nik Wheeler; 443 (tr) Bibliothèque Nationale de France; 443 (b) The Newark Museum/Art Resource, NY; 444 Private Collection/Bridgeman Art Library; 445 (c) Sandro Vannini/Corbis; 445 (t) Denis Rouvre/Musée des Arts d'Afrique et d'Océanie, Paris/Réunion des Musées Nationaux/Art Resource, NY; 446 Bernard and Catherine Desjeux/Corbis; 448 Michael Holford Photographs; 449 Janet Wishnetsky/Corbis; 450 The Granger Collection; 451 The British Library; 451 (t) Private Collection/Bridgeman Art Library; 452 The Metropolitan Museum of Art, Purchase, Bequest of Dorothy Graham Bennett, 1993 (1993.256) Photographs copyright 1997 The Metropolitan Museum of Art; 453 (inset) Kadokawa Shoten Publishing/Ancient Art & Architecture Collection, Ltd.; 453 (tr) British Library/The Art Archive; 454 Scala/Art Resource, NY; 455 David Kelly Crow/PhotoEdit; 456 (l) Mike Yamashita/Woodfin Camp & Associates; 458 (b) Bridgeman Art Library; 459 Mike Yamashita/Woodfin Camp & Associates; 459 (t) Philadelphia Museum of Art/Corbis; 460 (cl) Field Museum of Natural History; 460-461 Ferdinando Scianna/Magnum Photos; 461 (t) Werner Forman/Art Resource, NY; 462 (bc) The Granger Collection; 462 (bl) Jonathan Blair/Corbis; 462 (br) The British Museum/Topham-HIP/The Image Works, Inc.; 463 (br) Natural Science Academy Kiev/Dagli Orti/The Art Archive; 463 (tr) Prado, Madrid, Spain/Bridgeman Art Library; 463 (bc) Werner Forman/Art Resource, NY; 463 (bl) Werner Forman/Art Resource, NY; 464 Private Collection/Bridgeman Art Library; 465 Scala/Art Resource, NY; 466 (bl) The Granger Collection; 466 (tc-florin) Ted Spiegel/Corbis; 466 (tc-ducat) Erich Lessing/Art Resource, NY; 469-470 Neil Setchfield/Lonely Planet Images; 469 (b) Color Point Studios/Index Stock Imagery; 469 (cr) Gail Mooney/Corbis; 469 (c) Gail Mooney/Corbis; 470 (tr) Jon Davison/Lonely Planet Images; 470 (bl) Charles Walker/Topfoto/The Image Works, Inc.; 470 (tl) Giraudon/Bridgeman Art Library

UNIT 7

Opener (object) Museo degli Argenti Pitti Palace Florence/Dagli Orti/The Art Archive; Opener (bg) Scala/Art Resource, NY; Opener (spread) Scala/Art Resource, NY; 473 Museo degli Argenti Pitti Palace Florence/Dagli Orti/The Art Archive; 482-483 Photri-Microstock; 484 Mary Evans Picture Library; 485 Weldon Owen Publishing; 486 (tl) Archivo Iconografico, S.A./Corbis; 486 (b) Chronicle of France or of St. Denis (14th century) British Library, London, UK/Bridgeman Art Library; 487 Lauros/Giraudon/Bridgeman Art Library; 488 (c) The Stapleton Collection/Bridgeman Art Library; 488 (b) Mary Evans Picture Library; 490 Erich Lessing/Art Resource, NY; 491 Archivo del Stato, Florence, Italy/Bridgeman Art Library; 492 (b) Private Collection, London/Reuters/SuperStock; 492 (inset) Private Collection, London/Reuters/